A HISTORY
OF EDUCATION
IN THE
TWENTIETH CENTURY
WORLD

A HISTORY OF EDUCATION
IN THE TWENTIETH CENTURY WORLD

W.F. Connell

TEACHERS COLLEGE PRESS
Teachers College, Columbia University
New York

TO
MARGARET

Published simultaneously in the U.S.A.
and Australia by Teachers College Press
and the Curriculum Development Centre

Library of Congress Cataloging in Publication Data

Connell, William Fraser
A history of education in the twentieth century world

Includes index
1. Education - History. 2. Education
Philosophy. I. Title.
LA11.C66   370′.9′04   78-2947
ISBN 0-8077-8024-3

Edited by Beth Cooper
Designed by Chris Makepeace
Typeset in Australia by G.T. Setters Pty Ltd, Kenthurst, N.S.W.
Printed in Australia by Griffin Press Limited

ACKNOWLEDGMENTS

A large work on a wide canvas written over a period of many years incurs innumerable debts which are impossible to acknowledge in detail. Some, however, are of particular importance. I am especially grateful to the University of Sydney for providing financial support and research assistance, the University of Illinois for a period as an associate in the Center for Advanced studies and as a George H. Miller Visiting Professor, the University of Cambridge for a fellowship at Wolfson College, and the University of London for accommodation as a Visiting Scholar. The co-operation of the librarians in each of these institutions has been superb. To several research assistants I am greatly indebted, particularly to Sonja Standley who for several years worked on the project with great zest, and to Wendy Edgar who is responsible for many of the photographs and illustrations which appear throughout this publication. Betty Johnson has been invaluable in organising the secretarial side of the venture, Helen Connell has been responsible for the onerous job of proof reading, and Vija Sierins has supported it throughout with many suggestions, translations, and the compilation of the index. My academic colleagues in various countries have been most helpful with patient advice and criticism, particularly Professor D. Spearritt, Dr R. Petersen, and Dr Phillip W. Jones, at the University of Sydney, V. Aransky of the U.S.S.R. Academy of Pedagogical Sciences, Professor B.O. Smith of the University of Illinois, and Professor R.W. Connell and Dr P.M. Selkirk of Macquarie University; but above all I value the contribution of the many graduate students whose company I have greatly enjoyed and who have provided continuing intellectual challenge and exchange in successive seminars during the past twenty years.

FOREWORD

In this major work of scholarship and interpretation, Emeritus Professor Connell has produced a landmark in historical and comparative study of modern education. He adds immeasurably to our understanding of the nature, role and significance of educational theory and practice as it has evolved and changed through the twentieth century. The book is a significant contribution to the base of knowledge and understanding of contemporary education in its social and historical setting. This knowledge and understanding need to be built up by research and critical scholarship if effective practice, including curriculum development, is to occur. The Curriculum Development Centre is pleased to publish this book by one of Australia's leading educators and a foremost scholar in comparative and historical studies.

The canvas of the book is remarkable and Professor Connell has chosen to approach his subject by identifying and analysing major developmental themes, ideas and movements. Education and the social, political, economic and cultural forces working on it, are examined from a world-wide perspective. The rise of progressive education, educational change in communist countries, main trends in theory and research, the emergence of new patterns of education in developing countries and trends in teaching practice and curriculum development are among the wide array of themes which are examined in depth as well as breadth.

Material in the book is organised into three sections: the educational awakening that occurred in the early years of the century; educational changes and aspirations between the two world wars; and educational expansion and reconstruction in the period since 1945. Within each section, particular trends and themes are analysed in individual chapters. A general overview chapter introduces the whole work and each section is summarised through a review of major themes. The contents are carefully organised for study and reference purposes, supported with comprehensive reading references and index and illustrated by charts, diagrams and drawings of eminent educators. Thus, although the subject matter is vast it has been marshalled into a readable text which the Centre believes will be attractive to a wide audience. The whole study is a substantial, comprehensive interpretation of one of the most impressive of modern human achievements — the world-wide creation of organised, universal education.

Few writers could have encompassed the width of coverage of this book. Professor Connell, however, has gone far beyond a broad overview. Each topic is handled with depth and lucidity based on the author's mastery of the field. Thus what is most distinctive about the book is the combination of breadth of understanding and interpretation with exact scholarship; what is most fascinating about it is the author's demonstration of the centrality of education in the life and culture of all societies bent on their own change and development. The reader of this book will be left with an indelible impression of the interweaving of educational thought and practice with the main trends of modern life.

The book will be of value to all those involved in teaching, lecturing, educational administration, research and development who need to understand the overall shape, directions, achievements and frustrations of the field in which they are studying and working. Because it is written in a non-technical language the book will also be of interest to anyone outside professional education who wishes to understand the direction and impact of educational change in the contemporary world.

M. SKILBECK
Director.

CONTENTS

LIST OF FIGURES

LIST OF TABLES

**Ellen Key (1849-1926), a Swedish writer and teacher, who in 1900 wrote *The
Century of the Child* dedicated to 'all parents who hope to shape the new man
in the new century'.**

INTRODUCTION

Education in the Twentieth Century

SUMMARY

Education at the End of the Nineteenth Century
    (i)   The Provision of Education
    (ii)   Curriculum
    (iii)   Methods of Teaching

Three Periods of Education
    (i)   Educational Awakening c.1900-16
    (ii)   Educational Aspiration, 1916-45
    (iii)   Educational Reconstruction and Expansion,
            1945-75

Education and the Twentieth Century Revolution
    (i)   The Politicising of Education
    (ii)   Education for Individual and Social Betterment
    (iii)   From Instruction to Education

The twentieth century has been a time of profound revolution, and education has played an increasingly important part in fostering and shaping the transformation.

In many countries, changes have involved the forcible overthrow of existing authority and the destruction of selected aspects of traditional practices and cultures. Education, in such cases, has often been brought deliberately into the service of the new society to widen, deepen, and perpetuate the revolution. In many other places, profound changes have occurred through the process of silent social revolution.[1] Industrial development, scientific and technological progress, and increasing urbanisation have brought substantial changes in social organisation and cultural habits. In these societies material comfort has increased, and measures to secure the welfare of all have been considerably extended. In this transformation, education has played a central role. It has been required to interpret the new forces of the twentieth century and their effects to the young people growing up within them, it has taken on the task of searching out and providing the intellectual and social knowledge and skills by which the understanding, maintenance, and extension of the revolution can be achieved, and it has succeeded in raising human aspiration for more education and the better social and economic conditions that go with it.

Schools from kindergarten to university lie at the centre of a modern society's educational efforts. Obviously there are many other educational influences at work, but, in the twentieth century, the school is the one educational institution that has been deliberately set up on a large scale and fostered by much public and professional effort. Its programs, its organisation, the educational processes within it, the theory behind it, its association with related institutions such as youth organisations, and its impact on social, cultural and political life, together form a large and important body of material about the growth and development of contemporary human society. This is the subject of this book. It is an

---

[1]   The phrase is used as the title of one of the most widely read histories of recent education in England: G.A.N. Lowndes, *The Silent Social Revolution*, Oxford University Press, 1937, 2nd edn, 1969.

effort to show, by studying the work of schools, the part that education has played in moulding the mind of the twentieth century and in transforming itself incidentally in the process.

EDUCATION AT THE END OF THE NINETEENTH CENTURY

(i) The Provision of Education

At the beginning of the twentieth century formal education for the majority of people in the world scarcely existed. Three-quarters of the world's population were in agricultural countries where the educational changes of the past thousand years had made no significant impact on them. It is probable that in 1900, 70 per cent of all the inhabitants of the world over fifteen years of age and 95 per cent of those in underdeveloped countries were illiterate. The continuing intractability of the problem of merely achieving literacy was shown by the fact that, half a century later, in 1950, the figures were respectively about 44 per cent and 64 per cent, and, in 1970, 34 per cent and 50 per cent.[2] In some countries, such as Iran, India, and China, where illiteracy was rife, there was also a well-developed literate culture of long standing, but, at the beginning of the twentieth century, it was still confined to the very few. Japan alone of such countries had made substantial advances in the latter half of the nineteenth century and was a much studied example to the rest of Asia.

In the more developed and industrialised nations of North America, Western Europe, and the British colonies of Australia and New Zealand, universal education was well established. Six or more years of compulsory primary education for all children was common by the beginning of the twentieth century, a substantial expansion of public secondary education was under serious consideration, and a restricted but growing system of tertiary education was in operation. In the U.S.A. about 72 per cent of the age group 5-17 were in school in 1900, in England 64 per cent, and in Australia 52 per cent.

In Europe and Latin America primary and secondary education were not necessarily sequential. Primary education was for the masses, and, although, in some higher primary schools, it might extend upward for two or three years into the secondary level, it did not prepare pupils, except a few outstanding ones, for a full secondary education. Primary education was terminal and separate from secondary education; if it led to anything it led to some form of lower level vocational education. The two systems, primary and secondary, were based on and helped to maintain social class differences. Primary education was usually free and compulsory, secondary education was available to those who could pay, and it had its own system of preparatory schools separate from and parallel to the primary schools. The preparatory and secondary schools trained the children of a middle and upper class elite to move eventually into positions of professional or managerial responsibility.

The school systems of North America were structured differently. There, as a general rule, primary education was the first stage, leading to secondary education; the numbers completing a full secondary course, however, were still small, and attendance at high school was related to social class. Despite the claim by a school administrator that '... it is the children of the plain people, in city and country, who are crowding our school-rooms today...',[3] the masses were not staying on to complete the high school course. In 1900 the proportion of secondary school pupils in the U.S.A. was higher than that in any other country, but the drop-out rate was still extensive and was not determined solely by educational considerations. For many years to come both the opportunity for a full secondary and for a tertiary level education, and also the level of achievement and of measured intelligence reached by students were to be associated with such socio-economic status factors as the place of residence, the kind of occupation, income, and aspiration of a student's parents.

The nineteenth century saw the establishment in Germany of a comprehensive system of technical schools which in the last quarter of the century attracted the attention of educators and public-spirited citizens in many other countries. Technical and commercial education was meagrely provided for outside of Germany, but in countries where commerce and industry were expanding or well-established, such as France, England, the U.S.A. and Japan, there was much discussion, and, by 1900, a modest effort to develop more facilities for technical training. Tertiary education, for both professional and general studies, was also on the move. Universities and teachers' colleges particularly had multiplied in the last quarter of the nineteenth century in all the developed countries. Universities continued, however, to provide for an elite selected competitively from secondary schools; and teachers' colleges, though less selective, were, in the future, to look to the secondary schools for their entering students.

---

[2]   UNESCO, *Statistical Yearbook*, 1965, Table 1-3, and 1970, Table 1-4. The figures do not inlcude China, North Korea, or North Vietnam.

[3]   Charles R. Skinner, State Superintendent in New York, 'The Best Education for the Masses', Presidential Address, National Education Association, 1897, p.53, quoted in E.A. Krug, *The Shaping of the American High School 1800-1920*, University of Wisconsin, Madison, 1969, p. 175.

By 1900, it had become clear to educators in the most developed countries that secondary schooling was the most critical area of education. The nineteenth century had solidly established universal primary education. Further progress in technical, professional, and all forms of higher education depended on the effective organisation of the secondary level of schooling. The rethinking of the functions and the means of securing a rapid expansion of secondary education became, therefore, the most widely discussed task for educators in the early years of the new century in the industrialised countries of the world. In the underdeveloped countries there was little movement at either the secondary or tertiary level.

(ii) Curriculum

In content, primary education in all countries was designed to produce pupils who had command of the fundamental processes of literacy and numeracy, and who were persons of good character, honest, hard-working, and patriotic. The program of studies and the ideal of character were both somewhat limited, but, by the turn of the century, had already started to expand. The rigid and restricted ways exemplified by the English payment by results system of the latter half of the nineteenth century had begun to dissolve, and a richer view of the function of the primary school had for some time been slowly coming into being under the influence particularly of the Froebelian and the child study movements.

In secondary education the traditional curriculum of classics and mathematics had not yet been broken down; it had, however, been under threat for half a century. The virtues of the traditional curriculum were that it provided mental training and that it was the basis of a liberal education. Other subjects might offer interesting and useful information but were not admitted to have the fundamentally educational qualities of the classics and mathematics. To displace them, new subjects had to demonstrate that they could offer as sound an intellectual training, and as comprehensive an entry into the culture. By 1900, science and modern languages, both native and foreign, were establishing their claims. History, too, was becoming increasingly important. It was beginning to be thought of as a source of intellectual training, and also as an efficient vehicle of nationalism and moral education. In the U.S.A. the tradition had been eroded much further than in Europe. In Asian countries the established curriculum had begun to feel the impact of western thinking, and, notably in India and Japan, was steadily being remodelled to take in the more recent tendencies in Europe and America. One of the most recent of these interests was the wider development of secondary and post-secondary technical education.

(iii) **Methods of Teaching**

Methods of teaching in primary and secondary schools assumed that schools would be divided into classroom groups of pupils of approximately the same age, and that pupils would be taught together in each of these groups. Techniques of classroom teaching for groups of thirty or so children that, in exceptionally crowded schools, might range up to one hundred were the special concern of the educators in the nineteenth century while primary education was rapidly expanding. By 1900, teaching typically proceeded on the view that the teacher's principal task was to manage a classroom efficiently, that, in doing this, he should be able to instruct his pupils clearly, methodically, and thoroughly in a group, that the pupils should be directed by the teacher in what they learnt and how they learnt it, that the principal sources of their information should be the teacher and the textbook selected by the teacher, and that they should accept and reproduce the ideas and knowledge prescribed for them in a quiet and well-disciplined manner.

The classroom of 1900 was meant to be a still and orderly place where the teacher's voice predominated. It should not be thought, however, that this pattern of teaching went unchallenged. Progressive education which did more than any other movement in the twentieth century to undermine the received orthodoxy and to introduce a radically different view of pupil-teacher relationships did not spring suddenly into being in the first decade of the century. It had important forerunners of several kinds who worked in the later nineteenth century to modify the existing mould and to introduce more flexible procedures. Early in the century, Pestalozzi, and later Froebel had laid both a theoretical and practical foundation for educational reform which many educators had expanded by their various interests, in practical and manual work, in studies of children's play and growth, in encouraging non-book learning, in substituting problem-solving for memorisation, or in widening the range of subjects studied in school. In such ways innovative schools and teachers helped slowly to build up a climate of expectation which would enable their twentieth century successors to take bolder and more concerted steps to break out of the prevailing pattern.

Of the forthcoming changes there were two harbingers.

First, an interest developed during the last quarter of the nineteenth century in the application of systematic psychological theory to education. Herbart, early in the century, had started the trend with a theory of learning and teaching based on the association of ideas; his German successors in the second half of the century developed it and applied it carefully to classroom practice. At the same time Wundt had put experimental psychology on the map, and several of his students had begun to interest themselves in educational psychology. So far had the tendency progressed that in 1889 a well-known encyclopaedia stated firmly that psychology was the 'chief source of the principles or laws which make up the science or theory of education'.[4] In that same year, John Dewey published a textbook on *Psychology*, and started to move into an exploration of educational problems that was to continue throughout his long career and was to provide many of the basic ideas for the educational reformers of the twentieth century. The upsurge of interest in experimental psychology, the systematic application of psychological ideas and findings to educational practice by some leading educators, and the willingness of many teachers to seek for a connection between their methods of teaching and the course of their pupils' development, were important late nineteenth century anticipations of the first quarter of the twentieth century.

Secondly, the nation-state in western countries had, during the course of the nineteenth century, replaced the church as the principal educational authority. Church schools continued to flourish in most countries, but the principal task of providing the money and the educational facilities for mass elementary education, and for a good proportion of secondary and tertiary education had, by 1900, fallen to the public authorities. Education had not yet become a matter of great and continuing public importance. Occasionally, communities would divide excitedly on educational questions, and national elections might involve important educational issues, but, by and large, about 1900, the leading politicians and public figures did not give much time or thought to education. It had, however, come firmly into the public domain. As the nation's needs changed, so they could be translated into new educational developments; as public attitudes changed, so, too, they could be reflected more readily in school programs. Increasingly, in the twentieth century, as new ideologies came into play, as rivalries between nations intensified, as the growth of technological society called for higher levels of educational competence, there was an interest in the more effective provision of education by public authorities. By mid-century education had become a major public concern. The political, social, and economic effects of public education were widely seen and painstakingly, if not always accurately, calculated, and the impact of public control on the provision and conduct of schools had become an important part of the educational history of the twentieth century.

THREE PERIODS OF EDUCATION

In the course of the twentieth century, education has passed through three recognisable stages:

(i)   The Educational Awakening, c.1900-16

From the 1890's to World War I there was a general stirring in educational theory and practice. The impelling forces of industrial expansion, middle class ambition, and nationalism had begun to direct attention to the possibility of making more extensive use of education to promote these rising interests. New tasks were explored, fresh approaches to education were canvassed, and reforms, usually modest and conservative, but occasionally radical, were introduced to meet the new situation.

(ii)   Educational Aspiration, 1916-45

The second period began about the time John Dewey wrote his classic statement of educational faith, *Democracy and Education* in 1916, and continued until the latter years of World War II. The trends of the first period were consolidated, and the conflict between mass and elitist education was heightened. The optimism that flowed from World War I, and the fundamental re-examination of social, political, and economic questions brought about by the depression of the 1930's were a challenge and stimulus to educators. It became a time of heady aspiration in which ideals were formulated, the relationship of education to society carefully scrutinised, and a wealth of new practices and experiments introduced which began to put into operation wide and substantial changes in the objectives, content, and methods of teaching.

(iii)   Educational Reconstruction and Expansion, 1945-75

Following World War II there was initially a period of solid reformulation, as ideas expressed in the 1920's and 1930's were built into new structures to cope with the insistent demands of the mid-century. It was an era of planning in which the world's underdeveloped areas emerged rapidly into national consciousness and sought to use education as a means of developing social cohesion and economic strength. The second part of the period was characterised by continued expansion in both developed and underdeveloped countries, and by a wide range of projects to reconstruct school curricula in an effort to match the revolutionary changes that were occurring in science, in technology, and in social organisation.

---

4   A.E. Fletcher, (ed.) *Sonnenschein's Cyclopaedia of Education*, Sonnenschein, London, 1889, p. 290.

EDUCATION AND THE TWENTIETH CENTURY REVOLUTION

Education throughout most of human history, has been concerned principally with handing on an established intellectual and moral tradition, with adjusting conservatively to new circumstances, and with preparing young people to earn a living. Twentieth century education is an animal of a different colour. It has not abandoned its conservatism entirely, but it has sought more actively to question and to break with established traditions. Its task has been not only that of preservation but also that of criticism and reconstruction.

In an age of revolution, old information and old principles lose their relevance, old standards fade, and old forms of organisation become inappropriate. Even basic methods of thinking come under challenge. The schools, since the beginning of the century, have entered into their new role with varying degrees of consciousness, ability, and zeal. Where political revolution has been abrupt, they have quickly applied themselves to teaching the ideas, producing the kinds of persons and qualifications, and supporting the aspirations that would further the cause of the new society. Where revolution has been more gradual, they have remodelled their curricula, often slowly and reluctantly, to take account of and to provide a more satisfactory interpretation of the new trends, they have expanded their activities to the cultivation of the whole person of their pupils in the changing society, and they have encouraged the hopes and ambitions of a steadily increasing number of young people to seek, through education, for individual advancement and general social betterment.

In educational method and through the pattern of their organisation, schools have tried to meet the demands of the new era. Their role, in consequence, has been both destructive and creative. The teaching, for example, of scientific method and the techniques of literary and historical criticism, the provision of a richly varied primary education and of comprehensive secondary schools, and the vast widening of educational opportunities have been solvents of established modes of living and thinking. On the other hand, the association that has been encouraged between intellectual and practical activity has given a new dimension to social and cultural life, the link that has been forged between political aims and educational processes has been a significant factor in shaping the various kinds of mass society that have flourished in the twentieth century, and the general lifting of the cultural level achieved by the extension of education has created, in many nations, a new consciousness of human possibilities and has raised expectations of higher standards of social welfare.

It has not, however, been a case of unbroken progress. Several factors have produced delays and difficulties.

Teaching in schools has been imperfect and uneven. Ambitious aims have been frustrated by imperfect instruments. Frequently, worthwhile reforms have been proposed only to founder because teachers were inadequately prepared to put them into practice or the public were not ready to accept them.

Inspiration has faltered in the face of inescapable routine. The teaching profession has always been inclined towards order and system, and has not usually looked with favour on innovations that upset established practice. The tendency to resist the new and to put a brake on change was reinforced in the course of the twentieth century with the vast enlargement of educational responsibilities. The very considerable growth in the scale of educational organisations was accompanied by bureaucratic procedures and controls that sometimes, because of their great range, could speedily implement widespread reform but generally tended to slow progress down and inhibit the introduction of radical change. Large educational institutions tended to place an emphasis on stability and promotion by seniority. Their concern was for the efficient maintenance of day-to-day administration, and they had little time or money to spare for innovation.

Some political and social trends which were responsible for substantial educational change proved also, in some ways, to be inhibiting. Nationalism, for example, a powerful spur to development in both western and ex-colonial countries, gave to education under fascism a one-sided emphasis that crushed several other promising developments. The search for equality of opportunity stimulated the spread of education, but also, in many countries, led to a uniformity in school programs in an effort to avoid discrimination, and to a great dependence upon prescribed syllabuses and examinations to ensure fairness in the selection of students for further education.

From time to time, also, reaction has set in. American business interests, the demands of Russian planners, the predilections of French literary intellectuals, the attitudes of African nationalists — all, in some ways, radical influences — have at times effectively and conservatively protected their own interests to the detriment of the advances cherished by some contemporary educators. But, by and large, the teaching profession has steadily remodelled its procedures and the content of its curricula to match, and sometimes to outpace, the general movement of the century, and education has managed to play an interestingly varied role in the continuous reconstruction of society.

Throughout the century there have been three basic and related trends:

- a politicising of education;

- a concern with betterment through education;

- a reorienting of the educational process from instructional work to an interest in the cultivation of a wider range of human behaviour.

(i) The Politicising of Education

The politicising of education passed through three phases:

(a) Solidarity was the object of the first phase. The efforts to make good Americans out of a wide range of European immigrants, the use of the imperial rescript of 1890 in schools to unite all Japanese in loyal obedience to the emperor, the national day celebrations, memorial services, patriotic songs, literature, and history texts of England, Australia, France, Italy and of almost every nation were designed to instil common sentiments and attitudes which would cement the people of a particular country together into a common allegiance. Cubberley, writing in 1909 on changing conceptions of education in the U.S.A., expressed the current position very well: 'the task is thrown more and more upon the school of instilling into all a social and political consciousness that will lead to unity amid diversity, and to united action for the preservation and betterment of our democratic institutions'.[5] The school's task of building conviction in the young generation was intensified during World War I, and again, in response to the various political revolutions of the inter-war period and the independence movements in developing countries after World War II.

Nationalism was the strongest force making for solidarity and the one most assiduously cultivated in schools. The national rivalries of the early twentieth century prompted educators to devise ways to increase their pupils' knowledge of their own country and determination to further its interests. Intellectually, by increasing the national content of the school curriculum and emotionally, by patriotic speeches, symbols, displays and ceremonies, pupils were bound to their own nation. In the two world wars and the period between them, nationalistic teaching grew to excess. Again, in the 1950's and 1960's, new nation-states, released from colonialism and needing to build new ties and loyalties, enlisted the help of the schools. In consequence, there was much seeking after appropriate local material for the curriculum, and an enthusiastic cultivation of indigenous and patriotic music, songs, and ceremonies.

In the process of securing the loyalty and devoted service of the population to the particular way of life or political party that was in power an elaborate apparatus of persuasion was set up. The school, and often associated with it, a youth organisation, were at the centre of the operation. The twentieth century, with its variety of revolutionary movements and competing ideologies, became an era of persuasion in which the resources of education were substantially and often ingeniously involved. Mao Tsetung, whose country 'put politics in command' and became one of the most thoroughly committed to the saturation of education by politics, summed up the position when he declared: 'Not to have a correct political view is like having no soul, and, therefore for Chinese youth, the basic aim of education is to serve proletarian politics.'[6]

(b) Social, economic, and political justice was the object of the second phase of the politicising of education. It is closely related to the second major trend of education in the twentieth century, that concerned with general betterment. Most social welfare and general betterment policies had political overtones, if not active political associations.

Social efficiency was a much discussed aim of education in the first half of the twentieth century. It usually meant three things: that pupils should grasp the essential ideas and understand the civil organisation of their country, that they should have an adequate and sufficiently flexible general and vocational education to fit them to become useful citizens, and that, as good citizens, they should be aware of the weaknesses and strengths of their society and be prepared to help make it work as efficiently as possible. To achieve the last objective, that of advancing the public welfare, pupils must be in a position eventually to act as good and efficient citizens. There must therefore be adequate opportunity to prepare for and to provide service to society. The search for equality of opportunity became the principal feature of this phase. Initially it was important to

---

[5] E.P. Cubberley, *Changing Conceptions of Education*, Houghton Mifflin, Boston, 1909, p. 55.

[6] Mao Tsetung, *On the Correct Handling of Contradictions Among the People, The Question of the Intellectuals*, pocket edn Foreign Language Press, Peking, 1967, p. 202.

provide universal primary education. In developed countries this was largely achieved soon after the beginning of the twentieth century. As civilisation multiplied its complications, however, and it required more time and greater maturity to come to an elementary understanding of it, the new century found that its task was to provide universal secondary education.

At the beginning of the century primary education was regarded as the form and level of education suitable for the mass of pupils; secondary education was for the elite. Already, however, substantial moves had been made in the U.S.A. to make the high school into a normal continuation of the elementary school. The development of six-year elementary schools, the establishment of junior high schools in 1909-10 and their subsequent growth in popularity helped considerably. Nevertheless, until World War I, secondary education in the U.S.A. was far from universal and was popularly regarded as being principally concerned with the preparation of students for entry to tertiary colleges. In Europe, secondary schools tended to be fed by their own preparatory schools, and secondary and primary schools operated, for the most part, as two separate systems with a small amount of transfer between them.

The proliferation of the middle class, particularly the growth of the education-hungry salaried and professional middle class, brought larger numbers of interested pupils to secondary education. By the 1920's middle class educational expectations were beginning to be shared by many individuals in the lower classes, and the great twentieth century transformation was beginning. Education was starting to become a mass phenomenon. It was leaving the stage of primary education for the masses, and secondary and higher for the elite, and was entering the period in which it was to be the general expectation of everyone that they should have the opportunity of as much education as they could manage and might wish to avail themselves of. The transformation was not brought about quickly or easily. There was a long and often bitter struggle between the advocates of elite and mass education, the elitists groundlessly fearing that a loss of quality would accompany an increase in quantity.

The critical battles were fought over secondary education in the developed countries. The colonial administrators of underdeveloped countries tended to reflect the controversies of the developed countries, and, on the occasion of independence or revolution, their successors were inclined to opt for as much mass education as they could afford.

The obvious socio-economic class bias of secondary schools was initially broken down by admitting pupils of high ability from the primary schools; gradually, entry was extended to all pupils who could profit by a secondary education; and evidence of their ability to profit in this manner was demonstrated by selective entrance examinations. In due course all pupils proceeded automatically to some form of secondary level schooling, and in some countries, types of secondary schools were multiplied to cater for the variety of abilities and interests that followed the increase in number of pupils. By the 1940's serious questions were being asked about the allocation of pupils into different kinds of secondary schools.

Discussion on the most suitable means of providing opportunity for all pupils to receive secondary education grew in intensity up to about the 1960's.

Soon after World War II, in the 1940's, tertiary level education began to expand rapidly, and the consideration of wider opportunities for tertiary education vied in interest with that of the discussions in secondary education. By the 1970's the question of whether to establish sufficient facilities for universal secondary education in developed countries was settled; the matter, however, of the most appropriate content for secondary education was not. Nor was it yet clear what form wider opportunity in tertiary education should take.

It had, by then, become apparent that providing universal facilities did not necessarily equalise educational opportunities throughout the community. Discrimination and expectation were also important factors. Sex, social class, and race were important determiners of the amount and kind of education received by individuals in most countries. Educational opportunities for girls were restricted, in comparison with those available for boys, in some places by an active policy of discrimination, and in others, effectively but less obviously, by society's lower expectations for girls.

Similarly, and especially in the colonial territories, the native population received an education inferior to that of the white colonisers and were thought to be less capable of profiting by equal educational facilities. Lower socio-economic status was also a handicap to children: there was less ability to pay when fees were required, there was less ambition to progress up the educational ladder, the children were less favoured in health, nutrition, sleep, clothing, study and recreational circumstances, and, generally speaking, their educational facilities were inferior. Lower class children, in consequence, had a somewhat restricted opportunity to succeed. Middle class children, on the other hand, tended to receive more encouragement from parents and from the circumstances of their environment.

Attempts to compensate for inferior educational opportunities, and to ensure that available educational opportunities were used to the best advantage, were begun in some countries early in the century by associating some social welfare services with the schools. Thus, in England national legislation enabled educational authorities in 1906 to provide for hot midday meals for necessitous children, and, in the following year introduced a national school medical service. Before the end of World War I several educational authorities in the U.S.A. and in England were employing school psychologists to test children and, in due course, to develop guidance services for schools. The early educational psychologists began to accumulate data about individual differences among children that was extended and enriched in the 1920's and 1930's by their successors. It was not, however, until the 1940's that it became widely realised that differences in children's school performances were closely associated with their social and cultural environment. The full subtlety of the discrimination was gradually revealed and documented by educational sociologists in a large number of studies in many countries during the 1940's and subsequently. The matter then became very much an open political issue.

In order to provide genuine equality of educational opportunity it was necessary for a governmental authority to intervene with measures to improve the social and cultural condition of the disadvantaged. In essence, it meant an abridgement of liberty in the interests of fraternity. The social solidarity, in pursuit of which education was already engaged, had to be extended from something largely emotional and sentimental, to the practical reform of social relationships and conditions of living. Education thus became inescapably involved in a general program of social reform, often halting, piecemeal, and reluctantly entered into by conservative governments, but sometimes willingly and systematically undertaken by governments which welcomed the growing trend toward collectivism that marked the course of the twentieth century.

(c) The reconstruction of society was the object of the third phase of education's marriage with politics. John Dewey in 1916 had announced 'the reconstruction of man in society' as the aim of the educational revolution that he was trying to achieve. His fellow progressives in Europe and the U.S.A. seconded his efforts with a variety of programs that would encourage pupils to inquire into current social practices, to examine their own role in society, and to build up knowledge, habits, and attitudes that would make them into dedicated and responsible democrats. In reconstructing their own views, the pupils would also be taking part in the reconstruction of society.

If it was possible and desirable to teach pupils to examine their society critically and think of ways in which some aspects of it might be improved, why should not schools play a more active part in the process of social change? By teaching pupils to formulate their ideals for society, and by involving them in practical operations that would help to bring the ideal closer to realisation, schools could contribute directly to the reconstruction of society. *Dare the Schools Build a New Social Order?* was the title of a widely discussed book by a leading American educator in the early 1930's. It brought to notice the dramatic extension of the role of education during the first three decades of the twentieth century — from unappreciated Cinderella pursuing the humdrum work of elementary instruction to possible fairy godmother bringing a new civilisation into being.

The transformation was not a dream. It could be seen to be actually happening. The schools were not, unaided and alone, building up a new society, but they were, at least, giving vigorous aid to the process. The nursery schools of Deptford, for example, were slowly changing the child-rearing practices and the health habits of the slum parents in East London; primary and secondary schools in most countries had opened a new range of activities and recreational interests that were causing a widespread change and enrichment of later adult interests; the technical schools of Germany had been instrumental in building a powerful industrial nation and in rebuilding it after World War I, and Kerschensteiner's special version of them in Munich had combined solid citizenship with technical proficiency; the universities had been doubling the output of scientists in every decade since the beginning of the century, affecting by this and by their research the face and nature of the current technological revolution; the universities had also, by the 1930's, begun to establish substantial faculties in the social sciences from which came critical and constructive work that affected the general climate of the times and was sometimes responsible for engineering new governmental social policies and practices.

For the most part these were indirect and unsystematic influences that the schools exercised on society, and, obviously, they were not generated uniquely and solely by the educational system. The schools were part of the social fabric, and they were affected by current social trends.

What was unique about the situation, as it had developed by the 1930's, was that the schools had become not just a part of national social policy but active instruments of the policy. It was an inevitable result of the widening of the functions of education that had been taking place since the beginning of the century.

Education had never in its history been solely concerned with intellectual development. Schools had always supervised their pupils' manners and tried to influence their character and general development. When once they extended their care to the pupils' environment, they became involved in social policy. The extension took place at the time when educational facilities were being greatly expanded and the state had begun to become involved in providing education on a widespread scale. The schools were inescapably caught up in national social policy as instruments through which a society or its leaders could attempt to correct what might be regarded as undesirable social habits or reinforce a positive change in a forward direction. From the 1930's on, the social function of education became clearly one of importance, and was widely accepted by legislators and school administrators. If, for example, consumers' habits were unsatisfactory, then consumer education should be taught in the schools; if young people appeared to be more careless than older ones in driving cars and cycles, then driver education in schools was advocated; if society desired to expand and speed up its technological progress, then special programs for training science teachers were introduced and pupils were encouraged to take more science courses; if a change in the distribution of a country's manpower was sought, controls could be placed on the numbers of persons entering various secondary and tertiary institutions and courses, and government money could be distributed in such a way as to encourage one part of the educational system rather than another; if opportunities for various sections of society to develop and contribute effectively to social progress appeared to be lacking, then programs of compensatory education and social assistance could be tried out. Moves of these kinds became the commonplace of educational policy in the post-World War II period.

What was still more fundamental was the move to use the schools on a large scale to help to make a radical change in the social and cultural complexion of a country. Basic Education inspired by Gandhi in the 1930's, and, in a halting way, by some of the mission schools established in underdeveloped countries attempted this task. Without doubt, the most widespread and successful effort was that of the communist countries after their respective revolutions. Russia, starting in 1917, set the pattern which was taken up by the countries of Eastern Europe after World War II, and developed into a most thorough politicising of education by the Chinese in the People's Republic established by the revolution of 1949. The aim in each case was to bring about a total reconstruction of society. This implied a complete re-education of the whole population, so that it became a communist society in which the people not only accepted a communist way of life but actively and strenuously took part in the building and strengthening of it. The fundamental task was that of political education to ensure the total political commitment of the population. To that end all educational work was permeated with appropriate ideological content, and every opportunity was taken to educate the community. The country became an educative society in which every activity and every communication tended to have an educational purpose or, at least, some educational reference.

The direction and pace of the new society's growth were controlled by a process of state-wide economic and social planning within which education had an important role to fill. To meet the specific requirements, material and ideological, of successive plans, the organisation of the school system and the curriculum were appropriately redesigned. Beyond the basic tasks of political persuasion and manpower production the schools and the youth movement associated with them had other important responsibilities, such as the preparation of teachers for the new society, and the discharge of urgent social and educational tasks required in the program of reconstruction. In this fashion, education entered directly and deliberately into the reconstruction of society, sometimes leading the process, sometimes directed by it and supplementing the work of other agencies, and sometimes itself undergoing transformation and reconstruction.

(ii) Education for Individual and Social Betterment

The process of betterment through education had both an individual and a social side.

(a) Individual Betterment. Throughout its history, education has been one of the ways by which poor but talented children were sometimes able to rise to positions of influence, and the schools have always had the responsibility of maintaining a supply of adequately trained recruits for the community's work force. The functions of social elevation and vocational training continued to be part of the task of education in the twentieth century. Ambition, social pressure, and national interest, however, played more substantial parts than in the preceding centuries.

By World War I it was apparent that the strong competitive push of the middle classes was affecting their attitude to schools. In England, for example, the *Public Schools Year Book* bore witness to the recent foundation of a substantially increased number of highly esteemed, independent secondary schools for the aspiring sons of middle class parents; and in the U.S.A. in the 1920's there was wide discussion of studies which showed that the life earnings of individuals increased with the number of years completed in school, elementary school leavers earning less than high school graduates who, in turn, were outpaced by the college men.[7] The cash and prestige value of education continued to be an important incentive to middle class children to better themselves by extending their schooling, and by endeavouring to attend schools and universities which they regarded as offering the best education. To pressure to attend was added pressure to achieve, as increasing numbers entered the competition during the course of the century. Individuals, in order to profit fully from their schooling, needed to be able to produce evidence not only that they had attended but that they had also been proficient. Over and above well-known scholarship and matriculation examinations, tests at entry and exit, and intermediate tests on the way through school multiplied. By the 1920's certificates from a variety of public examining bodies had become important educational currency, and were playing an increasingly significant role in education.

It became clear in the inter-war period that the requirements of examining bodies, usually external to the school, were tending to dominate school work, dictating the aims of the school and determining much of its curriculum. During this period substantial investigations were made into the nature and conduct of examining. The reliability and validity of examinations came into serious question, and methods of testing were reappraised. Educational psychologists, who had been interested in devising various kinds of tests in a variety of fields since Meumann and Lay had brought Wundt's experimental attitude into educational research at the turn of the century, expanded their efforts to develop more satisfactory testing procedures, to relate tests of ability to tests of achievement, and to assess the impact of examining on the process of teaching. In the post-World War II period, researchers were to develop considerable sophistication in the analysis of data from tests, and in relating the form and content of testing to educational objectives.

The great interest in the testing and sorting of pupils that grew up in the twentieth century was attributable in large part to the multiplication of educated people. Never before, except in rare communities, had more than a small fraction of the population received any but the most meagre of educations. In the twentieth century, education became a major industry. Initially in developed countries and eventually in underdeveloped ones, every person came to have an extensive concern in it. The effect of this phenomenon on twentieth century life has been considerable and widespread. In this context, it is clear that the increase in the educated population stimulated the demand for new products and services and provided reasonably suitable occupants for the new jobs that were created. In this way it enlarged both an individual's and a society's opportunity for economic advancement. At the same time, it made more necessary the use of testing devices and selective procedures that would discriminate between well-educated applicants, and it entailed a greater degree of competition for the kind of education that would bring the highest rewards.

(b) Social betterment and the expansion of education were closely related from early in the century. Some of the clearest indications of a growing interest by the educated public in the betterment of society came from American literature at the turn of the century. It was the muckraking period in which the deficiencies of current living were forcefully and mercilessly exposed by public-spirited novelists and journalists. Thus, J.M. Rice, in a series of articles in 1892, made known the imperfections of American schools,[8] Lincoln Steffens and Jacob Riis uncovered the scandals of New York and other large cities, and Upton Sinclair and Thorsten Veblen made big business their target. They demonstrated the effect of the social environment on the behaviour of individuals, and they argued the moral duty of society to improve the condition of those whose opportunities were curtailed by corruption, mismanagement, or poverty of circumstances. Their campaign was a foretaste of the intellectual and moral

---

[7] For a summary of these studies, see H.F. Clark, *Cost and Quality in Public Education*, Syracuse University Press, 1963.

[8] J.M. Rice, *The Public-School System of the United States*, Century, New York, 1893.

commitment to social betterment that the growth of education brought with it during the course of the century in many parts of the world.

The twentieth century became a meliorative century. Notwithstanding periods of violence and total war, constant individual greed and exploitation, most nations steadily pursued a policy of improving the social and cultural conditions of their inhabitants, and, at times, even embarked on spectacular ventures of international betterment. From time to time scepticism and disillusion set in, but the spirit of beneficence managed to hold on remarkably well through the course of the century. Crises brought out new enthusiasm. The muckrakers and liberal reformers of the turn of the century were merely the start. Out of World War I, for example, emerged a band of optimistic European revolutionaries and reformers; the great depression of the 1930's threw up the New Dealers in the U.S.A.; from World War II came England's Beveridge Report and a packet of social legislation; and in the 1960's and 1970's, crises in colonial countries accelerated social reform, and independence brought a further large expansion of it.

Betterment was of two kinds, improvement in welfare, and increase in economic production. In both, education was an important factor. Early in the century arguments were advanced principally on the importance of vocational education as a means of improving industrial production, later the claims of general education received more attention, and after World War II, in the period of organisation and expansion, moves were made towards more careful planning of specific kinds and levels of education to fit national economic development plans. This progress was a political as well as an economic movement, and involved the schools both as participators in political re-education and national planning, and as trainers and producers of suitable human economic units who would help to raise the productive level of the country. One of the main problems of the twentieth century state was to effect a marriage between social welfare and high economic production. To the partners of such a union education was both maid of honour and best man.

(iii) From Instruction to Education

Within the classrooms of the twentieth century there was a steady movement from an instructional to an educational process. At various times during the first half of the twentieth century, in a large number of countries, the national departments concerned with the administration of schools changed from Ministries of Public Instruction to Ministries of Education. It was a significant change of name. It indicated the wider functions that teachers were expected to perform, and gave recognition to a changed concept of the nature of the teaching process.

The characteristics of an instructional process are formality, orderliness, arrangement of teaching procedures in advance, transference of information from an authoritative source to a pupil, and a concern for the logical arrangement of the material to be learnt. Education may share some of these characteristics, but it places its emphasis on inquiry, pupil activity, relevance, and a wide range of possible pupil growth.

The change from an instructional to an educational process in schools was a humanising process which moved the focus of teaching from subject-matter to the pupil. The teacher became a person whose principal skill lay in understanding children and the ways of assisting them in the development of their abilities. Without ceasing to be interested in solid learning, the teacher was no longer a pedant. His professional knowledge was not merely the content of a subject; it was also, in this 'century of the child', the behaviour of children and the meaning and means of educating persons in a society.

Though for the most part an unspectacular growth, the change had several periods of great vitality. The Herbartian movement which dominated the turn of the century was a mine of stimulating ideas on education, but, paradoxically, by providing a method of teaching that could be systematised, it helped to set up an instructional procedure that proved to be popular and lasting. The discussion surrounding Herbartianism, the development of Dewey's experimental school in Chicago, the initial spread of the activity movement, and the beginning of the study of educational psychology helped to make the first decade of the century a stimulating and productive one for the science of education. The next spurt came in the 1920's with an intensification of interest in providing ways of catering for individual differences among children. The Dalton and Winnetka plans became widely known and tried in many countries, the New Education Fellowship began a series of conferences that attracted leading educators from all parts of the world, and serious curriculum studies were made, leading to radical proposals for reform, notably in the U.S.A. and the U.S.S.R. In the 1930's efforts to relate school curricula to relevant social purposes and individual needs increased, and were responsible for producing the most interesting and important theoretical and practical proposals of the century. Curriculum work was again prominent in the 1960's stimulated by the development in the 1950's of the first man-made earth satellite. In that period teams of educators and scholars worked together to try to produce disciplined and relevant subject-matter in all fields of the school curriculum. There was also a revival of interest in the individual programming of pupils' work. Studies of children's growth were extended, teacher-student relationships became more relaxed, and pupils were encouraged to participate more actively in the learning process.

The change throughout the century was a slow, chequered growth which had three principal aspects to it. It was associated intimately with the growth and serious study of educational psychology; it was characterised by a move towards more active pupil participation in the educational process; and it was a fairly continuous passage towards producing a curriculum which would have more relevance for the pupil and his society.

(a) The growth of the study of educational psychology. There were two main lines in the development of educational psychology that bore on the movement in education from an instructional to an educational process.

First there was a general searching examination of existing educational procedures by educational psychologists interested in the functions of human behaviour. Starting with the work of Meumann and Lay, and extended by the efforts of Claparède and Thorndike and their associates in many countries, there was, in the first forty years of the twentieth century, a multitude of studies on educational ideas and on the proficiency of educational practices in all the subjects of the curriculum. The testing of school performances and teaching procedures was supplemented by a widespread and increasing interest in testing pupils' capabilities, intelligence being the main target. In the post-World War II period, studies in cognitive processes became popular, and major efforts were made to apply their often abstruse results in the classroom. Theories of learning, and teaching techniques in line with them, emerged from time to time from these studies and collections of data. Their general purport was to encourage the kind of teaching that involved pupils in situations in which they had to inquire, seek for meanings, and learn how to make use of information and skills they had discovered for themselves.

Parallel with this kind of trend in the work of educational psychologists there was another movement in the field. It was the impact of the various schools of dynamic psychology on educational activities. Bergson made the idea of *élan vital* popular with educational reformers early in the century, and it reinforced their efforts to encourage creativity and more active participation by pupils in the educational process. McDougall persuasively argued the case for a hormic or drive psychology

which inspired some educators to regard children's felt needs and interests as the baseline for learning and teaching. Freud and the psychoanalytic school exposed a world of hidden motivation and early childhood experiences which induced educators to take more account of non-intellectual factors in the development of children.

Interest had been introduced as an important element in education by the Herbartians; by the 1920's, educators had deepened and extended their views of it and were beginning to replace it with concepts such as motivation, satisfaction, and emotional tone. They were stimulated by the dynamic psychologists also to think of the learning and teaching process as a more complex fabric of emotional, conative, and cognitive forces than they had customarily allowed for. In consequence, teachers tended to become more perceptive in observing children's activity, more inclined to relate the various aspects of children's behaviour together, more interested in trying to develop integrated persons, and more prone to search through the children's social environment and seek its effect on their performance. Discipline in schools became more informal, and schools, in general, more humane and attractive places in which children and adults might work and enjoy their time together.

By the 1940's and 1950's the psychological study of human relations had become popular, and the dynamics of classroom behaviour, teacher-pupil relationships, and the social psychology of the schools had become objects of study. The effect of this trend on teaching was to increase its complexity still further. The teacher who had been trained in 1900 had had to study a program directed mainly to the management of the classroom; his counterpart in 1970 was expected to learn how he might foster the development of children in a nurturing social environment.

(b) The growth of an activity approach in education. Nineteenth century schools had cultivated both knowledge and character. The educators of the twentieth century continued with the same responsibilities. They endeavoured to introduce into them, however, a greater sense of participation. Educators in the twentieth century had a greater realisation that, as man does not merely think, but also acts and cares, the educational process should go beyond intellectual training, to assist young people to learn how to act effectively and responsibly.

Teachers during the course of the twentieth century aimed at encouraging pupils to acquire understanding rather than mere knowledge, and came increasingly to realise that understanding without action was an incomplete understanding. Dewey was the first to make this point in his experimental school at Chicago (1896-1903) where he developed a curriculum of social occupations. Decroly created a great deal of interest in Europe, in the immediate pre- and post-World War I generation, by developing a curriculum based on centres of interest; and, in the 1920's and 1930's, project work which, in theory and occasionally in practice, involved pupils in intellectual inquiry, collection of data, analysis, and consequential action, became popular in primary schools in many parts of the world. Current aspirations were summed up in the English Board of Education Report on *The Primary School* in 1931: 'the curriculum is to be thought of in terms of activity and experience rather than of knowledge to be acquired and facts to be stored.'[9]

Although the ideal was never realised, the efforts of progressive educators, and their experimentation with activity methods and activity curricula, left a substantial deposit. The 1953 English Ministry of Education statement of advice on primary schools was able to repeat the words of its predecessor of twenty years earlier and to refer to them as being close to reality in many English schools. At the secondary school level the principles and some of the practices of the radical revision of curricula for junior and senior high schools in the U.S.A., that were worked out along activity lines in the 1930's, appeared in the education textbooks of the 1950's, and were incorporated in many of the new programs that were developed in the 1960's and 1970's in many parts of the world.

The most dramatic effort to combine action with intellectual work were the programs in productive work that communist countries developed at all levels in their schools. After much experimentation in the 1920's with projects and various forms of labour education, and in the 1930's and 1940's with ways of putting polytechnic ideas into the curriculum, the U.S.S.R. and the countries of eastern Europe devised a variety of ways, with which they have continued to experiment, of ensuring that all pupils have various kinds of experiences of productive work. The Chinese in the 1950's made productive work an even more substantial part of the school program, seeing the practice of teaching pupils the virtue and habit of working productively on behalf of their society as a mainspring of education. During the Cultural Revolution of the late 1960's the practice was intensified in schools and was extended to adult intellectual workers who were required to spend appropriate periods in manual labour.

The activity movement in education was a central part of a new view of the task of education that developed in the twentieth century. Herbartianism had started it by presenting the teacher as a person who, piece by piece, formed and built the mind of a pupil. The general trend of thought in many fields early in the century supported the effort and ambition of human beings to take firmer control of their environment and to fashion their own future. Educators, responding to the mood of the times, began to seek ways in which they could increase their command not only over the training of their pupils' intellectual processes but also over the shaping of whole human beings. Educators became more and more interested as the century progressed in the conscious and deliberate shaping of human behaviour. It was this that progressive educators sought to do with their activity schools.

The pattern for the shaping was usually a loose one. It generally meant an encouragement of expressive behaviour associated with a tolerance for expressiveness in other people. They sought to develop authenticity and responsibility, helping pupils to find the best way to build up a genuine character and express a solidly formed opinion. Where optimism in human potential for building its own new personality and new world was married to a strongly held political philosophy, as happened often in socialist circles, and was exemplified particularly in Makarenko's work, the constructive drive was less tolerant of deviance and more inclined to work towards a recognised ideal in personal character and public social organisation.

(c) The search for relevance. Lack of relevance was a phrase widely used during the twentieth century as a criticism of educational practices that were traditional or were unrelated to current personal or social needs. Since change was the very tissue of life, and education was a vital and determining part of contemporary life, for some aspects of education to lack relevance was a powerful criticism of it. Relevance was also used constructively, and as a guide towards the improvement of current and future practice.

In respect to the school curriculum the criterion of relevance implied the need for two kinds of changes. First, there was a shift in emphasis in most school subjects from a knowledge of facts to a grasp of principles and then to a command of methods of work. The explosion of knowledge, which characterised most fields in the twentieth century and showed up spectacularly in the

---

[9]   Great Britain, Board of Education, *The Primary School*, Report of the Consultative Committee (Hadow), H.M.S.O., London, 1931, p. 93.

sciences, resulted in a great increase in the factual content of the subjects taught in schools. It was recognised in due course that an indefinite extension of subject-matter was not feasible, and would not, in any case, lead to a mastery of the subject. Accordingly, generalisations and principles were seen by some curriculum makers by the 1920's to be the important constituents. A grasp of them provided the network of inter-connections and related ideas that were the essence of a subject; and the intellectual exercise involved in working them out and in relating them to each other was important basic mental training. It was found, however, that principles also had a habit of changing, of being superseded, and of becoming irrelevant. What was left in the subject discipline, and was found to remain reasonably constant, were its methods of acquiring, analysing, and expressing its data. Writers such as Dewey had argued since the turn of the century for the teaching of scientific method, and some educators before World War II had sought to emphasise the methodological sides of their subjects. To this view many curriculum makers and teachers turned in the curriculum revival of the 1960's and 1970's. Particularly in the physical, biological, and social sciences, while not neglecting current trends and current knowledge in the subjects, teachers encouraged their pupils to spend more time on activities such as experiments, field excursions, using original documents, and carrying out social surveys, through which they would learn, in the various subjects, how to gather data and what conclusions they could draw from it.

Within the traditional subject framework, to be relevant meant to be concerned with and capable of handling the method which the experts in the subject habitually used. A world of change was to be controlled not by an accumulation of facts and principles but by mastering the best methods of acquiring, understanding, interpreting, and using facts and principles.

The second kind of change in the direction of greater relevance was a utilitarian trend. What was relevant to the prosperity of European, American, and Japanese society in the early years of the century was a good supply of technicians, hence much interest was taken in vocational education, and some in the teaching of science and mathematics. Latin and Greek which had been at the centre of the nineteenth century secondary school curriculum began to wane and were replaced by a greater interest in the national language. In the 1930's the great depression and the growing connection between education and politics gave greater significance to the study of social questions, and, in consequence, the social sciences began to assume a larger role in

all levels of education. The rapid extension of science teaching at secondary and tertiary levels in the 1950's and 1960's in both developed and underdeveloped countries was associated with a recognition of its utility for national defence and industrial progress. The expansion of education, particularly tertiary education at the same period, was generally attached to some form of national planning through which it was hoped to produce the most useful types and levels of manpower.

In a wider and fundamentally more important sense the schools were concerned with relevance in the kind of person they sought to produce. Education, which in the past might operate primarily for the extension of scholarship or for the cultural, vocational, or social interests of a particular group, became attached, in the twentieth century, to the interests of society in general. The trend affected the conduct of schools. Not only were subjects and methods of teaching modified and recast, but the atmosphere and discipline of the schools were also gradually changed. An important result was the growth in pupils' responsibility for their own conduct. Teachers became interested in producing self-directive and socially sensitive pupils. Interesting and notable experiments in self-government were made, of which those of Homer Lane in the U.S.A. and England and those in the U.S.S.R. became the most widely known. By the 1920's almost every primary and secondary school was experimenting with some form of pupil participation in school government. It was intended to be a training in self-direction, and a means of preparing pupils in a more relevant way for the greater and more evenly distributed responsibilities of marital and social life that the more equalitarian circumstances of the twentieth century brought to many people. During the next half-century, pupils' opportunities for exercising responsibility were steadily increased, sometimes beyond the level intended and planned by teachers and school programs.

At the tertiary level, university students' interest and participation in current affairs was indicated by their occasional intervention in political crises, most frequently in South American and Asian countries in pre-World War II decades. The great expansion in numbers, an increasing interest in the study of the social sciences, and a growing political sophistication among students led in the 1960's and 1970's to a series of explosive student protests and uprisings in many countries throughout the world. The movement was designed to put into their hands more responsibility for the government of their own universities and colleges and to draw public attention to the inadequacy and irrelevance of particular national policies of which they disapproved.

While school pupils and university students were learning to become more interested and participant in school and public affairs, teachers too were changing. From the work of the early educational psychologists, teachers became aware of differing patterns of child growth and very conscious of individual differences among the children whom they taught. Efforts to ensure that each child managed to get the education most stimulating and appropriate to him led to the development of educational guidance services and the practice of specially devised remedial teaching. Out of the attention given to studying children and to analysing and experimenting with the educational process, a substantial impetus was given to the study of education, particularly among the western nations.

The development of education as a professional discipline has been substantially an achievement of the twentieth century. The coincidence of the Herbartian and the child study movements at the turn of the century provided a growing body of knowledge from research, school practice, and theory relevant to the changing situation of the time. The subsequent expansion of educational psychology and later additions from educational sociology increased the body of knowledge. Like the study of engineering and medicine, the study of education has usually been carried on in institutions concerned with the training and refreshing of members for the profession. The needs of the practice of teaching have therefore generally had an effect on the nature of the research and thinking that has gone into the study of education. This has been a reciprocal exercise in relevance. While the needs of the profession have kept theorists and researchers reasonably close to the classroom, the theorists and researchers have helped to push the classroom teacher into breaking with the traditional recipes for classroom practice which are inclined to linger on in a conservative profession. The general effect was that, during the course of the twentieth century, a very considerable change was taking place in the competence and interests of the teaching profession.

As the study of education grew in western countries, so too did the influence of western-type schools expand rapidly throughout the world. In non-western countries, few indigenous schools survived to the middle of the century. Where they did, such as in Islamic countries and in India, their influence was somewhat restricted and specialised, and they were outdistanced by their western rivals. The western school, with its carefully organised grades and classroom procedures, its hierarchy of teachers and administrators, and its readily recognisable standards, certificates, and sequences of studies, established a pattern suitable for a program of mass education. It was a pattern that was easily grasped and readily exportable. Migrants from Europe and America and colonial administrators helped to set it up throughout the world and it was also actively sought and introduced by non-colonised countries such as Japan, China, Thailand, and Turkey. It was seen as an essential instrument of national development. It took root because it met a current need. Through the western school, education had been systematically institutionalised and packaged; and in that form it could be readily distributed to the mass audiences that were seeking it throughout the world. It was not, however, an inflexible pattern. Although it was stable, and at times, in its critics' eyes, deadened by routine, it was still capable of adjustment in new environments and of improvement at home. It was possible to export to new customers both the established pattern and the innovations of the reformers. What the world got was not just a machine for transmitting education in an orderly way; it was not just a matter of blackboards, gym periods, training colleges, headmasters, and high schools. It was an instrument of considerable power, not a god from a machine but a machine from the gods, through which the ordinary opportunities of the common man might be speedily widened, and new ideas of force and value might be generated in the economic, social, and political world.

PART ONE

EDUCATIONAL AWAKENING
c. 1900-16

Ovide Decroly (1871-1932), a distinguished Belgian educator, who for a quarter of a century ran *L'Ecole de l'Ermitage*, Europe's most noted activity school.

L'Ecole de l'Ermitage.

INTRODUCTION

The early years of the twentieth century, in the view of some social thinkers and educators, were the dawn of a new period in history requiring a new view of the function of education. Sidney Webb, for example, whose painstaking analyses of English social and political life were to make a solid and enduring impact on several generations of English men and women, wrote in 1901 that, 'during the last twenty or thirty years, we have become a new people'.[1] His remarks were echoed throughout the western world and in the emerging countries of Asia. Not all the writers who were conscious of the dawning of a new era would have agreed precisely with Webb's analysis of what was happening and what should happen, but they would have accepted the idea that the world was changing radically and that the time had come for a careful review and possible recasting of education.

The educational awakening of the early twentieth century grew out of the flux of the 1890's. There was a *fin de siècle* spirit abroad usually typified by the provocative aestheticism of an Oscar Wilde or a Toulouse Lautrec, but the spirit had also other elements of novelty and vitality. It was an expression of dissatisfaction with nineteenth century society and its culture, an encouragement to question conventional behaviour, and a stimulus to develop new responses. The Scots schoolmaster-poet, John Davidson, summed up the probing current of the age.[2]

These are times
When all must to the crucible — no thought,
Practice or use or custum sacro-sanct
But shall be violable now.

The nineteenth century had never been calm and unruffled, and, for many intellectuals, it ended in tormenting doubt, criticism, and an abundance of new fashions and untried ideas. It was the time of the new realism, new drama, new criticism, new fiction, and the new education. The world of Ibsen, Cézanne, Tolstoy, and Debussy was a world of protest against existing social and cultural conventions, and it was also a world of strenuous and imaginative effort. Artists, scholars, educators, and social thinkers sought to provide new and fruitful perceptions of what was seen to be a world of shifting standards and unprecedented demands.

THE IMPACT OF SCIENCE

Colouring much of the speculation of the 1890's and early twentieth century was a feeling that the future lay with science and scientific thought. For many who were concerned with various aspects of the state of society, the science to which they looked was biology. 'Doubtless', wrote Dewey in 1909, 'the greatest dissolvent in contemporary thought of old questions, the greatest precipitant of new methods, new intentions, new problems, is the one effected by the scientific revolution that found its climax in the *Origin of Species*'.[3] In the study of biology social thinkers found two features of principal interest.

The heart of biological method was felt to lie in its systematic approach to the observation and classification of the biological world. The precise observation and orderly arrangement of data was regarded as the essence of scientific method. An emphasis on careful observation implied that nothing was to be accepted at its face value. Not only natural phenomena but ideas and customs also were, in a scientific world, to be scrutinised with care and objectivity. An attitude of questioning, an urge to search for adequate evidence, and an effort to fit one's observations into a logical and systematic framework were characteristic of the approach that science appeared to embody. Training in that version of scientific method became common in schools where science was seriously taught, and the method became the basis of research also in the social sciences, lending a scientific air to the social surveys which were influential moulders of public opinion in the early part of the century.

More important than the impact of scientific method, however, was the effect of Darwin's biological writings on social thinking. Social Darwinism in the 1890's and the first decade of the twentieth century was an effort by writers and thinkers on social questions to apply the notions of natural selection and the survival of the fittest to human society. Two diametrically opposed schools of thought emerged.

The first reaction was to see in it an encouragement to individual ruthlessness. The world was a highly competitive one in which the nation or the individual that trained and equipped itself most efficiently to compete with others would succeed while its rivals would go under. Competition was the best incentive to development, competition was

---

[1] S. Webb, 'Lord Rosebery's escape from Houndsditch', *Nineteenth Century and After*, September 1901. p. 368. An interesting collection of and commentary on the educational writings of Sidney and Beatrice Webb is to be found in E.J.T. Brennan (ed.), *Education for National Efficiency, the Contribution of Sidney and Beatrice Webb*, Athlone, London. 1975.

[2] J. Davidson, 'A Woman and Her Son', *New Ballads*, 1897.

[3] J. Dewey, *The Influence of Darwin on Philosophy*, Smith, New York, 1951 (1910), p. 19.

inherent in the nature of things, and competition ought to be fostered by all who were interested in getting the best out of the human race. Competition was regarded as having both a factual support from Darwinian biology and a moral sanction from the general interest of the future of mankind. Those who succeeded were the ones most worthy of support and encouragement. That view of social Darwinism therefore favoured the cultivation of an elite of those best endowed in intellect and attitude to succeed. Its advocates encouraged selective and restrictive policies in schools; they supported eugenic practices of selective breeding and the sterilisation of the unfit; and they were somewhat race conscious, giving a higher status to the currently more successful white peoples. Efficiency was based on struggle and competition; and social efficiency could be properly regarded as an important aim for a society's schools if it meant that the schools adopted a rigorous examination and promotion system so that only the individuals best fitted to succeed were encouraged to progress into secondary and higher education.

Altruism, co-operation, and the capacity to be guided by supra-national ethical principles were the basis of the other school of thought of social Darwinism.[4] Because human beings were capable of deliberate, sustained, and varied co-operation in a way that no other animal had found possible, they had the opportunity to control their environment and to direct the course of evolution. By co-operation, by pooling their resources, and by harnessing individual competitiveness to social ends, they could reach a higher level of fitness and achieve a greater success than by the process of wasteful individual rivalry. Social efficiency was the basis of human progress; but it was an efficiency produced by expanding educational opportunities, by selflessness rather than selfishness, and by altruistic service in the interests of all rather than by seeking for individual advantage. In opposition to the cultivation of an elite, this school of thought proposed more extensive measures of social welfare. It was interested not in restricting and delimiting but in trying to improve the condition of those currently less successful in human society, and in raising human potential by equalising social, cultural, and educational opportunities throughout the community.

An important element in current thinking was the notion of creative evolution whose most eloquent advocate was the philosopher, Henri Bergson.[5] His most influential book was *Creative Evolution* published in 1907. In the universe, he suggested, there was a life-force (*élan vital*) which was the essence of all things, and its function was that of creation. Evolution therefore could have no predetermined path or end; it followed the creative urge of the vital force. Man because of his capacity for intuition could tune into and make creative use of it. He could apply to the material world the promptings of the *élan vital* and build his life and society in the most suitable direction.

Three lessons were drawn by educators from Bergson's views. First, rational, scientific thinking was important but it was not enough; creative work came from extra-rational intuitive thought. Progressives, fascists, and Marxists, were all, in various ways during the course of the twentieth century, to take up that approach and make much of it in their educational programs. The school curriculum should be much more than a collection of intellectual disciplines; it should provide scope also for non-intellectual experiences and for deepening the pupils' enjoyment of life. 'Nature', wrote Bergson, '...has set up a sign which apprises us every time our activity is in full expansion; this sign is joy.'[6] Secondly, human beings were dynamic and had a drive towards creativity; freedom and encouragement of creative expression, therefore, should be an essential aspect of all educational programs. Thirdly, man by using his intuitive powers and applying himself diligently and purposefully could rearrange his own world. Cézanne, for instance, the creator of a new era in art, demonstrated how, by painstaking reconstruction and intuitive under-standing, nature could be brought into a thoroughly co-ordinated whole of new relationships to express the vision of its human creator. Similarly, by appropriate education and experience, pupils could learn to express themselves more creatively, work more purposefully, and exercise a greater control over their environment.

Both the social Darwinists of the altruistic persuasion, and those educators who sympathised with Bergson's vitalism emphasised the active side of children's nature. They criticised the verbalism of current education and agitated for more active kinds of experiences for pupils. They were interested in studying children's growth and development, and put forward educational programs that would foster a great range of children's activities, would contribute to child growth, would meet children's interests, and would encourage children to express the vital spirit within them. Many of the progressive educators, such as Montessori and Ferrière, who first came into prominence in the pre-World War I

[4] It was popularised by the writings of Benjamin Kidd whose *Social Evolution* was published in 1894, and Peter Kropotkin whose *Mutual Aid* appeared in 1902. Both were widely read in the early years of the century, and the general trend of their argument was supported by many of the political theorists and sociologists of the day.

[5] Henri Bergson (1859-1941) was born in Paris and educated at the Ecole Normale Supérieure. He taught in several schools, and from 1900 to 1921 was a professor of philosophy at the Collège de France. An inspiring lecturer, a picturesque and lucid writer, his views were widely discussed during the early decades of the twentieth century. His principal publications were, *Matter and Memory* 1896, and *Creative Evolution* 1907. In 1928 he was awarded the Nobel Prize for literature. Olive A. Wheeler, *Bergson and Education*, Manchester University Press, 1922, and R.M. Mossé-Bastide, *Bergson éducateur*, Presses Universitaires de France, Paris, 1955 are the most substantial studies of the educational implications of his views.

[6] H. Bergson, Life and Consciousness, *Hibbert Journal*, October, 1911, pp. 41-43.

period, took that line.[7] Not all came to it, however, through Bergson or even through Darwinian literature. Some absorbed their interest in dynamic psychology from Dilthey, Croce, or, later, Freud; others could point to no obvious source. It was the mood of the time, widely reflected in literature, art, and the general conversation of educated people.

THE DOMINANCE OF THE MIDDLE CLASS

By about 1900 the western world had become a middle class world. Industry, trade, and commerce had become the principal source of national wealth, and power lay in the hands of the middle class who provided ownership and management. The focus of life was becoming urban, commercial, and industrial. The movement of agricultural population into the cities had increased in the later nineteenth century and was to accelerate throughout the twentieth century. Clerical and service occupations associated with urban commercial life had begun by the early 1900's to absorb large numbers of the population, and to add substantially to the middle class.

In education, therefore, there was evidence of the business mind at work, examining the efficiency of schools, economising in school organisation, and demanding value for money spent. But, without any doubt, the principal concern and interest was to ensure that there should be an adequate provision of schools of an appropriate type and curriculum to meet the requirements of the middle class. It was, of course, an amorphous mass of large and small entrepreneurs, administrators and clerks, members of professions and self-trained executives, managers and salesmen, writers, publishers, and housewives. The list of members was wide-ranging and almost endless; their tastes, interests, knowledge, and skills diverse; their wealth and personal circumstances enormously varied. Upon education, however, they were agreed. Secondary education was essential. Current provision for it was inadequate in quantity and in content; therefore an expansion and a reform of secondary education were both needed and were by far the most important matters to be undertaken in education. Hence, around the turn of the century, there was a wave of modest secondary school reform designed to make secondary education more accessible to middle class children and its curriculum more consonant to their needs in the early twentieth century. In the U.S.A. the Committee of Ten in 1893 and the Committee of Fifteen in 1895, in England the Bryce Commission Report of 1895 and the Board of Education's memorandum of 1904, in Prussia the reform of 1900, in Japan the Imperial Rescript of 1890 and the attendant reforms, and in France the Ribot Commission of 1899 and the 1902 reorganisation were solid and concerted attempts to examine secondary education, to lay the basis for its expansion, and to set in motion a program of cautious and influential reform.[8]

THE ACCELERATING INDUSTRIAL REVOLUTION

Interest in science was not confined to its methods and its somewhat theoretical applications. For most people its achievements and its industrial applications were its most significant features. Science was not only changing the processes and content of social philosophy, it was also changing the nature of society itself.

The new industrial state was built upon science and its handmaiden, technology. Behind the engineer who designed, built, and installed the equipment, and the industrial entrepreneur who financed and managed the plant, lay the chemists, physicists, and biologists whose work made the process possible, and behind them, again, the schoolmasters and schoolmistresses teaching the coming generation of young scientists and general public to understand and to contribute to the advancement of the scientific age in which they were growing up. Or such was the ideal picture. Germany, at the beginning of the century, was probably closest to it. Germany's appreciation of science and devotion to scientific and technical education was widely considered to be one of the main reasons for its recent rapid industrial progress. Other nations, such as Britain, suffered from a 'want of scientific spirit'[9] not only in the training of scientists and industrial workers but in all walks of life. It was increasingly asserted by writers on education and politics that vastly greater resources should be put into scientific research and into the teaching of science in schools. It was of particular importance too that vocational education should be fostered as a solid educational support for industrial expansion. A systematic strengthening and expansion of vocational education for occupations at all levels was, therefore, undertaken by many nations. Power in the contemporary world was thought to lie with the nation possessing the industrial resources supported by scientific research. Comparisons between nations in industrial progress and scientific education were part of a wider rivalry.

---

7   See below, Chapter 5.

8   See below, Chapter 1.

9   N. Lockyer, *Education and National Progress*, essay on the influence of brain-power on history, Presidential Address at the British Association meeting, 1903, Macmillan, London, p. 178.

The mass school systems of primary education that had arisen out of the industrial revolution in the nineteenth century were also affected by the acceleration of technological progress. They continued to expand and they began to widen their functions. The efficient production of literate workmen remained an important task, but the schools' curriculum also began to display more social relevance and relationship to the local urban community. The urban development that was part of the industrial revolution built up conglomerations of working class families thrust together in overcrowded conditions. Recognition of the social and educational disadvantages under which many urban dwellers suffered stimulated programs of social welfare. Improving nutrition through school meals, health through medical inspection, and educational opportunity through special schools for disadvantaged children were substantial ways in which social welfare, early in the century, became closely associated with the educational system.

NATIONALISM AND EDUCATION

The end of the nineteenth century and the early years of the twentieth century were a period of intense nationalism culminating in World War I. The United States' conflict with Spain in 1899, the Japanese war with China in 1894 and subsequently with Russia in 1904-5, the smouldering rivalry of the Triple Alliance and Triple Entente provided continuous occasion for the expression of jingoistic sentiment during the period.

The rivalry between nations had two important effects on education. First, it greatly increased the tendency to use the school, particularly the primary school, to foster patriotism and support for a particular national way of life. Most nations had already started to do this. With the burgeoning nationalism of the turn of the century those kinds of programs were intensified in all nations. The twentieth century era of persuasion was born in the patriotic exercises of the schools of the first decade of the century. In subsequent years, partly because of a growing relationship between school and society and partly because of a deliberate political effort to build up loyalty to a particular regime or ideology, political education through the schools was to be regarded as a normal part of the persuasive apparatus of the state.

Secondly, the nationalism of the times engendered comparisons between educational systems, and a serious consideration of the relationship between education and national welfare. Out of these studies there eventually came proposals for social betterment and increased national efficiency, to be achieved by improving the nation's educational

structure. Later in the century, the same trend gave rise to considerable research on the relationship between education and economic progress, and an effort in many countries to fit educational development into a framework of national economic planning.

SOCIAL EFFICIENCY

The progress of science, industry, commerce, and technology, the growing interest of the middle class in education, the educational demands of nationalism and national advancement, and a new consciousness of the relatedness of education to society, brought forth a strong and continuing demand that education should aim at social efficiency.

The position was neatly analysed in 1909 by Cubberley who was to become America's most well-known historian of education. 'We are standing', he wrote, 'on the threshold of a new era in educational progress'.[10] A radically new society was being created by the recent upsurge of cities, by the development of large scale commerce and industry, by the immigration of semi-literate workers, and by the growing interdependence of nations throughout the world. The new society was complex, fluid, and often irresponsible. It had to be made comprehensible, efficient, and securely democratic. There was a growing trend to see education as an instrument that could be used toward this end, and one which could make a significant contribution to the task. 'The school must grasp the significance of its social connections and relations, and must come to realize that its real worth and its hope of adequate reward lies in its social efficiency.'[11]

Social efficiency meant three things. The public school had the task of developing in its students a general political and social consciousness of the need for acting through democratic processes and for building a unity of feeling among the people of a nation; secondly, the school's curriculum should become more relevant to the needs of society, be fitted to the requirements of the various social classes, and paternalistically reflect the increasing interest that the state was assuming for the development and welfare of its children; and, thirdly, education should give a lead towards and be a means 'of improving the state and of advancing the public welfare'.[12] In this, Cubberley spoke not merely for

[10] E.P. Cubberley, *Changing Conceptions of Education*, Houghton Mifflin, Boston, 1909, p. 52.
[11] *ibid.*, p. 54.
[12] *ibid.*, p. 59.

educators in the United States but for many also in Europe and throughout the industrialised world. The public schools, in short, were becoming and should continue to become more socially conscious, relevant, and directive.

Social efficiency was a two-edged weapon.

Though Cubberley thought that social efficiency would work in the interests of greater democracy and social justice, it was not necessarily so. The alliance between big business and government that had been built up in Europe and America in the late nineteenth century was greatly strengthened in the early twentieth. It was an integration of economic and political interests that was socially and politically conservative. It was an effort to achieve a steady and orderly expansion within the existing social organisation without resort to radical change; it endeavoured to build co-operation and social efficiency into all aspects of life; and it sought to construct by every reasonable means a responsible social order. 'The key word in the new corporate vision of society was responsibility.'[13] The vision and the quiet movement towards its realisation continued on and underlay the whole of the post-World War I period in all the western democracies, emerging from time to time in sharper and more productive form in activities such as the early policies of the Weimar Republic, the Roosevelt New Deal, and, later, the Johnson Great Society.

Social efficiency on such a model was to imply, usually, a gradual reform of social and political conditions, and an increase in general prosperity without any political change of substance or loss of economic and political power to the existing holders of it. Its supporters tended to favour the extension of primary and vocational education and efforts to make school curricula more utilitarian and nationalistic; and they opposed the kind of progressive education that shunned the usual ways of measuring school efficiency and taught the need for the reconstruction of society.

On the other hand, the movement towards social efficiency, by implying an expansion in the function of the school and an interest in developing a more relevant curriculum, gave heart and opportunity to progressively-minded educators. It was a stimulus to them to rethink educational aims and processes. It was an encouragement to them also to experiment with fundamental changes in the relationship between school and society and in the selection and organisation of the knowledge to be studied in school programs. Social efficiency was, thus, a concept cherished alike by progressives and conservatives. It was the most pervasive educational idea of the early decades of the twentieth century, a general, fundamental idea of wide acceptance that provided scope for much earnest discussion on the great range of opinion concerning the changes that were necessary in education.

The early twentieth century awakening of education was more than an agitation and a stimulus to inquiry. It produced solid, though modest, educational reform;[14] it endorsed, in its wide acceptance of Herbartianism, a systematic reorganisation of teaching procedures;[15] it fathered a radically new and influential philosophy of education;[16] it opened up an interesting range of educational experiments which inaugurated the progressive education movement;[17] and it began to expand its responsibilities in areas of social welfare and national interest hitherto little connected with it. It was starting to become a new education not merely in the matter of school organisation and practice, but in its whole conception and function. Education was beginning, in effect, to develop into a hitherto unknown force which would exercise a novel influence on human civilisation.

---

[13] J. Weinstein, *The Corporate Ideal in the Liberal State 1900-1916*, Beacon, Boston, 1968, p. x. For an expansion of this analysis see the works of T. Veblen especially *Absentee Ownership and Business Enterprise in Recent Times*, Huebsch, New York, 1923, and G. Kolko, *The Triumph of Conservatism. A Reinterpretation of American History, 1900-1916*, Free Press, New York, 1963.

[14] See Chapter 1.

[15] See Chapter 2.

[16] See Chapter 3.

[17] See Chapters 4 and 5.

CHAPTER 1

EDUCATION FOR SOCIAL EFFICIENCY: THE DEVELOPMENT OF EDUCATION FROM THE 1890's TO 1914

Margaret McMillan (1860-1931), an English educator who devoted her life to the improvement of the health and education of young children.

Portrait by John Mansbridge in G.A.N. Lowndes, *Margaret McMillan "The Children's Champion"*, Museum Press Limited, London, 1960.

SUMMARY

General Condition of Education in 1900

(i) Trends in Primary Education: Towards Social Efficiency

    (a) Improving the Curriculum
    (b) Raising the Level of Attendance
    (c) Efficiency in School Management
    (d) Social Welfare and Primary Education
    (e) The Development of Civic and Personal
        Responsibility

(ii) Trends in Secondary Education

    (a) Japanese Education and Modernisation before
        World War I
    (b) United States of America: Rapid Expansion
        and Conservative Reform
    (c) England: State Reorganisation and the Slow
        Modification of Tradition
    (d) France and the Pursuit of the Intellectual
    (e) Germany: Debate and Stability

(iii) Trends in Vocational Education

    (a) Occupational Levels
    (b) Vocational Education in 1900
    (c) Vocational Education from 1900 to World War I

GENERAL CONDITION OF EDUCATION IN 1900

By the beginning of the twentieth century, primary education was well established and was rapidly expanding in the industrialised countries; and, in the colonial non-industrial ones, it was slowly making its way, largely after the pattern of one or other of the western nations.

The organisation of the primary school system varied from place to place. Some schools began at the age of five, others at six or seven; some kept children at school until the age of twelve, others insisted on thirteen, fourteen, or fifteen; there were four, five, six, seven and eight year schools, and primary work might be divided from higher primary or secondary at the age of eleven, twelve, or thirteen. In all the well-established systems, however, there were a number of common features and a number of common questions that were being asked. Most children stayed to complete about four years of elementary school work. In that time they concentrated on the Three R's and most of them reached a level of literacy that enabled them to read newspapers and notices and to communicate in the ordinary business of life and work without much handicap. They were also inducted, in some measure, into the patterns of private and public behaviour and the commonly accepted beliefs and opinions of the national group to which they belonged. The primary school, where character formation was of great importance, became the main target for the development of national solidarity through patriotic exercises and the study of civic and social activities.

Primary schooling was for the mass of children, few of whom managed to make their way into a secondary school. In the countries following the American tradition, progress in schooling was arranged so that it was like climbing the rungs of a single ladder; secondary education followed directly on primary, and a child who completed the eight grades of the elementary school in the U.S.A. could, if he had sufficient aspiration and resources, move up to the first rung of a secondary high school. In Europe, the mass character of primary education was made clearer by the nature of its organisation. Primary education was a system kept distinct from the secondary education system. Secondary education was a second stage of education but it followed on from its own preparatory schools rather than from the general, mass primary schools. There were two parallel ladders. A child could start on the bottom rung of either and, once committed to one of the ladders, there was not much opportunity to change to the other. The mass of the children in Europe climbed the primary school ladder, and with few exceptions, did not manage to move into the secondary system.

The twentieth century Industrial Revolution made a substantial impact on primary education in two special ways. Business and industrial interests were concerned to make it more efficient and more pertinent in its content to the growing urban and industrial world. The same world, however, had created a nest of social problems associated with the bad housing, poor nutrition, overcrowding, and culturally impoverished environment in which many of the families of primary school children lived. Moves to improve education and to improve undesirable social conditions came to focus on the primary school which became an important social welfare agency. The two trends, the drive for efficiency, and the provision of social welfare, both conflicted with and supplemented one another. Sometimes they represented the two sides of social Darwinism. Efficiency bred economy and competitiveness; social welfare promoted co-operation and raised the level of public expenditure. On the other hand, efficiency was sometimes seen to be related more to relevance than to parsimony; an efficient primary school curriculum was one which dealt with matters relevant to the young pupil's life and which helped him learn skills and knowledge which might enable him to improve his everyday living and his performance in his future job. An efficiency drive could therefore, appropriately, show concern for a reform in primary school teaching that might lead to greater social efficiency; and it sometimes did not prove difficult to persuade advocates of efficiency that improving the children's health and nutrition by means of school health and meals services was likely to improve their performance, encourage them to stay longer at school, and raise the level of efficiency of the primary school system.

Middle class predominance went along with a desire for businesslike efficiency in primary schools. It showed itself particularly, however, at the secondary school level. Secondary education, at the beginning of the twentieth century, was largely a middle class preserve. The improvement and extension of secondary education, to a sufficient level to meet the needs of a demanding and expanding middle class was therefore the main task of governments at that time. The current sense of the importance of science also had some impact on secondary education. In the process of reforming the secondary schools the traditional study of the classics was challenged by educators who sought to modernise the curriculum. Modern languages and the mother tongue were the chief beneficiaries of the resulting revisions, but science also managed to make progress.

Secondary education varied in length but not greatly in content. The biggest contrast was between the American high school which was a four-year school, and the different kinds of German *Gymnasia* which had six or nine classes with a four-year preparatory course. In other countries, secondary schools might have six, seven, or eight classes and be fed by four to six-year preparatory schools. Characteristic of all the secondary schools was the teaching of foreign languages with, usually, a strong interest in the ancient classical languages of Europe. There was a close

relationship between secondary and university education, and in most cases the curriculum of secondary schools was directed towards preparation for university studies. Secondary education thus tended to be suitable for and available to a small minority of pupils. It catered for an elite distinct from the mass who were expected to have their wants met by a primary education whose pupils were generally excluded from secondary schooling by the prevailing pattern of educational organisation, and by social and economic factors governing their educational aspirations and opportunities.

Education at a tertiary level was well established only in western countries, and there, for the most part, in the fields of professional training and general education offered by traditional universities. Old-established universities had been supplemented in the nineteenth century by the addition of new disciplines to their own curricula, and by new foundations, notably the technical universities of Germany, the land-grant universities of the U.S.A., and the municipal university colleges of England. Growing particularly in the latter part of the nineteenth century, the newer foundations were the beginning of the expression of a challenge to the traditional functions of universities and a questioning of their adequacy in a time of great technological growth. At the beginning of the twentieth century, there was an uneasy relationship between university, secondary, and technical education. Technical institutions lay somewhere between the other two, and there was an uncertainty as to the extent to which technical studies should be admitted to secondary schools and universities. Hesitation and unease on the question was to continue throughout most of the twentieth century.

A greater concern for vocational education was one of the more obvious effects of the increased tempo of commercial and industrial activity in the early twentieth century. Efforts were made to provide more adequate educational preparation for the different occupational levels that had become apparent, and considerable interest was shown in increasing the scientific content of vocational courses. In assessing the adequacy of educational provision in various countries, the educators of the early years of the century invariably made much of the level and extent of vocational education, and the relationship which it bore to the speed of industrial and commercial progress and to the quality of production in the nations under comparison.

In the following pages those trends in primary, secondary, and vocational education will be explored in more detail, using examples of ideas and practices from the principal industrial countries of the time, viz. the U.S.A., England, Germany, France, and Japan.

In summary, the main concern in the quarter-century between 1890 and the beginning of World War I was to produce educational systems whose central aim was social efficiency. In pursuit of social efficiency educators had to think how to put the schools more effectively at the service of the community, how to make the program of the schools more relevant to contemporary life, and how to ensure that the work they did was performed with the utmost proficiency. To achieve the desired objective there were three principal tasks:

- to reform primary education so as to make it more efficient, more effective as an instrument of social welfare, and more concerned with moral development and civic responsibility;
- to organise and expand secondary education;
- to meet the vocational needs of the technological revolution.

(i)   Trends in Primary Education: Towards Social Efficiency

Criticism of schools for inefficiency had two sides, an argument for a more practical and realistic curriculum, and a condemnation of the retardation and wastage of pupils in schools.

(a) Improving the Curriculum

The clearest and most strenuously put arguments for a more practical curriculum in the elementary schools came from those who considered that a country's material progress was related to the quality of the work force, which, in turn, depended on the efficiency and appropriateness of the elementary education that the working class received. In each of the western nations, without exception, that point of view, sharpened by local business competition and international commercial rivalry, received strong advocacy. Probably the best example of persistence and influence in the area was to be found in England in the person of Philip Magnus who was described early in his career as 'probably the greatest living authority on industrial education'.[1]

Magnus was much exercised about the inefficiency of English commerce and industry in competition with other nations, especially Germany and the U.S.A. A vital part of the remedy, as he saw it, was the improvement of vocational education, and of 'the training given in our public elementary school'.[2] In the elementary schools it was necessary to try to adapt the work to the practical needs of the life of the working man. To that end all subjects should undergo revision to ensure their practical usefulness; arithmetic, for example, was full of numerous difficult problems concerned with simplifying complex fractions or finding the greatest common measure, that were 'to a large extent time wasted'. If we were to consider 'the kind of problems that we are required to solve in our ordinary work', we would realise how abstract and unnecessary was much of the arithmetic curriculum.

In pursuance of his aims, Magnus was keen to introduce manual training through school workshops into English elementary schools, and to expand the study of science. His efforts were successful on both counts. In the case of science he insisted that science implied method as well as content. It was essential to learn how to discover scientific facts for oneself by practical means.[3] It was a method of inquiry similar to that advocated by his American contemporary, John Dewey, and it was designed to develop thinking and scientific habits of mind. Magnus thought that science teaching of that kind, if begun in elementary school, would help produce future workmen who were more intelligent, and more capable of solving problems in their daily work, and hence more efficient, more productive, and more capable of being trained to higher levels of technical expertness. The change in teaching method was part of a movement towards an approach — activity teaching — that was to become popular in various forms throughout the twentieth century. 'This great change of method', wrote Magnus in 1910, 'is tersely expressed in the phrase, now generally accepted as a pedagogic principle "Learning by doing".'[4] It was also to be a fundamental part of the contribution to educational theory and practice made by the progressive education movement throughout the next half-century.

A second aspect of the efficiency of the elementary school curriculum that was subject to considerable investigation and discussion was the question of economising both in time and in methods of teaching. The most part of the early research of European educational psychologists described by one of the leaders, Edouard Claparède, in a widely read handbook in 1910 was concerned with the measurement and elimination of fatigue in children's learning, and the most efficient methods of

[1] *Educational News*, 2 February 1889, quoted in F. Foden, *Philip Magnus. Victorian Educational Pioneer*, Valentine Mitchell, London, 1970, p. 195. Philip Magnus (1842-1933) was a Londoner, graduating in arts and science from University College, London. He was secretary and organising director of the City and Guilds of London Institute from 1880 to 1915, and served on a Royal Commission on Technical Education 1881-1884. He was a member of the London School Board and the governing body of the University of London, and became a member of Parliament in 1906. He spoke and wrote widely on educational topics. His best known publication is *Educational Aims and Efforts 1880-1910*, Longmans Green, London, 1910.

[2] P. Magnus, *Educational Aims and Efforts*, p. 209: quotation from the Presidential Address to the Educational Section of the British Association, 1907.

[3] The leading advocate of this 'heuristic' method at that time was H.E. Armstrong (1848-1937) who became a lecturer in applied chemistry at the City and Guilds College, London, in 1879, and, subsequently, professor in 1884. For several years he taught experimentally in schools and developed his heuristic method, a method of directed inquiry in training children 'to work out problems for themselves'. In the course of his long career he vigorously advocated the teaching of scientific method and, in particular, his heuristic version of it. He published a collection of his writings and speeches on education entitled *The Teaching of Scientific Method and Other Papers on Education*, Macmillan, London, 1903.

[4] P. Magnus, *op.cit.*, p. 138. A comprehensive description of the reforming efforts of the 'practical educationists' in England is given in R.J.W. Selleck, *The New Education*, Pitman, Melbourne, 1968.

learning and memorising. In those fields the educational psychologists of Germany and the United States were the most prominent.[5] The most substantial and prolonged investigation was the work done in the United States by a joint committee of the National Education Association, and the National Society for the Study of Education which sat for more than a decade and made four substantial reports between 1915 and 1922 on ways of economising in time in public school education.[6] It took the view that there was a great amount of wasted time in elementary school programs, and that by eliminating non-essential subject-matter and by improving methods of teaching much of the waste could be eliminated. The committee was guided in its task by two basic considerations:

- that the material to be offered to any age group should be comprehensible by them;
- that the material should relate to the social needs common to ordinary American children.

All the usual subjects of the elementary school curriculum were examined, viz. reading, handwriting, spelling, language, arithmetic, geography, history, civics, literature, physical education, drawing, and music, and recommendations were made about each. In formulating their reports, the authors relied heavily on their knowledge of current research in each subject concerning the grade placement of items, the sequencing of topics, and the most economical methods of learning. In their selections, the authors, like Philip Magnus in England, were also guided by a strong sense of social utility. In arithmetic, for example, a study was made of the arithmetical problems actually solved in daily life by a large sample of farmers, housekeepers, businessmen, and professionals; and, from a look at factory payrolls, sales advertisements, banking procedures, a cookbook, and a hardware catalogue, a list of problems and processes was compiled that the ordinary citizen might be expected to have to master.

The reports did not furnish final and definitive answers, but they did provide a stimulus to all those interested in education, to look to the most appropriate means 'to insure, with the assistance of the other institutions of society, the acquisition on the part of elementary-school children of those habits, skills, knowledges, ideals, and prejudices which must be made the common property of all, that each may be an efficient member of a progressive democratic society.'[7]

(b) Raising the Level of Attendance

During the same period there was considerable interest in the extent of school drop-out and retardation. The most well-organised expression of

it, again, was to be found in the United States where the recent rapid expansion of cities and the flow of European migrants to them had highlighted problems of school attendance. J.M. Rice, after spending five months in the early 1890's visiting the classrooms of the public schools of thirty-six cities in the United States pointed out in a series of articles that there were marked variations in the quality of schooling in different cities, and that many of the pupils in the cities would receive no more than three or four years of schooling.[8] At the same time, Jacob Riis had startled Americans with his stark descriptions of the brutalising conditions under which migrants lived in the downtown New York slums, where truancy was rampant and schools overcrowded and ineffectual. Riis's findings were reiterated by other writers from Philadelphia, Boston, Chicago, and Detroit. Ten years later, in 1902, in his *The Battle with the Slum* he proposed that the fight had to be centred in and around the public school.[9]

In 1909 L.P. Ayres published an important and influential study, *Laggards in our Schools*.[10] He traced the progress through school of twenty thousand New York children, and examined the records of most of the larger cities of the country. He found that a large proportion of school pupils were not completing an elementary course. Figure 1.1 indicates the

[5] See below, Chapter 4.

[6] National Society for the Study of Education, *Fourteenth Yearbook, Pt I, Minimum Essentials in Elementary School Subjects — Standards and Current Practices*, University of Chicago, 1915; NSSE, *Sixteenth Yearbook, Pt 1, Second Report of the Committee on Minimal Essentials in Elementary School Subjects*, Public School Publishing Co., Bloomington. Ill., 1917: NSSE, *Seventeenth Yearbook, Pt 1, Third Report of the Committee on Economy of Time in Education, ibid.*, 1919; NSSE *Eighteenth Yearbook, Pt II, Fourth Report of the Committee on Economy of Time in Education, ibid.*, 1922.

[7] NSSE, *Fourteenth Yearbook*, p. 15.

[8] J.M. Rice, *The Public-School System of the United States*, Century, New York, pp. 25, 97-8, 100, 101. In the St Louis schools, for example, there was an 'absolute lack of sympathy for the child... The unkindly spirit of the teacher is strikingly apparent; the pupils being completely subjugated to her will, are silent and motionless; the spiritual atmosphere of the classroom is damp and chilly.' In the schools of Indianapolis, on the other hand, 'the teacher uses every means at her command to render the life of the children happy and beautiful, without endangering its usefulness'.

[9] Jacob A. Riis, *How the Other Half Lives*, 1890; *The Children of the Poor*, 1892; *The Battle with the Slum*, 1902. See also S. Cohen, *Progressives and Urban School Reform: The Public Education Association of New York City, 1895-1954*, Teachers' College, Columbia University, New York, 1964.

[10] L.P. Ayres, *Laggards in Our Schools*, Russell Sage Foundation, New York, 1909. Two other extensive studies were also made. In 1907 Thorndike, using evidence from twenty-three cities, pointed out that 25 per cent of white children stayed at elementary school only long enough 'to learn to read simple English, write such words as they commonly use, and perform the four operations for integers without serious errors', and only about one-third managed to complete seven grades of elementary school. See E.L. Thorndike, *The Elimination of Pupils from Schools*, U.S. Bureau of Education, Washington, D.C., 1907. Using the returns from 318 cities in 1908, G.D. Strayer found that only 73 per cent of children reached sixth grade, and most left between the ages of 13 to 15. See G.D. Strayer, *Age and Grade Census of Schools and Colleges*, U.S. Office of Education, Washington, D.C., 1911.

Figure 1.1:   United States of America: Drop-out of Pupils in City School Systems, 1909.

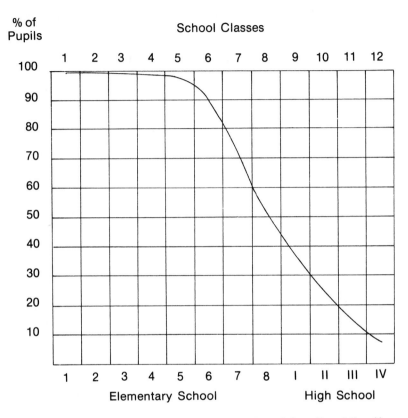

Adapted from L.P. Ayres, *Laggards in Our Schools*, Russell Sage Foundation, New York, 1909, p. 60.

unusually bright one'. Most children just could not make normal progress through the ordinary school syllabus. 'They fail repeatedly. They are thoroughly trained in failure.'[11]

(c) Efficiency in School Management

From his study, Ayres proposed an index of efficiency for school systems which would be the percentage of eighth grade pupils to beginners each year. Comparing a school system with a factory, he suggested that if 'a factory which instead of utilizing all its raw material (100 per cent) embodied only 50 per cent in its finished product', 50 per cent would be the measure of its efficiency. So, in a school system, if 'for each 1000 children who enter only 50 per cent reach eighth grade', the 'efficiency from the viewpoint of product is ½ or 50 per cent'.[12]

Not all the educators of the time would have cherished the business comparison, but the connection of business with studies of efficiency was in the air. It was the era of Taylor and Gilbreth, the efficiency experts, with their programs of scientific management. Once educators, therefore, became efficiency-conscious they began to think about scientific management. Bagley already in 1907 had said that 'classroom management may be looked upon as a business problem',[13] and the educational administrators of the era of efficiency responded by seeking ways in which not only the classroom but whole school systems might be made subject to the kind of scrutiny and measurement that produced effective products in the business world.[14]

Efficiency was more openly discussed in the U.S.A. than elsewhere, but in the European countries where there were central authorities with some measure of direction over education there was also considerable interest. By regulation, financial control, and constant inspection, the central authorities sought to ensure that local authorities and their schools were efficient. It was especially the case in the early twentieth century with a rapid expansion of population and school facilities. The chief executive officer from 1911 to 1925 of the recently established Board

extent of drop-out through the elementary and high school. It shows among other things, that only fifty per cent of fifth grade pupils could be expected to complete the eighth grade. Ayres found, also, allowing for great variation among schools and cities, that, on the average, about 33 per cent of children were retarded, i.e. they were older than they were expected to be for the grades they were in. Ayres reported that for every one child making normal progress, eight to ten children were making abnormally slow progress, and he concluded that 'our courses of study as at present constituted are fitted not to the slow child or to the average child but to the

[11]   L.P. Ayres, *op. cit.*, pp. 5, 220.

[12]   *ibid.*, pp. 176-7.

[13]   W.C. Bagley, *Classroom Management*, Macmillan, New York, 1907, p. 2.

[14]   Some measure of the importance given to the efficiency campaign can be found in the titles of the yearbooks published by the National Society for the Study of Education. Included in the eleven published between 1914 and 1918 were three reports of the economy of time committee, and a yearbook each on organising school surveys, on methods for measuring teachers' efficiency, on standards and tests for measuring the efficiency of schools and school systems, on the relationship between persistence in school and home conditions, on the efficiency of college students, and on the measurement of educational products. For a substantial treatment of the efficiency theme in United States education, see R.E. Callahan, *Education and the Cult of Efficiency*, University of Chicago, 1962.

of Education in England wrote, for example, that two of the central authority's major functions were the securing of minimum efficiency and value for money.[15] Efficiency was sought by drafting and enforcing appropriate regulations, by careful scrutiny of the schools by a team of inspectors, and by constant encouragement to the schools to raise their aspirations and 'to pursue a higher or broader objective'.[16]

Efficiency clearly had two sides. Administrators were interested in seeing that schools were well and economically organised and that there was full attendance and a minimum of retardation. Wherever the movement stopped at that point, however, it tended to be sterile, and to make little contribution to the improvement of education. It was possible for a school to be efficient 'in the sense that it does what it sets out to do, but what it does may be worth little.'[17] To keep abreast of current needs, to seek to do more for their pupils, and to rethink the curricula, as Magnus and like-minded educators suggested, were significant ways for schools to improve their efficiency and at the same time raise the quality of the education they provided. Efficiency in management needed to be supplemented by what educators had begun to refer to as social efficiency.

(d) Social Welfare and Primary Education

There were three principal areas in which elementary schools were closely associated with the improvement of their pupils' social conditions, and, in effect, became pioneers of public social welfare programs: the provision of meals at school, medical services for school children, and the development of special schools for children with handicaps of various kinds.

In France volunteer committees had begun in several cities to provide midday meals for poor children at school on a substantial scale in the 1880's. By the beginning of the twentieth century two-thirds of the meals were provided free of charge and the greater part of the cost was being borne by the local municipalities. During the pre-World War I period the same pattern continued, and in several areas breakfasts and suppers also, together with supplements such as codliver oil, were supplied. Germany followed a somewhat similar pattern, some cities relying on voluntary effort, others providing financial support, and in several cases taking the whole burden for school meals on themselves. In the United States, Philadelphia led the way with a well-organised voluntary society providing low cost meals with the co-operation of the teachers and school administrators. By 1912 similar schemes were operating in thirty other cities.

England was the first country in which the national legislature established a universal scheme for the provision of school meals and made it a possible charge on public funds. As in other countries, school meals,

for some years, had been provided for necessitous children by voluntary bodies. The efforts of a determined educational reformer, Margaret McMillan, and a socially conscious Labour Party recently returned in small but growing numbers to parliament, secured the passage in 1906 of the Education (Provision of Meals) Act.[18] The Act was a significant forward step but it was no social revolution. It was permissive not mandatory, allowing the recently established local educational authorities to provide premises for school meals and to supplement voluntary efforts or themselves to provide school meals out of public funds. It was, nevertheless, the beginning of a lasting program that expanded steadily in scale and effectiveness during the century, receiving a particular boost in England, as in other countries, during the world wars.

The same group in England pressed for the establishment of a national school health service and succeeded in having an act of parliament passed in 1907 requiring Local Education Authorities (LEA) to provide medical inspection of schoolchildren. A central school medical service was established in the following year to encourage and supervise the work of the local authorities. It was the culmination of twenty years of voluntary and piecemeal effort. London had appointed a school medical officer in 1890 and, soon after, several other school boards had followed suit. The Boer War (1899-1902) was a great incentive to further effort by drawing attention to the defective physical condition of potential recruits, more of whom were rejected than accepted.[19] Several surveys of the health of schoolchildren followed, and the reports both confirmed the desirability of providing a more effective medical service for schools and helped to arouse public opinion. The service, when established, found a daunting accumulation of ailments — lack of hygiene and cleanliness, defective eyesight, ear trouble, dental decay, throat and lung complaints, and infectious disease. As the medical service grew, inspection was supplemented by treatment. The service was

---

[15] L.A. Selby-Bigge, *the Board of Education*, Putnam, London, 1927, p. 30. His full list of functions were: the securing of (1) school provision; (2) school attendance and accessibility; (3) minimum efficiency; (4) value for money; (5) organisation; (6) systematisation.

[16] *ibid.*, p. 46.

[17] *ibid.*, p. 43.

[18] Margaret McMillan (1860-1931) joined the Labour Party in its early years, took part in the great dock strike of 1889, and worked with her sister Rachel in the 1890's in Bradford to improve children's health and the condition of schools. She lobbied successfully for the Education (Provision of Meals) Act 1906, and the Act of 1907 establishing the school medical service. In 1908 she set up a school clinic in London, and in 1910 the two sisters moved it to the dockside suburb of Deptford. There they also developed camp or open schools, and a nursery school. Rachel died in 1917, and Margaret established a training college in her memory. Margaret McMillan's publications were *Education through the Imagination*, 1904, *Labour and Childhood*, 1907 and *The Nursery School*, 1921.

[19] B. Simon, *Education and the Labour Movement, 1870-1920*, Lawrence and Wishart, London, 1965, p. 278; G. Leff and V. Leff, *The School Health Service*, Lewis, London, 1959, p. 21.

without doubt one of the factors contributing to the raising of the common person's standard of living. As the standard rose, the health of schoolchildren improved remarkably, and following generations of the mid-twentieth century could be clearly seen to be enjoying better health and to be capable of dealing more effectively with the school's educational program.

All other western countries by the end of the nineteenth century had some form of school medical inspection. France, making a start in the 1830's, had provided by law in 1886 for medical inspection in all elementary schools. The service was effectively maintained in Paris and several other cities, but up to the beginning of World War I had not become universal. In Germany, without formal governmental requirement except in the case of a few states, many cities had begun to employ part-time doctors for schools and by 1908 some four hundred cities had developed efficient systems of school medical service that were much studied by visiting educators. Japan in 1898 required schools to provide

At the nursery school established by Margaret and Rachel McMillan, the staff took care of the children's health as well as their physical, social and intellectual development.

G.A.N. Lowndes, *Margaret McMillan "The Children's Champion"*, Museum Press Limited, London, 1960.

medical inspection and gradually extended medical examination and attention throughout the country. By the end of World War I almost half the primary schools employed a doctor and offered physical and health education programs in which he took part. The United States, less systematic than the principal European countries, had developed regular medical inspection in the schools of the larger cities by the beginning of the twentieth century and by 1910 some four hundred cities had some form of school medical inspection and ten of the states had passed laws either requiring or encouraging local school authorities to establish some form of school medical inspection.

There was a moderate interest displayed during the nineteenth century by educators in providing special facilities for blind, deaf, sub-normal, and crippled children, and notable contributions to their education were made by people such as Braille, Itard, and Séguin. In the early years of the twentieth century, the child-study movement[20] led to a greater awareness of individual differences and the need to give special attention to children suffering from some handicap. That realisation together with the growing social conscience of the time led to a considerable increase in the kind of provision already being made, and to the addition of special classes in many elementary schools. In many countries, legislative provision accompanied these moves.

Those years saw also the introduction of a new kind of establishment. In 1904 an open-air recovery school was begun in Charlottenburg, a suburb of Berlin, for children who were below par, and, in particular, suffering from tuberculosis. The venture was successful, and was taken up elsewhere with great enthusiasm. Open-air schools spread throughout Germany and central Europe. In France they were generally associated with school colonies established in the country area for city children; and in the U.S.A., from 1908 to 1911, no less than forty-four were established in conjunction with hospitals and charitable associations. In 1907 one was opened in London, and others soon after in the main industrial towns where they were designed to provide a more healthy environment for deprived children of the slums, and became, through the efforts of the McMillan sisters, one of the bases on which England's nursery schools developed.

Thus, during the first decade of the twentieth century, the responsibilities of elementary education authorities had been substantially extended into an important aspect of social welfare, the health care of young children. By providing facilities and financial support for school meals they were taking serious steps to improve the nutrition of the underprivileged classes; by establishing a medical service for the

---

[20] See below, Chapter 4.

study, inspection, and treatment of school children they were becoming committed to a policy of trying to upgrade the health of the nation's children and of spreading more enlightened health practices throughout the community; and by expanding the provision of special schools and classes for atypical children they were giving to such children a greater chance to improve in health, happiness, and educational achievement. The schools, as Jacob Riis had hoped in his campaign to reform the slums of New York, had become pioneers in social welfare. Because they saw the need to improve their own educational outcomes, and because they were agencies that had a special responsibility for minors, they became vehicles for protective and educational measures that were to be of substantial benefit to the children and, incidentally, of considerable service to the whole adult community as well. Margaret McMillan neatly characterised the process as she saw it in the pre-World War I era: 'But the History of Education is the History of Democracy, and as the people advanced slowly in social hope and faith the level of their demands in education and nurture rose with the tide.'[21]

(e) **The Development of Civic and Personal Responsibility**

Popular education 'is universally considered a necessary pre-supposition of national strength and prosperity, and, above all, in our times, an essential means to the enjoyment of social peace', a leading German educator wrote in 1898, and few educators would have questioned his judgment.[22] Elementary education had in the nineteenth century made the western countries literate and numerate, provided more capable recruits for industry and commerce, and been the essential basis of vocational education. Such a general and indirect contribution to national prosperity, however, was not enough for most educators. They were interested in using the elementary schools directly to build solidarity of national feeling. The saying that the German victory over France at Sedan in 1870 was a triumph for the Prussian schoolmaster exemplified the part that the common schools had been playing in the development of patriotism.

Public systems of education, largely the product of the nineteenth century, were inevitably affected by public opinion, sometimes speedily and directly, but usually slowly and with many checks and balances. The moral beliefs and standards of behaviour of the schoolchildren, particularly, were matters that were related to the character and conduct of the community. Every school in some way concerned itself with the personal behaviour and morality of its pupils, and it also endeavoured to teach them their duties to their neighbours, fellow-citizens, and their country. Moral education thus had two sides, a private and a public

element. The pre-World War I years were a period in which there was much discussion of both aspects of moral education and an obvious and increasing interest in the kind of public opinion and behaviour that was associated with patriotism. Germany was widely seen as a country in which the schools had made a vital contribution to the high level of nationalism that characterised many of its citizens. The teaching was atmospheric and pervasive, and although apparently effective, was not based on a specific syllabus of moral and civic instruction as was the case in two other countries, France and Japan, which were also highly motivated in that area of teaching. It was, therefore, to the example of France and Japan that most educators who were interested in moral and political education directed their attention in the first decade of the twentieth century.

France in the process of its educational reorganisation in the 1870's and 1880's developed an enduring course of moral and civic instruction taught throughout the elementary schools which inducted young French pupils into their family and civic duties and into the virtues of the republican form of government and French nationalism. The course, and the textbooks and readers which accompanied it, dealt, often very interestingly, with everyday manners and morals, and with the responsibilities of French citizenship. In one well-used textbook, the development of social solidarity was offered as the main aim and directing idea of the course. The most popular of the elementary school texts, however, tended to move on from the notions of duty and solidarity to the attractions of heroism and patriotic behaviour.[23] The course in moral and civic education, as these texts demonstrated, was designed to be both an intellectual experience and an emotional one. Pupils were expected to deal with moral ideas, to argue about moral principles, and to learn intellectual virtues such as honesty in thinking and love of truth.[24] Intellect was supplemented by 'an appeal to the heart', by an emotional impact that made a more deep-seated impression. Thus intelligence motivated by sentiment would, it was hoped, lead to the goal of moral and civic education, moral action.[25]

[21] M. McMillan, *The Nursery School*, Dent, London, 1921, p. 21.

[22] W. Rein, Tendencies in the educational systems of Germany, in Great Britain, Department of Education, *Special Reports on Educational Subjects*, vol. 3, M.E. Sadler (ed.), H.M.S.O., London, C8988, 1898, p. 452.

[23] e.g. J. Payot, *La Morale à l'Ecole*, Armand Colin, Paris, 1907; and G. Bruno [pseud. for Mme A.J.E. Fouillée (1836-1912)], *Le Tour de la France par Deux Enfants*, 291st edn, Belin, Paris, 1900, and *Les Enfants de Marcel*, instruction morale et civique en action…, 70th edn, Belin, Paris, 1896. The 138th edn of *Les Enfants de Marcel* was published in 1925.

[24] G. Séailles, L'éducation intellectuelle et l'éducation morale, in G. Spiller (ed.), *Papers on Moral Education*, 2nd edn, London, First International Moral Education Congress, Nutt, London, 1909, p. 294.

[25] F. Buisson, *L'enseignement laïque de la morale en France*, p. 192.

Japanese education had always placed great importance on moral education. In the latter part of the nineteenth century Japan entered a dramatic period of change and modernisation, and, in new circumstances, found a need to rethink the basis and content of moral behaviour. The problem was not peculiarly Japanese; it was common to all the nations passing through the industrial revolution of the time and it proved to be a continuing problem in the twentieth century. Both private and public morality were affected, the one inevitably impinging on the other.

In Japan, with its close-knit and enduring family traditions, the pressing task was that of providing a public basis for morality which would ensure common ideals and the maintenance of national solidarity. The solution was found in the form of the Imperial Rescript on Education of 1890. It was a short two-paragraph statement of the principles underlying education that was to guide the views of educators for the next fifty-five years. The moral virtues of loyalty to and affection for family, friends, emperor, and nation were to be regarded as fundamental; building upon them, pupils should learn to advance the public good and respect the nation's laws; and, within such a framework of morality and service, learning should be vigorously pursued. The Rescript was an inspirational document, much read and reverenced in schools, which fortified teachers in their task of joining traditional moral character with modern learning.[26]

'Our whole moral education consists in instilling into the minds of our children the proper appreciation of the spirit of this rescript,' wrote a Minister for Education in the early years of the century.[27] The Rescript formulated the public ideal, making intense national feeling centred in the emperor a moral obligation, and it suggested an indissoluble connection between family and personal morality on the one hand and loyalty to the state and emperor on the other.

The courses in moral education given in all elementary schools came to occupy the foremost position in the curriculum.[28] They followed a series of textbooks and teachers' guides carefully prepared for each grade. In 1903 the Japanese government decided to publish national textbooks for use in all elementary schools in morals, history, geography, and Japanese literature. The monopoly lasted for the next forty years. Moral and patriotic teaching was included in each of the subjects, and given in greater depth and concentration in the subject of morals. The books were planned to emphasise the two complementary sides of moral teaching, personal virtue through filial piety, and civic duty. The fourth year, for example, which was the final year for most children, demonstrated the balance, by including topics such as: The Great Japanese Empire, patriotism, loyalty to the emperor, tenacity of purpose, benevolence, the duties of a man and the duties of a woman, and a good Japanese. The Russo-Japanese War of 1904-5 tended to strengthen Japanese patriotism and the ensuing revision of textbooks issued in 1910 intensified the nationalism of the teaching in them.[29]

The English-speaking nations were less direct but their interest increased in the early part of the twentieth century. The tendency of countries such as France, Germany, and Japan was to rely not solely on the general influence and atmosphere of family, school, and society, but to add to it direct instruction on moral and patriotic behaviour through a specified school syllabus. English and American educators placed more reliance on developing the desired traits of character through the influence of the corporate life and atmosphere of the school, the personality and example of the teacher and special visitors, and the occasional opportunities for improving discourse afforded by topics in various subjects. It was supplemented from time to time by formal exhortation in assemblies and ceremonies, on the sports field, or in other appropriate places. In the early years of the twentieth century, interest in using the schools to stimulate patriotism increased. In particular, the teaching of national history grew in popularity. History emerged from a study of chronology, wars, and political disputes into a study of the growth of a national society, and the history books of the period showed an understandable tendency not to understate the successes and virtues of the historian's own country: British seamen fought with true British pluck, and colonial administrators were ever devoted, trustworthy, and honourable; American explorers were intrepid, and the typical American

[26] K. Yoshida and T. Kaigo, *Japanese Education*, Board of Tourist Industries, Tokyo, 1937, pp. 2-3. The Imperial Rescript on Education, 1890: 'Know ye, Our subjects:

Our Imperial Ancestors have founded Our Empire on a basis broad and everlasting and have deeply and firmly implanted virtue; Our subjects ever united in loyalty and filial piety have from generation to generation illustrated the beauty thereof. This is the glory of the fundamental character of Our Empire, and herein also lies the source of Our education. Ye, Our subjects, be filial to your parents, affectionate to your brothers and sisters; as husbands and wives be harmonious, as friends true; bear yourselves in modesty and moderation; extend your benevolence to all; pursue learning and cultivate arts, and thereby develop intellectual faculties and perfect moral powers; furthermore advance public good and promote common interests; always respect the Constitution and observe the laws; should emergency arise, offer yourselves courageously to the State; and thus guard and maintain the prosperity of Our Imperial Throne coeval with heaven and earth. So shall ye not only be Our good and faithful Subjects, but render illustrious the best traditions of your forefathers.

The Way here set forth is indeed the teaching bequeathed by Our Imperial Ancestors, to be observed alike by Their Descendants and the subjects, infallible for all ages and true in all places. It is Our wish to lay it to heart in all reverence, in common with you, Our subjects, that we may all thus attain to the same virtue.

The 30th day of the 10th month of the 23rd year of Meiji. (Imperial Sign Manual. Imperial Seal.)

[27] Baron Kikuchi, 'The spirit of Japanese education', in M.E. Sadler (ed.), *Moral Instruction and Training in Schools*, 2, Longmans Green, London, 1909, p. 320.

[28] World Federation of Education Associations, *Proceedings of the Seventh Biennial Conference*, 1937, Japanese Education Association, Tokyo, 1938, p. 390.

[29] Japan, National Commission for UNESCO, *Development of Modern Textbook System in Japan, 1868-1961*, Ministry of Education, Tokyo, 1961, p. 53.

pioneer full of energy and initiative. Books on the method of teaching history deplored the introduction of bias, and praised objectivity, but classroom textbooks continued for many years quietly, persistently, and without undue distortion to present to the children an image of what the authors would like the readers to have of their nation's accomplishments and characteristics.

Though the English-speaking world did not develop special courses in morals and patriotism, many educational authorities at the beginning of the century did introduce patriotic ceremonies such as beginning the school day with a salute to the flag and a patriotic song. In the United States, most authorities required the study of basic national materials such as the constitution and various aspects of American history, and some compiled manuals for the use of teachers.[30]

Patriotism was one aspect of moral training. It was the most striking and appealing side, and in the early twentieth century it was clearly the side which blossomed and attracted attention. But, among educators, there was an intense interest in the kind of moral education that was concerned with cultivating virtues such as honesty, diligence, tolerance, and compassion. Germany, France, and many other European countries had long since committed themselves to a program by which such matters were deliberately taught. In England and the United States an unequivocal decision had not yet been taken on methods though their importance was acknowledged. Sadler, in England, felt strongly enough on the matter to write in 1912 that 'the question of moral instruction and training is the fundamental problem in education.'[31] In its first *Handbook of Suggestions for Teachers*, the English Board of Education in 1905 stated that moral training should not be left to chance, and in the following year incorporated in its regulations a statement that moral instruction should form an important part of every elementary school curriculum, and might be offered incidentally or given by a systematic course of instruction.[32] The desire by many people to keep religion out of the public elementary schools in England and in the United States, and the growing influence of the Herbartians who emphasised the ethical side of their teaching[33] reinforced the movement for moral education and at the same time proved to be a weakness. Advocates of the teaching of a secular morality were joined by religiously minded supporters as long as it was a matter of generally enthusing the schools to teach morals, but when the question of means was raised — whether, for example, morals were to be taught within a religious framework — the alliance fell apart. Similarly, teachers who could not give their adherence to Herbartian doctrine found that they could not consistently support their Herbartian colleagues when it came to a matter of practical teaching. The development of formal moral education in the English-speaking world was, in consequence, a piecemeal affair despite support from the central

authorities. The most notable point in its pre-World War I history was an international investigation which led to an extensive report in 1908 and an international moral education conference held in London in the same year,[34] and a subsequent one in The Hague in 1912.

There was always a danger, too, that sectional interests would identify the content of moral education with their own views and seek to have them generally taught throughout the national school system. That was clearly what happened with various religious groups and some of the influential sections of the business community. On occasion, the two combined. The most striking example of such an alliance was to be seen a little later, just after World War I, when a popular book appeared in the United States which described Jesus Christ as the forerunner of the modern businessman. 'Wist ye not that I must be about my father's *business*' was the quotation that set the pattern for the book.[35]

Despite the vested interests that became apparent as discussion and controversy developed, the attention given to the possibility of more effective moral education forced educators to rethink their views on the general purposes and aims of education. That exercise was associated in due course with a general reform and recasting of the content and methods of primary education during the next generation. Leading the way in the process of reconstruction were the progressive educators who first came into prominence in the pre-World War I period.

(ii) Trends in Secondary Education

Writing in the first year of the new century, Michael Sadler expressed the view that 'educational opinion all over the world is in rather a feverish

30 New York State, for example, in 1900, produced a substantial *Manual of Patriotism*, for use in the public schools on the principle expressed by the state superintendent that 'our schools should be nurseries of patriotism'. See C.R. Skinner (ed.), *Manual of Patriotism*, Albany, New York, 1900, p. 1. Songs, poetry, quotations, and ceremonies connected with the American flag formed the bulk of the volume which was rounded off with literary selections on topics such as patriotism, liberty, union, citizenship, and our country, and an annotated list of important dates in American history arranged for every day in the school year.

31 M.E. Sadler, Moral Instruction and Training in Schools, in A.P. Laurie (ed.), *The Teachers' Encyclopaedia*, Caxton, London, 1912, p. 35.

32 Great Britain, Board of Education, *Suggestions for the Consideration of Teachers and Others Concerned in the Work of Public Elementary Schools*, HMSO, London. 1905. cd2638, p. 8: *ibid., Code of Regulations, Prefatory Memorandum, 1906*, HMSO, London, 1906.

33 See below, Chapter 2.

34 Both projects collected and published descriptions of ideas and current practices in most European countries and several others overseas and discussions of the main problems by a number of leading educators from different nations. See M.E. Sadler (ed.), *Moral Instruction and Training in Schools*, 2 vols., Longmans Green, London, 1908-9, and G. Spiller (ed.), *Papers on Moral Education*, First International Moral Education Congress, Nutt, London, 1909.

35 B. Barton, *The Man Nobody Knows*, Bobbs-Merrill, Indianapolis, 1924.

state'.[36] Education was given an importance never previously accorded it and its current offerings were being widely and radically criticised. 'All over the world educational questions are coming fast to the front. In France, Germany and Russia, in Norway and Sweden, in Holland and Belgium, in Austria-Hungary and Switzerland, in Canada, Australia, and New Zealand, in the United Kingdom, and the United States of America, in Japan, and even in China, educational problems are demanding an ever-increasing share of national thought.'[37] Comparisons between nations were frequently made, and criticisms unfavourable to their own country's efforts were offered by educators anxious to catch up with overseas educational progress. Typical of the situation was the increasing frequency with which English educators, for example, were expressing the opinion that England had dropped behind, and had reached a state where it could no longer ignore the advantages achieved by its competitors through the skill with which they had harnessed 'education in the service of business and of other tasks of modern life'.[38] Similar views could be heard from educators in most other countries, and, where a particular country might be seen to be clearly ahead, its educators and politicians anxiously expressed the view that it should not slip behind.

Of all the educational problems of the early twentieth century, that of trying to determine the function and organisation of secondary education was probably the most important. It was the subject of investigation by many committees of considerable prestige, it was widely discussed in the professional and lay press, and the decisions made on it had important repercussions, on the one hand on primary, and on the other on university and vocational education. Primary education had been substantially established in the course of the nineteenth century; the systematic provision and reorganisation of secondary education was to be a major task of the twentieth.

(a) Japanese Education and Modernisation before World War I

Of all the countries that were to play leading roles in the twentieth century, Japan was one of the first to move towards rethinking its ideas on education. Since the 1850's it had been consciously and speedily recasting its economy in an effort to match the powers of the western world, and by the 1880's had entered its take-off stage. The process of modernisation had been held back from time to time by strenuous opposition from traditionalists, vested interests, and a lack of relevant education. The 1880's saw the firm development of a system of national education whose framework had been first laid down by the educational code of 1872. A national Ministry of Education was set up, and in 1886 a series of ordinances divided primary education into a four-year primary and a

four-year higher primary school, established a five-year middle secondary school, and created the Imperial Tokyo University. A significant reconciliation between the demands of modern industrial progress and the traditional Japanese way of life was effected by the Imperial Rescript on Education issued in 1890.

In 1899 secondary education was reorganised in an effort to ensure that each prefecture had at least one secondary school. It was thought of by its authors as part of a dual-structured system. Basic education for the people was given in four or six years of primary education in which moral education to strengthen family and imperial loyalties was of the greatest importance. On the other hand, a limited provision was made for educating an elite who would move into administrative and technical positions in the government service and industry. Secondary schools accordingly were selective, and higher secondary schools, of which there were few, were preparatory to university. The structures, however, were not separate systems but were end-on; all pupils were first educated to become good and loyal citizens, and those who had the ability and the wealth could move on into secondary and higher education.

Japan thus embarked at the beginning of the century on a system which would turn out leaders who 'are qualified to influence the thought of society, such as higher officials in the civil service, directors of commercial enterprises and specialised scholars in science', and the masses who 'are people of sound disposition serving the State, faithfully and diligently, according to their ability'.[39] The progress of industrialisation, however, made it impossible to maintain the distinction in the rapid expansion after 1900. The demand of industry was too great, and the number of aspirants too numerous. From 1900 secondary school enrolments escalated side by side with Japan's mounting industrial growth. As can be seen from Figure 1.3 enrolments rose from one hundred thousand in 1900 to seven hundred thousand in 1910, and continued upward to 1,200,000 in 1920.

[36]   Great Britain, Board of Education, Special Reports on Educational Subjects. vol. 9, *Education in Germany*, M. Sadler(ed.), Cd836. HMSO, 1902, p. 2. M.E. Sadler (1861-1943), educated at Rugby and Oxford, member of the royal commission on secondary education 1894-5, director of special inquiries and reports in the Education Department, 1895-1903, professor of education in the University of Manchester, 1903-11, vice-chancellor of the University of Leeds, 1911-23, president of the Calcutta university commission, 1917-19, and master of University College, Oxford, 1923-34. Sadler was one of England's most distinguished educators who wrote voluminously on a wide range of educational questions.

[37]   *ibid.*, p. 4.

[38]   *ibid.*, p. 11.

[39]   Makoto Aso & Ikuo Amano, *Education and Japan's Modernization*, Ministry of Foreign Affairs, Tokyo, 1972, pp. 22-3. The authors were quoting the words of the then Minister of Education Arinori Mori.

Figure 1.2:   Japan: Simplified School System, 1900.

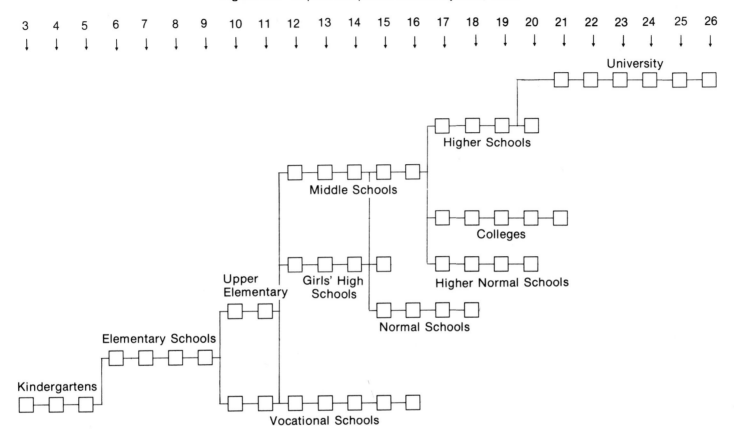

The successful war against China by which she acquired Korea and Formosa in 1894-95, and the defeat of Russia in 1904-5 boosted Japanese confidence and spurred her efforts to modernise and further expand her educational system. Six years of schooling became compulsory in 1907, the Herbartian method of teaching currently popular in the west[40] and not incompatible with the Imperial Rescript, was introduced and widely used, secondary schools for girls as well as boys were developed, normal schools for teacher education multiplied, and several more state or imperial universities were founded. The decade before World War I, therefore, witnessed the development of a new and well-articulated system of national education at primary, secondary and tertiary level that was sustained by an accepted purpose and educational ideal, was able to meet the new industrial and social demands made on it, and was to require little modification until the end of World War II.

(b)   United States of America: Rapid Expansion and Conservative Reform

The first of the western countries to look systematically at the new educational situation that was emerging about the turn of the century was the United States. By that time American education had been generally

---

[40]   See below, Chapter 2.

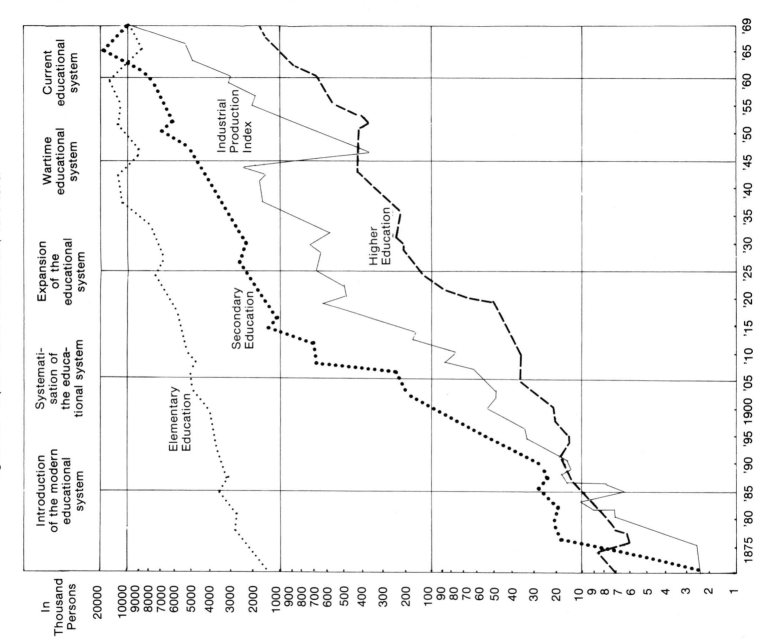

Figure 1.3: Japan: Trends in Enrolment, 1870-1970.

Adapted from, Japan, Ministry of Education, *Education in Japan: A Graphic Presentation 1971*, Tokyo, Government Printing Bureau, 1971.

organised into a sixteen year pattern of three consecutive stages, 8-4-4: eight years for elementary school, four years for high school following directly on the elementary school, and four years leading to a bachelor's degree in college.

In 1890 it was still a rare thing to go to high school; only two-hundred thousand or one per cent of the total population of the U.S.A. was in attendance.[41] Within twenty years the situation had dramatically changed. By 1900 the number had increased two and a half times to half a million, and, by 1912, the million mark had been passed.

Somewhat as a preparation for the coming deluge but also as a recognition of the fact that secondary education had already become well but rather untidily established in the United States, the National Educational Association (NEA) set up, in 1893, a Committee of Ten who were commissioned to report on high school programs. The result, according to the chairman of the NEA was 'the most important educational document ever issued in the United States.'[42]

Committee of Ten. The committee was a mixture of leading academics and school principals and was an interesting and successful exercise in school and university co-operation. Four important recommendations emerged in the final report:

- All subjects in the high school curriculum should be taught in the same way to all pupils irrespective of their probable destination. There should be no differentiation, for example, into college preparatory courses and shorter different courses for the students who might leave school early.

---

[41] E.A. Krug, *The Shaping of the American High School*, Wisconsin University Press, 1964, p. 11.

[42] National Education Association, *Report of the Committee of Ten*, American Book Co., New York, 1894, p. iii. The committee was chaired by President C.W. Eliot of Harvard University, and was organised into sub-committees each of ten well-known academics and schoolteachers in what the chairman regarded as the nine main subject groupings of the high school curriculum.

Figure 1.4: United States of America: School System, 1900. (simplified and generalised diagram)

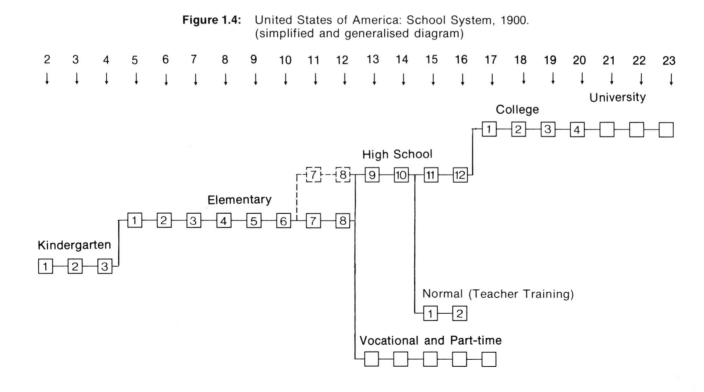

- A small number of subjects thoroughly studied was to be preferred to a large number superficially tasted. Where feasible it was desirable to correlate subjects together to form, as far as possible, a well-knit interrelated course of studies.

- All subjects should be regarded as of equal value. The value of a subject was to be found not primarily in its content but in the mental discipline achieved by the pupils who studied it. The committee, nevertheless, when producing sample curricula, showed a clear preference for language studies.

- High school courses might be put into a limited number of groupings based on the languages taken by students. Four patterns were given: Classical with three foreign languages (one modern); Latin-Scientific with two foreign languages (one modern); Modern Languages with two foreign languages (both modern); and English with one foreign language (ancient or modern). The committee's classification was typical of contemporary European thinking, and was almost identical with the bases on which Prussia had divided her secondary schools.[43]

The impact of the committee's report was considerable. It was a timely contribution to the 'deluge of discussion'[44] that was beginning to build up on secondary education throughout the world.

It was not a fundamental examination of secondary education, as, for example, the Bryce Commission was to be. Instead the committee appeared to make the assumption of a general agreement on educational aims that, in the event, subsequent developments were to show to be false, and it concentrated merely on ways of tidying up existing practices and giving firm advice within the accepted framework. It therefore proved very useful to the many teachers who were seeking an authoritative guide in the confusion and expansion of the next two decades.

The committee's influence was a modestly liberal one, and somewhat contradictory. By declaring all subjects of equal weight, it undermined the traditional position of languages and paved the way for an elective, free choice curriculum; at the same time it showed its preference for language study and, by its prestige, did much to maintain the popularity of languages and a curriculum for high schools that was basically a college preparatory one. The committee's work was a last strenuous effort to maintain in American schools the linguistic, humanist curriculum that had served the secondary schools of western culture for the past four hundred years. The utilitarians and progressives of the early twentieth century were to seek a new humanism with a substantially changed emphasis to match the changing times.

Reforms in Educational Organisation. The Committee of Ten was the forerunner of several more committees of note. The Committee of Fifteen reported in 1895, in a fairly conservative way, on elementary schools, outlining, much as the Committee of Ten had done, a fairly acceptable timetable of school-work, and pointing out, among other things, the need for more effective teacher training, and for more attention to the correlation of subjects. Striking a newer and more fundamental note than its predecessor, it started to explore the educational problems of city school systems affected by the recent acceleration in urban growth and the influx of immigrants.

The recommendations of the Committee of Ten were further developed by a committee on college entrance requirements which reported in 1899. It suggested the development of a six-year high school following a six-year elementary school in which students should be allowed to elect their own pattern of subjects, and that tertiary institutions should base their entrance requirements on the completion of a certain number of units in the subjects offered by high schools. By 1909, the unit, which came to be known as the Carnegie Unit, had been developed and was to be widely accepted.[45] The unit and the elective system were to remain distinctive and lasting aspects of the reorganisation of American secondary education. An accrediting system had been introduced by the University of Michigan in 1871, and, by the end of the century, about two hundred colleges and universities had adopted the plan which enabled graduates of approved secondary schools to be admitted to the university on the recommendation of the school principal. The development of the Carnegie Unit simplified the process of assessing credits and helped to spread the accrediting system.

The principal criticism that might be aimed at the numerically named committees of the 1890's and the subsequent activities that flowed from them was that they concerned themselves almost solely with the

[43] For a comprehensive study of the Committee of Ten, see T.R. Sizer, *Secondary Schools at the Turn of the Century*, Yale University Press, 1964 and E.A. Krug, *The Shaping of the American High School, 1880-1920*, Wisconsin University Press, 1964. The celebrated Kalamazoo case had defined high schools as schools in which languages other than English were taught. Michigan, *Annual Report of the Superintendent of Public Instruction, 1874*, Decision of Judge Cooley of Michigan Supreme Court on Appeal from Kalamazoo Circuit, W.S. George, Lansing, 1875, pp. 409, 411.

[44] A.F. West, Is there a democracy of studies?, *Atlantic Monthly*, December 1899, 821.

[45] The Carnegie Unit was developed through discussion in committees set up by the Board of Trustees of the Carnegie Foundation for the Advancement of Teaching which was established in 1905. The unit was, initially, to be regarded as five periods weekly for an academic year or one-fourth of a year's work. In 1971, when two American scholars made a study of educational change in the United States since 1895, they found that the Carnegie Unit, the elective system, and the junior high school were three of the relatively small number of 'changes that were highly successful and are firmly imbedded in the schools'. D.E. Orlosky and B.O. Smith, *A Study of Educational Change*, mimeo, U.S.O.E. Grant No. OEG-0-71-3958, September 1971, p. 38.

mechanics of educational organisation. Their reports showed little consciousness of the more fundamental social or intellectual changes that were beginning to press in on education. The Committee of Fifteen which did show a slight tendency to look at the more substantial problems was the least regarded and the least effective of them all. The teachers who, by and large, welcomed the reports, accepted the view that high schools were primarily concerned with the development of intellectual discipline and that existing subjects, with some adjustment, provided the most satisfactory way of achieving that aim. They were interested in learning ways of rearranging and reordering existing programs to make them more workable and more logical. They were not primarily interested in making a fundamental re-examination of educational aims. That was to be a longer process both of persuasion by the more perceptive and adventurous among them, and of eventual conviction by force of circumstances.

The beginning of the change became apparent in the United States about 1910. By that date, the educational climate had altered significantly from that in which the Committee of Ten had worked in 1893. Schools both in Europe and America found a variety of influences propelling them towards wider social responsibilities. Utility and social efficiency, supported by a growing and more intense study of education and of children, were beginning to become important considerations in determining the expansion, organisation, and content of education.

Junior High School. The concrete and most striking embodiment of a changed attitude to education in the United States was the establishment of the junior high school. For some ten years or so various school districts had experimented with a form of middle school, intermediate between elementary and high schools. In the school year 1909-10, in both Columbus, Ohio, and Berkeley, California, a three-year junior high school was established which attracted national attention and began a widespread movement to reorganise public education. By 1920 there were eight hundred and eighty-three recognised junior high schools and they were widely and rightly regarded as the representatives of a new and different kind of school. Because it was a new institution educators were not bound to established patterns and felt inclined to innovate. With its establishment, the existing 8-4 pattern of organisation was broken and a six-year elementary, three-year junior high, and three-year high school structure (6-3-3) began to develop which, thirty years later, by the 1940's, had become the common pattern.

The junior high school during the first ten years of its existence was seen as an institution in which:

- the impact of recent research in child development, especially into the needs and interests of adolescents, could be translated effectively into educational practice;
- more careful attention could be paid to the variety of backgrounds, abilities, and aptitudes of pupils, by providing a wide range of courses — general, special, and vocational — in which they might explore and seek guidance;
- without the pressure of college preparation bearing down on the school, its activities could develop a more social flavour by giving the social sciences more prominence in the curriculum and by expanding extra-curricular activities and those that linked the school with the community.

(c) England: State Reorganisation and the Slow Modification of Tradition

The Bryce Commission on Secondary Education, 1895. In England much of the initial discussion of educational issues was to be found in the investigations of the Royal Commission on Secondary Education which reported in 1895. The Bryce Commission, as it was known from the name of its chairman, took a comprehensive view of the function of secondary education. It was not a mere ways and means committee as the Committee of Ten had been for schools in the United States. Its intention was to give a lead to thinking about the general development of secondary education and its importance for the future of England and Englishmen. 'It is not merely in the interest,' it reported, 'of the material prosperity and intellectual activity of the nation, but no less in that of its happiness and its moral strength, that the extension and reorganisation of Secondary Education seem entitled to a place among the first subjects with which social legislation ought to deal.'[46] The commission remarked on the growing influence of the state in education, the recent increase in secondary education, and the expansion of the curriculum to include, as well as the classics, modern languages, physical sciences, and technical and manual education.

The principal needs, according to the report, were for greater unity of administrative control in secondary education, preferably by local authorities under the supervision of one central authority, for a change in the nature of teaching from that of the purveying of mere information to

---

[46] Great Britain, *Royal Commission on Secondary Education*, c. 7862, HMSO, London, 1895, I, p. 327. James Bryce (1838-1922) was regius professor of civil law at Oxford University, 1870-93, member of parliament, 1880-1906, and British ambassador to the U.S.A., 1907-13. He published *The American Commonwealth* in 1888, and *Modern Democracies* in 1921. He was a friend of President Eliot of Harvard, and in close touch with Eliot's work on the Committee of Ten.

the genuine cultivation of the mind, and for a wider view of the nature of secondary education to include commercial and technical education. The commission recommended the use of municipal government bodies as local educational authorities, the establishment of a central policy-formulating authority with an advisory council of professional experts, and the inspection of all non-state schools. On the curriculum, it advised that there should be a balance of three elements, literary, scientific, and technical. Secondary education, it thought, should not be free; it was not yet expected that it was to be provided for all, but schools in receipt of public money should provide a number of free places. To staff the expected expansion and improvement of secondary education, secondary school teachers should be prepared by a course of professional training given in the universities, and the central authority should keep a register of qualified teachers.

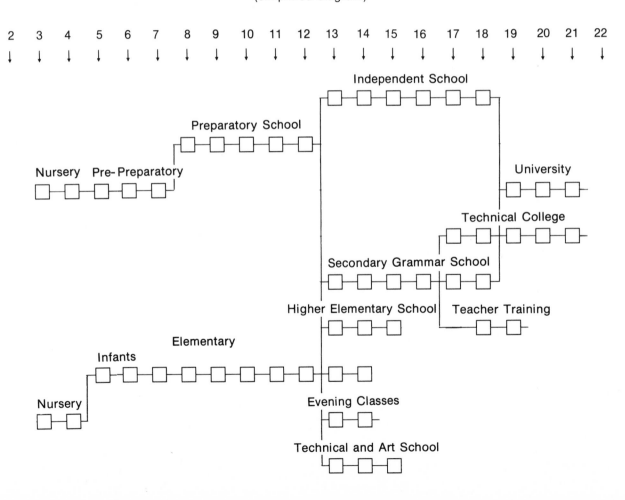

Figure 1.5:   England: School System, 1905.
(simplified diagram)

'The epoch-making Report,' as *The Educational Times* described it, was widely discussed, and made an impact on educational thinking and administration that was to last for many years. Its suggestions on administration were, for the most part, adopted in the legislation of the next ten years; and its ideas on curriculum remained a source of interesting discussion, pointing as they did to the need to find a modern substitute for the traditional emphasis on classics. In the years leading up to World War I the science subjects progressed as the commission had anticipated, but technical education remained firmly excluded from the secondary area.

The Education Acts of 1899 and 1902. The Education Act of 1899 set up a new central authority, the Board of Education, with a consultative committee of persons interested in education. The Board had a general power of supervision and inspection over elementary, secondary, and technical education, and some influence over tertiary education. It was the instrument through which government funds and policies found their way into the nation's schools. The Board, in its forty-five-year history, until it was superseded by a Ministry of Education in 1945, never actually met; it was simply a convenient administrative device for organising a segment of the central government. The consultative committee met from time to time over the period and published, on a wide range of significant matters referred to them by the Board, a series of reports which ranked among the best analyses of educational problems appearing in any country up to the end of World War II.

The year 1899 was noted for a second event of significance for the structure and organisation of English education. In that year the auditor disallowed expenditure of public money made by the London School Board on items beyond the elementary school curriculum.[47] The action raised doubts about the legality of some of the common educational practices of public authorities and forced a re-examination of the administrative structure of education in England. The eventual outcome was the Education Act of 1902.[48]

The Act abolished the *ad hoc* school boards of the late nineteenth century and gave educational authority to existing local government bodies. The whole of England and Wales was thus divided into about 420 local education authorities (LEA's), the larger of which had power to maintain secondary and technical as well as elementary education, to raise money by rating for their 'provided' schools and for the maintenance of the 'non-provided' schools established in their area by other bodies, and, above all, in conjunction with the central authority, to plan and co-ordinate all the forms of education in their area. During the next five years many LEA's commissioned educational surveys of their areas and developed plans which became the basis on which a comprehensive national but decentralised system of education was built up.

Regulations for Secondary Schools, 1904 and 1907. In 1904 the Board of Education issued their initial set of regulations for secondary schools. It was a first and authoritative attempt to define the field and to give a reasonably firm direction to its development. A secondary school was 'a Day or Boarding School offering to each of its scholars up to and beyond the age of 16, a general education, physical, mental and moral, given through a complete graded course of instruction, of wider scope and more advanced degree than that given in Elementary Schools'. The principal subjects of study were to be English; a language other than English, preferably Latin; history; geography; mathematics; science; and drawing. To these should be added manual work and physical exercise, and, in the case of girls, practical housewifery.[49]

The traditional, academic, secondary grammar school oriented towards preparation for university work was the model that the regulations proposed to encourage. Technical or vocational education, and the practical scientific and non-linguistic education recently evolved in higher elementary schools were firmly discouraged. English secondary education became grammar school education. Thus the Independent Public School tradition which provided the pattern for denominational and proprietary grammar schools was adopted also by the new foundations that the LEA's created in the course of the twentieth century. The tradition gave them ready-made 'standards of scholarship and internal organisation and an ideal of corporate spirit' and an aspiration towards the university and the learned professions.[50] It also had the effect of confirming the sharp distinction that had developed between primary and secondary education. Secondary education was for the relatively few, primary education and such continuation classes as might be organised in conjunction with it was for the mass.

---

[47] The view of Mr Cockerton, the local government board district auditor, was upheld by the courts in 1900 and, on appeal, in 1901. The Cockerton judgment was on a matter similar to that of the Kalamazoo High School case in Michigan, 1874, but the decision went in the opposite direction.

[48] It is commonly named after its political author and prime minister of the day, the Balfour Act.

[49] Great Britain, Board of Education, *Report of the Consultative Committee on Secondary Education*, (Spens Report), H.M.S.O., 1939, Chap. 1, Historical sketch (R.F. Young), pp. 67ff. Good short accounts of this period are to be found also in G.A.N. Lowndes, *The Silent Social Revolution*, O.U.P., 1937; E.J.R. Eaglesham, *The Foundations of 20th Century Education in England*, R.K.P., London, 1967; A.M. Kazamias, *Politics, Society and Secondary Education in England*, University of Pennsylvania, 1966; and D. Wardle, *English Popular Education, 1780-1970*, C.U.P., 1970.

[50] *Report of the Consultative Committee on Secondary Education*, 1939, p. 72.

The grammar school was the living tradition of secondary education that suited the expanding middle class of Edwardian England. The quasi-vocational trend evolved in the type of schools produced by the general upward extension of elementary education in the interests of the lower social classes was not yet to be the main line of secondary school development in England. In 1911-12, however, it was to get a fresh impetus with the establishment of four-year central schools for children from eleven to fifteen years in London and Manchester in which the curriculum was given a commercial or an industrial bias. The schools helped to reanimate the practical trend that, after the Hadow Report of 1926, was to merge with the grammar school tradition in the development of England's Modern Secondary schools.

In 1907 further secondary school regulations were introduced to encourage schools to offer 25 per cent of the enrolment as free places to children selected as a result of an attainment test set eventually for most schools at the age of eleven plus. It was the beginning of what was to become a fiercely competitive examination dominating the upper grades of the primary school for more than half a century. Secondary education was not free and the new regulations were an effort to widen opportunity to attend secondary schools. By 1920, about thirty per cent of children enrolled in secondary schools had free places, but only about six per cent of them had come from free state elementary schools. The trade union congress, as early as 1906, had adopted a policy of secondary education for all, and agitation for it was a factor in the development of the free place system, but the objective did not become politically feasible until the 1920's, nor a reality until after World War II.[51]

(d) France and the Pursuit of the Intellectual

The term 'intellectual' first became popular in the 1890's and was confirmed in its currency at the turn of the century in the poignant and long-drawn-out debates on the Dreyfus affair. An intellectual was a person of literary culture who felt impelled to enter into argument on contemporary issues of significance and to express a reasoned view with some depth of human concern. Thus, Anatole France called Emile Zola, for his outspokenness in the Dreyfus case, 'a moment of the French conscience'. It became a leading characteristic of French social and political discussion throughout the twentieth century that it should be fuelled by astute, quick-witted, and concerned contributions from the intellectuals.

The nurseries of the intellectuals of France were the classical secondary schools, the *lycées*, maintained by the central government, and the *collèges* established by municipalities.

Ribot Commission, 1899. Towards the end of the nineteenth century France found herself in the same state of unrest about education as the other countries of the world. In 1890 two parallel but unequal secondary courses — classics and modern — had been set up. Much dissatisfaction was caused by the fact that, in length, prestige, and as a qualification for further studies, the classics course was the superior, and that pupils who did not take the traditional curriculum were at a disadvantage. In order to sift the issues of secondary education thoroughly the French Chamber of Deputies set up a commission in 1898 presided over by one of its members, Alexandre Ribot. The commission took evidence from a large number of interested people and presented its report in 1899 in six substantial volumes. Never before had opinion been so thoroughly canvassed on every aspect of secondary education that the informants chose to deal with.

The uneasiness in secondary education, in Ribot's view, had arisen for several reasons: because the traditional culture could not meet the needs of the rising classes in the contemporary social and economic revolution; because science had acquired an enormous prestige and demanded more attention in secondary schools; and because modern conditions of living demanded intelligent persons with originality and a willingness to act, while the traditional curriculum inclined its pupils towards more intellectual analysis and contemplation.[52] The commission found that the main problem of interest was that of the content of secondary school studies, and that there were widely divergent views on the matter. One of the large local administrative authorities in central France, for example, made a spirited plea to maintain the classical curriculum on the ground that 'it trains the intelligence, stirs the feelings, nurtures the higher things of the mind, builds the finest character, and produces the intellectual elites which have raised the reputation of France so high'.[53] On the other hand, there were several strenuous opponents who saw classical education as the badge of upper middle class exclusiveness, who argued for subject-matter more relevant to contemporary life, and who wished to do away with the external final secondary school examination, the baccalauréat.[54] The general trend of the evidence before the commission, however, was for the retention of both classical and modern studies, and their task was to work out the best means of integrating the traditional literary with the modern scientific subjects.

[51] For an excellent analysis of labour views see B. Simon, *Education and the Labour Movement, 1870-1920*, Lawrence and Wishart, London, 1965.

[52] A. Ribot, *La Réforme de l'Enseignement Secondaire*, Colin, Paris, 1900, pp. 3-6.

[53] J.B. Piobetta, *Le Baccalauréat*, Baillière, Paris, p. 229.

[54] ibid., pp. 207, 225; Ribot, *op.cit.*, p. 193.

Figure 1.6: France: School System, 1902.
(simplified diagram)

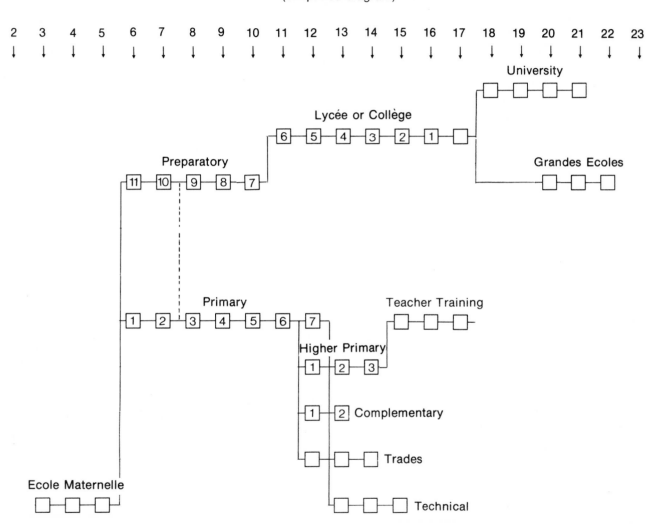

Secondary School Reform of 1902. The reform of secondary education that was accepted by the French parliament in 1902 following the Ribot Commission was, according to a leading French historian of education, more substantial than any that had preceded it, and could be regarded as the beginning of a new order of things.[55] The new approach offered a seven-year secondary course following a four or five-year preparatory course. The first four-year cycle of the secondary course provided a choice of two programs, a classical course in which Latin was compulsory from the first year and Greek was optional from the third, and a modern course with no ancient languages and with an emphasis on French and science. Each course was intended to be a complete and rounded general education. In the following three-year cycle, a pupil could choose one of four specialised courses: Latin and Greek; Latin and modern languages; Latin and science; and science and modern languages. with no Latin. In the final year in each of the four courses, there was the traditional concentration on philosophy or mathematics leading up to the award of the *baccalauréat*.

The curriculum reform of 1902 remained in force for over twenty years until its modification by the Bérard reforms in 1923-25. It accomplished four things. It abolished the individious duality of the previous curriculum by giving equal weight and reward to each of the options. It provided greater variety, in the expectation of catering for the greater range of aptitudes that contemporary educators were beginning to study and discuss. It recognised and fully accepted the possibility of achieving the traditional intellectual objectives of French secondary education in courses that were not dominated by the study of the classical languages or even, in some cases, did not contain the classics at all. And it acknowledged, as educators in other countries were also doing at the same time, that there had come into being a scientific as well as a literary culture, one modern and practical, the other traditional and linguistic. Judiciously mixed, they might be made to complement one another and provide an intellectual discipline highly relevant to the twentieth century that might orient pupils to some of the significant issues. Important in that regard was the inclusion of the study of ethics in the first cycle, and of philosophy in the second; ethics drew the students' attention to problems of behaviour in individual, social, and international situations, and philosophy provided a basic course in psychology, aesthetics, logic, ethics and metaphysics and gave the future intellectual an opportunity to compose and analyse the sorts of essays and arguments that he might soon be expected to deal with in a more public arena.

Despite the great amount of controversial discussion that led up to it, contemporary claims of its importance, and the subsequent concerted attempts by classicists to revoke it, the reform was far from radical or comprehensive. It was a moderate adjustment of content within an existing pattern of schooling. The curriculum of secondary education remained predominantly linguistic and not unlike the suggestions ten years earlier of the American Committe of Ten; and, while increased opportunity was provided for students to study in non-classical courses, the numbers studying Latin in the first cycle actually increased three and a half times during the next ten years.[56] It was not meant to be the beginning of a move towards universal secondary education; it was a move to update the education of a limited elite and to allow for some small expansion in it. Technical education, therefore, did not come into consideration, and the possibility of a general, upward, non-selective extension of primary education was not seriously thought of.

Growth of Secondary Education. The reform had been confined to boys' schools. Girls' secondary education, on any but a very small scale, had been a recent creation. In 1897 the program for girls' *lycées* had been reformed to provide a five-year course heavily weighted with modern language studies. Latin, except in translation in the final years, was not a part of a girls' education. During the ten years following the reorganisation, the girls' *lycées* increased rapidly and attendance at them doubled; but, by 1907, despite their growth, there were only forty-seven, with sixteen thousand pupils, compared with one hundred and thirteen boys' *lycées* with fifty-seven thousand pupils.

The years from 1902 up to World War I were a period of slow expansion in French secondary education. Attendance mounted, but at no great rate, increasing for all forms of secondary schools from approximately one-hundred thousand in 1900 to one-hundred and fifty thousand in 1920; smaller *lycées* which could not carry the full program steadily enlarged their facilities; and municipal *collèges* which followed the same courses as *lycées* grew in numbers and importance.

At the same time, a second system of schooling at the secondary level, but not designated secondary, was rapidly growing up with the development of higher primary schools. Organised originally in 1833, they had had a chequered career during the nineteenth century until the conditions of the early twentieth century gave them a new importance. They provided a three-year course with an entry age of about twelve. It was a general education similar to the modern course in the first cycle of the *lycée*, with pre-vocational courses available in industrial, commercial, agricultural, and domestic areas. The higher primary schools catered for a kind of second level elite — the more capable working class children who aspired to positions of minor responsibility in industry, commerce, and administration. The schools were somewhat similar to the central

[55] F. Vial, *Trois Siècles d'Histoire de l'Enseignement Secondaire*, Delagrave, Paris, 1936, p. 245.

[56] J.B. Piobetta, *Le Baccalauréat*, p. 193.

schools of England, the middle schools of Prussia, and, to a lesser extent, American junior high schools. Additional *cours complémentaires* were also attached in many places to primary schools and offered secondary education of the higher primary variety. The steady development of secondary level education of that kind was to induce the less conservative educators in the 1920's to rethink the objectives and provision of secondary education. After 1941, when the higher elementary schools were converted into *collèges*, the fusion coincided with concerted moves towards the development of comprehensive secondary schools that were eventually to bear fruit in the 1960's.

(e) Germany: Debate and Stability

Germany was generally regarded by the other developed nations as the pacesetter in education. So superior did a leading English educator regard Germany's achievement that, in admonishing his fellow-countrymen for their obtuseness and backwardness, he wrote, 'The ordinary middle class parent in Germany knows more about the real nature of education, and of the conditions which will make schooling successful, than our English Cabinet Ministers.'[57]

Nevertheless, in 1890, a German scholar wrote, 'The educational parties fight among themselves at the present time with the ardour of religious fanatics.'[58] It was a time of heated debate, and secondary education was the main issue. In that same year the German emperor entered the lists. In a rambling address to a special conference in Berlin on secondary school reform in Prussia he let it be known that he was dissatisfied with the current state of secondary education. Secondary schools, cramming and overtaxing their pupils, were producing a surplus of educated people, and, by neglecting character for knowledge, were creating a potentially disruptive element in the population. 'It is our duty to educate young men to become young Germans, and not young Greeks or Romans.' They were to be young Germans with two particular characteristics: they were to be loyal and patriotic, and they were to be familiar with modern German history and modern political issues, and thus, 'in some measure be practically equipped at school for actual life and its problems'.[59]

Secondary School Reform of 1892. The outcome of the 1890 conference was a modest reform introduced in 1892 similar to that in France in 1890, except that the different courses were to be offered in different schools. It was a compromise in which the classical secondary school, the *Gymnasium*, had the amount of Latin and Greek in its curriculum reduced, but still retained its central position in Prussian secondary education. The other two types of secondary school, the *Realgymnasium*, which taught Latin but no

Greek, was encouraged to place more emphasis on modern languages and science, and the *Oberrealschule* which taught no Latin also increased its teaching of modern languages, mathematics, and science. In all schools the time given to the teaching of German language and German history was increased. The scheme was a concession to the reformers whose views the emperor had voiced. It satisfied no one. The classicists felt deprived and unable to do their best on a restricted program, and the modernists were anxious for a more substantial change in spirit and content.

There was a double cleavage in German education as in the education of other developed countries. There was, in the first place, a conflict between the traditional and the up-to-date. The commercial, expansive Germany moving into the twentieth century was a different society from the scholar's dream of a romantic and artistic Germany of the early nineteenth century when the *Gymnasium* was first established. Berlin had replaced Weimar as the centre of affairs. Von Bülow, later to be Chancellor of Prussia, summed up the change in a speech to the Diet: 'The days when the German abandoned to one of his neighbours the earth, and to another the sea, and when he reserved for himself the Heavens above — the throne of pure doctrinaire theory — these days are past.'[60] And Paulsen, one of Germany's most lively academic minds of the period, pointed out the inference for secondary education: 'For the majority of our students, even those who are to proceed to a university, education in modern languages and in science is more essential, less dispensable than so-called classical education. They need a school more relevant to the present day, a modern *Gymnasium*.'[61]

The other cleavage was a social one. As the middle class increased in power and strengthened its claim for more and better secondary education, so, too, as primary education expanded, did the more ambitious among the mass of workers begin to look towards an upward extension of the primary school into a form of secondary education suitable to their needs. Their aspirations were to bring a new form of secondary education into being in European countries, taking it in many ways closer to the American pattern which was itself changing steadily under the pressure of the same force. The trend was discernible at the

[57] J.J. Findlay, The Genesis of the German Clerk, *Fortnightly Review*, 1899, 66, 534. J.J. Findlay was a professor of education at Manchester. See below, Chapter 2.

[58] P. Cauer, *Staat und Erziehung*, 1890, p. 6, quoted in Great Britain, Board of Education, *Special Reports on Educational Subjects, 3, The Continent*, HMSO, London, 1898, p. 103.

[59] Translations of the emperor's address are to be found in *Educational Review*, February, 1891, 200-208, and, in part, in Great Britain, Board of Education, *Special Reports on Educational Subjects, 3, op.cit.*, 108-9.

[60] Speech to the Imperial German Diet, 6 December 1897, quoted in Great Britain, Board of Education, *Special Reports on Educational Subjects, 3, op. cit.*, p. 114.

[61] F. Paulsen, *Geschichte des gelehrten Unterrichts*, 3rd edition, Gruyter, Berlin, 1921, 2, p. 649.

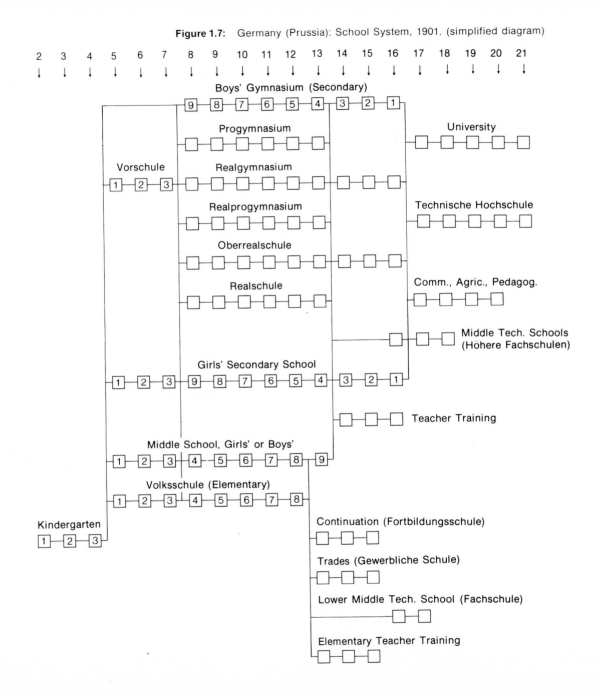

Figure 1.7: Germany (Prussia): School System, 1901. (simplified diagram)

beginning of the century; it did not gather force until after World War I; and it came into reality only in the 1950's and 60's.

Reorganisation in 1900. Meanwhile, at the beginning of the century, strenuous moves were under way to bring the curriculum of Prussian secondary schools up to date to meet the exigencies of Paulsen's modern Germany. In 1900 a general conference of educators was held which led to a substantial reform in the same year. All three types of school — *Gymnasium, Realgymnasium,* and *Oberrealschule* — were declared to be of equal status, capable of supplying students for most of the faculties of the university, and each henceforth endeavoured to concentrate on its own special brand of general education: the *Gymnasium* on ancient languages, the *Realgymnasium* on a balance of ancient and modern languages and science, and the *Oberrealschule* on modern languages and modern science. Though declared, in the decree of 1900, to be 'of equal value from the point of view of general intellectual culture', the *Gymnasium* continued to be the most popular school and the tradition that linguistic discipline was the basis of secondary education continued to be widely accepted. Each of the three main schools offered a nine-year course and parallel to them, there were also three six-year schools. The *Progymnasium* corresponded to the first six years of the *Gymnasium,* the *Realprogymnasium* to the first six years of the *Realgymnasium,* and the *Realschule* to the first six years of the *Oberrealschule.*

The reform accomplished little. It set the pattern of Prussian education up to the end of World War I, but it had actually made little change. Though German technical education had been built up to meet the demands of the industrial and commercial world, secondary education was still far from taking any serious account of practical utility and the interests of modern government and modern business.

(iii) Trends in Vocational Education

'A six year old lady who honours me with her friendship,' the writer of an article reported in 1901, 'came to tea with me one day recently, and being offered a choice of toys to play with afterwards chose unhesitatingly the typewriter.'[62] The choice may merely have reflected the poverty of the rival attractions that the author had to offer or the novelty of the mechanical toy. It could, on the other hand, be regarded as a symbol of the prevailing utilitarianism of the times.

The new utilitarian spirit, 'emphasises action rather than knowledge'. It looked to writers such as Bergson and aimed, through education, to produce the socially efficient individual.[63] One of the important elements of social efficiency was vocational competence. A growing number of educators were therefore becoming interested in working out ways in which vocational preparation could be incorporated more fully into the ordinary school program.

In the late nineteenth century, manual training had become an accepted part of the curriculum of primary and secondary schools in many countries and had been regarded as a useful part of general education or as a vocational preparation of a very general kind. With the beginning of the twentieth century there was a developing interest in specific vocational education given within the nation's schools.

(a) Occupational Levels

By 1900, in the industrialised countries of Europe and the United States, three levels of occupation with corresponding types of training had become apparent. The higher levels of management and scientific and technological research were well-established features of the industrial scene and offered positions which required an advanced level of training. It was to be obtained usually in a university or an associated institution.

Middle level management and technical skill were emerging as parts of an important segment of the structure of industry by the beginning of the twentieth century. Within the general grouping there were two sub-levels: the upper, of persons such as works managers and superintendents; the lower, of foremen and supervisors. Training for the middle level and for both its sub-levels was offered through courses both preparatory to and supplementary to industrial experience.

At the third level, most of the work force consisted of operatives of various degrees of skill. For them, lower level training was available through an apprenticeship system or short part-time training taken on the job or in special schools.

Higher, middle, and lower level occupations were reasonably distinguishable, and although there were possibilities of transfer and promotion from one level to another, there was a tendency for recruits to undergo separate initial training for each level. The distinction between the levels and the corresponding training was most clearly established and maintained in Germany and France, and, though discernible, was much

[62] Edward H. Cooper, Some Nurseries of the Twentieth Century, *Monthly Review*, November 1901, 145, collected in: Great Britain, Ministry of Education Library, *Education Miscellanies*, 29, 29. This is a large and invaluable collection of cuttings on education from English and foreign newspapers and periodicals put together by and held in the Ministry of Education Library. Of great value also for the student of technological education in Europe in the twentieth century is an unpublished thesis by V.J. Couch, *A Sociological Interpretation of the Development of Technological Education in England, France and Germany during the Twentieth Century,* Unpublished Ph.D. Thesis, University of London, 1955.

[63] A. Darroch, *Education and the New Utilitarianism,* Longmans Green, London, 1914, p. 3.

less distinct in England and the U.S.A. where training institutions and procedures were, consequently, less carefully differentiated.

(b) Vocational Education in 1900

By 1900, Germany had nine well-established *Technische Hochschulen* recently granted full university status which gave a lead to her interest in applying research and thorough training to the development of her industries. Their enrolment was approximately a quarter of all the university students in Germany. 'There is a close connection', wrote an appreciative foreign observer, 'between the enormous development of Germany's application of science and art to industry, and her astonishing industrial and commercial prosperity'.[64] At the middle level, technicians received their training in a multitude of specialist technical schools which provided, for almost every trade, upper grade courses for second level engineers and inspectors, and basic courses for overseers and foremen. Part-time continuation schools supplementing apprenticeship training and elementary education were well established and were rapidly expanding as an important aspect of basic training in all German towns, and, in many places, were compulsory. Trade schools and secondary technical schools also provided initial industrial and commercial training.

In France, the University of Paris and several of the regional universities had set up, by 1900, about ten institutes devoted to specialised study and training in various applied sciences, such as brewing, tanning, applied chemistry, radiology, and optics. In addition there were several *Grandes Ecoles*, independent of universities, to provide highly trained technical and administrative officers, such as civil and mining engineers, and colonial administrators, for the most part, for various government departments. That pattern was maintained and slowly expanded during the pre-World War I period. For middle grade technicians training was very diverse. Four regional schools for the training of second level engineers had been established; there were two post-primary technical schools for training foremen and workers for positions of intermediate management; and, in one or two industries, specialist schools after the German pattern were operating by the turn of the century. Trade teaching for the third level was introduced after 1892 into the public school system of France by the development of elementary vocational schools run by the Ministry of Commerce and Industry. Other trade schools were set up in the towns by individuals, industries, or public authorities to train skilled workmen, and to supplement the practice of apprenticeship which though declining was still the most popular means to learn a trade.

England, in 1900 had a dozen or so schools of engineering and applied science, some within the universities, others on the periphery. In addition, in London, three recently established colleges for science, mining, and engineering, respectively, were concerned with higher technological training and some aspects of research. A growing number of polytechnics and technical colleges provided by local authorities were responsible for the training of middle level technicians of various kinds. At the artisan level, evening continuation schools provided a low level of training for ex-elementary school pupils; and evening courses in technical schools and colleges were used to supplement apprenticeship and factory training for a small number of workers.

In the United States, higher technological education had been well established in the nineteenth century, first with the foundation of the Rensselaer Polytechnic Institute in 1824, then with the Massachusetts Institute of Technology in 1865, and, above all, with the stimulus of the First Morrill Land-Grant Act of 1862 which enabled numerous old and newly established universities to develop the study of agriculture and engineering. At the basic level of trade training the traditional approach through apprenticeship had been steadily declining in the latter part of the nineteenth century and there was much questioning as to its suitability for contemporary large-scale mass-producing industries.

(c) Vocational Education from 1900 to World War I

Nineteenth century vocational training, though providing for a variety of levels, concentrated most of its efforts on producing efficient workmen and clerks. The expansion and acceleration of the technological revolution in the twentieth century required, in addition, a supply of two other kinds of persons: higher level specialists, and managers of all levels. In the twentieth century there was to be a very substantial expansion in all forms of vocational education at all levels following somewhat the same patterns that were operating at the turn of the century. The main thrust, however, was to be at the middle level where technical and managerial responsibilities rapidly increased, and facilities for training were multiplied.

Germany. Between 1900 and World War I higher technical education in Germany did not actually expand, but rather consolidated and became increasingly specialised. While the number of students in other kinds of universities almost doubled, rising from thirty-four thousand in 1900 to sixty-one thousand in 1914, there was an increase only from 10,400 to 11,400 in the *Technische Hochschulen* over the same period. It was, nevertheless, a substantial enrolment. The total number of advanced students, by comparison, in English universities and technical institutes

[64] E.G. Cooley, *Vocational Education in Europe*, Report to the Chicago Commercial Club, 1912, p. 12.

was 2,500. Industry's demand in Germany was not for more high level technical recruits, but for individuals with a more professional and specialised training. Courses within the institutions, accordingly, became more professionally oriented, and each institution began to departmentalise and to specialise in selected areas.

In Germany, trades schools at both advanced and elementary level were greatly encouraged. The advanced schools followed a six-year secondary course and the two years of trade practice; they provided two to three year courses of both managerial and technical training of a standard somewhere between secondary and tertiary level education, and their products were in great demand. The lower schools catered for students who had completed an elementary school education and an apprenticeship; they provided one to two year courses for potential foremen and more highly skilled workmen. The advanced and lower level courses were offered in some states, in the same schools, and occasionally were to be found incorporated into secondary *Realgymnasien*.

In contrast with France, England and the U.S.A., Germany in the early years of the twentieth century consolidated her apprenticeship system. Training remained basically in the hands of master craftsmen in industry or special training schools set up in some of the larger industrial concerns, and was supplemented by compulsory education in continuation schools in which the trend was towards vocational rather than general education.

France. In France, between 1900 and World War I, the work of the regional technical schools was strengthened and their numbers increased. Of a similar standard to Germany's upper level trade schools, they required for entry some work experience and several years of post-primary education, and they were concerned with training 'intelligent and competent intermediaries between the engineer and the foreman'.[65] For lower level supervisory jobs the post-primary technical schools, comparable to the German lower level trade schools, were increased also by 1914. Each school served a wide region in France, admitting students at about the age of fourteen, and covering a variety of industries and businesses.

France from 1900 to 1914 experienced a crisis in apprenticeship training. Few employers were willing to accept responsibility for apprentices and baulked at the stringent conditions that accompanied their employment; at the same time, because of France's declining birthrate, the number of potential recruits dwindled, and trained foreign workers were engaged in increasing numbers. The result was the speedy disappearance of the apprenticeship system in France which up till 1900 had been the principal means of training young skilled workmen. The gap was not adequately filled. The number of elementary vocational schools was increased, but, as their courses were largely at a pre-

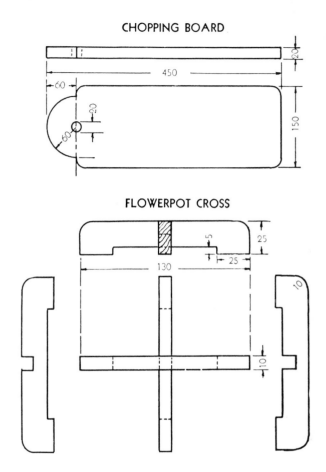

Typical sloyd exercises for first year secondary school students. The measurements are in millimetres.

Charles A. Bennett, *History of Manual Arts and Industrial Education, 1870 to 1917*, The Manual Arts Press, Peoria, Illinois, 1937.

---

[65]   E. Percy, Education for Industrial Vocations, *Yearbook of Education*, Evans, London, 1933, p. 117.

[66]   Philip Magnus, 'Some economic aspects of the application of science to industry', speech delivered in 1903 and reprinted in P. Magnus, *Educational Aims and Efforts, 1880-1910*, Longmans Green, London, 1910, p. 263.

apprenticeship level, they did not meet the real need. It was not until the *Loi Astier* was passed immediately after World War I, in 1919, that a serious solution to the problem was put forward.

England. In the pre-World War I period, England's higher technical education became even more heterogeneous. The three London colleges combined to become, in 1907, the Imperial College of Science and Technology and subsequently a school of the University of London; they provided the outstanding example of the absorption by universities of such higher level training. In some cities, however, colleges of technology developed parallel to the local university's technological faculties, and in several cities, too, polytechnic colleges developed higher level training courses comparable in some fields with those of universities. The emphasis in the higher level courses was on the study of science and its possible industrial application. It was the hope of persons like Philip Magnus, still England's leading advocate of technical education, that 'so intimate is now this relation, that one may truly say that no industry can be successfully pursued without some help from science'.[66] In reality, English industry in the pre-World War I period was in a state of technological starvation. To compete with its newer and flourishing rivals it needed re-equipping and restructuring. Capital, however, was not available for such activities. England's privileged trade position with its empire, and the attractions of overseas markets, meant that overseas investment was more profitable than investment in industrial improvement at home. In consequence, English industry and the technical education that could strengthen and invigorate it did not at that time receive the solid support they needed.

At the middle level the Board of Education in its regulations for technical schools in 1904 encouraged the development of full-time courses for students of about sixteen years of age who had completed three or four years of secondary school. Senior technical education of that kind had the same purpose as and was of similar standard to the higher trades schools of Germany and the regional technical schools of France. In England, however, the courses were usually not provided in separate technical schools but as a part of a technical college or polytechnic which also offered elementary trade courses and sometimes higher technological courses. Full-time education at the middle technical level did not flourish in England as it did in France and Germany, but tended to be restricted to part-time attendance and to be somewhat fragmentary. The lower level of middle technical training was undertaken mainly through works experience supplemented by evening courses.

For the lower levels of occupations, voluntary evening continuation schools and day technical classes were used to extend elementary education, especially in mathematics, technical drawing, science, and

English, and to give general introductory work in various trades, grouped in most schools into industrial, commercial, rural, or domestic occupations. The day technical classes were recognised by the Board of Education in 1913 as Junior Technical Schools, an institution which had no parallel in France or Germany. It provided full-time, general, pre-apprenticeship training, and did not attract many students. Skilled occupations were entered usually through an apprenticeship of up to five years begun at about the age of sixteen. Apprenticeship training was supplemented by specialised teaching in evening technical and commercial schools which generally formed part of a local technical college.

Technical education in England was the Cinderella of education. It was unplanned, inadequately financed, and looked on without enthusiasm by employers, employees, and educators. A government report in 1918 estimated that in 1914 only seven per cent of the male population was receiving any kind of technical instruction.[67] Technical education was seldom thought of as a substantial and well structured entity, effectively related to secondary and higher education and to the needs of industry as it could be seen to be in many parts of Germany. In England, it was generally regarded as predominantly a part-time education for technicians, craftsmen, and office workers, to supplement the experience of the workshop and office.[68]

United States of America. As a consequence of the current questioning of traditional methods of trade training in the United States, there was increased interest in formal courses of vocational training, full- or part-time, in schools. To further the movement, the National Society for the Promotion of Industrial Education was founded in 1906. The society became a focal point of all interested in vocational education. It worked hard during the next ten years to gather popular support, and eventually was instrumental in securing the passage of the federal Smith-Hughes Act of 1917 which provided a firm financial basis for vocational education in the public schools throughout the country. One of the principal questions for debate in those years was whether vocational education had a place in the public school curriculum, or whether a separate system of vocational schools should be established. Some educators expressed a fear that vocational education might be begun before the solid foundations of general education had been laid, and that the demands of trade rather than the cultivation of the mind might come to dominate the school

[67] *Report of the Committee, Appointed by the Prime Minister to Enquire into the Position of Natural Science in the Educational System of Great Britain* (J.J. Thomson, Chairman). HMSO, London, 1918, pp. 39-40.

[68] See M. Argles, *South Kensington to Robbins*, Longmans, London, 1964, pp. 58ff., and S.F. Cotgrove, *Technical Education and Social Change*, Allen and Unwin, London, 1958, pp. 67ff.

curriculum. A few, led by John Dewey, thought that vocational education could be a relevant aspect of general education in an industrial society. Eventually, the weight of opinion among educational administrators was in favour of retaining the high school as the sole secondary school, and of building commercial, industrial, agricultural, and home-making studies into its curriculum, gradually increasing the emphasis on them in the senior years.[69] For the most part, trade education in the high school was pre-vocational education. Vocational education, when it was sought, was obtained through apprenticeship or some form of trades school.

When an official monograph on education in the U.S.A. was prepared for the Paris Exposition in 1900, there was, in its 470 pages, no single mention of vocational education. The next ten years, however, produced a radical change. By 1910 more than half the states had established some kind of vocational education. A minority had set up technical high schools; many of the cities had grade schools for full and part-time education; and many rural areas had built agricultural high schools. In addition, there was a considerable number of vocational training schools established by individuals or large industries.

Despite the extensive discussion and substantial progress since 1900, a presidential commission reported in 1914 that less than 1 per cent of persons engaged in agriculture and in industry in the United States in 1910 had had an adequate vocational training, and that in the whole of the United States there were fewer trade schools of all kinds than in the small German state of Bavaria. The commission advised that in the interests of future national well-being the deficiency should be speedily remedied.

'Since commercial prosperity depends largely upon the skill and well-being of our workers, the outlook for American commerce in competition with our more enterprising neighbors, under present conditions, is not very promising.

'It is even more short-sighted of the State and Nation to neglect these investments, since national success is dependent not alone on returns in dollars and cents, but in civic and social well-being.' The commission's statement neatly illustrated the combination of political and economic consideration that entered into current thinking on education and was to be of fundamental importance in determining educational policies in all countries during the rest of the century.

---

[69] See A.B. Mays, *The Concept of Vocational Education in the Thinking of the General Educator, 1845 to 1945*, Urbana, University of Illinois Bulletin, 43, 1 July 1946, pp. 57-80; M.L. Barlow, *History of Industrial Education in the United States*, Peoria, Illinois, Bennett, 1967, pp. 51-66; C.A. Bennett, *History of Manual and Industrial Education, 1870-1917*, Manual Arts Press, Peoria, Illinois, 1937; and U.S.A. *Report of the Commission on National Aid to Vocational Education*, U.S. Government Printing Office, Washington, 1914.

CHAPTER 2

THE HERBARTIANS

Wilhelm Rein (1847-1929), the great German Herbartian, Professor of Education at the University of Jena.

At the beginning of the twentieth century Herbartianism was the ruling force in education. When Oscar Browning introduced the Felkins' translation of Herbart's *Letters and Lectures on Education* in 1898 he stated that the most prominent teacher-trainers in Germany and America were Herbartians, that Herbart dominated the training colleges at that time, and would probably do so even more in the future. Six years later, in 1904, Compayré, in a monograph *Herbart and Education by Instruction* expressed the view that, in Germany, Herbart had become 'the hero and ruling spirit of modern education', that his disciples were many and widespread, and, for the past fifty years, had succeeded each other in the chairs of pedagogy at the German universities and in *gymnasien*, normal schools, and primary schools throughout the country. Compayré went on to describe the Herbartian impact outside Germany, especially in the United States of America, concluding that it was an almost universal movement found throughout the whole world, and destined to endure and spread even more widely.

Browning suggested two reasons for the Herbartian ascendancy: it was the only complete and up-to-date system of education, and it was based upon a convincing and readily understandable theory of ethics and psychology which provided respectively the aim of education, and the method of teaching. These were the product not merely of the originator's work, but also of the theoretical adaptations and practical experimentations of a generation of disciples.[1]

THE EARLY HERBARTIANS

Herbart had died in 1841, leaving behind him a reputation as a German philosopher who had combined an interest in metaphysics and ethics with one in psychology and pedagogy. He had devoted much of his time to the theory and practice of teaching, and had written extensively on what he was pleased to call the 'science of education'. He suggested a method of instruction, supported by an associationist psychology, which

SUMMARY

The Early Herbartians

Wilhelm Rein

    (i)   Aim of Education
    (ii)   Method and Content of Teaching

Spread of Herbartianism

    (i)   France
    (ii)   U.S.A.
    (iii)   England

Characteristic Ideas of Herbartianism

    (i)   Apperception
    (ii)   Concentration
    (iii)   Interest

Significance of Herbartianism

---

[1] J.F. Herbart, *Letters and Education on Education*, trans. H.M. and Emmie Felkin, preface by Oscar Browning, Sonnenschein, London, 1898, p.ix; G. Compayré, *Herbart and Education by Instruction*, trans. Maria E. Findlay, Harrap, London, 1908, pp. 114, 125; W. Rein, *Encyklopädisches Handbuch der Pädagogik*, vol. 4, 2nd edn, Beyer & Sons, Langensalza, 1906. In Wilhelm Rein's *Handbuch* the range and importance of Herbartian influence was documented by listing and classifying with remarkable patience and thoroughness all the published Herbartian literature. In the German language alone there were 2,234 works by 141 authors; in the non-German Herbartian literature there was a list of 103 authors writing a great quantity of works in Armenian, Danish, English, French, Croat, Hungarian, Dutch, Rumanian, Swedish, and Serbian.

simplified the process by which teachers encouraged their pupils to build their impressions and observations into a systematic body of ideas. Intellectual instruction, he maintained, should have a close relationship to moral education and should contribute to the real and fundamental aim of education, that of character development.

For some twenty years after Herbart's death little attention had been paid to his ideas. The Herbartian movement may be said to have begun in 1865 with the publication of a significant book by T. Ziller, *Foundations of the Doctrine of Educative Instruction*. Ziller was a professor of pedagogy at the University of Leipzig, and there established a practice school and a centre for the development of Herbartian ideas.[2] In 1868 Ziller joined with Stoy, another prominent Herbartian, to found the Society for Scientific Pedagogy. That Society became one of the principal instruments for the dissemination of Herbartian ideas throughout Germany. It formed numerous branches in each of the German states, sponsored a Yearbook, and encouraged discussion, experimentation, and the publication of Herbartian ideas and practices.[3]

Ziller was a dynamic personality. He was an innovator with great enthusiasm and energy who, while committed to Herbart's fundamental ideas, developed, extended, clarified, and changed the emphasis of some of his master's views. Ziller continued to emphasise the moral aim of education and its relationship to instruction; he continued to explain the learning process by the association of ideas; and he gave practical and enthusiastic adherence to Herbart's view on the curriculum. Herbart had felt the need for more unity and relatedness in the content of school studies; Ziller developed the idea of concentration by which humanistic studies played a central role to which all other subject-matter was related. In the actual process of teaching, Herbart's suggested method was a little vague; Ziller refined it, made it into a more clearly recognisable series of formal steps, and emphasised it as a central part of the Herbartian approach to education. Herbart had pointed out that, for successful learning, children should be brought into a state of readiness to learn, and the material to be learnt should be appropriate to the children's stage of development. Ziller put forward the idea that, in the course of their growth, children passed through stages similar to that of the history of mankind, and that a course of studies might therefore be arranged as a series of culture epochs, corresponding in their degree of sophistication to the stages through which children developed in the course of their growing up. Interest, for Herbart, was to be a motivating factor in instruction and a link between instruction and moral behaviour. One of the principal aims of education was to produce a person of many-sided interests. That aspect of Herbart's doctrine Ziller accepted with enthusiasm. He wrote extensively on interest and made it a key concept in his theory. His ideas on concentration, formal steps, culture epochs, and

interest were taken up and further developed by his followers, and they became some of the most characteristic and enduring features of Herbartianism.

The practical impact of Herbartianism on the classroom and on schoolteachers was enhanced by the writing and work of a talented practising schoolmaster, Dörpfeld,[4] who taught for the whole of his career in primary schools, and developed a concentrated curriculum and instructional methods that were widely studied and commented upon. In 1866 he wrote a popular monograph on *Thought and Memory* which successfully explained the psychological principles of Herbartianism to classroom teachers.

The most comprehensive and widely read treatment of the psychological approach that underlay the Herbartian instructional process was a book by Karl Lange on *Apperception* which appeared in 1879.[5] In his book Lange made a strenuous plea for the scientific study of psychology and its intelligent application to education in a dawning era of mass education. Children, he felt, were ignorant and indifferent to education. Their companions and their environment did not encourage them to learn the things that school should teach. Educators, therefore, faced a challenge to devise ways to awaken a deep, permanent, and growing interest in the acquisition and possession of knowledge by such children. It was, he thought, a psychological problem which required the educator to put into the most effective combination his knowledge of the child's stage of development, the subject-matter to be learned, and the method of presenting the material. As a guide for the teacher, Lange set forth the Herbartian doctrine of apperception through which the subject-matter of education and the pupil's experience were brought into their most fruitful connection by the process of instruction.

Probably the most widely read and comprehensive statement of the Herbartian position was the *Introduction to Herbart's Pedagogy* by Christian Ufer. First published in 1882, it was described as 'the bridge

[2] Tuiskon Ziller (1817-1882) studied at the University of Leipzig, taught in the gymnasium of Meiningen, and became professor of pedagogy at Leipzig in 1864. In the next year he published his *Foundations of the Doctrine of Educative Instruction*, and in 1876 his *Lectures on General Pedagogy*. His seminar and practice school started in 1863 and continued throughout his professorship.

[3] K. von Stoy (1815-1885) was a conservative Herbartian who had studied under Herbart at Göttingen; he became a professor of pedagogy at Jena in 1843 and remained there for the next forty years. Stoy was a warm-hearted, inspiring teacher who attracted many students from Germany and abroad. He disapproved of the innovations of the Ziller school which was to become the mainstream of Herbartian thought.

[4] F.W. Dörpfeld (1824-1893) was from 1848 until his retirement in 1880, principal of the Lutheran Schools in Wuppertal in the Prussian Rhine Province. He was an indefatigable writer, whose principal contribution lay in the popularising of Herbartian ideas and in the design of the primary school curriculum. His book on *Thought and Memory*, published in 1866, was adapted and translated into English in 1895.

[5] K. Lange was born in 1849, and became director of a school at Plauen in Saxony.

over which thousands of teachers have passed'.[6] In his introduction to the 6th edition, ten years after the first publication, Ufer wrote of the great spread of Herbartian ideas during the past decade and claimed, with some justice, that his little book had played a significant part in the movement. By that time, Ziller and Stoy had ceased to be active and the dominant figure was Wilhelm Rein.

WILHELM REIN

Although Herbart's educational and psychological theories had been kept alive and developed by a steadily increasing band of theorists in Germany, it was not until Wilhelm Rein came to the chair at Jena and developed a seminar with a strong Herbartian bias in 1886, that Herbart's influence was felt much beyond the limits of his native land. For the next generation, the closing years of the nineteenth and the opening years of the twentieth century, Rein was the most important international figure in education. Jena in the 1890's and early 1900's became a new Yverdon, a centre of world-wide attraction. One of his American admirers wrote in 1895: 'Dr Rein has made the pedagogical seminary at Jena the most noted of its kind in Europe, to which students resort from every civilised country.'[7]

The Herbartians produced a well-articulated and systematic approach to education at a time when teachers and teacher trainers, particularly in the English-speaking world, were looking for just such a methodical and comprehensive view. Rein was the leading systematiser in German educational thinking. His presentation of education to his students and his readers was clear, well-ordered, and sequential; in it, theory was adequately related to practice, and practical implications were worked out in satisfactory detail. Rein's strength lay in the fact that he was clearly a professional educator. He was close to classroom problems; he could handle them in a realistic way, and, at the same time, he could demonstrate the systematic theory which could govern the activities of the classroom. He kept in touch with the movement of education and with the intellectual climate of his times. His views therefore represented a Herbartianism adapted to the needs of the early twentieth century.

(i) Aim of Education

Rein's ideas on education stemmed from his view of the nature of the ideal personality. The supreme purpose of education was to bring each pupil as close as possible to the ideal character that the educator accepted.

The educator's ultimate task was not to produce a person replete with knowledge or successful in his activities, but a person equipped with a good will. A good will has five characteristics: there is a harmonious relationship between the activity of the will and one's conscience so that one consistently does what one thinks to be right; the will is the judicious governor of all activities; unselfish devotion to the welfare of others is the central theme of its activities; the rights of others are fully and reciprocally recognised; and justice and equity should prevail in all relations with fellow human beings. Such are the characteristics of the most estimable of men, the man with moral strength of character. 'The educator should *so* educate his pupil that his future personality will be in keeping with the *ideal* human personality.'[8] Rein considered that this aim would be reached 'when the personality is constantly intent upon bringing its actual volition into correspondence with the ideal activity in the will, when it uninterruptedly inspects its own volitional acts with the purpose of determining whether they were made to accord with the moral ideas out of pure love for morality, and whether as much morality was always willed and practised as the ideals demanded or permitted.'[9] The ideal product, it appears, is a person who is conscientious, altruistic, self-critical, and high-principled — a man who combines probity with warm-heartedness.

(ii) Method and Content of Teaching

How is this object to be obtained by the educator? For the Herbartian this was a process of both training and instruction.

Training was the attempt to make a direct impact upon the formation of the pupil's character. It might be done by setting the pupil a good example, by working on his feelings, by redirecting his inclinations, by establishing desirable habits, and by whatever other means the educator may be able to employ in direct contact with his pupil.

---

[6] C. Ufer, *Introduction to the Pedagogy of Herbart*, trans. J.C. Zinser, (ed), C. De Garmo, Heath, Boston, 1894, p.vii.

[7] C. De Garmo, *Herbart and the Herbartians*, Heinemann, London, 1895, p.141. Wilhelm Rein (1847-1929) studied and worked with both Ziller and Stoy, taught in normal schools, and interested himself in a systematic study of the curriculum and teaching methods. In 1885 he succeeded Stoy as professor of education at Jena. From that time until his death forty-three years later, he was at the centre of the Herbartian movement, and his views, expressed in his many articles, books, and lectures, made a manifest impression on the educational world.

[8] W. Rein, *Outlines of Pedagogics*, 2nd edn, trans. C.C. and Ida J. van Liew, Bardeen, Syracuse, New York, 1893, p. 75.

[9] *ibid.*, p. 76.

Instruction was concerned with the acquisition and understanding of knowledge. It occupies most of the energies of the teacher and the time of the school. If the aim of education is to cultivate the will, and if the school is to carry out this effectively, then instruction and learning must be brought somehow into relationship with the development of the will. Instruction must somehow become educative. How is it possible for the acquisition of knowledge to have an influence on the formation of desire and will? This was a central problem for the Herbartians. What is the relation of instruction to character, of knowledge to virtue, of ideas to the good will?

The educator aimed to form the pupil's circle of thought by means of instruction, and through that process to educate the will. The Herbartians, for that purpose, were concerned to demonstrate a connection between the three traditional divisions of human behaviour: thought, feeling, and volition. Instruction, which produced knowledge, must be shown to arouse feeling, which, in turn, affected the will. For the Herbartians, knowledge consisted of ideas arranged in appropriate ways; the task of instruction was that of seeing that the right ideas were presented to the pupil's mind, absorbed by it, and organised in an effective manner. Feelings and desires do not exist independently of ideas. It is true that these ideas may sometimes be vague, but, separated from all ideas, feeling and will amount to nothing at all. To form a moral person, therefore, it is necessary to develop in the pupil ideas which stir his feelings in such a way as to arouse a wish to act in accordance with them. Not all instruction and knowledge produces this effect. What then is the ingredient in the process which touches off this train of development? The catalyst is interest. Interest is the feeling which gives knowledge a personal significance for us. It is present when knowledge becomes something that is felt as well as understood. 'The aim of instruction,' wrote Rein, 'may accordingly be defined as the training of the circle of thought by means of the interest, so as to render it capable of volition.'[10]

Interest could be of various kinds. Herbart had listed six — those arising from knowledge: empirical, speculative, aesthetic, and those arising from social intercourse: sympathetic, social, religious.[11] The aim of instruction may be described as that of producing, not a many-sided knowledge, but a many-sided interest. A man of many-sided interests is a man who is sensitive in a wide range of activities. It is the teacher's most important task to see that his pupil's sensitivity is directed to what is good in each of his many-sided activities. Thus, developing a many-sided interest can come to be synonymous with the development of a moral personality. By judicious instruction the Herbartian teacher may hope to build knowledge, through interest, into the good will.

To achieve his aims the Herbartian teacher should select his subject-matter on two principal bases. First, the subject-matter must be able to awaken the interest of the pupils. To do this it must be within the pupil's power of comprehension, and must have some similarity to the ideas that are already within the child's mind, so that the new knowledge may readily be linked with the old. Secondly, the subject-matter should be relevant to the present society and culture of the people among whom the pupil lives and intends to spend his life. The pupil's moral character should be developed in relation to the kinds of activities that he is likely to encounter in his present and future life. In Rein's view, probably the most suitable material for educative instruction, i.e. instruction aimed at developing character, was the history and literature of the national culture. He suggested that this should be presented from its beginnings up to the present time, following a succession of cultural epochs that corresponded to the stages of psychological growth observable among the children. There were, he suggested, three tasks to be undertaken in designing a course of study:

- The stages of development of the child's mind have to be determined;
- The cultural stages of mankind's development, or the stages of a nation's development, have to be decided upon;
- The latter have to be placed as far as possible parallel to and in harmony with the former.

Rein's view of an appropriate course in the moral-historical side of education for the first eight years of the common school is set out in Figure 2.1.

Not all the Herbartians, however, agreed that individual development ran parallel to that of society; and many consequently rejected the idea of building a curriculum out of the study of successive cultural epochs. They all agreed, however, that history and literature, whatever their arrangement might be, provided the soundest basis for moral education. There was a general agreement also that the curriculum might be divided into two main branches: the life of man; and the life of nature:

(a) **the life of man** comprised the historical and humanistic studies of which there were three sections:

- Those pre-eminently fitted for character training. They included biblical and ecclesiastical history, secular history, and literature.
- Art instruction. This included drawing, modelling, and singing.

---

[10] *ibid.*, p. 89.

[11] A fuller discussion of the place and importance of interest for the Herbartians will be found below.

Figure 2.1: Rein's Moral-Historical Curriculum for the First Eight Years of Schooling.

School Year	Content			
1 2	Fairy Tales *Robinson Crusoe*			
	Sacred	Profane		
	Religious Series	National Series		
		For German Schools	For English Schools	For American Schools
3	Patriarchs and Moses	Thüringer Tales	Old English Legends	Indian Legends
4	Judges and Kings	Nibelungen Tales	Settlement of England	Pioneer Stories
5	Life of Christ	Christianising of Germany	Christianising of England	Settlement of America
6	Life of Christ	Emperors; Kaiser Period	Great English Kings	Colonial History
7	Paul	Reformation	Renaissance, Reformation, Age of Discovery to 1763	Revolution
8	Luther, Catechism	Nationalisation	Development of Modern England	19th Century

W. Rein, *Outlines of Pedagogics*, 2nd edn, trans. C.C. and Ida J. van Liew, Sonnenschein, London, 1893, pp. 118ff. The suggestions concerning English and American schools were made by the translators who acknowledged the help of J.J. Findlay.

- Language instruction, including the learning of the mother tongue and foreign languages.

(b) **the life of nature** covered the natural sciences, and included geography, natural sciences, mathematics, and physical education.

Rein and his associates worked out a complete, sequential eight-year curriculum for the common school, giving in detail many model exercises planned according to the formal Herbartian steps.[12]

The ethical aim of instruction required that a pupil's ideas should not be dissipated throughout many unconnected subjects and topics, but should rather be concentrated in such a way that he could come to see a unity among his ideas, and could learn to develop a coherence and wholeness of character. An effort must therefore be made to centre the teacher's instruction around the kind of study that most lends itself to the development of moral character. Since, for the Herbartians, this material was to be found mainly in the literary and historical subjects, they became the centre of the curriculum, and the Herbartian teacher attempted with all the skill that he could command to relate the other subjects and topics of the curriculum to some central theme that he had chosen from the

---

12 W. Rein, A. Pickel, and E. Scheller (edd.), *Theorie und Praxis des Volksschulunterrichts nach Herbartschen Grundsätzen*, Bredt, Leipzig, 8 Bde. 1878.

historical and literary field. Concentration, the name given to that method of co-ordinating the material for instruction, became, in a somewhat modified form of correlation, a very popular approach to curriculum design in the early part of the twentieth century and has left a lasting impact.

Once the proper material for instruction had been chosen and suitably arranged, the next task was to present it to the pupils in the most effective way. The Herbartians were convinced that, for the purpose of instruction, there was one method that was clearly more suitable than all others; it was the method which conformed to the natural process of human learning. 'There can be but one natural method of instruction,' wrote Rein, 'viz. that which conforms exactly to the laws of the human mind and makes all its arrangements accordingly.'[13] Learning consisted in the association of ideas and their development into meaningful groupings by means of apperception and abstraction.

Under Rein's influence the various suggestions by earlier Herbartians about the process and sequence of learning and teaching were consolidated into a five-step general method which became widely known as the five Herbartian steps. Rein presented the sequence as follows:

1. preparation
2. presentation
3. association
4. generalisation
5. application

The teacher's first task was to arouse in the pupils' minds the ideas upon which he wished to graft the new material for his lesson: to indicate the aim of the lesson, to interest, and to focus the pupils' attention on matters from which he could lead into the lesson in hand. Having thus prepared the pupil's mind, the teacher presented his material clearly, succinctly, and attractively. He then proceeded to associate it with the ideas previously in the pupil's mind, knitting it skilfully in a variety of ways into the pattern which they form. Having established these relationships and tied them together securely, the next and fourth step, known variously as generalisation, assimilation, or condensation, was to examine the new pattern of old and fresh ideas which was then in the pupil's mind. What was the meaning of the new idea-mass that had been formed? What significance did it have? What was the essence of it? Could it be formulated into a general principle? The final step was that of applying the new knowledge in appropriate ways to establish command over it.

Figure 2.2 summarises the arrangement of the formal steps put forward by various German and American Herbartians.

Rein's work set the pattern and tone for the Herbartians of the late nineteenth and early twentieth century. It was systematic, it was practical, it could be easily understood and used by classroom teachers. It caught the spirit of the times. It was scientific in the sense that practice proceeded in an orderly way out of well-organised theory; it provided a firm, clear plan of instruction into which the training colleges multiplying rapidly at the turn of the century could induct their trainees with ease and confidence; and it offered a comprehensive view of education integrated in all its parts and yet capable of being summed up memorably in the few key concepts: for aim — education for moral development; for method — instruction through apperception and interest; and for content — a curriculum based on concentration.

Rein's influence made itself felt through his main publications. He collaborated on *The Theory and Practice of Instruction in the Elementary School* in 1878, he wrote *Outlines of Pedagogics* in 1890, he designed and edited the *Encyclopaedic Manual of Pedagogy*, 1894-1905, and he sponsored a bulletin entitled *From the Pedagogical Seminar at the University of Jena* that appeared almost every year from 1888 to 1918 and contained news and articles on theory and school practice.

SPREAD OF HERBARTIANISM

In 1886 Rein established his seminar with twenty-three students. On the occasion of the fiftieth semester in 1911, it was recorded that, 'Almost the whole world is represented in our list of old students, Japan as well as Australia and South Africa, Chile and Mexico, ... a large number of old and true friends from the United States ... In Greece there are more than 30 old seminarians, some 70 in Bulgaria, 20 in Rumania, more than 30 in Serbia, many in Russia, Armenia, Finland and Sweden, and Austria-Hungary, probably 30 in Switzerland, and 50 in England.'[14] Some two thousand students had, by 1911, passed through Rein's Jena seminar, many to go to positions of responsibility in schools and school-systems inside and outside Germany. Some were to become university professors and to set up, in their turn, their own Herbartian seminars, for example in Manchester, in several American universities, in Bucharest, Jassy, Belgrade, Athens, and in the normal schools and universities of Japan. News of their activities was reported in each number of the Jena Seminar bulletin.[15]

[13] *ibid.*, p. 136.

[14] *Jenaer Seminarbuch: Festschrift zum 50 Semester des Päd. Universitäts-Seminars unter Prof. D. Dr. W. Rein* (xiv Bd. der Mitteilungen *Aus dem Päd. Universitäts-Seminar*), Beyer and Mann, Langensalza, 1911, p. 241.

[15] W. Rein (ed.) *Aus dem Pädagogischen Universitäts-Seminar zu Jena*, Beyer and Mann, Langensalza, 1888-1918.

Figure 2.2: Herbartian Formal Steps.

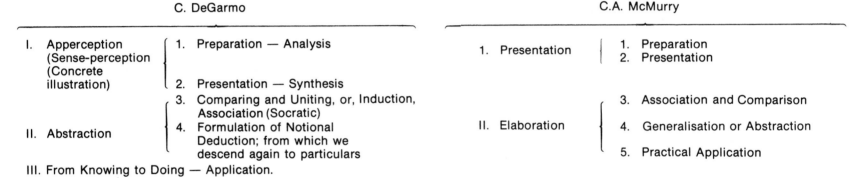

With the above may be compared the designations given to the 'formal steps' by the following American writers.

From W. Rein, *Outlines of Pedagogics*, trans. C.C. and Ida J. van Liew, 1893, p. 175.

(i) France

The one notable exception, a leading European country which felt the Herbartian impact only slightly, was France. The first work on Herbartianism appeared there in 1884;[16] it was followed by an introductory article in Buisson's *Dictionnaire* in 1887 and a series of four articles in the *Revue Pédagogique* in 1890-91 on the relationship of psychology to education. In 1894 the Herbartian contribution became more widely known with the translation of selected parts of Herbart's works.[17] A short and widely read exposition appeared in 1901,[18] and a small Herbartian movement may be said to have begun in France. Compayré published a monograph on Herbart in 1904, and Gockler in

1905; Roehrich produced a substantial volume on the philosophy of education with a Herbartian bias, and several other articles and books made their appearance.[19]

---

[16] E. Roehrich, *Théorie de l'Education d'après les Principes de Herbart*, Delagrave, Paris, 1884.

[17] H. Deureux, La Psychologie appliquée à l'Education d'après Herbart, *Rev. Ped.*, New Ser. XVI, 5 (1890), pp. 385-402, 497-513; (1891) pp. 137-49, 216-32. A. Pinloche trans., *J.F. Herbart, Principales Oeuvres Pédagogiques*, Alcan, Paris, 1894.

[18] M. Mauxion, *L'Education par l'Instruction et les Théories Pédagogiques de Herbart*, Alcan, Paris, 1900.

[19] G. Compayré, *Herbart and Education by Instruction*, Delaplane, Paris, 1904 (Eng. trans., 1908); L. Gockler, *La Pédagogie de Herbart*, Hachette, Paris, 1905; E. Roehrich, *Philosophie de l'Education*, Alcan, Paris, 1911.

All in all, it may be said that the Herbartian influence in France was weak; there were a few publications, some modest amount of discussion, and little practical impact either in the schools or the training colleges. In the French-speaking world it was in Switzerland that the influence was felt most strongly from the early 1890's, principally through the work of F. Guex who established a seminar at the University of Lausanne, wrote extensively, and edited several journals.

(ii) U.S.A.

The Herbartian movement started in the U.S.A. when three young men from Illinois Normal University returned from graduate study in Germany in the late 1880's. Each of them spent some time at Rein's seminar in Jena. Charles De Garmo visited Jena in the mid-1880's and soon after his return became president of Swathmore College, Pennsylvania. Charles McMurry studied at Jena from 1887 to 1888, and returned to work in practice schools in Illinois for many years before moving to George Peabody College for Teachers. His brother Frank McMurry spent the years 1887-88 with Rein, and wrote later that he had experienced there a pedagogical conversion equivalent to that at a religious revival.[20] He later became a professor of education at the University of Illinois and subsequently at Teachers' College, Columbia University.[21] Those three were the beginning of a small stream of American students of education who made their way to Jena during the next thirty years. The records of the Jena seminar from 1888 up to the beginning of World War I do not show a single year without an American in attendance, and in some years there were half-a-dozen or more. Many of the students returned to positions of influence in teacher training and transmitted their Herbartian convictions to their trainee teachers.

In 1892 a Herbart Club was formed. It sponsored translations of Herbart's works, and of leading expositions of Herbartianism such as Lange's *Apperception* which appeared in 1893, and Ufer's *Introduction* in 1894. Rein's *Outlines* was translated in 1893 by C.C. and Ida J. van Liew who had been at Jena in 1890-92, and had subsequently joined the staff of Illinois Normal. De Garmo wrote the *Essentials of Method* in 1889, and Charles McMurry *The Elements of General Method* in 1892. With those two books the movement may be said to have been fairly launched.

In 1895 the National Herbart Society for the Scientific Study of Education was organised. The three enthusiasts from Jena were members of its first committee, De Garmo as president, and Charles McMurry as secretary. John Dewey and Nicholas Murray Butler were also committee

members. In 1902 the title was changed to the National Society for the Scientific Study of Education, and, finally, in 1910, became the National Society for the Study of Education. Starting from the year of its foundation the society has published a Yearbook on some significant issue in American education, with chapters written by leading scholars and practitioners. The Yearbooks have maintained an enviable standard of excellence and have proved to be a significant vehicle for the analysis and expression of many of the leading ideas and practices that have shaped American education in the twentieth century.

So enthusiastically was the Herbartian campaign taken up in the early 1890's that W.T. Harris in his 1894-5 report as U.S. Commissioner of Education ventured the opinion that 'there are more adherents of Herbartian pedagogy today in America than in Germany itself',[22] and one of Herbart's translators was moved to write in 1895 that 'American educators have begun to live, move, and have their being in an atmosphere of Herbartianism.[23]

Most journals of the period carried articles with a Herbartian flavour, and the *Educational Review*, edited by Nicholas Murray Butler, provided space for several key expositions of Herbartian ideas such as a series of articles by De Garmo in 1891 on 'The Herbartian System of Pedagogics'. J.M. Rice, who published an influential investigation of American public schools in 1893, had also studied at Jena, and, in his report, commended the teaching methods practised there to the attention of American teachers.[24] Most books on teaching method written between 1895 and World War I were pervaded by Herbartian thinking. Herbartian terms

[20] F.M. McMurry, Recollections of Forty years of Education, *Peabody Journal of Education*, IV (May 1927), pp. 329-30, quoted in Dorothy McMurry, *Herbartian Contributions to History Instruction in American Elementary Schools*, Teachers College, Columbia University. New York, 1946, p. 47.

[21] C. De Garmo (1849-1934), graduated from Illinois State Normal University 1873 and Halle University 1886. He was professor of psychology at the University of Illinois (1890-1), president of Swarthmore College (1891-8) and professor of education at Cornell University (1888-1914). He wrote *The Essentials of Method*, 1889, *Herbart and the Herbartians*, 1895, *Interest and Education*, 1902, and *Principles of Secondary Education*, 1907-10.

Charles A. McMurry (1857-1929), graduated from Illinois State Normal University, 1876, and completed his Ph.D. at Halle 1887. He became principal of the practice school at Illinois State Normal, and in 1915 a professor at George Peabody College for Teachers, Nashville, Tennessee. He edited the *Yearbooks of the National Herbart Society*, wrote numerous books on special method, textbooks for schools, and *The Elements of General Method* (1892), *Method of the Recitation* (with F.M. McMurry, 1897), and *Teaching by Projects* (1920)).

Frank M. McMurry (1862-1936), studied at Illinois State Normal, Michigan University, and then in Halle and Jena 1886-9, where he obtained his Ph.D. in 1889, Geneva and Paris 1892-3. He was professor of education at Teachers College, Columbia University 1908-26. He was the author of a number of school textbooks, and *Method of the Recitation* (with his brother Charles, 1897).

[22] Report of the U.S. Commissioner of Education, 1894-1895, p. 322.

[23] J.F. Herbart, *The ABC of Sense-Perception and Minor Pedagogical Works*, trans. W.J. Eckoff, Appleton, New York, 1890, p.xiv; see also E.B. Wesley, *NEA: The First Hundred Years*, Harper, New York, 1957.

[24] J.M. Rice, *The Public School System of the United States*, New York, 1893, p. 119.

PREFACE TO THE FIRST EDITION

The papers included in this first *Yearbook* of the Herbart Society for the Scientific Study of Teaching, bring to a fuller treatment two of the questions that have already attracted the serious attention of teachers, and in the future are likely still more to call for thoughtful study and tests.

The problem of *Concentration* involves the whole school course in its influence upon child character, and treats the selection and arrangement of topics in the studies and the method of instruction that will establish the relations needed.

The *Culture Epochs* theory raises one of the most interesting and profound problems in education, and one, too, whose practical effects are quickly seen and felt.

The introduction gives a graphic account of the problems pressing for solution today, and touches in a lively way the questions which are more fully discussed in the other papers.

The course of study for first and second grades illustrates an attempt to select and arrange the materials of instruction, paying heed to the requirements of concentration.

Those interested in these papers will do well to read them carefully before going to Denver. The papers will not be read at the meeting, but the full time will be given to discussion. Those wishing to purchase copies at fifty cents, apply to the secretary.

CHARLES A. MCMURRY,
Normal, Illinois

From the first *Yearbook* of the National Herbart Society of the United States, 1895, this Preface summarised what the editor regarded as the main questions of interest to Herbartians at that time.

and practices became the general currency of educational discussion; and practices such as the use of the instructional steps, the cultural epoch curriculum, and correlation were tried in many schools.

The two Herbartian books which were probably the most popular, *The Elements of General Method*, and *The Method of the Recitation* reached the peak of their sales about 1906-7 and thereafter slowly declined.[25] *The Elements of General Method* was still sufficiently popular, however, to merit a further edition as late as 1922.

By about 1910 there was a noticeable falling off in the amount of literature appearing on Herbartian topics. It was an indication that Herbartianism as a defined movement was on the wane, but it by no means meant that the teachers in the nation's schools were giving up the methods and ideas that they had painstakingly acquired. Nor did it mean that the leading writers had abandoned Herbartian ways; they surrendered the cult because it was no longer necessary, and they retained much of the substance, modifying it as new influences came into operation. Thus, Herbartianism remained an important element in American thinking and classroom practice.

A leading American Herbartian attempted, in 1911, to sum up the impact of Herbartianism. He considered that it had been very extensive and that it was likely to endure. Many practices such as the instructional steps had been in vogue so long that many teachers had forgotten their origin. This meant frequently that Herbartian practices without the underlying theory had been adopted. The principal impact appeared to be on the teaching methods and curriculum of the elementary school. In particular, the thought, the moral aim of education was widely accepted, and so, too, were the formal instructional steps, concentration which tended rather to be a correlation, and the doctrine of interest. Dewey's influence and that of the newer educational psychologists such as Thorndike was growing and was being married in many ways into Herbartian theory and practice. The writer, however, saw Herbartianism as an important influence on American education for some time to come, principally through two agencies. There were quite a number of convinced Herbartians, many of them products of Rein's Jena seminar, in universities and teachers' colleges, who had set up training programs which maintained the spirit of Jena; their products would continue active in American schools for many years to come. And over the last ten years, since the beginning of the century, a large and increasing number of textbooks had been produced along Herbartian lines. In many cases these were substantial series from well-known publishers and were to be found in several subjects. Their use could be expected to ensure both the practicality and the durability of the Herbartian approach.[26]

In textbooks for teacher trainees also, aspects of Herbartianism were tenaciously preserved. In 1906 for example a superintendent of schools in

[25] Dorothy McMurry, *op.cit.*, pp. 50-1; see also H.B. Dunkel, *Herbart and Education*, Random, New York, 1969, Chapter 10.

[26] C.C. van Liew, 'Herbarts Einfluss in Amerika', *Jenaer Seminarbuch, Festschrift zum 50. Semester des Päd. Universitäts — Seminars unter Prof. D. Dr. W. Rein*, Beyer und Mann, Langensalza, 1911, pp. 309-14. For a further analysis of the Herbartian influence in the U.S.A., see H.B. Dunkel, *Herbart and Herbartianism: An Educational Ghost Story*, University of Chicago Press, 1970, and G.L. Moulton, 'The American Herbartian: a portrait from his Yearbooks', *History of Education Quarterly*, 3 March 1963, 134-42 and 187-97.

Pennsylvania wrote *The Recitation*, a book for the guidance of young teachers. It was vintage Herbartianism, with chapters on each of the five formal steps and an essay on interest, attention, and the association of ideas. The book was reprinted four years later, and, after World War I, in 1923, was revised and republished. The new edition retained the five formal steps and, with the addition of a chapter on 'the socialized recitation', it remained the same straightforward manual of Herbartian class-teaching.[27] Other texts used in the U.S.A. during the 1920's, while not as specifically Herbartian as Hamilton's, usually contained a description of the formal steps and had, as might well be expected, considerable Herbartian overtones.[28]

The Herbartian procedure was reported in 1933 as 'still current in textbooks on teaching' in the United States, and the writer of a widely used textbook devoted a section of his work to a revision of them.[29] In the same period, the well-known learning units devised by H.C. Morrison also had a distinctly Herbartian cast; these survived into the post-World War II period. The Herbartian steps were still to be found in standard text books used in the 1950's, suggested as suitable procedure for teachers to use in expository type lessons, and some authors even developed lesson plans which Rein would have been proud to acknowledge.[30]

(iii) England

The Herbartian movement in education appears to have been unknown in England before 1881 when Oscar Browning summarised Herbart's ideas in his book, *An Introduction to the History of Educational Theories*.[31] In 1880 J. Ward had contributed a widely read article on Herbart's psychology to the 9th edition of the *Encyclopaedia Britannica*, and in 1888 G.F. Stout, who was to become a leading English psychologist, started a series of articles which gave an extensive and appreciative account of Herbartian psychology in the journal *Mind*.

J.J. Findlay was the first English schoolman to become seriously involved with Herbartianism. In 1891-93, while still a young master in an English secondary school, he visited Germany and attended Rein's seminar. It was, for him, a critical and lasting intellectual experience. There he listened to a thorough and challenging exposition of a systematic educational theory from its leading interpreter, he took part in the task of putting theory to work in the practice school, and he rubbed shoulders with other men of experience and comparable intelligence who were eager to discuss, criticise, and learn to the full from the rich pedagogical atmosphere with which they were surrounded.[32] In 1902 Findlay wrote *Principles of Class Teaching* in which he handsomely acknowledged Rein's influence not only in the Herbartian ideas that were expressed in the book but in the very concept of his writing. The *Principles*, he claimed, was the first book by an English author to combine, in Jena fashion, a systematic, scientific approach to the subject with practical experience in the classroom. Findlay was made professor of education at the University of Manchester in 1903 and helped to make it an important centre for the diffusion of Herbartian ideas in England in the pre-World War I period. The primacy of the ethical aim of education, the usefulness of the formal steps in the instructional process, the process of apperception, the importance of interest, the centrality of the humanities in the curriculum, the necessity for concentration were significant parts of Findlay's view of education which he expressed in his *Principles*. They were not expressed, however, in exclusively Herbartian terms. Findlay's English experience and his reading of John Dewey, the new star that had recently appeared above the horizon in Chicago, led to interesting modifications in his views on theory and practice. 'It is not too much to assert,' he wrote, 'that a student of these topics may learn at Jena under Rein, and at Chicago, in the Institute of Education connected with the University, the best that has been offered in recent years as regards the teaching of young children.'[33] De Garmo and the McMurry brothers were, at the same time, experiencing a similar transformation. The synthesis which these men worked out well represents the course of educational thinking in the English-speaking world in the first two decades of the twentieth century.

Meanwhile, Catherine Dodd had joined the staff at Manchester. She too had studied with Rein, in 1896, and adhered more closely than Findlay to Herbartian doctrine. Her books were widely read and expressed lucidly and comprehensively the Ziller-Rein approach.[34] In the 1890's

---

27 Samuel Hamilton, *The Recitation*, Lippincott, Philadelphia, 1906, repr. 1910; Samuel Hamilton, *The Purpose, Preparation and Methods in the Recitation*, Lippincott, Philadelphia, 1923.

28 e.g., H. Foster, *Principles of Teaching in Secondary Education*, Scribner's, New York, 1921, and, in W.C. Bagley's best-selling *The Educative Process*, first published in 1905, the Herbartian steps were advocated as a model for inductive teaching; they were still being described in the 1920 and later editions.

29 W.C. Ruediger, *Teaching Procedures*, Harrap, London, 1933, pp. 54, 55ff.

30 T.M. Risk, *Principles and Practice of Teaching in Secondary Schools*, 2nd edn, American Book Co., New York, 1947, p. 374; 1st edn was 1941. See also G.A. Yoakum and R.G. Simpson, *Modern Methods and Techniques to Teaching*, New York, rev. edn, 1948, and Noble L. Garrison, *The Improvement of Teaching*, Dryden, New York, 1955.

31 Oscar Browning (1837-1923), taught for fifteen years at Eton, and became a lecturer in history at the University of Cambridge. From 1891 to 1909 he was principal of the Cambridge University day training college. He wrote *An Introduction to the History of Educational Theories*, Kegan Paul, London, 1881.

32 Findlay later wrote of the impact that the experience at Jena had on him in 'Professor Reins Einfluss auf einen englischen Schulmann', *Jenaer Seminarbuch*, 287-90.

33 J.J. Findlay, *Principles of Class Teaching*, Macmillan, London, 1902, p. 130.

three other important voices joined the Herbartian cause. Rooper, an inspector of schools who became a lecturer in education at Oxford University, spoke at many professional and lay meetings on a wide range of educational topics. He had a close acquaintance with contemporary German education and a sympathy with the Herbartian movement. One article, first published in 1891, 'A Pot of Green Feathers', was a lively, popular explanation of apperception that was stimulated by the remark of a young child who thought that a pot of fresh green ferns shown her by her teacher was a pot of green feathers; the essay was widely read and commented upon in both England and the U.S.A.[35] A systematic account of Herbart's views and their development along Zillerian lines appeared in 1895, as *An Introduction to Herbart's Science and Practice of Education* by H.M. and Emmie Felkin. The Felkins were also responsible for translating Herbart's *The Science of Education* in 1892 and *Letters and Lectures on Education* in 1898. Probably the most widely known, and certainly the most readable publication, was that by John Adams, *The Herbartian Psychology Applied to Education* which appeared in 1897 and remained in print for forty years. Adams' book was a sparkling and at the same time scholarly and subtle account — a thorough exposition of Herbart without tears.[36] It probably did more than any other book to introduce Herbartianism to England and the British dependencies. In Australia, for example, the book was recommended to teachers by several directors of education in the early years of the century; it became a standard text in the new teachers' colleges and did much to give teacher training and classroom practice a strong Herbartian flavour which they retained for the next fifty years.

In 1903 a new champion appeared. F.H. Hayward, an inspector of schools under the London County Council, wrote that 'Herbart's doctrines ... laid hold upon me powerfully',[37] and, within the six years from 1903 to 1909, he had published six popular and vigorously written books on Herbartianism. With some force he demolished opponents' arguments, and in dynamic phrases put forward his own. In *The Secret of Herbart* he summed up the new dispensation: 'The message of Herbart is Interest: the "secret of Herbart" is Apperception. Interest in almost *anything* is good — interest in nature, in art, in politics; and many Interests are *apperceptive*, dependent upon previous knowledge. But if there is one interest which is *above all others* important, and *above all others* dependent upon apperception, it is interest in moral goodness; and this will never be aroused in a living soul — even though the trumpet of Judgment be heard and the fires of hell burst open — unless the soul has known, in concrete form, what moral goodness means.'[38] Between the swinging broadsword of Hayward, and the darting rapier of Adams, the cause of Herbartianism in England was well served in the early years of the century.

CHARACTERISTIC IDEAS OF HERBARTIANISM

Rein was the central figure among the Herbartians at the beginning of the twentieth century and his views, summarised above, were the core of Herbartianism. Within the total pattern, three concepts were of particular importance, viz,: apperception, concentration, and interest. Rein had much to say on each of these, but others, too, took them up and wrote extensively on them. To understand the lines along which Herbartianism appealed to educators, and the kinds of ideas that were most commonly expounded and argued about, it is necessary to look in some detail at these three fundamentals.

(i) Apperception

The key process upon which the Herbartians based their educational methods was that of apperception. Pestalozzi had made educators aware of the importance of understanding the mechanism of sense perception in the learning process; Herbart extended Pestalozzi's idea of perception to include that of mental perception, and referred to the operation as apperception.

Lange, in his book *Apperception*, provided the most comprehensive statement by a Herbartian on this topic.

For the Herbartians a human mind consisted of ideas associated together in groups of similar ideas. Each group was knitted together by a complicated pattern of relationships, and acted more or less as a united force. Learning was a process of building new ideas into existing groups and developing richer and more dynamic relationships within the mind.

[34] Catherine I. Dodd, (1860-1932), studied extensively in Germany, was lecturer in education at the University of Manchester (1892-1905), headmistress of Milham Ford Secondary School (1905-1917), and principal of Cherwell Hall, a training college for secondary teachers at Oxford. She wrote *Introduction to Herbartian Principles of Teaching*, 1898 and *The Child and the Curriculum*, 1906.

[35] T.G. Rooper (1847-1903), an inspector of schools, published *A Pot of Green Feathers: A Study in Apperception*, Kellogg, New York, 1892; and *School and Home Life*, Brown, London, n.d.

[36] John Adams (1857-1934) was a graduate of the University of Glasgow, taught in Scotland, and in 1902 became the first professor of education at the University of London. After his retirement in 1922 he travelled widely and taught for some time at the University of California at Los Angeles. He published many books and articles, including *The Herbartian Psychology Applied to Education* in 1897, *Exposition and Illustration in Teaching*, 1909, *The Evolution of Educational Theory*, 1912, and *Modern Developments in Educational Practice*, 1922.

[37] F.H. Hayward, *The Meaning of Education as interpreted by Herbart*, Ralph, Holland, London, 1907, p. vii. Hayward was an inspector of schools from 1905 to 1937. In 1903 he published his polemical *The Critics of Herbartianism*.

[38] F.H. Hayward, *The Secret of Herbart*, Sonnenschein, London, 1904, pp. 65-6.

We come in contact with the world around us by receiving sensations, e.g. of touch, sight, sound, from it. The simple perception encounters ideas that are already in the mind. When it fuses with similar ideas, it may be held in consciousness, clarified, and properly related to a range of other ideas in the mind. This second level process of mental assimilation is called apperception. 'The mind,' wrote Lange, 'apprehends outer impressions in accordance with its wealth of knowledge gained through former activity. The process of perception becomes one of apperception.'[39] First there is a perception which becomes an idea in our consciousness; then one or more groups of ideas rise in our minds to enter into relationship with the perceived idea; in consequence, new thought combinations are formed; these combinations called apperception masses eventually stabilise into new patterns which give the original perception a wider significance, and add to the general enrichment of the mind.

The process of apperception was not one to be left to chance; 'it must be regarded as the highest art of the teacher and educator, rightly to induce the process of mental assimilation in the pupil, and to conduct it to a sure conclusion.'[40] Teachers should not merely convey knowledge, they should awaken, stimulate, and guide the course of apperception. To do this, teachers must make themselves aware of the ideas, feelings, and interests that the pupils bring to school, they must link their instruction with the experience of the pupil, and they must try to see to it that the pupils have the experience and the ideas which will readily relate to the material of instruction. 'One great art of teaching,' wrote T.G. Rooper, 'is the art of finding links and connections between isolated facts, and of making the child see that what seems quite new is an extension of what is already in his mind. Few people would long remember the name and date of a single Chinese king picked by chance from a list extending back thousands of years. Facts of English history are not much easier to remember than this for children who are not gifted with strong mechanical memories. Hence the value of presenting names, dates, and events, in connection with external memorials, such as monuments, buildings, battlefields or with poems and current events, and the like.'[41]

Specifically, teachers could, in most situations, follow a regular instructional pattern designed to make the best of the apperceptive process. Lange, like Rein, concluded that there were 'five methodical steps which must be taken in the treatment of a lesson. The preparation (analysis), the presentation (synthesis), the combination (association), the recapitulation (system), and the application. They indicate the method by which a complete apperception of culture-material is accomplished.'[42]

Lange and his colleagues were convinced that learning was, in the main, apperception, and that it was feasible and desirable to derive the general rules of teaching from this one fundamental process. The chief task of the teacher was to introduce the pupil to the process of apperception, exercise him constantly and skilfully in it, and to make it of absorbing interest to him.

(ii) Concentration

The Herbartians' psychology was an associationist one. Everything turned on the association of ideas. The emphasis on relatedness which, in teaching method, led to the development of the five instructional steps, had an important implication also for the curriculum. Taking their cue from Ziller, several leading Herbartians suggested curricula in which one topic or group of topics was made the centre of the curriculum and all the other matters to be studied were grouped round, made subordinate, and connected to it. The central material might be historical and literary as it was in Ziller's case, or geographical in Parker's Chicago curriculum, or even a triple core of humanistic, scientific, and economic studies as De Garmo suggested.[43] Although the theory behind the idea of concentration was vigorously argued, there does not appear ever to have been any strong support in practice for a pure form of it. Even the enthusiast, Hayward, thought that it was unattainable, and argued that correlation rather than concentration was more truly Herbartian.[44] Certainly, most of the proposals put forward by Herbartians, after the turn of the century, were ones involving correlation rather than concentration, and the Herbartian books and articles of the period on curriculum design argued the case for correlation.

The term correlation was used to indicate the deliberate establishment of a relationship between subjects or topics in the school curriculum. This relationship could be of varying degrees of closeness. It could be a mere juxtaposition of studies by timetabling American history and American literature for study on the same days or weeks. It might mean the seeking of deliberate relationships between subjects such as a study of the geography of Russia concurrently with the history of Peter the Great; or it could produce new broad subjects such as general science or general mathematics or broad interdisciplinary topics such as that given by McMurry: 'The treatment of the falls of Minneapolis, for example, would bring in, by way of necessary explanation, the rock strata

39 K. Lange, *Apperception*, C. De Garmo (ed.), Heath, London, 1893, p. 8.
40 *ibid.*, pp. 108-9.
41 T.G. Rooper, *School and Home Life*, Brown, London, n.d., pp. 58-9.
42 K. Lange, *op.cit.* p. 228.
43 C. De Garmo, *Herbart and the Herbartians*, Heinemann, London, 1895, pp. 243ff.
44 F.H. Hayward, *The Meaning of Education*, Ralph, Holland, London, 1907, pp. 123-31.

and the canyon below the falls (geology); the mills and turbine wheels (physics); sawmills and pineries (pine trees); the early history (Indians and Hennepin); besides the strict geographical relations of commerce, railroads, Minneapolis, etc.'[45]

An interest in correlation was not the peculiar privilege of the Herbartians. It was a strong feature of the Froebelian tradition and, from that source, was well-known to educators of the early twentieth century. It was the Herbartians, nevertheless, who brought it forward, popularised it, and made it one of the organising principles of curriculum construction. The idea of correlation was important to the Herbartians for a number of reasons. Strength of character went along with unity of personality, and some unity within the study material might be expected to further the Herbartian aim of developing firm, moral character. Well-articulated knowledge was the object at which the apperception process aimed, and knowledge of this kind facilitated its future use and retention, and the acquisition of further knowledge. The current expansion of knowledge and multiplication of studies required for its comprehension what McMurry called 'trunk lines of thought' connecting up and providing paths of communication between the various studies.[46] Correlation was a study of things-in-relationship; all study, for the Herbartian, was really a study of relationships, of the way in which ideas might be associated with a range of other ideas, and of the way in which our perceiving and learning them are affected by past associations. The Herbartian interest in teaching pupils to seek, understand, and build up relationships fitted well with a growing tendency in twentieth century thought; it had a strong initial attraction for John Dewey who eventually developed relational thinking far beyond Herbartian limits, and it was one of the factors that made it not too difficult for educators like Findlay and De Garmo to produce a workable synthesis of Herbart and Dewey.

(iii) Interest

One of the most enthusiastic of Herbartians, Hayward, regarded interest as Herbart's central thought and wrote of it as 'the fundamental concept of the theory of Educative Instruction'.[47] Across the title page of his *The Critics of Herbartianism* there appeared in capitals 'Interest is the Greatest Word in Education'. Hayward's sentiments were echoed less spectacularly but nonetheless sincerely by other Herbartians, several of whom wrote at length on the topic of interest. It was a beginning, by educators, of an interest in interest that was to have a vital effect on the process of education in the twentieth century. 'Interest,' wrote Ufer, 'is the lamp by which Herbart once and for all has brought the clearness of day in the dark and labyrinthine passages of didactics.'[48]

It was not easy to define what was meant by interest.[49] It was a wide term for an inclination towards an object, idea, or activity that led to some kind of close association with it. McMurry suggested that it was what gave knowledge personal significance for us. Most writers agreed that it included an intellectual perception that an object was related to an existing tendency or state of knowledge, that it was accompanied by a feeling of pleasure or pain, and that it led an individual to pay attention to the object. Interest undoubtedly involved feeling; it could be thought of as a particular kind of feeling tone, or as a mental state which involved pleasure or pain. In any case, it was a concept in which emotion was combined with some intellectual element. By giving emotion an important place, through their accent on interest, the Herbartians introduced a new dimension into school-life. 'It is suggestive to note,' Charles McMurry wrote, 'that in the whole catalogue of ideas which ancient and modern pedagogy have brought to the attention of teachers, the doctrine of interest is the only one which gives special emphasis to the emotional life.'[50]

Interest had two main functions: it was an essential part of the process of education, having a very important bearing on the effectiveness of learning, and, over and above this, it could be regarded as the aim of the educative process.

Each of the main parts of the learning process, the Herbartians argued, is vitally affected by the presence or absence of interest. An interest in something causes us to pay attention to it; generally speaking the more a thing interests us, the more attention we give it. Attention is the first step in the learning process. Closely associated with it is motivation; again the impelling force is interest which gives direction to our thoughts and sustains them. After motivation comes comprehension of meaning; by understanding, we mean that we see the relation of the new knowledge to what we already know, or, put another way, that we have developed an intelligent interest in it. To be effective, learning must be retained; the more interest we have, the more surely do we remember. What only flickers through our mind leaves little trace; what is attended by a strong

[45]   C.A. McMurry, *The Elements of General Method*, Macmillan, London, 1903 (1892), pp. 173-4.

[46]   *ibid.*, p. 199.

[47]   F.H. Hayward, *The Critics of Herbartianism*, Swan Sonnenschein, 1903, p. 196.

[48]   C. Ufer, *op.cit.*, p. 62. Probably the most comprehensive and distinctly Herbartian statements were those of Ostermann who wrote a book *Interest in its Relation to Pedagogy*, published in an English translation in 1899, and contributed a lengthy article on interest to Rein's *Encyclopedic Manual*, Adams whose final chapter in *The Herbartian Psychology Applied to Education* was entitled 'The Doctrine of Interest', and C.A. McMurry whose widely-read *The Elements of General Method Based on the Principles of Herbart*, 1903, contained a lengthy chapter on the subject.

[49]   Lucinda Bloggs, for example, a former student of Rein's seminar, worried over the matter in several successive articles in the *American Journal of Philosophy* in 1905-6.

[50]   C.A. McMurry, *op.cit.*, p. 105.

interest we retain more readily and more securely. Attention, motivation, understanding, and memory depend for their effectiveness on interest. Interest was, thus, an important pillar of intellectual education.

The Herbartians held, further, that interest was an essential part of moral education. To have an interest in something is to indicate that it is valued; interest is a value-judgment on the object or idea in question. 'We could describe interest,' wrote Ostermann, 'as consciousness of value.'[51] Moral education consists in teaching pupils to know what is good, to value what is good, and to act in accordance with what is good; it is a combination of knowledge, judgment, and action. Moral behaviour involves both intellectual activity, and an act of the will. Interest is the driving force throughout this process. Interest rouses desire, desire leads to decisions, and decisions to actions.

Interest, however, was to be something more for the Herbartians. '. . . the new standpoint asserts interest to be the highest aim of instruction, and ideas to be the means by which that object can be reached; that is, interest is the end and knowledge is the means.'[52] The test of a course of education was not to be the amount of knowledge acquired, but the range and depth of interests developed. A person of many-sided interest was the Herbartian ideal. The mastery of skill and knowledge was important, but what was of overriding value was the possession of a well-balanced range of accomplishments, a versatility of mind, a purposeful engagement in a range of significant matters, that came from the judicious development of a many-sided interest.

What were the educational implications of this doctrine of interest? Should work be made interesting? In the sense that an artificial attention might be attracted by spicing it with fun and games, or motivating it by extrinsic rewards or punishments, the answer was no. How then was school work to become interesting?

There were important implications for the curriculum. It should be carefully adapted to the children's level of achievement and their interests. The pupils cannot become interested if their lessons are beyond their capabilities, or if they have not been adequately prepared for them. The material must be within the range of the pupils' power of apperception, and it must follow from and connect up with the ideas that have already been built up in the pupils' minds. The curriculum should at the same time, be adapted to the level and type of children's interests at their different ages. Herbart's classification of interests into six categories was accepted by most Herbartians as a reasonable working guide. C. McMurry, however, echoed the current thinking of many teachers, especially those of the growing activity movement, when he suggested the addition of motor interests. Curriculum makers required more than a mere classification; they needed to know at what stage of child development the various interests emerged, what form they took, and

what experiences they gave rise to. In the period up to World War I there was considerable research and speculation on the emergence and patterning of interests. As the notion of instincts became more popular and fundamental in general psychology, educators such as C. McMurry and Dewey in the United States, and Cyril Burt and Nunn in England, argued that interests were purposes that arose out of inborn tendencies. Instincts were the basic framework on which patterns of interests developed. Accordingly various educators suggested that as each of these instinctive interests emerged the teacher should seize it at the time of its greatest intensity, build his program upon it, and gain for his teaching the force and direction which it imparted.

The first main implication, then, of the doctrine of interest for the school curriculum was that the curriculum should adapt itself to the child's level of achievement and to his emerging interests. A child should, in effect, be ready for the instructional material presented to him and it, too, should be appropriate to his state of readiness. The idea of readiness for learning was one which was to retain its popularity, and, linked with developmental psychologies, was subsequently to give birth to the idea of developmental tasks, the concept of the teachable moment, and the use of special readiness programs in subjects such as reading, mathematics, and science.

A second important implication for the curriculum lay in its bearing on moral education. Interest, which was a central factor in character development, could be, if undirected, morally good, bad, or indifferent. The curriculum maker, therefore, should see to it that the program furthered the kinds of interests that led to good desires and actions. These, every Herbartian knew, were to be found mostly through a selective study of the humanities, especially of history and literature.

A third significant educational implication was one for teaching method. A proper use of interest meant three things. In every lesson, each pupil should be motivated in a suitable way to learn the material presented to him; a purposeless lesson was a wasted lesson. Secondly, there should be as much scope for self-activity as possible. The teacher should encourage curiosity, inquiry, imagination, and reflection. Activity of this kind breeds interest, and is, in turn, stimulated by it. Thirdly, in learning, there should be a constant drive towards the mastery and permanent acquisition of the material or skill being learnt. Interest-pedagogy was not soft-pedagogy; it was purposeful and thorough, because it was willing and zestful. 'Interest,' wrote C. McMurry, 'is a quiet, steady undertone of feeling which brings everything into readiness

[51] W. Rein, *Encyclopädisches Handbuch der Pädagogik*, 2nd ed., 1906, article by W. Ostermann, 'Das Interesse', vol. 4, p. 559.

[52] F.M. McMurry, 'Interest: Some Objections to It', *Educational Review*, February 1896, 5, p. 147.

for action, clears the deck, so to speak, and even begins and vigorously supports the attack.'[53]

It was inevitable that there should be criticism on the ground that interest was subversive of proper discipline. To emphasise interest, its opponents suggested, was to make things easy for the pupils and, morally, to do them injury. The development of character required effort of will, self-denial not self-indulgence. Drudgery, hard work, and determination were the elements out of which high performance and good character were forged. The controversy over the relationships between interest, effort, and will was fought out to the satisfaction of neither side throughout the 1890's and the first decade of the twentieth century. The most notable statement on the problem was John Dewey's *Interest and Effort in Education*, published in 1913 as an expanded version of an essay first published in 1895 in which he handsomely resolved it into a relationship of mutual dependence. But perhaps the neatest statement of the Herbartian position was that of Adams who remarked that, 'The theory of interest does not propose to banish drudgery, but only to make drudgery tolerable by giving it a meaning.'[54]

SIGNIFICANCE OF HERBARTIANISM

Herbartianism made important in education several terms and ideas that henceforth, though with somewhat changed meanings, have become the stock in trade of educational thinking and writing. Interest, correlation, and the instructional steps were the three of most significance.

Until the Herbartians made it so, interest had never been an integral part of educational theory. Every good teacher had long acted on the assumption that a pupil learns better when he is interested in his lesson, but none had previously tried to explore precisely the way in which interest facilitated learning, and none had been bold enough to suggest that interest, in the form of an interested person, could actually be regarded as the aim of education. From the time of the Herbartians, interest has been a concept of importance in education. Educational psychologists have analysed its complicated structure and much research has been done on attention, motivation, mind-set, and satisfaction. Interest as a single concept, and indeed the term itself, had disappeared from textbooks of educational psychology by the 1940's and has not yet reappeared. In the literature on teaching procedures, however, interest has maintained a place of importance. Most progressive educators found interest to be vital in their work; Decroly, for example, built a program out of 'centres of interest'; and 'pockets of interest' were used to spice the Dalton Plan. Subsequently, 'felt interests' were regarded by many teachers as one of the bases upon which school curricula should be constructed, or,

at the least, upon which good teaching should be built, and this view has continued to remain one of the generally accepted principles used in designing school programs.

The Herbartian insistence on concentration stimulated activity among educators to effect if not a unity, at least a relatedness among school subjects. The twentieth century, consequently, has seen continuous efforts to use some form or other of integration in school programs. The idea of using one subject or one topic as a centre to which all other activities were related early dropped out of consideration; it was favoured by several of the progressive educators but never gained widespread acceptance. It did, however, soon become commonplace to integrate several related subjects into one broad field such as general science or social studies. The 'complex method' which was popular in the U.S.S.R. in the 1920's was an extension of this practice. Consistently, also, in most countries, efforts were made to correlate one subject with another, e.g. in geography, to study Italy when, in history, the topic was Roman history, and this has become a lasting and widely acceptable procedure.

A fuller form of correlation, closer to the Herbartian idea of concentration, was developed in the U.S.A. in the 1930's and was widely discussed and experimented with in the 1940's and 1950's. This was the core curriculum which maintained that there was a core of social values within each society which should be studied by every pupil and should become the nucleus or core round which the study of society should be made, integrating subject-matter from all appropriate fields.

The strong Herbartian interest in the humanities which, for them, included literature and the social sciences, undoubtedly stimulated progress in these subjects in schools. It fitted well with the growing general interest in the social sciences that was apparent at the beginning of the twentieth century, and it contributed to the upsurge in the popularity of history and civics that was characteristic of the schools of the United States and of most European countries at that time.

The humanities were important because they were the subjects which were thought to contribute most to the development of moral character. The emphasis which the Herbartians placed on character formation met with a ready response from educators in the early years of the twentieth century. They were very keen to develop the best of the national character in school pupils, and especially encouraged patriotism through civics and history programs, but they were also interested in general moral development. Much was written on moral education in the early years of the century. Signs of the times were the holding of the two congresses, in London in 1908, and in The Hague in 1912, and the production in 1908 of

[53]   C.A. McMurry, *op.cit.*, pp. 158-9.

[54]   J. Adams, *The Herbartian Psychology Applied to Education*, Isbister, London, 1897, pp. 262-3.

the monumental two-volume work on *Moral Instruction and Training in Schools*, edited by M.E. Sadler, who put together contributions which demonstrated the programs and arguments used in many different countries for the advancement of moral education.[55] The Herbartians were closely linked to this movement. Their distinctive contribution, apart from their deep sense of the importance of moral education, was their demonstration that morality could be taught; the instructional process, they held, could lead, when knowledge and interest were properly blended, to the development of moral ideas and moral activity. A view such as this, especially when accompanied, as it typically was, by practical examples, was of great influence with teachers and administrators.[56]

They also threw their weight on the side of the cultivation of social rather than individual morality. Certainly it was important for individuals to learn how to lead virtuous lives, but the principal need was to teach people to live together in mutual respect, sharing common duties and responsibilities. The Herbartians favoured current moves to strengthen education for citizenship in the schools, and saw this as involving the 'formation of right social ideals, the cultivation of adequate social disposition, and the formation of efficient social habits'.[57] On the whole they tended also to support the work of the social reformers of the early twentieth century.

The theory of apperception which lay behind and justified the instructional process did not long survive in the textbooks of educational psychology. A different form of associationism, the connectionism of Thorndike, new schools of behaviourism and organismic psychology, and the work of experimenters such as Meumann, Lay, and Claparède drove Herbartian psychology out of the market. The instructional process, however, retained its popularity.

The Herbartians had succeeded in giving to teaching a rationale out of which a methodical instructional process was built. But to operate the method it was not necessary to understand the rationale. When, therefore, the rationale became outmoded and neglected, the method could and did remain popular. The Herbartian steps were the basic pattern taught to trainees in pre-World War I teacher training colleges, samples of Herbartian lessons were made widely available for teachers in method textbooks, and they became the typical teaching procedure of primary and secondary school teachers. Inevitably, without the rationale, the method became sterile in the hands of many a teacher who was accustomed 'to insist pedantically on the Steps, the whole of the Steps, and nothing but the Steps.'[58] Nevertheless, 'The Herbartian pedagogy,' as an Australian educator put it in 1909, 'is a mine from which education may dig for many a day to come,'[59] and it was still to have its advocates and satisfied practitioners well after World War II in the 1950's and 1960's.

From the heyday of its influence, from about 1880 to about 1910, the outstanding general books on education, such as those by Rein, Adams, Findlay, and the McMurrys, which remained in print through several editions over many years, helped to mould the ideas and practices of several generations of teachers. Supplemented by many first-rate practical handbooks for teachers and school textbooks designed on Herbartian lines, it became a great industry of educational book production from whose influence few teachers were immune. It left an enduring deposit on the classroom habits of twentieth century teachers, many of whom have probably always been Herbartians without being aware of it.

Herbartianism, in Dewey's words, was 'the Schoolmaster come to his own'.[60] A child's character and knowledge were built up in him by education. By controlling the perceptions, by promoting this association and suppressing that, by cultivating particular interests, and by carefully superintending the whole apperception process, the teacher was, in actual fact, making men. He was in a position of great power and responsibility. 'Herbart,' wrote Findlay, 'showed us that our wares, the stuff we had to offer to children, were of supreme value.'[61] The Herbartians enhanced the status of the teacher and provided him with practical, workable tools to achieve his objects. They not only conferred great authority on the teacher, they also showed him in unmistakable detail how to use it.

Soon after the beginning of the century, although Herbartianism remained in the saddle, the current of educational thinking, particularly in the English-speaking countries, began to move slowly and steadily away from Herbartianism towards the views that Dewey represented. De Garmo, when he wrote his book *Interest and Education* in 1906, dedicated it to John Dewey; and J.J. Findlay's *Principles of Class Teaching* which first appeared in 1902 was an early thoughtful synthesis of both Rein's and Dewey's viewpoints. In subsequent works both writers absorbed more and more of Dewey, and even those staunch Herbartians, the McMurry brothers, had, by 1910, become as much Deweyan as Herbartian. In 1913 an anonymous reviewer in the English *Journal of Education* formally declared the end of the Herbartian era and the apotheosis of its founder:

[55] See above Chapter 1.

[56] R.J.W. Selleck, *The New Education*, Pitman, Melbourne, 1968, Chapter 9 has a good account of the movement for moral instruction in England.

[57] C. De Garmo, 'Social Aspects of Moral Education', *The Third Yearbook of the National Herbart Society*, C.A. McMurry (ed.), University of Chicago, 1897, p. 47; G.L. Moulton, 'The American Herbartian: A Portrait from his Yearbook, *History of Education Quarterly*, 3, p. 141; N.R. Hiner, Herbartians, history, and moral education, *School Review*, 79, 4 August 1971, pp. 590-601.

[58] J. Adams, *Exposition and Illustration in Teaching*, Macmillan, London, 1910, p. 153.

[59] A.J. Schulz, 'Herbart', *The Education Gazette* (South Australia), 12 October 1909, p. 235.

[60] J. Dewey, *Democracy and Education*, Macmillan, New York, 1916, p. 83.

[61] J.J. Findlay ed., *Educational Essays*, Blackie, London, 1910, p. 8.

'... it is no longer worthwhile to deal in detail with the Herbartian controversy. It has had its day, and now the works of Johann Friedrich have won their way among the classics of pedagogy.'[62]

Herbartianism was a timely development. The expansion of knowledge and multiplication of school pupils at the beginning of the century brought with them a demand for an effective and well-organised method of instruction, and the growing popularity of Darwinism generated an interest in the ways of using the driving forces of human will and character to best advantage. The Herbartians met the situation by providing a systematic form of instruction, by showing how volitional and intellectual training could be combined, and by demonstrating the motivational force of interest in every aspect of the educational process.

Herbartianism was the first phase through which twentieth century education passed. It was a complete and systematic doctrine in itself, but it was also a rich and diverse stimulus which led educators in many different directions. Dewey passed through a Herbartian period and absorbed and transformed many of its ideas; the early progressives, Lietz and Reddie, were students of Rein's seminar and kept in close contact with him. Progressives and conservatives all found satisfaction in some aspects of Herbartianism. Those interested in intellectual education found in it an instructional pattern which they could cherish; those who looked for more emphasis on emotional factors in education had, in the doctrine of interest, a justification for their faith; those who put a study of child development first could point, in both curriculum and method, to the Herbartians' insistence on understanding and charting the phases of children's growth. It appealed widely because it had something for every taste, and yet, was, at the same time, coherent and orderly. It was the end result, the solid culmination of much thought and methodical school practice, and, at the same time, a launching pad of educational ideas for the twentieth century.

---

[62] *The Journal of Education*, September 1913, 45, 530, p. 622.

CHAPTER 3

JOHN DEWEY AND EDUCATION FOR DEMOCRACY

John Dewey as a young professor in the 1890's, about the time that he established the Laboratory School at the University of Chicago.

In 1916 the most important educational treatise of the twentieth century was published. This was John Dewey's *Democracy and Education*. It was a careful and deliberate attempt to show the connection between education in a democracy and what Dewey thought to be the three newly significant cultural forces of the early twentieth century, 'experimental method in the sciences, evolutionary ideas in the biological sciences, and the industrial reorganization'.[1] It brought education into connection with contemporary life and fostered a re-thinking of the whole fabric of administration, teaching, and curriculum design. The book became a statement of importance and of wide reference not merely for American educators but for educators throughout the whole of the democratic world.

Dewey was fifty-seven at the time when he wrote *Democracy and Education* and his career was already distinguished for his contributions to philosophy, psychology, and the theory and practice of education. He was to live until 1952, and in the remaining thirty-six years his international reputation was enhanced by further important written contributions in several fields, by a number of significant overseas visits that he made, and by the widespread discussion that his works provoked among educators and philosophers.[2]

---

[1] J. Dewey, *Democracy and Education*, Macmillan, New York, 1916, Preface.

[2] John Dewey was born in Burlington, Vermont, in 1859. The son of a storekeeper of old New England stock, he was educated in the local high school and graduated in 1879 from the University of Vermont. For three years he taught school, and then entered the recently established Johns Hopkins University from which he obtained his Ph.D. degree with a thesis on the psychology of Kant. He taught philosophy at the University of Michigan, with a brief interval at Minnesota, from 1886 to 1894. For the next ten years, 1894 to 1904, he was chairman of the Department of Philosophy, Psychology, and Education at the University of Chicago. While there he helped to found a Laboratory School in connection with his work, and out of this association produced *The School and Society*, one of the most widely read of all his books.

From 1904 to 1930 he was professor of philosophy at Columbia University, New York. During this period he gave a stimulus to educational psychology by writing *How We Think* in 1910, *Interest and Effort in Education*, 1913, and *Human Nature and Conduct*, 1922. The general theory of education and the fundamentals of his philosophical views were expressed also in this period in a widely read series beginning with *Democracy and Education* in 1916, and continuing with *Reconstruction in Philosophy*, 1920, *Experience and Nature*, 1925, and *The Quest for Certainty*, 1929. Between 1918 and 1928 he visited for varying periods Japan, China, Turkey, Mexico, and the U.S.S.R.

After his retirement in 1930 he continued to write, giving a definitive statement of his views on aesthetics in *Art as Experience*, 1934, and on logic in *Logic: The Theory of Enquiry*, 1938. In *Experience and Education*, 1938, Dewey's last substantial work on education, he analysed the conflict between traditional and progressive education that had developed during the past generation, and summarised his own views on the means and ends of education. The most comprehensive biography of Dewey is G. Dykhuizen, *The Life and Mind of John Dewey*, Southern Illinois Press, Carbondale, Illinois, 1973.

THE REFLEX ARC

Dewey's first original and influential contribution was made in the field of psychology and appeared as an article entitled 'The Reflex Arc Concept in Psychology' in the *Psychological Review*, July 1896. He had, in the previous ten years, argued for a dynamic approach in psychology that would link an individual functionally to his environment.[3]

The basic unit of psychological explanation that had recently become popular was the reflex arc, subsequently known as the stimulus-response mechanism. Behaviour, it was suggested, proceeds from sensation to idea, and thence to action; or, put in physiological terms, sensory stimulus leads to central nervous activity and thence to motor discharge. Dewey expressed some concern that those three parts of behaviour might be regarded as distinct and separate from one another. The underlying reality, in Dewey's view, was an organic co-ordination.[4] The stimulus and the response were parts of the same experience; the final activity of the experience was a reconstruction of the first activity. The stimulus-response circuit should be regarded as a co-ordinated experi-ence, and could be understood only in relation to the purpose of the experience and the background of the person having the experience. Suppose a child on reaching for a bright light sometimes found something good to eat and sometimes burnt himself, 'the question of whether to reach or to abstain from reaching is the question of what sort of bright light have we here? . . . the discovery of the sensation marks the establishing of the problem.'[5] What purpose does the child have in mind in responding to the stimulus? And, further, what are the circumstances and the background of the experience? 'If one is reading a book, if one is hunting, if one is watching in a dark place on a lonely night, if one is performing a chemical experiment', in each case, the stimulus of say, a loud noise, has a different psychical value; 'it is a different experience'.[6] Stimuli were loaded with value and meaning depending upon the background experience of the individual encoun-tering the stimulus. 'The child,' Dewey pointed out, 'gets very few naked stimuli.'[7]

In the early writings on psychology, there was much that was characteristic of Dewey's later, developed thought. His concern with the nature of experience, and his view that it was not a series of discrete happenings, but was composed of organic co-ordinations, was widely expressed in his subsequent writings in social and educational philosophy. His view that conflicts, leading to problems, arose within experience, and called for the reconstruction of behaviour, became the basis of the instrumental logic and the method of teaching that he consistently emphasised. And his constant reference to a growing individual immersed in a social context flavoured all his subsequent writings on education.

It is possible to detect also, at that early stage, what he later wrote of, in a short autobiography, as 'the importance that the practice and theory of education have had for me; especially the education of the young . . . This interest fused with and brought together what might otherwise have been separate interests — that in psychology and that in social institutions and social life.'[8]

'MY PEDAGOGIC CREED'

In 1897 Dewey published *My Pedagogic Creed*. In that short pamphlet, Dewey stated incisively the essence of his educational theory: that education was not a preparation for future living, but was a 'continuing reconstruction of experience', that experience was saturated with social reference, that individuals were 'social individuals', and society an 'organic union of individuals', that the school was a community engaged in a social process of enriching the children's own activities, that the school taught the children to control their activities and their environment by well-disciplined thinking and intelligently co-operative behaviour, and that education was 'the fundamental method of social progress and reform'.[9]

Those ideas were later to be developed more fully and argued more closely in books such as *How We Think* and *Democracy and Education* and they were to find immediate expression in the work of Dewey's Laboratory School.

---

[3] J. Dewey, 'The New Psychology', *Andover Review*, September 1884, II, pp. 278-89; J. Dewey, *Psychology*, Harper, New York, 1887, p. 10; J.A. McLellan and J. Dewey, *Applied Psychology: An Introduction to the Principles and Practice of Education*, Educational Publishing Company, Boston, 1889.

[4] J. Dewey, 'The Reflex Arc Concept in Psychology', *Psychological Review*, July 1896, Ill. p. 358. This article is reprinted in John Dewey, *The Early Works, 1882-1898, 5: 1895-1898 Early Essays*, W.R. McKenzie (ed.), Southern Illinois University Press, Carbondale, Illinois, 1972, pp. 96-109.

[5] *ibid.*, pp. 367-9.

[6] *ibid.*, p. 361.

[7] J. Dewey, *Lectures in the Philosophy of Education*, 1899, R.D. Archambault, ed., Random House, New York, 1966, p. 46.

[8] 'From Absolutism to Experimentalism', in R.J. Bernstein (ed.), *John Dewey on Experience, Nature, and Freedom*, Liberal Arts Press, New York, 1960, p. 14.

[9] J. Dewey, *My Pedagogic Creed*, Washington D.C., The Progressive Education Association, 1929, reprinted, pp. 5,6,7,11,12,14 and 15.

THE LABORATORY SCHOOL, 1896-1903

In his presidential address to the American Psychological Association in 1899, Dewey referred to teaching as a 'mixture of empiricism and inspiration'.[10] It was the thought of being able to give it a sounder psychological and sociological basis that led to his establishing a laboratory school. The new school was not designed as a training or a practice school; it was to be a research centre in which theory could be tried out in action.

(i) Organisation

The Laboratory School was established at the University of Chicago in 1896 and lasted for seven years until 1903. It was supported by fees, private subscriptions, and some assistance from the University of Chicago. The number of children attending was never large, from sixteen pupils at its opening to a maximum of 140, and, in age, from four to fourteen. The school was at all times well supplied with staff and drew a number of part-time specialists from various university departments. In consequence, classes were small. They were based upon common interests and social compatibility and, in turn, were divided into small working groups so that much individual attention was possible for the benefit of all children. There were no formal examinations and no comparisons or rankings among the children.

Dewey was at all times very closely associated with the running of the school. He led discussions among the staff and parents on school policy, he sketched out his views on the aims of the school, and he gave much thought to the program and methods of teaching to be used at all levels. His book, *The School and Society*, published in 1900, was one of the important fruits of the lectures and discussions which he held in connection with this Laboratory School.

(ii) Social Emphasis

The aim of the school was 'to discover, in administration, selection of subject-matter, methods of learning, teaching, and discipline, how a school could become a co-operative community while developing in individuals their own capacities and satisfying their own needs'.[11]

Co-operation, co-ordination, sharing, and social responsibility are the kinds of words and ideas that constantly recur in the descriptions of the work of the school. There was much more freedom of choice and activity for the pupils than could be found in contemporary American schools, and that gave rise to an expression among some observers that the

MY PEDAGOGIC CREED

ARTICLE I—*What Education Is*

I Believe that

—all education proceeds by the participation of the individual in the social consciousness of the race. This process begins unconsciously almost at birth, and is continually shaping the individual's powers, saturating his consciousness, forming his habits, training his ideas, and arousing his feelings and emotions. Through this unconscious education the individual gradually comes to share in the intellectual and moral resources which humanity has succeeded in getting together. He becomes an inheritor of the funded capital of civilization. The most formal and technical education in the world cannot safely depart from this general process. It can only organize it or differentiate it in some particular direction.

—the only true education comes through the stimulation of the child's powers by the demands of the social situations in which he finds himself. Through these demands he is stimulated to act as a member of a unity, to emerge from his original narrowness of action and feeling, and to conceive of himself from the standpoint of the welfare of the group to which he belongs. Through the responses which others make to his own activities he comes to know what these mean in social terms. The value which they have is reflected back into them. For instance, through the response which is made to the child's instinctive

The first page of John Dewey's *My Pedagogic Creed*, 1897.

J. Dewey, *My Pedagogic Creed.* Republished in M.S. Dworkin (ed.), *Dewey on Education: Selection etc.,* Teachers College Press, New York, 1957.

---

[10]   J. Dewey, *Educational Essays*, J.J. Findlay ed., Blackie, London, 1910, p. 142.

[11]   K.C. Mayhew and A.C. Edwards, *The Dewey School, The Laboratory School of the University of Chicago, 1896-1903*, Atherton, New York, 1966, Introduction by John Dewey, p. xiv.

school 'was devoted to personal liberty and that it advocated rampant individualism'.[12] This view was wholly mistaken. The school certainly aimed to develop better individuals, but they would be better because they had deeper social contacts, because they were being educated in a rich community life, and because they were learning to contribute responsibly to co-operative activities. The aims, curriculum, and methods of work at the school were saturated with social significance. 'The school's ultimate social ideal was the transformation of society through a new, socially-minded individualism.'[14]

(iii) Activity Program

Besides the social emphasis, the other characteristic feature of the school was its interest in activity. Dewey related how, when he was looking for desks and chairs suited to the needs of the children and was having difficulty finding what he wanted, one dealer remarked to him: 'I am afraid we have not what you want. You want something at which the children may work; these are all for listening,'[14] The school was an *Arbeitsschule* or 'activity' school having much in common with the contemporary progressive school movement in Europe.

Dewey had put forward the view in his article on the reflex arc that the unit of human behaviour was an act. Each act was a co-ordinating of sensation, ideas, and expression. The first phase of an action was impulsive. When impulse met with difficulties or resistance, ideas were generated for dealing with the situation. Ideas redirected the course of the action, made provision for a choice between different possible actions, and gave opportunity for deliberation on the outcome of the action. Impulsive activity thus became meaningful activity.

The educator's task was to make all activity as meaningful as possible. To achieve this, two things were necessary:

First, the impulse to action should arise from the felt needs in the life of the children; the child was thus placed at the centre of the educational problem. This was in line with the change that was taking place in European countries at the same time, and which Ellen Key had described as the beginning of the century of the child. Dewey wrote of the change as 'the shifting of the centre of gravity. It is a change, a revolution, not unlike that introduced by Copernicus when the astronomical center shifted from the earth to the sun. In this case the child becomes the sun about which the appliances of education revolve; he is the center about which they are organised.'[15]

The second thing necessary was the planning of situations which would require children to deliberate in order to solve problems and use their intelligence as an instrument to improve their activity. Ideas were thus used to clarify and select activities, and activities in turn provided both the occasion for the ideas and the outcome of the deliberative process. In that way, progress was made by the children in understanding their environment and in building up their own ways of coping with it. The development of understanding through meaningful activities led to further understanding and expression in action and ideas. This was the process of human growth, over and above mere physiological development.

Growth was a progressive acquisition of meaningful ideas. Meaningful ideas stem from activity which is interesting, which rests on intelligent analysis, and which involves a thoughtful acceptance of responsibility for acting upon one's considered decision. 'The controlling principle of growth, ... became the guiding principle of the school's theory.'[16]

(iv) Curriculum

The curriculum of the Laboratory School was gradually worked out in its first three years and then consolidated and improved in its remaining four years. It was based upon social occupations related to Dewey's view of the basic impulses of children. These were sometimes called interests, desires, urges, or even instincts, and were classified under four heads:

- The *social* impulse was shown in children's conversation, communication, and desire to share their experiences with other people, especially with their family. An interest in the use of language was a part of this social impulse.

- The *constructive* impulse involved a desire to make things and to express oneself through play and through the shaping of various materials.

- The *investigative* impulse involved an interest in inquiring into and experimenting with the environment. It could be closely associated with both the social and constructive impulses.

- The *expressive* impulse was an urge to communicate and construct in an artistic way.

12   *ibid.*, p. 467.

13   *ibid.*, p. 436.

14   J. Dewey, *The School and Society*, rev. edn, University of Chicago Press, 1915, p. 32.

15   *ibid.*, p. 35.

16   K.C. Mayhew and A.C. Edwards, *op.cit.*, p. 413.

The four impulses or interests, Dewey wrote, 'are the natural resources, the uninvested capital, upon the exercise of which depends the active growth of the child'.[17]

The task of the Laboratory School was to devise a curriculum of studies which harmonised with the development of these impulses and with the growing experience of the children. The answer was found in a graded curriculum of social occupations.

An occupation was a form of activity on the part of the child which reproduced or ran parallel to some form of work carried on in social life. Woodwork, cooking, sewing, and textile work were the basic kinds of activities involved in each of the occupations. They were placed within a framework of social history.

In essence, the curriculum of the Laboratory School was 'the study of social life at various selected periods as mirrored in its occupations'.[18] Three groups of studies were made within this framework:

- *Science and mathematics.* The development of scientific knowledge and mathematical skill was continually cultivated at all ages in order to ensure a grasp of elementary scientific concepts, and to develop in the children the habit of using scientific procedures.
- *Skills in communication and expression.* They included reading, writing and discussing in one's native language, and, after about the age of ten, a study related to English, or a foreign language. Drama, music, modelling, painting, and other expressive activities in wood, metal, or fabric were constantly cultivated as an integral part of all the typical school experiences.
- *Social Studies.* The social activities of the children's present society and family, and the history and geography of mankind's developing occupations were the setting into which all the studies of various kinds were integrated.

There was a considerable emphasis on the study of history throughout the Laboratory School curriculum. There were two reasons for it. History, for Dewey, was a kind of indirect sociology; it was a study of present society by making known the forces that have woven the present pattern and by providing, especially in primitive history, the fundamental elements of the present situation in immensely simplified and more readily understandable form.[19] History was vital in another important sense in Dewey's thinking during his Chicago period. In ethics, it is not easy to see how experimental methods can provide the control and understanding that they supply in the physical sciences; history, however, can act as a substitute for experiment. We can look at an aspect of human behaviour and see how it came to be, taking it apart in its primitive manifestations, and building it up into its subsequent more

synthesised and complicated form. This is very much what the scientific experimenter is engaged in doing. History, therefore, can be an important vehicle in the study of morality, not by offering examples for imitation, but by providing a method of analysing moral situations, of understanding them in their developing social context, and of controlling them through this understanding.[20]

Throughout all years, the program correlated the three groups of studies into the pattern set by the social studies, allowing for a greater degree of specialised work for the older children.

(v) Methods

The methods used in teaching and learning were varied and flexible. They were designed to give appropriate expression to the four basic impulses of communication, construction, inquiry, and artistic expression.

In the activities, initiative, as far as possible, rested with the children, and responsibility for the completion of the work was in large part also theirs, under the sensitive guidance of the teachers.

Each substantial activity normally involved three kinds of work: motor, intellectual, and co-operative planning. They gave a balance and completeness to the work:

- *Motor.* Motor activities such as weaving, cooking, handiwork and painting were important, not primarily because of their utilitarian value, but because they were an essential part of a completed action and necessary to the understanding of that action, and because action undertaken in its completeness was regarded as the central element in personal and social development.
- *Intellectual.* All activities involved strenuous intellectual work. 'The choice by the school of intelligence as the preferred method of action'[21] meant that there was an insistence on planning and thinking through activities and, above all, on the use of and training in experimental or scientific methods. From their earliest

[17] J. Dewey, *The School and Society*, p. 45. A further account of these impulses is given in Mayhew and Edwards, *The Dewey School*, pp. 40ff. These authors write: 'These fourfold desires — to communicate, to construct, to inquire and to express in finer form — are the child's natural springs for action.' See also J. Dewey, *Interest and Effort in Education*, pp. 65ff.

[18] K.C. Mayhew and A.C. Edwards, *op.cit.*, p. 164.

[19] J. Dewey, *Democracy and Education*, Macmillan, New York, 1916, pp. 250ff; A.G. Wirth, *John Dewey as Educator. His Design for Work in Education, (1894-1904)*, Wiley, New York, 1966, pp. 138-47.

[20] M. White, *Social Thought in America*, Beacon, Boston, 1957 (1947) pp. 20-1.

[21] K.C. Mayhew and A.C. Edwards, *op.cit.*, p. 438.

years at the school, children were encouraged to inquire, research and experiment. Scientific method was the constantly used tool at all times and in all situations in which it could possibly be used. A few years later, the process and its importance in education were analysed in detail by Dewey in *How We Think* and, some forty years later he felt the need to voice his opinion strongly again. 'What we need is a type of education that will start very early to develop the spirit of inquiry, of willingness to weigh the evidence, of experimentation — in short, the scientific spirit. We also need to pay more attention to the application of the scientific spirit in the social sciences, and to emphasise the social aspects of science in our schools.'[22] It was a method which combined experience, problem solving, hard thinking, and action.

- *Co-operative planning.* It was customary in each classroom to spend the first part of each session in a general consultation among the pupils and teachers, reviewing existing work and planning future activities. It was an essential part of the school's approach that all activities were co-operatively planned by pupils and teachers.

(vi) Results

The effects of the Laboratory School are not easy to judge. It was not evaluated independently, and all that is available is a small selection of the impressions formed by teachers, parents, and children, as to the outcome of the work.

On that evidence, the scientific emphasis appears to have left a permanent deposit in the behaviour of the pupils. In those who spent some considerable time at the school, there was an ingrained objectivity in their thinking, and a readiness to inquire and to conduct appropriate research into matters which engaged their attention. Through their extensive social science programs, the children came to understand the developing pattern and importance of human occupations and gradually to become aware that the function of thinking is to manage experience. The most important effect of the expressive work appeared to have been a noticeable growth in the power of self-expression and in self-confidence. Each individual boy or girl felt increasingly capable of conceiving, evaluating, and executing activities of which he was the author. He developed thereby a general attitude of confidence towards life, which was an amalgam of his consciousness of his ability to meet and cope with circumstances as they arose, and his growing capacity to link his work with that of others in concerted and fruitful action.

The school was well known to educators in the U.S.A. and Europe. A contemporary observer remarked that 'More eyes are now fixed upon the University elementary school of Chicago than upon any other elementary school in the country, or probably in the world.'[23] It did not, however, have any immediate imitators. Its influence was probably felt mainly through the descriptions and ideas that were to be found in Dewey's popular little book, *The School and Society.*

The Laboratory School was an example of Dewey's own theory in action. It was a substantial practical activity directed by the educational theory which Dewey was then formulating. In turn, the experimental work of the classroom helped to mould and modify the theoretical position. In Dewey's writings and speeches during his Laboratory School period, the ideas on education that he was to explore later at greater length and the characteristic vocabulary of his educational writings emerged clearly, were related to one another through practical trial, and took an articulate shape.

DEWEY'S GROWING INFLUENCE

Dewey's ideas did not develop in isolation. He regarded himself as taking part in a 'general movement of intellectual reconstruction',[24] which the publication of Darwin's *Origin of Species* had made necessary. Of particular importance in the movement of ideas was the work of William James whose pragmatism Dewey came more and more to share. James' *Principles of Psychology*, published in 1890, made a profound impression on him and accelerated his movement into the functional and instrumental school of thought.

During Dewey's ten-year period at the new University of Chicago, he found himself in a sympathetic and invigorating environment.[25] In his own department he had the stimulus of working with G.H. Mead, who was to become one of America's most seminal social philosophers, and

[22] R.L. Straker *et al., Educating for Democracy: A Symposium*, Antioch Press, Yellow Springs, Ohio, 1937, p. 146.

[23] Quoted in G. Dykhuizen, 'John Dewey: The Chicago Years' *Journal of the History of Philosophy*, 2, 2, October 1964, 252.

[24] J. Dewey, *The Influence of Darwin on Philosophy*, Indiana University Press, Bloomington, 1965 (1910), p. iv.

[25] Thomas, Small, Boas, Starr, and Veblen in anthropology and sociology, Chamberlin in geology, Loeb in physiology, and Michelson in physics were his colleagues. Many of them were interested in Dewey's work and offered courses suitable for education students, or took some part in the work of the Laboratory School.

J.R. Angell, whose work in experimental psychology helped to lay the foundations of the functionalist school.[26]

Outside the university Dewey had a close and refreshing contact with Jane Addams who had established in 1889 an adult social and educational centre, Hull House, in a poor immigrant area of Chicago. Liberal individuals interested in social reform joined the activities of Hull House and Dewey found there an atmosphere and an audience sensitive to his ideas and, in addition, practical social work on which to test out his reconstructive theory. Another figure of importance was the embattled principal of the Cook County Normal School, Francis W. Parker.[27] After eighteen years of struggle with a conservative school board, Parker was eventually able to transfer to the University of Chicago his progressive elementary training school in 1901. On his death in the following year, it was amalgamated with the Dewey Laboratory School.

By about the turn of the century, Dewey's efforts at reconstruction were beginning to be recognised as something of significant weight in psychology, education, and philosophy, and as important expressions of the pragmatist viewpoint that William James and C.S. Peirce had begun to build into an approach distinctive of much of American philosophy for several decades to come.

Dewey's departure from Chicago for Columbia in 1904 meant the end of his close connection with a School of Education. Henceforth, his contact with schools and education students was to be an indirect one. The Chicago experience, however, had left a permanent impress on his work. In all his subsequent thought and writing, education was a constant concern and his most substantial contributions to the literature of education were still to come.

His early works were steadily being read both in the United States and abroad. In England, for example, Findlay, a respected and influential educator, edited two volumes of Dewey's essays, and recorded, in 1910, in the introduction to the second, his opinion that 'we have here a system emerging which will catch on, which will secure discipleship, among many perhaps who do not half understand its philosophic foundation'.[28] In Germany, *The School and Society* appeared in translation in 1905 and Kerschensteiner's approval of him helped to keep Dewey's ideas fresh in the minds of German educators. The Swiss educator, Claparède, then one of Europe's most influential educational researchers, and Decroly, the Belgian leader of the progressive movement, were attracted by Dewey's work and made his name more widely known in educational discussion in Europe. In 1909 his monograph on *Moral Principles in Education* dealt with the theme that had become the most widely discussed topic during the last three or four years. In the next year *How We Think* was simultaneously published in London and New York. Three years later, in 1913, *Interest and Effort in Education* reinterpreted a central concept of

the predominant Herbartianism. In 1915 *Schools of Tomorrow* set out, in readable fashion, with practical examples, the ideas that Dewey hoped to foster. In 1916 *Democracy and Education* capped seven years of substantial and almost continuous production. Those years were the core of his writing on education. It was through those works that he chiefly became known overseas and it was those works which provided the basic material for his followers at home.

Dewey had neither the character nor the oratorical equipment to inspire and lead a movement. He was described at the time of his appointment to Chicago as 'simple, modest, utterly devoid of any affectation';[29] he remained always, quiet, humane, contemplative, and a little shy. He was, nevertheless, persistent, ingeniously argumentative, and immensely hardworking. For sixty years he wrote constantly, producing an immense stream of articles and books, each one on some aspect of the human condition, arguing persistently and striving continually to bring his readers to 'the realisation that intelligent action is the sole ultimate resource of mankind in every field whatsoever'.[30] His style of writing in popular articles was clear and forceful; in the majority of his technical works, it was turgid and convoluted. The books were like his lectures — exercises in feeling his way through a problem, searching for the exactness of definition and idea that best expressed his absorption in the topic. The style was nicely summed up by Mr Justice Holmes: 'But although Dewey's book [*Experience and Nature*] is incredibly ill-written, it seemed to me after several re-readings to have a feeling of intimacy with the inside of the cosmos that I found unequaled. So methought God would have spoken had He been inarticulate but keenly desirous to tell you how it was.'[31]

[26] A more extensive account of Dewey's relations with his colleagues at Chicago is to be found in: G. Dykhuizen, 'John Dewey: The Chicago Years', *Journal of the History of Philosophy*, 2,2, October 1964, pp. 227-53; A.G. Wirth, *John Dewey as Educator. His Design for Work in Education (1894-1904)*, Wiley, New York, 1966, pp. 42-52; R.L. McCaul, Dewey's Chicago, *The School Review*, 67,2, Summer 1959, pp. 258-80; and R.L. McCaul, A preliminary listing of Dewey letters, 1894-1904, *The School and Society*, 87,2157, October 10, 1959, The John Dewey Centennial Special Issue, p. 396.

[27] J. Dewey, 'How Much Freedom in New Schools', *New Republic*, LXIII, 9 July 1930, p. 204. Dewey made a brief assessment of Parker's work in: 'In Remembrance: Francis W. Parker', *Journal of Education*, LV, 27 March, 1902, p. 119; and J. Dewey, In Memorium: Colonel Francis Wayland Parker, *The Elementary School Teacher*, II, June 1902, pp. 704-8.

[28] J. Dewey, *Educational Essays*, J.J. Findlay, (ed.), Blackie, London, 1910, p. 10.

[29] W.W. Brickman and S. Lehrer, *John Dewey: Master Educator*, 2nd edn, New York, Society for the Advancement of Education, 1961, p. 168; Professor James H. Tuft's letter recommending John Dewey to President Harper, 1893/4.

[30] J. Dewey, *The Quest for Certainty*, Capricorn Books, New York, 1960 (1929), p. 252.

[31] O.W. Holmes, *Holmes-Pollock Letters: The Correspondence of Mr. Justice Holmes and Sir Frederick Pollock 1874-1932*, M. De W. Howe (ed.), Harvard University Press, Cambridge, Mass., 1941, vol. 2, p. 287.

DEMOCRACY AND EDUCATION

AN INTRODUCTION TO THE PHILOS- OPHY OF EDUCATION

BY

JOHN DEWEY

New York

THE MACMILLAN COMPANY

1916

The title page of John Dewey's book that influenced the pattern of thinking of many educators throughout the world in the first half of the twentieth century.

J. Dewey, *Democracy and Education*, Macmillan, New York 1916. (Copyright 1916 by Macmillan Publishing Co., Inc., renewed 1944 by John Dewey.)

Similarly, in university lectures, his style was flat and unexciting, but for those who had the patience it was intellectually stimulating; it was an exercise in dogged intellectual exploration and honest, penetrating analysis into some pertinent issue or problem. Dewey, wrote one of his hearers, 'does not pound. He quietly loosens the hoops and the bottom insensibly vanishes.'[32]

In due course, however, he did not lack supporters with a more popular appeal. By about the time of World War I a number of the leading educators in the United States were beginning to express themselves in Deweyan terms. Foremost amongst them were B.H. Bode and W.H. Kilpatrick. Bode from 1910 made important contributions, from the pragmatist viewpoint, to the discussion of logical theory and subsequently became a strenuous supporter of Dewey's viewpoint in education. Kilpatrick was caught in the Deweyan net after reading *Interest as Related to Will*, began working with Dewey in 1907, and remained in close contact with him at Columbia for the next forty years. A striking and popular lecturer, he did much from his position of influence at Columbia Teachers' College to make Dewey's ideas known and widely acceptable.

JOHN DEWEY ABROAD

During the 1920's Dewey had the opportunity to visit and study several countries — Japan (1919), China (1919-21), Turkey (1924), Mexico (1926), and the U.S.S.R. (1928) — whose traditions were markedly different from those of his own country, and who were in the process of re-examining their accepted values and building new societies to cope with changed conditions and expectations of the post-World War I years.

In 1919 he spent two months in Japan, speaking to teachers and lecturing at Tokyo University. His lectures were subsequently published as *Reconstruction in Philosophy* and became one of his most widely read books. Throughout the 1920's he was somewhat in vogue among Japanese educators and his ideas stimulated some experimentation with progressive methods. His visit appears also to have influenced several young educators who, later, after World War II, were to become of considerable importance. These men helped to stimulate a revival of interest in his work which was seen to have particular appropriateness both to the American ideas then flooding the country, and to the democratically oriented social reconstruction that took place at that time.[33]

[32] G. Dykhuizen, 'John Dewey: The Chicago Years', p. 247.

[33] V.N. Kobayashi, *John Dewey in Japanese Educational Thought*, Ann Arbor, University of Michigan School of Education, 1964, Chapters 2, 3, 5 and 6.

From 1919 to 1921 he was in China at the invitation of several educational bodies to lecture principally at universities and teachers' colleges in Peking, Nanking, and Shanghai. During his two-year stay he toured widely, lecturing on and discussing education and its connection with science and democracy in the modern world. He was well received, made intimate contact with Chinese intellectuals to an extent seldom previously achieved by a western scholar, and took a devoted personal interest in the prospects of the new society. He arrived at a critical time, at the beginning of the May Fourth new cultural movement initiated at Peking University in 1919. He appears to have caught the sense of the moment admirably and to have made a considerable impression at the time and during the course of the 1920's. One later Chinese commentator even went so far as to write that his visit was the beginning of a new era in Chinese education.[34] In education, particularly, his impact can be seen in the general program of reform adopted in 1922, in the establishment of experimental schools, in the upsurge of new reform literature on social and educational affairs to which he contributed and in the widespread currency of his ideas among educators for many years thereafter.[35] Eventually his influence appears to have been absorbed into and transformed by the strong upsurge of Marxist thinking among Chinese scholars in the 1930's.

What struck him particularly in each of the countries was the basic similarity of the problem, that of constructing a new community for the newly industrial society into which they were thrusting, sometimes with 'incredible' consequences and speed.[36] He was stirred by the *élan* with which the developing countries were proceeding. There was an abundance of 'vitality, energy, sacrificial devotion'[37] and eagerness to build the new mind and the new society. In each country there was a clear realisation that education had a key role to play in the transformation. In China, for example, he wrote 'there is nothing one hears so often from the lips of the representatives of Young China of today as that education is the sole means of reconstructing China'.[38] During the depression of the 1930's in America he was to experience the same sense of the urgency and importance of education and he was to discuss in *The Social Frontier* the same kind of journalism that he had seen started in the May 4th Movement during his visit to China.

In Russia in 1928, he found the reconstructive work intrinsically educational; what was taking place was not to be grasped in political or economic terms, but in educational. It was the building of a 'new collective mentality'.[39] The function of the new education in Russia was to create persons who would act co-operatively rather than individualistically. This necessitated a very close relationship between the school and contemporary political and social life. The task for intellectuals was not one of criticism as in most western countries, but one that was constructive; they were an important part of the collective mentality working creatively for the new society.

In keeping with this association of school and community Dewey found that the activity principle was being widely advocated, especially in Mexico and Russia, and he himself suggested more attention to it in China and Turkey.

DEWEY, THE POLITICAL AND SOCIAL LIBERAL

Up until World War I, when Dewey was in his late fifties, he had written very little on political and social affairs outside of education. From then on, especially in the inter-war period, he contributed articles and books continuously in that field and by his actions demonstrated his liberal convictions in practice.[40] Dewey's liberalism was an alliance of democracy, social planning, and the scientific spirit. He maintained that social and political thought had not caught up with two major factors in the twentieth century life, the massive development of science and technology, and the growing interdependence and corporateness of personal, social, and economic life. His activities were designed to make the public aware of this anomaly, and to suggest the way of remedying 'the chief problem — that of remaking society to serve the growth of a new type of individual'.[41]

The new individual that the times required should have four principal characteristics: his behaviour should habitually rely on and be

---

[34] Ou Tsuin Chen, *La Doctrine Pédagogique de John Dewey*, Vrin, Paris, 1958 (1931), p. 253.

[35] J. Blewett (ed.) *John Dewey: His Thought and Influence*, Chapter VIII; T. Berry, 'Dewey's Influence in China', Fordham University Press, New York, 1960; Ou Tsuin Chen, *op.cit.*, pp. 251-4; C.A. Moore (ed.), *Philosophy and Culture East and West*, Hu Shih, 'John Dewey in China', pp. 762-9.

[36] J. Dewey, *Characters and Events*, 1, Allen & Unwin, London, 1929, pp. 155, 359.

[37] *ibid.*, p. 370.

[38] *ibid.*, p. 306.

[39] *ibid.*, p. 400.

[40] Dewey helped to organise and became the first president of the American Association of University Professors in 1915; he was an original member of the first Teachers' Union in New York, 1916; in 1929 he was made president of the People's Lobby to further progressive policies in Congress, and national chairman of the League for Independent Political Action; in the presidential elections of 1932 and 1936 he publicly supported the socialist candidate, Norman Thomas; and in 1937 he presided in Mexico over a Commission of Inquiry into the charges made against Trotsky in the current Moscow trials. In the liberal journal, *New Republic*, and in whatever other journals would give him a sympathetic hearing, he supported the principles of freedom of inquiry and expression, equality of opportunity, and social and economic planning, and he expressed his views on the current happenings which violated or illustrated these principles. In *The Public and its Problems* (1927), *Individualism Old and New* (1930), *Liberalism and Social Action* (1935), and *Freedom and Culture* (1939) he explained his particular brand of liberalism.

[41] J. Dewey, *Individualism Old and New*, Allen & Unwin, London, 1931, p. 77.

regulated by a belief in the experimental character of life and in intelligence as the finally directive force in life; he should be devoted to freedom of thought, expression, and inquiry; he should develop his capabilities in the interest of the general enrichment of society; and he should work towards the kind of social organisation that will best promote the collective good. This individual was the true liberal and democrat of the twentieth century.[42]

Those habits of mind and character had to be built up steadily and soundly by an appropriate program of education. Thus, for Dewey, the interests of social reconstruction and educational reconstruction coincided.

DEWEY'S EDUCATIONAL PHILOSOPHY

Out of the background of pragmatic philosophy and his experiences in and reflections on his Laboratory School and the world of liberal politics, Dewey matured his educational theory. It was an amalgam of three strands of his philosophical and psychological thought: functional psychology, instrumental logic, and an organic social philosophy.

His functional psychology was expressed in his fundamental assumption that children were active, functioning organisms reaching out into their environment and interacting with it. He held that children learn through their activity and build their minds through the kind of behaviour in which they participate. The function of their learning and of their 'minded behaviour' is to co-operate more fruitfully with their social and non-social environment.

Dewey's instrumental logic was an effort to explain the method of this interaction with the environment, this 'continuing reconstruction of experience'.[43] It operated through the resolution of the difficulties, and the solution of the problems encountered in the adjustment process. The world for Dewey is a tissue of changing, unfinished, indeterminate, and problematic experience. Man makes his way through it by moving from problem to problem, seeking to bring it under tentative and workable control. The ideas and processes of human thought are called into play in problematic situations and become the instruments for the reconstruction and redirection of human activities. Training, therefore, in problem-solving and the techniques of critical thinking was of central importance in school programs.

The 'minded behaviour' that is being built by experience in problem-solving Dewey thought of as 'a function of social life — as not capable of developing by itself, but as requiring continued stimulus from social agencies and finding its nutrition in social supplies'.[44] By participating in the group life each individual builds the meanings and ways of behaving

that constitute his mind. Similarly, the self is socially built. The individual 'has no existence by himself. He lives in, for, and by society, just as society has no existence except in and through the individuals who constitute it.'[45] The school, therefore, as the educator of this social animal must be thoroughly a part of society. 'The only way to prepare for social life,' he held, 'is to engage in social life.'[46]

His functionalism, instrumentalism, and social organicism were interrelated and fundamental aspects of the thought that saturated his writing on education.

At one stage, in *Democracy and Education*, he summarised the basic concepts found in his views on education: the biological continuity of human impulses and instincts with natural energies, the dependence of the growth of mind upon participation in conjoint activities having a common purpose, the influence of the physical environment through the uses made of it in the social medium, the necessity to use individual variations in desire and thinking for a progressively developing society, the essential unity of method and subject-matter, the intrinsic continuity of ends and means, and the recognition of mind as thinking which perceives and tests the meanings of behaviour. He considered that 'these conceptions are consistent with the philosophy which sees intelligence to be the purposive reorganisation, through action, of the material of experience'.[47]

The way in which these concepts were fitted together and applied coherently to the field of education can best be understood by studying five key topics in his educational thinking: interest; reflective thinking; experience and its relationship to intelligence; education as a social function; and education and social reconstruction.

(i) Interest

One of the significant things that the Herbartians had done was to make interest an important concept of education. Dewey's work reinforced its position.

---

[42] Justice Holmes appeared to come closest, in Dewey's view, to his ideal; see 'Oliver Wendell Holmes', *Characters and Events*, pp. 100-6.

[43] J. Dewey, *My Pedagogic Creed*, p. 11 (art. 3). Dewey's instrumental logic first appeared publicly in *Studies in Logical Theory*, 1903, by Dewey and seven of his associates. In his preface, he wrote of 'the intimate connections of logical theory with functional psychology', and of the 'pre-eminent obligation' which the writers owed to William James.

[44] J. Dewey, *The School and the Child*, J.J. Findlay (ed.), (article on 'The Psychology of the Elementary Curriculum', 1900), Blackie, London, 1906, p. 109.

[45] J. Dewey, *Educational Essays*, J.J. Findlay (ed.), (article on 'Ethical Principles underlying education', 1897), Blackie, London, 1910, pp. 22-3.

[46] *ibid.*, p. 34.

[47] J. Dewey, *Democracy and Education*, p. 377.

One of the controversies of the early twentieth century took place over the relationship between interest and effort in education. Hard work at matters of importance in which there was not necessarily anything interesting, it was suggested, was a plain fact of human life. Children, therefore, had better learn to discipline themselves to uninteresting work. On the other hand, it was contended that work was better done by people who were interested in it and that, for children, the learning process was more efficient when they were interested in what they were learning.

Dewey pointed out that the word interest was used in various senses.[48] A person's occupation, pursuit or employment might be referred to as his interest, as when we say that his interest is in banking or journalism. We might also think of interest as some personal advantage or disadvantage through an association with some activity, as a person, for example, might have an interest in a local government proposal to make a footpath outside his property. Interest might also be thought of as a personal attitude towards some object which he cared about, was attentive to, and found himself absorbed in. The interest with which Dewey was concerned and which he referred to as genuine interest, was the third kind, the absorption of one's self in an object; but where the first kind, a pursuit or occupation, was an active, comprehensive and absorbing development, it, too, was a genuine interest.

In teaching, Dewey stated, 'The fundamental principle is that the child is always a being, with activities of his own, which are present and urgent, and do not require to be 'induced', 'drawn-out', 'developed', etc.'[49]

Interest stemmed from those active impulses. It was the emotional state which accompanied the channelling of a child's activities and impulses to achieve an end purpose desired by the child. It therefore involved attention, effort, and purpose. It also implied that the facts to be learnt, the object to be made, the action to be taken or the end to be mastered became an integral part of the growing mind and self of the child. 'The genuine principle of interest is the principle of the recognised identity of the fact to be learned or the action proposed with the growing self; that it lies in the direction of the agent's own growth and is, therefore, imperiously demanded, if the agent is to be himself.'[50]

It was false pedagogy to have to make things interesting. The important thing was to bring to consciousness the bearing of the new materials to be learnt, to connect it with the growth of the learner in such a way that he could see the significance of it for his development and that it contributed to an end which commanded his attention. Effort and disciplined work were also thereby assured.[51]

Interest was the link which lay between the human mind and the object of its attention. Mind was purposeful action; subject-matter was the resource material used in this purposeful action; interest was the dynamic force of an activity which engaged a person in a whole-hearted way. Wherever there was genuine interest, mind and subject-matter were indistinguishable. This was a situation whose factors were continually changing and developing. The constant factor was a self, engaged in and absorbed by the process. The self grew through the course of the activity; it was in continuous formation and was to be found in the interests generated by purposeful activities. Interests 'can be employed as vital terms only when the self is seen to be in process and interest to be a name for whatever is concerned in furthering its movement'.[52] Interest and self were inseparable; 'the kind and amount of interest actively taken in a thing reveals and measures the quality of selfhood which exists'.[53] And the kind and amount of interests actively taken up revealed and defined the nature of the self.

(ii) Reflective Thinking

Dewey was convinced that the central factor in all teaching should be an endeavour to develop in the pupil 'that attitude of mind, that habit of thought, which we call scientific'.[54] The Laboratory School was thoroughly concerned with building a habit of scientific thinking into the behaviour of all its pupils, and, throughout all his educational writings, Dewey never tired of arguing that scientific method, which was synonymous with his view of reflective thinking, should permeate all school activities.

To think scientifically or reflectively, it was necessary to be able to form concepts and to use them. Nothing was more important to teaching than the question of the way in which concepts might be formed.[55] Concepts were standardised meanings, that is, meanings that were general and constant. The simplest form of a concept is a common noun such as table, carpet, house, animal or tree; a more sophisticated form is a generalisation derived from the analysis of data on some topic. Concepts for Dewey were the building blocks of all the edifices of our thought.

[48] Dewey's work at the Laboratory School was closely concerned with the place of interest in education and he wrote a contribution for the *National Herbart Society Yearbook* for 1895 on the relationship of interest and will. This he expanded into the substantial monograph in 1913 entitled *Interest and Effort in Education*. His ideas on the matter were further developed in *Democracy and Education*.

[49] K.C. Mayhew and A.C. Edwards, *op.cit.*, p. 475.

[50] J. Dewey, *Interest and Effort in Education*, Houghton, Boston, 1913, p. 7.

[51] K.C. Mayhew and A.C. Edwards, *op.cit.*, p. 421.

[52] J. Dewey, *Reconstruction in Philosophy*, Beacon, New York, 1957 (1920), p. 195.

[53] J. Dewey, *Democracy and Education*, p. 408.

[54] J. Dewey, *How We Think*, Heath, New York, 1933 (1910). Preface to 1st edn, p. v.

[55] *ibid.*, p. 154.

Experiences could not be understood until they were conceptualised and it was this that made them educationally worthwhile. Constantly in every lesson, at every stage of development, there should be some conceptualising of impressions and ideas.

Reflective thinking in Dewey's view began with a forked-road situation. Where there was a choice of activity, where one might go in more than one direction, where there was ambiguity, reflective thinking was called into play. It started from a state of doubt, a problem, and was an act of searching to try to reach a settled conclusion. Reflective thinking was a means of controlling a perplexing situation. It involved an orderly and consecutive chain of ideas, a controlling purpose, and systematic inquiry.

Dewey argued as follows. An actual situation in which the person experiences some doubt or some need to make a choice is the beginning of reflective thinking. A teacher who wishes to stimulate thought should involve the pupils in a situation which engages their interests and which has in it factors that are new, uncertain, or problematic and yet sufficiently connected with their previous experience to be able to call out effective responses from them. When this perplexing situation is carefully studied, the problem it poses can be defined and clarified. To present a pupil with ready-made problems is to deny him the opportunity of analysing problematic situations and of discovering his own problems. The finding and defining of problems is an integral a part of the process of reflective thinking as is the solving of problems.[56]

To operate effectively, the process of reflective thought requires a supply of both data and ideas. The data or facts are the material that has to be interpreted and utilised, the ideas are the suggested solutions for the difficulties that arise during the course of the process of thinking. To acquire the appropriate data, observation is necessary. These observations must be accurate, pertinent and sufficiently comprehensive to deal with the situation under review. They may come from the direct use of the senses, from memory of past activities, or from books and other records. In addition to noting the conditions and facts that have to be dealt with, it is necessary to make suggestions about possible courses of action in dealing with them. These are ideas inferred from the data or conjectured by the mind as ways of manipulating the data. The suggestions or inferences that are brought forward have to be tested to see how well they fit the situation. They may be tested in thought to see whether the various elements in the suggestion are logical and coherent; and they may be tested in action to see whether the consequences that are anticipated by them occur in fact. This process of checking inferences, of proving their validity, lies at the heart of scientific or reflective thinking.

Throughout all of the processes, judgment is necessary as a constituent part of every aspect of reflective thinking. Judgments must be made as to the pertinence of the data. They must be made about the feasibility of various suggestions. They must be made about the appropriateness of the testing procedures and they must be made, finally, on the validity of the solution to the problem under consideration.

Dewey summed up the essentials of reflection by saying: 'They are, first, that the pupil has a genuine situation of experience — that there be a continuous activity in which he is interested for its own sake; secondly, that a genuine problem develop within this situation as a stimulus to thought; third, that he possess the information and make the observations needed to deal with it; fourth, that suggested solutions occur to him which he shall be responsible for developing in an orderly way; fifth, that he have opportunity and occasion to test his ideas by application, to make their meaning clear and to discover for himself their validity.'[57] He was careful to point out that the five phases were not necessarily separate and distinct, nor did they necessarily follow one another in a set order.

Intellectually, the main task of the school was to teach children to think reflectively. They should learn the skills involved in this process and exercise them until they become habitual. This method of thinking Dewey also referred to in various places as the scientific or experimental method, and he regarded it as applicable to every kind of subject-matter.

Skill in those processes needed the support of certain attitudes. Hence the teacher, while cultivating the pupils' skills in observation, suggestion, testing, judgment, and the various phases of reflective thinking, had also to try to develop in the pupils attitudes of open-mindedness, wholeheartedness, and responsibility. Knowledge of the methods alone was not enough. There must be an inclination to use them; hence the need for building up attitudes favourable to the adoption and use of reflective thinking in all appropriate situations. A freedom from partisanship and an open-minded willingness to consider new problems and entertain new ideas was a basic requisite. To this must be added a whole-hearted absorption in the process of problem-solving and a buoyant enthusiasm for the task of suggesting, inquiring, discussing, testing, and judging. A further trait necessary, too, was that of integrity or intellectual responsibility, which was a willingness to acknowledge and stand by the logical consequences of the process of thought upon which one has entered. Once the requisite skills have been attained, these attitudes provide the power to carry through to completeness an activity of reflective thinking.

---

[56] Dewey's advocacy of problem-solving as a basic method in teaching was parallelled at that time by H.E. Armstrong's campaign in England for the use of the heuristic method (see above, Chapter 1).

[57] J. Dewey, *Democracy and Education*, p. 192.

The teacher, according to Dewey 'is the intellectual leader of a social group'.[58] His task was to take the natural tendencies of children towards curiosity and imaginative expression and use them in an orderly way to build the skills and attitudes that will produce in them the habit of reflective thinking.

(iii) Experience and Intelligence

In 1917 Dewey wrote: 'If changing conduct and expanding knowledge ever required a willingness to surrender not merely old solutions but old problems it is now.'[59] The key to the new departure in philosophy that Dewey was making, lay in his view of the nature of experience and of its association with intelligence. For him experience was not primarily concerned with what has happened, but rather with what is about to happen. It was characterised by projection, by reaching forward into the unknown rather than with a contemplation of past activity. Experience is not characterised by particularism, but by connections and continuities, and a striving to control the new directions in which the environment may develop. It is not something to be contrasted with thought, but is impregnated with it and, rightly conceived, controlled by it.

Experience is both active and passive. It is an attempt to accomplish something, and it is a suffering of the consequences of an activity. It is personal, and it is a transaction which involves other persons and objects. When the transaction becomes meaningful to a person, experience becomes an experience.

An experience is experience with a pattern and structure in which doing and undergoing are seen to be in a relationship. An experience is therefore a three-fold activity. It is practical, emotional, and intellectual. It is a practical transaction between an organism and the events or objects which surround it; it is felt to be a unity; and it acquires meaning as thought is incorporated into its process. Thought is the instrument by which experience can be controlled. The great task of our times is to learn to control human experience by the application of intelligence to it.

Intelligence is the main instrument in giving experience its future projection. 'We live forward'[60] wrote Dewey, and therefore anticipation and the projection of future behaviour are of fundamental importance to us. Intelligence enables us to forecast, to anticipate to redirect the course of our experience. To illuminate and control experience in a creative way by intelligence is the fundamental educational task.

Dewey spoke of 'education of, by, and for experience'.[61] Educative experience was to him the material out of which all educational programs were built. To be educative, experience had to become an experience or a series of experiences characterised by three things.

A primary characteristic of an experience is that it is felt. One has an experience. It may, for example, be beautiful, or humorous, or comfortable, or poignant, or annoying, or splendid, or have any of a number of qualities that are directly felt. 'Having' an experience is different from 'knowing' an experience. The first characteristic of an educative experience is that it should be known as well as had. To know an experience an individual must perceive the relationship between its parts and the consequences to which they lead; in other words, he must apply thought to his experience. This helps him to grasp whatever meaning it may have and enables him in some measure to control the direction of that experience and of subsequent experiences, so that he may enter into 'more effective and more profitable relations' with his environment in the future.[62]

The second characteristic of an educative experience is that it must have continuity. The principle of continuity implies that there must be recognisable order and sequence within the experience, and that it should lead on to further experiences that are both deeper and wider, securing, in this way, the growth of the individual.

The third characteristic is that of interaction. In his later writings Dewey preferred to use the word transaction because it expressed more clearly the unity of an activity. The common process, the community of action, the creative reconstruction that takes place in an experience was what Dewey wished to emphasise rather than the relating together, as interactions, items which might be viewed as separate components.[63] An educative experience involves a transaction between an individual and his environment in which due weight is given both to the needs, interests, and state of development of the individual on the one hand, and the persons, events, and objective conditions selected as a suitable environment on the other. As the social content of a transaction increases, so too is its educational effect widened.

Educational experiences, if they have continuity, if they are genuine transactions, and if they are brought under intellectual control, are the means for 'the achieving of a life of rich significance'[64] for individuals and for society, as they grow together through the continual reconstruction of experience.

[58] J. Dewey, *How We Think*, p. 273.

[59] J. Dewey *et al.*, *Creative Intelligence. Essays in the Pragmatic Attitude*, Holt, New York, 1917, pp. 4-5.

[60] J. Dewey *et al.*, *Creative Intelligence*, p. 12.

[61] J. Dewey, *Experience and Education*, Macmillan, New York, 1938, p. 19.

[62] J. Dewey, *Philosophy and Civilization*, Capricorn, New York, 1963 (1931), p. 30.

[63] J. Dewey and A.F. Bentley, *Knowing and the Known*, Beacon, Boston, 1960 (1949), p. 304.

[64] J. Dewey, *Democracy and Education*, p. 297.

(iv) Education as a Social Function

In his *Democracy and Education* Dewey took a comprehensive look at education, developing fully his views on what he felt to be the most significant aspects that needed examination. In particular he explored the social role of education, using his views on its social function as a touchstone in his analysis of educational problems.

The continuity of human society is made possible only by the continual transmission of its ideals and practices from generation to generation. 'Education, in its broadest sense, is the means of this social continuity of life.'[65] It enables the young to share the common life of society, and to enter into communication with the great variety of forces that exist in modern society. Society is the relationships that exist between individuals; it exists *in* communication. Every communication is at once social and educational to the participants. While every social arrangement is educative in effect, its educative value is proportional to the extent to which it promotes a social disposition. The ultimate value of every social institution lies in its human effect, that is to say, to the extent to which it promotes and enriches the common life, or, in other words, educates society. The principal formal institution for this purpose is the school.

The social environment educates by stimulating certain ways of acting, and by making the individual a partner in a form of associated activity, engaging him in it so that he feels its success as his success and its failure as his failure. He becomes involved emotionally, intellectually, and physically in some shared activity. In this way he learns the emotional, mental, and physical habits of his society and becomes a committed contributor to them.

The school is an institution set up for the deliberate control of the social environment of the young, to ensure that the young members of society encounter the kinds of experience that will make them productive members of their society.

In a complex society the school has to provide a special social environment which has three functions. In the complications and confusions of modern society, a school's first function is to provide a simplified environment. It has to choose the fundamental features that are capable of being responded to by its pupils, and arrange them in an appropriate order, gradually building its environment into more complicated patterns. Secondly, it has to establish a purified environment, eliminating the more trivial and undesirable things. It is responsible for helping to transmit not the whole of society's existing activities, but only such as will make for a better future society. Thirdly, it is the function of the school to balance the various elements in the social environment. It has to provide a wider environment than any individual otherwise unaided would encounter. It should enable each individual to share in the activities of a selected number of the many associations and groups within society, which he might not encounter without assistance from the school. As part of this function, the school has the task of co-ordinating the influences of the various social environments into which its pupils enter, and thereby, exercising an integrating and steadying effect throughout society.

To say that education has such social functions is to say that education will vary with the kind of society of which it forms a part. The life of one kind of society will require a different kind of education from that of another.[66] Dewey's concern was with a democratic society and the part education might play within it.

Democracy 'is primarily a mode of associated living, of conjoint communicated experience'.[67] Democracy is the form of a relationship in which there is the fullest and freest interplay among the members of the society. 'From the standpoint of the individual, it consists in having a responsible share according to capacity in forming and directing the activities of the groups to which one belongs and in participating according to need in the values which the groups sustain. From the standpoint of the groups, it demands liberation of the potentialities of members of a group in harmony with the interests and goods which are common. Since every individual is a member of many groups, this specification cannot be fulfilled except when different groups interact flexibly and fully in connection with other groups... It is the idea of community life itself.'[68] A society of this type must have the kind of education which gives individuals a personal interest, and 'the habits of mind which secure social changes without introducing disorder'.[69]

What should be the aim of education in a democratic society?

Democracy is a condition of society in which social relationships are equitably balanced and conducted. This means that, in so far as the society is genuinely democratic, the aim of every individual's activities is decided within the context of the social processes of which he has a full and free part. His aims are not determined by some external authority, but by him acting within the framework of a society whose purposes he fully shares. The aim of education, therefore, is to be found within the democratic process of living. The democratic society is progressive in the sense that it aims at a greater variety of mutually shared interests among its members. It is engaged consciously and continuously in reconstructing its activities, to provide for all its members increasing opportunities to achieve a life of rich

---

[65] *ibid.*, p. 3.

[66] *ibid.*, p. 12.

[67] *ibid.*, p. 101.

[68] J. Dewey, *The Public and Its Problems*, Holt, New York, 1927, pp. 147-8.

[69] J. Dewey, *Democracy and Education*, p. 115.

significance. This, too, is precisely the task of education within a democracy.

The aims of education and the aims of a democratic society are one and the same. A society, in so far as it is democratic, is an educative society. Dewey considered that 'the educational process has no end beyond itself; it is its own end;...and the educational process is one of continual reorganising, reconstructing, transforming'.[70] If we think of growth as the process of discovering more and more meaning in one's activities, and of extending the sharing of the new meanings with one's fellow individuals, then growth is education and education is growth. Education 'is that reconstruction or reorganisation of experience which adds to the meaning of experience, and which increases ability to direct the course of subsequent experience'.[71] It is not a preparation for a remote future or an unfolding of hidden potential, or a forming of persons to an agreed pattern; it is a continuous reconstruction of experience. The aim of education in a democratic society is for Dewey the continuous and meaningful reconstruction of man-in-society.

This aim takes full account of the needs of individuality, and the requirements of society. Individual variations are precious contributions to the growth of society. Education in a democratic society therefore encourages intellectual freedom and caters for the development of diverse interests. The qualities which characterise creative individuality are the same as those which are essential for a progressive democratic society. Open-mindedness, single-mindedness, sincerity, breadth of outlook, thoroughness, assumption of responsibility for developing the consequences of accepted ideas, are the basic traits of character required in productive individuals and productive societies. It is no accident that this should be so. An individual does not build in isolation a mind with such characteristics, but builds it through living in a society which values these traits. An individual grows up in a social medium and his actions acquire meaning as he sees them in relation to the activities and attitudes of others. Through sharing in the activities, he gradually builds up a mind of his own out of the relationships and meanings that he has incorporated into his own behaviour.

(v) Education and Social Reconstruction

In the mid-30's Dewey was one of the moving spirits behind an interesting new journal, *The Social Frontier*. It was started in 1934 during the depression, and was one of the vehicles for the expression of the upsurge of social liberalism that accompanied the early stages of Roosevelt's New Deal. Dewey and his fellow-writers saw the need for community planning both to retrieve the current situation, and to build better for the future. For the first two and a half years he contributed a monthly John Dewey's Page, and, throughout its ten-year existence, he continued to write occasional articles. His theme from the very first number was that of education's contribution to social reconstruction. The schools, he felt, could not in any literal sense build a new social order, but they could be one of the main instruments in fashioning it. If the teachers actively aligned themselves 'with the forces and conditions that are making for change in the direction of social control of capitalism — economic and political',[72] they could help to create a favourable climate, and could constantly find ways to express their choice through their approach to teaching methods, selection of subject-matter, school discipline, and school administration.

The school could not avoid having a social orientation of some kind; it had, he thought, a choice between two orientations — one looked to the past and to the interests of a small class maintained by selfish individualistic economics at the expense of the masses, the other to the future, and, through the harnessing of scientific and technological forces, to the possibility of freedom, security, and cultural development for the masses. In furthering the trend 'toward a socialized co-operative democracy'[73] teachers must start by systematically encouraging the use of intelligence, 'a popular intelligence that is critically discriminating',[74] able to combat prejudice and propaganda, and capable of understanding the social forces that point to the new social orientation which will produce 'more just, equitable, and human relations of men, women, and children to one another',[75] and will make 'democracy a living and effective reality in the minds of the youth who form the future citizenship of the country'.[76]

The heart of the social problem of our times was that intelligence, as Dewey defined it,[77] had been applied scientifically and with great effect to the physical world, but 'has hardly been used to modify men's fundamental acts and attitudes in social matters'.[78] Dewey whole-heartedly accepted the modern world. He did not cling to established traditions, nor yearn

---

[70] *ibid.*, p. 59.

[71] *ibid.*, p. 89-90.

[72] J. Dewey, 'Can Education Share in Social Reconstruction', *The Social Frontier*, October 1934, 1, 1, 12.

[73] J. Dewey, 'The Crucial Role of Intelligence', *ibid.*, 1, 5, 10.

[74] J. Dewey, 'Toward a National System of Education', *ibid.*, 1, 9, 10.

[75] J. Dewey, 'The Social Significance of Academic Freedom', *ibid.*, March 1936, 2, 6, p. 165.

[76] J. Dewey, 'Education, Democracy, and Socialized Economy', *ibid.*, December 1938, 5, 40, 72. Between December 1936 and April 1937, Dewey reviewed *The Higher Learning in America* in the pages of *The Social Frontier* and had a short and controversial exchange of views with its author, J.M. Hutchins, the president of the University of Chicago. Against Hutchins' traditional metaphysics Dewey set out his own emphasis upon experimental method, social reconstruction, and the schools' role in the production of social change.

[77] See above p. 82ff.

[78] J. Dewey, *Philosophy and Civilization*, Capricorn, New York, 1963 (1931) p. 324.

nostalgically for past societies; he looked for ways to make the best future out of the present. He accepted change, and made a philosophy out of mutability. The fact that 'process' was the universal in our world he regarded as 'the most revolutionary discovery yet made'.[79] It was acknowledged by scientists; it had yet to be recognised and applied in social and political behaviour. To control and improve human relations by scientifically directed intelligence was the first and vital step towards building a first-rate culture out of our present concern for technological and commercial progress. The reconstruction would not come by trying to develop a higher cultural life independent of the material forces of our age, but only by accepting our material civilisation, by using the scientific intelligence characteristic of it, and by turning, thereby 'a machine age into a significantly new habit of mind and sentiment'.[80] That was the immense educational challenge of our times, to achieve the genuinely modern outlook that 'has still to be brought into existence'.[81]

Writing at the end of World War II, in 1945, at the age of eighty-six, he referred to the disappointment of the generous hopes of earlier years. Instead of universal peace, the twentieth century had witnessed two destructive world wars: instead of a steady growth of democratic freedom, the development of several powerful totalitarian states; instead of economic security, an increase in industrial crises; instead of social stability, the possibility of widespread revolution. These illiberal and anti-democratic tendencies were evidence of our failure to use, in the field of human relations, the methods of intelligence to which we owe the conquest of the physical world. The remedy lay in a continued optimistic application of intelligence to the planning of human affairs, and especially in a persistence in developing through education the habitual use of reflective thinking and democratic procedures. Science, education, and democracy meet as one in the cause of social reconstruction.[82]

DEWEY'S INFLUENCE IN EDUCATION

On the occasion of Dewey's ninetieth birthday the editors of *New Republic*, in a special issue, summed up his influence in the United States with the statement: 'If any other individual has equalled Dewey's effect on the intellectual life today, we do not know his name.'[83] With this estimate each of the contributors very largely agreed, one even suggesting that 'there is no one of the present generation of Americans who can have escaped the influence of John Dewey'.[84]

How does one account for this influence? It can be attributed fundamentally to the timeliness and relevance of his ideas. In a period of great expansion and social change, he made change and growth central

features of his thought; in a society propelled forward by science, he accepted the probabilism of science and insisted upon the efficacy of scientific method in all human activities; in an increasingly collectivist world, he emphasised co-operative planning as the essential way to develop a viable democracy; and to educators conscious of a rapidly changing society and of new psychological and sociological explanations of human behaviour, he offered a systematic functional relationship between individual, school, and society. His work dealt with vital and relevant issues in his field, clarifying current problems, constructing general principles in his discussion of them, and developing ideas which continued to be pertinent and effective throughout the whole of his long and productive life.

He was engaged, in Smuts' phrase, in bridge building.[85] He connected knowledge with action, logic with inquiry, science with human conduct, experience with education, school with society, and collectivism with democracy. It was an impressive feat of interrelating throughout the social sciences, and it helped many of his readers to see fresh associations and to arrive at a coherent method of interpreting their experience. This was particularly true of his main reading public, the teachers,[86] who, in a period of exceptional and almost continuous curriculum revision, were interested in fundamental and vital ways of interrelating subject-matter.

One cannot help thinking also that good health and literary persistence played an important part in building up and maintaining his influence. During the course of his ninety-two years he published a massive amount. Throughout much of it the same ideas recur. It was a distinguished body of original work, but much of it is repetitive and some of it consists of the republication of earlier materials. Nowhere in his educational theory does he praise the virtues of repetition, but at least his own educational effectiveness probably depended in some measure on the frequency with which his readers encountered the same ideas patiently expounded and applied to a great variety of situations.

[79] J. Dewey, *Reconstruction in Philosophy*, enlarged edn., Beacon, Boston, p. xiii.

[80] J. Dewey, *Individualism Old and New*, p. 115.

[81] *ibid.*, p. xxxv.

[82] J. Dewey, 'The Democratic Faith and Education', *The Authoritarian Attempt to Capture Education*. Papers from the Second Conference on the Scientific Spirit and Democratic Faith, King's Crown Press, New York, 1945, pp. 1-9.

[83] *New Republic*, 17 October 1949, p. 10.

[84] *ibid.*, p. 26.

[85] *ibid.*, p. 13.

[86] C. Wright Mills, *Sociology and Pragmatism*, Oxford University Press, New York, 1966, Chapter 17, makes a useful analysis of Dewey's reading public.

What was the nature of Dewey's influence in education? Perhaps the most important effect was that he established a particular climate of thinking. In its literature, if not yet in its practice, education moved between the beginning of the century and World War I from an era of Herbartianism to one of Deweyism. It was a shift from a static to a mobile view. Dewey's educational world was one of activity and process in which the real content of schooling was to be found not in the acquisition of facts, but in the intellectual processes of acquiring them, and the consequential attitudes and habits.

The new educational climate also had a strong social orientation. From the time when Dewey's impact began to be felt, educational administration, curriculum, and teaching method have become saturated with social reference. Educators have thought automatically of the social bearings of whatever aspect of policy or practice they were concerned with. Dewey, however, made education pertinent not to society in general, but to democratic society in particular. Nor was the association between the school and society simply an imitative one. The school was not the mere reflection of society; it had a creative and reconstructive role. But Dewey was not a revolutionary. His new individual and new society were to be brought into being by education, intellectual persuasion, and co-operation. His more radical critics considered that he underestimated the power of vested interests, and that his suggestions could often be turned to the support of conservative forces in American political and economic life.[87] On this matter, as White has pointed out, there seem to have been two Deweys: the one who revolted against formalism in education and feared the consequences of a systematic program, and the other who wanted to be a social engineer.[88] This ambivalence produced a division among his followers, the social engineers developing in greater theoretical and practical detail the political, economic, social, and educational requirements of reconstructionism, the anti-formalists tending to work for improved methods of thinking and behaving among their pupils that would in due course produce a more fully democratic society.

The Deweyan climate gave a new dignity and importance to education and educators. Dewey provided a vision of a humane education for the modern era. Horne, by no means an admirer, nevertheless described Dewey and his work as 'humanism at its best'.[89] His temper was considerate, sane, rational, and optimistic, and the Deweyan teacher is of the same mould. The teacher had, also, a social task of consequence; he was not merely educating children, he was changing the nature of society, building a fuller democracy, and producing a new type of culture.

Important though it was to have created such a climate, Dewey's influence was substantially more than that. It could be seen concretely in his effect on individuals and institutions. He reinforced the impact of his fellow-liberals such as Beard, Robinson, Holmes, and Veblen. James Harvey Robinson's best-selling and influential *The Mind in the Making*, published in 1921, might almost have been written by Dewey, so close are the sentiments and expressions of the two authors. Dewey was the centre of a prominent and productive group of educators such as Kilpatrick, Childs, Rugg, Counts, Bode, Brunner, Charters, Raup, and Newlon whose influence, radiating principally from Teachers College, Columbia University, was spread deeply throughout the United States; a second generation of educators such as Goodwin Watson, Hand, Caswell, Hullfish, Axtelle, Benne, Smith, Stanley, Hanna, and Brameld, again largely moving through Teachers College, cemented and extended the impact of the first. Particularly affected by Dewey's ideas also were a number of pioneering institutions such as the Bank Street Schools, the Lincoln School of Teachers College, Bennington College, Sarah Lawrence College, and the New School of Social Research.

Dewey's influence, however, was more pervasive than it is possible to indicate by a select list of names and schools. He had always been interested in what he called the 'New Education'. In his lecture, *Construction and Criticism*, he spoke of education as 'one of the great opportunities for present day pioneering'.[90] At Chicago in the initial years of the new education he was one of the early leaders, and he continued to play a vital part in its development until the end of his career. In 1899, for instance, he announced the new dispensation as one in which the child becomes the centre about which education is organised,[91] but a centre connected with the main line of current social development.[92] In 1933, he analysed the main characteristics of progressive schools and found three essential principles which differentiated them from traditional schools: they paid more attention to individual needs, they used the expressive activities of their pupils more abundantly, and they aimed at an unusual amount of co-operation of pupils with one another and of pupils with teachers.[93] His final statement on the matter, in 1938, made a neat comparison of traditional and progressive practices: 'To imposition from above is opposed expression

---

[87] C.J. Karier, P. Violas, & J. Spring, *Roots of Crisis*, Rand McNally, Chicago, 1973.

[88] M. White *Social Thought in America*, Beacon, Boston, 1957 (1947), p. 244. Cf.H.H. Horne, *The Democratic Philosophy of Education*, Macmillan, New York, 1932, p. xi, '...though Dr. Dewey has a method, he lacks a plan.'

[89] H. Horne, *The Democratic Philosophy of Education*, Macmillan, New York, 1932, p. 159.

[90] J. Dewey, *Construction and Criticism*, Columbia University Press, New York, 1930, p. 9.

[91] J. Dewey, *The School and Society*, p. 35.

[92] *ibid.*, pp. 4-5.

[93] J. Dewey, 'Why Have Progressive Schools?' (July 1933) *Education Today*, Putnam, New York, 1940, pp. 280-1.

and cultivation of individuality; to external discipline is opposed free activity; to learning from texts and teachers, learning through experience; to acquisition of isolated skills and techniques by drill, is opposed acquisition of them as means of attaining ends which make direct vital appeal; to preparation for a more or less remote future is opposed making the most of the opportunities of the present life; to static aims and materials is opposed acquaintance with a changing world.'[94] In that statement he summarised the attitudes and ideas that his own work had, for about half a century, been instrumental in developing in the minds of large numbers of teachers.

Dewey's connection with the progressive education movement was continuous and substantial, yet ambiguous. In 1927, after the Progressive Education Association had been operating for eight years, he accepted the honorary presidency of it but did not become very active in it. His main contribution to the movement was nevertheless a vital one: he provided a systematic philosophy for it. *Democracy and Education* was the central statement of policy for the reform of education in American schools in the first half of the twentieth century. The progressive educators did not always give his ideas the same emphasis and balance that he would have wished, and he was therefore both sympathetic and critical of the association's work and of the conduct of progressive schools. Where they simply represented a protest against traditional schooling, as seemed to be the case with child-centred schools, he condemned their negativism, and their absence of intellectual control; where, on the other hand, they were constructively trying to work out and experiment with programs that made effective the positive principles that he discerned within the movement, he encouraged and defended them to the full.

Democracy and Education, however, was more than a manifesto for teachers in schools that were labelled 'progressive'. It was, as its sub-title indicated, An Introduction to the Philosophy of Education, suitable for all teachers, and it became in the inter-war period the most popular text in educational philosophy in the United States, and probably in the whole of the English-speaking world. It was the ordinary teacher's rationale for reform in the traditional school. Dewey's writings were supplemented by the widely read texts of men such as Kilpatrick, Counts, and Rugg, who built Deweyan theory into educational principles, methods of teaching, curriculum practices, and textbook construction. In that way the ordinary school absorbed much of his teaching, and gradually but substantially adapted its ways to the Deweyan climate. The most significant example of this process of adjustment was to be seen in the effect on school curricula during the 1920's and 1930's. It was a movement away from academically oriented subject-matter towards materials impregnated with social reference, integrated round social problems, and studied by the method of inquiry.[95]

Dewey summed up his own aspirations, and his sense of the importance of the teaching profession in a final paragraph of *A Common Faith*, written with his usual optimism and dedication in the depths of the great depression of the 1930's: 'Ours is the responsibility of conserving, transmitting, rectifying, and expanding the heritage of values we have received that those who come after us may receive it more solid and secure, more widely accessible and more generously shared than we have received it. Here are all the elements for a religious faith that shall not be confined to sect, class, or race. Such a faith has always been implicitly the common faith of mankind. It remains to make it explicit and militant.'[96] It was to be a New World

'... borne by new life within
Out upon the far reaches of untrav'lled space.'[97]

There he expressed his own deep sense of obligation to his society, and his hope that all mankind would share that feeling with him. It was a faith in the power of education, directed by human intelligence, to build a democratic community in which mutual obligation should reign.

A democratic society required behaviour that was intelligent, innovative, and socially responsible. In pursuit of this 'we may say that the kind of experience to which the work of the school should contribute is one marked by executive competency in the management of resources and obstacles encountered (efficiency); by sociability, or interest in the direct companionship of others; by aesthetic taste or capacity to appreciate artistic excellence in at least some of its classic forms; by trained intellectual method, or interest in some mode of scientific achievement; and by sensitiveness to the rights and claims of others — conscientiousness.'[98] To achieve these experiences, the school must concern itself with education rather than mere instruction. It must itself become a community in the full sense of the word, and its activities must be connected in a direct and meaningful way with the life of society outside the school. In this fashion an educative society, which Dewey conceived democracy to be, would be built — a society marked by disciplined thought, creative imagination, and social sensitivity.

---

[94] J. Dewey, *Experience and Education*, Macmillan, New York, 1946 (1938) pp. 5-6.

[95] See below, Chapter 11.

[96] J. Dewey, *A Common Faith*, Yale University Press, New Haven, 1934, p. 87.

[97] Jo Ann Boydston (ed.), *The Poems of John Dewey*, 'The New World', Southern Illinois University Press, Carbondale, Illinois, 1977, p. 58.

[98] J. Dewey, *Democracy and Education*, pp. 285-6.

A. Binet
(1857-1911)

E.L. Thorndike
(1874-1949)

G. Stanley Hall
(1844-1924)

Pioneers in the study of child development and educational testing.

CHAPTER 4

THE BEGINNING OF A SCIENCE OF EDUCATION

SUMMARY

Child Study

- (i)   Main Areas of Child Study
- (ii) Method of Child Study
- (iii) Importance of the Child Study Movement

The School Survey Movement

- (i) Early Influences
- (ii) Early School Surveys in the U.S.A.

The Importance of Science

- (i) E. L. Thorndike
- (ii) E. Claparède

Experimental Laboratories and Classes

- (i) E. Meumann
- (ii) Wilhelm Lay

Fundamental Research Problems

- (i)   Economy of Work
- (ii) Mental Testing
    - (a) The Work of Alfred Binet
    - (b) The Nature of Intelligence
    - (c) Intelligence Testing
- (iii) Transfer of Training
    - (a) Research by Thorndike and Woodworth
    - (b) Research on Transfer of Training 1900-30's
    - (c) Review of Research on Transfer of Training

Achievements of Early Educational Research

By the beginning of the twentieth century European society had reached the stage of being interested in and to a certain extent capable of planning its own evolution consciously. To build his own future, man had to control the tools and instruments of the natural sciences, and to understand and reconstruct the social sciences. Education aspired to be one of the significant new social sciences, and the serious study of it as a social science began from about that time. In the period before World War I the new educational aspirations were expressed in three distinct but related movements: the child study movement, the school survey movement, and the development of experimental studies in education.

CHILD STUDY

Early in the 1880's three works appeared which gave a new direction to studies in psychology. A classic analysis, *The Mind of the Child*, by Wilhelm Preyer, a German psychologist, appeared in 1882; two interesting articles on children's imagination and children's language were written by an English psychologist, James Sully, in 1880 and 1884; and an American, G. Stanley Hall, in 1883, produced a lengthy article, 'The Content of Children's Minds', and a pamphlet *The Study of Children*. Those publications marked the beginning of what came to be known as the child study movement. As a separate and definable movement it lasted for some thirty years, approximately up to the beginning of World War I. Beyond that point it merged more fully with the study of tests and measurements, learning processes, and clinical investigation to become a normal part of the subject of educational psychology and to help to preserve the developmental trend of that discipline.

Throughout the 1880's progress in child study was slow. Interested teachers and medical groups made a number of studies of children's interests and mental development, and gradually a movement gathered force. In the 1890's it developed quickly and extensively. It acquired vigorous leadership, a forum for discussion in the shape of numerous child study associations, and a vehicle for the wider distribution of research and ideas by the foundation of a number of learned and popular journals.

The most prominent leader in the field was G. Stanley Hall.[1] Hall was a complex man, a person of great dynamism and appeal. He was among the earliest of American psychologists to insist on a scientific approach but his own work lacked precision and objectivity. Up to the early years of the century, he had done more than any other American to bring psychological research to bear on and reform the methods of education, yet in many important matters his own educational views were extraordinarily conservative. Hall's great achievement, for education, was to pioneer genetic, developmental psychology, apply it to the study of children, and, for twenty years from 1891 to 1911, to give a vigorous leadership in America to work in that field. After his initial publications on child study in 1883, he had begun to lecture on pedagogy and to build up an interest in applying scientific procedures to the study of educational problems and child development. In 1891 he founded *The Pedagogical Seminary*, a journal which was to become the principal organ of the child study movement, and in the same year he began to lecture publicly and to offer summer courses on child study. When, in 1894, the National Education Association established a Child Study Department with Hall as its first president, the movement in America may be said to have been firmly launched.

In Europe, similarly, there was a slow build-up of interest until the mid-1890's, and then a considerable increase in activity for the next twenty years. Every country of eastern and western Europe from Portugal to Russia was involved with varying degrees of enthusiasm. Outside of Europe and North America, Latin America became involved, and Japan also had its quota of supporters.

The movement produced several studies of lasting interest and outstanding merit. Sully published, in England, a widely read *Studies in Childhood* in 1895. Karl Groos wrote two seminal books on play in 1896 and 1899. Ellen Key, a Swedish reformer, caught the spirit of the times in 1900 with a rousing call for a more sensitive consideration of children and their individual needs. In France, Alfred Binet, in 1900, put together his ingenious and penetrating researches of the preceding ten years in a book on suggestibility in children, in 1903 produced one of the most interesting accounts of the evolution of intelligence in *The Experimental Study of Intelligence*, and in 1909 gave his considered and stimulating reflections of the progress of child study in *Modern Ideas on Children*. Antonia Marro from Italy made the first substantial study of adolescents in 1897, and was followed in 1904 by G. Stanley Hall's widely read work on *Adolescence* in America. Millicent Shinn in 1893 and 1907, in California, painstakingly documented by careful observation the sensory and motor

development of a child from birth to the age of three. Clara and William Stern's monograph from Hamburg in 1907 opened up the study of children's speech as an index to the development of thought and in 1914 William Stern's *Psychology of Early Childhood* made a systematic summary and review of what had been accomplished in the thirty-two years of child study since the appearance of Preyer's pioneering work.[2]

Most countries established a child study journal of which the most widely known were Hall's *The Pedagogical Seminary* founded in 1891 and later called the *Journal of Genetic Psychology*, the *Zeitschrift für Kinderforschung*, 1896, the English *The Paidologist*, 1899, which later became *Child Study* in 1907, and the *Bulletin* of the French society, 1900.

To encourage discussion and research most countries formed child study associations, the first to be established being the American one in 1894. England followed soon after in 1896, Germany in 1897, and France in 1899. Many of the associations had enthusiastic branches. In the U.S.A., for example, twenty-three of the states formed branches, and one, the Illinois Society for the Study of Children, boasted of an attendance of three thousand at one of its summer congresses in 1896. Membership in most countries consisted mostly of interested teachers, under the leadership of professors of psychology and education; school administrators, doctors, and a sprinkling of parents made up most of the rest of the members.[3] In 1909 an international association of child study and experimental education was established at a meeting in Paris, initially presided over by the Belgian educator, M.C. Schuyten, and supported by the leading educational researchers in Europe and America. In all, between 1890 and 1914, about twenty separate journals, and twenty-five national associations were established to promote the study of the behaviour of children.

---

[1] G.S. Hall (1844-1924) studied philosophy and psychology in both America and Germany, and was heavily influenced by the newer trend towards laboratory experimentation. He taught briefly at Harvard and Johns Hopkins, and in 1888 became president of Clark University where he remained until his retirement in 1920.

[2] J. Sully, *Studies in Childhood*, Longmans Green, London, 1895; K. Groos, *Die Spiele Der Tiere*, Fischer, Jena, 1896; K. Groos, *Die Spiele des Menschen*, Fischer, Jena, 1899; Ellen K.S. Key, *Barnets arhundrade*, A. Bonnier, Stockholm, 1900; A. Binet, *La Suggestibilité*, Schleicher Frères, Paris, 1900; A. Binet, *Les Idées Modernes sur les Enfants*, Flammarion, Paris, 1909; A. Marro, *La Puberta*, Bocca, Torino, 1897; G.S. Hall, *Adolescence*, 2 vols, Appleton, New York, 1904; Millicent W. Shinn, *Notes on the Development of a Child*, Berkeley, University of California Studies, 1, pt.I, 1893, pt.II, 1894, pts III & IV, 1899; Millicent W. Shinn, *Notes on the Development of a Child II, ibid.*, Education, 4, 1907; C. and W. Stern, *Die Kindersprache*, Barth, Leipzig, 1907; William Stern, *Psychologie der Frühen Kindheit*, Quelle and Meyer, Leipzig, 1914.

[3] See, for example, accounts of the activities of the associations in Theta M. Wolf. *Alfred Binet*, University of Chicago, 1973, pp. 288ff. and Dorothy Ross, *G. Stanley Hall, the Psychologist as Prophet*, University of Chicago, 1972, pp. 297ff. Two international associations were established on the same date in Paris, one presided over by Schuyten, the other by Binet. A merger was subsequently negotiated.

(i) Main Areas of Child Study

The child study movement was a sustained effort to discover more about the development of children and adolescents, to explore their physical, mental, and emotional growth, to chart their behaviour, and to investigate their interests and attitudes. It was also an effort to make the discoveries known and to encourage all who were connected with the education and upbringing of children to learn more about them and to join in the program of investigation to the best of their ability.

Many of the research workers were interested in children's health and physical development. The English association, for example, grew out of an initial interest among doctors and teachers in hygiene and the conditions under which the poorer city children were being brought up. Mental fatigue was a particular interest to European educators in the 1890's. Ebbinghaus made an extensive study of it in the Breslau schools; and one of Binet's most notable contributions, in 1898, was a comprehensive critique of the work already done in mental fatigue, and a demonstration of the use of appropriate experimental techniques of investigation. Hall and his associates in America had a great concern for physical health and undertook a considerable amount of research on muscular function in children's activity.

A second important area of concern was that of children's emotions, attitudes, and interests. Many inventories of children's and adolescents' interests were compiled, and efforts were made to put them into categories and to try to establish a developmental pattern that would be useful to teachers who wished to relate the sequence of their teaching to their pupils' interests. Many students collected examples of children's games and play activities and gave consideration to the way in which teachers could use these activities in the classroom, and to the general significance of play in a child's development. Was play, for example, a kind of rehearsal for the more serious activities of adult life, as Karl Groos suggested, much as a kitten by playing with a wind-blown leaf or cotton reel may be learning the hunting skills it may later have to use? Or was play, on the other hand, as Hall suggested, a progressive recapitulation, by children as they grow up, of the stages through which civilisation has passed in the course of its long development, and may not children by parallelling in their play the history of the human race bring themselves steadily up to the point where they can cope with modern civilisation? In the early years of the century rival views of the nature of play were much discussed, and, though never resolved, did help to underscore the growing recognition of the educational value of play activities that Froebel's kindergartners had first brought seriously into consideration. Children's attitudes to many other things were studied in various situations, for example, their views on and feelings about light and darkness, clouds, flowers, and animals, their lies and fears, their anger, and their pleasures.

From the time when Preyer had written the initial study in the movement, *The Mind of the Child*, there was, also, a continuing interest in the intellectual development of children. Memory and imitation were the mental processes that most frequently came under scrutiny in all countries. They lent themselves particularly to investigation by psychologists and teachers who were influenced by the associationist psychology which prevailed in the late nineteenth century and was reinforced in educational circles by the popularity of the Herbartian movement. As the child study movement, however, took form and substance by the beginning of the twentieth century, its leaders, attracted to current biological thinking, began to develop a genetic or developmental approach. This change was promoted particularly by Hall, Stern, and Binet, and led to an interest in studying children's mental processes and their evolution. Binet's *Experimental Study of Intelligence* which he published in 1903 was an important pointer to this trend. It was an investigation of the intellectual development of his two daughters. His study was a search for the 'directing ideas' or purposes that lay behind and gave a particular orientation to the way in which each individual's thought processes developed. Though still much involved in testing his children's powers of mental association, he had begun also to look at the functional nature of intelligence and to draw attention to it as a process of adaptation, an adjusting of means to ends. Stern carried the functional trend still further.[4] The developmental approach to child behaviour linked the movement more closely in the early part of the century with the pioneers of progressive education who tended to favour a dynamic and developmental view of child growth. In the pre-World War I years a number of the leading research workers, such as Decroly in Belgium, Claparède in Switzerland, and Binet in France, became identified with movements for educational reform.

(ii) Method of Child Study

Information on children's behaviour was gathered, during the course of the child study movement, chiefly by means of questionnaires and personal observation. Teachers, students in training, and college lecturers

---

[4]   William Stern (1871-1938) graduated from the University of Berlin in 1892, taught at the University of Breslau, and in 1916 went to Hamburg where he became professor (1919) and director of the Psychological Institute until 1933 when he migrated with his wife Clara to the U.S.A. Stern was one of the leading European psychologists of his era, known particularly for his theory of personalism. His work was an important part of the tradition out of which Lewin and Piaget respectively developed their ideas. His most widely read book was *Person und Sache (Person and Thing)* 1906-24, 3 vols.

were encouraged, particularly in the United States, to devise question-naires or use those distributed by Hall and his associates on every aspect of children's activity that could be thought of. Between 1894 and 1915 Hall circulated questionnaires on no less than 194 subjects. He had, according to a contemporary psychologist, gone 'mad on child business and the questionnaire'.[5]

Often the instruments were poorly constructed, the sampling inadequate, and the responses ineptly analysed. In consequence there was much criticism of the procedures and findings. At a time when the leading educational psychologists were interested in making a science out of education, the looseness and amateurishness of the methods of many contemporary child studies was an irritant to the researchers who were working with greater depth and precision. One American psychologist put it as '...all this seductive but rude and untrained and untechnical gathering of cheap and vulgar material means a caricature and not an improvement of psychology'.[6] Fortunately there was a sprinkling of good work, especially among the observational studies.

There was, also, a connection continuously maintained between child studies and experimental investigations in education. After 1900, in the United States, as Thorndike's influence increased, and in Europe where experimental work with children had remained an integral part of the child study movement, a more scientific approach began to take over, and by World War I the study of children was taking its place as an accepted, and reasonably precise, empirical area within the field of educational psychology.

(iii) Importance of the Child Study Movement

For all its shortcomings, the child study movement made a considerable impact on contemporaries and left a substantial legacy.

It was the central part of a more general interest in children that developed at the beginning of the century and gave Ellen Key hope that the world was entering into the century of the child. The child study movement spilled over into and reinforced similar and associated interests such as the child welfare movement. Many who studied the growth of children became interested in improving the children's performance and the conditions in which they developed. The provision, therefore, of better health services, recreational facilities, children's libraries, school meals, and the improvement of school classrooms and conditions of juvenile labour were tasks that many who were interested in child study were easily persuaded to undertake. Social and educational reformers in many countries, such as Jane Addams, Julia Lathrop, Margaret McMillan, and Pauline Kergomard, tended, in their various countries, to

be interested in the work done by the child study movement and to receive warm support from many of its members.

It was evidence of an important trend in psychology, towards developmental psychology, and it probably helped to confirm and extend the trend. Researchers and teachers concerned with the study of children tended to look at and arrange their observations of children's behaviour in a sequential way, building, wherever possible, patterns of development through which children might move as they were growing up. They were interested also, particularly in the later stages of the movement, in thinking of children's behaviour in dynamic terms, and they tended to seek to discover the motivation and drive associated with the behaviour they were studying. Thus the child study movement became connected with the more biologically inclined, dynamic psychologists, and looked with great sympathy on men such as Bergson, Dewey, McDougall, and later Freud.

The most significant change that the movement effected was in the concept of the child. It brought three vital things about children clearly and firmly into the stream of educational and psychological thinking.

In the first place, the numerous studies served to demonstrate the very considerable differences between children. Every mother has always known that no two children are the same. The child study movement documented the differences. It showed that there were wide variations among children in the rate of their intellectual, emotional, and physical growth, in their interests and enthusiasms, in the way in which they expressed themselves, and in the quality of their work and play. For the first time, individual differences among school pupils were carefully measured, and the extent of them made apparent to the reading public, to practising teachers, and to students in training. Henceforth, there was an increased and informed interest in providing for the educational needs of children with clearly definable differences such as subnormal, physically handicapped, and exceptionally bright children. There was, at the same time, a continuing effort to cater more effectively for the range of individual differences found in the primary classroom, to introduce more variation in teaching method and content, and to break the lock-step by which schools required most children to progress at a common rate through a common body of material.

In the second place, the thirty years of child studies had revealed that children were complicated and many-faceted creatures. To understand a child it was necessary to look at many different aspects of his behaviour. Teachers who tended to be interested primarily in the intellectual and

---

[5] D. Ross, *op.cit.*, p. 270.

[6] H. Münsterberg, *Psychology and Life*, Houghton Mifflin, Boston, 1899, p. 116.

physical development of children, discovered, in the course of the movement, much more about their emotional and social development. The progressive education movement placed emphasis on this wider view and made a point of incorporating social and emotional activities in its school programs to such good effect that, in varying degrees, they shortly became customary in most schools. Of most importance, however, was the realisation that all of the different aspects of a child's behaviour were related to one another. To understand intellectual development, for example, it was necessary to take account of related aspects of physical, social, and emotional development. There was a recognition that every individual was a unity, that all the various aspects of his behaviour converged to form a single interrelated whole, and that teaching anything to a child meant changing not just a single function in his behaviour but, in some measure, developing the child as a whole.

In the third place, out of the work of the child study movement came the realisation that young people grew up through a series of stages which not only had recognisable characteristics but also were related successively to one another in important ways. One of the main concerns of the leaders of the movement was to find a suitable basis on which to determine the successive stages. It was obvious that, chronologically, it was possible to speak of infancy (from birth to about two years), early childhood (about two to five), childhood (about six to eleven), puberty or early adolescence (about twelve to fourteen), and later adolescence (about fifteen to eighteen). Some such division occurred in most of the textbooks then in use. But what was characteristic of each age? And was it possible, by not relying merely on age, to arrive at a more significant set of stages?

Hall, for much of his career, held to a recapitulation theory by which he contended that the successive periods of children's growth paralleled the development of civilisation; later he moved into the Freudian camp, and based the stages on the psychic development of children. Stern proposed a sequence of personality development: the first, early childhood from birth to seven years, was characterised by play and by the progressive acquisition of the power to express and communicate ideas in speech; the second, childhood from seven to fourteen years, by the systematic development of memory and conscious learning; and the third, youth from fourteen to twenty years, by a self-conscious effort to relate the outer world to a growing, independent personality. The most elaborate analysis of stages of growth was that of Claparède. It took account of the great variety of work done in the course of the child study movement, and was something of an overall analysis and summary of research findings up to 1910. Claparède based his proposed stages on mental development as exemplified in the interests that became most apparent at particular periods:

I *Stage of Acquisition and Experimentation*

1. Period of perceptive interest, first year.
2. Period of glossic (language) interest, second and third year.
3. Period of general interests and intellectual awakening (questioning age), third to seventh year.
4. Period of special and objective interests, seventh to twelfth year.

II *Stage of Organisation and Evaluation*

5. Period of sentiment, ethical and social interests, specialised interests, and sexual interests, twelfth to eighteenth year.

III *Stage of Production*

6. Period of work and subordination of various interests to some superior interest, adult age.

Claparède's classification obviously reflected the times. He caught both the current preoccupation of educators with children's interests, and the beginning of a concern for the study and measurement of children's intellectual development. There was also more information about and more interest in young children; hence the careful division of periods of development at that level, and the comparative neglect of the older years.[7] Adolescence had begun to emerge as a topic of study in the early years of the century at a time when the reform of secondary education was receiving increased attention, but a substantial and sustained study of both adolescence and the possibility of universal secondary education was not to come until the 1920's and 1930's.

Much of the subsequent work in child study during the course of the twentieth century was concerned with modifying prevalent views on the stages of development and with finding new bases on which to suggest different and sounder patterns. The work done early in the century drew the attention of educators not only to the differences among individual children but also to the similarity of progression through which children passed in the course of their growth. In consequence, teachers were alerted to look for evidence in a child's behaviour of the stage which he might be expected to have reached, and, particularly, to try to ensure that the child had the experiences which made him ready to pass on to the next appropriate stage. The later interest of educational psychologists in

[7] Dorothy Ross, *op.cit.*, Chapters 16 and 18; William Stern, *Psychology of Early Childhood*, Anna Barwell trans. Holt, New York, 1926 (1914), Chapter 1; E. Claparède, *Experimental Pedagogy and the Psychology of the Child*, 4th edn, Mary Louch & H. Holman, trans. Arnold, London, 1911 (1910) p. 174.

readiness and in developmental tasks at the mid-century was anticipated by Judd in 1903 who summed up the importance for teachers of a knowledge of child development: 'The really important question for the teacher is this: What are the conditions that must be fulfilled before the mind is prepared for a new step in development? ... If we know the conditions and can control them, we can then produce the phenomenon at such a time as we may deem appropriate.'[8]

The child study movement flourished during an upsurge of interest in developmental processes and in the activity of children. It was stimulated by the current popularity of the biological sciences and the theory of evolution. In that sense it was connected with science but it was not necessarily scientific in its methods. Many of the best studies of children were carefully and methodically done, but it could not be said that the movement as a whole was primarily interested in being rigorously scientific.

Some educators, particularly in the United States, combined an interest in child development with a desire to improve social organisation. They saw the need to get accurate information on the children's social and educational environment and on the effectiveness of their schooling. They joined forces with school administrators who were looking for more efficient ways of assisting the pupils' educational progress, and began what came to be known as the school survey movement.

THE SCHOOL SURVEY MOVEMENT

Organised and systematic investigations to discover the facts and to assist in the diagnosis and clarification of social problems started to become a fashionable pastime in the period of rapid urban growth at the end of the nineteenth century. By World War I an American sociologist commenting on its current popularity, wrote, 'The social survey is new. Its very rapid rise and immense popularity almost designate it a fad. The prominent part it has recently played in reform movements suggests that it may be a new sort of religion.'[9] Social surveys covered many fields from urban poverty, health, industry, and housing, to rural social conditions, and agricultural prospects. The social survey probed current social issues, and exposed the community itself to examination.

One important branch of the general movement was the educational survey which eventually achieved great popularity in the United States. It began in the early years of the century and developed into substantial proportions after World War I.

(i) Early Influences

The movement was a product of three factors:

First, the welfare movement that had blossomed in the latter years of the nineteenth century encouraged researchers to investigate and assess the social conditions of the areas in which they were interested. The outstanding example of that form of investigation was Charles Booth's fifteen-year study of *Life and Labour of the People of London*, finally completed and published in 1902. Booth saw his and other such studies as the means of providing an accurate and well-analysed picture of the actual situation of London life. Such information would enable interested people to understand the position and to see the possibilities of change. He wrote, in a vein that many were to echo later in the century in their bewilderment at the growing intricacy of bureaucracy and urbanisation, of 'the sense of helplessness that tries everyone';[10] wage-earner, manufacturer, legislator, all alike did not know how to manage the situation. The first step towards establishing control, he suggested, was a careful and thorough survey of the facts.

A second factor lying behind the development of the survey movement in education was a growing interest in the social relationships of the school. Since the publication of Dewey's *School and Society* in 1899, the social purposes of education had become the centre of much discussion in many educational circles. Increasing industrialisation and urbanisation directed attention to current social changes and the need to examine whether the school's work was appropriate in the changed society; and various special circumstances, such as the influx of migrants mostly from southern and eastern Europe into the United States at the turn of the century, or the move towards a wide expansion of secondary education characteristic of many developed countries early in the century, stimulated a rethinking of the social purposes and practices of education. Those kinds of considerations induced many educators to seek out the facts of the various situations.

A growing interest in efficient management, not unrelated to Booth's thoughts on overcoming contemporary feelings of powerlessness, was a third important factor behind the survey movement. Taylor and Gilbreth in the first decade of the century had successfully started a reform in industrial and business management which emphasised the elimination

8 C.H. Judd, *Genetic Psychology for Teachers*, Appleton, New York, 1903, pp. 305-6.

9 C.C. Taylor, *The Social Survey, its History and Methods*, University of Missouri Bulletin 20, 28, Social Science Series 3, Columbia, Mo, October 1919, p. 5.

10 C. Booth, The inhabitants of Tower Hamlets (School Board Division), their condition and occupations, *Journal of the Royal Statistical Society*, 50, pt. 2, 1887, p. 376.

of waste and the adoption of efficient and economic methods of work. To achieve efficiency it was necessary to have an accurate knowledge of one's resources, objectives, methods, and output. Information on those aspects of a school or an educational system could be sought through a carefully conducted survey, which might be regarded as a first step towards the scientific management of the institution. In educational philosophy, educational research, and educational administration the scientific fashion was strong. In essence it meant that the work should be coherently structured and subject to measurement. The scientific movement added its weight to the other major factors in the interests of producing more precise, quantified, and well-organised material on schools, and the educational surveys that were undertaken were generally regarded as a contribution to a more scientific approach to education.

Various countries from time to time had conducted wide educational investigations. In the twentieth century it became a regular practice to survey not only broad educational areas and problems, but also smaller units such as country and city systems and individual schools. Michael Sadler was the first in the field in undertaking between 1903 and 1906 a succession of careful and judicious surveys of several English cities and counties. His lucidly written work was widely read both at home and abroad, 'and without doubt wielded a significant influence' in the United States where the survey movement was to have its most substantial development.[11] Sadler's work was brought on by the need for the various English school authorities to think out and propose efficient ways of expanding their efforts to meet the terms of the recently passed Education Act of 1902. He had the great merit of combining a shrewd eye for efficiency with an excellence of educational judgment and a facility for making appropriate suggestions for further development.

(ii)   Early School Surveys in the U.S.A.

The survey movement was launched in the United States at Boise, Idaho, in 1910 when the local school board invited an educational administrator from the east coast to investigate and report on their schools and to advise on future developments. During the next ten years surveys were conducted in many of the major city school systems in the United States such as Baltimore (1911), New York (1912), Portland (1913), and a substantial study at Cleveland (1915-16). In the same period hundreds of surveys were made of individual schools and small systems.

The Cleveland survey, undertaken by L.P. Ayres and a large team of assistants, was the most comprehensive one of the period. It demonstrated more clearly than any of its predecessors the two characteristics of surveys that encouraged their supporters to think they were making a

contribution to the science of education, viz. a well-structured and comprehensive account of the facts on education in the area under review, and an extensive use of objective measuring instruments in gathering the data presented by the investigators.

The Cleveland survey team produced twenty-five volumes, each dealing with a different aspect of urban life and education. They had a comprehensive look at the vocational and social structure of the city, reporting in detail on the educational needs of the major occupations. They painstakingly compared Cleveland's financial resources and expenditures with those of ten other large American cities. They then made an assessment of the school system and the work of the local Board of Education in the economic and social setting that they had systematically analysed.

A flavour of their work can be got from looking at some of their general findings. In regard to the general administration of the schools they found that, on the business side matters were run efficiently, but on the educational side the schools lacked professional leadership and supervision. The schools and teachers tended to be conservative and formalistic, 'rather than liberalistic and progressive', untouched by 'the stirring developments in education that have brought about new and better equipped buildings, an enriched course of study, and scientific methods of supervision'.[12] In the elementary schools there was a decided emphasis on the 3 R's, and little attention to subjects such as history, civics, and science. Despite the formality of the methods of teaching, however, there was considerable variation in the children's actual performance in different schools. Especially worrying to the surveyors was the educational provision made for immigrants. Three-quarters of all the inhabitants of Cleveland were either foreign born or of foreign parentage, and half of the children in the elementary schools and one-third of those in high schools came from homes in which English was not regularly spoken. Neither in the schools nor in the adult evening classes were the methods of English teaching very satisfactory. Cleveland, like most cities, also had a considerable retardation and drop-out problem. Almost all pupils completed fifth grade, but only 63 per cent reached eighth grade; 41 per cent went on to high school, and only nineteen per cent completed it. Along the way, some 32 per cent of pupils were retarded in their progress by one or more years. The survey team, while recommending a number of changes in administrative procedures, supervision, curriculum, and methods of teaching, gave the impression that Cleveland's schools were for the most part a fair sample of the nation's educational

---

[11] H.L. Caswell, *City School Surveys*, Teachers' College, Columbia University, New York, 1929, p. 23.

[12] L.P. Ayres, *The Cleveland School Survey (Summary Volume)*, Survey Committee of the Cleveland Foundation, Cleveland, 1917, pp. 54, 60.

efforts; their working and their results were not far from the average, and, with the co-operation of an enthusiastic and aspiring community, which Cleveland appeared to be, the schools might expect substantial progress in the near future.

In coming to their various conclusions, the members of the survey team used a variety of investigative techniques and instruments. They used rating scales to assess the quality of school buildings and library facilities. They used standardised tests to determine the effectiveness of the teaching of reading, and they devised several new tests for assessing handwriting, spelling, and arithmetic. They compared the performance of the immigrant population with the native, the Cleveland schools with those in other cities, and various systems of teaching with one another. They quantified their data wherever they possibly could, they made an extensive use of graphs and tables in presenting it, and they recommended that the Cleveland schools should establish the practice of scientific supervision by adopting and continuing with the methods of the surveyors.

The survey movement grew in popularity in the 1920's and 1930's, and techniques were refined and improved as more and better tests of aptitude and achievement became available. The educational psychologists who devised the testing instruments were products of the interest in educational measurement that began about the turn of the century. It developed out of the researches of a group of experimental educators who were not merely interested in the accurate measurement of educational phenomena, but were trying also to develop a scientific approach to the solution of all educational problems. They sought to apply scientific method in their work, and to build up a body of carefully researched data about educational practices.

THE IMPORTANCE OF SCIENCE

In 1892 Karl Pearson[13] wrote his influential *The Grammar of Science*. In it he argued with much force that science, properly conceived, was competent to tackle all fields of knowledge, that it was essential for the proper conduct of any investigation, and that its goal was to provide a complete interpretation of the universe. Not only were scientists busy contributing to our physical comfort by revolutionising our practical life, our means of transport, and our treatment of disease, they were also affecting our social conduct by their attention to social problems.

In the arrangement and analysis of scientific material the key concepts were those of probability, variability, and contingency. The prediction of behaviour, and, therefore, the usefulness of it in practical application, depended upon the probability of its future occurrence. Hence the need to understand and to sharpen the tools by which probability could be assessed. The universe as the scientist saw it was a sum of phenomena, some more, others less closely associated with or contingent on each other. Variability was the characteristic of these phenomena; and the fundamental problem of science, therefore, was to discover and measure the extent to which the variation in one class of phenomena was correlated with or contingent on the variation in a second class.

Pearson's book expressed his conviction that the study of science could and should embrace all fields of knowledge, that the disciplined study of science was a particularly suitable training for the citizens of modern society, and that the study of science meant, primarily, the study of scientific method.

The ideas expressed by Pearson in his *The Grammar of Science* were widely current in the 1890's, and his book served to crystallise them and to encourage like-minded individuals interested in the social sciences to apply them in their field. Two such persons well acquainted with Pearson's work were E.L. Thorndike in America, and Edouard Claparède in Europe. For the forty years from the beginning of the century to the outbreak of World War II both Thorndike and Claparède were key figures on their respective continents in the movement for the application of scientific methods to the study of education. By their tireless advocacy, and by the example of their own research, they helped to build and maintain a supply of material and skilled research workers, and a body of professional opinion favourable to the scientific study of educational problems.

(i) E. L. Thorndike

Thorndike worked from 1899 till 1940 as a member of the faculty of Teachers College, Columbia University, and was the most prominent educational psychologist of his time. For him science was 'the only sure

---

[13] Karl Pearson (1857-1936), mathematician, and biologist, and one of the great names in the history of statistical method, became professor of applied mathematics and mechanics in 1884 and subsequently of eugenics in 1911 at the University of London. He was the founder (1901) and editor until 1933 of *Biometrika*. His major contributions throughout his lifetime were to the refining of the mathematical tools of scientific method. He was, for example, the first to use the terms 'normal curve' and 'standard deviation'. In particular, he contributed new techniques to the measurement of contingency and probability; he showed the value of the product-moment formula for correlation and the method of bi-serial correlation. In 1900 he introduced the chi-square test of goodness of fit, and a few years later developed the contingency coefficient. He had, in effect, by the early years of the twentieth century given notice that scientific work had an important part to play in the study of social phenomena and he provided some of the fundamental tools which would enable it to do so.

foundation for social progress'.[14] In the early years of the century, according to Michael Sadler, one of England's wisest and most well-known educators of that period, America was stirred to its depth by experiencing 'a great outburst of physical and intellectual energy' carrying the nation forward 'in an exhilarating rush of common effort'. The guiding principle of this upheaval was a common feeling that scientific knowledge and scientific method could be so applied to the affairs of men as to produce great and desirable changes.[15]

Education was infected by this movement. Thorndike rejoiced in it, and devoted his life to the cause. 'The science of education,' he wrote in 1903, 'when it develops will like other sciences rest upon direct observations of and experiments on the influence of educational institutions and methods made and reported with quantitative precision. Since groups of variable facts will be the material it studies, statistics will everywhere be its handmaid. The chief duty of serious students of the theory of education today is to form the habit of inductive study and learn the logic of statistics ... We conquer the facts of nature when we observe and experiment upon them. When we measure them we have made them our servants.'[16]

By encouraging the movement to quantify educational data, by writing textbooks on statistical procedures, by designing ingenious experiments in a wide variety of fields in education, and by devising and using improved methods of testing achievement in the basic subjects, Thorndike, for half a century, exercised an important influence on American education, moving its professionals more and more into empirical research, and building up a general current of opinion favourable to the application of scientific methods to educational problems.

(ii) E. Claparède

In Europe, Claparède's contribution to research was less extensive than Thorndike's, but his advocacy of scientific procedures was no less determined. Brought up in Geneva, he studied there and in Leipzig, and graduated in medicine. Through research in Paris and Geneva he became interested in neurology and thence psychology. In 1900 he began to turn his attention to educational psychology. He was asked to assist in training teachers for subnormal children, and he visited and was impressed by the work of Decroly, in Brussels. In 1901 he gave a lecture to the Medical Society of Geneva on what he called 'L'Ecole sur Mesure' — the school made to measure. 'We are not,' he said, 'as careful of our children's minds as we are even of their feet. Shoes are made of different sizes and patterns to suit their feet. When shall we have school made to measure?'[17] In 1920 an enlarged version of the lecture, with associated papers, was published, and in it can be seen the requirements that Claparède thought necessary for the establishment of a science of education. Meanwhile he had become, in 1915, professor of experimental psychology at Geneva, had founded the J.J. Rousseau Institute for Child Study and Educational Research in Geneva in 1912, and was established as an internationally known figure in psychological and educational circles.

A made to measure school was one in which the school program was adapted to the intelligence and aptitudes of its pupils. Just as a tailor needs a tape measure, a customer to measure, and material to shape, so the bespoke educator needs measuring instruments, a knowledge of child development, and an application of the measurements to the teaching program which he is shaping. In his book on *Experimental Pedagogy and the Psychology of the Child* written in 1905 he explained that this could be achieved only by using the result of scientifically designed experimentation in education, and he gave in considerable detail his ideas on the nature and range of scientific research necessary to equip the educator to carry out his task.

The prime necessity was to study children, and to study them as developing, growing beings. A reading of Karl Groos' books on play revealed to Claparède the significance of childhood — that full development throughout it was necessary for the full development of an adult human animal. Childhood was not to be interpreted in adult terms, but had its own successive stages, balances, and levels of articulation and performance that had to be worked through in the course of healthy development. Unique activities arose in connection with the children's various stages of growth; to understand them one must ask what function they performed in furthering the various developmental processes. This genetic, biological approach to human behaviour was, wrote Claparède, 'the thread of Ariadne in my work'.[18] The research worker who studied children must constantly ask two questions: Of what use or significance is the behaviour he is observing, and to what does it lead?

The second requirement of a science of education was the use of experimental methods. 'Open some pedagogical treatise,' wrote Claparède, 'and see if you can find any really definite directions as to the

[14] G. Joncich, *The Sane Positivist. A Biography of Edward L. Thorndike*, Wesleyan University Press, Middletown, Conn., 1968, p. 4.

[15] M. Sadler, 'Impressions of American education', *Educational Review*, 25 (March 1903), pp. 217ff.

[16] E.L. Thorndike, *Educational Psychology*, Science Press, New York, 1903, p. 164.

[17] C. Murchison ed., *A History of Psychology in Autobiography*, Clark University Press, Worcester, Mass., p. 74.

[18] C. Murchison, *op.cit.*, p. 75.

education of the senses, the power of observation, or memory; as to fatigue, or to the teaching of spelling or arithmetic. You will find how feeble is the treatment of these subjects.' What strikes one most is that the author never has recourse to *facts* but always to *opinions*; he quotes the teaching of Rousseau, Herbart, Spencer, of this, that, and the other person; often he cites the opinions of literati, but never does he make it his business to know whether these different writers have based their opinions on facts, and whether these facts have been observed by sufficiently careful methods...

For this dogmatic method, the worthlessness of which is always in evidence, must be substituted the experimental method, which consists in interrogating facts. In order that the desired answer may be obtained, these facts must be collected, compared, and investigated as to cause and effect.[19]

Careful, objective investigation by observation and by experiment was the only sound way to provide the body of facts and relationships through which the developmental patterns of children's behaviour could be understood and brought to bear on the process of education. Research of this kind, which came generally to be known as Experimental Education developed an array of typical instruments and procedures. For sensori-motor functions, apparatus such as aesthesiometers, dynamometers, ergometers, telegraphic keyboards, chronoscopes, stopwatches, and other instruments common in the laboratories of contemporary experimental psychologists; for studies of affective and intellectual functions, introspection, questionnaires, a great variety of pencil and paper tests, puzzle-boxes, and mazes became the stock-in-trade. For analysis of the data, statistical methods of increasing refinement were necessary. An understanding of the possibilities and meaning of new statistical techniques as they developed and competence at a modest level came to be required of all educational researchers.

EXPERIMENTAL LABORATORIES AND CLASSES

The scientific movement in its early phase established three agencies new to the educational scene: experimental education laboratories, research associations and journals, and experimental schools and classes.

Probably the first pedagogical experiment in the history of the movement was undertaken by Sikorsky, a Russian child psychologist, who investigated the effect on schoolchildren of fatigue caused by mental work. This was in 1879, and was carried out in the schools of Kiev.

Twenty years later the first educational laboratory was established at the University of Chicago in 1899 in John Dewey's Department of Education. In 1900 Antwerp established a pedagogical laboratory for child study of which Schuyten later became the director. Nechayev opened a laboratory in St Petersburg in 1901, Binet established one in a primary school in Paris in 1905, and Claparède in 1912 established the J.J. Rousseau Institute in Geneva which during the next half-century built up an enviable reputation for its contribution to child study and education. In the ten years preceding World War I many more laboratories were opened in Europe, in North and South America, and in Japan. Much of the experimental work, however, was done not in specifically educational laboratories but in laboratories for experimental psychology. It was an interesting sign of the times that, in 1904, the British Association, a leading forum for scientific discussion, established a section on Educational Science; and the English Board of Education, at the same time, in its new regulations for the training of teachers, advised that the scientific spirit should be infused into every branch of their curriculum.[20]

Experimental education in these early years was closely associated with the experimental movement in psychology to which Wundt had given a great impetus in the later years of the nineteenth century. Some of the early educational experimenters the most notable of whom was Ernst Meumann, were trained at Leipzig under Wundt. Meumann and Wilhelm Lay, a schoolteacher and professor of pedagogy, were the founders of experimental education in Germany, and, with Claparède, Binet, and Thorndike, were the five outstanding figures of the movement in the first quarter of the twentieth century.

(i) E. Meumann

Meumann (1862-1915) studied at Leipzig for six years from 1891 to 1897, became a devoted experimentalist, and was regarded by Wundt as one of his most promising pupils. In 1897 he moved to the University of Zurich and started to become interested in educational problems. Four years later, in 1901, he published a series of articles in *Deutsche Schule* outlining the content and aims of the new field of experimental education. His interest in learning and memory was expressed by the publication of a book on the psychology of learning entitled *Economy and Technique of Learning* in 1908. In the introduction to the American

---

[19] E. Claparède, *Experimental Pedagogy and the Psychology of the Child,* trans Mary Louch and H. Holman, Arnold, London, 1911, pp. 74-5.

[20] E. Fry, 'Science and Education', *Contemporary*, March 1905.

Meumann's substantial volumes contained a definitive account of educational research up to that point, indicating the results obtained, the experimenter's inferences, and the inferences which Meumann considered to be justified. It covered all aspects of educational research — mental and physical development, individual differences, memory, imagination, feeling, will, intelligence, and the teaching of the subjects of the elementary school curriculum. The book indicated the bearings of the research results in each field on school practice.

Meumann's own experimental work was acute and suggestive. His use of statistical techniques, however, was weak and his contemporaries were rightly suspicious of some of his results. He excelled, nevertheless, in isolating and analysing research problems, indicating the key elements in the problem and the appropriate means of tackling it. His work covered a broad compass, as might be expected of a pioneer, and he was not loath to tackle live, contemporary issues such as sex education, co-education, and the ethical development of school pupils. Probably his most considerable research was on aspects of intellectual development, particularly the problems concerned with mental fatigue involved in learning, and with memorisation.

His work was laboratory research. He pointed out in his *Introductory Course* that the current movement had two sides. It rested, on the one hand, on the work of academic experimenters working away in their laboratories, distinguishable from experimental psychologists, if at all, only by the fact that they were dealing with items involved in the educational process; on the other hand, it was sustained by a body of professional researchers and teachers who found their problems in the classroom and conducted their experiments there.

(ii) Wilhelm Lay

Wilhelm Lay's work was of the second category. Lay (1862-1926) was a teacher in Karlsruhe, his native city, who, after studying at Freiburg and Halle, returned to the normal school at Karlsruhe where he spent the rest of his life. In 1897 and 1898 he published two experimental studies on school work that were among the first undertaken in Germany, and, for his doctoral work at Halle in 1903, he wrote *Experimental Didactics* in which he argued the case vigorously for schoolroom experimentation. He followed this in 1908 with a book entitled *Experimental Pedagogy*, and,

Ernst Meumann (1862-1915), who with Wilhelm Lay, laid the foundations for the empirical study of education in Europe.

edition of it he expressed the opinion that experimental education was the joint product of workers in the U.S.A. and Germany, and that in his writings, he constantly kept the American reader in mind. His book was a timely contribution to the current concern in the United States with means of economising in time and effort in school learning. The 1901 articles were subsequently expanded in 1907-8 into a multi-volume work, *Introductory Course in Experimental Education and its Psychological Foundations,* and supplemented in 1914 by a *Handbook of Experimental Pedagogy.*[21] The *Introductory Course* and Thorndike's earlier (1903) and more modest *Educational Psychology* became the two standard textbooks in educational psychology throughout the pre-World War I period.

21   E. Meumann, *Vorlesungen zur Einführung in die experimentelle Pädogogie,* Engelmann, Leipẑig, 3 vols. 1907-8; E. Meumann, *Oekonomie and Technik des Gedächtnisses,* 1908, J.W. Baird, trans.; *The Psychology of Learning,* Appleton, New York, 1913; E. Meumann, *Abriss der experimentellen Pädagogie,* Engelmann, Leipẑig, 1914.

jointly with Meumann, founded in 1905 the journal, *Die Experimentelle Pädagogik*.[22] The two men complemented each other with their different orientations, but unfortunately their differences developed into a display of unseemly backbiting, more perhaps on the part of their disciples who claimed the one or the other as the true founder of experimental education, and the classroom or the laboratory approach as the one true method.

Wilhelm Lay (1862-1926), co-founder of the empirical study of education in Europe.

FUNDAMENTAL RESEARCH PROBLEMS

There were four basic educational topics with which the pre-World War I researchers were concerned: economy of work; mental testing; transfer of training; and moral education.

'The first duty of the educator,' wrote Claparède, 'every one will agree, is to do no harm.' He therefore has to learn not to make undue demands upon his pupils such as will damage their health. Two problems arise from this. First, that of mental fatigue: what causes it? How can it be overcome? What level of fatigue is associated with each school subject and each age group of children? Second, that of *economy of work*: how can pupils accomplish their work efficiently with the least effort in the least time? e.g. what is the most economical method of learning poetry or spelling? What is the best time to introduce dates in the teaching of history, or formal reasoning in science and mathematics? Problems of these kinds were very much to the fore in the work of the educational researchers of the early years of the century and there was a continuous and mounting body of empirical evidence produced by workers such as Thorndike, Meumann, Lay, and their followers. A concerted effort was made in that direction just before World War I by the American National Society for the Study of Education, which appointed a committee on Economy of Time in Education. The committee produced four monumental and influential reports from 1916 to 1919 which appeared as *Yearbooks* of the society.

Every teacher is conscious of the fact that the children he teaches differ in their capacities to learn, and perform with differing degrees of success. On his impression of their brightness, he may classify them, perhaps promote them, and perhaps select them to take particular courses or to go to particular kinds of secondary or higher institutions. In doing so, he is inferring their potential from his observation of them or from their performance in the examinations he sets them. Some objective way of assessing their potential, which could be applied to children with whom he was unfamiliar as well as those he knew well, would have great value for the teaching profession. As the educators about the turn of the century thought about this problem, they concentrated on trying to develop a means of testing what they regarded as the central factor in school success, the mental capacity possessed by the child. The key to grading, classifying, and catering for individual differences lay in the development of an objective and scaled *test of general intelligence*.

---

[22] Lay's main publications were: W.A. Lay, *Experimentelle Didaktik*, Wiesbaden, 1903; W.A. Lay, *Experimentelle Pädagogik*, Teubner, Leipzig, 1908, A. Weil & E.K. Schwartz trans, *Experimental Pedagogy*, Prentice-Hall, New York, 1936; W.A. Lay, *Die Tatschule*, Zickfeldt, Leipzig, 1911.

You cannot teach in school everything that is useful or potentially useful. You try therefore to teach knowledge, skills, and attitudes that can be useful in a variety of situations. You try to provide basic ideas that can be applied in a variety of fields, you try to teach skills, for example, intellectual skills that can be used in every situation and with all kinds of materials, and you try to develop attitudes that will persist and guide pupils in all their work. In teaching these things, you must, of course, use particular materials and methods and particular situations that have been specifically selected and inserted in the school curriculum. Can what is learned on these particular items be transferred to other situations at other times and places? This is a fundamental question for educators. If there is no transfer, then the whole business of educating is a hopeless one. But, granted that transfer does take place, what is the extent of it? and is the process an automatic one? or are there some conditions more favourable to it than others? This basic problem of transfer of learning, or, as it was more usually called, *transfer of training*, was taken up and extensively argued and investigated by these early experimenters.

The most delicate and difficult task, but one which all educators have regarded as central, is that of *moral education*. Beyond the acquisition of knowledge lies the development of character. The children have to be taught to make decisions, and the basis upon which decisions may be made. With the greater availability of formal education at primary level, and the growing popularity of secondary education, a new educational dimension, an educated populace, was beginning to make itself felt in the early part of the century. The new educational researchers were most interested in the problems of moral education; but because of the intractability of the subject, little of significance was contributed by them. A summary of the work and of current educational practices on a world-wide basis was made at a World Congress in 1908, and there was a separate substantial report edited by Michael Sadler, in 1908-09.

Of these four problem areas which the pioneers regarded as fundamental, the fourth, that on moral education, proved too elusive to provide satisfactory examples of experimental research. The other three fields, economy of work, intelligence, and the problem of transfer of training were their fruitful lines of work. It is possible in these areas to see some concrete and significant achievement by them, and, in each case, their efforts were responsible for stimulating a very considerable amount of research and discussion by their successors.

(i)   Economy of Work

An early and substantial example of research on economy of work was that by Lay published in 1897 on the learning of spelling. It is one of the earliest pieces of work in the movement, and can be contrasted with the more sophisticated technique used by Meredith in his transfer of training experiment twenty-five years later.

Lay's aim was to determine the best method of teaching spelling in the elementary school. He started by analysing existing opinions and methods. Some emphasised the need to hear and form an auditory impression of the word; others discounted the importance of hearing, and stressed, instead, visual appearance; some insisted upon the learning and understanding of rules; others rejected rules; some insisted upon pronunciation while others opposed its use; and finally, others again emphasised the importance of motor images from writing. Hearing, speech, sight, and writing were all favoured. Which single or combined approach was the most effective? There was plenty of argument but no firm evidence. Lay endeavoured to provide the empirical evidence.

He hoped to secure material of uniform difficulty by devising nonsense material graded for the different class levels that he wished to test. The fourth class, for example, had a series which started

Libug,	Bollis	Gohlin,	Seufil
Labog,	Bulles,	Gihlan,	Saifol
Lubag,	Billas,	Gahlen,	Seiful
Ribog,	Mallis,	Kahlun,	Teufar

and so on, like the witches of Cawdor.

These and other nonsense syllables were used to test four main patterns of learning, with several sub-groups: writing after merely hearing the words dictated, writing after seeing, spelling the letters aloud from the words written on the blackboard, and copying. The tests were given on an extensive scale to children in school in classes 1 to 6 of the elementary school, and to a group of older students in training at the normal school at Karlsruhe. All told, there were 4,800 results to analyse.

Lay rated the various methods by the number of errors made per pupil and his results in summary were as follows:

1.	Writing after hearing without vocalising	3.04
	hearing with speaking in an undertone	2.69
	hearing with speaking aloud	2.25
2.	Writing after seeing without vocalising	1.22
	seeing with speaking in an undertone	1.02
	seeing with speaking aloud	0.95
3.	Spelling aloud	1.02
4.	Copying	0.54

Thus copying down, and seeing with speaking aloud gave the best results, and hearing without vocalisation the worst.

Lay drew from the work the implications that, for learning to spell, seeing is more useful than hearing, and that the combination of motor activity with seeing in the process of copying is the most useful procedure of all.

This early investigation by Lay is good evidence of the current state of research and an indication of coming trends in twentieth century educational research.

His sampling procedures were unsatisfactory. His statistical procedures were elementary, amounting only to the calculation of simple means with no indication of the dispersion of scores. Several important variables were not taken into account, e.g. time taken over each procedure — the greater length of time taken in copying and spelling aloud would probably favour both these processes. Nevertheless it was a brave attempt. It was functional and it was in the school room. It took up an important area of school teaching, analysed the various unexamined methods in use, isolated the aspects of it that could be researched, and designed an appropriate and comprehensive experiment. It showed the way in which experimental data, rather than untested opinion, could be accumulated to provide a more solid foundation for the practice of school teaching.

Lay's work was followed by many others in many fields, and the results were made known through the new associations and research journals that came into being in the early years of the century to cater for the new movement.

An interesting study of the relative performance of girls and boys in school work was carried out in Central Europe. It was a unique, long-term piece of research conducted by Körösy in Hungary.[23]

For twenty-seven years, from 1873 to 1900, the schools of Budapest sent to him a report on the progress of each pupil, giving a total of 808,350 cases. In the elementary schools, ages six to twelve years, he compared the number of boys and girls who had to repeat a year's work instead of proceeding to the next standard. Of 412,758 boys 16.8 per cent repeated, and of 350,382 girls 15.8 per cent repeated. The higher the standard of work the greater appeared to be the superiority of the girls' performance. When the relative frequency of gaining the best marks was compared, the same pattern emerged and was maintained in every subject. Körösy realised that the boys were a less select group than the girls, but still felt puzzled by the result. He concluded: 'The results are all in favour of the female sex, but relate only to children. Since not only in sciences, but also in poetry and (with the exception of the stage) in arts, the great work of human progress has been accomplished by the male sex, one is obliged to suppose that with the age of ripening the female intellect develops itself more slowly than the masculine.'

(ii) Mental Testing

The greatest achievement of the experimentalists of the period was the development by Binet of an intelligence test in the form of an age scale.

In 1883 Galton in England had suggested the possibility of measuring intellectual abilities by means of simple laboratory tests and had designed some pieces of apparatus for the purpose. McKeen Cattell in the U.S.A. refined Galton's methods, and encouraged among his students of psychology, of whom Thorndike was one, an interest in individual testing and in the development of appropriate and improved statistical procedures. Early in the century Spearman in England began to apply correlational methods to combinations of tests of various abilities. By looking to see the amount of agreement between two sets of such measurements he was able to suggest that in each ability there was a common factor which he called g or general ability, and also something specific which he called an s factor. From the time when he first published his results in 1904 his methods were widely adopted and his views intensively discussed. His work provided a basis for thinking that some general ability which might be called intelligence could be abstracted and measured by a number of tests which probed several different abilities. A Frenchman, Alfred Binet, was the one who succeeded in accomplishing this task.

(a) The Work of Alfred Binet

Binet (1857-1911) became the director of the psychological laboratory at the Sorbonne in 1894 and speedily became interested in a range of problems that bore on the practice of education. He remained at the Sorbonne and contributed to this field constantly up to the time of his death. Some of the most serious of investigators, however, appear at times to have had their lighter moments, and we find him, at one stage, counting loaves of bread and examining the waste returns in boys' normal boarding schools. He was interested, at that time, in the relation between intellectual work and appetite, appetite being measured by the consumption of bread. Binet found that consumption decreased during the course of the year, and drew the conclusion that intense intellectual work injured appetite. The study was solemnly published in 1900.[24]

[23] J. de Körösy, A comparison of the intellectual power of the two sexes, II, *Report of the British Association for the Advancement of Science 1904*, Murray, London, 1905, 841-2.

[24] Binet's study was followed up in Belgium by Schuyten who found that children were eating less bread in summer, a time when he considered their growth rate to be at its highest. He concluded that there must be some disturbing factor in their environment. This he did not find in the bakery but in the school, and he suggested the interesting conclusion that whenever a phenomenon in child development differs in the course of its evolution from what one has a right to expect one may rightly suspect the pernicious influence of the school.

Psychological testing in the laboratories and schools at the turn of the century was concerned mostly with sensori-motor functions. There were, for example, tests for sensory discrimination of sound or of weight, tests of reaction time, and of strength of movement. These were often related to mental development and used as possible measures of mental fatigue, a topic widely studied at the time. Higher level functions such as memory, suggestibility, and imitation interested a growing number of investigators, some of whom tried to put tests of various functions together into tests of general intelligence. Binet worked on this problem for many years, being particularly interested in trying to isolate the principal ingredients of intelligence, and in devising a method which would enable educators to discriminate between normal and mentally defective children.

Although he did not fully accept either Spearman's methods or his views on general ability, he did suggest a number of different functions which intelligence performed: these, he thought, could be tested separately and the results combined to give a score which represented an individual's general ability. The four principal functions of which intelligence was a synthesis were those of giving a direction to thinking, comprehending meaning, discovering, and making judgments. 'Comprehending, discovering, directing, and judging, intelligence is contained in these four words,' he wrote. 'Consequently we can conclude ... that these four functions, which are basic, ought to be the ones to be studied by our method and to be the object of special tests.'[25]

In 1905 he and Simon produced a revolutionary intelligence test in the form of an age scale. Binet summarised how it was done: 'The main idea of this scale was the following: think up a large number of tests, both quick, accurate, and of increasing difficulty; try out these tests on a large number of children of different ages; note the results; find the tests which match a given age, and of which the children a year younger cannot get half right; put together a metric intelligence scale, which will enable you to decide whether a particular subject has the level of intelligence for his age, or is above or below it, and how many months or years he is above or below.'[26]

The new intelligence scale had several important characteristics. It was concerned with general intelligence. It did not measure simple sense perception or attention; it was designed to measure the higher mental functions, and, in doing so, to take into account a broad spectrum of functions that Binet had outlined. He was of the opinion that previous tests were too fragmentary and did not cover the whole range of intellectual functioning; his new scale made use of a wide spread of experiences. As far as possible he used everyday situations taken from the ordinary life and culture of the children he was dealing with. The tests were administered individually to each child. He required verbal responses to most of the tests, and thus gave a considerable weighting to facility with language as an indicator of general intelligence. The items were arranged in order of increasing difficulty, and Binet indicated what children of three, five, seven, nine, and eleven might be expected to do.

'Our scale,' wrote Binet, 'is rather like a tape measure, which, instead of measuring height, aims to measure intelligence, but just as the ordinary tape measure gives no information about the normality of physical development (you can record the same number of centimeters for a normal child and an adult hunchback), so our intelligence scale gives the actual level of intelligence without analysing it and without comment on the degree of intellectual brightness.'[27] But Binet did intend the scale to be used as a help in discriminating between persons of different levels of mental performance. Just as he expected children of different ages to pass tests of a certain level of difficulty, so, too, he expected to distinguish between individuals of different levels of intelligence by the number of tests they might pass. Thus, in Binet's terminology, an idiot could not go beyond test six, and an imbecile's score ranged from seven to sixteen.

The fundamental notion here was that the stages of mental growth of a normal child might be used to measure differences in mental brightness. Once you indicate the level expected to be reached by children of certain ages or by adults of certain levels of intelligence, you can use the tape measure as an indicator of intellectual brightness. Binet's treatment of the scale made it possible to relate age to mental development.

In 1908, three years after the first publication of the scale, Binet and Simon produced a revision in which the items were arranged in successive age groups from three to thirteen years, with the number of tests for each age varying from three to eight. In 1911, a further revision was made in response to the criticisms and studies that had been made in many countries since the publication of the 1908 scale. Binet made the new scale more uniform by using five tests for each age level, and by readjusting the levels by placing in a given age group the items successfully passed by 75 per cent of the age group on which he tried them out. Tests were arranged in successive age groups from three to twelve, omitting eleven, with additional tests for fifteen-year-olds and adults.

Examples of some of the groups are as follows:

---

[25] A. Binet, *Les Idées Modernes sur les Enfants*, Flammarion, Paris, 1911, pp. 118ff, 242ff.

[26] *ibid.*, p. 125.

[27] A. Binet and Th. Simon, 'Nouvelle theorie psychologique et clinique de la démence', *L'Année Psychologique*, XV (1909) p. 183.

Examples of Binet's 1911 Scale, Test of General Intelligence

Three years

1. Understands simple commands, e.g. on request, points to nose, eyes, and mouth
2. Repeats two numbers
3. Enumerates at least two objects or persons in describing a picture
4. Gives surname
5. Repeats a sentence containing six syllables.

Ten years

1. Arranges five weights in order
2. Copies two simple designs from memory, e.g. Greek key pattern, and a truncated pyramid
3. Explains the absurdities in several nonsensical statements, e.g. 'I have three brothers — Jack, Tom, and myself.' What is silly in that?
4. Understands and answers some difficult personal questions, e.g. Suppose a boy does something that is unkind. Why do we forgive him more readily if he was angry than if he was not angry?
5. Uses three given words in two sentences, e.g. Paris, gutter, money.

To determine the child's mental age, the tester took as a basic age the point at which the child passed all but one of the tests, and then added one-fifth of a year for every further test passed. Binet regarded as of superior intelligence a child who scored two years in advance of his chronological age, and, as retarded, one who was two years behind. He did not work out any more closely the relationship between mental and chronological age. That task was undertaken by William Stern in 1913 who produced what he called a mental quotient, by dividing the child's mental age by his chronological age. Thus a child whose mental age was seven and chronological age five would have a mental quotient of $7/5 = 1.4$. Terman then suggested that the quotient could be expressed more conveniently as a whole number if it were multiplied by one hundred. Thus a child whose mental age was equal to his chronological age would have a quotient of one hundred, and the five-year old with a mental age of seven would have a quotient of 140. This relationship he renamed intelligence quotient or IQ.

The IQ was a measure of intellectual brightness. It expressed the relationship between the level of a child's mental development and what was expected of him at his age. If he maintained the same mental performance from year to year he would keep the same intelligence quotient. The IQ was a measure, therefore, through which the intellectual brightness of children of different ages could be compared. For example two five-year-old children (A and B) with mental ages respectively of four and six would have IQ's of 80 and 120; two other children (C and D) aged ten with mental ages of nine and eleven respectively would have IQ's of 90 and 110. Using their IQ scores it would be possible to rank them in order of mental brightness as A, C, D, B.

Two related lines of research developed out of Binet's work on intelligence.

(b) The Nature of Intelligence

There was a continuation of the interest in investigating the nature of intelligence and the processes of thinking. By the end of World War I there were three main schools of thought concerning intelligence. The first, associated with Binet, regarded it as a convenient term for the effect of several functions such as the powers of adaptation, self-criticism, and direction; the second, championed by Thorndike, considered that mental traits were all specific and independent abilities, and that intelligence was some sort of average of them; and the third, advanced by Spearman and Stern, held that there was a central complex quality of general adaptability that was common to all intellectual processes. These diverging ideas on the nature of intelligence were closely associated with mental testing. They arose out of an interest in devising methods of quantifying the mind's output, or expressing this in manageable functional relationships.[28]

In contrast to the involvement with mental testing, interest in the analysis of the growth of thought processes in children produced, as it had also with Binet, ideas about the nature of mental activity and the characteristics of the stages through which it passed in growing children. It was a line of thinking heavily influenced by the language and ideas of Darwinian biology. In the U.S.A., Dewey and Baldwin were the two principally interested in this trend of ideas about children's mental development. Dewey regarded intelligence as an instrument for controlling and extending experience. Thinking arose out of a problematic situation, and its function was to work out the action that would resolve the problem and make a more effective adaptation between the individual and the environment. Baldwin, whose books were widely read by educators, was, like Dewey, excited by the idea that mind was a growing and developing activity. Mental processes, in his view, developed through three stages: pre-logical in which the mind of young children dealt with concrete objects and imagery; logical in which the more mature

---

[28] Shelley Phillips, *Thinking about Thinking*, unpublished Ph.D. Thesis, University of Sydney, 1972, vol. 2, p. 468. Dr. Phillips has made a thoughtful analysis of the contrasting contributions of the American neo-behaviourists and the European traditionalists to the study of cognitive processes.

processes of conceptualising, generalising, and reflecting on one's own thoughts become possible; and hyperlogical in which abstract ideas and moral issues could be manipulated by the mind. Thought originated in children's activities, especially social ones, and was instrumental in furthering their activities which develop together with thought by a process of accommodation to new activities, assimilation of new into established patterns, and association of appropriate mental and motor elements.

In Europe, Claparède, who had worked with Binet, and Stern combined an interest in experimentation and mental measurement with analysis of thought processes in the functionalist tradition. Claparède's views resembled those of Dewey. Thinking was a purposive activity which aimed to re-establish the equilibrium between the organism and the environment disturbed by some difficulty or problem. By play and imitation, the individual assimilated and accommodated to the environment, acting always in accordance with his strongest interest which propelled him into a dynamic contact with his world. Much of this world was social, and by his consciousness of and comparison with others the child gradually forged his own personality. The purposive striving which characterised human development, and the process of mental growth through certain discernible stages and by means of particular intellectual activities characteristic of each stage, were integral parts of the functional tradition upheld also by William Stern. He was supported by contemporary anthropologists such as Lévy-Bruhl who published the first of a series of books on the thinking processes of primitive peoples in 1910.[29]

Maria Montessori, too, whose ideas on early childhood education were immensely popular in the first quarter of the century, followed a similar line of ideas. What she eventually called the absorbent mind was a purposive way of thinking, developing out of appropriate activities by assimilating ideas and using the mental processes that the individual was ready for at each stage of his development. For her, as for the other functionalists, activity was the basis on which intelligence developed, and other progressive educators made activity a central part of their school programs.

This functionalist trend provided the backdrop for the subsequent work of Claparède's younger colleague, Piaget, whose substantial contributions to the study of cognitive processes in children and adolescents, during half a century from the 1920's on, were built on the foundations laid by the pre-World War I theories and discussions.

(c) Intelligence Testing

The second impact of Binet's research was an upsurge in the amount of work put into improving, adapting, and standardising the intelligence tests for use in many different countries. The most notable efforts were those of Terman and Otis in the United States. Out of the many discussions and modifications of the Binet material that took place after its introduction to America in 1910, Terman produced, in 1916, the *Stanford Revision of the Binet Scale of Intelligence*. It was a rearrangement of the order of the tests, a considerable extension in the number of them, an adjustment of the vocabulary and material, and a standardisation on a large sample of American school students. It became the most widely used age scale for intelligence testing in the English-speaking world for the next twenty years. It was then revised, in 1937, and the new version continued to be of central importance until it, too, had a further revision in 1960.[30]

Parallel with Terman's work there was an effort to produce an instrument which could be administered to a group and could be more simply scored than the Binet individual age scale tests. Otis, one of Terman's students, in the years preceding World War I produced, in two parallel forms, a battery of pencil and paper tests which could be answered with a minimum of writing by each individual, could be scored objectively by allotting a point for each correct answer and simply adding the total points, and could be given simultaneously to a group of individuals. During World War I, Otis was a member of the psychology section of the U.S. army and assisted in producing the Army Alpha group intelligence test used on a mass scale to test about one and three-quarter

[29]   J.M. Baldwin (1861-1934), an American psychologist who studied at Berlin and Leipzig with Wundt, established a psychological laboratory at Toronto and subsequently at Princeton in 1893. In 1908 he went to Mexico and in 1913 to Paris where he spent most of the rest of his life. He was a lucid and elegant writer, was deeply influenced by Darwinism, and became a leader of the functional school of psychology. See particularly J.M. Baldwin, *Mental Development in the Child and the Race*, Macmillan, New York, 1895; and J.M. Baldwin, *Darwin and the Humanities*, Swan Sonnenschein, London, 1910.

E. Claparède (1873-1940) — see above p. 100 — a native of Geneva, qualified as a medical practitioner and became interested in psychology, child psychology, and the reform of education. He taught in the psychological laboratory at the University of Geneva from 1899 to 1920. In 1912 he founded the J.J. Rousseau Institute. His main contributions to educational psychology were *Experimental Pedagogy and the Psychology of the Child*; Mary Louch & H. Holman trans. Arnold, London, 1911; *L'Ecole sur Mesure*, Delachaux and Niestlé, Neuchâtel, 1953 (1920); and *L'Education Functionelle*, Delachaux & Niestlé, Neuchâtel, 1931.

L. Lévy-Bruhl (1857-1939) was a professor at the University of Paris from 1896. Between 1910 and 1938 he published six volumes on primitive mentality, the first of which was his *Functions Mentales dans les Sociétés Inférieures*, translated into English as *How Natives Think*.

[30]   L.M. Terman (1877-1956) was one of G. Stanley Hall's graduate students at Clark University. He taught high school, and then became a professor of psychology at Stanford University in 1910. He remained in California, at Stanford, until his death in 1956. In addition to his work on mental testing he was particularly interested in giftedness and produced *Genetic Studies of Genius* in 5 vols published between 1925 and 1959. His principal books dealing with intelligence were: *The Measurement of Intelligence*, Houghton Mifflin, Boston, 1916; *The Intelligence of School Children*, Houghton Mifflin, Boston, 1919; with Maud A. Merrill, *Measuring Intelligence*, Houghton Mifflin, Boston, 1937; and *Stanford-Binet Intelligence Scale: Manual for the Third Revision, Form L-M*, Houghton Mifflin, Boston, 1960.

million American recruits. Modifications of the Army Alpha and Otis' own group tests were widely used in the early 1920's, spread to many other countries, and increased in popularity in succeeding years.[31]

One fundamental assumption in the construction of mental tests was, as Nunn pointed out, 'the implicit theory that from measurements of a person's ability to do certain kinds of things — namely, the things which the tests require him to do — it is possible to infer his ability to do other things apparently quite different from those'.[32] Obviously the measure must be a measure of some level of performance and the performance must relate to material with which one already had some familiarity. The purpose of measuring intelligence, however, was not to have a measure of present achievement in some field or other, but to have some measure of potential achievement from which it might be possible to predict future success in a different field of endeavour. This object was related to the problem of transfer of training — of whether it is possible by training and by learning material in one field to improve one's performance in another field.

(iii) Transfer of Training

Transfer of training was the third major interest of the early educational experimenters. It was the great educational problem of the time, a centre of controversy in educational research and teaching during the period from 1900 to 1930.

By the end of the nineteenth century it was widely held that, because of a process of formal discipline or training, ability gained in dealing with one set of subject-matter was automatically applicable to any other field in which it might be required. To what extent was this true? Can we, by learning and exercising a skill on a particular subject, strengthen that skill as a whole, and make it available for other subjects and situations?

Confidence in formal training had a large influence on the school curriculum. Arithmetic and geometry taught with an emphasis on accuracy and logic, and Latin and modern languages grammatically based were the favoured subjects. Mathematics developed reasoning ability; languages, especially Latin, cultivated the memory and the habit of verbal accuracy. Thorndike well summed up the main points of the doctrine when he wrote: 'It is clear that the common view is that the words, accuracy, quickness, discrimination, memory, observation, attention, concentration, judgment, reasoning etc., stand for some real and elemental abilities which are the same no matter what material they work upon; that these elemental abilities are altered by special disciplines to a large extent; that they retain those alterations when turned to other

fields; that thus in a more or less mysterious way learning to do one thing well will make one do better things that in concrete appearance have absolutely no community with it.'[33]

Thorndike quoted examples of the prevailing attitude from statements by contemporary educators, e.g. Joseph Payne, the first professor of education in England, who held his chair at the College of Preceptors in London, wrote: 'Arithmetic ... if judiciously taught, involves a genuine mental discipline of the most valuable kind; ... it forms in the pupil habits of mental attention, argumentative sequence, absolute accuracy, and satisfaction in truth as a result, that do not seem to spring equally from the study of any other subject suitable to this elementary stage of instruction';[34] and Woodrow Wilson, then President of Princeton University and later to be President of the United States, declared: 'We speak of the "disciplinary studies" ... having in our thought the mathematics of arithmetic, elementary algebra and geometry, the Greek-Latin texts and grammars, the elements of English and of French or German... The mind takes fiber, facility, strength, adaptability, certainty of touch from handling them, when the teacher knows his art and their power.'[35]

(a) Research by Thorndike and Woodworth

The first substantial questioning of this view came from a research program undertaken by Thorndike and Woodworth, reported in three articles in 1901.[36] They tested a small number, between four and six, of their students at Columbia University in various mental functions, then trained them in some other functions until a certain amount of improvement was noted, and finally tested again their performance in the first set of functions. The functions investigated in that way were fairly simple matters of perception and discrimination in estimating areas,

---

[31] A.S. Otis (1886-1964), a graduate of Stanford University, worked with the U.S. army and war department, and subsequently the civil aeronautical department. He produced texts on educational measurement, and several widely used group tests of intelligence. For a summary of the early testing movement see Kathryn W. Linden & J.D. Linden, *Modern Mental Measurement: A Historical Perspective*, Houghton Mifflin, Boston, 1968; F.N. Freeman, *Mental Tests. Their History, Principles and Applications*, rev. edn, Harrap, London, 1938; P.E. Vernon, *Intelligence and Attainment Tests*, University of London Press, 1960.

[32] T.P. Nunn, *Education. Its Data and First Principles*, 2nd edn, Arnold, London, 1930, p. 126.

[33] E.L. Thorndike, *Educational Psychology*, Science Press, New York, 1903, p. 84.

[34] J. Payne, *Lectures on the Science and Art of Education*, Longmans Green, London, 1880, p. 262.

[35] Woodrow Wilson, 'Princeton for the nation's service', *Science*, 7 November 1902, p. 726.

[36] E.L. Thorndike and R.S. Woodworth, 'The Influence of Improvement in one Mental Function upon the Efficiency of Other Functions', *Psychological Review*, 8, 3, May 1901, pp. 247-61; 8, 4, July 1901, pp. 384-5; 8, 6, November 1901, pp. 553-64.

lengths, and weights, and in picking out letters or words in selected passages. For example, in one experiment the subjects practised marking the letters *e* and *s* in a number of selected passages. They were tested, before and after their training, for the accuracy and speed with which they marked words containing other combinations of two letters, mis-spelled words, and the capital letter *A* in a page of randomly arranged capital letters. Thorndike and Woodworth then compared the improvement between the first and last tests with the improvement made in the training sessions. If transfer of training was substantial and automatic, the gain between tests should have approximately equalled the gain in training. They found this to be far otherwise. Despite the close similarity of the test and the training tasks, transfer did not exceed 52 per cent in the most similar tasks, ranged down to zero for others, and in several instances was negative.

The researchers concluded that the experiments showed that: 'It is misleading to speak of sense discrimination, attention, memory, observation, accuracy, quickness etc., as multitudinous separate individual functions are referred to by any one of these words. These functions may have little in common. There is no reason to suppose that any general change occurs corresponding to the words "improvement of the attention", or "of the power of observation", or "of accuracy"...'

Improvement in any single mental function need not improve the ability in functions commonly called by the same name. It may injure it.

Improvement in any single mental function rarely brings about equal improvement in any other function, no matter how similar, for the working of every mental function-group is conditioned by the nature of the data in each particular case ...

'The general consideration of the cases of retention or of loss of practice occurs only where identical elements are concerned in the influencing and influenced function.'[37]

These experiments and the conclusions drawn from them had a considerable impact on the educational world, initiated a dispute that continued for many years, and generated a wide range of experimentation.

(b) Research on Transfer of Training, 1900-30's

Research on transfer of training until the end of the 1930's covered mainly four fields: memory, sensory discrimination, attitudes, and school subjects.[38]

Memory training was the target of many of the early experiments. Ebert and Meumann in 1904 at the University of Zurich assessed the effect of learning nonsense syllables on the efficiency of memorising other material such as numbers, geometrical forms, foreign language vocabu-

lary, poetry, and prose. Their results showed a considerable gain for all the kinds of memory examined in the final test.[39] The absence of a control group, however, made it difficult to assess how much of the gain could be attributed to transfer from the training program.

This methodological deficiency was remedied by Sleight in an extensive and careful series of experiments with twelve-year-old school children in England in 1911. Eighty-four pupils from three schools were divided by testing into four groups of approximately equal memorising ability. One group was trained in learning poetry, the second in arithmetical tables, the third in reproducing the thought content of prose passages, and the fourth, a control group, had no special training. In the final test on a wide range of materials, the trained groups showed only slight gains over the control group. Sleight concluded that: 'There appears to be no general memory improvement as a result of practice, nor any evidence for the hypothesis of a general memory function.'[40]

In 1927, however, Woodrow, by introducing an interesting variable into the pattern, obtained rather different results. He used three groups of university students: the 'training' group were given specific instruction and practice in various techniques of memorising, the 'practice' group were given practice with no instruction, the 'control' group had neither practice nor instruction. In the final tests the differences between the control and the practice groups was insignificant, the training group, on the other hand, showed a decidedly greater improvement than either of the other groups in every test. The issue in this experiment was not between memory practice and no memory practice, but between practice supported by intelligent teaching, and practice that was unenlightened. The experiment demonstrated that little transfer followed from unintelligent memory drill, but that considerable transfer occurred when general principles and techniques were applied.

In the area of *sensory discrimination*, a similar conclusion had been reached by Judd in 1908 in one of the earliest experiments on transfer with a motor skill. Judd reported rather sketchily on an investigation of the effect of an understanding of the principle of refraction upon learning to hit a target under water. He and Scholskow took two groups of fifth and sixth grade boys, giving to one group a full theoretical explanation of refraction, and leaving the other group to depend on their own

[37] E.L. Thorndike and R.S. Woodworth, *op.cit.*, 8, 3, May 1901, pp. 249-50.

[38] See particularly, W.B. Kolesnik, *Mental Discipline in Modern Education*, University of Wisconsin, Madison, 1962, pp. 30-61.

[39] E. Ebert & E. Meumann, 'Über einige Grundfragen der Psychologie der Übungsphänomene im Bereiche des Gedächtnisses', *Archiv f.d. ges. Psychol.*, IV, 1905, 1-232. This study was summarised in E. Meumann, *The Psychology of Learning*, trans. J. W. Baird, Appleton, New York, 1913, pp. 353-5.

[40] W.G. Sleight, 'Memory and Formal Training', *British Journal of Psychology*, iv, 1911, p. 455.

Table 4.1: Significant Transfer of Training Experiments, 1901-33.

Person	Date	Subject	Sample	Method	Results
Thorndike & Woodworth	1901	Perception & sensori-motor discrimination	4-6 university students	Two of T. & W..s many tests 1(a) with pieces of paper cut to various sizes and shapes, subjects were asked to estimate areas, (b) practised on similar material, and (c) then tested on original material 2(a) subjects were tested for speed and accuracy in marking certain letters, mis-spelled words, capital *A* in prepared passages, (b) practised in marking the letters *e* & *s* (c) retested on original material.	Gain between tests was much less than gain in training. Improvement in any single mental function need not improve ability in functions commonly called by the same name.
Memory					
Ebert & Meumann	1904	Memory	6 adults	Various types of memory tested, trained for 36 days on nonsense syllables, retested.	Every kind of memory was considerably improved.
Sleight	1911	Memory	84 pupils from 3 schools in 4 groups 12 y.o.	4 groups of equal memorising ability: 1st trained on poetry 2nd on arithmetic tables 3rd on prose content 4th control, no training. Final test on many materials	Only slight gains in training groups. No general memory improvement as result of practice.
Woodrow	1927	Memory	University students	1st group — instruction and practice in techniques 2nd group — practice but no instruction 3rd group — neither (control group) Final test.	Practice-with-instruction group ahead of others; no distinction between simple practice and control groups.
Sensory Discrimination					
Judd	reported in 1908	Perception	5th & 6th grade schoolboys	1st group — theoretical training in refraction 2nd group — no explanation. Required to hit target, underwater, with dart; practised at 12″ depth, tested at 4″ depth.	Group with theoretical training performed better.
Wang	1916	Sensori-motor discrimination	Small number of school pupils	Trained in discriminating lengths of vertical lines; tested ability in other fields, e.g. pitch, shades of colour.	Transfer only if pupil could develop an efficient method and generalise it.

Person	Date	Subject	Sample	Method	Results
Attitudes					
Mrs Squire	1904	Neatness & accuracy	3rd grade elem. school pupils	Trained in neatness and accuracy in arithmetic	Neatness not transferred to language work.
Ruediger	1908	Neatness	7th grade school pupils	1 of 3 classes given conscious training in neatness in arithmetic and as ideal in life	Neatness as ideal transferred to other subjects.
School Subjects					
Winch	1910	Skill in arithmetic	School children	Test in problem-solving, practice in computation, retest	No transfer of skill in computation to skill in problem solving, but when principles stressed, transfer occurred.
Briggs	1913	English grammar, logical reasoning	9th grade school pupils, large sample	1 group trained on grammar for 6 months, 2nd group studied language and composition; 54 tests of reasoning	No improvement by 1st group over 2nd group.
Whelden	1933	Effect of Latin on quality of academic work	Yale university students	Analysis of student records	No support for view of Latin as a superior intellectual discipline.
Thorndike	1922-3 (repeated 1925-6; repeated by Wesman 1945)	Disciplinary value of various high school subjects	8,564 high school pupils	Intelligence tests given at a 12 months' interval; Test gains were related to subjects studied by pupils	Transfer not nearly as important as native intelligence. Book-keeping, maths, and physical science most successful subjects.
Meredith	1923	Magnetism; consciousness of method	60 boys; 13-14 y.o.	3 groups matched in intelligence; test on ability to define in correct way 20 words A. control, no training B. discussion of definition of magnetism C. lessons on principles of definition, Retest on alternate list of words	A & B same; C showed a marked gain.

experience. The two groups practised throwing a small dart at a target twelve inches under water. In this session while all the boys were learning how to control the dart the two groups 'gave about the same results'. Then the twelve inches were reduced to four, and the difference between the groups was striking. The boys without theory were confused, and their errors were large and persistent; those with theory adjusted themselves very rapidly. Judd suggested that the greater success of those with a knowledge of the general theory showed that transfer depended on the extent to which experiences were consciously generalised.[41]

Again, in the sensori-motor field, Wang, a Chinese student of educational psychology at the University of Michigan, trained a small number of pupils in discriminating the lengths of vertical lines, and tested their ability to discriminate in other fields, e.g. pitch, shades of colour, and sizes of figures. He concluded that transfer occurred only when the children developed an efficient method in the training series, and generalised this sufficiently to use it in the test series.[42]

In the transfer of *attitudes*, Bagley in 1905 reported an experiment by Mrs Squire in which neatness and accuracy practised in arithmetic by third grade elementary school pupils did not transfer to language work.[43] Ruediger, soon after, extended this experiment by having the arithmetic teacher in one of the classes talk to the children about neatness as an ideal to be applied in the home and in daily life. Small gains from transfer appeared, leading Ruediger to conclude: 'Neatness made conscious as an ideal or aim in connection with only one school subject does function in other subjects.'[44]

In looking at *school subjects*, in relation to transfer of training, Winch, an English inspector of schools, who had been one of the first to tackle the problem in the classroom with studies on memory transfer, undertook, in 1910, several studies on aspects of arithmetic. He found that even though there was a high positive correlation between skill in computation and skill in problem-solving, skill developed through practice in computation did not transfer to skill in problem-solving. In a later study on reasoning, however, he found that when there was a conscious development of principles, for example, on the nature of reasoning in mathematics, there was considerable transfer to wider situations.[45]

In the teaching of English grammar, Briggs in 1913 carried out a careful and extensive investigation to assess whether training in grammar should improve children's ability to see likenesses and differences in language forms, to apply definitions, to seek full evidence before drawing conclusions, to test reasons, and to use logical reasoning in other fields. He concluded that it did not.[46]

Arithmetic, grammar, and Latin were among the favourite discipli- nary vehicles. At the secondary school level, Latin especially was defended on disciplinary grounds. 'Far above every other subject,' wrote Gonzalez Lodge, a leading classicist whose Latin grammar was for many years an important source of reference for budding scholars, 'it trains (1) the process of observation, (2) the function of correct record, (3) reasoning power and general intelligence in correct inference from recorded observation. To this should be added its great value in developing the power of voluntary attention.'[47]

After World War I research on transfer continued along the lines already mapped out, and two or three notable and well-designed contributions were made which supported existing findings.

The study with the most bearing on Lodge's contentions was one by Whelden who, in 1933, investigated the effect of Latin on the quality of academic work done at Yale University; it was a well-conceived, carefully controlled, and statistically sophisticated piece of work. Whelden concluded that, taking Latin and other subjects as currently taught, there was no support for a view of Latin 'as an intellectual discipline serving to extend the scope of intellectual capacity in whatever field it might be applied'.[48]

Thorndike, meanwhile, had entered the lists again with an extensive study in 1922-23, nearly a quarter of a century after his initial study. This was repeated in 1925-26, and followed up by Wesman in 1945 with similar conclusions in each case. Thorndike gave a battery of intelligence tests to

[41] C.H. Judd, 'The Relation of special Training to General Intelligence', *Educational Review*, 36, June 1908, pp. 28-42. An attempt to repeat Judd's experiment was made in a Cincinnati school some thirty-four years later, in 1941. The results were somewhat hilarious. The dart used by the boys bounced off the water, rippling obscured the target and slowed the experiment to a snail's pace, and the boys just couldn't throw a dart accurately. The experiment was eventually undertaken with an air-gun, and the results were rather less striking than might have been anticipated on Judd's report. It was found that the theoretical group did best at all stages, but the differences between the groups was small, and the variation among individuals considerable. G. Hendrickson & W.H. Schroeder, 'Transfer of Training in Learning to Hit a Submerged Target', *Journal of Educational Psychology*, 32, 1941, pp. 205-13.

[42] C.P. Wang, *The General Value of Visual Sense Training in Children*, Educational Psychology Monographs, No. 15, 1916.

[43] W. C. Bagley, *The Educative Process*, Macmillan, New York, 1905, p. 208.

[44] W.C. Ruediger, 'The Indirect Improvement of Mental Functions through Ideals,' *Educational Review* 36, 1908, pp. 364-71.

[45] W.H. Winch, 'Accuracy in School Children. Does improvement in numerical accuracy transfer?' *Educational Review*, 2, 1911, pp. 262-72; 'The Transfer of Improvement in Reasoning in School Children', *British Journal of Psychology*, XIII, 1923.

[46] T.H. Briggs, 'Formal English Grammar as a Discipline', *Teachers College Record* 14, September 1913.

[47] P. Monroe (ed.), *Principles of Secondary Education*, Macmillan, New York, 1914, p. 388.

[48] C.H. Whelden, 'Training in Latin and the quality of other academic work', *Journal of Educational Psychology*, October 1933, p. 497.

8,564 high school pupils in May 1922 and again a year later, and analysed the gains made during the year. By relating them through an elaborate statistical procedure to the subjects studied during the course of the year, he was able to assess the contribution made by each subject to the traits measured by the intelligence tests. Bookkeeping, mathematics, and the physical sciences did well in comparison with Latin and French which were rated about equal with physical education and slightly above English and history; dramatic art and the biological sciences came off least well. The amount of transfer, however, from any subject was small. The transfer gains, in Thorndike's view, played such a small role when compared with the contribution of native intelligence that he concluded that: 'If our inquiry had been carried out by a psychologist from Mars, who knew nothing of theories of mental discipline, and simply tried to answer the question "What are the amounts of influence of sex, race, age, amount of ability, and studies taken, upon the gain made during the year in power to think?" ... he might even dismiss "studies taken" with the comment: "The differences are so small and the unreliabilities are relatively so large that this factor seems unimportant." The chief reason why good thinkers in the past seem to have been made such by the school subjects they have taken is that good thinkers have taken such subjects. When the good thinkers studied Latin and Greek, these studies seemed to make good thinking ... If the abler pupils should all study Physical Education and Dramatic Art, these subjects would seem to make good thinkers. These were, indeed, a large fraction of the program of studies for the best thinkers the world has produced, the Athenian Greeks. After positive correlation of gain with initial ability is allowed for, the balance in favor of any study is certainly not large.'[49]

At about the same time, a well-designed study on consciousness of method as a means of transfer of training was conducted by Meredith on a group of thirteen to fourteen year old pupils in England. Meredith matched three groups of twenty boys in intelligence, and tested them on their ability to define in a correct and formal way twenty words in everyday use. Group A became the control group without special training, Group B was given three lessons on elementary magnetism which included a discussion on the definition of a magnet. Group C was given similar lessons to which the form and principles of making definitions were added. All groups were then retested in defining a second list of twenty words. Meredith found that there was no significant difference in the performance of Groups A and B in the tests at the beginning and end of the study, but that Group C showed a marked gain in the final test. He concluded that when science was taught so that pupils became conscious of the methods they were expected to use in defining scientific terms, this training will transfer to the definition of ordinary terms.[50]

(c) **Review of Research on Transfer of Training**

Orata in 1928 reviewed the ninety-nine transfer experiments that he could find up to that date, and subsequently in 1935 and 1941 published further reviews.[51] He showed clearly that the evidence from the studies was conflicting. It is clear that there were two reasons for this. In the first place much of the research was badly done. Hamley remarked somewhat mildly in 1939, 'On reviewing the literature on this subject one is struck by the dearth of well-planned and carefully executed research.'[52] Many of the researchers used too small a sample and too short a time-span, many confined their investigations to adults in a laboratory situation, many lacked adequate control groups, and most of them had an inadequate grasp of the appropriate statistical procedures. As an exercise in scientific educational research, the studies in transfer of training were, for the most part, academic disasters. In the second place, the various studies were attempting to answer different questions. There were four main problems:

1. *Does transfer of training take place?* Overwhelmingly the answer was, yes. Orata estimated that in over eighty per cent of the researches published up to the time of his survey in 1927 there was evidence of at least appreciable transfer. Even when the questionable studies were eliminated there was still a considerable body of good evidence to show that transfer of some kind did take place. Indeed, it is difficult to conceive how, without transfer of training, education even in its narrowest sense can take place. The important question, therefore, was to what extent knowledge, skills, and attitudes could be generalised without conscious effort being taken to this end. Hence question 2.

2. *Does transfer of training take place without deliberate intent on the part of the teacher?* Clearly the answer was, no or hardly at all. This was the question to which Thorndike and Woodworth had directed their attention in their original investigation. For the sensori-motor field they had given an unmistakably negative answer. In this they were supported by

[49] E.L. Thorndike, 'Mental discipline in high school studies', *Journal of Educational Psychology*, 15, 1, January 1924, pp. 1-22; *ibid.*, 15, 2, February 1924, pp. 83-98.

[50] G.P. Meredith, 'Consciousness of Method as a Means of Transfer of Training', *The Forum of Education*, V. 1, February 1927, pp. 37-45.

[51] P.T. Orata. *The Theory of Identical Elements*, Ohio State University Press, Columbus, 1928; 'Transfer of Training and Educational Pseudoscience,' *Mathematics Teacher*, 28 (1935) pp. 266-7; 'Recent Research Studies in Transfer of Training with Implications for the Curriculum, Guidance and Personnel Work', *Journal of Educational Research*, 35 (1941), pp. 81-2.

[52] Great Britain, Board of Education, *Report of the Consultative Committee on Secondary Education with special reference to Grammar Schools and Technical High Schools* (Spens Report) HMSO, London, 1939, H.R. Hamley, Memorandum on the Cognitive Aspects of Transfer of Training, Appendix V, p. 444.

Sleight's work in memorising, by Briggs and Whelden in the subject fields of English grammar and Latin, and eventually by Thorndike's massive study of all high school studies. It was this work that disposed of the disciplinary claims of various subject specialists. It appeared that any subject, suitably taught, could probably provide as good mental discipline as any other, and good teaching could deliberately insure as general a transfer of intellectual skills from it as from any other subject. The principal interest of educational researchers, therefore, from as early as Judd's and Ruediger's studies in 1908, was in trying to establish the conditions under which transfer takes place.

3. *Under what conditions does transfer of training best occur?* The work by Woodrow on techniques of memorising, Wang on method of sensory discriminating, Judd on theorising in the sensori-motor field, Ruediger on the generalising of neatness, and Winch and Meredith on the conscious development of general principles of reasoning and defining in mathematics and science were indications of the way in which transfer could be consciously encouraged in teaching. It appeared from these studies that when there was a conscious formulation of principles of organisation or procedures, or when there was an emphasis on building desirable traits into ideals, there was a good possibility of wider transfer. Burt summed up the position well in 1930 in a report to the British Association: 'Transfer of improvement occurs only when there are *common usable elements,* shared both by the activity used for the training and also by the activity in which the results of the training reappear. The "common elements" may be elements of (i) material, (ii) method, (iii) ideal; they are most "usable" when they are conscious. A common element is more likely to be usable if the learner becomes clearly conscious of its nature and of its general applicability: active or deliberate transfer is far more effective and frequent than passive, automatic or unintentional transfer. This seems especially true when the common element is an element of method rather than of material, an ideal rather than a piece of information.'[53] If these seem to be the conditions under which transfer occurs, what then can be said about the transfer process itself?

4. *What is the nature of transfer? What happens in the transfer process?* Thorndike suggested in his earliest paper, and maintained thereafter that transfer takes place through identical elements. A change in one mental function alters another only in so far as the second function shares a common element with the first. In Thorndike's view all abilities were individual and specific; mind, for him, was a convenient name for a collection of countless special operations. You train one or several of these, but never a faculty or function in general, such as memory in general, or reasoning in general, or neatness in general. The process of transfer, therefore, 'consists in doing over again what we have learned to do before

except that it is part of another situation'. What are the common factors or identical elements through which transfer may take place? Thorndike regarded them as associations involving facts which may be common to two or more situations, and associations about aims, methods, and general principles. Orata objected to this theory on the ground that it was not a theory of transfer at all: there is nothing transferred, it simply explains transfer away. He regarded it as part of Thorndike's mechanistic view of intelligence, which, in effect, cannot account for intelligent behaviour. Orata suggested that the essence of transfer was to be found in the detaching of meanings from one situation and the application of them to another. This is consonant with Judd's explanation of transfer as the generalisation of experience.

Judd's theory, the principal rival of Thorndike's, was expressed in connection with his early work on transfer in 1908, and it was reinforced by the kind of experimentation that Ruediger, Woodrow, Winch, and Meredith did. The teacher's task is to establish general modes of thought and action in every possible way, and it is through this constant press for generalising that transfer takes place. He was critical both of Thorndike's over-particularism, and of the subject-specialists' over-inflated claims. 'If there is anyone,' he wrote, 'who asserts that mathematics or Latin or science will train the general powers of discrimination or observation or reasoning, that person is wrong. If, on the other hand, anyone asserts that all training is particular, that the mind is made up of many independent special modes of thinking, that person is just as wrong as his opponent... It is not far from the truth to assert that any subject taught with a view to training pupils in methods of generalisation is highly useful as a source of mental training and that any subject which emphasises particular items of knowledge and does not stimulate generalisation is educationally barren.'[54]

If generalisation can be regarded as the conscious recognition of common elements — facts, ideas, procedures, attitudes — in as many situations as possible, the two approaches to the problem of transfer may be reconciled. This is what they both implied in practice. It is doubtful, however, whether their supporters would have accepted the reconciliation in theory. Each fundamentally stemmed from a different view of the nature of intelligence: Thorndike's an atomistic connectionism, Judd's somewhat closer to the Gestaltists.

After the 1930's experimentation which previously, for the most part, had stemmed from the practical needs of the classroom teacher, became

[53] C. Burt, *Formal Training,* Report of a committee appointed by the British Association and presented at Bristol in 1930, pp. 3-4, quoted in H.R. Hamley, *op.cit.,* pp. 446-7.

[54] C.H. Judd, *Psychology of Secondary Education,* Ginn, Boston, 1927, pp. 432-3.

the interest of psychologists of various theoretical persuasions. Henceforth the work became much more technical in nature, and much more interested in the mechanism of the transfer process and its relation to aspects of current research on learning theory. Since the early 1940's little of the research had any direct reference to the schoolroom, or was interpreted and applied in practice by teachers.

ACHIEVEMENTS OF EARLY EDUCATIONAL RESEARCH

What was achieved by the educational researchers in the early part of the century? Despite much triviality and inaccuracy they did manage to offer useful, if not definitive, empirically researched answers on problems of classification, transfer, and methods of teaching, and they steadily improved the design of experimentation and the statistical techniques used in educational research. In that way they made a considerable practical contribution to education.

But beyond that, they had a more pervasive effect. Their work reinforced the new education, the progressive, activity education that developed in the early years of the century and left a lasting deposit on twentieth century thinking and practice in education. Most of the leaders in the scientific movement wrote in support of progressive education and were associated with some aspect of it. Both by their research and their public advocacy they did much to promote the eventual development of the 'made to measure' school.

In a more general sense, too, their work ensured that future educational discussions could not be adequately held without taking account of or searching for all the available empirical evidence appropriate to the question being considered. They made it impossible for anyone to talk intelligently about educational theory without taking into account the findings of empirical educational research.

They did not succeed in making education wholly into a science. They did, however, demonstrate that much of the data of education could be usefully quantified, and that most of the problems of education were susceptible to objective analysis and perhaps experimental research. And they did ensure that the scientific methods which they pioneered would be expanded and applied in future educational studies.

Cecil Reddie (1858-1932), founder of Abbotsholme.

CHAPTER 5

PROGRESSIVE EDUCATORS
BEFORE WORLD WAR I

SUMMARY

The Nature of Progressive Education

Spread of Progressive Education

Developing the Deweyan Tradition in the U.S.A.
  (i)   Francis W. Parker School
  (ii)   Marietta Johnson (1864-1938)
  (iii) Schools of Tomorrow

The Progressive Country Boarding Schools of Europe
  (i)   Abbotsholme and Bedales
  (ii)   Landerziehungsheime
  (iii) The Contribution of the Progressive Country
         Boarding Schools

European Progressive Educators
  (i)   Marie Montessori (1870-1952)
  (ii)   Georg Kerschensteiner (1854-1932)
  (iii) Ovide Decroly (1871-1932)
  (iv)   The Trend of Montessori's, Kerschensteiner's and
         Decroly's Work

THE NATURE OF PROGRESSIVE EDUCATION

One of the characteristics of the twentieth century has been the constant effort to develop new forms, new methods, and new content in education that would be appropriate to the demands of the new era. Among educators the consciousness of living in challenging times and the desire to make a new start were strong. Many of them saw the early twentieth century as a period of more rapid material and social change, a period in which scientific thinking would assume a great importance, a period in which communication and co-operation among mankind would be more highly developed, and, above all, a period in which there would be much greater opportunity for all human beings to get satisfaction from their life and to express themselves more freely and more humanely.

The new education, therefore, was to be re-designed to produce people who could take full advantage of the coming opportunities, people who were aware of rapid social change, the importance of scientific thinking, the facilitation of communication and co-operation, and the new opportunities for the expression of humanity.

Current educational practices and ideas were referred to as the old education and came under severe criticism. The new educators mounted their protest on four main grounds.

It was a protest against intellectualism, against the schools' over-concern with mental cultivation. The new educators were interested in intellectual development, especially in encouraging their pupils to solve problems and to learn to use scientific methods, but they were concerned also with educating a whole person, a person of feeling, taste, responsibility, and thought, and they objected to a one-sided emphasis on intellectual performance. It was a protest about the relevance of the traditional school's program. The new educators held that existing school curricula had very little connection with the needs of a technological society and provided inadequate preparation for a possible democratic society of the future; there was little in the school programs about current society, small encouragement to study science, and almost no opportunity to practise the skills and activities characteristic of life in the twentieth century. It was a protest against the inflexibility of existing schools. The desks for listening, that Dewey found so difficult to replace with furniture suitable for working, were symbolic of the inflexibility of the school in its administration, its organisation, its pupil-teacher relationships, its curriculum, and its examinations. It was immensely difficult to break through the hard cake of custom in the schools, and yet among the new educators, there were those who thought that not only should the school be responsive to social change, it should also be a leader of change. Finally, it was a protest against the deadening effect that schools had on the pupils' spirit. In a widely read book, a converted inspector of schools in England, Edmond Holmes, condemned the practice of shepherding the pupil along the 'path of mechanical obedience'. 'The aim of his teachers,' he wrote, 'is to leave nothing to his nature, nothing to his spontaneous life, nothing to his free activity; to repress all his natural impulses; to drill his energies into complete quiescence; to keep his whole being in a state of sustained and painful tension...Blind, passive, literal, unintelligent obedience is the basis on which the whole system of Western education has been reared'.[1] The preference of schoolmasters for routine and conformity rather than ingenuity and spontaneity irked the new generation who looked to provide their pupils with rich and widening opportunities to express themselves.

In protesting against those things — the over-intellectualism, the lack of relevance, the inflexibility, and the deadening effect of existing education — the progressives helped to establish a climate suitable for reform, and gave themselves the task of putting into practice alternate new ways of educating that would compensate for the defects of the old.

The progressive movement, however, was much more than a protest movement. It was a creative educational effort by thoughtful, sensitive, adventurous men and women, alive to the importance of their calling and dedicated to its improvement. Nothing like it had ever previously occurred in the history of education. The progressive movement was an effort by many educators in many countries to come to grips with their perception that the new world of the twentieth century was causing substantial changes in social organisation and in human relations, and that education in these circumstances had a new dimension and importance.

The progressives felt moved not merely to analyse and argue about the current situation, but also to act so as eventually to bring it under control. The instrument of adjustment was education. Education was seen as a process of many-faceted growth both for individuals and for societies. The century of the child that Ellen Key proclaimed meant that the extent and direction of both an individual's and a society's growth were limited by the style and extent of the education available. The progressives did not all agree on what was the most suitable kind of education. Each made his own characteristic contribution, sometimes spiced with quaint fads, sometimes innocent of practicalities, but always with dedication and self-sacrifice. Not all of the progressives, of course, were saints, though some in hostile environments came close to being martyrs.

Early in the movement Adolphe Ferrière founded the International Bureau of New Schools in 1899 to act as a documentation centre. By 1913 he had one hundred schools on the register, and two years later he essayed a definition: 'The new school is, above all, a country boarding school with a family atmosphere, a place where the personal experience of the child is the foundation both of intellectual education, which is developed particularly in association with manual work, and of moral education through pupil self-government.'[2] Ferrière aptly characterised an important group of new schools, the progressive country boarding schools, whose development had been the most substantial achievement by the European progressives in the early years of the movement. Progressive education, however, was wider and more radical than that view of it. The definition was already out of date when Ferrière formulated it. The type of school which he described, while providing more up-to-date and more humane education than most of its contemporaries, did not always incorporate the central ideas of the new educators which made them vital and important contributors to twentieth century civilisation. Subsequently, in writing his book on the activity school, he came to realise this.

Meanwhile Claparède, his colleague in Geneva, pointed out that the heart of the new education was to be found in the process with which it was concerned; this was the activity process. *L'école active* was the name coined by Pierre Bovet for the school which expressed it. In Germany it was known as the *Arbeitsschule*, and sometimes the *Tatschule*;[3] in the English-speaking world it was the activity school.

Writing in 1912, Claparède suggested that the new approach to education was characterised primarily by the 'replacement of passive obedience by the activity and initiative of the child', and that this implied the use of teaching methods based on a psychological study of child development, the encouragement of co-operative work, and the organisation of schools along democratic lines with an opportunity for pupil self-government.[4] A few years later he summed up his perception of the activity school in an essay in which he described it as 'functional education'. Needs, pupil's and society's, are the basis of the educational process; they give rise to and are expressed in interest which leads to the pursuit of the knowledge that is concerned with the satisfaction of the

---

[1] E. Holmes, *What is and What Might Be*, Constable, London, 1911, p. 48.

[2] A. Ferrière, *L'Ecole Nouvelle et le Bureau International des Ecoles Nouvelles*, 3rd edn, Les Pléiades sur Blonay, Vaud, 1919, p. 3

[3] E. Claparède, *L'Education Functionnelle*, Delachaux et Niestlé, Neuchâtel, 1931, p. 153, refers to Bovet, the first director of the Jean-Jacques Rousseau Institute of Geneva as the originator of the term *'école active'*. W. Lay, one of the German pioneers of the scientific study of education, wrote a widely studied book, *Die Tatschule*, Zickfeldt, Leipzig, 1911.

[4] E. Claparède, *L'Ecole sur Mesure*, new edn, Delachaux et Niestlé, Neuchâtel, 1953, p. 83.

needs. Knowledge acquired in this way is functional; it is not knowledge for its own sake, it is knowledge for the sake of solving a problem or building a machine or for some other purpose. Its acquisition is an active process, and it forms the basis for the further activity of achieving and expressing the satisfaction of the need. The activity school, then, involves felt needs, interest, functional knowledge, and expression. Together they form a chain of purposeful activity.[5]

Claparède's American contemporary, W.H. Kilpatrick, described a characteristic product of the American progressive education movement, the project method, in very similar terms. The project was an activity that evolved out of and gave practical and popular expression to John Dewey's view that education was the continuing 'reconstruction of experience'. When, in 1924, Boyd Bode tried to analyse the meaning of the activity school,[6] he thought that it was essentially a new view of the learning process and was best summed up in that phrase of Dewey's. It implied a view consonant with that of Claparède who frequently acknowledged his affinity with Dewey. Education was a process of living by developing and redeveloping one's needs and interests and expressing oneself intelligently and sensitively in an active and productive relationship with others. This was the kernel of the activity school idea.

The insistence by the progressives on looking at needs and developing pupils' interest was another form of their view that education should be relevant to twentieth century conditions. They did not all have the same sense of what was relevant, nor did they have a common emphasis. Two principal tendencies stood out; these were represented by the community-centred and the child-centred educators respectively.

Those who started by considering the needs of the community, by thinking of the kind of national or world society that was possible and desirable, and by giving importance to the kinds of human, political, and economic relations that they wished to foster, developed schools which encouraged co-operation, altruism, internationalism, group life, and an interest in social studies. Those, on the other hand, whose ideas and practices arose out of a conviction that individual freedom was the most important part of human life, developed schools in which there was a minimum of prescription, where self-expression, individual initiative, and an absence of curriculum prescription were the fashion. Those were the child-centred schools, the products of what in Germany was known as the movement *vom Kinde aus*. Most progressive schools were neither wholly one nor wholly the other. They mixed their intentions and their practices; they were interested in both community and individual development, emphasising the one or the other in varying degrees.

In short, the education that was called progressive, tended: in content to emphasise the nature of current society and the needs of the society and the individuals within it; in method, to involve each individual in problem-solving and actual experiencing; and, in organisation, to foster self-government and community living. Those were the cardinal features of the new education, matching as far as was conceivable the progressives' general sensitivity about the new era and the new society that was coming into being.

The progressive movement aroused immense enthusiasm among its adherents. It was an enthusiasm born of the conviction that they were engaged upon important work, and a buoyancy tinged with a somewhat utopian expectation that their venture could really succeed in producing a new order in education and, perhaps, a new approach to human living. Ferrière caught this spirit when he wrote: 'It is more than a reform, it is a transformation. A new spirit is abroad in the world; the old traditional school with its substructure of routine, its walls of prejudice, and its roof of social conformity, will not be able to resist it.

'In its place will be constructed a vaster edifice, founded on scientific knowledge, refined by experience; and some day we shall perhaps see men who no longer hate the school of their childhood days, for in it they will have learned health of body, harmony of spirit, and enrichment of mind.'[7]

And the German author and schoolmaster, Adolf Rude, proclaimed: 'The new school is on the way; it is coming; it must and will come! And it will bring salvation to our people.'[8]

SPREAD OF PROGRESSIVE EDUCATION

The movement had no geographical centre. In its earliest years, in the 1890's, it was most prominent in England and the United States; after the turn of the century, Germany, and subsequently Italy, Belgium, France, and Switzerland made substantial contributions. In the beginning a progressive education movement developed towards the end of the nineteenth century simultaneously and independently in both Europe and the U.S.A. Two separate traditions emerged, which began to meet and mix from about 1910 on.

In Europe the movement began with the establishment of progressive country boarding schools, first in England and subsequently in other

---

[5] E. Claparède, *L'Education Fonctionnelle*, pp. 150-64, 'La Psychologie de l'école active'. This article first appeared in *L'Intermédiare des Educateurs*, 97, 13 December 1923.

[6] National Society for the Study of Education, *The Thirty-Third Yearbook, Part II, The Activity Movement*, Public School Publishing Co., Bloomington, 1934, pp. 78-81.

[7] A. Ferrière, *The Activity School*, trans. F.D. Moore and F.C. Wooton, Day, New York, 1927, pp. 13-14.

[8] W. Flitner & G. Kudritzki (edd.), *Die Deutsche Reformpädagogik*, Düsseldorf, Küpper, 1962, Bd. 2, p. 233. A. Rude was a teacher, educational administrator, and author of books and articles on teaching method widely read in the 1920's.

countries. The leaders were practical teachers interested in a curriculum and in a pattern of behaviour for their pupils more relevant to the times. In some of the more democratically-minded schools in England, Germany, and Switzerland, wider opportunities were eventually developed for individual self-fulfilment, and ideas emerged on cultural and social reform. In the U.S.A., by the turn of the century, Dewey had been involved in educational experiment and had begun to develop a body of systematic educational theory. He found a sympathetic fellow-worker in F.W. Parker who had a reputation as an innovator and whose books had had a wide readership. Parker's ideas and his supporters were readily absorbed, after his death in 1902, into the Deweyan stream, and in the early twentieth century it was Dewey's theory and practice that appeared best able to meet the conditions of the time and provide a comprehensive basis for the reconstruction of education. Individuals such as Flora Cooke and Marietta Johnson, while pursuing their own particular educational preferences, worked within the broad framework of Dewey's ideas and contributed through the reputation of their schools to the strengthening of the Deweyan tradition among progressive educators in the U.S.A.

Meanwhile, in Europe, progressive educators such as Decroly and Kerschensteiner, outside the country boarding school tradition, were putting forward and experimenting with ideas similar to those of Dewey whose works were beginning to find an audience among European readers. By World War I there was a substantial degree of communication among progresssive European educators. There was also a general realisation that, whether they were within country boarding schools, state elementary schools, kindergartens or special experimental schools, they were working on the same problems, that there was a common social and pedagogical content to their work, and that there was a substantial community of ideas and practices among them.

The growing sense of shared involvement in a common educational campaign led eventually to the formation in 1921 of the New Education Fellowship.

Transatlantic contacts were developed by visits, correspondence, and the spread of publications. By World War I the Deweyan approach was well known to many European progressives, and was accepted, in many of its features, by leaders such as Claparède, Decroly, Otto, Natorp and Kerschensteiner as a basic and systematic statement of progressive educational theory. The two movements, by that stage, had thus come to share a range of common experiences and to have developed a varied but sufficiently common platform for them to be regarded as part of a single international movement.

In the subsequent period, between World War I and World War II, the influence of progressive education spread more widely still, the U.S.S.R. during the 1920's, the United States, and the United Kingdom

providing the most fertile ground; and the two associations of progressive teachers, the New Education Fellowship which held periodical conferences in various European countries, and the Progressive Education Association in the U.S.A., tended to become focal points.

The first period, up to World War I, before the movement became general, was characterised by the activities and ideas of several outstanding individuals or interesting innovative schools. In Europe, the progressive country boarding schools, stemming from Cecil Reddie's foundation of Abbotsholme, gave a definitive start to the movement. The possibilities subsequently offered to progressive teachers in the first two decades of the century can then best be seen by looking in detail at the contributions of the three outstanding innovators of the period, Maria Montessori, Georg Kerschensteiner, and Ovide Decroly. In the United States, John Dewey was of central importance,[9] and the growing impact of his and similar ideas was illustrated in the work of the Francis W. Parker School in Chicago, and of Marietta Johnson in Fairhope, Alabama.

DEVELOPING THE DEWEYAN TRADITION IN THE U.S.A.

(i) Francis W. Parker School

'Colonel Parker,' according to John Dewey, 'more nearly than any other one person was the father of the progressive educational movement.'[10] Parker had first shown his remarkable ability as superintendent of schools at Quincy, Massachusetts, from 1875 to 1880. His Quincy schools became widely known for their unconventional methods and for their undoubted success. In 1883 he became principal of the Cook County Normal School in Chicago, and remained there until 1901, developing in the 1890's a friendship with John Dewey to whom 'he turned over the philosophy of the new education'.[11] At Chicago he was able to formulate his ideas more

9 See above, Chapter 3.

10 J. Dewey, 'How much freedom in new schools', *The New Republic*, 9 July 1930, p. 204. F.W. Parker (1837-1902) started his career as a country schoolmaster in New Hampshire, took part in the Civil War, was discharged as a colonel, and returned to schoolteaching. He travelled in Europe and studied pedagogy in Berlin. From 1875 to 1880 he was superintendent of schools at Quincy, Mass., then at Boston and from 1883 to 1901 was principal of the Cook County Normal School in Chicago. For the year before his death in 1902 he was head of the School of Education of the University of Chicago. He published two widely read books *Talks on Teaching* (1883), and *Talks on Pedagogics* (1894).

11 J.K. Campbell, *Colonel Francis W. Parker: The Children's Crusader*, Teachers College, Columbia University, New York, 1967, p. 146.

systematically, and see them in action in the practice school; he was able, also, to train a wide band of enthusiastic and talented teachers who spread his ideas and his spirit to many parts of the United States. His ideas were continued in some measure in the Francis W. Parker School that came into being in 1901, and for the next thirty-three years was under the direction of one of his leading disciples, Flora J. Cooke.

Parker's contribution was a fourfold one. He insisted that the child should be the centre round which the school's work was planned. Secondly, the child's development should take place in a warm community atmosphere, where there was a constant and united effort 'for the upbuilding of democracy'.[12] Thirdly, the school curriculum should arise as far as possible out of practical activities, e.g. from geography excursions, observations of nature, readers made by the children; and the activities in the curriculum should be interrelated by being built around broad strands that straddled several conventional subjects. Parker was very much interested in a sort of Herbartian concentration which put nature study, geography, and history at the centre of the program. Finally, he had an immense interest in encouraging expressive work through art, literature, and physical movement; his teachers and their pupils developed great enthusiasm for creative art work, which permeated the whole school program and reached a high level both in individual work and in the production of school pageants, plays, and dances.

The Francis W. Parker School under Flora J. Cooke followed a pattern in which both Parker's and Dewey's ideas could be found together in a harmonious blend. The school, in its methods, emphasised:

- Interest: 'Interest is the root law of attention and educative effort,' wrote Flora J. Cooke in reviewing the school's work in 1912.[13] Interest was the spur which urged pupils on to work hard, and their interests were the best starting point through which to develop worthwhile activities. It was the teachers' constant function to see that old interests evolved into new interests on an even higher plane.

- Social activity: Wherever possible the pupils worked together for the benefit of the group or the larger community. They designed and made school curtains together, they compiled a history of Chicago as a group, and, above all, they took part in a communal morning exercise in which all the school came together for common activities when, among other things, the high school pupils would attempt an exercise for the whole school, such as making some aspects of current events intelligible to the younger children or explaining to them the proportion of different gases that make up the air.

- Task oriented learning: The school controlled the direction and pace of learning by setting a list of minimum requirements from first through to eighth grade in the basic tool subjects such as English and mathematics, a practice that Washburne, one of Parker's students, was later to develop more systematically at Winnetka. In their work the pupils proceeded from task to task or problem to problem. This meant that the work in various subjects would be integrated round a particular task, and the basic English or mathematical knowledge would be taught and, if need be, drilled, as the need for it arose in connection with the wider task. For example, in working on the history of Chicago, the third grade pupils had the task of reconstructing the Chicago of a hundred years earlier; it involved work in science in studying swamp life and the making of candles and the use of gas as a fuel, work in geography through mapmaking and excursions to the dunes and the harbour, work in English in writing up their findings and recreating stories about pioneer life, and various kinds of hand work in making wheels, rollers, ox carts and other forms of early transportation.

The school was 'attempting the difficult task of training human beings into freedom coupled with responsibility'.[14] It showed the union of child development and community service, the regard for interest and relevance in the curriculum, and the use of activity and expressive work, that were characteristic of well-rounded progressive schools.

(ii)   Marietta Johnson (1864-1938)

In 1902 C.H. Henderson, a gentle, erudite, and thoughtful teacher, wrote a book suggesting the need for an 'organic education' which would aim to develop the whole human organism with all its sensory, physical, intellectual, and social powers towards the perfection of life and culture 'which is the most abiding impulse of the human spirit'.[15] Marietta Johnson was immensely influenced by Henderson's work which aptly expressed the aspirations of humane and thoughtful educators who were dissatisfied with current society and the education which served it, and looked forward to the possibility of developing higher and fuller levels of

[12] F.W. Parker, *Talks on Pedagogics*, Barnes, New York, 1894, p. 421.

[13] Flora J. Cooke, 'Colonel Francis W. Parker as interpreted through the work of the Francis W. Parker School,' *The Elementary School Teacher*, 12, 9, May 1912, 407.

[14] *ibid.*, 419.

[15] Charles H. Henderson, *Education and the Larger Life*, Houghton Mifflin, Boston, 1902, p. 97.

human behaviour through a more widely based organic education. She was at that time an experienced public elementary and high school teacher concerned with teacher training, interested in Dewey's work, and critical of contemporary public schools.

In 1907 she founded a private school, the School of Organic Education, at Fairhope, Alabama, which Dewey later described in very favourable terms.[16] Starting with young elementary school children, the school eventually embraced a full range of elementary and secondary students. She remained with the school for the next thirty years, lecturing on her views each summer in teacher training courses in New England, helping in several branch schools in various parts of the United States, and gradually building a substantial reputation for her ideas and her school.

The quality of life rather than material achievement was, in Marietta Johnson's view, the concern of education. To improve the quality of life, it was necessary to try to produce a better person. This, she hoped, could be done consciously and deliberately through improved education.

The kind of education that was needed was one which ministered to the growing child, which did not prepare him for a remote adulthood, which did not restrict his natural growth, which regarded him as important in himself at his own unique stage of human development, and which acted on the principle that 'childhood is for childhood'.[17] This was an organic education. It had four principal features:

- Needs: We should start by asking at all stages of education, What are the needs of the children? By first seeking their needs and then devising a program to satisfy them, the new school aimed to foster the children's natural growth. Closely associated with needs are interests. Like the Herbartians, Marietta Johnson regarded interest as a vital factor in education. It was not a matter of trying to make previously concocted material interesting to the pupils, but rather a matter of seeking out the material in which the children were already interested and building on it in interesting ways. Need and interest produce concentrated, well disciplined, and creative work.

- Activity: School is a place to work. 'All schools should be workshops,' Marietta Johnson wrote,[18] but there is a difference between the worker and the labourer. The worker is artistic, gets joy and satisfaction from his activity, and sets his own standards of excellence. He is a creative person. The Fairhope school was an activity school in which the work was to involve the full energy and resource of each pupil and was to be a creative experience, one 'in which the work attracts, which grows under one's attention and,

then, when the end is reached, gives us an inner satisfaction and a consciousness of power'.[19]

- Discipline: A well-educated child was a well-disciplined child. Ministering to the children's growth did not mean that the children should do as they please. Children had to grow through childhood in the way most advantageous to them. The teacher, therefore, had an important task to ensure that the children encountered the experiences that were best for them and that they did not, by lacking adequate guidance, suffer the consequences of their ignorance. Conformity and obedience were necessary, provided that they were part of a process that develops unselfishness, willing co-operation, and self-discipline. The school process should develop the whole human organism in a balanced and disciplined way.

- Social consciousness: The Fairhope school was co-educational because its founder thought that men and women should be accustomed from childhood to work together. Human beings she regarded as fundamentally and irretrievably social, though they might act in selfish and greedy ways. The school should therefore regard the development of appropriate social relations as one of its most important tasks. Human relations she described as the one great comprehensive art. It rested upon a highly developed social consciousness characterised by selflessness, open-mindedness, co-operativeness, and an ability to make creative rather than critical suggestions.

The Fairhope school was divided into life classes instead of regular grades, roughly equivalent to two- or three-year age groups from kindergarten to senior high school. The subjects of study were, in the younger years, music, handwork, nature, and stories. Formal work was postponed as long as possible, so that reading and writing were not commenced until the age of eight or nine. As the children grew older, the subjects were multiplied, growing out of the original four. Thus, from music developed the dramatic arts and folk dancing which Marietta Johnson regarded as providing some of the most important educational experiences; from nature came general science and later more specialised work; from stories came literature, history and geography. At junior high school level, formal mathematics was added, and at senior high school the

16   J. and E. Dewey, *Schools of Tomorrow*, Dutton, New York, 1915, pp. 17-40.
17   Marietta Johnson, *Youth in a World of Men*, Day, New York, 1929, p. 145.
18   *ibid.*, p. 76.
19   *ibid.*, pp. 78-9.

curriculum followed the conventional pattern. The curriculum, as far as she could manage it, grew from the lower classes up. The requirements of college and high school did not determine the content and standards of the lower grades; the way the children grew and the levels that they reached, without pressure of examinations or competition, determined the work that they were to tackle progressively up through the elementary and high school.

It was a school in which the pupils learnt to be sincere, unself-conscious, creative, and socially responsible. It was child-centred and it was also socially conscious. Marietta Johnson summarised her view of her school's task in very Deweyan language: 'If education ministers to growth, the reward at each step will be capacity for more growth. This capacity will be evidenced by keenness of interest, by strength of concentration, by spontaneity and sincerity, and by a growing appreciation of others and a consciousness of interdependence — the development of the socialized mind.'[20]

In 1919 she became one of the founders of the Progressive Education Association, and remained throughout the 1920's and 1930's one of its leading members, developing in that period an association with like-minded European progressives whom she met through the New Education Fellowship. Her ideas and her work at Fairhope were fairly central to the progressive tradition. In her concern for child growth, her interest in children's needs, her encouragement of spontaneity and creativity, her balance of children's interests and social responsibilities, and her centring of the educational process upon activity she gave practical expression to much of Dewey's theory. Her work in the U.S.A., and that of Ovide Decroly in Belgium, had much in common. She was, perhaps, a less precise and more dramatic Decroly, but nevertheless one who had caught much of the essence of the new movement, and had made a challenging and successful attempt to put it into practical form. Together, they demonstrated the community of progressive educational thought and practice that had developed across the Atlantic by the second decade of the twentieth century.

(iii) Schools of Tomorrow

In 1915 John Dewey and his daughter Evelyn wrote a book in which they examined twenty or so of the new schools, including those of Flora Cooke and Marietta Johnson, as examples of what they took to be 'the general trend of education at the present time'.[21] They concluded that the new schools shared four principal features:

• They attached considerable importance to the physical welfare of their pupils. They paid close attention to the children's health and they considered that intellectual growth had an important relationship to physical development and bodily activity.

• All the schools were involved in activity programs in which children learned by actual experience, and became involved in situations 'which reproduce the conditions of real life.'[22] Particularly significant, in the light of twentieth century urban and industrial development, was the way in which schools in industrial and commercial centres such as Chicago, and Gary, Indiana, had planned to involve their pupils comprehensively in urban occupations and problems, and to give them the general scientific and industrial training to cope with contemporary life. Activity education, with the freedom and responsibility which it brought to pupils, was seen to be a vital and positive means of promoting both intellectual and moral growth.

• Interest was a main criterion in selecting the work pupils were to do and the way in which they should do it. The most effort-producing kind of interest emerged when pupils were challenged to solve problems that had some significance in the activity on which they were engaged.

• Above all, the schools were committed to forwarding democratic values and practices. 'The spread of the realization of this connection between democracy and education is perhaps the most interesting and significant phase of present educational tendencies.'[23] The trend was exemplified by the schools' interest in allowing children freedom to develop both initiative and responsibility, and by extending the schools' programs to meet the needs of and provide more equality of opportunity to all classes in society.

Activity, relevance, interest, and democratic involvement were the characteristics of the new education that the Deweys saw to be steadily spreading throughout the schools of the United States, and providing the foundation for the schools of the future. Meanwhile, a similar pattern was emerging in Europe.

[20] ibid., p. 303.
[21] J. and E. Dewey, Schools of Tomorrow, Dutton, New York, 1915, p. 287.
[22] ibid., p. 292.
[23] ibid., p. 304-5.

THE PROGRESSIVE COUNTRY BOARDING SCHOOLS OF EUROPE

(i) Abbotsholme and Bedales

One of the main trends in the early development of progressive education had its beginning in England with the establishment in 1889 of a country boarding school for boys known as Abbotsholme.

The founder of the new school, Cecil Reddie, a young chemistry teacher, had absorbed some of the more advanced ideas on social and intellectual reform current in late Victorian England. He became interested in some kind of social reconstruction out of which a new and better England might arise, and he canvassed the possibility of building a new intellectual synthesis resting on a harmonious union of ethics, aesthetics, philosophy, and religion. He was a visionary and an eccentric. He was a part of the utopian, mildly socialist movement of the times that bred a generation of ardent social reformers or sent its adherents back to nature away from the complications of industrial life. Reddie was both reformer and recluse. He set his educational experiment in the countryside, remote from the contagion of the cities, and he endeavoured to use it as a basis for the eventual reform of English society.[24]

Reddie saw the school, particularly the English public boarding school type, as potentially a great force in the remodelling of civilisation, but thought it currently fell far short of what it might be. It had little to do with the needs of present-day life, its classical curriculum was not adapted to the requirements of a scientific age, it placed an undue emphasis on competition in games and examinations, and it was ignorant and neglectful of social and personal relationships. Reddie determined, therefore, to found a new-model public boarding school.

Abbotsholme was a secondary school for boys from eleven to eighteen years of age. It was intended to provide 'an all-round *Education* of an entirely modern, and rational character'[25] adapted to the needs of the 'directing classes' of society. The school, Reddie reported to the Bryce Commission, that 'I am endeavouring to organise is not intended to suit the whims of a few faddists, but the normal wants of the Directing Classes of a Reorganised English Nation'.[26]

[24] Cecil Reddie (1858-1932) was educated at Fettes College, a boarding school in Edinburgh, with the traditional public school and classical training, graduated B.Sc. at the University of Edinburgh, and in 1884 took a Ph.D. in Chemistry at the University of Göttingen. In his university years he developed a strong leaning towards socialism, and subsequently was much influenced by Edward Carpenter who advocated and practised a return to a simple democratic country life. Reddie taught briefly in several schools, and founded Abbotsholme in 1889 where he remained as headmaster until 1927.

[25] From the revised prospectus of 1894, reproduced in C. Reddie, *Abbotsholme*, Allen, London, 1900, pp. 133-4.

[26] *ibid.*, p. 191.

Abbotsholme School, established in 1889, the first of the progressive boarding schools of Europe.

Photograph by Herr Karl Neumann. First published in B.M. Ward, *Reddie of Abbotsholme*, George Allen & Unwin Ltd, London, 1934.

The curriculum had five main parts. First, it covered physical and manual activities. The boys were required to work in an agricultural plot in the extensive school grounds of 133 acres. They prepared their own cricket pitches and tennis courts, they built their own pavilion, they chopped their own trees down for firewood, they disposed of their own refuse, and, in addition, they had a carefully organised program of manual work on the farm, and in wood and metal workshops. The second aspect of the curriculum was artistic and imaginative. The boys were exposed to the best of traditional and modern art, they were expected to learn some artistic skill and craft, and in particular they were to cultivate music and singing. Thirdly, the curriculum was literary and intellectual, but it was different from the classical curriculum. It was said that, at that time, about 1890, Eton had twenty-four classical masters, six mathematics masters, one history master, and no master for science or modern languages. Reddie wanted to reverse that kind of preference. His first and most important subject was English. To it he added modern languages — French and German, mathematics, the three branches of sciences — physics, chemistry, and biology, and the social sciences of history and geography. Fourthly, social education was a vital part of the Abbotshol-mian's experience. The school was intended to be a warm and closely knit community. Classes were kept small with not more than fifteen pupils in each, and given as much of a family atmosphere as was possible in an all-male school with few women on the premises. Social recreation was encouraged in the evenings and weekends; clubs and dramatic and musical performances were fostered; and co-operative work projects were a leading characteristic of the school. And finally, the fifth element in the curriculum, moral and religious education, was given an important place. It was for the most part taught informally by the influence of the teaching staff and the general environment in which they lived, and by undenominational ethical services of a semi-religious kind that were held in the chapel, and which were intended to build up in the boys a religious feeling that was rather wider than a series of denominational services would be able to produce.[27]

The five aspects of the curriculum were not regarded as distinct and separate segments. Reddie had a close contact with Rein and had learnt a little from the Herbartians. The school made every effort to bring each boy's 'knowledge, power, and skill into harmonious interrelation'.[28] English was regarded as the central subject. The other subjects were correlated with one another in some degree and, wherever possible, the curriculum was related to the actual facts of the local neighbourhood or the work activity that the boys had in hand.

The school day was divided fairly neatly into three parts. In the morning the boys were concerned mainly with their academic work, in the afternoon with physical exercise and practical outdoor work, and in the evening with recreational and artistic activities such as play-reading and music.

The ideas that Reddie principally emphasised throughout the school were co-operation, balance, and leadership. He provided opportunities as widely as he could for the boys to work together in groups on a variety of activities and for them to seek out occupations which required more than one person so that they would have to co-operate actively in order to complete them. Art, writing, and play-acting could be co-operative work enterprises, and so too were the tasks of getting in the hay from the fields, or building fences, sheds, earth closets, glass-houses, boats, and other equipment. Balance, the second fundamental idea, was to be seen in the even weighting given to the five parts of the curriculum, designed to produce a 'complete and harmonious life'.[29] Reddie was also fond of pointing out to the boys various dualities in life that they should seek to reconcile and balance, such as co-operation and competition, the pioneering force of the male and the home-loving of the female, the disintegrating power of liberty and the unifying power of law, the regenerating strength of the countryside and the corrupt industrial atmosphere of the city. The third main emphasis, leadership, was obviously a central feature of an institution which advertised itself as a school for the sons of the directing classes. They clearly had to learn how to direct. Reddie began by teaching boys to be self-reliant in a range of small tasks and responsibilities allotted to them. Later they would be elected to school offices and receive greater responsibilities. Along with self-reliance, they had to learn to act with initiative and to develop a willingness and ability to co-operate. Above all, they had to learn that leadership was not a plum and an opportunity for self-gratification; it was a form of service. 'At the present day, above all, he is to be taught that social regeneration is only possible through education, and in particular that of the directing class. That they must aim not at climbing on to a snug perch above the weltering chaos of our modern life, but at battling with it until we have again social order. If boys are taught to work for the work's sake, their eyes will be not on the prize, but on the goal.'[30]

The school had its heyday from about 1889-1899. It started with sixteen pupils, and ten years later had reached its highest number under Reddie's headmastership, sixty-one. It was never intended that it should go beyond a hundred. In the next period, from 1900 to 1914, the school

27 For example on Good Friday the headmaster read three lessons: one dealt with Plato's account of the death of Socrates, the second dealt with the end of Oliver Cromwell, and the third was on the crucifixion.

28 C. Reddie, *op.cit.*, p. 230.

29 *ibid.*, p. 75.

30 *ibid.*, p. 601.

faltered badly. As Reddie got older he became more and more eccentric; he would quarrel with his staff continuously and in consequence the turnover of masters was probably the fastest of any school in England. The school, hard hit by World War I, continued to decline, and by the time Reddie left it finally in 1927, there were only two boys in attendance. The new headmaster, however, proved to be a wise choice, and within about ten years the school was well back on its feet.

Abbotsholme:
A Pioneer School at Work

Time Table.

6.55 Rise [in Summer—Rise, 6.10; Drill, 6.30; School, 6.45-7.30].
7.15 Military Drill, Dumb Bells, or Run (according to the weather).
7.30 Chapel.
7.40 Breakfast—after which Dormitory Parade (bed-making and teeth-cleaning), and Violin Practice.
8.30 to 10.45 School (during the first Period, 8.30-9.15, the boys visit, in batches under captains, the earth cabinets in the garden).
10.45 to 11.15 Lunch, and, if *fine*, Lung drill in the open air, stripped to the waist (to teach breathing).
11.15 School.
[In Summer, if fine and warm enough, 12, Singing; 12.20 Bathing in the River.]
1.0 Dinner.
1.30-1.45 Music Recital in Big School.
2 to 6 Drawing, Workshop, Gardening, Games, or Excursions on Foot or Bicycle, &c., &c.
6.0 Tea—after which Violin Practice.
6.45-7.30 Singing [in Summer the work omitted at 12].
7.30 Shakespeare Reading, Lecture, Rehearsal of Play, Concert, &c., each upon the appointed day.
8.30 Supper.
8.40 Chapel.

A sample of the time-table from the early years at Abbotsholme.

C. Reddie, *Abbotsholme*, George Allen, London, 1900, p. 63.

Abbotsholme, while never itself a great success as far as pupil numbers went, set a pattern of new thinking and new practice that other pioneering schools took up and progressively developed. Reddie's idea that, through properly arranged schooling, it would be possible to reconstruct society by creating 'a higher type of human being, able to cope with the increasing extent and complexity of modern knowledge and modern life, and able by a better development of the affections to seek to develop a more wholesome type of human society',[31] was to become one of the important strands of progressive educational thinking. Reddie, however, for all his forward thinking, did not adapt his school to the new conditions and educational ideas that evolved in the twentieth century. He remained a revolutionary of the 1890's, while people such as Badley, Geheeb, and Wyneken, who had learnt the Abbotsholme message, managed to add to it in their several schools by introducing a number of relevant and timely innovations.

Abbotsholme's first offshoot was Bedales, a flourishing school which J.H. Badley,[32] one of Reddie's staff, founded in 1893. Bedales was established in the south of England in Sussex and in 1900 moved to a new site a little north of Portsmouth where it remained. The school was initially for nine to fifteeen year old boys; it began with three and had increased to twenty-one at the end of the first year. In 1898 it began also to accept girls. Henceforth, the fact that it was co-educational was its most obvious difference from Abbotsholme. Badley designedly built much of his educational program around the relationships between adolescent boys and girls, believing that the 'co-operation of the sexes adds greatly to the range of what can be accomplished' and that a school comradeship nourished on the sharing of common responsibilities was the soundest foundation for future adult relationships between the sexes.[33] Attendance at the school rose fairly steadily, passing one hundred in 1903, and reaching two hundred in 1921 with an approximately equal number of boys and girls.[34] The age range of the pupils was also increased. By World War I, Bedales had ceased to merely be a secondary school, and was accepting pupils from kindergarten to nineteen years of age.

---

[31] *ibid.*, p. 16. For the English progressive school movement and especially the country boarding schools, see particularly W.A.C. Stewart, *The Educational Innovators:* Volume II; Progressive Schools 1881-1967, Macmillan, London, 1968, and R. Skidelsky, *English Progressive Schools*, Penguin, 1969.

[32] J.H. Badley (1865-1967) was educated at Rugby and Cambridge University, following a traditional classical curriculum. He was a good scholar and athlete, and developed an interest in social reform with some sympathy for the growing Labour Party. For two years he taught at Abbotsholme, and then left to found Bedales which he ran for the next forty-three years, retiring eventually in 1935 at the age of seventy.

[33] J.H. Badley, *Bedales*, Methuen, London, 1923, pp. 64-5.

[34] W.A.C. Stewart, *op.cit.*, p. 311, reported that in 1965 Bedales had 389 pupils and Abbotsholme 195. By 1977, four thousand pupils had passed through Bedales, see J.L. Henderson, *Irregularly Bold*, Deutsch, London, 1978, p. 152.

Badley had the same kinds of aims as Reddie. The practical work, expressive activities, the academic programming of English, modern languages, science, and social sciences, the social occupations and rich extra-curricular experiences, and the solid but unorthodox moral education were all a part of Bedales; but the teaching staff was more secure and stable, and, over the years, the school program was more effectively carried out.

Badley was a gentler and more understanding person than Reddie, and he was more democratic in his dealings with his staff and pupils. In consequence, Bedales displayed a more progressive character in the matter of student government. Where Reddie designed his school specifically for the sons of the directing classes, Badley was less concerned with producing persons who could be seen to be leaders; he was more interested in trying to get the pupils to work out ways and means of governing the school so that they would have an opportunity to see what government meant and how persons might set about developing a form of government. Eventually they instituted a school parliament with general elections, involving all the pupils in some measure in the government of the school.

A further interesting feature of Bedales that differentiated it from Abbotsholme was that Badley was more interested in teaching processes than was Reddie. Even in the very first year of operation he wrote of attempting to adapt new methods of teaching foreign languages and woodwork for use in the school, and, when Montessori started to become popular in the years before World War I, Badley saw that she was providing a method of educating young children which would fit in with his ideas of self-direction. He therefore incorporated the Montessori method into the lower classes of the school. When in the 1920's the Dalton laboratory plan of individualised learning was developed, again he saw the usefulness of that kind of method, and began to use it for much of the work in the secondary school.

Reddie's interest at Abbotsholme had been to produce generations of new leaders who would reconstruct English society. Badley did not lose sight of that ideal, but he leaned more towards the production of creative individuals who would live a fulfilling life through which a more humane and culturally enriched society might emerge. As the school developed, his attention tended to be directed more to the new individual than to the new society. 'To combine freedom and responsibility, to reconcile the claims of individuality with social obligations'[35] was a fundamental problem of life in a community, and one with which schools had to grapple.

To develop adequately, pupils needed three things: opportunity to work at matters through which they could give full expression of themselves; a community of people interested in encouraging one another

to fulfil their needs; and an ideal of human behaviour towards which to direct their efforts. Bedales was designed to provide those three things. The individual educated through those opportunities and influences would be able to turn fresh attitudes and understandings to the task of bringing a new society into being.

(ii) Landerziehungsheime

In Germany Hermann Lietz[36] established a private country-home boarding school, like Abbotsholme, in the Harz mountains at Ilsenburg in 1898 for children from six to twelve years old. Two other schools, Haubinda in Thuringia for boys from thirteen to sixteen and Bieberstein in the old castle at Fulda for boys from sixteen to nineteen came into existence in the next six years. Girls were admitted in small numbers at Ilsenburg, and occasionally at the other schools. Lietz ran the three-tiered organisation along lines similar to those of Reddie, whom he had visited and reported on approvingly in his book *Emlohstobba*.[37] The schools were a protest against the restricted view of schooling practised in the ordinary schools. They were therefore established in carefully selected locations in the depths of the country and, while retaining the subjects and content of an equivalent state school, they offered an additional range of activities to facilitate the pupils' all-round development. In the program for Ilsenburg published in 1898, Lietz spoke of the physical, practical, intellectual, and artistic sides through which he hoped to produce pupils who would 'think clearly and incisively, feel warmly, and act with courage and determination'.[38] To achieve this aim he adopted a curriculum similar to that of a *Realschule*, emphasising the study of German, and including French, English, history, geography, nature study, and mathematics. Latin and Greek could also be taken by those who wished. Two features were of note. Lietz insisted that all the work should build on the pupils' interests and experiences and should be oriented towards understanding contemporary society. Secondly, showing the influence of his study with Rein at Jena, he adopted the

---

[35] J.H. Badley, *Bedales*, *op.cit.*, p. 208.

[36] H. Lietz (1868-1919) was born on the Baltic island of Rügen, brought up on a farm, was unhappy in his schooling at the town of Greifswald, and studied at the universities of Halle and Jena. He was influenced by Rein, and visited and taught at Abbotsholme. Politically conservative, but educationally liberal, the founder of the *Landerziehungsheime* movement was a man of considerable personal charm and great determination who continued to teach until his death in 1919.

[37] H. Lietz, *Emlohstobba: Fiction or Fact*, with Preface by Wm Rein, trans. in C. Reddie, *Abbotsholme*, Allen, London, 1900, pp. 259-380. Emlohstobba is Abbotsholme written backwards.

[38] H. Lietz, *Die Erziehungsgrundsätze des Deutschen Landerziehungsheims von H. Lietz bei Ilsenburg im Harz*, in W. Flitner and G. Kudritzki, *op.cit.*, pp. 73ff.

Figure 5.1: Progressive Country Boarding Schools.

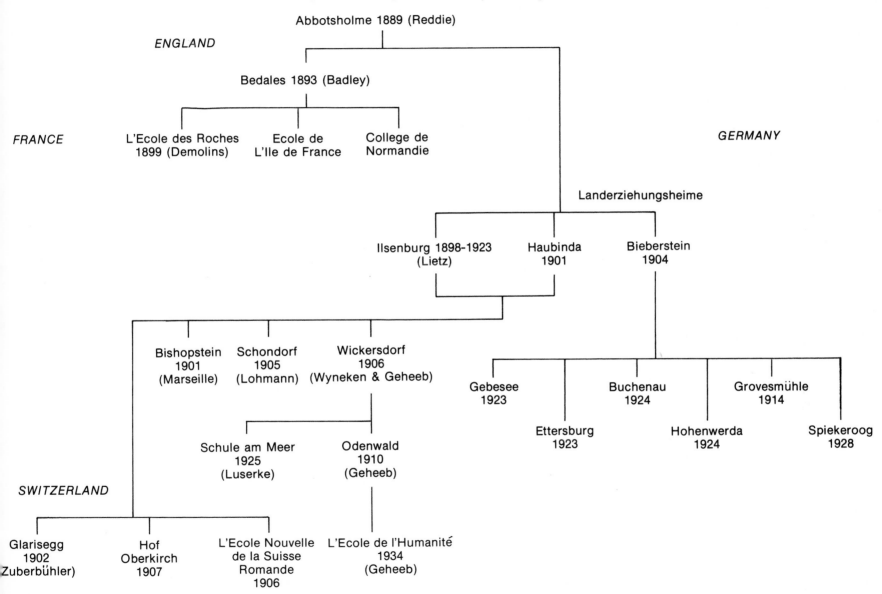

Herbartian practice of concentration. The subjects were placed in two groups, the humanities and the natural sciences; geography was used as the link between them and the basis on which the concentration took place. In addition to academic work the schools made a feature of agricultural work, and used the neighbouring villages and countryside extensively for rambles, picnics, and school meetings. The arts, too, especially music, were widely cultivated, and craftwork was taught with great skill and enthusiasm.

Lietz summarised the daily program at Ilsenburg as 'about 5 hours of academic work; 5 hours of physical work, physical exercise, and craftwork; 10 hours sleep; 4 hours for meals, bathing, leisure etc.'[39]

The overall characteristic of the Lietzian schools was their corporate life. As they were boarding schools it was possible every evening for the school to gather together for general discussion, reading, music, and leisurely entertainment in a relaxed and family atmosphere. Formal rules were kept to a minimum, and the boys were organised in small groups which made for intimate contact between them and the master who looked after them.

Besides the original three, six other schools were eventually established. In 1914 an orphanage was founded at Veckenstedt in the Harz; in 1923 Ilsenburg was closed and replaced by Gebesee near Erfurt, and Ettersburg was opened near Weimar; in 1924 Buchenau for boys and Hohenwerda for girls were started near Bieberstein; and in 1928 Spiekeroog on a Friesian island near Bremerhaven was set up for senior boys.[40]

Lietz's schools showed, in the highly intellectualised atmosphere of the contemporary German schools, that it was possible to combine intellectual work successfully with extensive physical activities, social education, and artistic appreciation.

In a letter written in 1918, the year before he died, Lietz reviewed his twenty years of experience with his schools, and suggested the following recipe for success in such ventures:

'To put these ideas into operation the Homes need, from their leadership, creativity, judgment, courage, straight-thinking, and perseverance, from their staff, ability, sincerity, and devotion, from the parents or their representatives, trust and understanding, and, last but not least, from those of you who have come to us, flexibility, receptiveness, and enthusiasm.'

Some would think it placed too much emphasis on the adult leadership of the schools, and left too little initiative to the pupils. At all events the schools brought together many talented and inventive teachers of whom two of the most radical were Gustav Wyneken and Paul Geheeb.[41] Their innovations made for greater pupil initiative and responsibility. Together they established the Wickersdorf school in 1906 in Thuringia; Geheeb left in 1910 to set up the Odenwald school, and subsequently, after the Nazi party came to power in Germany, moved into Switzerland and established, in 1934, L'Ecole de l'Humanité.

Wickersdorf, Odenwald, and, later, the Schule-am-Meer founded in 1925 by Luserke on the North Sea island of Juist, were more experimental than the Lietz schools. They took children from nine to nineteen, and were co-educational, much more pupil-centred, and more flexible in their academic programming. Wickersdorf was known as the free school community because the school met as a community on frequent occasions to discuss and decide upon the conduct of the school. It was genuine self-government, subject to the ultimate veto of the principal; at Odenwald the school community was sovereign. Small, all-age comradeship groups were centred around each teacher, the pupils themselves selecting the group to which they wished to belong. Wyneken's contribution to the progressive movement was his conviction that youth should have the opportunity to develop its own culture, and, through it, to build a new way of life. 'It seeks a new way of life which will correspond to its youthful living, but which, at the same time, will enable it to take itself and its creations seriously and help it to link itself as a distinct factor with the work of civilization.'[42] Wyneken rejected the world of materialistic standards in favour of co-operation and humaneness, and he wished the youth of his day to have the opportunity to start to remake the values and the patterns of living in the world into which they were moving.

---

[39] W. Flitner and G. Kudritzki, *op.cit.*, p. 323.

[40] At the time of writing, the Hermann Lietz Schools Foundation of German Country Boarding Homes consists of four schools in West Germany: Buchenau, Bieberstein, Hohenwerda, and Spiekeroog. Haubinda, Gebesee, and Ettersburg are in East Germany.

[41] G. Wyneken (1875-1964) in 1900 became a teacher and then director of Lietz's Ilsenburg school, and subsequently moved to Haubinda. In 1906 he and Paul Geheeb broke with Lietz and, taking also two outstanding teachers, the musician Halm, and the dramatist M. Luserke, founded the new school of Wickersdorf. In 1909 Wyneken and Geheeb fell out, and Geheeb left. In the following year Wyneken resigned in favour of Luserke. He returned in 1919, lost his post after a year and a half, but remained in the neighbourhood and had an influence on the school until 1931 when he settled as an author in Göttingen. He had a considerable interest in the pre-Nazi youth movement in Germany. A creative and progressive mind, his principal influential publication was *Schule und Jugendkultur*, Jena, 1913.

P. Geheeb (1870-1961) was educated at Giessen, Jena, and Berlin universities, and became a teacher at Lietz's school, Haubinda, in 1902. He taught for a short while at Abbotsholme, and became the director of Haubinda, moving in 1906 with Wynekan to Wickersdorf. In 1910 he left to found the Odenwald school near Heppenheim in the Rhine valley. He migrated to Switzerland in 1934 where he sought to set up L'Ecole de l'Humanité in various places until he finally settled in the Bernese Oberland where he remained until his death in 1961. Geheeb was a man of great understanding and humanity who developed one of the great progressive schools of the twentieth century.

[42] G. Wyneken, *Wickersdorf*, Lavenburg, A. Saal, 1922, trans. in A.E. Meyer, *Modern European Educators and their Work*, Prentice-Hall, New York, 1934, p. 123.

Geheeb was of like mind, and even more adventurous in the conduct of his school. At Odenwald there was liberty and equality throughout the community. Above all, there was a rare quality of fraternity expressed in the relationships between boys and girls, in the internationalism of the school's outlook, in the untrammelled power of the school community to make its own rules and organise its own discipline, and in the frequent art festivals excitingly planned and participated in by the whole school. In the school's academic work the pupils exercised considerable responsibility for the choice and completion of their work. With a scheme somewhat similar to the Dalton Plan, all children over ten years of age worked on a program of academic and craft courses which they re-selected each month. The choice of work was their own, and the school community saw to it that each person completed his task in a responsible way. The younger children under ten worked in a more informal way at an integrated centres-of-interest approach somewhat resembling that of Decroly.

Other teachers from the Lietz schools also moved off to found their own variations of the country boarding school, and by World War I there were about a dozen of them in existence in Germany alone. Ferrière assessed them on their contribution to the progressive movement, and judged Odenwald to be the foremost. The movement spread both from England and from Germany into several other European countries.

In France, the Ecole des Roches was founded in 1899 by Demolins. Three years earlier, after studying Abbotsholme and Bedales, Demolins had written a widely-read book in which he attributed Anglo-Saxon superiority to the educational practices found in English boarding schools. He established L'Ecole des Roches as far as he could along the lines of Bedales, on a country property about one hundred kilometres west of Paris. The school opened with eighty boys and had grown to almost two hundred boys and a few girls by the outbreak of World War I. Organised team games, careful attention to each pupil's health, small classes, close association between staff and boys, and a curriculum of modern languages, science, history, geography, and practical manual work were the main characteristics of the new education in Demolins' school. It was a protest against over-intellectualism in French education, and an effort to provide a more balanced moral, physical, social and intellectual experience.[43]

In Switzerland, early in the century, there were several country boarding schools of which two achieved a wide reputation. Glarisegg, founded in 1902 on Lake Constance was a small school for boys from nine to eighteen, much after the Abbotsholme model. It had a strong family atmosphere, a large degree of pupil self-government, and a curriculum which combined academic with outdoor and productive work. Not far away, near St Gall, the school of Hof Oberkirch was founded by Hermann Tobler in 1907.[44] The school accepted pupils between the ages of seven

and seventeen, and emphasised vocational work and character building. Tobler was an alert and flexible educator who, like Badley, adapted new ideas and practices from various quarters for his own purposes. Within the country boarding school framework he developed Kerschensteiner's activity school ideas, he used Decroly's centres of interest as a basis for his curriculum at both primary and secondary level, and he introduced some of the insights from analytical psychology into the conduct of the school.

(iii)   The Contribution of the Progressive Country Boarding Schools

The pioneering country boarding schools were a prominent feature of progressive education in the period before World War I. They and their successors continued, after that, to be important centres in England and Germany, but elsewhere the movement was better represented by other kinds of schools and educators. The country boarding schools, nevertheless, did succeed in drawing a reasonable amount of attention to a range of new ideas in education and to the need to re-examine traditional practices. They gave to the new education an international flavour by building up a close and enduring connection between related schools in various countries. Through mutual visits, the organisation of conferences, exchanges of pupils and teachers, and a sharing of successful practices, they eased the way for the movement of educational ideas between countries in a manner that was to be characteristic of progressive education and was to become more common in all educational circles as the twentieth century wore on.

The country boarding schools, however, were necessarily somewhat exclusive. They were expensive and small in size, drew their pupils from upper social and income groups, and lay outside the state system of education. They had a direct effect, therefore, on only a small proportion of children of school age,[45] and their pupils tended to be the sons and daughters of more radically minded upper middle class parents. Their great virtue was that they demonstrated in a concrete way that it was

---

[43]   E. Demolins, *A Quoi Tient la Supériorité des Anglo-Saxons?*, Firmin-Didot, Paris, 1897; E. Demolins, *L'Education Nouvelle: L'Ecole des Roches*, Firmin-Didot, Paris, 1898; C. Brereton, *Studies in Foreign Education*, Harrap, London, 1913, pp. 152-9.

[44]   H. Tobler (1872-1933) a Swiss educator, studied in England and taught languages in several schools in St Gall. He became an active and well-known member of the New Education Fellowship.

[45]   W.A.C. Stewart, *op.cit.*, p. 309, calculated that in 1965 the total number of secondary pupils at twenty-five English progressive schools, mostly of the country boarding type, was only .2 per cent of all the secondary pupils in England.

possible to rethink educational traditions and adapt them radically and deliberately to the circumstances of a new era. They gave a new emphasis to corporate life in schools and changed its nature by making it a community life of great warmth and width of participation. They enriched the educational opportunities available for every individual by the range and quality of the expressive activities which they provided to suit a great variety of tastes. They moved ahead of their times with a reasonably sure step, and saw many of their ideas slowly absorbed into the general body of educational practice. The kind of curriculum which they first worked out in 1900 received wide endorsement in the heady educational discussions of the 1930's, and had, by 1950, passed in large measure into the commonplace thinking of educational writers and teacher-educators, and was becoming the customary practice of both state and independent schools.[46]

EUROPEAN PROGRESSIVE EDUCATORS

In Europe before World War I, three persons achieved an outstanding reputation for developing new educational ideas and putting them into successful practice. Maria Montessori discovered ways of encouraging individual development, and she trained several generations of teachers to use her methods and materials with young children; for her, spontaneity, activity, and individual freedom were essential in the educational process. Georg Kerschensteiner was also interested in activity methods, but he saw education to be concerned not primarily with individual freedom but with the welfare of society; not that the two were incompatible — but Kerschensteiner's interest was in producing a good citizen. His educational ideas were community-centred, Montessori's child-centred. Between the two stood Ovide Decroly, an original mind, who gathered together the leading educational ideas of the period and fashioned a child-cum-community-centred synthesis that went into effective operation in his own school and that of his many admirers.

(i)   Maria Montessori (1870-1952)

In a letter to the *Times Educational Supplement* of 4 February 1913 E.G.A. Holmes wrote, 'What is quintessential in the Montessori System is its author's emphatic affirmation (or reaffirmation) of the master truth that children can neither develop themselves properly nor be "studied" profitably except in an atmosphere of freedom!' Montessori was dedicated

Maria Montessori (1870-1952), an Italian educator whose methods of encouraging spontaneity and activity in children's learning became popular throughout the first half of the twentieth century.

to this proposition. She held that a child should be treated not as an object but as a person; not as a vessel to be filled by an adult but as a being striving to develop itself; not as a creature to receive identity at the hands of a parent or teacher but as a living, active, unique person.[47]

---

[46]   See W.A.C. Stewart, *op.cit.*, p. 343.

[47]   M. Montessori, *The Secret of Childhood*, B.B. Carter trans., Longmans, London, 1936, p. 13.

Early Career. Maria Montessori was born near the Adriatic town of Ancona and moved at an early age to Rome. The 'beautiful, gifted girl-student'[48] eventually entered the medical faculty at the University of Rome, and in 1896 graduated as its first woman doctor of medicine. Not unnaturally she soon became known as a strong feminist, championing the cause of working women in Italy and at meetings in various European countries. She thus gained an early experience of public meetings and of the necessity for the persistent advocacy of social causes. Immediately after graduation she worked as an assistant at the psychiatric clinic of the University of Rome and there came in contact for the first time with defective children. She grew to be immensely interested in the education of feeble-minded children, spent some time in Paris and London studying current ideas and practices, and from 1898 to 1900 became the directress of a newly established state Orthophrenic School. The experience gained during those two years and some of the methods which she devised were to form the basis of her later educational work. In 1900 she delivered and published a series of lectures in which she briefly summarised her approach: 'The child should be led from the education of the muscular system to that of the nervous and sensory systems; from the education of the senses to concepts; from concepts to general ideas; from general ideas to morality. This is the educational method of Séguin.'[49]

For the next seven years she studied to widen her knowledge and to increase her understanding of the education of young children, and for part of the time lectured at the University of Rome in anthropology. She had already become acquainted with the writings of Itard who, early in the nineteenth century, had devised methods of teaching the wild boy of Aveyron, and with Séguin who had further developed Itard's ideas. Montessori thoroughly read and digested Séguin's work, and throughout her career she was to remain faithful to his general approach and to many of the details of his technique and apparatus.

In January 1907 she became the directress for the Children's Houses, (Case dei Bambini) opened for the first time in a slum improvement project near the main railway station in Rome. She remained in this work until 1911. It was the first time that she had had the opportunity to apply her thinking to the education of normal children, and it was, in consequence, through these Children's Houses that she laid the foundation and provided a demonstration of her methods of educating ordinary pre-school children. Within the first two years of starting, three Children's Houses were set up in Rome. Each consisted of a large room at the bottom of an apartment house, with some garden space, for children from the ages of three to seven of parents who were away at work during the day. The Children's Houses were free, were equipped with light tables, chairs, and apparatus designed by Maria Montessori, were staffed by a resident directress, and visited by a doctor.[50]

Her writings, her speeches, and her practical work in the Roman Children's Houses show a curious mixture of perceptive and liberal ideas with traditional and mystical nonsense. Though tentative in her first approaches to education, as she gained in confidence she became dogmatic. This was part of what one of her admirers had called 'a massive and unassailable strength of character — like a mountain unmoved by the storms which beat against it'.[51]

From her earliest years she showed herself to be a woman of determination and, once having formulated her educational ideas and techniques, she displayed great tenacity and extraordinary ability in the task of propagating them. She commanded great loyalty and devotion from her immediate associates, and was able to stimulate lasting enthusiasm among many thousands of teachers who attended the courses or listened to her speeches. The secret of her influence was to be found in the sincerity of her love for children. She was acutely sensitive to their needs and interests and gave them the central position in her life. A good example of her sympathetic understanding of children is to be found in her description of the way adults continually interfere in the activities which the children would prefer to cope with on their own in their smaller and slower world.

'What should we do if we were to become the slaves of a people incapable of understanding our feelings, a gigantic people, very much stronger than ourselves? When we were quietly eating our soup, enjoying it at our leisure (and we know that enjoyment depends on being at liberty), suppose a giant appeared, and

---

[48]   Dorothy C. Fisher, *A Montessori Mother*, Constable, London, 1913, p. 213.

[49]   Maria Montessori, *The Advanced Montessori Method*, II, A. Livingston trans, Heinemann, London, 1918, pp. 413-14.

[50]   Montessori reported on her work in the Children's Houses and on the ideas and methods that grew out of and developed beyond that experience in three basic books: *The Montessori Method*, first published in Italian as *The Method of Scientific Pedagogy Applied to Infant Education in the Children's Houses* 1910; *The Advanced Montessori Method*, vols I and II, 1918-19; and *Dr. Montessori's Own Handbook*, 1914. In subsequent years she produced many books, pamphlets, and articles on various aspects of child development, the most widely read of which were *The Secret of Childhood*, 1936, and *The Absorbent Mind*, 1949. After World War I much of Montessori's time was spent outside Italy, organising schools in Europe and America. She lived in Spain from 1915 to 1918 and at various times afterwards, establishing a substantial centre at Barcelona. During the Spanish Civil War she moved to Holland and set up headquarters near Amsterdam; meanwhile she spent a good deal of time helping to organise schools and training courses for teachers in England. In 1939 she went to India, and during World War II helped to found a considerable number of Montessori schools in India and Ceylon. After World War II she again became active in many European countries, returning for a while to try to re-establish her influence in Italy after the fall of the fascist regime which, through showing an initial interest, especially from about 1924 to 1930, had eventually proved unsympathetic to her efforts. She died in 1952 in Holland.

[51]   E.M. Standing, *Maria Montessori, Her Life and Work*, Mentor-Omega, New York, 1962, p. 83.

snatching the spoon from our hand, made us swallow it in such haste, that we were almost choked.'[52]

Aim of Education. Montessori stated that her educational aim for very young children was 'to aid the spontaneous development of the mental, spiritual, and physical personality'.[53] The educator's job was to understand the process of the child's natural development and to provide the means by which the child can steadily increase his own control of the environment and the process of his development. She hoped, by her methods, 'to produce a better type of man, a man endued with superior characteristics as if belonging to a new race: the superman of which Nietzsche caught glimpses'.[54] Children, educated in freedom, growing vigorously and spontaneously in an ordered way, would become a new generation of 'powerful men'[55] with the ability and the equipment to maintain the scientific progress of our civilisation. She did not sketch in detail the utopia which the new form of education was to bring about, but she did at least join her hopes with those of the other reformers of her generation, that a new and better world might emerge through their efforts.

Scientific Method in Education. Montessori worked immensely hard to design and perfect her methods of teaching. She claimed that her work was scientific and that she was helping to found a new scientific pedagogy. Her work at the Children's Houses in Rome was contemporaneous with the early experimental work of Claparède, Binet, Lay, and Meumann, but she was not at one with them. Her work was of a different kind and quality. For Montessori, scientific method consisted of three things: observation, experimentation, and analysis. Observation was the objective collection of facts, and Montessori never tired of exhorting her followers to observe and understand the growth of children. Adequate measurement of behaviour she acknowledged also to be part of the observational process. Her mastery, however, of current statistical procedures was slight. She did not have Decroly's competence in this area, and she tended to rely more upon her acute intuition than upon measurement.[56] Montessori experimented in education in the sense of trying out her ideas in her schools and modifying her procedures according to her judgment of the degree of success with which they were meeting. She did not experiment in the scientific sense of selecting appropriate samples of children and attempting to control the variables with which she was dealing. Her conclusions, for instance, concerning sensitive periods appear to have been based upon anecdotal material acutely selected and observed rather than upon a careful program of controlled experimentation. Science for her was largely the art of observing and ordering. Observations must be analysed, classified, and

synthesised; and, from that process of ordered analysis, generalisations and conclusions might be drawn. She adopted that procedure in her own work, and she devised ways of teaching it to young children as a basis for their intellectual development.

Education for Independence. She was interested in providing in her schools an environment in which children could grow independently of adults, where they would be free to do things for themselves, and to proceed at their own pace.

She criticised contemporary schools for their lack of freedom and general unsuitability for growing children. The children were 'reduced to slavery'[57] in an unlovely and depressing environment where they had to remain motionless, passively obedient to a teacher. They were prohibited from helping one another, curbed and stimulated by punishments and prizes, and compelled to follow a program which had little reference to the course of their own development and which changed every half-hour or so from subject to subject:

'. . .this environment, where free exercise is prohibited, as also the choice of work, and meditation, where every sentiment is oppressed, and from which every external stimulus which might enrich the intelligence with spontaneous acquisitions is eliminated . . .'[58]

Montessori's method was one based on freedom for the child in a prepared environment. In the preface to her *Handbook*, she pointed out that Helen Keller's remarkable education[59] demonstrated the possibility of liberating the human spirit through the education of the senses, and

---

[52]   Maria Montessori, *The Advanced Montessori Method*, I, trans. F. Simmonds & L. Hutchinson rev. edn Heinemann, London, 1919, pp. 20-1.

[53]   Maria Montessori, *The Montessori Method*, trans. Anne E. George, Heinemann, London, (1912) 1920, p. 232.

[54]   Maria Montessori, *Peace and Education*, Montessori Society, London, 1932, p. 13.

[55]   Maria Montessori, *The Montessori Method*, p. 101.

[56]   In her book *Pedagogical Anthropology* published in 1913 she included a chapter on statistical methodology, which showed a much more elementary view of sampling, measures of dispersion, and correlation than might have been expected of one writing a textbook in scientific pedagogy at that time.

[57]   Maria Montessori, *The Advanced Montessori Method*, I, p. 270.

[58]   *ibid.*

[59]   Helen Keller (1880-1968) born in Alabama, became blind, deaf, and dumb at an early age as a result of scarlet fever. From the age of seven she came under the care of a gifted teacher, Anne Sullivan, from whom she learnt to talk, type, and read Braille. Helen Keller graduated from Radcliffe College in 1904, and embarked on a distinguished literary and lecturing career which made her one of the foremost women in America in the first half of the twentieth century.

that that was the basis of her own method. She considered that, in the course of his development, the child had to establish effectively three functions: motor functions, sensory functions, and the function of physical adaptation. The child was naturally active and interested in work; his basic education therefore should aim to develop his three functions through activity and work of a carefully graduated kind. She therefore developed motor, sensory, language, and intellectual exercises, carefully graduated and for the most part self-corrective that the children could undertake with the minimum of adult guidance. Using Séguin's material as a basis, she constructed apparatus by which muscular, sensory, and psychical training was to proceed in an orderly and sequential fashion; and she placed her pupils in a school environment in which there was a minimum of adult interference, and a maximum of opportunity for self-education by the children. Her efforts were, for the pre-school, an early twentieth century version of the programmed instruction that was to become popular in the 1960's at the elementary and secondary school level. It is not surprising to find that there was a revival of her influence at that time in the United States when programmed instruction was most popular.

Sensitive Periods. She held the view that children grow because of some life force within them. She seems to have accepted in very general terms the notion that there is a natural striving — what Bergson popularised as an *élan vital*, and Nunn, whose term Montessori later accepted and used, as *horme* — to develop tendencies with which one is born. She wrote somewhat quaintly of the mysterious powers which lie within the child and 'unfold according to mysterious laws'.[60] The principal indications of the unfolding are to be found in what she refers to as the 'sensitive period'. As a child developed, certain periods of special sensitivity appear from time to time, and disappear. When they are present the child shows a particular interest in certain objects and exercises, and is able most readily to cope with and learn the matters to which his special sensitivity applies, and 'so infancy passes from conquest to conquest, in a continuous vital vibrancy'.[61] Montessori drew attention to an important sensitive period for order which lasts for about two years, beginning in the child's second year, and to sensitive periods for the refinement of the senses, the time at which it was most appropriate to teach such things as discrimination of colour, taste, sound, touch; there was also a sensitive period for learning good manners, covering approximately the same period as the sensory one from two-and-a-half to six years of age. Her definitions and descriptions of these periods were vague and ill-substantiated, but the educational point that she made as a result of her analysis was a vital and important one. She pointed out that there was a psychological moment, a best time, a point at which children

are most sensitive to undertake various tasks and to learn them most effectively. A good teacher was the one who was aware of this phenomenon, who prepared the right kind of material to capitalise on the child's sensitivity, and who patiently waited and, where possible, helped to make the child ready to profit fully when the right time came. In her views on sensitive periods she anticipated and stimulated an interest in the study of children's readiness for learning that was later to be an important aspect of the work of educational psychologists and to become an essential basis of teaching method.

Sense Education. At the beginning of a chapter on the education of the senses Montessori wrote: 'In a pedagogical method which is experimental, the education of the senses must undoubtedly assume the greatest importance.'[62] The aim of educating the senses is to refine a child's perception of stimuli by the exercise of attention, comparison, and judgment.

Muscular exercise was an important basis for sensory training. Montessori's pupils, therefore, were given appropriate exercises to develop their muscular functions generally, and also those which were specially important for the sensory exercises that she had devised. Her work covered the tactile, thermic, and baric senses and the senses of taste, smell, vision, colour, and hearing. Those singly and in various combinations were exercised by means of her specially devised didactic apparatus. She hoped through such sense education to do three things: to make children more acute observers of phenomena by exercising them in discriminating between carefully graduated sense stimuli; second, to develop and improve their sensory functioning in general; and third, to get various senses in a more satisfactory state of readiness to perform complicated acts such as reading and writing. The third function was a straightforward preparation for a concrete and useful task dependent in some measure on sensory acuteness. Montessori appears to have managed this skilfully and successfully.

The other aims, training in observation and in sensitivity in general, appear to stem from her acceptance of the theory of formal discipline in its old form. 'It is exactly,' she wrote, 'in the repetition of the exercises that the education of the senses consists; their aim is not that the child shall *know* colours, forms, and the different qualities of objects, but that he refine his senses through an exercise of attention, of comparison, of judgment. These exercises are true intellectual gymnastics. Such

[60] Maria Montessori, *Dr Montessori's Own Handbook*, p. 90; *The Absorbent Mind*, trans C.A. Claremont. Holt, Rinehart and Winston, New York, (1949) 1962, pp. 83 *et seq.*

[61] Marie Montessori, *The Secret of Childhood*, trans. B.B. Carter, Longmans Green, London, 1936, p. 41.

[62] Maria Montessori, *The Montessori Method*, p. 168.

gymnastics, reasonably directed by means of various devices, aid in the formation of the intellect, just as physical exercises fortify the general health and quicken the growth of the body.'[63] Montessori appeared to assume the validity of a general transfer of training, expecting, from the particular materials on which the children were exercised, an all-round improvement in sensory performance. At the time she was writing, however, this assumption was very much in question and was subject to considerable research during the first four decades of the twentieth century. Montessori did not take this research into account, nor did she attempt experimentally to establish the validity of the general transfer that much of her work of sensory training assumed. Accurate perception and practice in discriminating, comparing, and classifying perception was for her the basis upon which intellectual education should rest. Imagination had the same basis. The introduction into schools of imaginative games and stories not based on reality, e.g. fairy tales, could lead only to credulity, not to creativity. Creativity came from accurate and perceptive observation, and the path to it was through graduated and well-ordered sensory education.

Didactic Apparatus. For the motor education of young children Montessori thought that proper management and exercise within a well-prepared environment was sufficient; for sensory education, however, and for education in language and number, specially provided didactic materials were necessary. The materials took the place of the chalk and talk of the traditional teacher and made auto-education possible for each child. The didactic materials were expected to attract the spontaneous attention of the children and to contain a rational gradation of stimuli. The systematic education of the senses rested, therefore, not on the ability of a teacher, but on the proper and orderly use of the didactic apparatus.

The didactic material for pre-school children consisted of items for education in practical life activities, for the education of the senses, and for preparation for writing, reading, music, and arithmetic. Among the practical life materials were frames for lacing and buttoning to help children develop skill in dressing and undressing. Among the sense education apparatus some of the most widely used items were three sets of solid insets. They consisted of three pieces of wood in each of which was a row of three small cylinders, in one case, of the same height but diminishing in diameter, in the second case, decreasing in diameter and height, and in the third case, diminishing in height only. The children's exercise consisted of taking out the cylinders, mixing them and putting them back in the right place, so that they fitted into their holes exactly. For developing the tactile sense preparatory to writing, there were cards on which sandpapered letters were pasted. A child repeatedly ran his first and

second fingers over the surface of the sandpapered letters, tracing out their form.

The child learned to use the materials by watching other children at work or from a brief and unobtrusive demonstration by the teacher. He was required to use them in the way Montessori prescribed. She insisted on this. The materials had a specific training purpose. They were not to be played with in some imaginative way but to be used in the matter-of-fact exercises for which they were designed. She did not regard this as an infringement of a child's liberty, but, on the contrary, the very means to it, by helping him step by step to master the reality around him and the potential within him.

The Montessori Program. The program of the Montessori school consisted very largely of following a series of graded exercises in conjunction with the didactic apparatus. At the pre-school level the exercises were concerned mainly with practical life, writing, and arithmetic.

To help children to learn to co-ordinate their movements and to perform daily tasks around the house and school, there were a series of practical life exercises. The youngest children learned to button and unbutton their clothes and to move their seats in silence; later they learned to walk with rhythm and balance on a chalk line on the schoolroom floor, set about dusting and tidying the room and waiting at table for the midday meal. They learned to get order and control into their movements by walking quietly on tip-toe and standing from time to time in complete silence.

The sensory exercises started usually with the cylinders. These exercises helped to fix the children's attention and exercise their judgment in an elementary way in comparing the dimensions of the various cylinders. Progressively then the children moved through tactile, chromatic, hearing, and weight exercises, learning through them to discriminate among fine gradations of touch, weight, colour, and sound, and establishing greater control of their hand movements. Such activities merged gradually into language and arithmetic exercises. The children traced written letters of the alphabet with their fingers, then with a pencil on a piece of paper, and filled in the design with coloured pencils. They composed words and phrases with a movable alphabet, and then exploded spontaneously into the writing of words and phrases. Montessori held that the accomplishment of writing was the culmination of constant practice with the various preparatory exercises, and that the achievement came upon the children 'not gradually, but in an explosive way'.[64]

[63] *ibid.*, pp. 362-3.
[64] *ibid.*, p. 290.

Montessori gave a delightful description of one such dramatic moment in one of the Children's Houses at Rome. She was sitting on the roof of the apartment, surrounded by the children on one sunny December day, when one of them 'looked at me, smiled, remained for a moment as if on the point of bursting into some joyous act, and then cried out, "I can write! I can write!" and kneeling down again he wrote on the pavement the word "hand". Then, full of enthusiasm, he wrote also "chimney", "roof". As he wrote, he continued to cry out, "I can write! I know how to write." '[65]

Writing preceded reading. Children began by recognising names of familiar objects, and then practised with cards on which there were the names of a large variety of other objects. In that way the mechanism of reading was established. Elementary composition developed spontaneously after that and was followed by continuous exercises in reading short passages for meaning. Little by little the children discovered that language transmitted thought, and that, by improving their competence in it, they could enlarge their ideas, and make rapid intellectual progress.

Parallel with the work in language there were exercises in numeration leading to the learning of arithmetic. Again the process was through tactile sensations such as the feeling and the manipulation, often blindfold, of regularly shaped geometrical figures, followed by the use of graduated rods and the building of Long and Big Stairs with prisms which were part of the didactic apparatus, finger tracing of sandpapered numbers, and number games with counting boxes and movable numbers. Montessori extended her language and arithmetic program upwards to the elementary school grades, and in the second volume of *The Advanced Montessori Method* she described the material and its use for children from seven to eleven years in the learning of grammar, reading, arithmetic, geometry, drawing, music, and metre in poetry.

Montessori considered that all her exercises, besides being a training in skill, were exercises in will-power. They were a training in perseverance, determination, obedience, and inhibition. They were designed to produce disciplined and orderly persons. Thus her teachers in the Children's Houses did not report that a child was developing or progressing, but that 'the child *is becoming disciplined*, or *is not becoming disciplined*'.[66] Discipline was not imposed by the teachers; it was learned by the children through their own work. The child made himself better, disciplining himself by achieving a succession of conquests over the graduated work that he took in hand. As he grew in competence he increased his freedom to achieve what he wished. His discipline and his liberty grew side by side and depended upon each other. Montessori's view of discipline is not unlike that of Rousseau's 'well-regulated liberty'.

Moral education ran parallel to the education of the senses. It was in essence a disciplining of the feelings in the way already described, and a

process of habitual acceptance of authoritative moral judgments. Pupils developed sensibility to what is right and wrong in the same way as they developed sensory and intellectual skills. Instead of the teacher simply saying: This is red. This is green; she would say This is right. This is wrong. The child was to learn by constant repetition and practice to distinguish between right and wrong and to prefer the right. The task was to establish an ordered set of accepted ideas. Approval from other pupils or from a teacher was important and stimulating, but, for the most part, Montessori hoped to arrange the children's working environment in such a way that the children would not feel the need of an incentive from the teacher.

The Montessori Teacher. 'The instructions of the teacher,' Montessori wrote, 'consist then merely in a hint, a touch — enough to give a start to the child. The rest develops of itself.'[67] When a teacher gave a lesson or demonstration it was to be brief, simple, and objective, guiding the child along his path of natural development with the least amount of effort on his part. Montessori preferred the name directress to that of teacher and used it to indicate that she thought that the teacher's job should be largely one of passive observation of the children and the work. She must observe constantly and intelligently and keep the children's work flowing without being unduly intrusive. The directress, however, could not really remain passive; she had several positive functions to perform. She should try to take a scientific interest in education by experimenting with new procedures and equipment within the framework of Montessori's principles. She had also the task of hindering such things as disorderly movement, incorrect use of materials, and attempts at work which she judged to be too difficult. Another important task was that of recognising the readiness of children for the particular steps in their training. She had to be alert to provide opportunities at the appropriate time. Montessori summed up the qualities of a directress by suggesting that she should have a capacity for scientific observation and for sustained and accurate application, that she should possess patience and humility, that she should have a quiet and calm manner, and that she should have a deep sense of respect for the children and their freedom.

Auto-education — Liberty, Activity, and Order. By restricting the activity of the directress, Montessori emphasised the liberty of the pupil.

[65] *ibid.*, p. 289.

[66] Maria Montessori, *The Advanced Montessori Method*, I, p. 122.

[67] Maria Montessori, *Dr Montessori's Own Handbook*, p. 26.

Her system was designed to give responsibility as far as possible to the children for their own education. Nothing was to be done for a child which he could do for himself. All the exercises and apparatus that Montessori devised were designed to promote a child's auto-education. The Montessori program was a path to independence. 'The child who does not do, does not know how to do.'[68] We must see to it therefore that he does whatever he can for himself to enable him through his own efforts to master himself and his environment. By working steadily through Montessori's materials the child guided himself, corrected himself, and gained the satisfaction of self-achievement. In pursuit of his independence through auto-education each child was in large part an isolated worker. The typical picture of a Children's House showed a room in which a dozen or more children were working quietly on their own with some piece of apparatus. Although Montessori did say that human activity was an eminently social activity,[69] she concentrated her efforts upon individual development. From time to time, nevertheless, the children played together with toys or read together or listened to a story; they sometimes also formed an interested audience when one of the children was doing something novel or intricate. In that way, Montessori suggested, there developed a feeling of fellowship, an attitude of mutual aid, and an interest on the part of the older children in the work and progress of the younger.

If liberty was the first characteristic of Montessori's approach, activity was its second. It was 'founded on work and on liberty'. Her school was a genuine activity school. She started from the premise that a child has an instinct for work, 'the characteristic instinct of the human race',[70] and her exercises were planned to ensure that the child worked diligently along the line of what she took to be his natural development. Her rationale is a basic principle of the activity school. She argued that the pursuit and use of an object was more important to a child than the object itself. In the course of his self-development he prefers the act of dressing himself to the state of being dressed; he prefers the act of washing to the satisfaction of being clean; he prefers to make a house rather than merely own it. The pupil's prime satisfaction does not come from possessing a piece of information, but from the process of learning it. And, in turn, to have learned something, is only a point of departure. Enjoyment comes from actively using and working on what has been learned. Thus it is the getting and the using, not the having, that is important for the child as an active, working being.

Activity, however, should not be haphazard. Montessori called the child 'a passionate lover of order and work'.[71] Liberty, work, and order were the three main props of the house that Montessori built for children. From their very earliest years the children were performing exercises in orderly arrangement; and, capitalising on the sensitive period for order,

her didactic apparatus was designed to build order constantly and permanently into the various impressions which a child absorbed. In her program Montessori regarded the silence exercises as among the most important. To stand silent, listen to a whisper, and carry out a command quietly, was, she contended, an excellent basis for developing order and a disciplined mind. Orderly behaviour, in her view, was akin to moral behaviour. By eliminating disorder, which is bad, her school provided for the children liberty for what is orderly and good.[72]

Influence of Montessori. Montessori's influence was widespread. She made some impact in probably every country of the world, and, in the education of young children, hers was the greatest influence since the time of Froebel. Her work appealed more strongly to teachers in English-speaking countries than elsewhere. There was a Montessori Society established in England in 1912, and many of the progressive schools such as Bedales established Montessori classes. By 1920 there were many Montessori classes throughout England, and a well-known English educator testified to her influence in the 1920's with his remark that 'there is little doubt that the most vital movement in education today is the movement towards individual work ... "auto-education" has become a watchword and a battle-cry'.[73] In the United States, triumphantly visited by Montessori in 1914, classes were set up with great enthusiasm and, with the erection of a Montessori school in Philadelphia, the movement got well under way; by the mid 1920's, however, the Montessorian influence was fading.

In 1919 Montessori established a six-month international training course; one course was given in London every second year from 1919-38, and in various cities in Europe, America, India, and Ceylon in the other years. The courses were well attended by teachers and parents from the United States, Australia, India, and many European countries. The trainees on their return in many cases succeeded in establishing classes and in spreading Montessori's influence. Thus, several of her students set up schools in Czarist Russia at St Petersburg and Moscow, and the impact was continued into the early years of the Soviet regime.[74] International

---

68 Maria Montessori, *The Montessori Method*, p. 98.

69 *ibid.*, p. 224.

70 Maria Montessori, *The Secret of Childhood*, p. 230, in chapter which she entitled 'Homo Laborans'.

71 Maria Montessori, *Peace and Education*, p. 13.

72 Maria Montessori, *Dr Montessori's Own Handbook*, pp. 129-30.

73 P.B. Ballard, *The Changing School*, University of London Press, London, 1925, p. 183.

74 Nadia Labriola, 'Report from Russia', *The Call of Education*, 2, 1, 1925, pp. 57-64, R.C. Petersen trans.

Montessori Congresses were also established. Beginning at Helsinki in 1925 and presided over by Maria Montessori until the Ninth Congress in London in 1951, the year before her death, they served to bring together interested persons and trained Montessori teachers from all parts of the world. The congresses were a continual demonstration that the method had as one writer put it, 'universal application'.[75] Montessori did not approve of adaptations to existing materials or practices, but she was interested in promoting the development of further materials and ideas that were consistent with the fundamentals of her approach. Probably the two most striking developments made by her trainees were in the adaptation of her ideas to secondary school work, viz. the Howard Plan of individual timetabling developed by M. O'B. Harris in the Clapton Secondary School, London,[76] and the Dalton Laboratory Plan worked out by Helen Pankhurst and first used in the high school at Dalton, Massachusetts.[77]

Montessori's work met with great enthusiasm, but it also touched off considerable controversy among her contemporaries. Two criticisms stand out, both by leading educators of the time.

Wilhelm Stern, whose *Psychology of Early Childhood*, first published in 1914, and continually republished for the next twenty-five years, was a landmark in European child development study, took Montessori to task on four main grounds. He thought that the Montessori school did not have a broad enough range in its activities; it was too exclusively intellectual. Play, the cultivation of a wide range of interests, and the development of the imagination were unfortunately neglected. Secondly, he thought that her claims to scientific knowledge and procedure were wide of the mark. Her practices were basically unsuited to what was known of the nature of the development of young children, and were a premature transference of school methods to a period of a child's life for which they were inappropriate. Thirdly, he thought Montessori unduly restricted the way in which the child could use her material. Although she spoke much of spontaneity, freedom, and independence she straitjacketed her children by confining them to apparatus which she had designed and by insisting that they make use of it only in a specified way. Stern's final criticism was of the lack of adequate social education. The children in Montessori schools did not work in groups. Each was concerned with his own activity, other children were 'only NEAR, and BESIDE, but not as a fact WITH each other'.[78]

An American educator, W.H. Kilpatrick, writing as a convinced Deweyan, endorsed the criticisms made by Stern, but found Montessori's re-emphasis on freedom in education to be highly commendable. He was particularly critical of the theoretical basis of her sensory education, on the ground that it rested on an outmoded view of the transfer of training. In summing up his views he wrote, 'we feel compelled to say that, in the content of her doctrine, she belongs essentially to the mid-nineteenth century, some fifty years behind the present development of educational theory.'[79]

Despite such criticism, Montessori's impact on twentieth century education was considerable. Because of its simplicity, its precise material, its limited scope, and its tangible results, the Montessori method appealed to many teachers who were looking for some firm guidance in their work; and it appealed also to teachers with scanty resources, such as those in underdeveloped countries where a firm pattern with a modicum of equipment proved to be a very expedient approach. Maria Montessori's main contribution , however, to the stream of twentieth century education lay not in the convenience of her suggestions, but in the more general impact that her ideas had on the attitudes of the teaching profession to children and to the educational process. She was a worthy successor to Ellen Key who had proclaimed the twentieth century as the century of the child. As a result of Montessori's work, teachers came to pay more attention to the observation and the study of the children whom they were teaching. And, furthermore, they began to move the emphasis in the teaching process away from the teacher to the children. The twentieth century trend towards greater independence and individual responsibility on the part of the pupils probably owed more to Montessori than to any other single educator.

(ii) Georg Kerschensteiner (1854-1932)

'The German School,' wrote an English observer in 1904 'is really one of the most effective factories in the world.'[80] It was against such an assessment that a lively group of German educators, early in the century, entered a sharp and sustained protest. Schoolmasters such as Lichtwark in Hamburg began a movement for more artistic and creative work in schools; Gläser, in the same city, propounded and eventually experimented in the public school system with an open, ungraded, child-centred system of education; Otto in Berlin ran, from 1906, a self-governing school with an integrated and highly individualised program; Sickinger in Mannheim reorganised the primary grades to provide courses for a

[75]   E.M. Standing, *The Montessori Revolution in Education*, Schocker, New York, (1962) 1966, p. 204.

[76]   M. O'B. Harris, *Towards Freedom*, University of London Press, London, 1923.

[77]   Helen Parkhurst, *Education on the Dalton Plan*, Bell, London, 1924.

[78]   W. Stern, *op.cit.*, p. 529.

[79]   W.H. Kilpatrick, *Montessori Examined*, Constable, London, 1915, p. 85.

[80]   C. Brereton, *Studies in Foreign Education*, Harrap, London, 1913, p. 253.

variety of abilities and to make both accelerated and more leisurely progress possible; and educational writers such as Gurlitt argued for the free development of personality, and Gaudig for more individual self-expression and creative activity in schools.

The pleas to give more attention to the cultivation of individual needs and interests in children were parallelled by other substantial voices arguing for more attention to the social content of education. The chief among the educational philosophers with a highly social approach was Paul Natorp.[81] Plato, Fichte, and Pestalozzi were the educational writers whom he most esteemed; for they were the ones who were most interested in a transformation of society in which a transformed education was to be one of the principal agents of the change. Natorp was critical of contemporary Herbartians and individualistically-minded educators because they did not give sufficient attention to that kind of objective. 'Man,' he pointed out, 'is man only in human society and through his participation in the life of society.'[82] Organised society educates and is, in turn, dependent on education. Education must go hand in hand with social reform to ensure the improvement of society. Educators must, therefore, try to secure equality of educational opportunity, must make their pupils socially competent, and must see that their pupils participate in socially useful activities. Natorp was widely studied in Germany, and had a sympathetic reader in Kerschensteiner who eventually found himself in a position to put the theory into practice.

Kerschensteiner was born in Munich, the chief city of Bavaria, and spent all his working life in the schools of that southern German state. He trained as an elementary school teacher and, while teaching, developed an interest in science. He returned for further study at a gymnasium and subsequently graduated in mathematics and science at the University of Munich. In 1883 he began work as a secondary school teacher, taught for twelve years in various Bavarian towns, and in 1894 was appointed Director of Education for Munich. He occupied that post until his retirement almost a quarter of a century later, in 1919.[83]

Kerschensteiner's main responsibility was for the elementary and continuation schools of the municipality. He made his name through the reforms that he introduced into both of these kinds of schools, as a result of which he became the most widely-known German schoolman in the first two decades of the twentieth century.

Continuation Education. The continuation schools in Munich, as in most places in Germany at the end of the nineteenth century, were compulsory classes offering to pupils who had left the elementary school a general education for two to four years five to eight hours a week in the evenings and on Sundays. Kerschensteiner succeeded in having the pupils released

from their employment to attend continuation education during the daytime for a full or half day as well as in the early evening, for about nine hours per week for a period of four years.

He abandoned general education, and substituted for it special continuation schools for particular trades. His schools were compulsory for all apprentices from the age of fourteen to eighteen, and they covered all the existing industrial, commercial, and agricultural trades of the area. The courses involved practical and theoretical instruction in a particular trade, arithmetic, drawing, bookkeeping, and business composition associated with the trade, religion, hygiene, and civics.

The curriculum was a successful and popular blend of technical, economic, and social material of clear interest and usefulness to young people beginning to earn their living and to take a responsible part in society. It was intended to be both a vocational education and an education in citizenship. Kerschensteiner was particularly interested in its civic aspects. He endeavoured to promote the education of the citizen by encouraging a close association between local trade organisations and his courses, by emphasising the social character of the work done in the school workshops, and by introducing a compulsory civics course. This course included: German history; a history of particular trades; health and first-aid; industrial organisation; elementary economics; a study of

[81] Alfred Lichtwark (1852-1914) was one of the founders of the art education movement in Hamburg. Johannes Gläser coined the slogan *vom Kinde aus* (child-centred). Berthold Otto (1859-1933) called by another educator 'the most influential of our German educators', ran his experimental school in Berlin from 1906 to 1933, and wrote *The Reformation of the School* in 1912. J. Anton Sickinger (1858-1930) was the school superintendent in Mannheim from 1895 to 1923. Ludwig Gurlitt (1855-1931) taught in Berlin and Munich, and was one of the most severe critics of traditional education, and an advocate of educational freedom. Hugo Gaudig (1860-1923) was, from 1900 to 1923, director of a girls' college and teacher training institution, and was a widely read writer on education and personal development. Paul Natorp (1854-1924) became a professor at the University of Marburg. His major works in education were *Sozialpädagogik* (1899), and *Philosophie und Pädagogik* (1909).

[82] P. Natorp, *Religion innerhalb der Grenzen der Humanität*, quoted in F. de Hovre, *Philosophy and Education*, E.B. Jordan trans., Benziger, New York, 1930, p. 118.

[83] In 1918 Kerschensteiner became a professor of education at the University of Munich and retained this position until his death in 1932. During his directorship, in 1912, he became a member of the federal Reichstag and regularly attended its meetings in Berlin. He travelled widely in Europe and America and wrote several comparative studies on aspects of education in Germany and the English-speaking countries. Throughout his career he wrote extensively on educational questions, notably in the years from 1907 to World War I, and during the 1920's after his retirement. His most significant works were: an essay on Education for Citizenship that gained him a public prize in 1900 and was described by M.E. Sadler as 'a landmark in the history of education' (G. Kerschensteiner, *Education for Citizenship*, A.J. Pressland, trans. Harrap, London, 1912, introd. by M.E. Sadler, p. ix.); a speech at Zurich honouring Pestalozzi in 1908, 'The School of the Future, an Activity School' (G. Kerschensteiner, *The Schools and the Nation*, C.K. Ogden, trans., Macmillan, London, 1914. This volume is a collection of speeches and articles); The Idea of the Activity School *(Arbeitsschule)* (G. Kerschensteiner, *Begriff der Arbeitsschule*, Teubner, Liepzig, 1912. A substantial chapter on work in its educational context was added in 1925. The English translation is *The Idea of the Industrial School*, R. Pintner, trans., Macmillan, New York, 1913); his comprehensive *Theory of Education* (G. Kerschensteiner, *Theorie der Bildung*, Teubner, Leipzig, 1926).

the individual, community and state, and the interrelationships between them; and personal and civic behaviour. Voluntary continuation schools were also available for tradesmen who were interested in further improving their qualifications.

Reform of Elementary Education. In the elementary schools Kerschensteiner changed both the curriculum and the tone. The work in the schools was 'based on the principle that the treatment of the various separate subjects must always keep in view one single end, the education of the future citizen, and in order to attain this object, the material was selected, and its treatment prescribed in such a manner as to render possible the encouragement of the elementary civic virtues, independent work and creative power, and the development of productive capacity in the spirit of perseverence, thoroughness, and conscientiousness.'[84]

From 1900 the elementary schools of Munich became eight-year schools for pupils from six to approximately fourteen years of age. The course of studies consisted of religion, language work, arithmetic and geometry, geography, history, science, manual work and gymnastics. Kerschensteiner's contribution to its reorganisation was to encourage a more thorough and thoughtful study of the material. He fostered activity methods in the schools, especially by supplying them with laboratories, workshops, school kitchens, and school gardens, and by supporting the idea that the pupils' learning should be based on their observation, personal experience, and productive work. He gave a greater emphasis to the teaching of science, manual work, gymnastics, and sport. Through all subjects, and particularly through these latter ones, and through experience of group work and self-government in the schools, he hoped to interest the pupils in matters of social and civic importance such as health, trade, technology, and community relationships, and to provide them with the intellectual skills and the moral virtues that could become the foundation of good citizenship.

Education for Citizenship. Kerschensteiner's work was a challenge to contemporary education in several ways. He criticised the barrenness and superficiality of existing education. He vigorously repudiated the Herbartian general education of 'many-sided interests', then entrenched in educational thinking. He rejected the egoistic competitiveness of the traditional school and the individualism of many contemporary reformers, and argued strenuously for co-operation and altruism. He put forward the activity school to replace the book school. He advocated and

Georg Kerschensteiner (1854-1932), noted German educational administrator and supporter of the activity school.

---

[84]   G. Kerschensteiner, *The Schools and the Nation*, p. 301.

endeavoured to show in his Munich schools an education relevant to the twentieth century in which the pupils would be engaged in productive rather than reproductive work, in which knowledge and action should be brought into a close and fruitful relationship, and in which education for effective community living would go hand-in-hand with up-to-date vocational preparation. The technological society of the twentieth century needed, he believed, better scientific knowledge for all, better technical education particularly for lower and middle level workers and better education in civic responsibilities.

'The aim of all education,' Kerschensteiner wrote in his early prize essay, 'is to produce a society, consisting, as far as possible, of persons characterized by independence of mind, harmonious development, and freedom of action which springs from high principles.'[85] The principal function of the public school was the education of the citizen for that kind of society. It had three features:

- To fit an individual for carrying out some useful function in society;

- To accustom the individual to regard his vocation as a duty not merely to his own welfare but to the interests of the community in which he lived;

- To develop in the pupils a desire to contribute to their society in such a way that it might progress further towards its ideal condition.

To achieve the aims, it was necessary, Kerschensteiner thought, to change the book schools into work communities, to convert the values acquired by mere habit into values meaningfully associated with citizenship, and to provide experience of government and civic affairs.

Kerschensteiner's ideal society was a technological social democracy, a society probably not unlike that sought by Dewey whom, about 1910, he began to study and found both congenial and illuminating. 'Many of my ideas,' he wrote in his autobiography, 'hitherto unclear, I have been able to clarify as a result of an intensive study of his writings.'[86] Kerschensteiner's ideal community was clearly not yet in being; it was, nevertheless, an important aspiration and educational guide. It was a state of universal altruism in which each individual got his satisfaction from working for the common good, a state in which service to others was the first of virtues. One of Kerschensteiner's main criticisms of contemporary schools was that they actively encouraged the reverse. They cultivated, in their pupils, personal advantage and egoism. 'They are schools where the selfish desire for knowledge, and not — or hardly at all — the social nature, undergoes a systematic development...The modern

school is not constituted or directed so as to make the social forces co-operative through suitable work.'[87]

The ideal to strive for was the situation in which the aims of the individual coincide with the common good. This was the end towards which civic education was to be directed: it was not aimed at the preservation of the existing state but at the realisation of the ideal. Nevertheless, the existing community, and the national state which was its most prominent form, were worthy of loyalty, especially as one of the duties of the modern state is to work 'towards a state of humanity among mankind'.[88] Service to them would give opportunity for co-operativeness, and bring out the altruistic attitudes that express the real purpose of human life.

In his continuation schools, therefore, he sought first to appeal to the pupil's interest in his vocation, and then to show its social implications. He supplemented this approach with a subject called civics which introduced the pupil to the history, current state, and values of his society. He encouraged practical work in science and handicrafts that involved small teams working together on a common task or problem, and he fostered schemes of self-government in the schools in the hope that they would develop into work communities. He held the view that 'one cannot educate people to be men without educating them to be a community',[89] and that the fundamental problem of public education is how to provide 'the systematic training and organisation of the people to take pleasure in active constructive work for the common good'.[90]

Activity School. Kerschensteiner's reforms were designed to give the schools of Munich more of the character of what he called the school of the future, the *Arbeitsschule* meant, for most educators in Germany, a work school, in the curriculum of which manual work had a prominent place. It implied also that direct experience beyond the vicarious experience of book learning was an important ingredient of education. Kerschensteiner's lecture in Zurich in 1908 and its subsequent enlargement into his book *Begriff der Arbeitsschule* (1912) gave to the word a fresh popularity and a more sophisticated meaning. *Arbeitsschule*, henceforth interpreted as

[85] G. Kerschensteiner, *Education for Citizenship*, p. 18.

[86] E. Hahn ed. *Die Pädagogik der Gegenwart in Selbstdarstellungen*, Felix Meiner, Leipzig, 1926, p. 75. For Dewey see chapter 3.

[87] G. Kerschensteiner, *The Schools and the Nation*, pp. 11-12.

[88] G. Kerschensteiner, *The Idea of the Industrial School*, p. 14.

[89] G. Kerschensteiner, *Theorie der Bildung*, Teubner, Leipzig, 1926, p. 213, quoted in D. Simons, *Georg Kerschensteiner*, Methuen, London, 1966, p. 132.

[90] G. Kerschensteiner, *The Schools and the Nation*, p. 14.

'activity school', became a catchword for the next fifteen or so years to rally the school reformers of continental Europe.[91]

He envisaged an activity school as one in which work was the central feature, work which should give pleasure, gain the pupil's interest, arouse effort, and be conducted efficiently.[92] Work did not necessarily have to be vocational. This was the obvious kind of work which held the interest of young apprentices in continuation schools; in much of the elementary schools, however, vocational work was out of place. He therefore spoke of 'productive' work, contrasting it with play. The job of the school was to turn play into work, 'earnest, intensive, practical activity'.[93]

Productive work was full of purpose; its purpose imposed a discipline on the worker and set up duties that must be performed; its accomplishment gave rise to fresh ideas and provided an impetus for further learning; and the whole progress developed strength of character and gave satisfaction with life. Truly productive work, Kerschensteiner suggested, might be undertaken in all the different subjects of the school curriculum, e.g. in history, through the use of original documents; in literature, by acting in plays; in physics, chemistry, and biology, by undertaking experiments; and in social studies, by experience in responsible social service.

The activity for which the *Arbeitsschule* stood was the necessary basis of education in three important aspects:

- Effective learning, in Kerschensteiner's opinion, depended upon a proper combination of thinking and action.[94] Deploring the superficiality of the study of numerous subjects, especially in German secondary schools, Kerschensteiner exclaimed, 'We need men, not lexicons.'[95] Kerschensteiner was aware of the knowledge explosion that was already making it impossible for any one person to become competent and knowledgeable over a wide field. Intellectual education, he concluded, must concentrate upon three things. It must teach the structure of subjects — the essential ideas, the method of thinking, and the characteristic modes of operation of each subject; it must teach economy of thought — how to organise one's ideas and activities simply, logically, and comprehensively; and it must teach ways of putting thought into action. Intellectual skill, spontaneity, and productive application were to be prized far above the accumulation of knowledge.

- The activity approach was necessary in education for character development. There were four traits of character necessary for successful citizenship: will-power which produced initiative to undertake activities, and patience and perseverance to see them through; discernment to judge the issues clearly and objectively; sensitivity to others' feelings and points of view, and the tact to adapt readily and suitably to a variety of situations and people; and an inner involvement, an ability to involve oneself wholly in a task, an idea, or a cause, so as to become committed to a set of worthwhile values through which the person and the community could find fulfilment. Such traits of character could be developed only through earnest and sustained activity which made serious intellectual and moral demands on the pupils, for 'action is the only foundation of virtue'.[96] Productive work was 'one of the strongest moral agencies in the education of mankind',[97] more particularly when it was put to the service of society.

- To accomplish the principal task of the schools, that of educating for citizenship, it was necessary to develop in the pupils social and civic skills. For that task activity methods were indispensable. Concrete practical examples and exercises in social and civic duties, participation in law-making and committee work, involvement in situations in which community must come before personal interests, were the kinds of ways in which co-operative skills and altruistic attitudes might be developed. Wherever possible, to this training Kerschensteiner added experience in group work.

Importance of Kerschensteiner. Kerschensteiner's practical contribution lay in the fact that he was able to bring progressive education on a wide scale into a public school system, and to demonstrate there its workability over a sustained period of time. His success undoubtedly encouraged other public authorities later to make interesting attempts, notably in Hamburg, Vienna, and the U.S.S.R. in the 1920's.

In the Activity School movement he stands midway between the advocates of individual creativity with their unplanned programs of

---

[91] H. Schloen, *Entwicklung und Aufbau der Arbeitsschule*, Union Deutsche, Berlin, 1926, pp. 226-7; see also A.E. Meyer, 'The *Arbeitsschule* in Germany', *Pedagogical Seminary*, XXXIII, 1926, pp. 508-20.

[92] G. Kerschensteiner, *Education for Citizenship*, p. 56.

[93] G. Kerschensteiner, *The Idea of the Industrial School*, p. 65; *The Schools and the Nation*, p. 49.

[94] In his autobiography he confessed to an admiration for Goethe's educational insight, and quoted a passage from *Wilhelm Meister's Travels*: 'Thought and action, action and thought, that is the sum of all [educational] wisdom...Whoever makes it a rule for himself...to test action against thought and thought against action cannot go astray, and, if he should stray, he will soon find himself back on the right path.' This Kerschensteiner affirmed, was the fundamental idea he had always kept in mind. J.W. Goethe, *Werke*, Bk. VIII, *Wilhelm Meisters Wanderjahre*, 2, 9, Wegner, Hamburg, quoted by Kerschensteiner in E. Hahn, *Die Pädagogik der Gegenwart in Selbstdarstellungen*, p. 91.

[95] G. Kerschensteiner, *The Schools and the Nation*, p. 257.

[96] G. Kerschensteiner, *Education for Citizenship*, p. 25.

[97] *ibid.*, p. 63.

experiences, and Blonsky's *Arbeitsschule* centring on industrial production. He commanded an audience by his obvious practical success, and by his moderate but convinced advocacy of activity school work.

Kerschensteiner brought the twentieth century into education. He saw a new democratic force coming into being, and he embraced the social philosophy that Natorp and Dewey put forward to cater for the new educational situation. He remodelled and popularised continuation education for the working classes, and built the elementary school into a common school for all. He saw the need to build new social and civic skills for the new society, and, above all, the need to reconstruct the schools, to change them from the cultivation of selfish individualism, competition, and reproduction to the nurture of co-operation, altruism, and productive work. He saw the increasing technological revolution and the knowledge explosion that was accompanying it, and he advanced the cause of science, technical training, and intelligent specialisation to cope with these developments. In 1916 he summed up his own efforts and aspirations when he wrote: 'The transformation of the school from a place where "personal ambition" is cultivated into a place where pupils are trained for social duty; its transformation from a place where theoretical intellectual many-sidedness is practised into a workshop of practical human many-sidedness; its transformation from a place where solid knowledge is acquired into a school where the judicious use of knowledge is acquired: here we have the fundamental reform that is both necessary and indispensable to our whole school organisation.'[98] In short, he suggested an intellectual, moral, and civic education that was rigorous, stimulating, practicable, and designed to be abreast of the times.

(iii) Ovide Decroly (1871-1932)

Decroly is the representative man of progressive education. In his work he effectively incorporated a wide range of the new tendencies of the early twentieth century and skilfully built them into an attractive, workable, and distinctive program that became known as the Decroly method.[99]

Decroly was not a prolific writer. His books and articles, often written in collaboration with one of his fellow-teachers or research workers, dealt with the development of tests of intelligence and other abilities, and with the various methods of teaching and the educational programs developed for normal and for atypical children at his schools. Decroly's great strength came from the effective combination of his three main occupations: he was a doctor of medicine, an educational psychologist, and a practical schoolteacher. In each of his roles he was both practitioner and theorist, and he had the capacity to combine his interests in a stimulating and fruitful way. Scholar and man of action, Decroly was dedicated to the task of humanising and enlivening the

education of children. He had the commonsense of a scientifically trained person, and the democratic feeling of a devoted social worker. He was a modest, unassuming man, who could enter empathically into the concerns of children, and find ingenious and satisfying ways of catering for their needs and interests. With persistence, enthusiasm, and the staunch support of a talented staff, his ideas were developed and tested from the beginning of the century for over thirty years through his school for atypical children which he established in 1901; through his school in the *rue de l'Ermitage* founded six years later, and through the classes that the local educational authorities, motivated by his example, were prompted to set up.

L'Ecole de l'Ermitage. Claparède in 1922 wrote of 'that humming, working hive' that was the school in the rue de l'Ermitage.[100] It was an activity school, offering education for life by living.[101]

Established in 1907 with a few pupils in a modest house, the school grew to two hundred and fifty to three hundred in the 1920's and moved out to more spacious premises on the outskirts of Brussels. The new building was a large, rambling, turretted house set in extensive and beautiful grounds which lent themselves to a variety of exciting activities for children. In this place there was 'nothing monastic, nothing of the barracks or the academic prison. Children breathed pure air, lived in the bright house or in the full sunlight of the smiling garden; they frisked

---

[98] G. Kerschensteiner, *Deutsche Schulerziehung im Krieg und Frieden*, p. 88, quoted in F. De Hovre, *Philosophy and Education*, E.B. Jordan trans., Benziger, New York, 1931, p. 132.

[99] Decroly was born at a small town in Belgium in 1871, was successful in school and entered the University of Ghent where he studied medicine. After graduation he worked for a short while in Paris and Berlin, decided to concentrate on neurology and mental diseases, and joined a clinic in Brussels. There, in Brussels, he worked for the rest of his life. In 1901 he established a school for defective children attached to his own residence. In 1903 he became an inspector of special classes for Brussels, and gradually built up a reputation throughout Europe as a leading authority on the education of defective children.

In 1907, being persuaded to apply his experience to normal children, he founded a school in the *rue de l'Ermitage*, in a well-to-do suburb of Brussels. The school, generally known as *L'Ecole de l'Ermitage*, was an experimental venture through which Decroly made his main contribution to educational thought and practice. It remained his constant concern for twenty-five years until his death in 1932. His interest in education and his influence on current thinking were extended by his joining the staff of the higher normal school in Brussels in 1913, and by his appointment, in 1920, as professor of child psychology in the University of Brussels. In the following year he also became head of the department of school hygiene in the university medical school. Throughout the 1920's he was a regular attender and speaker at the biennial international conferences of the New Education Fellowship, and he travelled throughout Europe, the United States, and Latin America observing and advising on educational practices.

[100] Amélie Hamaïde, *The Decroly Class*, preface E. Claparède, Jean L. Hunt trans., Dent, London, 1925, p. xxvii.

[101] 'L'ecole de la vie pour la vie', see E. Flayol, *Le Dr. O. Decroly Educateur*, Nathan, Paris, 1934, p. 152.

about on the lawns, or ran till they were out of breath along the pathways. Couches were set up in the sun for a quiet rest or siesta. Everywhere there were pet animals: cats, dogs, sheep, tortoises, birds, all cared for as attentively as the fowls, rabbits, and garden plants. Nature surrounded them on all sides . . .'[102]

For most of Decroly's life the school received pupils of both sexes from about the age of four to fifteen; in 1930 the age range was extended upward to eighteen, thus providing for its pupils a range of schooling covering kindergarten, primary, and secondary work, and enabling them to proceed from *l'Ecole de l'Ermitage* to the university.

The aim of the school was to develop an active life in the pupils to its greatest extent. The school catered for their intellectual, physical, social and aesthetic life by arranging their educational environment in such a way that they could follow their interests with the maximum zest and educational profit to themselves and their society. Like Dewey's school in Chicago, *l'Ecole de l'Ermitage* and its gardens was a laboratory. It was one in which the children could work at their interests with joy, persistence, and intellectual and aesthetic benefit. Each classroom was equipped like a studio, and the staff were trained to observe and stimulate.

The daily school program was in three parts:

● The morning started with work on the 3R's, the techniques of written and spoken language and of number, taught by what the Decroly staff called an ideovisual method.

● Following the 3R's came a Centre-of-Interest program which was the central part of the school work.

● Finally, in the late morning, or after the school-provided midday meal, there was opportunity for the pupils to pursue their own manual interests or to learn a foreign language.

The methods used in the initial stages of the teaching of reading illustrated Decroly's use of interest, wholeness, relevance, and expressive activities to motivate learning. By starting with short sentences, and teaching children to recognise whole sentence patterns, by relating reading to everyday experiences and to play activities, by building up a systematic structure of words and sentences, and by encouraging pupils to make up their own stories, Decroly's teachers met with great success in initiating children into reading, and preparing them for the activities of the centres-of-interest program.

Decroly had four important criticisms to make of contemporary school education. It took too much account of academic specialties and too little of the psychology of children's learning and development, with the result that school work was not well enough adapted to the age, the

competence, and the interests of children. The subjects for study were isolated from one another, and the relationship of ideas between them was not usually grasped by the pupils. Too much of the time and effort of the school pupils was put into acquisition and too little into expression, as if children were purely receptive, rather than vitally active creatures. And, finally, as a consequence of the other defects, there was an enormous amount of backwardness in the schools. Decroly estimated that in 1921 eighty-five per cent of the school children of Brussels benefited only minimally from their education and left school with a small amount of half-assimilated knowledge, with a distaste for intellectual activity, with an aversion to work, and with an ingrained sense of discouragement.[103] In several of his studies on school achievement he was able to show that backwardness was rampant in the schools, in the same dimension that Ayres in the U.S.A. and Burt in England had dramatically demonstrated. From that evidence Decroly became convinced of the need to organise school classes into ability groups and to introduce active, individualised school programs suited to the needs and interests of the children.

His principal contribution towards overcoming the shortcomings of contemporary education was his centre of interest program developed at *L'Ecole de l'Ermitage*. It arose out of his study of children; it was an integrated approach with no separate subjects; and it had a careful balance of observational, associative, and expressive activities.

Centres of Interest. 'Interest,' wrote Decroly, 'is the sluice gate. By means of it the reservoir of attention is opened and directed.'[104] Since the early years of the century interest had become an important word in the vocabulary of education. It was the fuse that the Herbartians had to activate in order to set their instructional process in motion, and for Dewey it was an indicator of the direction of a child's growth. Decroly's viewpoint, in this as in many other matters, resembled that of Dewey. Interest was not something to be aroused more or less artificially; it was an expression of the child's very being. As an educational psychologist Decroly was concerned principally with the study of child growth. His orientation, like that of Montessori, was that of the emerging dynamic school of Bergson in France, and McDougall in England. For Decroly, children had an *élan vital* that educators should capitalise on; it was expressed most distinctly in the interests that arose out of their basic needs. The most fruitful path of child development, therefore, was to be found by cultivating interests through

[102]   E. Flayol, *Le Dr. O. Decroly Educateur*, p. 155.

[103]   O. Decroly and G. Boon, *Vers L'Ecole Rénovée*, Office de Publicité, Bruxelles, 1921, p. 11.

[104]   Amélie Hamaïde, *The Decroly Class*, p. 32.

which basic needs could be satisfied. The appropriate educational program was one which centred round the needs and interests of the child.

'I believe,' wrote Decroly, 'we must say this; the knowledge most necessary to the child is, in the first place, knowledge of himself...

After knowledge of himself follows logically that of the world about him, the environment in which he as a child finds himself...

I consider the environment solely from the child's point of view, and I discard so far as possible, whatever does not relate directly to his life...

Thus it is the needs of the child that serve as a pivotal fact and all that society and nature, living and inanimate, supply for their satisfaction may be used as the subject matter of learning, in the measure, let it be said, in which the mind of the child is able to assimilate them.'[105]

Accordingly, Decroly first set out three major divisions of the environment within which children's needs may seek for satisfaction: the human environment — family, school, and societal life; the living environment of animal and vegetable life; and non-living environment. He then listed four primitive needs with which clusters of interests are associated: the need to feed oneself, the need to protect oneself from the elements, the need to defend oneself against dangers and enemies of various kinds, the need for activity, for example, for work with one's fellows, for recreation, and for self-development.

From these needs he specified four major centres of interest:

1. food
2. protection from the elements
3. defence against enemies
4. work, and mutual dependence.

The major part of school time was spent on the study of those centres of interest, each one of which was linked, where appropriate, to as many aspects as possible of the various divisions of the pupils' environment. They took the place of school subjects and were studied with different content and in varying degrees of depth from year to year according to the level and range of interest developed by the pupils. In the early years of the school's existence topics taken from several centres of interest were studied in all classes each year. After 1921 this practice was retained for the younger children only; from the third grade upward the work for each year was organised about a single centre of interest.

Each centre was divided into manageable topics, and in the study of each topic there were three phases, viz. observation, association, and expression. These, in Decroly's view, were the three central educational activities of a school. His activity school, therefore, developed its teaching methods around them in a sort of tripartite process.

Observation and its corollary, measurement, were, for Decroly, the activities upon which an understanding of the environment and sound

intellectual growth were based. 'Observation exercises,' he wrote, 'consist in making the intelligence work on material gathered at first hand.'[106] His scientific training and interests inclined him to introduce much more biological and physical material into the school program than was usual at the time, and also to encourage pupils to use scientific procedures. The term observation implied first-hand direct experience of things, places, and people; hence there was an extensive use of the gardens at *L'Ecole de l'Ermitage*, an accumulation of pets, aquaria, and children's collections, and frequent excursions to see places and people of interest. Observation usually starts with a general impression; it is a globalisation, and through it an overall meaning is grasped or an attitude conveyed. Globalisation sets a pattern of interest which helps a pupil to persist with the study of a topic and fill out the meaning of the preliminary understanding he has gained. One should therefore tend for the most part to teach from the whole to the part rather than from the part to the whole. But for accurate perception it is necessary also to analyse and measure what has been observed. Out of elementary comparisons and measurements of materials used in their centre-of-interest program, the children learnt arithmetic. For their teachers and for students of education, Decroly co-authored in 1929 an *Introduction to Quantitative Pedagogy* dealing with statistical procedures that would help educators observe more rigorously the relationships among the factors which operate in their pupils' performance. He was responsible also for the development of questionnaires, and tests of intelligence, reading, and number through which his own experimentation in the teaching of reading, arithmetic, and interest-centred topics was improved.

Association followed observation. If the significance of the observed data is to be thoroughly understood, it must be assembled, classified, compared, and made the basis for generalisation. This series of associative and constructive processes one author has compared with Karl Pearson's analysis of scientific method. 'What is this but "The Grammar of Science" in terms of the elementary school?'[107] The procedures, however, as Amélie Hamaïde, Decroly's collaborator, described them, were also distinctly Herbartian. 'We begin by sense experiences, proceed by comparisons and noting of differences, and so by a process of elaboration arrive at some generalisation... This is followed by some application of the newly acquired ideas, sometimes in the form of a graphic resumé, sometimes as free work in composition, or as some practical application to his everyday life, or to his life in the school group.'[108] Most of the work

---

[105]   *ibid.*, p. 180.

[106]   E. Flayol, *Le Dr. O. Decroly Educateur*, p. 115.

[107]   Jean L. Hunt in Amélie Hamaïde, *The Decroly Class*, p. xiii.

[108]   *ibid.*, pp. 30-1.

listed in the school program under the heading of association was designed to meet the pupils' curiosity to know whether the activities they observed around them existed also in other places and at other times. Their curiosity on those matters became a vehicle for the teaching of geography and history, and in that way much of the content that the ordinary schools of Brussels taught was brought into the work of the Decroly classes.

Expression, the third of the school's fundamental educational activities, could be either concrete or abstract. Concrete expression might involve clay work, cutting, painting, drawing, and a variety of manual activities; abstract expression involved primarily language activity such as writing, original composition, and discussion. Manual activities were plentiful and varied and were regarded as important ways in which children could express their interests. Practice in expression helped to consolidate what had been learnt by observation and association, especially when it took the form of compiling notebooks and albums of work done. It helped also to expand the meaning of what was being learnt, and to enlarge the range of the pupils' interests. In their expressive activities the children were encouraged to develop their emotions in song, verse, dance, and drama; and they were stimulated to put themselves freely into whatever they wrote or built, and to express themselves creatively in whatever medium most interested and suited them.

The following is an example of a centre-of-interest program introduced during World War I and in use in Brussels schools in the early 1920's. It was a guide to work rather than a program to be formally adhered to.

Outline for Centre-of-Interest Program for Fourth Class.[109] The following is an abbreviated outline developed by the children of the fourth year (primary school) themselves with the aid of their teacher.

Centre of Interest: Plants.

Observation: Different parts of plant, pot-herbs, wild plants, uses of plants, plants used for medicine...

Association: Plants that grow in foreign lands, food plants of foreign lands, plant life throughout the ages, Ardenne and its forests, cactus plants of Mexico, sacred plants of the ancients...

Expression: Find words belonging to the word-families: plant, flower, leaf etc.; dialogue between a flower and a plant; the story of a flower girl and her violets; telling time by the flowers in my garden; conversation between the lotus flower and an Egyptian; drawing of fruit, flower and leaf designs; modelling flowers in clay; discussions on flower festivals; poisonous plants; growing cork etc.

Freedom and Solidarity. Decroly's centres of interest introduced a considerable measure of freedom into the school curriculum. Within a general pattern, they put forward wide areas in which the children could seek and choose their interests. They offered material that could be readily adjusted to the children's age, capability, and level of previous achievement. They did not prescribe a fixed amount of material to be covered by each child in each school hour. They provided a diversity of intellectual, affective, and physical activities, and the children were encouraged to add their own suggestions in a responsible way to the construction of the curriculum.

His flexible curriculum made it possible to provide more readily for individual differences among the pupils. Decroly, with his interest in Binet's work and his leaning towards measurement, was keenly aware of the variety of growth patterns among young children, and he sought to provide an educational environment that would stimulate the growth of every individual and at the same time preserve his spontaneity. Decroly never lost sight, however, of the individual as a member of society. The pupils' experiences at school were designed to contribute to the development of their social knowledge, skills, and attitudes. The class and the school were regarded as simplified societies. To show the children social life in simple form Decroly preferred a rural environment for schools and tried to maintain such an atmosphere at *L'Ecole de l'Ermitage*. The children were made partly responsible for the effective operation of the school society through the election of monitors, through the assignment of duties such as the feeding of pets or the maintenance of a nature collection, and through consultations on the discipline and conduct of the little society. Each centre of interest had social aspects to it, and many of the activities, e.g. excursions, involved the children both in the social experience of planning and arranging them, and in the study of social institutions.

Parents were encouraged to participate in the school's affairs, and at *L'Ecole de l'Ermitage* played a regular and important part in the organisation of the school. Thus the work of the school was knitted in some measure into the life of the community, and the children at school learned to feel that their work was part of that of the general society. The feeling of solidarity was carefully cultivated within the school also by the use of co-operative activities, such as the building of class nature collections, and by the development of a tradition of mutual assistance among pupils.

Education was oriented to the social realities of the present day.[110] The child was to be prepared for life by living to the full in existing society.

[109] Amélie Hamaïde, *The Decroly Class*, pp. 109-14.

[110] O. Decroly and G. Boon, *Vers l'Ecole Rénovée*, pp. 23-4.

Decroly hoped that people educated along his lines would help in due course to develop a better society, but his desire for social reconstruction had no strong influence on his educational aims and practices. It was enough for the children to learn to live joyfully, smoothly, and responsibly in the school community, and to grow steadily in understanding the great society of which their school was seen to be an integral part.

Decroly's Contribution to Education. Decroly in his work and thought united in an elegant and becoming synthesis the main trends that affected the growing edge of education in the early twentieth century. The Herbartians contributed to his method of association and to his use of interest which he transformed into the central feature of his thinking on the curriculum. From the scientific movement in education he plucked the processes of observation and measurement, and grafted them on to the process of association to form fundamental parts of his teaching method. The importance of studying and utilising children's needs to secure their effective and complete education he learned from the child study movement to which he was a distinguished contributor. From the same source came his keen sense of individual difference among his pupils, his desire not to suppress spontaneity, and his wish to give to all opportunity for variety and fullness of expression. He was a vital part of the activity school movement, voicing its protests about current education, and expressing its wish for a lively connection between school and life. Tinged with a faint utopianism, he was hopeful like most progressive educators that his work would contribute to a more vitally democratic society.

Many progressive schools in various countries have been outside the government systems and have remained relatively isolated from and of little influence on the main stream of education. It has always been a problem to devise ways in which their ideas and experience could be brought to bear on the teachers and pupils within the state system. Educators such as Decroly, therefore, who worked in person, or through their followers, within the state schools are of particular significance. They were able to show the workability of the new practices for ordinary pupils and teachers, and to leaven traditional schools with progressive ideas.

One of the virtues of Decroly's contribution was that he was able to maintain, though with a changed method, the teaching of the 3R's and much of the traditional primary school subject-matter, and that his pupils were able to acquire that knowledge and skill with no less success than in the traditional school. To these acquirements the Decroly pupils added a variety of other useful knowledge and skill, and considerable zest

for learning and living. It was not a difficult matter, therefore, for public authorities to become interested in Decroly's work and to seek to incorporate it into their own programs.

Decroly's influence in the schools made itself felt in the inter-war period. His school was given a government subsidy in 1921; in 1917 Mlle. Hamaïde started to introduce his work into the state schools, and by 1924 there were forty-six Decroly classes in the Brussels elementary school system. It was clear that his methods were not just for the sons and daughters of the well-to-do in the *rue de l'Ermitage*, but were applicable on a wider scale to the ordinary pupils and teachers in the ordinary schools.[111]

Several of Decroly's disciples became school inspectors, school principals, and lecturers in teacher training institutions, and spread the effect of his work more widely throughout Belgium. Official bulletins containing suggested programs were produced, and guides for teachers were written. The author of one of the guides was moved to commence the preface to its second edition in 1931 with the remark that the success of Dr Decroly's principles of education was by then beyond contention. For ten years they had been the subject of numerous official reports and investigation both in Belgium and abroad, and had managed to stand up to the examination.[112]

Beyond Belgium Decroly became widely known and *L'Ecole de L'Ermitage* was visited by educators from many countries. In the 1920's there were many examples of attempts to dispense with traditional subjects and to build integrated curricula. The most widely known of these efforts were the project method developed in the U.S.A., and the 'method of complexes' in the U.S.S.R. Both had affinities to Decroly's 'centres of interest', but there is no evidence that either was influenced in its original development by his work. In Austria and in Spain the republican governments in the 1920's used a centre-of-interest approach in their primary schools that was related to and affected by Decroly's work. Latin American countries proved to be most receptive to his ideas; and, in almost every country of that area in the 1920's and 1930's, his influence was felt in some measure through training programs in normal schools or experimental classes at primary level.[113]

Decroly and his disciples demonstrated clearly for primary school classes the feasibility and benefit of an approach to the curriculum that largely dispensed with traditional subjects, and took its stand on observational, associative, and expressive activities organised around

[111]   Amélie Hamaïde, *op.cit.*, p. 234.

[112]   L. Dalhem, *Contribution à la Méthode De Croly*, 2nd edn, Lamertin, Bruxelles, 1932.

[113]   E. Flayol, *op.cit.*, pp. 210-12.

pupils' needs and interests. Experimentation with pupils in the secondary school above the age of fourteen had hardly got under way before Decroly's death in 1932. Decroly's work in Belgium was the forerunner of the movement, developed especially in the United States in the inter-war period, to use the needs and interests of children as the basis of curriculum construction and teaching method. His centres of interest anticipated the experience-based curricula developed by many public authorities, and the core curricula produced by some of the secondary schools in the Progressive Education Association's Eight Year Study of the late 1930's.

(iv) The Trend of Montessori's, Kerschensteiner's, and Decroly's Work

All three — Montessori, Kerschensteiner, and Decroly — despite their different emphases, came out of the same matrix. They were a part of the same movement for educational renovation; they experienced the same social and cultural trends; and they absorbed and, each in his own way, reacted to the educational climate of the early twentieth century.

The biological tone of Montessori's work reflected the prevailing sense of the importance of science and, in particular, of the contribution that biology might make to the understanding of human development and human behaviour. Bergson had made current the idea of an *élan vital*, a dynamic and expressive force in human nature. Montessori took a similar stand and argued for the desirability of providing an educational environment which would encourage the expression of the individual's 'inner drives'. It was a 'conception of biological liberty, in other words, the triumph of the free and peaceful development of life', which, she contended, 'constitutes, in my opinion, the very essence of the new pedagogy.'[114] As sensitive periods emerged in a child's development they were to be taken up, and the individual was to be encouraged to move purposefully on to the next stage of this development. Purposive behaviour, expressed through the children's interests, was a central part also of the process of learning and developing, in the theory and practice of Ovide Decroly, whose career as doctor, authority on defective children, educational psychologist, practical schoolteacher, and university lecturer was remarkably similar to that of Montessori. For both of them freedom and spontaneity had a biological basis and justification. Both of them, too, liked to regard themselves as scientists, who were helping to forge a science of education for the new age. Kerschensteiner also was attracted to science, but his concern was to expand the teaching of it, and relate it to the work and the civic interests of society.

All three educators were part of the growing activity school movement. Kerschensteiner's insistence on the educative value of productive work, Montessori's view that satisfaction came from the active process of acquiring rather than from the product, and Decroly's belief that expression was the culminating activity in learning, were key ideas in the activity school movement that they developed and strengthened by their work.

The contributors to the child study movement and the developmental psychologists, popular at the turn of the century, had made detailed studies of the process of child growth, and had experimented extensively with sense discrimination and the motor functions associated with sensory perception. Individual differences in growth patterns among children were widely noted, and the need for curricula, materials, and teaching methods adapted to individual needs was canvassed by many educators. Montessori and Decroly shared the current concern, and the one, by her advocacy of auto-education, and the other, by his centres-of-interest approach, sought to meet the rising demand. The relation of intellectual education to various sensory processes was also a popular topic for discussion and research among educational psychologists. Montessori and Decroly were both widely acquainted with current activity in that field; and their own work and ideas reflected their interest. Montessori made sensory training a cardinal feature of her method of cognitive and moral education, and Decroly built the associative part of his teaching process on sense experience.

Above all they sympathised with the prevailing desire of the progressives to form a new generation which might develop a higher order of personal and social experience. The altruistic side of social Darwinism affected all three. Notably, Kerschensteiner made co-operation and service of the common good the central feature of the new character and the new society that might emerge from the reform of education. Montessori and Decroly, while also looking towards an eventual Utopia, shared the interests, though not necessarily the politics, of the prominent social worker-educators such as Margaret McMillan, Pauline Kergomard, and Jane Addams, in improving the educational opportunities of deprived and handicapped children. From their experience with children outside the usual pattern of schooling, they gained not only a heightened sense of the need to improve educational opportunities, but also some unusual insight into children's needs and developmental processes that they were able to apply to the improvement of the education of all children.

---

[114] M. Montessori, *Pedagogical Anthropology*, F.T. Cooper trans., Stokes, New York, 1913, p. 477.

PART TWO

EDUCATIONAL ASPIRATION
1916-45

**From a Frieze of Industry made by eleventh grade pupils in Horace Mann
School, New York, 1936.**

Progressive Education Association, *Progressive Education*, vol. xiii, no. 1, January 1936, p. 57.

INTRODUCTION

The period between World War I and World War II was, educationally, an exciting one. It saw an intensification of the effort to provide universal secondary education in the industrialised nations, the first sustained effort by any nation to use education in the construction of a new society, the development of several comprehensive and influential theories of education, and the heyday of progressive experimentation and curricular innovation. It was a period of political, economic, and educational crisis which heightened tension and conflict, nurtured both scepticism and utopianism, and stimulated a closer examination of human experience and an intensive search for more relevant educational practice.

CONTINUANCE OF TRENDS FROM THE FIRST PERIOD

The educational demands of the middle class continued, in the inter-war period, to be of great importance. Secondary education was further extended largely within the existing competitive pattern and with a traditional university preparatory function. In England the independent Public Schools continued to flourish and to impart their tradition to the state secondary schools that were established. In other European countries secondary education still continued to be separated from primary and to be highly selective. In the U.S.A. attendance was greatly increased, and the range of offerings in high schools greatly widened, but success, it was found, still came mainly to the sons and daughters of the middle class. In underdeveloped countries secondary education began to develop in a small way, mainly along the lines of various European models and with the intention of developing a limited administrative elite.

Educators were still attempting to graft universal education on to old nineteenth century structures. Mass education was slowly being implemented by adjusting an elite system to accommodate the larger numbers and different aspirations of the new pupils. It was not until after World War II that most countries devised and put into operation a new structure to cope with the requirements of mass education. In doing this they had the example, which they studied with care during the 1920's and

1930's, of a radical break with the past in the U.S.S.R. and of an evolving, flexible educational ladder in the U.S.A.

The deep interest in science and technology that educators professed in the early years of the twentieth century began to appear more clearly in educational organisation and practice. Technical education, for example, was stimulated and given form by key enactments such as the Loi Astier in France and the Smith-Hughes Act in the U.S.A. Technological development, in the minds of the earlier advocates, had always been associated with national prosperity and prestige. In the inter-war period it continued to be so, and nationalism, dampened momentarily by an interest in internationalism in the early 1920's, surged back in the 1930's larger and livelier than ever. The totalitarian regimes in Italy, Germany, and Japan encouraged patriotism of an extreme kind, and, with varying degrees of cohesion, harnessed industry, science, and scientific education to the interests of national aggrandisement. The resurgent nationalism of the 1930's eventually coloured every aspect of education, throwing politics and the schools into a close and mutually supportive union.

THE EDUCATIONAL IMPETUS FROM WORLD WAR I

The inter-war period started with great optimism. World War I generated many comprehensive educational plans for the extension and improvement of existing educational systems. Among the main combatants in the war, the Fisher Act in England, the *Cardinal Principles of Secondary Education* in the U.S.A., the 1918 reorganisation in Russia, the *Reichsschulkonferenz* in Germany, the manifestos of *Les Compagnons* in France, and the founding of the New Education Fellowship and the Progressive Education Association were examples of fresh educational moves tinged with the utopianism of the war and immediate post-war years.

Physical and intellectual tests, conducted on a widespread scale among recruits in World War I, revealed striking inadequacies and inequalities. The results were used to point to the great range in the patterns of development among young people, and to support moves to cater more adequately in schools for individual differences. Greater opportunities for education in general, and especially secondary education for all children, were strongly advocated in the 1920's. The middle class widened and consolidated its educational opportunities, but Caliban was also astir. The masses were beginning to value education beyond the elementary level, and spokesmen for workers' parties were pointing out in the 1920's the importance of developing a secondary and tertiary organisation of education that would be relevant to and available for all young people. The encroachment of the masses upon the classes did not occur without protest from the advocates of elitism, and the problem of maintaining quality in education while increasing quantity was extensively argued throughout the period.

Characteristic also of the interest in post-war reconstruction were the moves made to use education as a means of changing current patterns of living. The outstanding example was that of Soviet Russia where the new society and its educational underpinnings were objects of great interest and attention by educators in most parts of the world. A similar expectation at a much reduced tempo and on a less ambitious scale could be seen in the colonial territories of the European powers. There, missionary education aspired modestly and with meagre resources to convert populations not only to a particular religious belief but also to a changed form of social and economic life; and government-provided education helped in some small part to train a nucleus of the people in vocational and professional skills which helped slowly to modernise those regions and to provide them eventually with the leaders who, after World War II, pushed each country rapidly into independence and a new social pattern. In Western Europe, North America, Australia, and New Zealand, liberal democracy was in the ascendant and was expanding into new countries such as Czechoslovakia and the Weimar Republic of Germany. The writers and thinkers of the liberal democratic movement had a sense of the importance of improving educational opportunities as part of the development of the kind of society and way of life which they favoured.

THE IMPACT OF THE DEPRESSION IN THE 1930'S

With the Wall Street crash of 1929 and the world-wide economic depression of the 1930's, education altered its mood. The buoyancy of the early 1920's was exchanged for a sense of imminent crisis. The world was obviously adrift, and serious, realistic work was required to re-educate and re-direct it.

The 1930's nevertheless were education's golden years. The crisis forced educators to look critically at fundamental objectives, to examine in depth the religious and ethical traditions with which they had long been associated, and to sift sceptically and mercilessly the inert and irrelevant from the actual and useful. They had also to devise curricula that could be seen to be pertinent and appropriate and which made students face up to the crucial issues of the social, political, and scientific

ferment in which they lived. In the educational journals and books of the 1930's in which educators explored and argued through their problems is to be found the finest and most seminal literature of probably any period of educational history. It was penetrating, it was wide-ranging, it was detailed, and it was imaginative. It covered every mood and every range of opinion; it probed extensively and deeply; it produced ideas and practical, well-tested innovations of great significance for the future. The great bulk of the writing was American but substantial contributions came also from the U.S.S.R., England, and Switzerland.

THE INTER-WAR PERIOD AS AN EDUCATIONAL WATERSHED

Most of the educational argument of the inter-war era was set within a framework of educational theory that was consolidated near the beginning of the period by three influential writers, Dewey, Nunn, and Gentile, and supplemented in mid-period by the work of the fourth important writer of the time, Makarenko. Dewey, the American, wrote the educational classic of the twentieth century in 1916, *Democracy and Education,* which balanced the demands of social and individual life in a progressive, pragmatic view of education functioning as a personal and social reconstructive force; Nunn, the Englishman, published his popular and enduring *Education: Its Data and First Principles* in 1920, applying the contributions of dynamic psychology to the cultivation of the individual potential of each child; Gentile, the Italian, provided in 1923, in *The Reform of Education,* a less influential but nevertheless solid and coherent statement of the role of the teacher and the school in promoting spiritual solidarity in a totalitarian state; and Makarenko, the Soviet citizen, in *The Road to Life,* in 1932, set forth the fundamental principles and provided a lively discussion of the way in which education set about the task of building the new man and the new society in the U.S.S.R.

Each of the writers, in his own particular way, challenged the received educational tradition. They were part of the twentieth century literature of protest and reconstruction. They sought, as did the artists and creative writers of the period, for the form and content that would express their new world in a way that would stimulate active participation and would have contemporary relevance.

The 1920's and 1930's were a watershed in the educational history of the twentieth century. The teachers of the period built on to the general theories put forward by writers such as Dewey, Nunn, and Makarenko. Some looked into the new regions of the unconscious, cultivated individual creative impulses, and encouraged emotional as well as intellectual expression; others were more interested in intellectual rigour and emphasised the need to learn with thoroughness the techniques of sifting evidence and solving problems; and others, again, placed most importance on understanding and dealing with social issues, and on learning how to discuss, co-operate, and reconstruct situations for the advantage of all participants. The importance of the inter-war period was that each of these lines of educational effort was carefully and systematically pursued. Previously they had been ideas which sometimes issued in inspired practice; after World War I they were subject to deliberate experiment in many different places. Hence, it was from that time that creative activities, problem-solving techniques, and the school's social significance began to become important aspects to consider in a school's program. The educators of the 1920's and 1930's were thus changing the balance of studies in primary and secondary schools to an extent that had not occurred for several generations. The primary school stepped out beyond the 3R's into a rich mixture of educational experiences, and the secondary school began to lose its identification with language teaching as the physical and social sciences and the arts gained in importance.

The nature of the teacher's activity also began to change. He was ceasing to be primarily an instructor of set school subjects, and was beginning to be much more cognisant of and interested in the full range of his pupils' activities in school and out, and of the emotional as well as the intellectual aspects of their growth. Educational psychology had grown by the 1930's into a substantial field with a considerable body of pertinent research on ability and achievement testing, on the intellectual, social, and emotional growth of children and adolescents, on experimentation with various methods of teaching school subjects, and on learning and the nature of the cognitive processes involved in it. Developments in each of these areas improved the teacher's professional competence and enlarged his activities. He became more skilled in assessing his pupils' performance, he became more aware of the pupils' need for psychological and educational guidance, and he became more practised in devising materials and methods that would suit each pupil and contribute to greater efficiency in learning.

CHAPTER 6

WORLD WAR I AND POST-WAR EDUCATIONAL REFORM

THE GOAL OF EDUCATION IN A DEMOCRACY

Education in the United States should be guided by a clear conception of the meaning of democracy. It is the ideal of democracy that the individual and society may find fulfillment each in the other. Democracy sanctions neither the exploitation of the individual by society, nor the disregard of the interests of the society by the individual. More explicitly—

The purpose of democracy is so to organize society that each member may develop his personality primarily through activities designed for the well-being of his fellow members and of society as a whole.

This ideal demands that human activities be placed upon a high level of efficiency; that to this efficiency be added an appreciation of the significance of these activities and loyalty to the best ideals involved; and that the individual choose that vocation and those forms of social service in which his personality may develop and become most effective. For the achievement of these ends democracy must place chief reliance upon education.

Consequently, education in a democracy, both within and without the school, should develop in each individual the knowledge, interests, ideals, habits, and powers whereby he will find his place and use that place to shape both himself and society toward ever nobler ends.

Extract from the *Cardinal Principles of Secondary Education*, published in the U.S.A. in 1918.

The first world war broke out in Europe in August 1914 and continued until November 1918. Never before in the history of the world had there been a war so widespread, so severe, and so protracted. It was not a war of mercenaries and professional soldiers; it was fought with all the resources, human, economic, and military, that the combatants could muster. For four years most of the nations of the world were completely dedicated to the struggle; their manpower was encouraged or directed into the military and civil occupations where it would be of most value to the war effort; their industry was supervised in the interests of national victory; their commerce and banking were brought under wartime control; and their informational and social services were oriented towards the building of a state of mind and body through which the conduct of the war could best be furthered. It was total war, not organised as thoroughly perhaps in all its phases as World War II, but nevertheless involving and integrating the whole community in a manner and to an extent that had never before been achieved.

DISRUPTION OF EDUCATION

Thorough involvement in the war meant a complete organisation and redirection of all of each nation's intellectual and physical resources. This, amongst other things, meant the disruption of many activities regarded as normal in peacetime. One of the first and most important of these activities to suffer was the work of the schools. In every belligerent country, and in the neutral countries, such as the Scandinavian ones whose economies were greatly affected by the war, the schools were seriously handicapped throughout the whole course of the conflict.

In the first place, large numbers of teachers volunteered or were drafted into the armed services. 'Of the teachers of the Berlin public schools, for instance,' wrote a German educator, reviewing the situation at the beginning of the last year of the war, 'two-thirds have gone into the army. The remainder are overworked. Dropping class periods, or combining classes together is the order of the day. In the higher schools half of the teachers are in the army.'[1] In France, the situation was similar. In England and Russia it is probable that about fifty per cent of all male

[1] *Vossische Zeitung*, 23 January 1918, Dr Paul Hildebrandt, 'War Effects on the Schools', Victor S. Clark trans.

school teachers served in the armed forces,[2] and in the United States the Federal Commissioner of Education reported that 'almost one-third of all American teachers were drawn out of their regular work by war conditions'. Even in India the chronic shortage of teachers was exacerbated by the drying up of the supply of trained European teachers upon whom the secondary schools, both government and missionary, were heavily dependent.

Many teachers, both men and women, in all countries were attracted into other civilian occupations.[3] Higher pay and more attractive conditions of work prevailed with some, others moved out into newly created posts in various expanding wartime civil service departments or, in the case of women, into nursing and social service work, because they felt they could serve their country best in those positions. Universities especially were denuded by the part-time advisory and full-time administrative posts which new ministries and intelligence sections created. More women teachers were recruited to replace the men in schools, but many classes remained over-large, and many schools held multiple sessions to try to cope with the teacher shortage.

To the shortage of teachers was added a shortage of school accommodation. Building programs were slowed down in all countries, and, as the backlog in school plans mounted, school buildings were requisitioned in large numbers as hospitals, barracks, and offices for the use of the armed and auxiliary services. Many schools had to limp along throughout the war with the assistance of church halls, 'sometimes in a barn, where the schools have been converted into hospitals, sometimes in a cellar as in Rheims'.[4]

WARTIME DEMANDS ON SCHOOLS

At the same time enlarged demands were made on the schools. In school time and out, pupils and teachers organised many practical activities to further the war effort. Girls knitted and sewed for relations or for other soldiers and sailors adopted by schools, classes, and individual pupils; boys made crutches, bed-boards, and splints; all the pupils made up comforts parcels for the men in the trenches and for prisoners of war. To supplement the nation's diminishing food supplies, they collected rose-hips, blackberries, thistles, and chestnuts in the fields, and devoted much energy and time to school vegetable gardens and to the cultivation of playing fields and vacant allotments. War loans were widely supported by the schools, and substantial sums of money were subscribed through the efforts of schoolchildren who made this work part of a general thrift campaign which helped to conserve the resources of each of the nations at war.

In addition to these ventures into part-time manufacturing, food-gathering, and money-raising, the schools became important centres in many communities for the organisation of social services, for the distribution of public information, and for the promotion, among the general public, of various national campaigns on matters such as diet, censorship, economy, and the care of refugee families.

School attendance was obviously sometimes irregular and uncertain in the areas of southern and western Russia, in the Balkans, in northern Italy, in north-east France and in the other places that from time to time became battlefields. But attendance even at schools, such as those in England and neutral Norway and Sweden, well away from the centres of fighting, was affected by war conditions. Calls were made sometimes by industry, and more often by agriculture, for juvenile labour to meet particular emergencies, and thousands of children interrupted their studies temporarily to help to deal with the situation. In some parts, however, school attendance actually increased. This was the case with the grant-aided secondary schools of England. While attendance at elementary schools showed a slight decrease, the numbers of children between the ages of twelve to sixteen in secondary grant-aided schools almost doubled between 1914 and 1921, the biggest increase occurring in the later years of the war. As the upward swing continued, it helped to focus attention in the post-war period on the need for re-thinking the pattern of secondary education, but during the war period it proved to be an embarrassing exacerbation of the already perilous staffing and accommodation position.[5]

---

[2] C. Birchenough, *History of Elementary Education in England and Wales from 1800 to the Present Day*, University Tutorial Press, London, 1927, p. 208. As the detailed collection of statistics by the Board of Education was suspended for the duration it is difficult to give accurate figures of educational activities in Great Britain during the course of the war. P.N. Ignatiev, D.M. Odinetz and P.J. Novgorotsev, *Russian Schools and Universities in the World War*, Yale University Press, New Haven, 1929, p. 63; L.P. Todd, *Wartime Relations of the Federal Government and the Public Schools 1917-1918*, Bureau of Publications, Teachers' College, Columbia University, 1945, p.201.

[3] See for example, P.N. Ignatiev, D.M. Odinetz and P.J. Novgorotsev, *op.cit.*, p. 88, and L.P. Todd, *op.cit.*, p. 200.

[4] This is taken from an address by the French Minister of Public Instruction, Paul Painlevé, 21 May 1916; see F. Buisson and F.E. Farrington, *French Educational Ideals Today*, New York, World Book Co., Yonkers-on-Hudson, 1919, p. 323. Rheims, for two years, while under fire, had ten underground elementary schools; see O. Forsant, 'L'Ecole primaire à Reims pendant le Bombardement', *Revue Pédagogique*, 69, 11 November 1916, pp. 519-33. Several of the schools were held in wine cellars. In one, the classrooms were separated by partitions made of cases of champagne piled on top of each other, and the school itself was marked off by a double row of casks! (p. 521). O. Forsant, *L'Ecole sous les obus*, préface de Leon Bourgeois, Hachette, Paris, 1918, contains accounts of the schools under the successive bombardments suffered by Rheims from 1914 to 1917.

[5] Board of Education, *Report of the Board of Education for the year 1920-21* (Cmd. 1718), HMSO, 1922, pp. 28-9. See also the remarks of the President of the Board of Education, H.A.L. Fisher, *Parliamentary Debates*, 5th series, vol. XCII, House of Commons, 1917, col. 1891, in which he claimed that the increased enrolments were the result of the increased prosperity of the working classes during the war.

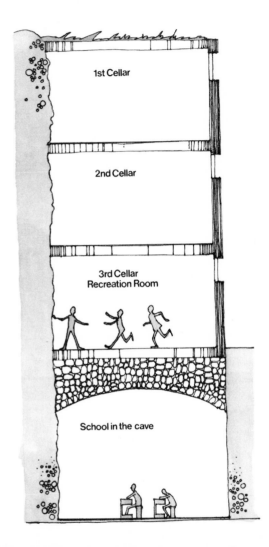

1st Cellar

2nd Cellar

3rd Cellar
Recreation Room

School in the cave

L'Ecole 'Joffre', wartime school in the wine cellars at Rheims. Four floors down and protected by reinforced concrete platforms and a thick concrete vault, the students worked and played, throughout heavy bombardments, in their underground classrooms among stacked cases of champagne.

With typical English understatement the English Board of Education in 1917 summarised the position in words that would have applied to most countries: 'The continuance of the war has inevitably imposed an increased strain upon the public educational service. Further calls have been made upon the administrative and teaching staffs of local education authorities and school governing bodies for service in Your Majesty's forces, and an increased burden has been placed on those who have remained to carry on the work of the schools; difficulties of school accommodation have been intensified, owing to shortage of labour and materials; supplies of school equipment have had to be still more severely restricted; and in many other ways sacrifices have been required which are bound to react unfavourably upon the work of education.'[6]

Those, then, were the kinds of services rendered by the schools, and the kinds of war-caused disabilities that everywhere accompanied them.

PATRIOTISM AND THE EDUCATIONAL WORLD

There was, however, a further and deeper sense in which the war affected the schools and even coloured the whole of the intellectual world.

In reviewing the exhibition 'The School and the War' staged in Paris in May 1917, a French inspector of schools remarked on the importance of the daily classroom reading of the official news of the war situation. The *communiqué* was read to the children, commented upon by the teacher, and became a topic for class discussion. In keeping with this tendency, contemporary public speeches, patriotic appeals, factual war stories highlighting the valour of the French soldiers and the heroism of their allies, tended to become the material commonly used for reading, dictation, and composition work, and for lessons in morals. 'The war therefore has frequently been,' the inspector wrote, 'the centre of interest and the source of inspiration for the school.'[7]

A similar exhibition in Berlin in May 1915 revealed that the same trend had developed in German schools. There, the children were to be impressed with 'the unique grandeur of contemporary events', and to be made conscious of the fact that they were living in 'the greatest epoch' of German history.[8] Children were encouraged to write and make speeches

---

[6] Board of Education, *Report of the Board of Education for the year 1916-17*, [Cd.9045], HMSO, 1918, p. 1. The successive annual reports of the Board of Education for the wartime years give details of the typical activities and difficulties of schools under wartime conditions.

[7] Lacabe-Plasteig, 'L'ecole pendant la guerre,' *Revue Pédagogique*, 71, 10, October 1917, p. 356. See also Albert Sarraut, *L'Instruction Publique et la Guerre*, Didier, Paris, 1916, pp. 220-1 *et passim*.

[8] *Schule und Krieg*, Weidmann, Berlin, 1915, described and commented on the Berlin exhibition; *cf.* Ausstellung, Schule und Krieg im Zentralinstitut für Erziehung and Unterricht, *Deutsche Schule*, 19, 191, pp. 394-6 and pp. 325-6; *Zeitschrift für den deutschen Unterricht*, 29, 1915, pp. 799-800; F.W. Forster *et al.*, *Der Weltkrieg im Unterricht*, Perthes, Gotha, 1915, p. 87. This book was reviewed at length by E. Victor, 'La Guerre Mondiale et l'Enseignement,' *Revue Pédagogique*, 69, 10 October 1916, pp. 323-59; see also *Zeitschrift für den deutschen Unterricht*, 29, 1915, p. 542.

about the heroes of the army and the U-boat campaigns, and about events such as the battle of Tannenberg and the sea battle off the Chilean coast. They made a careful study in school of the official war reports and some classes learned by heart current poems about German military exploits in the Great War. There was also a patriotic 'speak German' campaign to eliminate foreign words from German speech. Those kinds of activities were spread throughout all school levels in the hope that 'this great period will long be a vivid memory even for the youngest children'.[9] When the United States declared war in 1917, private societies and public authorities encouraged the schools to foster in the children a line of patriotism just as vigorous and uncompromising as that of the schools of Europe. Even the teaching of German, which had declined in popularity in England and France, was banned by some state legislatures and school boards in parts of the United States, and the proportion of secondary school pupils studying German fell from 24 per cent in 1915 to sixteen per cent in 1922. Courses in patriotism were formulated, even more thoroughly than in Europe, and patriotic textbooks in history, geography, and social studies, and pamphlets flooded the schools.[10]

The war had the effect of knitting people more closely together within each nation, emphasising 'the responsibility of each individual for the whole'.[11] The collective patriotic feeling was deliberately and assiduously fostered by the schools.

The schools of each of the belligerent countries became, in effect, agents of patriotism reflecting the intense feeling of the time, blending it throughout their school-work, and focusing, intensifying, and imprinting it unforgettably in the minds of the children. Never before in the world's history had there been such a universal outburst of extreme patriotic fervour, as each nation glorified in its own exploits and condemned the culture and the activities of its enemy. From this contagion few persons were immune.

PROPAGANDA AMONG THE INTELLECTUALS

In the first year of the war when excitement was at its highest pitch, the intellectual leaders — academics, artists, writers, and ecclesiastics — in each country engaged in a crossfire of claim and counter-claim about the origins of the war, the behaviour of their armed forces, and the value of their respective national cultures. The great French writer, Romain Rolland, standing aside from the conflict, wrote in September 1914: 'There is not one amongst the leaders of thought in each country who does not proclaim with conviction that the cause of his people is the cause of God, the cause of liberty and of human progress. And I, too, proclaim it.

'Strange combats are being waged between metaphysicians, poets, historians—Eucken against Bergson; Hauptmann against Maeterlinck;

Rolland against Hauptmann; Wells against Bernard Shaw. Kipling and D'Annunzio, Dehmel and de Regnier sing war hymns, Barres and Maeterlinck chant paeans of hatred. Between a fugue of Bach and the organ which thunders *Deutschland über Alles*, Wundt, the aged philosopher of eighty-two, calls with his quavering voice the students of Leipzig to the holy war. And each nation hurls at the other the name "Barbarians".'[12]

In the first three months of the war several manifestos were issued by leading intellectuals, theologians, and university authorities. The most widely canvassed was the *Appeal to the Civilized Nations*, a statement of nine short paragraphs signed by ninety-three leaders of German cultural life. These included scientists such as Max Planck, Ernst Haeckel, Wilhelm Röntgen, and Paul Ehrlich, leading scholars in the humanities and social sciences such as Ulrich von Wilamowitz-Moellendorf, Eduard Meyer, Gustav-Adolf von Harnack, and Rudolf Eucken, and writers and artists such as Max Reinhardt, Richard Dehmel, and Gerhart Hauptmann. The *Appeal* claimed that it was not true, as the enemies of Germany put out, that Germany had caused the war, that she had violated the neutrality of Belgium, misused the inhabitants of that country without provocation, and brutally destroyed Louvain, and that the German armies paid no respect to international law. Rather, 'those who have allied themselves with the Russians and the Serbs, and who do not flinch from inciting Mongols and Negroes against the white race, presenting thus to the world the most shameful spectacle imaginable, are certainly the last to have the right to claim the title of the defenders of European civilization'. And finally, 'it is not true, as our enemies hypocritically claim, that the struggle against what is called our militarism is not directed against our culture. Without our militarism, our civilization would long ago have been annihilated. For its protection this militarism was born in our country, a country exposed as no other to repeated invasions over the centuries. The German army and the German people are one.'[13] Three thousand teachers in universities and higher institutions

[9] Th. Valentiner, 'Aus dem Deutschunterricht in grosser Zeit' *Zeitschrift für den deutschen Unterricht*, 29, 1915, pp. 51-60 and p. 56; Walther Hofstaetter, 'Der deutsche Krieg und der deutsche Unterricht', *ibid.*, p. 1-11; Willy Strehl, 'Schulaufsatz, Kriegserlebnis, und Kriegsliteratur', *ibid.*, 30, 1916, pp. 328-35; Katı Lotz, 'Kriegsdiktate. Anregungen aus der Ausstellung Krieg und Schule in Berlin', *Archiv für Pädagogik*, 4, 1915-16, October 1915, pp. 17-19.

[10] *School Life*, 1, 1, 1 August 1918, p. 10; 1, 4, 16 September 1918, p. 13; 2, 8, 16 April 1919, p. 14; 2, 11, 1 June 1919, p. 13; J.D. Deihl, 'Adjusting instruction in German to conditions imposed by the war', *Monatshefte für deutsche Sprache und Pädagogik*, 19, 5, May 1918, pp. 128ff.

[11] Walther Hofstaetter, *op.cit.*, p. 3.

[12] Romain Rolland, *Above the Battle*, trans. C.K. Ogden, Open Court, Chicago, 1916, pp. 43-4.

[13] *Aufruf an die Kulturwelt. 'Es ist nicht Wahr'*. This and similar documents can be found in a French translation with commentary in T. Jaulmes, *Ignorance? Inconscience ... ou Hypocrisie?* Attinger, Paris, n.d., pp. 18-20, and in an English translation in J.J. Chapman, *Deutschland über alles or Germany Speaks*, Putnam, New York, 1914, pp. 37-42.

and a group of leading theologians mounted a similar protest against the distinction drawn by their enemies between the spirit of Prussian militarism, and the scientific and humane spirit of well-educated Germans.[14] Each of the declarations provoked considerable discussion in intellectual circles among friends, foes, and neutrals. Many refutations and counter-refutations were written. The intellectual battle raged hotly for many months, and simmered on throughout the remainder of the war.

The German pamphleteers made two basic points throughout all their submissions: first, that they saw the war as a struggle to save German civilisation and, through it, the civilisation of the world, and, secondly, that the nation as a whole was animated by this common purpose and that the military, scientific, humane, and religious aspects in which it expressed itself were integral parts of a common German *Kultur*.

There can be no doubt that those who wrote such statements were sincere, and were convinced of the justness and the importance of their cause.[15]

But so were their enemies. It is a significant feature of the controversy that those enemies, too, made somewhat the same points in their own favour, and with the same air of conviction. 'It is an indisputable fact,' wrote the celebrated French sociologist, Emile Durkheim, in 1915, 'that since the beginning of the war France has gained for herself an incontestable moral position in the eyes of the world... The moment the country was in danger, all individuals found themselves united in one common aim.' It was to further 'the moral greatness of France'.[16] For Henri Bergson, the noted philosopher and psychologist, France's 'cause is that of humanity itself'.[17] It was in vain that Wundt wrote that 'M. Henri Bergson' was a person 'whom no reputable philosopher in Germany has ever taken seriously',[18] other scholars elsewhere did listen to him, and did support his point of view. A thousand Russian writers and academics issued a statement roundly condemning 'what the Germans call culture'.[19] A group of English theologians, replying to the German manifesto to evangelical Christians, took the view that 'the contest in which our country has engaged is a contest on behalf of the supremest interests of Christian civilization'.[20] According to A.V. Dicey, one of England's best-known legal historians, the war was a contest of ideals between militarism and freedom, a Holy War against 'the whole German nation, trained to the belief that the greatness, the glory, and the existence of the Empire depends upon the triumph of German arms'.[21]

It is not to be wondered at, therefore, that a group of representative men from neutral Holland, after reading the great number of pamphlets and manifestos scattered by the warring nations throughout the neutral states, pointed to the fact 'that the spokesmen of the opposing nations are equally convinced of the justice of their cause'.[22] And the scholars were equally vehement and patriotic in expressing their convictions.

KULTUR

Initially it was a fight for and against German *Kultur*. In its broadest meaning, *Kultur* as it was conceived by its German exponents was the sum total of all human activities and human creations within the life of a nation. All nations, in that sense, possessed it. If it was to be expressed in its truest and deepest form, it must be the product of the conscious striving of individual men and women to realise and to express the best that lay within the nation.[23] A nation, however, was more than the sum of the individuals within it; it was an organism of which the external form was the state and the internal lifeforce was *Kultur*. '*Kultur* is the heart, the State is the protecting thorax of the national organism.'[24] But the state was more than a mere protector; it had the task also of providing the best conditions for the realisation of the nation's *Kultur*, of raising the level of the citizens' efforts, and of nurturing every endeavour to express effectively the nation's values. *Kultur* and the state thus became intimately related to one another, and out of their association was produced the *Kulturstaat* which laid claim to the devotion of its citizens and was a vehicle for their enthusiasm. Similarly the army with its activities fitted well into the pattern. It offered the most complete example of service to the national state. It embraced all persons within the nation,

[14] See Jaulmes, *op.cit.*, p. 21, and *To the Christian Scholars of Europe and America*, A Reply from Oxford to the German 'Address of the German theologians to Evangelical Christians Abroad', Oxford Pamphlets 1914, no. 2, Oxford University Press, 1914, p. 20. An English translation of the German address is given on pp. 19-24.

[15] They could also draw comfort from the fact that their former nationals working in universities in neutral countries fully supported their stand, e.g. Kuno Francke, 'The True Germany', *Atlantic Monthly*, 116, 4, October 1915, p. 553.

[16] Emile Durkheim, 'The School of Tomorrow', pp. 18-19, in F. Buisson and F.E. Farrington (edd.) *French Educational Ideals of Today*, World Book Co., Yonkers-on-Hudson, New York, 1919.

[17] H. Bergson, *The Meaning of the War, Life and Matter in Conflict*, Unwin, London, 1915, p. 44.

[18] W. Wundt, *Concerning True War*, trans. Grace E. Hadow, Oxford Pamphlets, 1914-15, Oxford University Press, London, p. 14.

[19] Two Russian manifestos each signed by more than a thousand leaders in the arts, literature, and science are reproduced in French translation. T. Jaulmes, *op.cit.*, pp. 39-40; cf. P.N. Ignatiev, D.M. Odinetz and P.J. Novgorotsev, *op.cit.*, pp. 156ff.

[20] *To the Christian Scholars of Europe and America*, A Reply from Oxford to the German Address to Evangelical Christians Abroad, Oxford Pamphlets no.2, 1914-15, Oxford University Press, London, p. 15.

[21] A.V. Dicey, *How We Ought to Feel about the War*, Oxford Pamphlets, 1914-15, Oxford University Press, London, pp. 13, 17, 19.

[22] Quoted in R. Rolland, *op.cit.*, p. 131.

[23] Hugo Münsterberg, *The Peace and America*, Appleton, New York, 1915, pp. 150ff. Münsterberg was a leading German and American psychologist.

[24] F. de Hovre, *German and English Education*, Scribners, New York, 1917, p. 28.

it surrounded them with an atmosphere of duty and moral seriousness which was the very foundation of *Kultur*. Thus German militarism was to be regarded not as a militaristic force, but as a devoted harnessing of force to the service of the *Kulturstaat*.

The unity of purpose which their *Kultur* provided, the solidarity which flowed from the all-embracing state, and the heightened spirits produced by an efficient and enthusiastic military force gave to the German nation 'an immense and deep-seated consciousness of strength',[25] and a conviction of being the leader among the nations of the world.

That view of the *Kulturstaat* Germany's opponents regarded as undesirable and dangerous. Germany's unity of purpose they regarded as mere uniformity, and her solidarity as a lack of freedom imposed by an autocracy; her heightened spirits, they considered, led to sabre-rattling, her consciousness of strength to boastfulness, and her conviction of leadership was a threat to the independence of all non-German peoples. *Kultur*, in their view, was destructive of individual liberty, domineering, and dangerously militaristic. England and France, and later the United States of America, declared that they fought against it on behalf of freedom and democracy. And each nation was at pains to clarify its view, express it forcibly and repeatedly, and to see that its schools impressed it upon the nation's children.

EDUCATION FOR NATIONAL EFFICIENCY

The war was a struggle between nations. It was not merely a battle of opposing armies, it was a contest which involved every person in each of the belligerent countries. Each nation felt that it was fighting to maintain its way of life and that this responsibility was something that had to be accepted by the whole nation. It was no mere war for petty aggrandisement, it was thought to be a war between two different outlooks on life, between German *Kultur* on the one hand, and the tradition of Anglo-French democracy on the other.

It was, therefore, in the fullest sense a struggle between rival educational forces. If it had been possible to suggest that the Prussian schoolmaster had triumphed at Sedan, it was even closer to the truth to suggest that the schoolmaster's work was to be seen behind that clash of nations not only in the firing line at Mons, Verdun, and Jutland but even in the factories of the Ruhr and the English Midlands, in the wheatfields of Saskatchewan, and the coal mines of Silesia. The nations were convinced that they were fighting for a cause — a cause that emerged from the texture of each nation's life and had been shaped and focused by the nation's schoolmasters. As the war developed, it was the job of the writers and artists throughout the community, and of the schoolmasters within

the schools to keep the nations conscious of their cause, to explain, enlarge upon, and justify their ideals, and to strengthen them in their determination to persist until victory was secured.

Thus it came about that the schools, universities and all other educational agencies and influences became securely tied to each nation's war effort. Their intellectual resources were put at the nation's service, and their training programs were adapted to war needs. They became the special instruments by which the nation's war aims and ideals were assembled and passed on to the rising generation, and they provided the means of buttressing and reassuring the nation in its beliefs. That had been the function of the school for many years in Germany; it had been a growing tendency among the other nations for the past half-century. National education had been a term of wide currency for many years, but the full force of its meaning was not realised until the war was seen and widely spoken of 'as a test of the efficiency of national education'. 'The war,' wrote a Belgian educator in England in 1917, 'has opened people's eyes to the national meaning of education. Many for the first time now understand that education is an organ of national life as vital as its economic and political organization; many now are convinced that the power of education for the woe or weal of the nation is not eclipsed by that of any other province of national activity.'[26]

The educational campaign was intense but by no means wholly successful. In the first year of the war in the European countries it probably met with its greatest response, and again in 1917 when the United States entered the war. But the harsh realities of sub-human existence in the trenches, prodigal expenditure of human lives in battle, and deprivation on the home front, made it difficult to keep the lamps of idealism alight. As the war progressed, many soldiers went into battle not knowing why they fought, others speedily became disillusioned, and the thoughts of people at home were often distracted by discomfort and mismanagement from the ideals by which they had earlier been fortified. Nevertheless the sense of fighting for a cause managed to persist, though in the course of time the meaning of the cause was changed.

DISCOVERY OF DEFICIENCIES

In the early years of the war there was, on both sides, much self-satisfaction about the effectiveness of the schools which had produced the trained and steadfast warriors required for the armed services of each

---

[25] W. Sanday, *The Deeper Causes of the War*, Oxford Pamphlets 1914, no.1, Oxford University Press, London, pp. 8-9.

[26] F. de Hovre, *op.cit.*, p. 18.

nation. And, even as late as 1917, the president of the Board of Education in England, H.A.L. Fisher, spoke admiringly of the contribution of the elementary schools.[27]

As reports on recruits to the services accumulated, however, from physical and psychological examinations, and from tests of literacy and general knowledge, self-congratulation gave way to a concern which led to considerable questioning and eventually to widespread criticism. The most careful and most extensive investigation undertaken by any of the belligerents into the mental and physical condition of its troops was that done in the United States. The results were surprising and disquietening; but so were the results among the other nations even though they were not as systematically documented. The American findings were not unique; they served as an example of the deficiencies found in all the nations. They were summarised as follows: 'The exigencies of the Great War have revealed and emphasized the following serious defects and weaknesses in the citizenry of the United States of America, *viz*.:

1. A startling percentage of physical defects and weaknesses, largely remediable under suitable treatment.

2. A large percentage of adult illiteracy, approximately 25% of the men of the first draft failing to pass a literacy test based on the ability to read a newspaper readily and intelligently and to express one's thoughts fairly clearly in writing.

3. The number of men adequately trained in the various skilled processes of industry, agriculture, commercial organization, and control grossly insufficient to meet the needs of the state, civil as well as military.

4. Generally inadequate preparation for civic responsibilities to insure the safety and progress of the nation in war and in peace.[28]

(i) Illiteracy

Soon after the entry of the United States into the war in 1917, a Division of Psychology was established to undertake an extensive program of intelligence testing among the army draftees. By the end of the war 1,726,966 men had been tested, and classified. Two batteries of group intelligence tests were developed, known as Army Alpha and Army Beta, the first for literate, the second for illiterate recruits or for those who could not understand English. The reports of the testing showed clear discrepancies in mental ability between whites and negroes, between northern and southern negroes, and between literates and illiterates, and

further, that length of schooling was associated with these discrepancies. They provided detailed information, also, about length of schooling. 'The facts reported by white recruits may be stated in this form: Of 100 white recruits who entered the first grade in this country, 95 remained in school till grade two, 92 till grade three, 87 till grade four, 79 till grade five, 70 till grade six, 59 till grade seven, 45 till grade eight; 21 of them entered high school, 16 kept on till the second year, 11 till the third year, and 9 of the 100 graduated from high school; 5 of these entered college, and 1 graduated from college.' The equivalent figures for negro recruits were: 'of 100 negroes of first grade age, 87 entered first grade, 79 second, 71 third, 59 fourth, 45 fifth, 32 sixth, 24 seventh, 17 eighth; 8 entered high school, 6 second year, 4 third, 3 fourth; 2 entered college, and 0.4 graduated.'[29]

It was not easy to decide upon an acceptable standard or to devise a suitable test of literacy. The somewhat imprecise definition of 'an ability to read and understand newspapers and write letters home', was used as the level at which recruits could cope with the verbal Alpha test; the remainder took the non-verbal Beta test. Those latter constituted approximately 25 per cent of all the recruits.[30]

The army findings were widely publicised, and were brought to public attention at a time of intense and patriotic feeling. The National Education Association promptly formed a Commission on Illiteracy which, reporting five years later, in 1923, was of the opinion that there were about twenty million persons who should be taken into account in any consideration of illiteracy. The Commission described the worst affected areas with indignation and a sense of outrage: 'In the most illiterate sections of the United States conditions approach the barbaric. Marriage has no sanctity whatever, and commerce is carried on through trade and barter, as when America was roamed over by savage Indians. In these densely illiterate communities the currency of the country is an unknown medium of exchange, neither silver, gold nor paper money being used anywhere in the locality.'[31] Such evidence of educational inequality was a further ground for the growing agitation for democratic educational reform which would help to raise the social and economic standards of the community.

In countries such as the United States, France, Germany, and Great Britain, however, by world standards, the illiteracy rate was comparat-

[27] *Parliamentary Debates*, 5th series, vol. XCII, House of Commons, 19 April 1917, col. 1893.

[28] National Education Association of the United States, *Addresses and Proceedings of the Fifty-Seventh Annual Conference*, New Education Association, Washington, 1919, pp. 58-9.

[29] R.M. Yerkes, (ed.), *Psychological Examining in the United States Army*, Memoirs of the National Academy of Sciences, vol. xv, Government Printer, Washington, 1921, pp. 762-3.

[30] R.M. Yerkes, *op.cit.*, p. 743.

[31] National Education Association of the United States, *Addresses and Proceedings of the Sixty-First Annual Meeting*, 1923, vol. LXI, New Education Association, Washington, p. 267.

ively small. The recognition that illiteracy existed above what might reasonably be regarded as a minimum level stimulated educational reform but was not the main feature upon which reform was concentrated. In the southern and western European countries, on the other hand, and throughout most of Asia, Africa, and Latin America, the elimination of illiteracy was still one of the most important educational tasks. In Italy, for example, according to its 1911 Census, the percentage of illiteracy was forty-seven; this excessively high rate received wide publicity as the youth registered for service in 1916, and gave rise both to the development of special hospital schools for the wounded and illiterate, and to a considerable agitation for the spread and improvement of elementary education.[32] And in an underdeveloped country such as India, with an illiteracy rate of 94 per cent, and only 4 per cent of the total population under instruction, the fundamental educational task in the view of the Montagu-Chelmsford Report of 1918 was simply the provision of adequate elementary education for the whole population.[33]

(ii) Physical Fitness

Another feature of the examination of recruits that caused concern was the state of their physical fitness. The provost marshal-general for the United States reported in 1918 that approximately one-third of all draftees medically examined had been classified as unfit for ordinary and regular military duties.[34] The rejection rate, when it became known after the provost marshal-general's first report, was a topic of considerable moment. 'Out of the ensuing accusations and recriminations came an awakened conscience. People were now ready to give backing to a real program of physical education in the schools.'[35]

A similar concern for physical fitness, and criticism of existing facilities for physical education were expressed in other countries. England had had its shock earlier, at the turn of the century, when large numbers of volunteers for service in the Boer War had been rejected as physically unsuitable. The ensuing public debate had led to a considerable extension of physical education in the schools. World War I strengthened the trend. Children's play centres multiplied, holiday camps were extended, and attention to children's health and physical development became a matter of considerable importance. In Germany, where physical education had long been prominent in schools, the emphasis was increased early in the war by the establishment of Youth Companies to provide further training for older youths in physical activities and in exercises that would equip them more effectively for war service.

(iii) Juvenile Delinquency

Similar concern to that felt in England for the welfare of children was also expressed in Germany. It became particularly marked later in the war as living conditions worsened and home life and parental discipline deteriorated to the point where juvenile delinquency became a matter of serious concern. Early in 1918, Professor Paul Hildebrandt, wrote, 'The sixth grade pupils of 1914 are now about to be promoted to the upper third. They have become accustomed to the war. Who can wonder, then, that now in the fourth year of war our children exhibit signs of change? Too many of the restraints have been removed which should shape their development: the loosening of family ties, the father at the front, the mother employed away from home, and in the lower ranks of society doing the work of men; the relaxation of school discipline ... Already the total number of violent crimes committed by youths in the city of Berlin is more than three times the number reported by 1914.

'Thus, dark shadows are falling over the brilliant picture of 1914. Every disciplinary influence, every effort of the still fundamentally sound German nation must be exerted to oppose this tendency, and to lead the children back to the path of rectitude.'[36]

The 'dark shadows' of juvenile delinquency matching the general increase in the German crime rate as the war progressed were no new nor isolated phenomena.[37] They were to be expected in time of war, and they had been noticed and commented on even in the early years of the war in more than one of the belligerent countries.[38] They emphasised the need for close attention to the needs of the children in wartime, and gave a somewhat dramatic point to criticisms of the inadequacy of existing educational provision. They were clear indicators of the difficulty of maintaining morale on the home front where, with resources strained to the utmost, a nation's social services had to defer to the demands of war.

---

[32] *Annuario Statistico Italiano*, Anno 1916, Seconda Serie, vol, VI, Ufficio Centrali di Statistica, Rome, 1918, p. 83; Walter A. Montgomery, *Education in Italy*, Department of the Interior, Bureau of Education, Bulletin 1919, no.36, Government Printer, Washington D.C., pp. 4, 13.

[33] East India (Constitutional Reforms), *Report on Indian Constitutional Reforms* (Montagu-Chelmsford Report) [Cd. 9109], HMSO, 1918, pp. 149-54.

[34] *Second Report of the Provost Marshal-General to the Secretary of War in the Operations of the Selective Service System to December 20th, 1918*. Government Printer, Washington D.C., 1919, p. 162.

[35] Emmett A. Rice, John L. Hutchinson, Mabel Lee, *A Brief History of Physical Education*, 4th edn, Ronald, New York, 1958, pp. 293-4.

[36] *Vossische Zeitung*, 23 January 1918, 'War Effects on the Schools', trans. Victor S. Clark, *op.cit.*, pp. 3-4.

[37] *Vorwärts*, 9 June 1918: 'Nearly four years ago, when world catastrophe broke over us, there were some enthusiastic war prophets who fondly predicted an ethical renaissance of the country through the steel bath...Since the fourth of August, 1914, we have been enjoying the blessings of this bath of steel in an increasing degree and the result is a moral status of the German population faithfully portrayed in the statistics of criminality. These tell of a steadily increasing score of violent offences — of serious attacks upon property...'

[38] e.g. *Frankfurter Zeitung*, 5 February, evening, 1916, leading article; *Archiv für Pädagogik*, 1915-16, 4, 3, February 1916, pp. 141-3.

(iv) Civic Education

The maintenance of morale by assuring that both the fighting men and their non-combatant support at home understood and were committed to their nation's cause was essential if the war was to be waged effectively for any protracted period. This task was an immensely difficult one.

In the case of the illiterates who joined the forces, it might be expected that few of them had any thorough grasp of the war issues or of the duties, responsibilities, and ideals of citizenship. What came as somewhat of a shock, however, was the discovery that many literate and intelligent recruits were similarly ignorant. Many appeared to have little idea of what the war was about and no notion at all of the deeper issues of freedom, democracy, and the nature of *Kultur* that the intellectuals were spending a great deal of time and effort in discussing. Many, further, did not know the nature of their own nation's government, or the civil organisation of their own town or district, and many could not even sing the words of national or patriotic songs.[39]

In consequence, the armed forces of each nation undertook to provide in various ways supplementary civic and political education for the troops under arms.[40] To inform the fighting man and the nation as a whole, propaganda and information departments were expanded, and the resources of private associations, schoolteachers, and university lecturers were widely called on. This was a special feature of the work of the universities and tertiary level colleges during wartime. In general the part played by them in the war effort of each country was noteworthy. Their professors and lecturers served both in the forces and in many branches of the public service; they provided military training for potential officers; they expanded the opportunities for special courses of particular value to the war effort; and, through their extension services, they helped spread information and sustain public morale. Not every university or college was in a position to engage in all these activities, and some countries used their university resources to better advantage than others. All, however, in some measure, engaged in the work of informing and encouraging the general public.[41] The more these activities had to be developed, the more conscious did the university extension lecturers, the pamphleteers, and the organisers of classes become of the basic deficiency in civic knowledge and understanding shown by the general public, and many became concerned that this vital element should not be omitted from the future schooling of the nation.

(v) Technical Training

A shortage of well-trained technical men for service in skilled sections of the navy and army, and in wartime industry and agriculture was a further deficiency to become apparent as the war progressed. It was true that many intelligent young men with a good general education were trained effectively for service in technical positions by well-designed short courses. But there were many basic jobs, for example, in both military and civil engineering fields which required substantially trained technicians and professional guidance. Throughout the whole war there was a noticeable lag in the supply of such people despite the acceleration in technical education that had taken place since the turn of the century.[42]

The shortcomings in health and physical development, in literacy and general education, in civic knowledge and responsibility, and in scientific and vocational skills which the war made apparent in many of the nations became the springboard for the launching of criticism against the inadequacies of the schools.

EDUCATIONAL CRITICISM AND PLANNING

In the last two years of the war and for the next five or six years of the post-war reconstruction period, there was probably more widespread discussion of fundamental educational questions than in any previous period in history. It was a time of challenge to received tradition and existing organisation. To accommodate the multitude and variety of demands it made upon the schools, the war provided an incentive for educators to break away from traditional offerings and inflexible programs, and to respond to the emergencies of the moment with improvisation, imagination, and originality. The deficiencies which the war highlighted challenged educators and other interested persons to look afresh at educational aims, and at their order of priorities. In consequence, education assumed in public discussion an importance rarely accorded to it at other times. The press devoted substantial space to it, and opened its correspondence columns to a discussion of many of the issues; conferences and committees of investigation produced reports; legislation was drafted, debated, and placed on the statute books as a concrete expression of the new dispensation. Some of this legislation proved to be a somewhat timid expression of prevailing opinion, and some of it was never fully implemented; but whatever its shape, and whatever its fate, it did bear witness to the movement of the times, and it did embody in some measure the fundamental ideas that were in the air.

[39] Ernest C. Moore, *What the War Teaches about Education*, Macmillan, New York, 1919, p. 237.

[40] Lewis P. Todd, *op.cit.*, p. 49.

[41] See, for example, R. Thamin, *L'Université et La Guerre*, Hachette, Paris, 1916, 'Classes sur le Front'; Albert Sarraut, *op.cit.*, pp. 98-199; Samuel P. Capen & Walton C. John, *A Survey of Higher Education, 1916-1918*, Department of the Interior, Bureau of Education, Bulletin 1919, no. 22, Government Printer, Washington D.C., 1919; *Der Tag*, 5 February 1918 on university courses at the Front.

[42] S.P. Capen & W.C. John, *op.cit.*, pp. 51ff for U.S. shortages of technically trained men and the measures adopted to train them.

Out of this ferment three principal lines of development emerged. First, there was an increased desire for more utility in education which took the form both of an assault on traditional school programs and of moves for a greater extension of vocational education. Secondly, the development and maintenance of national solidarity, a feature of the war years, continued to be specifically planned and deliberately pursued in the years which followed. Thirdly, education became enmeshed in the movement for national reconstruction through which it was hoped a new and better world was to be born out of the grim and bloody labours of the old. Above and beyond the movements for more realistic content and practice in education and for more effective civic education, there was, in many of the countries engaged in the war, a widespread desire for more radical measures. In the minds of many sailors and soldiers there was a determination that out of their sacrifices would come a better society in the future. They fought not merely to repel the foreign enemy but also to dispel domestic inequalities and disabilities. In the mess decks and the trenches there was opportunity to mix, to talk, to dream, to study, and to plan with many others of various walks of life and a variety of backgrounds. The war experience shook millions of young men and women out of their accustomed ways, and set them thinking of the new society after the war. And in their thoughts the basis of the new dispensation was to be found in a substantial broadening of educational opportunity and a reconstruction of the existing educational system.

Speaking in 1917 in the House of Lords, no less a witness than the Archbishop of Canterbury, Randall Davidson, gave evidence of the new spirit of the times. 'Education,' he said, 'is not a subject which stands in isolation by itself. It is coloured by the Nation's social, economic, and religious traditions and aims. The returning soldier — that means, after all, the men of England practically today — will not be satisfied with some of the old conditions . . . At all events, whether we like it or not, these things are astir in the minds of men who are coming back with a wider horizon and with new thoughts in their minds.'[43]

Among many who fought on the battlefields of World War I or laboured on the home front there was a deep sense that they were participating in events of great significance, and a determination to see that their efforts would lead to a new and better world. The heritage was to be not merely the accumulated wisdom of the past, but also the new opportunities for future development made possible by the present sacrifices of the nations at war. The morning was breaking, it was hoped, on the new era.

The aspirations did, in some measure, bear fruit. Certainly, it was not true that Utopia was born out of the upheaval of the war; but it was true that the war period was an important nursery of new ideas. Politically it brought to an end long-established autocracies in Germany, Russia, and

Austria-Hungary; it cleared the way and established the climate for the extension of democratic practices in countries where democracy was already accepted, and for the introduction of democratic governments in many countries where it had not hitherto been tried. The war settlement, acting on the principle of national self-determination, was responsible for the establishment of many new nations — a multiplication of national units which subsequently spread from central and northern Europe to the Middle East, to South-East Asia, and throughout Africa. Thus a wider range and greater strength was given to the idea of nationality, and to the loyalties and practices associated with national states. At the same time, a moderately successful attempt to establish international institutions, and to develop an international orientation in the post-war world was undertaken with the establishment of the League of Nations and the agencies associated with it.

The war had the effect also of accelerating the social, economic, and technological changes that had been developing since the beginning of the century. Electrification for power, heat, light and communication was so rapidly and extensively developed as to revolutionise the life and economy of many parts of the post-war world. Means of transport were improved by the more widespread use of the motor car, and in the 1930's the aeroplane. Manufacture was rationalised and multiplied, industrial and commercial possibilities were enormously expanded, and investment became more varied and extensive. In the 1920's the Era of Business set in. Some of the business ventures were highly successful, others unduly speculative, and others again resounding failures. And this applied to the economic conditions of whole countries. The changing industrial pattern brought with it dislocation as well as advance; and with the dislocation went unemployment and labour unrest. In that situation labour and socialist political parties increased their strength, and in several European countries came into power for the first time. Their rise was accompanied by an increase in social welfare legislation, and by an extension of the franchise, the most notable of which was the granting of the vote to women.

To preserve and deepen a sense of nationality in the old and new countries of the post-war world, to ensure that the newly enfranchised might vote with discretion, to provide skilled and versatile workers for the developing economy, to widen opportunities for employment, to enable the newly conscious democratic masses to inherit the old and build the new culture with greater wisdom, and to raise the general level of human dignity, education was the great thing needed. In the post-war period there came the realisation that henceforth national welfare was indissolubly associated with education. But, for the tasks of the new era, it had to be a changed education.

[43] *Parliamentary Debates*, 5th series, vol. XXII, House of Lords, 19 July 1916, cols 794-5.

Paul Crouzet expressed the sentiments of his contemporaries in many countries when, in the midst of war in 1917, he wrote concerning French education: 'If there is a universally felt need in the country, it is the need to reform the nation's education in such depth as to produce for the France of tomorrow a new race of Frenchmen.' The basic problem, he suggested, facing all levels of education in the post-war period 'was that of reconciling the two cultures; the humane and the practical'.[44]

EDUCATIONAL REGENERATION

(i)   Rethinking Educational Principles

World War I generated many educational plans for the extension and improvement of existing educational systems. Two lengthy discussions on educational principles and school curricula produced conclusions that aptly summed up current thinking and had a lasting influence. The first, a debate on the content of a liberal education in England, signalled the end of the old secondary curriculum, traditionally dominated by the classics; the second, a report on the Cardinal Principles of Secondary

English Public School boys from Eton outside Lords cricket ground during the Eton v. Harrow match, watched by some working lads.

Education in the U.S.A., pointed the way to a future curriculum based on social efficiency that was to have a world-wide impact.

(a)   Liberal Education in England

In England early in 1916, there appeared in *The Times* a letter signed by thirty-six eminent scientists. They began with the blunt statement that: 'It is admitted on all sides that we have suffered checks since the war began, due directly as well as indirectly to a lack of knowledge on the part of our legislators and administrative officials of what is called "science" or "physical science".'[45] Yet England's success 'now and in the difficult time of reorganization after the war depends largely on the possession by war leaders and administrators of the scientific method and the scientific habit of mind'. The solution lay in recasting education in the schools and the universities of Oxford and Cambridge from which these officials were largely drawn. Despite fifty years of effort to introduce effective teaching of science into them, 'it is clear that the old methods and old vested interests have retained their dominance. ... Of the 35 largest and best known public schools 34 have classical men as headmasters. Science holds no place in the list.' Since the work of the schools was determined largely by the requirements of the examinations for entrance to Oxford and Cambridge, to the civil service and to the army, the writers suggested that the most effective means of promoting the study of science was to give it a much increased weight in those examinations.

The letter sparked off a series of discussions on the proper content of a secondary education which continued vigorously throughout the remainder of the year, and well into 1917.[46] The debate concluded with all parties declaring 'their faith in a liberal education as the foundation for all activities of mind and spirit in a civilised country.'[47]

The liberal education which was thus agreed upon took account of and summed up the movement in educational thought since the turn of the century. It was acknowledged that a liberal education could be achieved through a variety of subject-matter; that the sciences, modern languages, history, geography, and the national language too could each make a proper and appropriate contribution; and that a sound modern liberal education required a study of each of these fields.

[44] Paul Crouzet, 'Pour la revision d'ensemble de l'éducation nationale', *La Grande Revue*, 94, September 1917, pp. 393, 395.

[45] *The Times*, London, 2 February 1916, p. 10.

[46] Frederic G. Kenyon (ed), *Education Scientific and Humane. A Report of the Proceedings of the Council for the Humanistic Studies*, Murray, London, 1917, p. 6. This pamphlet was issued in August 1917 as a record of the discussions by the various associations and at the various conferences held during the preceding eighteen months.

[47] F.G. Kenyon, *op.cit.*, p. 23.

An exclusively classical education had tended to be identified with social class privilege; the broader concept of the secondary school curriculum cleared the way for the considerable expansion of secondary education which was about to take place. In the post-war period the study of Latin and Greek steadily receded throughout the English-speaking world, and even in the classical strongholds of Germany and France, despite vigorous attempts on its behalf, its importance was diminished.[48]

The subject which gained most from the decline of the classics was, interestingly enough, not science but the vernacular language. In the post-World War I period the humanities began to centre around modern languages. 'But progress, the inevitable factor in the life of nations,' said a teacher in France, 'has allowed French, English, German, and other languages to rival fully in lucidity and grace of expression the ancient languages. ... One would claim, therefore, that the study of modern languages can furnish an educational discipline of the first order.'[49] English for the English, French for the French, German for the Germans, Russian for the Russians speedily became the main source of humane education. The national language achieved for the first time, in the post-war period, a central position in the curriculum which it has continued to consolidate up to the present. Its promotion was in keeping with the determined nationalism of the period, but it was also an indication that, with the wider spread of secondary education, subject-matter that could be seen to be directly pertinent to everyday life was likely to get preference in the school curriculum.

Each subject, therefore, tended to justify itself on two kinds of grounds: first, disciplinary and sometimes cultural, and secondly, utilitarian. Each of the statements produced by the special committee reports commissioned by the British government on modern languages, natural science, classics, and English provided extensive evidence of the double kind of justification. Modern languages, for example, were found 'to subserve the purpose of industry and commerce; they are needed for scientific instruction and information ...' and they were also an instrument of that culture 'which tends to develop the higher faculties, the imagination, the sense of beauty, and the intellectual comprehension'. In the case of natural science, 'It can arouse and satisfy the element of wonder in our nature. As an intellectual exercise it disciplines our powers of mind. Its utility and applicability are obvious.' The committee on the classics affirmed that, in the teaching of the classics, the pupils should be brought to realise that the civilisations of Greece and Rome have not only an inspirational value but also 'have something to contribute to the problems of the present day and the permanent life of man'. They also stated realistically that 'we have no desire to restore Classics to their ancient predominance'.[50]

(b) Cardinal Principles of Secondary Education

The general enthusiasm for the reorganisation of education that was characteristic of the period was apparent also in the United States, and had its most effective expression there in the influential and lasting work of the National Education Association's Commission on the Reorganization of Secondary Education. The commission was first formed in 1913 and worked for the next twelve years throughout the war and early post-war period producing by means of its numerous sub-committees a number of well-considered, widely-read, and stimulating reports. Looking back on its work, an educator wrote in the late 1930's: 'The work of the Commission on the Reorganization of Secondary Education exerted profound influence. In numerous instances the special reports served as manuals to guide the work of high school teachers, of special committees on curriculum making, or of textbook writers. The famous *Cardinal Principles of Secondary Education*, published in 1918, which contained the views of the commission on the objectives of secondary education and a summary of principles for the reorganization of school systems, has been one of the most widely read educational documents ever published in the United States.'[51]

The report of one of its committees in 1916 stated that 'the keynote of modern education is "social efficiency", and instruction in all subjects should contribute to this end'.[52] That view permeated the whole of the commission and was best and most succinctly expressed in the Cardinal Principles: 'Education in the United States should be guided by a clear conception of the meaning of democracy, ... The purpose of democracy is so to organize society that each member may develop his personality primarily through activities designed for the well-being of his fellow

[48] The same period of controversy produced a magnificently written *A Defence of Classical Education*, R.W. Livingstone, Macmillan, London, 1916. The title itself is a significant indication that the classics were starting to lose power. Livingstone found it easier to justify the teaching of Greek rather than Latin which 'of the two limbs of the classical education ... can be easiest replaced' (p. 153). Since Greek had already been relegated to a minor status in schools with no prospect of revival, that kind of defence could not have been very encouraging to the Latinists who were responsible for most of the classical teaching.

[49] *The Classical Investigation, conducted by the Advisory Committee of the American Classical League*, Part 3, The Classics in England, France and Germany, University Press, Princeton, 1925, p. 107.

[50] *Report of the Committee appointed to inquire into the position of Natural Science in the Educational System of Great Britain*, H.M.S.O., London, 1918; *Report of the Committee appointed by the Prime Minister to inquire into the position of Modern Languages in the Educational System of Great Britain*, HMSO, London, 1918; *Report of the Prime Minister's Committee on the position of Classics in the Educational System of the United Kingdom, The Classics in Education*. HMSO, London, 1923, p. 57.

[51] Aubrey A. Douglass, *Modern Secondary Education*, Houghton Mifflin, Boston, 1938, p. 104.

[52] Arthur W. Dunn, *The Social Studies in Secondary Education*, Department of the Interior, Bureau of Education, Bulletin 1916, no. 28, Government Printer, Washington D.C., 1916, p. 9.

members and of society as a whole.'[53] In order for society to function efficiently, education must see to it that each individual understood his functions within the democratic society, and knew how to perform them. The first step therefore in determining the objectives upon which an educational program could be formulated was to analyse the activities of an individual.

The commission stated, in a way that would have rejoiced the spirit of Herbert Spencer, that secondary education 'must aim at nothing less than complete and worthy living for all youth',[54] and proceeded to an analysis reminiscent of Spencer's list of human activities upon which he had based his educational principles. The commission held that an individual's main activities could be found in seven areas. He was a member of several groups — family, vocational, and civic groups — and was called upon through them to undertake activities that promoted the welfare of all persons connected with these groups. Apart from duties such as these, each individual should also have an opportunity to cultivate interests that enrich his leisure time, and, in order to enjoy these interests and to perform his duties effectively, he should be ensured of good health. Underpinning all his personal, vocational and social activities, there were certain processes such as reading, writing, calculating, and oral expression that must be mastered by every potentially efficient citizen; and finally, it was necessary to develop the will 'to discharge the duties of life', and at the same time to ensure that those duties were discharged according to the highest ethical principles.[55]

The main objectives of education were, therefore, summarised as: Health; Command of fundamental processes, Worthy home-membership; Vocation; Citizenship; Worthy use of leisure; Ethical character.

They were to apply to education as a whole — elementary, secondary, and higher, but the commission's concern was merely to show their significance for secondary education. This they did by indicating their implications for school organisation, and for the curriculum. To achieve these objectives effectively, the commission considered and specifically recommended that the school system should be reorganised to provide for a six-year elementary school followed by a six-year 'secondary education designed to meet the needs of pupils of approximately 12 to 18 years of age.'[56] Secondary education should consist of a junior and senior level each of three years, to be undertaken in a 'comprehensive high school embracing all curriculums in one unified organization'.[57]

The *Cardinal Principles of Secondary Education* was an influential report. Its statement of objectives provided a pattern that was widely used in numerous subsequent reports on many aspects of education, in textbooks, and in educational discussions for many years to come. Abroad, too, it was widely read and extensively quoted, and its impact can

be seen in official reports, particularly in English-speaking countries, for the next half century.

It was important also for its declaration in favour both of the 6-3-3 school plan and of the comprehensive secondary school which were thus in some measure identified with the kind of education desirable for the development of a democratic society. But more important still was its advocacy of secondary education for all. It was one of the first unequivocal statements that a full secondary education was essential for all youth. During the next thirty years the other developed countries of the world also became persuaded of the truth of this statement, and the history of secondary education since 1918 could largely be written as a contemporary upon the phrase 'secondary education for all'.

It helped to set the pattern also for a utilitarian approach to educational matters. The function of education was to contribute to the betterment of the activities of a given society; by a process of job analysis it was possible to determine the activities within the society with which education would be concerned, and in consequence, the objectives at which it should aim. More clearly and consistently than in any previous report in English-speaking countries, the Cardinal Principles emphasised the social aims and content of education. The intimate relationship between education and society that was characteristic of the German view of *Kultur* was, with a somewhat different perspective, to be an important feature, henceforth, in democratic countries, and that was perhaps one of the most enduring effects of World War I on educational thinking.

(ii) Reform of Vocational Education

The first concrete example of educational reform and the most loudly and consistently agitated for was in the field of vocational education. The war made enormous demands on industry and agriculture, and made strikingly clear the many inefficiencies and the lack of trained manpower among all the belligerents. Germany was generally recognised to have the most efficient industrial work force, and this was attributed to the attention she had paid to the development of an extensive system of vocational

[53] *Cardinal Principles of Secondary Education*, A Report of the Commission on the Reorganization of Secondary Education, appointed by the National Education Association, Department of the Interior, Bureau of Education, Bulletin 1918, no. 35, Government Printer, Washington D.C. 1918, p. 9.

[54] *Cardinal Principles, op.cit.*, p. 32.

[55] ibid., p. 10.

[56] ibid., p. 18.

[57] ibid., p. 24.

education at both its lower and higher levels.[58] Among the other nations there was much self-criticism of their own inadequacies in this field.

The earliest substantial move, in this context, to support vocational education was taken in the United States with the passage of the Smith-Hughes Act in 1917. The Act was the outcome of a decade of agitation and growing interest in vocational education. In 1914 the Smith-Lever Act had enabled federal money to be paid to the states to help in 'diffusing among the people of the United States useful and practical information on subjects relating to agriculture and home economics, and to encourage the application of the same'. The Smith-Hughes Act went much further than its predecessor and inaugurated a new educational policy by bringing federal government influence to bear in a substantial way on high school programs. The Act provided federal money for the states to assist instruction in agricultural, trade, home economics, and industrial subjects, and to help prepare and pay teachers of vocational subjects. The Act stimulated a number of conferences and investigations on the aims of vocational education, on the preparation of teachers, and on general policy. Vocational schools were established, and part-time continuation schools were multiplied. One outcome of the increased interest in vocational education was a tendency to reinforce the practical element in all stages of education. An education that could be seen to be related to present-day life became increasingly popular, and led to modifications of curricula which would produce more realistic and more recognisably utilitarian school programs.

The same sentiments found expression in France in an ill-fated Bill put forward in 1917 by Viviani, then Minister of Public Instruction. Viviani proposed to develop 'good workers, good soldiers, and good citizens' by the introduction of compulsory and free part-time continuation education up to the age of twenty for boys and eighteen for girls, for all young people who had completed elementary school. It was to be physical, vocational, and general education. The proposals which were debated over the course of several years, reflected the opinion of many thoughtful people in France, and helped to direct public interest to the consideration of the country's need in vocational and civic education in the post-war period. Eventually, arising out of the discussions, a law of lasting significance, the *Loi Astier* was passed in 1919. Technical education had first been seriously and comprehensively organised as a result of the law of 1892; the *Loi Astier* made it effectively a part of public education. It provided a framework for the control of all technical education, encouraged a great extension of public facilities, and set the guidelines for courses, examinations, and the award of certificates for the various levels of provision beyond the school leaving age. The *Loi Astier* was the charter for technical education for France in the twentieth century, and every subsequent development was built on its foundations.

Similar considerations moved the English Board of Education to appoint a departmental committee on Juvenile Education in Relation to Employment after the War. The committee's recommendations in 1917 were a blueprint for the Fisher Act of the following year. They posed the question: 'Can the conception of the juvenile as primarily a little wage-earner be replaced by the conception of the juvenile as primarily the workman and the citizen in training?'[59] To help achieve this end they recommended, amongst other things, that a uniform elementary school leaving age of fourteen be established throughout the whole country, that every local education authority be required to provide part-time, day, continuation education which should be compulsory for all young persons between the ages of fourteen and eighteen, and that continuation education should contain physical, general, and vocational instruction, and, for the older children, citizenship training.[60]

The current emphasis on utility had two aspects. There was, certainly, a widespread interest in promoting vocational education, and in ensuring through the schools an adequate supply of trained craftsmen and technicians for the future needs of society. There was also a somewhat more generalised and pervasive view, brought to bear on education of every kind and at every level. It was the view that education should contribute primarily to the mastery of the present way of living and to its future improvement. To that end the things that were taught in school should be realistically and practically oriented. They should be seen to be useful in the everyday activities and in the future growth of society. Many educators who were chary about the extension of vocational education, especially if it impinged on the work of the secondary schools, were heartily in favour of the second kind of utilitarian emphasis, and much of the educational discussion of the later years of the war and of the early post-war years was concerned with getting the principle established, and with devising ways of putting it into practice.

(iii) Programs of Educational Reform in Western Europe

Among the European nations involved in the war, three levels of commitment to educational renovation emerged and were exemplified in the proposals and reforms of the three major powers. Germany, prostrated by the war, took the opportunity to recast its constitution and to set

[58] A heartfelt statement of this view is to be found in Paul L. d'Arc, *Pour L'Apres-Guerre*, vol. 1, *L'Education Française*, Grasset, Paris, 1917, chapters IX and XVIII, written while the author was a prisoner of war in Germany. See also Viscount Haldane, *Parliamentary Debates*, 5th series, vol. XXII, House of Lords, 12 July 1916, cols 661-2.

[59] *Final Report of the Departmental Committee on Juvenile Education in Relation to Employment after the War* (Lewis Report) (Cd.8512), HMSO, 1917, p. 5.

[60] *ibid.*, pp. 16-17, 27-8.

education the task of helping in the production of a revivified and democratic society. The effort was abortive. It was blighted by economic circumstances and conservatively nationalist forces in the mid-1920's. Its failure in the course of the 1920's was a prelude to the development of totalitarianism in the 1930's. In France, the change was less abrupt. During the war years and throughout the 1920's, criticism was active but sweeping reform was not the order of the day. The reform movement argued for adjustments of the existing structure and modest extensions of accepted principles and, in the ensuing round of compromises, a small measure of progress took place. Primary and technical education benefitted most; in secondary education there was a reversion towards pre-twentieth century practices. The English educational reformers, too, failed to achieve great changes in practice but, in the matter of educational thought and principle, succeeded in producing a substantial change of climate. The beginning of a serious commitment to open up all levels of education to the working classes took place in the discussions of the post-war years. The main topic of debate was the possibility of secondary education for all. The arguments put forward by the leading advocates, and the recommendations made in official reports in England were the clearest and most sustained examples of the change that was developing at that time in views about the purpose and function of education. But, although the argument for radical change was cogently put and widely appreciated in England, there was no correspondingly radical change in the structure and content of education. Among the major combatants of World War I, it was only in Russia that the educational tradition was thoroughly broken and remade. In that country, the pressures of political revolution and ideological conviction provided the driving force that generated fundamental changes throughout the whole theory and practice of education.[61]

(a) Educational Renovation in Germany

Disillusion. In Germany, there had been four years of a desperately fought and unsuccessful war, in the latter part of which much of the population was near starvation. It had been followed by a naval mutiny, the abdication of the emperor, a revolution, economic depression, and continuing unrest. It is not to be wondered at, therefore, that the buoyant confidence with which the war had been opened had somewhat evaporated by its close.

Feeling in Germany had clearly started to change after the disastrous and inconclusive battles of Verdun and the Somme in 1916 which had caused nearly a million German casualties. The following winter, one of the most miserable on record, with excessive cold, fuel shortage and crop failure, increased the disillusion. Stalemate on the front and distress at home could be endured if they could be seen to be the way to a brighter future. Unfortunately, no such prospect seemed apparent. The govern-

ment became more militarised, the class structure seemed to be getting more rigid, and the masses who fought and endured appeared to have little prospect of influencing either the course of the war or the subsequent settlement. Even the resolution of the Reichstag, the lower house of the national parliament, calling in 1917 for peace negotiations, was disregarded by the government.

The great intoxication of the time has died away
And a world of pain lies before me
The time of deep suffering looms ahead,
The mad springtime of slaughter has had its day.[62]

In these words, a poet expressed the growing feeling of the time.

An important consequence of the forlornness and disillusion was a deep heart-searching and a questioning of the traditional basis of society, government, and culture. The Expressionist writers and painters of the period well exemplified the trend when they delved into the inner spiritual resources of the nation, bemoaned existing circumstances, and called for a new society.

Germany's collapse in 1918-19 was a shattering one. It was followed by four years of unrest culminating in the invasion of the Ruhr by the French in 1923 and calamitous inflation in the same year. 'What we have and what we had has all suddenly vanished.'[63] It was an obvious material collapse and it was also a cultural one. The leadership of the educated class, which had become identified with the military officer class, had clearly failed. Its judgment and its aim had been unsound. As the nation began to fall apart at its seams, it could be seen that, despite the nationalistic emphasis and traditional *Kultur*, no solid and durable basis for national unity had been provided. If the nation was to fight its way up and out of the abysmal condition that the end-of-war convulsions had plunged it into, a much more profound basis of association and co-operative effort would have to be found. To supplant those 'powers, sanctioned by history, clad in the authority of inherited glory and glamour, and so compelling that it was but natural to support and preserve them',[64] to replace an aristocratic and exclusive orientation, and to give the working man of both the blue and the white collar variety a full stake in the country, were the crucial tasks facing the reformers. The new society was to have a much more generous measure of socialism, democracy, and educational opportunity. Indicative of this thinking was

[61] See chapters 7 and 8 for an account of the U.S.S.R. experience.

[62] Joachim Freiherr von der Goltz, 'Der deutsche Musketier, 1916' *Deutsche Sonette*, Cassirer, Berlin, 1916.

[63] Joachim Ringelnatz, *Be Quiet*, quoted and translated in R. Samuel and R.H. Thomas, *Expressionism in German Life, Literature and the Theatre*, Heffer, Cambridge, 1939, p. 173.

[64] Thomas Mann, 'The German Republic', a speech delivered in Berlin in 1923 and published in *Order of the Day*, Knopf, New York, 1942, p. 13.

a widely read book, *The New Society*, written in 1920 by Walter Rathenau, a prominent industrialist who was to become the foreign minister in the early years of the new republic and to die by assassination in 1922.

Germany's task, according to Rathenau, would be long and arduous. It was nothing less than the creation of a new society with a necessarily low material standard, but of high morality, based upon a common determination to succeed. A new awakening must come that would make a nation where none then existed and would, through a deeply-felt sense of collective solidarity, build an organic democratic society.

The sense of solidarity meant that each man considered first the general good and not his own and felt answerable for all, and all for each; it was a spirit built upon a thorough cultivation of the moral and spiritual resources of the whole people. Thus, the new society must be based upon a refashioning of the educational influences at work in Germany. 'Though we become as poor as church-mice, we must stake our last penny on this, and tune up our education and instruction, our models and outlook, our motives and claims, our achievement and our atmosphere, to so high a point that any one coming into Germany shall feel that he is entering into a new age.'[65]

Weimar Republic: The Constitution and Education. The first steps towards educational regeneration were taken in the national constitution of the new republic. Germany, under the Weimar constitution adopted in 1919, was to be a federation of nineteen democratic republican states with governments responsible to a popular assembly elected by a system of proportional representation through direct, equal, and secret suffrage exercised by all persons over the age of twenty. Universal adult suffrage and democratic institutions necessarily implied the provision of adequate educational facilities to try to ensure, as far as possible, a sufficiency of education upon which to base a proper exercise of voting power and popular decision.

Accordingly, the constitution declared that authority for education should be vested in the states which should provide for eight years of free, compulsory, elementary education and supplemented by compulsory part-time continuation education up to the age of eighteen. Provision was to be made for scholarships for pupils in poor circumstances to attend secondary and higher schools. Education was normally to be provided by public institutions; private preparatory schools, the special privilege of the wealthy classes, were summarily abolished. Other private schools, however, could be established subject to state permission and inspection. Teacher training was to be genuinely a tertiary level process.

Those were the general ideas written into the constitution, upon which, it was hoped, the new fabric of education was to be erected.

National Educational Conference. Although educational authority rested with the states, the Weimar constitution authorised the federal government to prescribe guiding principles for education throughout the federation.[66] Hence the general statements about education and the provision of schooling that appeared in the constitution.

To put the function into more effective operation and to provide the basis upon which well-considered policies might rest, the Minister for the Interior called a National Education Conference (*Reichsschulkonferenz*) in 1920. This 'first German parliament of educators', as one of its distinguished participants called it,[67] met on nine days from 11th June to 19th June. The seven hundred educators who attended came from every part of the country and represented every shade of educational opinion. They included ministers and senior educational officials from every state, local educational officials, school principals, teachers of public and private schools at all levels, university professors, representatives of youth groups and of technical and vocational institutions, persons from educational, religious and economic associations, and a goodly number of specially selected individuals. Well-known educators such as Rein, Natorp, Stern, and Spranger were there, progressives such as Gaudig, Tews, Wyneken, and Kerschensteiner, the conservatives Harnach and Binder, and the radicals Oestreich and Karsen.

Three issues occasioned the greatest interest and discussion among the participants: the organisation of the school system, teacher training, and the basis of teaching method.

The national law, passed a short while before the conference, establishing a common four-year elementary school was the background to the discussion on the general organisation of the school system. Prominent in the debate were the advocates of a unified plan of schooling (*Einheitsschule*). Tews, for instance, argued for a pattern which basically would consist of a six-year common elementary school, followed by a three-year common middle school leading to a three-year upper secondary school. His views were strenuously opposed by the stalwarts of the *gymnasium* who regarded the existing pattern of secondary education as substantially sound. Finally, the conference reached a compromise by agreeing that each state should think out its own pattern and might be expected to experiment with several designs. The day was thus saved for the traditional secondary school, but the advocates of the *Einheitsschule* had given substantial notice that they were an important force to be reckoned with.[68]

[65] Walter Rathenau, *The New Society*, Williams and Norgate, London, 1912, p. 104.

[66] Article 10.

[67] Oskar Frey, 'Die Reichsschulkonferenz', *Neue Bahnen*, 31, 7, July 1920, 242.

[68] Felix Behrend, 'Die Reichsschulkonferenz und das höhere Schulwesen', *Sokrates, Zeitschrift für das Gymnasialwesen*, new series, 8, 74, 1920, Berlin, 1920, pp. 218-21.

On the matter of teacher training there was long discussion and eventual wide agreement that, since all teachers were members of a common profession, they should have the same basic preparation, with additional study and training according to their particular specialties.

One of the high-points of the conference, according to one of its members,[69] was the discussion on the place of activity work in schools. There was considerable interest expressed in the ideas put forward by its advocates and in the implications for teaching at all levels of the elementary and secondary school. It is probably too much to claim, as one historian has, that the activity principle dominated the discussions of the conference,[70] but certainly its advocates were strong, enthusiastic, and persuasive. They had, at the conference, for the first time, a great public forum for the expression of their ideas, and their views were very pertinent to the educational tasks of the new democracy. They made an impressive showing and for the next ten years were to be accepted as important and stimulating contributors to the continuing educational debate.

School Reforms in the Early 1920s. Although no common detailed plan emerged, in the early 1920s five principal reforms were made which affected considerably the structure and spirit of education throughout the whole of Germany.

First, in 1920, in accordance with the requirements of the constitution, the national government enacted a law for the establishment of a common four-year elementary school (*Grundschule*) throughout Germany. This was but a partial response to the advocates of the *Einheitsschule*. It was, however, a considerable advance, enabling elementary school pupils henceforth to enter secondary schools, the door to which had previously been closed except for the few gifted children who had been admitted by a recent wartime reform.

The second substantial activity, again by the national government, was the Juvenile Welfare Law of 1923, requiring state governments to provide facilities for the development of every child's physical strength, moral capacity and vocational ability, for the supervision of children in need of care, for the protection of children against exploitation, and for the preservation of the health of mothers and children. This was a charter under which a wide range of socially desirable legislation was enacted in every state for the general welfare of all German children.

Thirdly, on completing the work of the *Grundschule*, pupils were henceforth provided with a wider range of choice of secondary level schools. Germany had for long tended to produce a somewhat bewildering variety of schools at that level and in the post-World War I period, she managed to multiply them still further.

The fourth aspect of educational reform that was undertaken in that period was a recasting of the teacher training programs for elementary school teachers. Up to the 1920's they had been prepared in normal schools with a restricted program that ran parallel to but lacked the liberal content of *gymnasium*-type courses. Thenceforth they were to be trained at a tertiary level in a variety of ways by the various states.

The fifth feature of the reconstruction was to be found not so much in actual regulations and institutional changes, as in the spirit that pervaded much of the legislation and reorganisation at all levels. The reorganisation of schools and teacher training provided a pattern through which a less class-ridden, more cohesive republican society could be more suitably developed. Into this pattern it was necessary to inject a renascent spirit — a spur and inspiration to the effort of refashioning such as that which had revived the Germany of a hundred years before, after the defeat at Jena. Consequently, in all school programs, an effort was made to emphasise German culture as the central feature of German education, and to concentrate in elementary and secondary school programs upon a thorough knowledge and appreciation of the social, political and economic activities of both the local environment and the nation as a whole.

The new approach, however, did not always succeed in promoting democratic ways and ideas. Perhaps the best illustration of the impact of the atmosphere of the Weimar period is to be found in the trend taken by the German youth movement. The movement was a twentieth century phenomenon originating in Germany and contributing substantially to the physical, social, and emotional education of young people in Germany.

Youth Movement in Germany. The youth movement started as a non-political organisation about 1896 and developed eventually in the 1920's into a series of groups with staunch political interests and affiliations. As a whole, the movement was never tightly organised and run to a set policy, but consisted of many small and large groups with somewhat similar characteristics and reasonably common aims. Parallel to it, there were youth groups run by churches and by various political parties. In its early years it had some similarity to the Boy Scout movement which started in England in 1907 and it subsequently provided a basis and somewhat of a model for the youth movements of Hitler Germany, Fascist Italy, and Soviet Russia.

The *Wandervögel* (birds of passage) was the first stage of the movement from 1896 to 1919; the *Bund* (Association) was the second from 1919 to 1933.

The *Wandervögel* movement was very much part of the progressive education movement and had close associations with the educators and the

---

[69] Oskar Frey, *op.cit.*, p. 271.

[70] Theodor Wilhelm, *Pädagogik der Gegenwart*, 2nd edn, Kröner, Stuttgart, 1960, p. 76.

students of progressive schools. It was never large — its members did not at any time exceed sixty thousand; it was very much a middle class affair, scarcely touching working class youth; and it remained peculiarly German, never spreading beyond the boundaries of the German language. The original members of the movement were the 'angry young men' of the turn of the century who could see little worthwhile in contemporary society and wished to develop their own way of life. They chose to move out from what they conceived to be a materialistic society into a simple, wandering, rural life steeped in traditional folklore and mediaeval customs and filled with a warmth of human companionship.

The first leader was Karl Fischer who had a simple uncomplicated interest in rambling through the German countryside. He was responsible for getting the association of *Wandervögel* formally established in 1901 in Berlin. During the next ten or so years, many groups of youths between twelve and nineteen years old were formed, especially in northern and central Germany and, after 1911, girls also were accepted for membership. They went off on bicycles in the school summer holidays and sometimes in the shorter vacations or weekends, cooking their own food and sleeping in the open; they put on their own theatricals, ran their own magazine, revived folksongs, and formed choirs and orchestras to sing them.

The hikes were, for many young people, deeply emotional experiences, producing lasting friendships and an abiding love of the German countryside. The groups tended also to establish a home meeting place where they might assemble for a weekly discussion or song night. Their attitude to society was more one of detachment than of revolt. They did not spend much time on the discussion of social questions and less on social action. The emphasis was on freedom for young people rather than on social responsibility and active citizenship. After about 1910, patriotism began to become an important element and to assume large proportions during the years of World War I. From that time on, the *Wandervögel* lost something of its earlier spontaneity.

A reaction to the growing nationalistic flavour came from a short-lived union of groups called the Free German Youth, who declared that they would shape their lives 'at their own initiative, on their own responsibility, and with deep sincerity'.[71] The declaration was associated with the well-known progressive educator, Wyneken, and was formulated at a mass rally on the Hohe Meissner mountain in Cassel in 1913 on the centenary of the Battle of Leipzig. Wyneken suggested that youth should seriously address themselves to the task of remaking the world. He pointed out that they had a style but no culture; they should endeavour to express themselves through a distinctive youth culture which might be the beginning of a more co-operative and flexible society.

After World War I the movement broke up into an even larger number of groups or *Bünde* of various sizes with characteristics decidedly different from those of the pre-war *Wandervögel*. Their popularity greatly increased and attendance rose considerably. The *Bünde* tended to wear uniforms distinctive of each group, they became more interested in sporting activities, and they often arranged expeditions abroad to places such as Lapland or the Sahara. In the 1920's their activities tended to take on a more military appearance and in their songs martial airs began to replace more innocent folk tunes. 'If the vagrant scholar might be said to have been the *Wandervögel* ideal, that of the *Bünde* was the soldier.'[72] The *Bünde* were more collectively-minded and more disciplined than the earlier, more amiable and comradely *Wandervögel*; and they became more immersed in politics, polarizing into right and left wing groups. Towards the end of the 1920's the right wing elements predominated, militant nationalism increased and the groups tended to become close-knit units serving a political cause. By the early 1930's it was not difficult for many of their members to transfer to the nazi youth organisation.

Impact of the Weimar Reforms. In the event, the effort of reconstruction did not meet with the success that its advocates had hoped for. Without doubt, it immeasurably increased the effectiveness of the educational systems throughout Germany and widened educational opportunity, but it did not succeed in laying an enduring foundation for the new society.

It had to struggle against increasing opposition and difficulty. It was born of defeat and associated with enemy dictation: 'a situation profoundly hated by considerable sections of citizens and young people, who will simply have none of it because, forsooth, it did not come to birth in triumph and the exercise of free choice, but in defeat and collapse, making it seem bound up for ever with weakness, shame and foreign domination.' Thus, in 1923, did Thomas Mann, the most distinguished contemporary German writer, describe the origin of the Weimar Republic, speaking on its behalf unconvincingly, in the *Beethovensaal* in Berlin to the jeers and catcalls of a hostile student gallery.[73]

The young people on whom the future of the democracy clearly rested were not universally imbued with the new spirit. No strong leadership came from the Youth Movement which, if it had been true to its founder's spirit, should have given powerful support to the new tendencies. Resentment at the situation in which defeat had placed the

---

[71] Quoted in W.Z. Laqueur, *Young Germany, A History of the German Youth Movement*, RKP, London, 1962, p. 31; see also H. Becker, *German Youth: Bond or Free*, RKP, London, 1946.

[72] W.Z. Laqueur, *op.cit.*, p. 235.

[73] Thomas Mann, *Order of the Day*, Knopf, New York, 1942, containing a speech, The German Republic, delivered in 1923, p. 16.

country and the remnants of militarism helped to rekindle a virulent nationalism opposed to the ideals and practices of the Weimar Republic. This was abetted by continuing economic difficulties up to the mid-1920's. By that point, the initial enthusiasm that had been generated was steadily running down. There were still a few choice spirits in the educational field and a number of them were interesting, talented, and first-rate educators who had worked for reform for many years and made a considerable contribution to the thought and practice of education. The movement, however, never had its Fichte. The final dampening influence in the mid-1920's was the advent of a conservative national government, part of a general trend in Europe towards conservatism, which succeeded in slowing educational development in Germany and many other countries for the remaining years of the decade.[74]

(b) Educational Ferment in France

Les Compagnons. In France some educators found, in the events and activities of the war, a justification to return to the solid virtues of the pre-1902 classical curriculum upon which they claimed France's intellectual culture was founded. Many university professors and teachers in the *lycées* were of that opinion. They formed a substantial and conservative group of respected and influential persons. They deplored the inroads made into classical studies by the reorganisation of secondary programs in 1902; they regarded the pupils since that time as 'a generation whose education had been sacrificed', and they firmly resisted any further move away from traditional programs.[75]

On the other hand, it was undeniable that 'certain ideas were in the air'.[76] The new ideas were to be seem most clearly and cogently expressed in the articles, letters, pamphlets, and books of *Les Compagnons,* a group of young university graduates who, early in the war, while serving at the front, had started to agitate for a complete reform of French education. Notable articles written by members of the group in 1918 brought them considerable support and in 1919 they formed their own association and started their own journal which continued publication monthly until 1925.

The work of *Les Compagnons* in the cause of educational reform was a sample of wartime thinking at its best — an example of high idealism sustained by solid theoretical argument and grounded in practical knowledge. They continued in being until 1933 and were the main driving force for the reform of French education throughout the inter-war period.

With the cry 'we will have fought in vain, during the war, if peace should conquer us,'[77] the group launched a carefully considered attack on the whole of French education and proposed a series of radical reforms.

Some of these were modified subsequently in the light of practical realities but the most significant remained intact.

To achieve their purpose, they argued for a reorientation of the civic education that had operated in French schools since the beginning of the Third Republic. In the view of *Les Compagnons*, it had tended not to distinguish between patriotism and citizenship, and to concentrate upon building patriots. Patriotism was important but not enough; it was possible to be a fine patriot and a poor citizen. French children must learn their social duties and develop a sense of responsibility for the public welfare. 'We want education to have a positive social content, a distinctly social spirit.'[78]

One consequence of that viewpoint, was their advocacy of *l'école unique*, the common school which they defined as 'the school of all and for all, the school which provides access to secondary education for all who are worthy of it.'[79] They suggested, as their fellow-spirits in Germany were also doing, a single primary school up to the age of fourteen to be attended by all children. At the end of that period children would proceed, on the basis of intellectual selection, to a variety of secondary level schools according to their several interests and talents. The fundamental reason for this was to break down the senseless exclusiveness associated with separate and parallel school systems. 'We want a democratic education. . . True democracy is a society which is governed by the common interest, one in which men do not live as if they came from different worlds.'[80] It was in the interest of democracy, *Les Compagnons* claimed, both that there should be wider educational opportunity for all children and that talent from whatever source it came should be selected and trained according to its capacity.

Beyond the primary school, they proposed a traditionally classical secondary school of five years. Their views were later modified to admit a modern stream of studies side by side with the classical stream and to push

---

[74] See I.L. Kandel, *Studies in Comparative Education*, pp. 153-4 for details of modifications and adjustments introduced into the reforms as a result of economic or conservative pressures.

[75] G.S. Weill, *Histoire de l'Enseignement Secondaire en France (1802-1920)*, Payot, Paris, 1921, pp. 234-5.

[76] G.S. Weill, *op.cit.*, p. 238.

[77] 'Les Compagnons', *L'Université Nouvelle*, vol I, Fischbacher, Paris, 1924, p. vi. The principal statement of their views appeared in a vigorous two-volume work *L'Université Nouvelle*, published in 1918-1919. The first volume was an outline of the general principles of their suggested reforms, the second a detailed practical analysis of the changes necessary at each level of education and of the problems involved in putting these changes into effect.

[78] *ibid.*, vol II, p. 15.

[79] *ibid.*, vol. II, p. 49.

[80] *ibid.*, vol. I. pp. 21, 24-5.

the age of entry down to thirteen years. The majority of pupils, however, would proceed from primary school to a flexible and widely available system of vocational education in which schools offering either full- or part-time education were to be free and compulsory for all children up to the age of eighteen.

Consistent with the general wartime interest in health and physical education programs. *Les Compagnons* insisted that in all schools a sufficient time must be given to physical education. They saw it not only contributing to the improvement of the health and physique of the French nation, but also providing opportunity for children to develop a taste for hard work, to experience an element of risk, to accustom themselves to discipline and, above all, to work together and develop common loyalties.

Higher education, also, was in need of some recasting. A university, they considered, had three functions. It must prepare people for their professions, especially for the teaching profession; it must further the progress of scholarship and scientific research; it must enrich the nation by making widely known and understood the knowledge it had accumulated. To accomplish those tasks, there was need of a better and more pertinent initiation of students into their professional courses, a more systematic approach to research with more generous financial support, the establishment of a closer relationship between scientific research and industry and a determined effort by the university professors to enlighten every section of the public through talks, books, journal articles and pamphlets.[81]

Reformed in that way, French education would be fit to meet the challenge of the new era. 'It is not the teachers and the ideas of 1900 who will make the France of 1950'; their tradition died in the Great War, it was necessary 'to rebuild the house from top to bottom'.[82]

Primary School Reform. The impact which *Les Compagnons* and like-minded people made on French educational thought was to be seen first at the primary school level in the steps taken to put the ideas of *l'école unique* into practice. The first significant change came in 1923 with a decision that, between the years of compulsory education from six to thirteen, all children were to follow the same syllabus of studies whether they were attending an elementary school or the preparatory classes of a *lycée*. The schools were not amalgamated into a common school but, at least, they were henceforth to follow a common program. The number of scholarships available for secondary education, for which fees were still charged, was steadily increased and, from, 1925, all candidates for higher elementary, secondary, or technical education were required to present themselves for a common examination on the basis of which awards would be made for

all post-primary courses. Parental income was taken into account in the award of scholarships and encouragement given to the bright children of poorer parents by the payment of maintenance allowances.

The courses of study for elementary schools had, in 1923, their first serious revision since 1887. For the most part, the modifications were not extensive, but they were in line with the views of *Les Compagnons*. Their principal function was to eliminate an accumulation of outmoded material which was overloading the curriculum, to endeavour to give a more realistic and concrete bias to the work of the classroom, to update the teaching of morals and civics, and to introduce a reasonable amount of physical education.[83]

Reaction in Secondary Education. The measure of reform was far from the complete reconstruction that had been argued for. It undoubtedly improved the conduct of the elementary schools and it provided additional though limited opportunities for more pupils of talent to move into a secondary school. At the secondary school level, however, reaction was the order of the day in the early 1920's. It took the form of a revolt against the reform of 1902 and culminated in the Bérard Reform of 1923. The Minister of Public Instruction, Léon Bérard, with the concurrence of a reasonable majority in the French parliament, replaced the parallel courses of the 1902 system with a single four-year common course which made Latin compulsory for all pupils, followed by a two-year course in which pupils could take either a classics or a modern languages specialty. In the following year, Albert, Bérard's successor, recast the reform, not reviving the 1902 position, but providing for a modern languages stream as an alternative to the classics in the first four years of the secondary school and strengthening the study of French in all streams as a central and vital part of the *lycée's* program of *culture générale*. That, with minor modifications, remained largely the position throughout the remainder of the 1920's. It had the effect that, whatever course a pupil studied during his first six years of secondary work, he would be required to spend approximately fifty per cent of his time in language study.

The reaction of the 1920's represented a stubborn refusal by French authorities to make much modification in the idea of *culture générale* that characterised their education, as it had that of most other European nations for centuries past. In the post-World War I period when most nations were broadening the range of school studies and revising their

[81] *ibid.*, vol. I, pp. 41-6.

[82] *ibid.*, vol. I, pp. 11-12.

[83] P.H. Gay and O. Montreux (ed.), *French Elementary Schools, Official Courses of Study*, trans. with introd. by I.L. Kandel, New York Teachers' College, Columbia University, 1926; see particularly pp. 56-64.

views of a general education suitable to the times, the French clung tenaciously to a literary education with a classical foundation and chose to remain educationally in 'that modern land of antiquity'.[84]

Reacting against the conservative success in the *lycée* reforms of 1923-26, *Les Compagnons* pushed for the extension rather than the contraction of secondary school programs. Paul Langevin, one of *Les Compagnons* and a member of a ministerial commission in 1925 on *l'école unique*, favoured a common primary school followed by a period of orientation leading to a secondary education of several strands; it was, in some measure, an anticipation of the subsequent 1945 Langevin-Wallon National Commission Report, widely debated in the post-World War II years. In 1933 all classes in secondary schools finally became free of tuition fees and, in 1936, the school leaving age was raised to fourteen.

Eventually, in 1937, a plan of reform was formally put before the Chamber of Deputies in a proposed abortive bill by Jean Zay, a young radical Minister for National Education.[85] In introducing the measure, he referred to it as an instalment of *l'école unique* which would be 'a work of justice and an instrument of social progress'.[86] By careful examination at the end of the common primary course at the age of twelve, children were to be selected for the *lycées* to pass into a one-year orientation class introductory to a whole range of secondary school studies which would enable the ex-primary school pupil to choose the course best suited to his abilities. In 1937, some 120 experimental orientation classes were started in forty-five centres throughout the country. They were an anticipation of the experimental *classes nouvelles* which initiated post-World War II reform in France. For the pupils who did not gain selection to work in a *lycée*, a separate 'complementary' education was to be provided, not unlike that in existing *écoles primaires superieures*.[87]

It is difficult to escape the conclusion that the advocates of *l'école unique* were not particularly concerned with the education of the mass of school pupils. In 1924, 2.7 per cent of the eligible age group entered the *lycée*; in 1938, the proportion was still only 3.8 per cent and the Zay reform was unlikely to change it significantly. In common with the traditionalists, the reformers were interested in the production of an élite. Their view of the elite, however, was a broader one and gave recognition to technical and scientific proficiency as well as to literary pursuits. Equality of educational opportunity for them meant essentially equality of opportunity to gain a place among the elite.

(c) Educational Reform in England

England was the first of the belligerents to attempt a general re-examination of her educational system. Interest in educational reform had been simmering since the first year of the war. It grew to considerable proportions in 1916, and by 1917 had become a ferment. The leader-writer in *The Times Educational Supplement* in January of that year declared that 'Schemes of educational reform, amounting in fact to educational revolution, pour today into the press.'[88] And H.A.L. Fisher, the new president of the Board of Education, recorded subsequently in his autobiography: 'As happens in any revolutionary age, the educational world was in a state of ferment. For the first time in our national history, **education was a popular subject and discussed in an atmosphere cleared of religious acrimony... I was sensible from the first that, while the war** lasted, reforms could be obtained and advances could be made which would be impossible to realize in the critical atmosphere of peace. I resolved to move forward at a hand gallop and along the whole front.'[89]

Fisher Act, 1918. A Bill was drafted and presented to parliament shortly before the summer recess in 1917. During the recess it was widely discussed in the country, encountering considerable objection on the part of the Local Education Authorities and employers who were apparently not as ready for change as the young men in the forces. 'I bowed to the storm,' Fisher wrote. 'The measure was carefully stripped of every feature which might make it obnoxious to the public bodies who would be required to work it in the event of its becoming law.' Fisher's hand gallop had slowed to a walk; and the Act that was eventually presented to and passed by parliament in 1918 turned out to be a somewhat mild reform rather than a root and branch reconstruction.

It did, however, incorporate some interesting and important features.

For the first time in English history, educational legislation was specifically declared to be enacted 'with a view to the establishment of a national system of public education available for all persons capable of profiting thereby'.[90] In actual fact, the Act was less comprehensive than the wording in its introduction implied and less deserving of the description 'national' than the Education (Balfour) Act of 1902 whose structure it

---

[84] W. Rathenau, *The New Society*, p. 89.

[85] Jean Zay (1904-1944) was a radical journalist and lawyer who, in his three years as Minister of Education from 1936 up to the outbreak of World War II, began a number of reforms that delighted his progressive supporters and anticipated post-war reconstruction. He was imprisoned by the Vichy government and died in 1944.

[86] Journal Officiel, Chambre de Députés, 16e Leg., Sess. Ord., de 1937, *Documents Parlementaires*, Annexe No. 2038, 2e séance du 5 mars 1937, p. 298.

[87] J.E. Talbott, *The Politics of Educational Reform in France, 1918-1940*, Princeton University Press, 1969, provides a lucid and thorough account of French education in the inter-war period. For the Zay proposals, see particularly pp. 209-44.

[88] *The Times Educational Supplement*, 4 January 1917.

[89] H.A.L. Fisher, *An Unfinished Autobiography*, Oxford University Press, London, 1940, pp. 94, 103. H.A.L. Fisher (1865-1940) was a well-known historian and vice-chancellor of the University of Sheffield, 1912-16. He was a member of parliament from 1916 to 1926.

[90] Education Act, 1918, 8 and 9 Geo. V. Chap. 39 #1.

maintained. The use of the word 'national' did, however, symbolise the newly-felt unity of the wartime era and undoubtedly helped to channel the thinking of the next two decades towards a concern with the whole range of educational activities in the country and with their interrelationships.

The Fisher Act introduced changes in several areas. Its provisions on the general administration of education made adjustments in the relationships between the central government Board of Education and the more than three hundred Local Education Authorities established by the Balfour Act,[91] thereby slightly increasing the possibility of more unified planning for the country as a whole. The Act fixed the ages of compulsory attendance without exemption at five to fourteen, empowering LEA's to fix an upper limit of fifteen if they so wished. No local authority, however, exercised its discretionary power in this matter. All public elementary education was henceforth to be free and it could be provided by an LEA for children up to the age of sixteen.

The war had brought an unprecedented increase in the number of pupils seeking a secondary education, probably as a result of the greatly increased earning power of wage-earning families employed in war industries. Those pupils were the first wave of the new generation with a different background who would replace the young secondary school men lost in the war and create a demand henceforth for a wider and more generous view of secondary education. It was to cater for that situation that the larger English cities, from 1911 on, started to develop central schools. They were the forerunners of the Modern Schools and represented the first substantial attempt in English public education to take a broader view of secondary level education. The Fisher Act recognised and encouraged central schools and their like and contributed much towards the development of the movement.[93]

For the children who did not remain at school beyond the school leaving age, the Act provided that LEA's should establish continuation schools, initially for pupils from fourteen to sixteen, and subsequently from sixteen to eighteen years of age. They were to be free and compulsory and instruction was to be an appropriate balance of general, physical, and vocational. That section was the principal innovation in the Act. It was the one which its author regarded as its most significant, and the one which created the greatest controversy and debate. In the event, the scheme was virtually stillborn. With few exceptions, the local authorities did not avail themselves of the power to make continuation education compulsory. Those who established schools soon abandoned them in the economic recession of the early twenties and one authority only, Rugby, managed to maintain a compulsory continuation scheme through to World War II.

The Act also made a substantial extension of the social services for children that had been steadily developing during the two pre-war

An English Public School. **In this aerial photograph of Harrow School the original schoolroom of 1611 is marked with an arrow. The expansion of the school began with the conversion of a number of private houses and, after about 1840, the school built its own boarding houses in an imposing Victorian style. The teaching accommodation was similarly increased, so that the old school is now completely overshadowed by the later development, and has been expanded into extensive grounds.**

decades. The child welfare provisions and the encouragement given to new forms of post-primary schools proved to be the most valuable and lasting aspects of the Fisher Act. It was a useful but somewhat disappointing outcome to the widespread public campaign for national educational reconstruction.

[91] W.O. Lester Smith, *Education. An Introductory Survey*, Penguin, London, 1957, pp. 91-3. Amongst other things, Fisher was able to implement the recommendations of the 1916 Kempe Report which had shrewdly devised a means whereby the central authority could, in a rational rather than in the former piecemeal fashion, enter into a real and enduring financial partnership with the local education authorities to the lasting benefit of education.

[92] See G.A.N. Lowndes, *The Silent Social Revolution*, Oxford University Press, London, 1937, pp. 113-15, and A.M. Kazamias, *Politics, Society and Secondary Education in England*, University of Pennsylvania, Philadelphia, 1966, pp. 211ff.

[93] See H.C. Dent, *Secondary Modern Schools*, Routledge and Kegan Paul, London, 1958, pp. 4-5.

The most effective of Fisher's activities while president of the Board of Education were not to be found on the statute book but in the reform which he secured in the public examination system, in the revision of the method of fixing teachers' salaries,[94] and in the establishment of a University Grants Committee which preserved for universities an acceptable degree of independence while guaranteeing them reasonable support from government moneys. The examination reform was of particular importance. By 1917 the secondary schools of the country were presenting candidates for a large number and variety of badly co-ordinated external examinations run by a multitude of authorities. Under Fisher's guidance, the number was reduced to two — a School Certificate to be taken at approximately the age of sixteen and providing evidence of general education, and a Higher School Certificate intended to be taken two years later by those pupils who had specialised in an advanced course. Initially seven, later eight examining boards in various parts of the country were recognised as competent authorities by the Board of Education. The reorganisation lasted until 1951 and the examinations were a major factor during that period controlling the curriculum and activities of secondary schools.

Fisher and his supporters recognised but did not grapple thoroughly with the new spirit of the times and the new social forces, the importance of which the Archbishop of Canterbury had foreshadowed in the mid-war years. After the war there was no doubting the new climate.

Towards Secondary Education for all. Caliban, the rough, ill-educated artisan and man in the street, was clearly astir.[95] As the world of privilege and tradition collapsed, Caliban became conscious of the possibility that the future might lie in his hands. To be effective in his impending role, he felt the need of a more extensive education. Elementary education was not enough, but was the existing secondary and further education appropriate? Where the culture of the secondary schools tended towards exclusiveness and a reverence for the past, it was inadequate and even harmful. To select a few to rise through this education as a leaven for the existing elite, or to submit the whole new mass to the old program, was merely to perpetuate existing privilege and a type of humanism insufficiently aware of the living present. Caliban, if he was to emerge most fruitfully from his chronically underprivileged state into a position of wisely and judiciously exercised power, needed an education which would be both humane and useful, and education which would make him fully a man in a modern setting.

The aspirations of the working class which Caliban thus expressed were channelled in the post-war years largely through the Socialist and Labour parties whose rise to importance and to some measure of legislative power in many countries was a feature of the 1920's. The expression of those aspirations and their connection with the socialist policy of the time was most apparent in Russia.[96] Among the other European countries, it could most clearly be seen in England through the movement, in the 1920's, for universal secondary education.

During the nineteenth century and in the years prior to World War II, post-primary education in England had, like much of the education of Europe, moved along three paths. There were the traditional, academically-oriented grammar and independent schools, to whom the name secondary was exclusively applied; there were 'recurrent upthrusts by the elementary school',[97] producing higher primary and central schools as a continuation, within the primary framework, of the elementary school; and there were, from about 1905 on, junior technical schools offering two to three years of general education spiced, according to the locality, with varying amounts of vocational education. In effect, there were in existence two systems — on the one hand, an elementary education established in the nineteenth century for the sons and daughters of the working classes slowly thrusting upward and extending its provisions in technical and general fields and, on the other, secondary education for the children of the well-to-do in schools which had no express connection with the elementary schools and drew often upon preparatory schools independent of the national system.

In these circumstances, there was a choice of three policies:

• To maintain the separation of the two systems;

• To compromise by selecting the most suitable children from the elementary schools and permitting them to enter the secondary system;

• To unify the systems, so that all children might pass, at a given stage, from elementary primary schools on to a secondary education which might have a considerable variety of courses.

Separation, selection, or unification were the issues debated by those interested in secondary education throughout the inter-war period.

---

[94] Fisher was responsible for establishing standing committees under the chairmanship of Lord Burnham in 1919 with the task of recommending salary scales for primary, secondary, and technical teachers.

[95] Jean Guéhenno, *Caliban Parle*, Grasset, Paris, 1928, used Shakespeare's ungainly and uncouth Caliban as a symbol for the rising lower classes and, in this book, analysed their aspirations, their possibilities and their need for an education in a culture that was different from that prevailing in the classical tradition of the French schools. See particularly pp. 85, 97, 166 and 220. Jean Guéhenno, born 1890, worked in a factory, attended l'Ecole Normale Superieure, taught in *lycées* at Lille, Sceaux and Paris and became inspector-general of public instruction in 1945. He wrote essays, monographs, and reminiscences and edited the reviews *Europe* and *Vendredi*. In 1962 he was elected a member of the French Academy.

[96] See below, Chapter 7.

[97] Harold C. Dent, *Secondary Education for All*, Routledge and Kegan Paul, London, 1949, p. 4. This book is an admirable treatment of the history of this question.

In Germany and France, the discussion largely centred around the possibility of establishing the *Einheitsschule* or *école unique*, a common primary school from which all pupils might have an equal chance to proceed by merit to some kind of recognised secondary school. In England, the debate first started seriously in the educational exchanges that preceded the Fisher Act. In August 1915 the leader writer of *The Times Educational Supplement* referred to the necessity of 'secondary education, of some sort or another, for all', and in the following months argued the case for terminating elementary education at the age of eleven years, and providing compulsory non-selective secondary education for all children thereafter.[98]

The Fisher Act did nothing to further the cause and, if anything, distracted and divided the advocates of universal secondary education by making provision for continuation education, which could be construed as a substitution for it. When the implementing of those provisions was at first postponed and later, for financial reasons, indefinitely shelved, agitation for more effective secondary education was revived.

The principal advocates were the members of the parliamentary Labour Party which in 1918 had decided henceforth to adopt a socialist platform.[99] In 1922 under the editorship of its principal educational spokesman, a distinguished economist and historian, R.H. Tawney, it produced *Secondary Education for All. A Policy for Labour* which presented a thoroughly argued and carefully documented case for the expansion of secondary education.[100]

There was at that time a considerable and increasing public demand for secondary education. 'The fact is,' wrote Tawney, 'that in the last fifteen years a revolution has taken place in the educational outlook of a considerable section of the population ...'[101] The recently increased numbers of secondary schools, the requirement since 1905 that all schoolteachers should have a secondary school education, the development, since 1907, of a system of free places in secondary schools for children from primary schools, and the increase in the affluence of many working class families during the war years — these were a series of factors which made the idea of secondary education more familiar, increased the opportunities for it, and stimulated the demand for more extensive facilities. It was a demand not for more part-time continuation schools but for full-time secondary education.[102] And it was clear that existing facilities were inadequate, even though in 1920 only between five and nine per cent of the children leaving primary schools entered secondary schools, and the majority of them left the secondary school before the age of fifteen after an average of two and a half years there. As a consequence of the lack of provision, and the high wastage rate, only two per cent of the boys and girls of the country completed a sufficient amount of secondary education to enable them to proceed to a university. 'In starving the

education of the adolescent,' wrote Tawney, 'the nation is sterilising itself.' It was depriving itself of a reservoir of educated intelligence which might form the basis of its future industrial and commercial progress; it was unduly restricting its supply of professional men; it was failing, by casting its net too narrowly, to discover and nourish the best available talent for the service of the community, and consequently, drawing for leadership upon 'an insignificant fraction of the whole population'.[103]

A drastic change in policy was clearly needed. Hitherto a policy of separation with a minor degree of selection had prevailed. Secondary schools had developed independently of the elementary school system and 'by means of free places, scholarships, and maintenance allowances a bridge, if a slender one, had been thrown between the primary and the secondary school'.[104] Henceforth the two systems should be one.

Tawney proposed a redefinition of national education. As first conceived in the mid-nineteenth century, national education in England meant a minimum of elementary education for the children of the working classes; by the time of the Balfour Act in 1902 it had come to mean a complete and compulsory elementary education; by the end of the World War I and the passing of the Fisher Act it meant a compulsory elementary education up to the age of fourteen with some encouragement in deserving cases to continue into secondary education. It was always, up to that point, regarded as an education provided publicly for the underprivileged, and it did not embrace schools recognised by contemporaries as secondary. Tawney's proposal, endorsed by the Labour Party, was to regard all elementary and secondary education as being within the one

---

[98] *The Times Educational Supplement*, 3 August 1915, p. 97; 7 September 1915, pp. 1, 107; 5 October 1915, p. 119.

[99] H.G. Wells, who was a labour candidate in the 1922 election, wrote of the intimate connection between education and socialism in the minds of his fellow-workers. 'Socialism implies education...'

[100] Two years later during the short period of England's first Labour government, in 1924, the party produced *Education: The Socialist Policy* written by Tawney, with a preface by the president of the Board of Education. In the following year in a volume of lectures on aspects of the Labour movement Tawney again summed up his party's views on the development of education in England.

R.H. Tawney (1880-1962) was professor of economic history in the University of London. He served on several government commissions and was described by a leader of the British Labour Party as '*the* Democratic Socialist *par excellence*'. His two most significant books were *The Acquisitive Society* and *Equality*. For his writings on education, see R.H. Tawney ed. *Secondary Education for All. A Policy for Labour Education:* The *Socialist Policy*, Independent Labour Party Publishing Department, London, 1924; *The British Labor Movement*, Yale University Press, New Haven, 1925, and *The Radical Tradition*, ed. Penguin, Rita Hinden, 1964.

[101] R.H. Tawney ed., *Secondary Education for All*, p. 36.

[102] R.H. Tawney, *op.cit.*, p. 102: " ... we assert that part-time continuation schools cannot be accepted by the Labour Movement as a substitute for the program of secondary education set out in this pamphlet."

[103] The above statistics and arguments are to be found in Tawney, *op.cit.*, Chapters 2 and 3.

[104] R.H. Tawney, *Education:* The *Socialist Policy*, p. 1.

system. National education was to mean education provided for all the children throughout the nation organised in such a way 'that instead of the vast majority — roughly 85 per cent — of the children ending their education at fourteen, all normal children may pass, as a matter of course, to one or another of several different types of secondary schools at the age of eleven or twelve (roughly at adolescence), and remain there till at least sixteen'.[105] In the future, secondary education should be part of the ordinary national provision of education for all pupils. The move was justified on the grounds, first, that it was the humane and proper thing to provide the maximum of educational opportunity to assist the development of every individual; secondly, that it was in the national interest to encourage potential talent from whatever source it might emerge, and, thirdly, that a high standard of understanding diffused generally throughout the community was 'the condition of the co-operation without which civilization is impossible.'

The third reason appears to have been the one that was of greatest importance in the minds of the leaders of the Labour movement. Where primary education might have been the sufficient level for a civilised community in the nineteenth century, secondary education was coming to be regarded as a minimum necessity for the democratic nation of the post-war period. It was argued optimistically that men's liability to succumb 'to the great modern art of organizing delusion might be overcome by a greater cultivation of the intellect from more extensive education.'[106]

Tawney thus sketched the pattern of argument for the general extension of secondary education — a pattern which persisted through the next half-century as secondary education for all gradually became a reality in the more developed countries of the world. He summarised his position in the final sentence of his 1924 booklet: 'The society based on the free co-operation of citizens, which is the ideal of the Socialist, depends, in short, on the widest possible diffusion of education.'[107] The extension of educational opportunity, and in particular the provision of universal secondary education, was a characteristic objective of the socialists of the time. They did not always achieve their aims even when in power, and men of other political persuasions sometimes were responsible for considerable educational progress, but it remained true that the reasoned planning which lay behind the movement and the thrusting enthusiasm which provided its momentum came very largely from persons with socialist interests.

Hadow Report, 1926. As a possible first step towards the recasting of English secondary education, the Labour government of 1924 commissioned a consultative committee of the Board of Education to investigate and report on a suitable form of full-time post-primary education for children who might remain at schools other than academic secondary schools up to the age of fifteen. *The Education of the Adolescent* appeared in 1926 and was generally known, after the name of the committee's chairman, as the Hadow Report.

The report confirmed the current rising interest in post-primary education, analysed its history, alluded to developments abroad in dealing with the same problem, summarised the existing position in England, and proceeded to sketch out what it considered to be the desirable 'lines of advance'.[108] If many of the recommendations were similar to those put forward by Tawney, it was not to be wondered at, as he was a member of the committee.

The main questions to be answered were the same facing all the developed countries of the world which without exception at that time were interested in planning for a post-primary expansion.

The committee did not strike out in any novel direction but decided to follow existing precedents and to build 'on foundations which have long been laid'.[109]

They suggested that there should be a clear break in schooling at the age of eleven+, dividing primary education, the education of childhood, from secondary, the education of adolescence. In Shakespearian tones they reported: 'There is a tide which begins to rise in the veins of youth at the age of eleven or twelve. It is called by the name of adolescence. If that tide can be taken at the flood, and a new voyage begun in the strength and along the flow of its current, we think that it will "move on to fortune".'[110] The term elementary should be discontinued in favour of primary, and the term secondary should be extended to cover all forms of post-primary education except technical. All normal children should proceed, as a matter of course, at eleven+ to secondary schools of which there should be four varieties:

- Grammar School, then commonly known as 'secondary', following in the main a predominantly literary and scientific curriculum, and carrying the education of their pupils forward to the age of at least sixteen+;

---

[105] R.H. Tawney, *The British Labor Movement*, p. 128.

[106] R.H. Tawney, *Education:* The *Socialist Policy*, pp. 3-4.

[107] *ibid.*, p. 58.

[108] *The Education of the Adolescent*, Report of the Consultative Committee of the Board of Education (Hadow Report) HMSO, London, 1926, Chapter 3.

[109] *ibid.*, p. 70.

[110] *ibid*, p. xix.

- Selective Modern Schools, the former Central Schools and their like, giving at least a four-year course with a practical trend in the last two years, the new name 'Modern' being chosen to convey to the public that the education, like that of the German *Realschulen*, 'which these schools offer, without being primarily vocational, gives a prominent place to studies whose bearing on practical life is obvious and immediate';[111]

- Non-selective Modern Schools;

- Senior Classes within public elementary schools where local conditions made the provision of one of the other types of school impossible.

To place each child in the school for which he might be thought to be best suited, a selective examination should be held at the transfer age of eleven+.

The committee's brief was for the most part concerned with the Modern Schools and Senior Classes. To enable them to develop worthwhile secondary courses the committee recommended the raising of the school leaving age to fifteen. These schools were to plan their courses for a three- or four-year secondary education along much the same lines as those of the Grammar Schools, except that their work would be more limited in scope, and would give more attention to handwork and similar pursuits, and would strive, in the last two years, realistically 'to connect the school work with the interests arising from the social and industrial environment of the pupils'.[112] In accordance with the views of current educational thought, the timetabling of subjects should be more flexible, the boundaries of subjects less rigid than in the traditional pattern, and, after consultation with local employing authorities, a connection should be established between the work of the school and that of local industry, due care being taken that the general education of the adolescents should not be prejudiced. The committee took pains to make a substantial body of suggestions about the content and method of teaching the subjects appropriate to the Modern Schools; and many of the ideas contained in their lengthy appendix on those matters were widely used by Modern School teachers in subsequent years.

Their general advice was that Modern Schools should approximate to Grammar Schools; care should be taken to prevent the development of inferior and superior types of secondary schools. Differentiation of schools in function but not in prestige was to be aimed at.

Thus did the Hadow Committee, somewhat hesitantly, father a conception of secondary education for all adolescents in England. It is a little surprising that a committee launched by a Labour government should not have looked more intensively at the possible relationships

between a humane education, described by the committee as 'one which brings children into contact with the larger interests of mankind', and some technical understanding of human occupations which constitute the distinctive interests of *homo faber*. They did not seriously examine the relationship between vocational and secondary education. There appears also to have been no thought of a single comprehensive secondary school. Both Tawney in his essays and the Hadow Committee in its Report refer to the necessity for a variety of courses to cater for the diverse needs of secondary school pupils, and assume that they had to be offered in a variety of schools. There was no discussion of the possibility of their being offered in a single school, or of the possibility of avoiding competition for prestige between types of schools by basing the new secondary system on an all-inclusive unit. Those questions, heavily freighted with social and educational implications, lay implicitly within the committee's original brief; they did not, however, assume any importance in their eyes nor did they become significant in English educational discussion until they were first tentatively explored by the Spens Report in 1938.

The substantive contribution of the Hadow Committee was threefold. First, it gave an official imprint to the idea of secondary education for all, setting a clear terminus to primary education beyond which all adolescents were to enter schools, all of which were, it hoped, thenceforth to be regarded as secondary.

In the second place the committee helped to consolidate secondary education into a bipartite pattern. Its fourfold division of schools was in reality a dual one — Grammar Schools on the one hand, and, on the other, Modern Schools of various kinds. The examination at eleven+ separated potential entrants into two types which, in practice, became the more and the less intellectual — the more intellectual, those in the Grammar Schools, being provided with a longer preparation which opened for them the way to tertiary education and to the more highly regarded and remunerative avenues of employment.

The Hadow Committee's policy was one of unification with selection. The divided streams of post-primary education were to be united under the banner of secondary education, and all children without selection were to proceed into secondary schools. The type of school to which they were to proceed, however, was to be decided by a selective examination. That was to remain the basic organisational principle of English secondary education for the next three decades, coming under criticism particularly in the post-World War II period, but not being challenged with any measure of success until the 1960's.

---

[111] *ibid.*, p. 100.

[112] *ibid.*, p. 175.

In the third place, it introduced a new tone into educational discussion. Hitherto, economic, political, sociological, pedagogical, or administrative considerations had prevailed throughout the arguments of commissions and committees of investigation. The Hadow Report did not neglect those approaches, but it added to them a fresh dimension, a psychological one.[113] In justifying the break between primary and secondary education, in recommending the use of psychological tests, and in making suggestions about the nature of the work to be done in Modern Schools, the committee continually had an eye to current knowledge of educational psychology, and to the pattern of child growth that might emerge. The Hadow Committee, in this report, in the next one on Psychological Tests of Educable Capacity, and in the two to follow on the Primary School, and on Infant and Nursery Schools, officially declared educational psychology to be of age in England.

As was the case with the Fisher Act, there was an enthusiastic reception in the press and among professional educators for the Hadow Report, but its actual impact up to the outbreak of World War II on the reorganisation of secondary education in England was slight. In 1928 the Board of Education issued a somewhat dampening summary of the Hadow recommendations and made suggestions about appropriate action by the school authorities: 'If we err at all, it should be on the side of caution.'[114] The Board's pamphlet made mention of the Modern School, and then consistently spoke of the Junior and Senior divisions of the elementary school. In the upshot, separate Modern Schools under a secondary administration did not come into operation until after World War II in 1945; and the post-eleven+ schools and classes that were in what was known as the Hadow reorganisation remained, throughout the late 1920's and 1930's, part of the elementary system and were generally referred to as Senior Schools. The recommendation that the school leaving age should be raised to fifteen years was defeated in parliament in 1929, and subsequently adopted in 1936 to come into force on 1 September 1939, only to be postponed by the outbreak of war. Just as the Fisher Act foundered in the recession of the early 1920's, so the Hadow Report, lacking enthusiastic support from conservative politicians and administrators, suffered a grievous blow with the onset of the depression in 1929, and, by the time that it was possible to resuscitate its spirit, a second world war temporarily diverted the nation's resources and thoughts away from educational reform. At that stage, by 1939, thirteen years after the Hadow Committee reported, only 69 per cent of urban and 22 per cent of rural educational authorities had organised separate senior departments.[115] Secondary education for all remained still an aspiration.

Spens Report, 1938. In the previous year, however, 1938, another important report of the consultative committee had appeared, putting forward ideas very much in the Hadow tradition. This was the Spens Report entitled *Secondary Education with Special Reference to Grammar Schools and Technical High Schools*. The Spens Committee, also assisted by Nunn, continued the Hadow Committee's psychological approach. By 1938, however, the more emphatic individualism that had characterised the writing of the early twenties had been mellowed by a more ample appreciation of the social functions of the school and of the contribution currently being made by social psychologists to the understanding of human behaviour. This affected the committee's views, particularly in regard to the curricular and extra-curricular activities of secondary schools upon which they wrote some of their finest paragraphs.[116] In the present context, the significant feature of the Spens Report was the manner in which it expanded the Hadow Committee's efforts towards establishing an organisation of schooling which would satisfactorily provide secondary education for all. It re-emphasised the distinction between primary and secondary education, gently chided the administrative system for its slowness in adopting the Hadow proposals, and emphasised the necessity for establishing parity between all types of secondary schools. The committee, taking into account the growth of junior technical schools, proceeded to extend the Hadow bi-partite scheme to a tri-partite one of Modern, Grammar, and Technical High Schools.[117] It was an important recognition of technical education as a part of secondary education, a principle suggested by the Bryce Commission in 1895 and subsequently disregarded. The Spens Committee went even further in suggesting the introduction of vocational work into the other kinds of secondary schools. The Technical High and the Grammar Schools were to be selective, most Modern Schools not. In such circumstances parity of esteem between the three types might prove difficult to maintain. The committee considered the possibility of multilateral schools, found the idea attractive, but decided that it could not recommend their general establishment, mainly on the grounds that the schools would have to be too large if a satisfactory number of pupils were to be maintained in each stream and at the top in the sixth form. To insure an adequate secondary education, whatever the

---

[113] It is significant of the new trend that the committee invited the co-operation of T.P. Nunn, one of England's leading educational psychologists, in the preparation of the report.

[114] Board of Education, Educational Pamphlets, no. 60, *The New Prospect in Education*, HMSO, London, 1928, p. 4.

[115] H.C. Dent, *Secondary Education for All*, pp. 70-1.

[116] See Chapter 10.

[117] *Secondary Education with Special Reference to Grammar Schools and Technical High Schools*, Report of the Consultative Committee of the Board of Education (Spens Report), HMSO, London, 1938, p. 377, #134.

school or stream, and parity among the secondary schools, the committee were of the opinion that the raising of the school leaving age to sixteen was inevitable.[118]

(d) Expansion of Middle Schools

The Hadow Report in England, and the debates on the *école unique* in France, and on the *Einheitsschule* in Germany were comparable examples of the way in which three leading European countries faced the growing demand in the inter-war period for equality of educational opportunity.

What emerged from the movement in each country for more post-primary education was the development of some form of middle school. The principal kinds of academic secondary school remained largely intact, serving restricted numbers and much the same purposes as in the previous generation. Once, then, the limits of primary education had been set, the upward expansion ballooned out into a middle school. In England it was the Senior or Modern School, in Germany the *Mittelschule,* and in France *l'Ecole Primaire Superieure.* In each case they were expansions and refinements of schools that had been growing slowly for a considerable time.

Although described here as middle schools, they were, for most pupils, terminal institutions. Opportunities existed on a limited scale for pupils to transfer from them to full secondary schools but that was an incidental feature. They were not placed like the American Junior High School as part of the normal progression between the elementary and senior high school; they were a continuation of the elementary system parallel to the selective secondary school having no special connection with any further kind of schooling.

The English Senior School offering a three- or four-year course overlapped the first two years of the Grammar School course and provided a pattern of general education which included the study of a foreign language. In the final years the courses were given a more practical bias. Throughout the inter-war period the nature of those schools and of their work changed little; they grew steadily in numbers and became increasingly recognised as separate and important institutions responsible for the post-primary education of the majority of the children of England.

The *Mittelschulen* of Germany differed from both the English Senior Schools and the American Junior High Schools in that they were intended neither to be the normal terminal continuation of the elementary school for the bulk of the population, nor an intermediate stage between elementary and higher secondary education. They were designed to provide a middling level of education for children destined for middle class occupations. Their function was defined in the Prussian regulations of 1925 as that of providing 'a suitable type of preparation for many sorts of intermediate positions in the administrative service of the State or municipalities, as well as in the larger industrial and commercial enterprises' and in agriculture.[119] The majority of children, on completing the four-year *Grundschule*, passed on to the upper four years of the *Volksschule*; a selected minority entered the various kinds of *Gymnasien* available, and the remainder, of middle-class and middle ability, about equal in number in Prussia to those entering the *Gymnasien*, proceeded to the *Mittelschule*. It was a six-year school with several varieties among the different German states providing, in some cases, work which could be continued in the non-classical *Gymnasien* but, for the most part, offering courses of general education diversified in the later years into vocational courses for commerce, industry, agriculture, and homemaking. The character of the work undertaken in the schools was not unlike that of a six-year American high school program.

In France, the *école primaire supérieure*, founded in 1833 and expanded since the 1880's in the years of the Third Republic, had for many years performed a function very similar to that of the German *Mittelschule* up to a slightly less advanced level. It offered a three-year course for pupils who had completed the final examination of the six-seven year primary school course and had reached the age of twelve. In a number of localities one- or two-year *cours complémentaires*, added to the primary school, provided a shortened course along the same lines. The higher primary school offered a general education, and, in the second and third years, provided a variety of vocational courses for industrial, commercial, agricultural, and homemaking pursuits. It could also offer preparatory courses for the normal schools in which primary school teachers were trained. For selected pupils, transfer to the non-classical course of a *lycée* or *collège* was possible. It catered, like the *Mittelschule*, very largely for children destined for minor administrative positions in the civil service and for lesser executive jobs in industry or commerce.

The great majority of French children completed their schooling by remaining in the primary school until the age of thirteen and, after 1936, fourteen. A small and select group continued their education in the secondary schools, the *lycées* and *collèges*; and another small, middle group went to the *écoles primaires supérieures*. Both groups grew by

[118] *ibid.*, p. 311.

[119] Weidmannsche Taschenausgaben von der Vergangenheit der Preussischen Schulverwaltung, Heft 26: *Die Mittelschule*, 2nd edn, Herausgeb. Thomas Stolze and Karl Remus, Berlin, 1927, p. 12. An interesting first-hand description of a girls' *Mittelschule*, in Lübeck in the mid-1920's is to be found in Thomas Alexander & Beryl Parker, *The New Education in the German Republic*, John Day, New York, 1929, pp.256ff. The comparison of *Mittelschulen* with American high schools has been made by I.L. Kandel, *Comparative Education*, p. 453, and Adolph E. Meyer, *The Development of Education in the Twentieth Century*, Prentice-Hall, New York, 1939, p. 331.

about 40 per cent during the inter-war period and by the late 1930's. The *écoles primaires supérieures* contained about half as many pupils as the regular secondary school system.

(e) Secondary School Traditions in Slow Transition

In each of the four leading democracies in western society during the inter-war period of the 1920's and 1930's — France, England, U.S.A., and Germany during the Weimar Republic — their most cherished educational ideas were embodied in the forms and procedures of the school which they regarded as the central part of their secondary tradition. The *lycée* in France, the *Gymnasium* in Germany, the public school in England, and the high school in the United States were the transmitters of a way of thinking and behaving that each nation considered to be representative of the best and finest aspects of its way of life. Strong emotions could be aroused when changes in their established procedures were suggested. Nevertheless, they did change. The schools were subject to criticism from time to time, and their practices were modified in various ways.

The tradition which they represented was a living and growing one; it had sufficient consistency to be recognisably different in each of the four countries and yet each school moved with the times. The *lycée* and the public school were the least subject to innovation. 'Winchester,' a nineteenth century headmaster had said, 'does not move much'; and in the twentieth century the English Public School, though more flexible than before, still made its adjustments with considerable caution to the revolution going on around it. The German *Gymnasium* was somewhat more susceptible, and after World War I was less certain of its heritage. Of the four schools, it was the American high school which was most open to change. The inter-war period in the United States was an exciting one for educators. During those twenty years educational theory was probed as never before, traditional ideas on curricula were criticised; and new and fruitful approaches were introduced, innovations in methods of teaching and school organisation were widely experimented with, educational psychologists made considerable advances in their knowledge of child behaviour and in the ways of measuring children's aptitudes and achievements, and the educational writers of the period produced a rich and stimulating body of educational literature that affected the practice and theory of education throughout the world. In the ferment, all levels of American education were affected; the elementary school was probably subject to the most experimentation but interesting changes occurred even in universities and colleges. The high school managed to preserve much of its pre-war tradition but moved forward into fresh patterns of teaching that fitted the new objectives emerging from contemporary discussion and re-evaluation.

The characteristics of the four secondary schools expressed what the inter-war generation thought to be best in their educational system at that time. The philosophy of the schools, their established practices, their various readjustments and reforms, and the views of their critics admirably convey the educational flavour of the period.

The French Lycées. The *lycées*, and the *collèges*, provided in the 1920's and 1930's the whole of French secondary education, which was considerably restricted in scope and number of pupils. They catered for about 20 per cent of youth within their age range which was approximately from eleven to eighteen years; and in the five years prior to World War II their numbers increased by almost 30 per cent. They offered facilities for day and boarding pupils and, except for the elimination of tuition fees by 1933, and the development of some experimental orientation classes, no change of any consequence took place in their organisation or programs between the reforms of the mid-1920's and the outbreak of World War II. A common course was provided for all pupils for the first four years, consisting of French, history, geography and science, with a choice of Latin or a modern foreign language. In the third year, Greek or a second modern foreign language was added to the curriculum; and for the next three years, leading to the first part of the *baccalauréat* examination, in the sixth year, the school was divided into three streams: A, classical, Latin and Greek; A[1], Latin and a modern foreign language; and B, modern foreign languages. Each stream continued its work in the common subjects but the bulk of time was devoted to literary studies. About 50 per cent of those presenting for the first part of the *baccalauréat* were successful, and proceeded in their seventh year to the final class which offered a choice between philosophy and mathematics. Those were the two sides of the second part of the *baccalauréat*, in which about 50 per cent of candidates managed to survive and become eligible for university. A special prize examination, the *concours général*, was held annually among pupils selected throughout France from those in the final two years of the course, and served as a stimulus to the maintenance of high standards of literary and general scholarship.

The task of the *lycée*, i.e. of French secondary education, was the production of an *élite* nurtured in the French view of *culture générale*. It was a constant, unchanging duty. 'The object of secondary education cannot vary. Its real nature and task is, above all, to prepare minds, by a good general education, either for higher studies, or for the speedy and profitable acquisition of the special knowledge required in the professions...'[120]

---

[120] Gaston Antignac, *Guide des Etudes, 1935-6*, vol. II, Enseignement Secondaire, Primaire, Technique, Préface de Mario Roustan, Ministre de l'Education Nationale, Paris, L'Information Universitaire, 1935, p. 8. Extract from Report of the Minister of Public Instruction, 13 May, 1925.

It was not, therefore, the kind of education that could be made widely available. Secondary education for all would, to a French educator, not have been secondary education at all. Certainly, more and further education was desirable for the mass of the people, but it was more education of a primary kind. Secondary education called for abilities above the ordinary, and a considerable length of time in which to absorb its discipline, so as 'to form, by the slow action of a course of extended and disinterested study, young people who, whatever their later specialty, will be noted for their high ability to interest themselves in and adapt themselves to the various creations of the human mind and human effort'.[121]

The amount of knowledge acquired in the program, outside that of literary history and usage, was not extensive. It was intended to be a careful, reflective study of the knowledge appropriate to a non-specialist and well-informed citizen. Montaigne's dictum, 'A well-made head is better than a well-filled head', was a guide often repeated and widely accepted. Secondary education was to be a commerce of young minds with the great minds and great works of human culture. Out of that continuing contact over many years there should develop an appreciation of first-rate work, a lasting taste for the best in art, literature, and thought, and a hard-won skill in written and oral expression. Elegance of style in communication was the criterion of a well-educated person. It was an elegance, however, that stood for more than verbal delicacy and skill; it implied, as well, a judicious balance of intellect and expression. The whole educational process was that of a sharpening of minds. By the study of words, by the dissection of ideas, by the criticism of style, by the close polishing of expression, the pupils slowly honed the rapiers of the mind. To criticise, to take nothing for granted, to exist through thought, to become a true Cartesian, that was the idea.

To the scrutiny of the works of others, self-examination was added, an examination not merely of the validity of argument or the aptness of expression but of motives, intentions, and personal decisions. Education was at all times concerned with morality, with building the good as well as the accomplished man. It should encourage 'the habit of introspection', and 'it will attempt to stimulate the inner life of the pupil and make it valuable to him'.[122] Out of constant intellectual exercise and self-criticism a habit of reflection was slowly matured. It was the proper and disciplined basis for the exercise of judgment upon human expression and human action. To command the power to judge accurately, knowledgeably, and penetratingly in all human concerns was the expectation of the successful product of that form of education.

The work of the *lycées* was concerned with the moral, intellectual, and aesthetic cultivation of its pupils. It was designed to produce, ideally, young men of cultivated taste, sound judgment, and elegant expression.

For that task there were three principal instruments: the classical languages, French literature, and philosophy.

From the study of Greece and Rome the pupil would gain an indispensable insight into the foundations of French civilisation, and would be brought into intimate contact with a people unmatched in the clarity and subtlety of their thought upon problems of human behaviour, and unrivalled in the aptness and beauty of their expression over a wide range of literature. Moreover, since the classics had been taught as the principal instrument of humanistic education for many centuries, the methods for carrying out the central purpose of the *lycées* had been tested and refined by many generations of successful schoolmasters upon whose work French culture had long continued to flourish. The study of French literature and the practice of French composition complemented the study of the classics. The analysis of structure, the use of words, and of the meaning of selected texts helped the pupils to acquire a better understanding of the literary masterpieces of French culture; constant practice in imitating their style and ideas produced an ability to argue subtly and originally, and provided pupils with the basis upon which to develop the artistry they sought in their own speech and writing.[123] The formal study of psychology, logic, ethics and the elements of metaphysics in the final year of the *lycée* was designed to broaden and sharpen the pupils' minds, and to encourage them in systematic reflection.

It was fundamentally a literary program: 'the service that can be rendered by these subjects is at once apparent, for the study of literature is observation of the human mind in action. Literary research considers individual minds, each one of which forms an entity at once complex and coherent. It proposes men for our analysis...'[124]

It did not go unchallenged. The reform of 1902 had unsettled the traditional program which the reaction of the early 1920's restored. But the grumblings of reformers continued. The modernists wished to replace the study of the ancient languages with that of modern languages, and they succeeded through the Albert reform of 1925-26 in re-establishing a modern languages stream. They did not doubt the efficacy of a literary education, they merely wished to place modern literature and language on an equality with the classics. More radical were those who advocated the development of streams which would not be based on literary studies

[121] Gaston Antignac, *op.cit.*, p. 8. Extract from the Report of the Minister of Public Instruction, 1923. See also C. Bouglé, The French Conception of 'Culture Générale' and its influences upon instruction, *Teachers' College Record*, 39, 8, May 1938, 692.

[122] Paul Desjardins, in F. Buisson & F.E. Farrington, *French Educational Ideals of Today*, World Book Co., Yonkers-on-Hudson, New York, 1919, p. 311.

[123] Alain, *Propos sur L'Education*, Presses Univ. de France, Paris, 1961 (1932), LIV, p. 120.

[124] Paul Desjardins, *op.cit.*, p. 312.

but on scientific or technical subjects, or on a more even distribution of work in all the major subjects. *Les Compagnons* were among those reformers. They held that, with the growth throughout the twentieth century of scientific knowledge, the multiplication of technical skills, and an increased understanding of society through the expansion of sociological studies, a new humanism, and with it, a new *culture générale* was emerging which called for the revision of traditional prescriptions. Those views were increasingly canvassed during the 1930's, and lay behind the proposed reforms of the radical Minister for National Education, Jean Zay, but they did not succeed in having any practical effect on the schools. They did, however, help to build up a climate of opinion which made reform more probable in the post-World War II period.

The German Gymnasien. It would probably have been true to say that, from the end of World War I up to the beginning of the Nazi period in 1933, most of the German secondary school teachers and administrators would have been agreed in applying to the various types of *Gymnasien* the French view of the function of the *lycée*, that it was a selective school designed to produce an elite through an extended period of intellectual, moral, and aesthetic education. There were however two significant differences. In the first place there was not one type but four types of schools, each with its own particular orientation. The *Gymnasium* catered specially for classical languages, the *Realgymnasium* for Latin and a modern foreign language, the *Oberrealschule* for mathematics and the sciences, and the *Deutsche Oberschule* for German language, literature, history, and geography. Each, moreover, was preparatory to particular tertiary level courses; their pupils did not achieve a general matriculation but rather tended to qualify in the special areas of their choice which had been made early in their gymnasial career. In the second place, although the study of languages was important in all four types of school, it did not loom as large as in the French *lycée*. Even in the *Gymnasium* proper which required Latin, Greek, and a modern foreign language, and in the *Realgymnasium* with Latin and two modern languages, the emphasis was less, and the distribution of subjects more even, allowing more time for mathematics, history, geography, and religion.

Although the division into four schools produced more specialisation, a wide program of general knowledge was provided in each. The Prussian Regulations of 1924 suggested that a common culture should be fostered throughout the schools, but that does not appear to have operated in practice. There was no equivalent in Germany, nor indeed in any country not modelled on the French pattern, to the French class in philosophy through which some measure of cultural synthesis might be achieved at the conclusion of the secondary school course. The *Gymnasium*, by the 1920's, appeared to have lost the central devotion to a general human culture, *allgemeine Bildung*, that had been its characteristic in the early nineteenth century. Many secondary teachers were hopeful of maintaining the tradition, but the unity between subjects and between schools was lacking. The *Gymnasium* was shedding its humanistic tradition and was becoming concerned, instead, with the development of scholarship to a high level in several fields, principally in classics, modern languages, mathematics, science, and history. The students who completed the program in one of the four types of schools should have acquired a scholarly knowledge of some of these subjects, and a good general understanding of most of the others.

Like the products of all secondary schools in Europe at that time, the students were an elite. They were selected from the final year of the *Grundschule* and, since secondary education, because of school fees and continued general living expenses, was a costly business, they tended mostly to be children of the middle and upper social classes, although by the early 1930's about one-third of the children, presumably from the lower income groups, had been granted a remission of fees. German class structure, however, in that period was somewhat difficult to define. Because of the inflation of the early 1920's which had a particularly disastrous effect on the income from salaries and investments of a great many of the middle class, and the depression of the early 1930's, it is quite likely that many parents who considered themselves members of the middle class and who normally would have expected to send their children to secondary school, would have needed considerable financial help to realise that ambition for their children.

The *Gymnasien*, like Germany in the 1920's, were in a somewhat indeterminate state, not only in the matter of their clientele, but also in the content of their programs. In their curricula they represented an interesting stage half-way between the general culture of the French *lycées* and the high degree of specialisation developed in the English Public Schools at that time. In effect, they were, in the Weimar period, schools which had lost their mission and had not yet developed a new conviction.

The English Public Schools. The English Public School for boys, which Graham Greene in 1934 prematurely regarded as doomed,[125] has been the most characteristic and influential development of the English educational world. The schools having grown as independent entities, showed considerable variation and were therefore difficult to define. Most of the leading ones, however, would come within

[125] Graham Greene ed., *The Old School*, Jonathan Cape, London, 1934, p. 7.

the scope of the statement: 'In its full-blown form what we mean by a Public School is an independent, non-local, predominantly boarding school for the upper and upper-middle classes.'[126] Eton, Harrow, Winchester, Rugby and perhaps ten or twelve more conformed to that broad definition and throughout the twentieth century were generally regarded as the central core and most influential of the schools. In 1926, 130, and in 1956, 218 secondary schools were members of the Headmasters' Conference which represented the broad limits of the Public School field.

The Public School took boys approximately at the age of thirteen, most of whom had attended an independent preparatory school, and retained them up to the age of eighteen or nineteen. It aimed to provide for them 'that education which trains a generation through religion and discipline, through culture of the mind and perfection of the body, to a conscious end of service to the community'.[127] It was, fundamentally, a character education. Whereas the French *lycée*, in general, symbolised intellectual education, and the German *Gymnasium* the acquisition of knowledge, the English Public School stood for the education of character as William Wykeham, the founder of the oldest of the great public schools, Winchester, had set forth in his motto, 'Manners makyth man'.

Through traditional routines, religious observances, and a common disciplined life, the desired behaviour was to be produced. It was a world of obedience to constituted authority, providing, for selected boys, opportunity for the exercise of considerable responsibility. 'The rule of discipline, then, is that you must do your duty, or pay the penalty: authority comes from above, but all share in delegated powers for the purpose of living a common life.... The business of a school is to work and to get on with its life without bothering about Whys, and Wherefores, and abstract justice, and the democratic principle.'[128] Its life was that of inculcating into the boys the Public School spirit, a way of behaving and a code of values summed up in the phrase, 'playing the game'. 'To say that an action is not sporting,' wrote an ex-headmaster of Harrow, 'or is not cricket, or that somebody does not play up, or does not play with a straight bat, or does not pull his weight, or that he hits below the belt, is an English method of indicating some defect of character. Perhaps one of the most difficult yet the most valuable habits which are formed as outcomes of the sporting spirit is the habit of obedience to the umpire; for it is a habit of self-restraint, of respect for authority and of confidence in the honourable spirit of one whose decision, whether popular or unpopular, must be unhesitatingly accepted.'[129]

After such a description of the outcome of a Public School Education, it comes as no surprise to find that a German observer of English life in the 1920's reported on the Public School that, 'the principal means of education is sport'.[130] Athletics were certainly of considerable importance. They were regarded as a means of promoting physical fitness, alertness, courage, and a sense of fair play. Team games such as cricket and rugby held pride of place on the ground that, besides possessing the usual virtues of sport, they encouraged a team spirit, an unselfish subordination of individual distinction for the benefit of the whole side. To do the best for one's side was the important thing. It did not matter whether the side won or not. It was not the prize that mattered, it was the game. The boy who could play the game whole-heartedly for his team and with scrupulous fairness in the true spirit and tradition of the gentleman amateur gave evidence of the kind of character which the Public Schools strove to encourage.

Sports, however, though important, were not all. The school curriculum, in the post-World War I period, was one of reasonable breadth for the first three or four years of the secondary course. It was a general education which usually involved a study of English with some history and geography, one or more foreign languages, of which Latin was the predominant one, and science and mathematics. The balance between subjects varied from school to school, and no general defence of the selection of them and the method of teaching them was worked out comparable with that of the French view of *culture générale*. The classics which had been the staple for many centuries had, since the mid-Victorian period, started to decline in importance but were still widely taught and highly regarded. Conformably with that situation, there was a tendency to think that the teacher's function was not to convey a wide range of knowledge but to teach some selected parts of it thoroughly so that the pupil might understand the virtue of fully mastering some aspect of knowledge, and experience the intellectual discipline involved in this process. The later years of the secondary school, accordingly, were devoted to specialised work to a degree well beyond that usually found in a *lycée* or *Gymnasium*. In preparation for university scholarships, the senior boys would spend two or three years working solely in the field of classics, modern languages, history, mathematics, physics, chemistry, or biology.

Of considerable importance for the development of accepted ways of behaving were the arrangements for self-government and extra-curricular activities of the schools. 'The small boy goes to his Preparatory School,' wrote Norwood, 'and after certain years he rises to high office, becomes a

---

[126] Vivian Ogilvie, *The English Public School*, Batsford, London, 1957, p. 8.

[127] Cyril Norwood, *The English Tradition of Education*, Dutton, New York, 1930, p. 243.

[128] *ibid.*, p. 75.

[129] J.E.C. Welldon, 'The Public School Spirit in Public Life', *The Contemporary Review*, vol. 132, November 1927, pp. 620-1.

[130] Wilhelm Dibelius, *England*, 5th edn., Deutsche Verlags-Anstalt, Stuttgart, 1929, vol. II, p. 175.

dormitory captain, perhaps captain of the XI: he is a Triton among the minnows. He goes on to his Public School: he is a new boy, a minnow among the Tritons. Again he climbs by the same methods, he reaches the VIth, he is a prefect, he represents the school. Twice over he has learned the qualities which others trust, and tasted the reward for work done. He leaves, and becomes nobody, a new boy in the outer world. Is it a bad preparation for the third stage, the ordeal of practical life?'[131] Art, drama, debating, naturalist, camera, stamp clubs and many others, chapel services, and the officers training corps provided further and extensive opportunities to develop interests, to accept responsibilities, and to make a contribution to the life of the school.

To be of service to the school, the community, and one's fellow-men was 'the inspiration of the English school tradition'.[132] The highest ideal, the essential quality produced by the Public Schools in each of its pupils was summed up by an appreciative writer as 'a readiness to be an officer',[133] that is to say, a willingness to take on necessary responsibilities, to set an example of unimpeachable conduct, and to serve to the best of his abilities at all times for the good of others. The ideal of service linked the long tradition of the English Public School, stemming from the chivalric practices of the later middle ages, to the practical necessities of a twentieth century England which drew the greater part of her senior civil servants, legislators, judges, and ecclesiastics from among the pupils of those schools.

Throughout the inter-war period there were no sharp-cut or dramatic changes, but there was a process of continuous change which, while not modifying the schools in their essential ideals and purposes, succeeded in altering, and to some extent modernising, their practices to a considerable degree.

They came more and more under the influence of external examinations, adjusting their courses to fit the 1917 reorganisation with its pattern of general education for the School Certificate, and specialisation thereafter for the Higher School Certificate. Specialisation steadily increased in the top form, the sixth, in which a boy might spend two or three years. In the 1930's their pupils came into competition with the growing number of publicly supported grammar schools for scholarships to the universities of Oxford and Cambridge. The competition increased the schools' interest in intellectual achievement, for lack of which they had been strongly criticised in the pre-war period. Boys would select a group of subjects, such as classics, modern languages, science and mathematics, or English and history, and would concentrate their studies on no more than about three related ones within the selected group in preparation for matriculation. The link between the sixth form and universities was greatly strengthened. Throughout the school in general, however, there was at the same time an enrichment of both curricular and extra-curricular activities. 'Before the war', wrote one headmaster, 'a boy might pass through a Public School without having a single hour's work in geography or English literature. Now a completely new type of English teaching has been introduced, with a genuine love of literature and a definite pride in the English language and its history, as its goal. The modern geography room also is an entirely new thing.'[134] Classes in economics, politics, current affairs, agriculture, metal and wood-working also found a place in some schools; and new art, craft, and music studios, staffed with talented and sensitive teachers, became more widespread. The breadth of the curriculum below the specialised sixth form, and the manner of its arrangement in many schools reflected their desire to adjust their educational program to the demands of current society and to educational trends developing throughout the English-speaking world. In many schools the traditional practice of appointing a clerical headmaster was abandoned; and laymen, often younger, brisker, more businesslike, and of a wider scholarship were selected to provide more flexible leadership.

Immediately following World War I the schools gained greatly in popularity, and even as late as 1930 it could be said that they were 'enjoying a period of unexampled prosperity'.[135] It was the result partly of the schools' traditional reputation, partly of the increased ability of many persons who had prospered during the war and its aftermath to pay the considerable fees charged by the Public Schools, and partly of the snobbery of middle class professional and business parents who, finding that the local grammar schools were patronised in larger numbers by ex-elementary lower class children, decided to send their own children off to boarding schools to prevent their picking up an undesirable accent, and to ensure that they could lay claim to the right background when, on leaving school, they sought the more favoured positions in the commercial world and the public service.[136] With the onset of the economic depression in the early 1930's, numbers started to drop; as the state-supported grammar schools increased in number and effectiveness they regained their attractiveness for many people in that straitened period and increased the drain on the Public Schools. In consequence, the

[131] C. Norwood, op.cit., pp. 78-9.

[132] ibid., p. 122.

[133] Bernard Darwin, The English Public School, Longmans Green, London, 1929, p. 22.

[134] Vivian Ogilvie, op.cit., p. 204, quoting Wyatt Rawson (ed.), The Freedom We Seek, 1937, pp. 103-4. Good evidence of the extent of the changes developed in the period is to be found in V.P. Nevill et al., The Headmaster Speaks, Kegan Paul, London, 1936, and C.D'O. Gowan et al., The Assistant Master Speaks, Kegan Paul, London, 1938.

[135] C. Norwood, op.cit., p. 129.

[136] Edward C. Mack, Public Schools and British Opinion since 1860, Columbia University Press, New York, 1942, pp. 381-3; C. Norwood, op.cit, pp. 129-32

1930's was a period of declining numbers for most of the schools, and of actual hardship for some of the less robust. It seemed as though they were being killed off by slow economic pressure. Nevertheless at the outbreak of war in 1939 the number of boys in the Public Schools was still greater than that at the outbreak of war in 1914.

The influence of the Public Schools was not confined to those who had been educated in them. Their tradition became also the inheritance of the state-supported grammar schools whose numbers were multiplying in the 1920's and 1930's. The influence penetrated further, into the senior and modern schools, and even into the primary schools. Every new playing-field that was incorporated into the design of a newly-built primary, senior, or secondary school, and every election of prefects that took place in them testified to and was redolent of the Public School spirit working its way through the whole of the English school system and penetrating even the schools of the British dominions and colonies overseas.

The influence that the training of the Public Schools may have had upon the conduct of English public and commercial policies had long been the subject of comment. For the year 1927, Tawney made a brief analysis of the schools attended by leading civil servants, judges, bishops, bank directors, and members of various professions. The high proportion of those persons educated at Public Schools, and even at a small number of the more celebrated of the schools, was readily apparent. Again, for the year 1961, Titmuss repeated part of Tawney's analysis and published Table 6.1.[137]

It was clear from this that the influence of the Public Schools had changed little during the intervening thirty-four years. If they were responsible for slightly fewer bishops, they had not lost ground in the more worldly professions, and one of them, Eton, was actually

[137] R.H. Tawney, *Equality*, with a new introduction by Richard M. Titmuss, Allen and Unwin, London, 1964, p. 248. The first edition of this book was published in 1931.

Table 6.1: English Public Schools and Selected Professions.

Profession	1927				1961*			
	Total number	Number for whom information is available	Educated at		Total number	Number for whom information is available	Educated at	
			English Public Schools (†)	Other schools or privately			English Public Schools (††)	Other schools or privately
Bishops	68	56	52 (38)	4	87	74	50 (19)	24
Lords of Appeal, Justices of Court of Appeal and High Court	39	25	17 (11)	8	63	59	45 (28)	14
Directors of five banks	165	82	62 (53)	20	149	133	94 (83)§	39

* Sources of 1961 figures: *Whitaker's Almanack* for 1962, the *Stock Exchange Year Book* for 1961, and *Who's Who*.

† Figures in brackets indicate, for 1927, numbers educated at 14 principal schools and, for 1961, at 15 schools attended by 3 or more individuals.

‡ The 182 schools represented at the Headmasters' Conference in 1943 (listed in the *Report of the Committee on Public Schools*, HMSO, 1944).

§ Includes Eton, 38; Harrow, 7; Winchester, 8.

responsible for nearly one-third of the directors of England's principal banks.

Perhaps the most striking evidence of the hold exercised by the Old School upon public life and the most prominent figure in it during the inter-war period was the statement by Stanley Baldwin, three times conservative Prime Minister of England, that, 'when the call came to me to form a Government, one of my first thoughts was that it should be a Government of which Harrow should not be ashamed. I remembered how in previous Governments there had been four or perhaps, five Harrovians, and I determined to have six.'[138]

Facts and statements such as those were the cause of considerable criticism during the 1920's and 1930's aimed both at the exclusiveness of the Public Schools, at the nature of their activities, and at their products.

An extensive controversy arose during the war years with the publication in 1917 of Alec Waugh's *The Loom of Youth*, which criticised the ultimate emptiness of Public School life. It was suggested that its inculcation of manners and its worship of insignificant customs were an inadequate substitute for what should have been an education in a lasting idea.[139] The controversy died away a little in the next few years, to be renewed with greater vigour in the 1930's. Most of the critics in the earlier controversy seem to have been interested in reforming the Public Schools. In the 1930's the reformers were still in evidence but there were, also, voices calling more powerfully for the elimination of the schools. Laski, for example, wrote on 'The Danger of Being a Gentleman', and, while appreciative of the sober virtues of the public school boy, pointed out the risk of having him in a position of leadership: 'For there is no field of activity in the modern world in which the amateur, however benevolent, can retain his function as leader without risking the survival of those who depend on him.' And an ex-Public School boy and master in a strongly-worded book, *Barbarians and Philistines*, roundly condemned the schools as anti-democratic anachronisms. 'The Public School Tradition,' he declared, 'has already served its turn. It had indeed already served it by the end of the last war at the latest. The perpetuation and, indeed, reinforcement of it in the years after the war, has been a major social as well as educational disaster.'[140]

The defenders of the tradition, however, were plentiful, and varied in their offerings. They ranged from a mawkish diary of *Antony*, an Eton boy, through the nostalgic reminiscences of ex-headmasters and sentimental novels of understanding and old-fashioned assistant masters such as *Good-bye, Mr. Chips*,[141] to formal presentations of the tradition by professional writers such as Bernard Darwin or by the principal apologist, Cyril Norwood. The Public Schools in their view epitomised the finest in English life. They held up before the youth of the country the ideal of service and fair play, the basis of true community life; and they claimed that in proper English fashion they were soundly adapting the best of the English tradition of education to the new ideas and circumstances of the twentieth century. Despite trenchant criticism and the adverse economic conditions in the 1930's which hit some schools very hard, the tradition in 1939 appeared still to have a good deal of life in it.

The American High School. 'The excellence of any state system of education,' a leading educational administrator wrote in 1909, 'must depend upon the excellence of its academic schools.' By academic schools he meant secondary high schools which gave a 'reasonably liberal education, a training in both efficiency and culture'.[142] That view, not unlike contemporary German and French ideas of the nature of the *Gymnasium* and *lycée*, was in the tradition of the Committee of Ten,[143] and was common and appropriate so long as the American high school was an elite and mainly college-preparatory institution. Efficiency, however, was already a modifying influence on the cultivation of traditional academic scholarship and during the next quarter of a century it was to grow considerably. A great expansion in high school enrolment and the changed social and educational climate of the post-World War I period helped to move the American high school towards a closer acceptance of the utilitarian Cardinal Principles of Secondary Education. While retaining a substantial academic allegiance, the high school became steadily more susceptible to considerations of 'social efficiency'. Its condition was painted in painstaking detail by a survey team in 1930.

The survey movement which had begun in the United States shortly before World War I,[144] spread vigorously during the 1920's and by the end of the 1930's some three thousand surveys of schools, state systems, special subjects, and building programs had been recorded. The most comprehensive was a national survey of secondary education commissioned by the U.S. Congress for the year 1930. In 1932 Leonard V. Koos and his staff

[138] Stanley Baldwin, *On England*, Allan, London, 1926, p. 267.

[139] Alec Waugh, *The Loom of Youth*, Richards, London, 1917. J.H. Whitehouse, *The English Public School*. A Symposium, Richards, London, 1919 contains a collection of some of the more significant correspondence aroused by the 'most powerful indictment of the conventional English public school that has appeared in our literature' (p. 34). E.C. Mack, *op.cit.*, pp. 305-452, gives an extensive account of controversies throughout the inter-war period.

[140] L.B. Pekin, *Public Schools, Their Future and Their Reform*, London, 1932, p. 24; Harold J. Laski, *The Danger of Being a Gentleman and Other Essays*, Viking, New York, 1940, p. 23; E.M. Forster, *Goldsworthy Lowes Dickinson*, New York, 1934, p. 25; T.C. Worsley, *Barbarians and Philistines. Democracy and the Public Schools*, Hale, London, 1940, pp. 10-11.

[141] The Earl of Lytton, *Antony, A Record of Youth*, London, 1935; James Hilton, *Good-bye Mr. Chips*, 1934.

[142] A.S. Draper, *American Education*, Houghton Mifflin, Boston, 1909, p. 157.

[143] See Chapter 1.

[144] See Chapter 4.

presented the first of the twenty-eight monographs that constituted the survey statement.

Koos reported that high school enrolments had increased rapidly during the twentieth century to the point where more than 50 per cent of the youth in the fourteen to seventeen year age group was at a public or private school. Part-time continuation schools and evening classes added to the number of older adolescents who were furthering their secondary education. Figure 6.1 illustrates the trend of fourteen to seventeen year old enrolments throughout the century up to 1960. From it can be seen the very considerable acceleration that took place between 1920 and 1940, at the mid-point of which Koos' survey took place.

The most popular form of school organisation continued to be eight years of elementary education followed by four years of high school. About a quarter of the public secondary schools, however, had incorporated a junior high school into the pattern, and tended to adopt a 6-3-3 or 6-6 scheme. As yet there were few junior high schools in rural areas, and the country high schools were predominantly very small institutions. In assessing trends in the high school curriculum, the surveyors found that there was at the junior high school level over the past ten years a tendency for the non-academic subjects to gain at the expense of academic ones, an increase in social-integration activities, such as clubs and home-room activities, and in general subjects such as general mathematics and social science, and a tendency for the junior high school to be used reasonably widely for curriculum innovation. At the senior high school level since the beginning of the century there had been a trend towards the introduction of more streams or groups of courses, with the result that by 1930 only a third of the programs being offered were college-preparatory ones, the remainder being divided between groupings such as general education, commercial, industrial arts, household arts and the like. There had been a great increase in the number of courses offered, from about fifty to three hundred, and an increase in interest in non-academic subjects largely at the expense of foreign languages, mathematics and science.

The accompanying graph (Figure 6.2) of the trend in subject enrolments from 1900 to 1950 indicates the substantial change in the high school program that was occurring in the inter-war period. The high popularity of a small number of subjects in the pre-World War I period is an indication of the fairly monolithic nature of the high school in which most students followed somewhat the same course towards college preparation. About 1910, as enrolments noticeably increased and an interest in education for social efficiency became more widespread, the trend began to change. From 1920 a new pattern was clearly emerging and by 1940 it had become well established. English, some social science, and physical education were taken by most students who, in addition, had

some experience of vocational subjects, and some mathematics and science. The high school had modified its college-preparatory requirements, and had also developed other streams, e.g. commercial, home economics and industrial arts.

High School building of the 1920's in the U.S.A.

One further significant finding by the survey team on school practices was the increased provision that the secondary schools made for individual differences among pupils. Not only was there a greater range of courses, and an attempt to design general subjects, but there were also many examples of special arrangements and projects within schools to deal with the problem. Three methods, in particular, were popular: ability grouping, special classes for the gifted or the slow, and the use of some form of unit arrangement such as the Dalton Plan, Winnetka Plan, Morrison Plan, problem method, project method, differentiated assignments, and various others. The schools appeared to be successful in using those methods and, in operation, made little distinction between the different kinds of units.

The American high school, by the 1930's, was making a very distinctive contribution to educational thought and practice. In providing a secondary education which followed directly on and grew out of elementary education, it had always been unique and different from the European pattern, though it had concentrated on preparing students for higher studies. It had not wholly freed itself from the academic tradition characteristic of European secondary schools but it had modified the academic influence considerably.

Figure 6.1:   United States of America: Number and per cent of
Population Age 14-17 in Public Secondary Schools,
1890-1959.

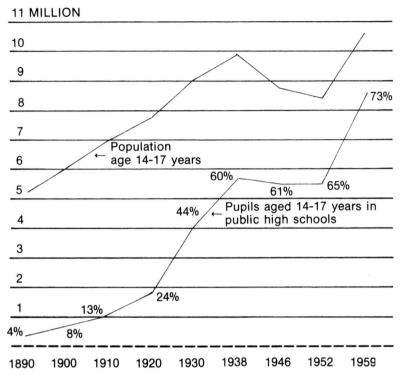

Adapted from *Statistics of Education in the United States, 1958-1959 series*

The high school was no longer an elite institution; it was a school which had to provide for the majority of America's adolescents. An investigation in 1920 had indicated that attendance at high school was related to social class; the sons and daughters of managerial and professional families appeared to profit most, and the proportion of upper middle class children completing a full secondary education was probably ten times that of the children of manual workers.[145] By 1940 inequalities had been greatly reduced; but there was abundant evidence to show that children of lower social class, non-white children, and children living in rural areas were at a disadvantage. White urban middle class children stayed on longer at school and were provided with better schools and

teachers. Nevertheless no other country could boast in 1940 of having two-thirds of its fourteen to seventeen year olds at school.[146] The United States still had a problem of equalising educational opportunities for all American youth, but it had already developed a school structure and a body of educational ideas and practices within which expansion and readjustment could· be reasonably undertaken.

The high school in the 1930's had come to be thought of as a vital training ground for democracy. To cope with the expansion of numbers and the responsibilities of providing a basis for democratic living, the school greatly widened its curriculum, and became a multilateral institution offering different arrangements of courses for several different streams of pupils.

The schools varied in size from a New York city school of ten thousand to many in rural areas of less than fifty pupils. The median school had an enrolment of about one hundred. In consequence, there was a great variation in the numbers of courses and kinds of patterns that were offered throughout the country. There was, nevertheless, a sufficient similarity among schools for it to be possible to regard the public high school as an institution with identifiable and unique features. By the 1930's it had developed several distinctive characteristics.

The public high school was a common, non-selective school available for all children who completed elementary school. It was concerned primarily with the general education of its students. In consequence they had some choice, and sometimes a very wide choice, of topics to study, and were not encouraged to specialise in one area of subject-matter; but breadth and versatility in study did not necessarily lead to the neglect of intellectual rigour in the high school. It was concerned very much with intellectual cultivation. Unlike its European counterparts, however, it did not place its main emphasis on style or comprehensive scholarship or depth of understanding; it looked for and cultivated initiative, self-direction, and problem-solving.

The American high school teacher was interested in encouraging individuals to seek, to find, and to act on the basis of reasonable conclusions. The high school program, in consequence, tended not to be wholly prescriptive but to leave opportunity for considerable individual variation and for activity that might develop out of students' interests from time to time. If a student was shorter on facts than his fellow-student in a European secondary school, he had a greater array of personally

---

[145] G.S. Counts, *The Selective Character of American Education,* University of Chicago Department of Education, Chicago, 1922.

[146] The evidence of educational inequality was summarised in W.L. Warner, R.J. Havighurst, and M.B. Loeb, *Who Shall be Educated?,* Harper, New York 1944, and in N. Edwards and H.G. Richey, *The School in the American Social Order,* Houghton Mifflin, Boston, 1947, pp. 686ff.

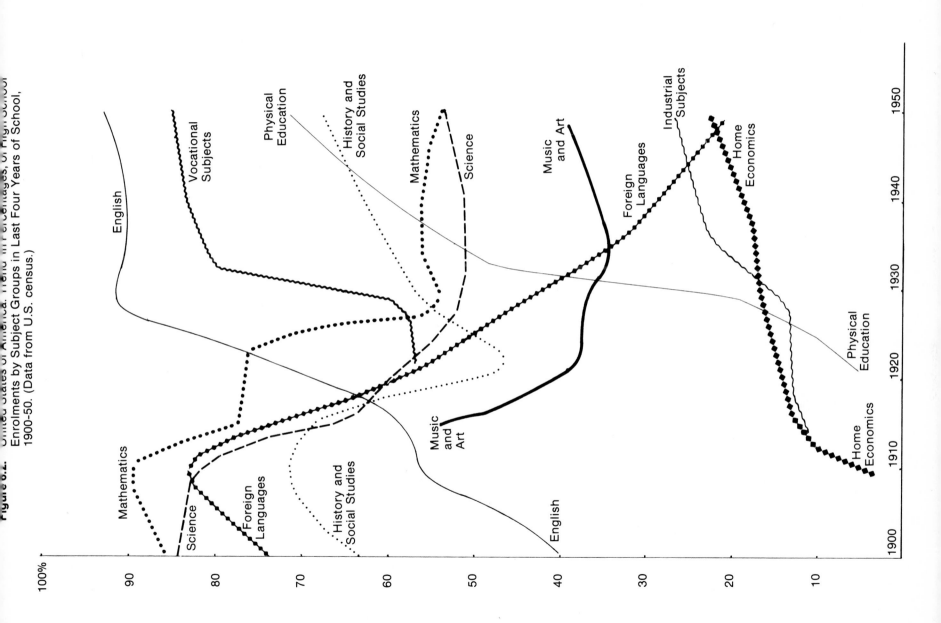

Figure 8.2. United States of America. Trend in Percentages, of High School Enrolments by Subject Groups in Last Four Years of School, 1900-50. (Data from U.S. census.)

researched facts that he had put to use, and he had a sharper appreciation of the intellectual process of discovery and the utilisation of data in the solving of problems. It was thought important also that the school should provide opportunities for students to participate in discussions, in sharing some of the planning of classwork, and in the government of the school, with the object of teaching students the skills and encouraging them to accept the kinds of responsibilities that would fit them for life in a democratic society. The American public high school also paid considerable attention to the general welfare of its students. The teacher's function, therefore, was regarded as a counselling as well as a pedagogical one. Educational and personal problems, and the health and physical welfare of the students were legitimate matters for the school staff to attend to as part of their day-to-day business or as specialists in one of the counselling fields.

Not every *lycée*, *Gymnasium*, English Public School, and American high school accepted and displayed to perfection all the characteristics which have just been attributed to them. But each was recognisable as one of its own type; and educators in each country were aware of their own and sought to maintain or modify it according to their judgment of the validity of its basic principles and the efficacy of its practices. It was, for each country, an institution of somewhat the same order as the monarchy, the republic, or the constitution. Only the boldest could seek its downfall and replacement by some other structure, but its failings could be discussed and even savoured a little by all interested parties. Foremost among the critics were the progressive educators. They offered a great range of new techniques and new ideas not only to secondary schools but to schools of every type and level. Their impact was felt in the 1930's on the American high school whose curricula and methods were steadily and increasingly affected.[147] Some English Public Schools also absorbed and encouraged progressive teachers. Among the *lycées* and *Gymnasien* there was scarcely a flutter; they were not to be seriously affected until well after World War II.

---

[147] See below, Chapter 10.

CHAPTER 7

EDUCATION IN THE U.S.S.R., 1917-40

A.V. Lunacharsky (1875-1933), the first commissar for education in the U.S.S.R. and his contemporary Stanislaus Shatsky (1878-1934), progressive educator and founder of the Colony of the Cheerful Life in the U.S.S.R.

THE EDUCATIONAL CHALLENGE

In 1913 Lenin said, 'With the exception of Russia, there is no other such savage country in Europe in which the masses of the people have been so *robbed* of educational enlightenment and knowledge.' Half a century later, communist Russia stood as one of the two great powers of the world, economically strong and technologically sophisticated — a land with three million students in higher education, flourishing technical and secondary education and a great spirit of collective ambition. The transformation was striking. The educational revolution that was accomplished was impressive in both quality and quantity. It was not, however, of even growth nor of constant direction. Its tasks, achievements, and vicissitudes provide an interesting view of the uncertainties of educational progress in revolutionary times, and of the role that education has played in reconstructing one of the world's leading societies.

When the Soviets came to power in November 1917 their educators' principal concern was with the manner in which education could contribute to the building of the new society. It was a society for which there was no previous model; and it was therefore an educational situation for which there was very little guidance. The challenge to the educators was an exhilarating one, to which they responded as whole-heartedly and imaginatively as did the politicians to their wider problems.

If they had no precedent, at least they had a vision — a Pied Piper which drew them hopefully and enthusiastically on to the new dispensation. This vision was well expressed by the first Commissar for Education in the RSFSR, Lunacharsky,[1] in a declaration of educational policy which he made on 11 November 1917, only four days after the outbreak of the Revolution.

The common people, in Lunacharsky's view, had ideas, sentiments, and characteristic approaches to life which were seeking release and expression. The educator's task was to help the mass of the people express themselves and to assist them to create a culture based upon their experiences and their aspirations. To open the way for the people, and to give them the opportunity and the power to develop creatively and

---

[1] A.V. Lunacharsky (1875-1933) was a leading literary critic, Bolshevik writer, and friend of Lenin. In his early years he engaged in revolutionary activity, was imprisoned, and subsequently spent much time on revolutionary propaganda in Switzerland, France, and Italy. In 1917 he became Commissar of Education. A scholarly, judicious, and tolerant man, devoted to the education of the masses, to the preservation of the cultural heritage, and to the promotion of science and good scholarship, he presided, during his twelve years of office, over a vital, interesting, experimental effort to combine the modern and the traditional in education and culture. He was dismissed in 1929, and was appointed ambassador to Spain in 1933, but died before he was able to take up his post.

collectively their own standards and values, and thus to release 'a mighty wave' of mass culture was the true task of the new Soviet educator.[2]

The general idea was one that had been eloquently expressed by Lenin and by his wife N.K. Krupskaya who, from the outset, became one of the most influential voices in shaping educational policy.[3] Speaking in 1920 to the third congress of the Young Communist League, Lenin made the point that the youth of the new country were to be the creators of the new society: 'the generation which is now fifteen years old will see communist society, and will itself build it. And it must realise that the whole purpose of its life is to build this society.'[4]

The new generation, in Krupskaya's view, must be imbued with a collective spirit, must grasp clearly the nature of the continuous class-struggle, and must understand the means of achieving the new collective society. In pursuing these purposes, the Soviet school 'furthers the personal development of each child, widens his horizons, deepens his consciousness, and enriches his experience.'[5]

The tasks which the educators faced in pursuit of their general aim were outlined by Lunacharsky in his 1917 statement.[6] Illiteracy and ignorance were the two main enemies that he saw. To combat them it was necessary to develop a network of schools, to make these schools compulsory, free, and generally available, to secure an adequate supply of teachers, and to establish a sufficient number of teachers' colleges in which to train them. Elementary education, however, was not enough; schools at all levels were necessary and were to be open to pupils on the basis of their quality rather than their religion or family background.

In establishing the new society five major educational tasks faced the Soviet Union:

- The elimination of illiteracy;
- The provision of universal general education of a kind that would be distinctive of the new communist civilisation;
- The education of the mass of the people to accept communist practices and ideas;
- The training of new leaders for the new society;
- The training of technicians and scientists in sufficient quantities and of sufficient quality to ensure the development of a modern, industrial, self-sufficient communist society.

THE LIQUIDATION OF ILLITERACY

It is difficult to estimate the extent of illiteracy throughout the U.S.S.R. in 1917 or to make accurate comparisons between the progress made in this field by communist or Tsarist governments. The collection of statistics

Table 7.1: Literacy in the Russian Empire and the U.S.S.R.

Year	% of literate population between the ages of 9 and 50
1897	26
1926	57
1939	89

Adapted from *Educational Planning in the U.S.S.R.*, UNESCO, International Institute for Educational Planning, Paris, 1968, p. 30.

appears to have been irregular and unreliable, and the standards used for judging illiteracy seem to have varied from time to time. It is, however, possible to say that illiteracy was very extensive in 1917, and that by the end of the 1930's, some twenty years later, it was well on the way towards being eliminated. The figures given in the accompanying table, though by no means dependable, provide a general picture of the magnitude of the problem and the pace of its liquidation.

Table 7.1 shows that in 1897 about a quarter of the population was literate, by 1926 a little more than half, and by the outbreak of the second world war about nine-tenths. The main body of the illiterates was to be found among the women of the U.S.S.R., among the non-European peoples, especially those living in the northern taiga and tundra, the central Asian republics and the areas around the Caucasus, and, of course, among the children of school age who were in insufficient attendance at

[2] Proclamation of the People's Commissar for Education, A.V. Lunacharsky, 29 October (11 November) 1917, reprinted and translated O. Anweiler and K. Meyer (edd.). *Die Sowjetische Bildungspolitik seit 1917, Documente und Texte*, Quelle and Meyer, Heidelberg, 1961, p. 57.

[3] N.K. Krupskaya (1869-1939) born at St Petersburg, joined Marxist circles in 1891, and married Lenin while they were both in exile in Siberia in 1898. After the Revolution she became a member of the board of the People's Commissariat of Education and of the Scientific Council of Education, and in 1929 assistant vice-commissar. In 1927 she became a member of the Central Committee of the Communist Party. She was instrumental in founding the Pioneer Movement, in developing kindergartens, and in fostering polytechnisation. She delivered many widely-read speeches on education and wrote several books.

[4] V.I. Lenin, *Lenin Speaks to Youth*, International Publishers, New York, 1936, p. 21.

[5] N.K. Krupskaya, *Ausgewählte Pädagogische Schriften*, Volk und Wissen, 'Aus dem Aufsatz "über die Ziele der Schule"', pp. 112-13.

[6] O. Anweiler and K. Meyer (edd.), *op.cit.*, pp. 56ff.

school. The conquest of prejudice and ignorance, the opening up of new economic and artistic possibilities, and the missionary zeal of those devoted to the development of a new literate society throughout the whole of the U.S.S.R. is one of the great sagas of modern educational history which found its echo after World War II in China and in many of the newly-developing countries of Africa and Asia.

At the end of 1919 Lenin signed a decree for the elimination of illiteracy among the population of the RSFSR. It stated that 'to enable the entire population of the Republic to participate consciously in the country's political life' the entire population between the ages of eight and fifteen incapable of reading or writing was obliged to study in their own or the Russian language. A date for the elimination of illiteracy was to be set by the provincial and city soviets in the area concerned, and the educational authorities were forthwith to draw up a general plan for the elimination of illiteracy in their particular area. In order to carry out their plan, educational authorities were given the right to conscript all the literate population of the country to teach illiterates and to enlist the active support of bodies such as the trade unions, Communist Party cells, and the Young Communist League.[7] They were authorised to use any public or private buildings deemed suitable for their purposes. Workers attending literacy courses were to be given two hours off each day without any deduction in wages.[8]

A class for illiterates in the Central Asian region of the U.S.S.R. in the 1930's.

The overall direction of the literacy campaign was in the hands of the Commissariat of Education which in 1920 appointed the all-Russian Extraordinary Committee for the Elimination of Illiteracy. That body, for the next ten years, until it was superseded in 1930, supervised the work in the RSFSR. The campaign throughout the 1920's generated enormous enthusiasm. 'People learned everywhere: at schools, at clubs, in the barracks, in the offices, in the open air.[9] But, partly because appropriate techniques had not yet been worked out, and partly because of the disturbed conditions and economic difficulties of the country, it met with somewhat limited success. The principal successes came through activity in the Red Army and Navy during the civil war, through the work of the trade unions in industrial establishments and state farms, and through the campaign of the communist party's Down With Illiteracy Society founded in 1923. Through the work of bodies such as these, a network of anti-illiteracy centres was set up, manpower was organised, propaganda campaigns were undertaken, new primers and news sheets were written, great quantities of literature were produced, educational films were made and widely distributed, and the basic ideas and organisation established which was to enable the campaign to go ahead to much greater success when it became associated with the first Five Year Plan in 1929. It was clear by then that the three different types of illiterates called for different modes of attack:

- The children of school age. The establishment of universal general education, still far from realisation, would in the long run be the only secure method for the permanent elimination of illiteracy. A considerable step forward was taken to implement widespread and compulsory education during the 1930's.

- Adult illiterates. The incidence of adult illiteracy, especially among the rural population and among women, was still enormous. The census of 1926 recorded, for example, that only 24.5 per cent of the population aged fifty and over were literate.[10]

- The peoples of remote nationalities within the U.S.S.R. These required unusual treatment and a variety of special services.

In the early 1920's the great aim was to achieve the elimination of illiteracy by the tenth anniversary of the revolution in 1927. The census of

[7]   See below pp. 220ff The Young Communist League is usually called Komsomol, and its junior, the Pioneers.

[8]   M. Zinovyev & A. Pleshakova, *How Illiteracy was Wiped Out in the USSR*, Foreign Language Publishing House, Moscow, nd., Appendix no. 1, p. 99; V. Aransky, *The Role of State Bodies and Public Organization in the Elimination of Illiteracy in the U.S.S.R.*, U.S.S.R. Commission for UNESCO, Moscow, 1965, pp. 2-3.

[9]   V. Aranksy, *op.cit.*, p. 4.

[10] N. De Witt, *Education and Professional Employment in the U.S.S.R.*, National Science Foundation, Washington D.C., 1961, p. 72.

1926, however, made it clear that this objective would not be reached or even remotely approached. 'We have succeeded,' said Krupskaya, 'in arresting illiteracy but not in eliminating it. Each year about a million illiterates receive instruction but about the same number come up from the school-age years.'[11]

The census showed that the proportion of illiterates among children of school age from nine to twelve years of age was still surprisingly high, varying from 36 per cent in the Ukrainian SSR to 91 per cent in the Uzbek SSR. It appeared also that probably only half the children of school age were in school and that the average duration of their schooling was from two to three years.[12] Clearly one of the main requirements for the future was the effective provision of compulsory four-year schooling for all children. It was clear also that the country people, the people of the non-European regions and nationalities, and the women throughout all the territories made up the bulk of the illiterates and that their position had not been greatly altered by the campaign of the early 1920's.

The first Five Year Plan, 1929-32, endeavoured to lay the foundation in heavy industry for the new soviet society. Industrialisation and collectivisation were to be pushed ahead rapidly, and were to be closely linked with the cultural revolution. In Central Asia the connection between education and economic development was made plain in the following appeal to teachers in 1929: 'Tajik teacher!... you are the only one with a higher cultural level in the villages. Encourage the backward peasants towards the new life and civilization. Guide them in new methods in the agriculture and technology of their economy.'[13] Thus the illiteracy campaign came to be associated closely with the objectives and activities of the Five-Year Plan.

'The tractor and the primer pave the way to collectivisation in the countryside' was a popular slogan of the period,[14] and, with improving economic prospects through the modernisation of industry and agriculture, the motivation hitherto lacking among many people to become literate and share in the economic advancement of the country gave the literacy campaign a new life and increased prospect of lasting success.

The first Five Year Plan undertook to have eighteen million literates and semi-literates under instruction by 1932-33; this called for progress at more than twice the rate of any previous period. In 1928 the Komsomol league proclaimed a culture campaign and in 1929 it was taken up throughout the whole of the U.S.S.R., and given high priority by all communist party organisations. During that period increased use was made of the youth organisations. In many areas they had the task of identifying illiterates and persuading them to attend organised classes. After 1936 they directed their efforts increasingly to adolescent semi-literates. For them they organised special schools from which the pupils could pass to adult schools and then through preparatory courses to

higher educational establishments. Many persons who had had only two or three years primary education were able in this way to proceed part-time to complete their general education and in many cases to undertake more advanced technological courses. Part-time, mostly evening schools, became and remained an important part of the educational program of the U.S.S.R. This appears to have been the turning point of the campaign. In 1931, twelve years after Lenin's 1919 decree, it was possible in the RSFSR to introduce a regulation requiring all illiterate persons in towns and in the countryside between the ages of fifteen and fifty to attend formal classes of instruction. What was achieved, however, was the barest of literacy for the majority of the students. 'The culture campaign,' said Krupskaya, 'has helped millions to read and write but this knowledge is of the most elementary kind.'[15]

During the first and second Five Year Plans every educational authority throughout the U.S.S.R. put a special effort into its literacy campaigns, receiving help on occasion from visitors and in particular from cultural teams sent by factories and trade unions in more literate areas. The work of these cultural teams and of the Komsomols lent to the campaign a strongly political and technological flavour. Reading was a skill to be acquired not simply for its own sake but to enable the new scholar to comprehend the new way of life that communist society was bringing into existence in the U.S.S.R. Nowhere was this more important than among the masses of illiterate women who were a great potential reservoir of contributing soviet citizens. They had to be shown their possibilities, awakened to their new responsibilities, and equipped with the appropriate education for their new life. The task was especially difficult in the central Asian republics where Uzbek, Turkmen, Tajik, Kazakh, and Kirghiz women occupied a lowly state which severely restricted their opportunities for education and for public service. With considerable difficulty and against sometimes violent opposition, literacy classes were opened for women, clubs and circles established to further their education and to provide better opportunities for social intercourse, and girls' and women's schools were multiplied. Mobile teams toured villages, and the local soviets joined in the work of emancipation. The

[11] Quoted in O. Anweiler, *Geschichte der Schule und Pädagogik in Russland*, Quelle and Meyer, Berlin, 1964, p. 217.

[12] O. Anweiler, *op.cit.*, pp. 220ff.

[13] M.M. Shorish, Education in the Tajik Soviet Socialist Republic 1917-1967, unpubl. Ph.D. thesis, University of Chicago, 1972, p. 233.

[14] N. Zinovyev and A. Pleshakova, *op.cit.*, p. 51.

[15] O. Anweiler, *op.cit.*, p. 348. A critical account of the effectiveness of the literacy campaign is to be found in a chapter contributed by Nina Nar, 'The Campaign against Illiteracy and Semiliteracy in the Ukraine, Transcaucasus, and Northern Caucasus, 1922-41', *Soviet Education*, ed. G.L. Kline, Routledge and Kegan Paul, London, 1957.

number of women literates increased considerably during the 1930's. For instance, where one per cent of the Tajik and seven per cent of the Turkmen women could read and write in 1926, by 1938 the proportions had risen to approximately 77 per cent and sixty per cent.[16]

It could be said that, by the outbreak of World War II, the U.S.S.R. was well on the way to realising in fact the aspiration set down in the constitution of 1936, that 'Women in the U.S.S.R. are accorded equal rights with men in all spheres of economic, state, cultural, social, and political life.'[17]

The literacy campaign among the peoples of the illiterate or semi-literate nations was a fascinating struggle to provide basic education for people who were in some cases nomadic, lacking a written language or even an alphabet, and with no knowledge of modern government or machinery. To help in the work with the people in the northern forests and Arctic lands of Russia and Siberia, the Institute of the Northern Peoples was established in Leningrad in 1923. In other places Regional National Minority Education Institutes were established and a central research institute for the education of national minorities was set up in Moscow.

Wherever possible the literacy campaign in each district became part of a wider movement centring around a cultural base which provided a combination of services. A medical team and sometimes a hospital promoted the health of the community; a veterinary station provided advice on animal management and agriculture; a co-operative store provided facilities for training and marketing; and a cinema and clubhouse within the adult education centre served as a common meeting ground for the district and provided opportunities for learning about and experiencing some of the practices of the new society. An integral part of the cultural base was the school, often a boarding school whose teachers were the chief promoters of the literacy campaign throughout the district. As the campaign succeeded, further experts would come into the district, to help, for example, to develop mining resources or to build new industries. The school would expand from an initial four-year school to a seven-year school, and technical and higher education would gradually be developed. The young people would become members of the Pioneer and Komsomol organisations, and some promising students might be sent to the Leningrad Institute of the Northern Peoples or to other suitable training centres throughout the U.S.S.R., returning in due course to provide political and technical leadership for their people.[18] In this way the literacy campaign helped in 'the creation of a people's intelligentsia'[19] in hitherto backward areas of the country.

The success of the literacy campaign in the 1930's meant however a great deal more than the creation of a new intelligentsia; it provided the foundation for a wide-based popular culture, for a widespread acceptance of communist practices and ideas, and for unprecedented social and economic progress throughout the U.S.S.R.

Adult literacy campaigns were useful but for the most part palliative. The development of a literate, educated population throughout the U.S.S.R. depended fundamentally upon the successful provision of universal education for the children. This too was a prime task for the first Five-Year Plan and was given special attention by the communist party from 1930 on. Through the vigorous prosecution of this double campaign for adult literacy and for compulsory general education for the children during the course of the first and second Five Year Plans, illiteracy as a mass phenomenon had vanished from the U.S.S.R. by the end of the 1930's. There were still too many illiterates and still too many with a very meagre education but the new society was no longer faced with the task of having to begin the education of a half to three-quarters of its citizens.[20]

THE DEVELOPMENT OF UNIVERSAL COMPULSORY EDUCATION

The early years of the new soviet government were alive with new expectations and with ideas about the development of the new society. In education these were expressed simply in Article 17 of the 1918 constitution of the RSFSR: 'to guarantee to the working classes real access to knowledge, the RSFSR takes on the task of providing a complete, all round, and free education for the workers and poor peasants.'[21]

Many decrees and resolutions were passed both by the committees of soviets and by the communist party concerning various aspects of education which would ensure the effective implementation of universal compulsory education. These were summed up in a comprehensive decree issued by the All-Russian central executive committee of the soviets for the RSFSR on 16 October 1918. The decree outlined a new pattern of general education:

[16] N. Zinovyev and A. Pleshakova, *op.cit.*, p. 78 and M.M. Shorish, *op.cit.*, p. 185.

[17] Constitution of the U.S.S.R., Article 122.

[18] T. Semushkin, *Children of the Soviet Arctic*, Hutchinson, London, n.d., describes graphically the establishment of a school and its workings at a cultural base in Chukotka, a national area in the north-eastern corner of Asia by the Bering Strait.

[19] N. Zinovyev and A. Pleshakova, *op.cit.*, p. 23. This expression comes from one of Lenin's last articles, 'Our Revolution'.

[20] O. Anweiler, *op.cit.*, p. 349.

[21] O. Anweiler and K. Meyer (edd.), *op.cit.*, p. 65.

- It declared the abolition of the previous organisation of schools and the elimination of the various types then existing;

- It gave complete authority for education to the state department of education;

- Education was to be compulsory from eight to seventeen years;

- Schools were to be co-educational;

- Education was to be free at all levels;

- It set up the Unified Labour School as the pivot of the system;

- The Unified Labour School was to have two levels — a five-year course for children from eight to thirteen years, and a four-year course for children from thirteen to seventeen;

- Below the general Unified Labour School, a two-year kindergarten might be established for children from six to eight, so that the whole school system might provide effective education for children from the age of six through to seventeen;

- No religious education or religious observances of any kind were to be permitted within the school premises;

- The basis of school life was to be found in productive work and collective activity;

- For each school a council was to be formed consisting of all school staff, a representative of the local education authority, and representatives of the local school district workers and of the school pupils over the age of twelve. The function of the council was to direct the activities of the school and to make decisions on details concerning the appropriate curricula and methods that might be used in the school.

On the same day that the decree was issued, a lengthy statement was published outlining the fundamental principles of the Unified Labour School. To say that it was a unified school, the statement affirmed, meant that the whole school system from kindergarten to university was to be a single, unbroken ladder which all children might climb as far as they were capable. To call it a labour school implied that productive work was to be introduced as a fundamental educational principle. For this, the statement suggested, there were two main reasons. The first was psychological, in the tradition of the progressive Activity School approach: children have an urge to be active, and they grasp thoroughly only the things that they learn in an active way. Productive labour caters for this view of the educative process by putting children into an active, mobile, and creative relationship with their environment. The second reason was a practical, political one. The future of the new society and of

the children in it simply required that the pupils become familiar with the range and the processes of agricultural and industrial work.[22]

In explaining these ideas Lunacharsky said in his first annual report in 1918: 'The labor character of the school consists in the fact that labor, pedagogical as well as productive labor, will be made a basis of teaching. In the primary schools it will be mostly work within the walls of the school: in the kitchen, in the garden, in special workshops, etc. The labor must be of a productive character — in this way, in particular, that the children serve the needs of the community so far as their strength will permit them ... [The older children's labor] should be an easy but *real* labor outside of the school — the participation in factory or shop work, the helping in serious farm work, the co-operation in some business enterprise, the co-operation in some social or state undertaking.'[23]

This program and the statements surrounding and supporting it were aspirations not to be realised for many years. They were an ideal and a guide for the future. Nevertheless, although the full program was beyond immediate reach, a number of the basic ideas were put into operation immediately and became integral parts of the developing soviet system of education. These were:

- the overall state control of education;

- the unified, single school;

- the free, secular, and co-educational nature of the schools.

The emphasis upon productive labour, and upon collective school work and school organisation, was to be tried out in varying ways with varying degrees of success during the course of the next two decades.

Four years of war communism, of cataclysmic disturbance, and experimentation under the Act of 1918, led to a modification of the Act in two directions during the period of modified capitalism known as the New Economic Policy (1921-28).

The new education was to be slightly less ambitious in organisation and it was to be tied much more closely to the aims and policies of the communist party. Accordingly a statute published on 18 December 1923 for the RSFSR superseded the Act of 1918 and outlined the organisation under which education was to operate during the remainder of the 1920's. The unified labour school was to provide an education for children from the age of eight to seventeen which was to be secular, co-educational, compulsory as far as it was possible to insist upon this, and directed by a school council in which teachers predominated but upon

[22]   O. Anweiler & K. Meyer, *op.cit.*, pp. 73-89, Declaration of the Unified Labour School, 16 October 1918. 1918.

[23]   This quotation comes from D.B. Leary, *Education and Autocracy in Russia from the Origins to the Bolsheviki,* University of Buffalo Press, Buffalo, 1919, pp. 113-14; See also G.Z.F. Bereday, W.W. Brickman, & G.H. Read (edd.), *The Changing Soviet School,* Constable, London, 1960, pp. 51-3.

Figure 7.1:   U.S.S.R.: School System in the NEP period, 1921-28.

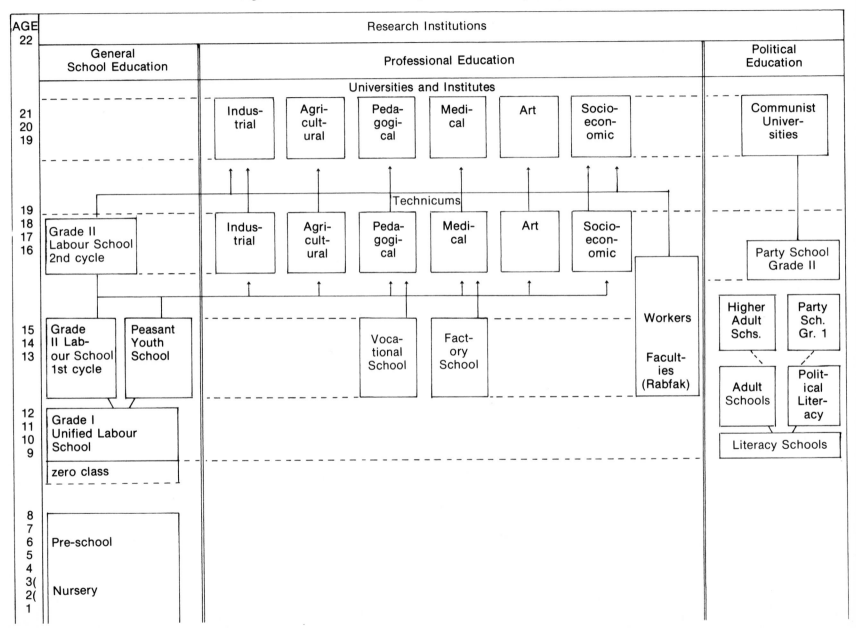

Adapted from T. Woody, *New Minds: New Men?*, Macmillan, 1932, p. 445, after A.C. Kalashnikov and M.S. Epstein (eds), *Pedagogical Encyclopedia*, Moscow, 3 vols., 1929-30.

which representatives of the communist party might sit. The principal, however, had a much more substantial authority than under the Act of 1918. The school was divided into two levels. The first level consisted of a four-year course instead of the previous five, and the second level of a five-year course divided into two sections of three and two years. This had the effect of reducing the standard elementary school program from five years to four years and of making the usual post-elementary one consist of three years.

Thus a network of four-year and seven-year schools grew up throughout the U.S.S.R. during the remainder of the 1920's and 1930's. The aim of the school was to be the same as that enunciated by the Act of 1918 but more emphasis was placed in the 1923 statute on the necessity for co-operation with the communist party and its youth organisations, to the end that 'the entire work and organization of the school must conduce to the development of a proletarian class consciousness of the solidarity of all working people in their struggle against capitalism and serve as a preparation for a useful productive life of social activity'.[24]

In the RSFSR during the NEP period the overall educational system developed as follows: there was a basic nine-year pattern, the Unified Labour School, divided into three stages (4-3-2) with four-year, seven-year, and nine-year schools, and, supplementing them, two other general schools with rather more vocational bias, the Schools of Peasant Youth and seven-year Industrial Schools. Below the nine-year schools, there was available a three-year Nursery School and a four-year Kindergarten. Starting at the second stage there was a pattern of vocational education: lower level training in vocational and factory schools, middle level in technicums, and upper level in universities and higher technical institutes. In addition there was a system of special Communist Party schools for political education starting at the second level of the general school and proceeding through to Communist Universities.

Meanwhile, advice had been issued to party members through a circular of 4 November 1921, dealing with the relationships between the party and the educational system. It suggested that the task of education within the soviet republic was not only that of developing economic strength but also of fostering a communist consciousness in the mass of the people and of the coming generation. Party members should pay special attention to the organisation of every aspect of education, must examine all educational decisions and do their utmost to forward those which contribute to the fundamental aims of education. It was not precisely clear, however, how these aims were to be realised. The general lines of the education system had been worked out, but the precise methods, the curricula, and the activities of the schools were by no means definitely settled. In consequence, the whole of this period was one of varied and luxuriant experiment, as educators searched for the most appropriate means of educating for the new society.

EXPERIMENT WITH EDUCATION

Before building the new society, it was necessary to shake off the old. The first ten years of Soviet education is very much a period of breaking with the old tradition. Whatever was traditional was wrong. Once this iconoclasm had had its due season, and the new and experimental had not shown themselves to answer to the new social and economic demands of communist society, educators turned back abruptly at first in the 1930's to a modification of the old European tradition, and then amalgamated it with a new native conception that a soviet school-master, Makarenko, had been painstakingly working on throughout the 1920's and early 1930's.

In the 1920's the European progressive tradition which had made an impact in pre-revolutionary times continued to exercise an influence on many educators. Ideas from American progressives were also tried out. In particular the Dalton Plan had a period of great popularity but met with mixed success.[25] It was enthusiastically taken up by Krupskaya in 1922, and in the secondary schools and higher institutions for several years was more widely experimented with in Russia than in any other country. It was modified by the introduction of collective, instead of individual, contracts, and by being set into a pre-arranged timetable. It finally dropped out of favour during the period of the first Five Year Plan.

The most popular of all overseas educators was John Dewey whose works were widely read during the 1920's. Dewey recorded, on his visit to the U.S.S.R. in 1928, his opinion that American influence had been at its height 'up to 1922 or 1923'.[26] His own works, however, remained popular throughout the 1920's, and one of Russia's leading educators, Pinkevitch, suggested that 'every contemporary student of education should study his writings'.[27] The leading progressive, S.T. Shatsky, was one of those most interested in Dewey's ideas; he had read and been impressed by him in the early years of the century, and after the Revolution he translated parts of *Democracy and Education* and wrote sympathetically about the suitability of Dewey's work for Soviet education.

[24] Statute on the Unified Labour School issued by the Council of People's Commissars of the RSFSR, 18 December 1923, Article 35, reproduced in O. Anweiler and K. Meyer edd, *op.cit.*, p. 132.

[25] N. Ognyov, *The Diary of a Communist Schoolboy*, trans. A. Werth, Payson & Clarke, New York, 1928, describes rather critically a pupil's experiences in a Russian school in 1923-4 which was experimenting with the Dalton Plan. See also S.M. Teitelbaum, 'The Dalton Plan in the Soviet Schools', *Harvard Educational Review*, 17, 2, Spring 1947, pp. 91-101.

[26] J. Dewey, *Characters and Events*, Allen and Unwin, London, 1929, vol. 1., p. 415. For Dewey's visit, see Chapter 3.

[27] A.P. Pinkevitch, *The New Education in the Soviet Republic*, trans. Nucia Perlmutter, Day, New York, 1929, p. 177.

On his brief visit to the U.S.S.R. Dewey saw something of the work of Shatsky and Pistrak[28] whose schools were experimenting with activity approaches to collectively creative work in rural and urban environments. In this matter, he shrewdly observed that it raised one of the 'burning points'[29] in Russian discussions on education. One school of thought held that educational principles should be derived from psychology and biology, and, with the recent progress in educational psychology and measurement, this pedagogical approach had strong support. The more orthodox Marxian view, he thought, was that social utility was the fundamental criterion in all educational practice, and that environments could be so reconstructed that, with this process, new people with new educational requirements would come into being. Dewey's sympathies clearly lay with the second viewpoint.

When the project method became widespread in 1929-30, Dewey's influence was at its height. Very soon, however, as the Five Year Plan gained momentum, it began to evaporate. Changed educational policies during the 1930's made the educational atmosphere less congenial to his views, and by the end of the decade he had dropped completely out of favour.

Throughout the 1920's the schools of the U.S.S.R. experimented in four main areas:

- With subject-matter, in an endeavour to break out of traditional subject divisions and provide material that was both in appearance and in fact more closely related to the pupils' present and prospective life;
- With methods of teaching and learning, with the object of encouraging pupils to engage in group work both in selecting the material for study and in the actual study of the subject-matter;
- With school organisation, in the hope of encouraging more self-government for the pupils, and more interest on the part of teachers, pupils, and the community in the administration of the school;
- With polytechnic education, in an effort to develop an approach to education distinctive to communism.

(i) Subject-Matter

In the reform of subject-matter the most widely attempted innovation was the introduction of the 'method of complexes'. The curriculum makers of the 1920's in all countries were interested in developing some form of correlation between the various subjects of a school curriculum. The method of complexes, somewhat similar to the project method, was an attempt on the part of Russian educators to design a correlated

Table 7.2: An Integrated 'Method of Complexes' Curriculum in Primary Grades in the U.S.S.R.

Nature	Work	Society	Year of Study
The seasons, aspects of physical geography	The family at work in a village or city	The family and its relations with the school	1st
Air, water, soil, cultivated plants, domestic animals	The village at work, or the city area where the pupil lives	Social institutions of the village or the city	2nd
Elementary aspects of physics, chemistry, agriculture, industry, mining, communications, human biology	Economics of the region	Regional institutions present and past	3rd
Geography of the U.S.S.R. and of other countries; human biology	Economics of the U.S.S.R. and of other countries	Political and social organisation of the U.S.S.R. and of other countries in the past and present	4th

28 For Shatsky, see below. M.M. Pistrak (1888-1940) was an early member of the Communist Party. Trained as an electrical engineer, he turned to teaching and became widely known as the principal of the experimental Lepeshinsky School in Moscow. He was a leading advocate of the collective labour school and one of the architects of the 'complex' program in the 1920's.

29 A.P. Pinkevitch, op.cit., p. 408.

curriculum appropriate to the tasks of the soviet school. It was an interesting attempt to relate the social and natural sciences together in an integrated program. Nature, work, and society were the three principal concepts around which study was organised and interrelated.

The scheme was set out in 1923 as in Table 7.2.

The program was a continually expanding one from year to year, moving from local geography and the family through to the village, town, larger region, the U.S.S.R., the world. In each step the three major concepts of nature, work, and society were interrelated, and the traditional subjects such as history, geography, arithmetic, and the native language were taught as the need for them arose in the study of the 'complex'. They were not valued as subjects in and of themselves but as a means to grasping thoroughly the ideas which the teacher wished to develop during the course of studying the 'complex'. The scheme could be developed appropriately for all levels of education. The 'complex' arrangement was an attempt to provide a new basis, divorced from the traditional subject program, through which a new orientation could be given to all studies throughout the Soviet school.[30]

Using the broad divisions, nature, work, and society, a detailed course of study for elementary and secondary level classes was worked out and built into a logical sequence. The course of study was divided into small units or centres of interest in which the work could be arranged around a theme or problem. These centres of interest or 'complexes' might be as various as the study of steam engines in the third year or autumn foliage in the first. Traditional subject-matter was to be learnt incidentally to the pursuit of the general theme; thus, on the theme 'trains', some elementary physics would be acquired in learning how the steam engine works, mapping practice in sketching the extent of the railways, a little chemistry in studying the fuel, and composition from the writing of reports of excursions. The overall theme which held the whole system of 'complexes' together was the understanding of human labour, of the productive forces which man uses, and of the social relations which grow out of the way in which they are organised. The Labour School had a labour-oriented curriculum, which, starting from an elementary study of production in the lowest grades, eventually worked its way through to the highest grades where, it was hoped, socially productive work would be combined with vocational training and a sophisticated understanding of the significance of labour.

There was much discussion and writing on the new approach and in 1923 a definitive statement was made by the State Scientific Council of Education for the RSFSR which was a leading influence towards experimental work, and of which Krupskaya was an important member.[31] It set out the general lines of organisation, as shown in the diagram above, worked out suggestive programs of work for the four primary

grades, with different content for rural and city schools, and listed the knowledge and skills that all pupils might be expected to have acquired after the four-year course. For example, in social skills, they should be able:

- to participate in and lead general meetings, to take and report minutes, to work as a member, president, or secretary;
- to execute individually and collectively various social obligations such as participation in commissions;
- to organise social undertakings such as circles, co-operatives, clubs, general holidays, and recreations;
- to prepare wall newspapers, reports, articles.

The council provided outlines also for the remaining grades of the nine-year school, dropping the 'complex' plan for the secondary level pupils and retaining traditional subjects organised around a number of themes which were designed to bring the subject into closer relationship with the life of labour.

The council's proposals were modified from time to time, notably in a comprehensive revision in 1927, but retained the same basic features throughout. The 'complex' method which they advocated and expanded was used in some form by most schools in the Soviet Union in the mid-1920's, and was popular in teacher training courses until the early 1930's. At the end of the 1920's many schools moved from a 'complex' curriculum to the use of projects which, though similar in practice were more flexible, in that they were not necessarily tied to a curriculum pattern.

(ii) Methods of Teaching

The 'complex' program was not precisely the same in every school. Although the general framework was preserved, variations developed in the topics and centres of interest in order to cater for the interests and social needs of pupils in diverse parts of the Soviet Union. In particular, encouragement was given to pupils to discuss the program with their teachers and to have a share in deciding upon and planning the work they were to undertake. Responsibility of this kind was exercised with increasing effect as the pupils grew older, and in some tertiary level

---

[30]   A diagrammatic presentation of the 'method of complexes' similar to Table 7.2 and a description may be found in Scott Nearing, *Education in Soviet Russia*, International, New York, 1926, pp. 94ff.; Lucy L. Wilson, *The New Schools of New Russia*, Vanguard, New York, 1928, pp. 170ff.; A.P. Pinkevitch, *The New Education in the Soviet Republic*, trans. Nucia Perlmutter, John Day, New York, 1929, pp. 305ff.; L. Volpicelli, *L'Evolution de la Pédagogie Soviétique*, trans. P. Bovet, Delachaux et Niestlé, Neuchâtel, 1954, p. 79.

[31]   This Council (G.U.S.) (a section of the Ministry of Education) was established in 1919, and discontinued in 1932. Its function was to advise on educational methods, and to prepare curricula for schools at all levels.

institutions students had a decisive role in the selection of the curriculum. Encouragement was also given to pupils to consult among themselves and to work in groups. Good evidence of this trend was provided by the change which overtook the Dalton Plan quite early in its use in Russian secondary grades. The Dalton Plan has two principal features: laboratories or workrooms for each subject, and individual assignments enabling each pupil to proceed at his own pace. After a short experience, the individual aspects of the Plan were dropped and the laboratories retained, but each laboratory was equipped with tables of a size sufficient for a small group, sometimes called a 'brigade', to sit together and work as a group on their assignment. In this way the interests of collective education were more effectively served.

(iii) Self-government

Most schools encouraged their pupils to extend their responsibility by a scheme of self-government through which they might learn to organise and discipline themselves. It was an important part of their social education, and a vital step towards developing collective attitudes and practices throughout the school. A teacher's job was, in essence, twofold: to stimulate an interest in scientific knowledge and to encourage group activity. The school curriculum was designed to emphasise a scientific approach to the physical and social environment, and the methods of teaching and organising in the schools provided wide opportunities for group work. Student organisation varied in effectiveness from school to school; in some it was highly developed, in others rudimentary. It was common practice to establish a classroom organisation and also one for the whole school. Committees were elected by pupils, and tended to assume responsibility for four areas of pupil activity: for the cleanliness of the school and the pupils, for school discipline, for cultural activities such as the organisation of wall newspapers and reading rooms, and for the management of clubs and extra-curricular activities. In the matter of student discipline the schools produced examples of outstanding successes as well as unruly failures. Where things went well, the tone of the school was exemplary, there was a pervasive sense of collective responsibility among the pupils, and their behaviour was regulated by a judicious use of social approval or disapproval.

For the general organisation of the school, two committees were often brought into existence. There was a wide policy-making body, the general committee, representing pupils, teachers, other workers at the school, parents, trade unions, youth groups, and the local soviet; in addition there was a small executive committee usually consisting of the school director, his assistant, and a representative of the teachers and of the pupils.

(iv) Polytechnical Education

In the *Manifesto of the Communist Party* published in 1848, Marx and Engels suggested that, in the school for the future communist society, there would be a 'combination of education with industrial production'. This thought Marx reiterated in *Capital*, forecasting 'an education that will, in the case of every child over a given age, combine productive labour with instruction and gymnastics, not only as one of the methods of adding to the efficiency of production, but as the only method of producing fully developed human beings.'[32]

Schools based on these principles were advocated by Lenin as proper for the new society, and he encouraged his wife, Krupskaya, to publish in her book, *Popular Education and Democracy*, in 1917, an account of current practices and of the views which they both shared on the subject. Lunacharsky's Act of 1918 formally established the Unified Labour School as the common, compulsory school for all pupils from eight to seventeen years of age, offering a general and polytechnical education. The statement issued with the Act set out the meaning and place of polytechnical education.

The pupils were to be made familiar with agricultural and industrial work in all its diversity. At the first or elementary school level (eight to thirteen years) they were to be introduced to work processes through manual work, at the upper level (thirteen to seventeen years) they would have experience of mechanised agriculture and industrial machine production. The aim of this education was not to train pupils in any particular manual skill, but to give them a polytechnic outlook through practical experience, partly in school workshops and farms and partly in factories and offices. A fourteen-year-old pupil, it was declared, with a polytechnical education was 'capable of taking up and making sense of any subject he chooses'; and, in the secondary level, provision was to be made for a systematic study of language, mathematics, and the sciences, to supplement general polytechnical education. In the following year, 1919, the 8th Congress of the Communist Party endorsed this position.[33] By 1921, however, Lenin had been forced to concede, as a temporary practical necessity resulting from the economic condition of the country, that the age of polytechnical education should be lowered to fifteen, and that the upper secondary grades should be merged with the work of vocational schools. For some time to come polytechnical work remained meagre and inadequate, and was little more than work in ill-equipped carpentry, shoemaking, sewing, and bookbinding workshops, and, in rural areas,

[32] K. Marx & F. Engels, *Manifesto of the Communist Party*, Foreign Language Publishing House, Moscow, 1952, p. 81; K. Marx, *Capital*, Foreign Language Publishing House, Moscow, 1957, 1, p. 484.
[33] O. Anweiler & K. Meyer (edd.), *op.cit.*, pp. 73-89, 91-2.

some attention to gardens and agricultural plots. Effective programs were to be found only in the special experimental schools. Lenin's wish that it should be an opportunity for all pupils to get a general industrial orientation, and an understanding, in particular, of the new basis of soviet economy, electricity, remained an aspiration.

The principle, however, was not surrendered, although the practice lagged. The most comprehensive statement on the principle came from Blonsky who in 1919 published a widely-read book *The Labour School* to which Lenin was greatly attracted.[34]

Blonsky pointed up the distinctively Russian contribution to the *Arbeitsschule* movement by drawing a distinction between his own program and that put forward by educators such as Kerschensteiner. The non-Russian approach made work an important feature of the school curriculum but work did not permeate every aspect of the program, and it was manual work, not productive, factory work. Blonsky's school was a 'daughter of city culture', a product of industrial life, which, for him, was the modern centre of intellectual stimulus and educational innovation.[35] His school was to establish a multitude of links with everyday economic and social life; productive work was to be the central idea of the school and to permeate the entire school curriculum. Only by such a thorough immersion in useful productive work could pupils become really acquainted with actual economic processes. School work was to be radically re-oriented, and the pupils to be steadily transformed in character and outlook by a complete absorption into a world of machine production and working class culture.

Blonsky and his fellow-educators believed that the worker in the U.S.S.R. had a role different from that of the worker elsewhere. He was not merely an employee blindly taking direction from a superior; he was the creator of a new world. As such, he had to understand the fundamental principles of production, and, at the same time, become skilled in various aspects of practical work. School pupils, by learning the basic ideas of productive work, and by actually working and producing, would learn to be and to think like workers, and would effectively enter into the new worker-culture that was coming into being.

The Labour School, the communist version of the Activity School, was an industrial school arising out of and responsive to the needs of an industrial society, with its machine production and its class conscious-ness. The experience of productive work in the school was felt to be the best way of merging children into industrial life, of inducting them into the feelings, aspirations, and habits of the world-wide working class, of saturating them with its ideology, of teaching them the discipline of work, and of giving them an understanding of contemporary life.[36]

How were objectives and aspirations such as these to be put into practice? Throughout the 1920's there was a range of prescriptions. Some schools were able to develop programs through which the whole of school life was integrated by productive work; others built a close association with a local factory, and their pupils shared their time between the factory and the school. Most schools acquired their own woodwork, metalwork, and sewing workshops and used them as additions to the school curriculum in which pupils spent part of their time working on their own hobbies or on prescribed work; a few, like Makarenko's schools, were kept completely separate from the program of productive work which was carried on, outside of school time, in separate factory premises. It was calculated that, in 1928, forty million of the seven to fifteen year old pupils were producing through their schools the equivalent of the work output of ten million adults.[37] Productive work of various kinds was certainly proceeding in Soviet schools in the 1920's but, as to the best methods of conducting it, there was no widespread agreement. The Labour School was not meant to provide vocational training; that was the function of the factory schools and the technicums.

In 1929 the First All-Russian Congress on Polytechnical Education was held. It was opened by Krupskaya who had already defined polytechnical education in 1928: 'This does not mean a school in which one studies several trades, but rather a school where children learn to understand the essence of the labouring process, the substance of the labour activity of the people, and the conditions of success in work.'[38] Polytechnical education, in this view, was general education.

During the period of the first Five Year Plan, the debate on polytechnisation was intensified. In the opinion of some educators, it could become so general that it was possible to dispense with formal education. For example, Shulgin, director of the Marx-Lenin Educational Institute in Moscow, in 1929 revived an interesting theory of the early 1920's that in due course factory work and the general social life of the worker-community could best provide the necessary education for children, and that the school, like the state, should wither away. Neither the state, however, nor the school showed any signs of withering away in the 1930's. On the contrary, they both significantly increased the strength of their activities. The prevailing view by the beginning of the 1930's was

[34] S.C. Shapovalenko (ed.), *Polytechnical Education in the U.S.S.R.* UNESCO Paris, 1963, p. 37. P.P. Blonsky (1884-1941) was a leading Soviet educator of the early period. His *The Labour School* was widely read, and he helped to design the 'complex' curricula of the 1920's. He was the principal of a large school in Moscow and a professor at the Krupskaya Institute of Social education. He was greatly interested in the testing movement, and lost much of his influence when pedology came under censure in 1936.

[35] P.P. Blonsky, *Die Arbeitsschule*, trans. H. Ruoff, Berlin, 1921, p. 23.

[36] See A.P. Pinkevitch, *The New Education in the Soviet Republic*, ibid., pp. 200-1.

[37] L. Sabsovitch, *L'U.R.S.S. dans dix ans, Plan general de la construction de Socialisme*, Paris, 1930, p. 138; quoted in E. Devaud, *La Pédagogie Scolaire en Russie Soviètique*, Brouiver, Paris, 1932, p. 110.

[38] Quoted in A.P. Pinkevitch, *op.cit.*, p. 200.

that polytechnic education and general education should be thought of as much the same thing; that general education for the society of the U.S.S.R. should have a polytechnic approach, and that it should provide and be carefully distinguished from vocational education. That was the decision of the Ministry of Education of the RSFSR, and it accorded with Krupskaya's view.

This attitude was to be changed, however, by a decision of the Central Committee of the Communist Party in 1931, which brought the experimental period to an end.

SHATSKY (1878-1934), AND THE COLONY OF THE CHEERFUL LIFE

The most versatile educator of the experimental period of the 1920's who, in his work, exemplified most of the new tendencies was Shatsky. The principles of the 'complex' curriculum reform, activity methods, pupil self-government, and productive work were all effectively practised in his experimental work.

The Colony of the Cheerful Life, founded in 1905 and run by Shatsky for the next thirty years, was one of the most extensive and long-lived experiments in the history of education, but one on which there is very little published data. It expressed in its work all the principal features of contemporary progressive education, and imparted to them at the same time a character that was distinctively Russian.

Shatsky was born in Smolensk in 1878, and educated in Moscow. He attended science courses at the university irregularly, and studied music at the conservatorium. He disliked the joylessness of his upbringing and the tedious restrictiveness of his schooling; and his subsequent educational work was, in part, a reaction against these uninspiring experiences. 'Whenever I fancy,' he wrote in 1903 when he was twenty-five, 'that I have enough strength left to achieve the desired goal to see around me a crowd of gay, healthy, human, free children's faces, and to know that I am storing up the capital deposited in them for their future life, then my soul becomes still with joy, and I desire nothing more in life.'[39] To achieve this goal he gave up a promising musical career to found the Colony of the Cheerful Life.

In 1905 he joined forces with A.U. Zelenko, a young architect recently returned from visiting European and American progressive schools and working for some time in Jane Addams' settlement, Hull House, in Chicago. Together, in a summer house on the outskirts of Moscow they founded a colony for children. In the following year a settlement was started in an industrial district of Moscow, and soon they were responsible for about 250 children in a kindergarten, primary, and secondary school, in clubs, workshops, and the summer colony. In 1911, at Kaluga, about one hundred kilometres south-west of Moscow, a summer colony was opened and named the Colony of the Cheerful Life; it henceforth was to become the focal point of Shatsky's work. In 1916 the colony was expanded into a general cultural centre and research station, and included programs of health, agricultural, and general adult education, a kindergarten, primary school, and training centre for teachers. It was a venture in community education through which Shatsky hoped to transform village life.

In building his work up to that point Shatsky had been greatly influenced by his study of the ideas of Dewey whom he regarded as the 'strongest and most refreshing voice' in contemporary education, and as 'the best philosopher of the school of today'.[40] He was abreast of the most recent developments in European schools also, and had visited and talked with people such as Decroly and Kerschensteiner. He acknowledged, too, his deep indebtedness to Tolstoy who had helped him understand the signal importance of education, had demonstrated the need for a reconstruction of rural education and culture in Russia, and had provided an inspiring example of educational work directed to this end.

In 1918 Shatsky approved of the decree and explanatory statement on the Unified Labour School issued by the new revolutionary government, and henceforth, for the next ten years up to the beginning of the first Five Year Plan, he became one of the leading educators in the Soviet Union. In 1921 he became a member of the Council of Education and found a sympathetic ally in Krupskaya. Together they were largely responsible for the design of the 1923 statement on 'complex' programs, and for continual encouragement to the schools during the next five years to put the programs into effect.

His colony was converted in 1919 into the First Experimental Station for the Education of the People, and gradually expanded in scope, until it eventually embraced thirty-five villages, and included seven kindergartens, fourteen primary schools, a secondary school, and several village libraries, in addition to the central plant at the children's colony, consisting of a kindergarten, nine-year boarding school, and a social and cultural centre. In Moscow a city section of the experimental station was added in the form of a kindergarten, two primary schools, and teacher training technicum. It was a substantial enterprise for educational experimentation. Eventually, in 1923, Shatsky was appointed head of the Central Pedagogical Laboratory of the Ministry of Education, and the First Experimental Station was merged into the new organisation.

[39]   Quoted in O. Anweiler, *op.cit.*, p. 55. There is a very interesting account of a visit to Shatsky's colony in T. Woody, *New Minds: New Men?* Macmillan, New York, 1932, pp. 43-60.

[40]   O. Anweiler, *op.cit.*, p. 60.

In 1925 Shatsky's influence on official educational policy was strengthened by his becoming a member of the communist party; and although after the end of the 1920's his views met with less enthusiasm, he was still a figure of importance at the time of his death in 1934. Shatsky's contribution was a fourfold one:

- Productive work as the basis of education. In Shatsky's view, a child's life had in it seven principal elements: physical growth, productive work, play, art, intellectual life, social life, and emotional life. Of those, two were of particular importance: productive work, and social life. The school, for Shatsky, was essentially a working community of children. In his country experimental station, equipped with a farm and workshops, the work of the school developed out of the children's interests in the agricultural environment of their village communities. They developed a 'complex' approach which fitted well with the official program based on the study of nature, work, and society. Shatsky's was an activity approach in which the local world was a laboratory, and the school a central preparation room within it. In their school program they took up the vital problems and themes of productive work in the local area, learning incidentally the necessary skills to improve their life in all its seven aspects, and gaining a drive towards accomplishment by their consciousness that what they were learning had a clear significance for their everyday life. Socially useful work was divided into four sectors, economic production, transport and communication, cultural enlightenment, and health and hygiene; and it was the educator's duty to see that the children had experience of all four. The colony was noted specially for its agricultural bias. Before the industrial acceleration of the 1930's it provided a well-tested example of the way in which the work in rural schools could be effectively made to centre round the gardens, agricultural plots, and workshops.

- Social and community education. The colony was also noted for the quality and keenness of its musical and dramatic work. Shatsky and his wife were both talented artists and encouraged the development of this kind of cultural work in the colony and its associated villages. It had the effect of bringing groups intimately together to stage performances, and of drawing large audiences to see them throughout all the villages. This artistic work was one important way in which Shatsky tried to build common interests among the villages, and, at the same time, to raise the cultural level of life within them. An extensive program of political and agricultural education for adults was a further part of the colony's work, essential to his Pestalozzian effort to raise the level of rural life. Within each school he tried to build a sense of community that was based on mutual affection, a generally agreed upon organisation, and a sense of shared interest. Learning to live cheerfully in a community was a moral education. And, for Shatsky, moral development was the heart of the educational process. He encouraged self-government in his schools, the formation of clubs run by the pupils, and the development of Pioneer and Komsomol activities. The children learnt by actual practice how to run a community and govern themselves. They learnt discipline through taking part in the forming of public opinion in the community and accepting its judgment on their behaviour.

- The place of the individual. Shatsky's earliest work was decidedly child-centred. He could conceive of no aim for education except that of enabling children to live their own lives as fully and freely as possible. From this program would come, automatically, better citizens and an improved society. 'To live now, to live this very moment, to know how to live in accordance with the needs dictated by the present is the best method of preparing one's self through a number of imperceptible steps for that form of life activity that is peculiar to the nature of man.'[41] This was a call to the joyous life, and one that he tried to put into practice in his educational experiments. In the course of his work, in the early 1920's he proposed as an experiment that some of the school gardens, hitherto worked as a unit for the benefit of all, should be handed over for private use. Before long a sharp distinction developed in the quality of work done on the individual and the social plots, and pupils started to complain about the extra activities in the colony such as singing and art sessions that used up time they could spend on their own plots; tools were hidden and relations between members of the community deteriorated. The authority of the general meeting was weakened and life in the colony became so uncomfortable that the experiment was given up. Shatsky concluded that the colony should be collectively organised in such a way that individual initiative should not be paralysed. And his views on educational aims began to change. He suggested, in 1923, that they were dependent on the general spirit of the times and, after his admission to the communist party in 1925 and as he started to play a more important role in official circles, he came to be of the opinion that his work was to educate a 'soviet citizen whose task was the building of socialism'.[42] In this way he reconciled his interest in

---

[41] A.P. Pinkevitch, *op.cit.*, pp. 189-90.

[42] O. Anweiler, *op.cit.*, p. 324.

individual productiveness with his concern for the improvement of society through education.

- Experimental education. Shatsky was a skilled and practical innovator, whose work was firmly grounded on his observation of and practical experience with children. His ideas started to grow from the first moment when, in 1905, he and Zelenko founded their colony with very little idea of what they were trying to do apart from bringing pleasure into the lives of some children. They continued to develop for the next quarter of a century, as he observed the activities of his pupils, expanded his interests over all levels of education, and became involved with rural and industrial communities. He was first and foremost a practitioner. His strength lay, not in expounding theory, but in trying out ideas in practice. He did not have to argue elaborately for innovations; he could show them working in actual practice. He had the courage to experiment and he developed his experiments on an extraordinarily large scale. His experimental temper fitted the spirit of the 1920's admirably. By the time he died, however, in the mid-1930's the educational climate had changed. It is probable that, in an increasingly industrialised community, a different approach to the connection between productive work and education was required. Certainly, Shatsky's integrated program based on pupil activity gave way to a demand for a more thorough study of subjects, especially maths and science, that could provide the basis for the vocational and technological training that was currently being accelerated. His social and community education, though a step in the right direction, lacked the strenuous political orientation and the sharp bite of collective discipline that the mid-1930's favoured. In these matters Makarenko eclipsed him, and Shatsky's work largely dropped out of sight.[43]

PEDOLOGY

Allied with the development of experimental work in teaching was a movement for child study and experimental work in educational psychology, known as pedology. These activities were a continuation of the pre-revolutionary movement and were closely associated with the European and American child study and experimental education movements. In the 1920's, for example, the biological and experimental interests of Edouard Claparède, the work of Wilhelm Stern on the development of intelligence in young children, and E.L. Thorndike's behaviourist approach to learning were widely known, and their

principal writings were used as texts in teacher training courses. The Russian pedologists tended to be behaviourists, and to favour the design and use of tests and measurements that would make the study of children and the assessment of educational processes as scientific and objective as possible. The leading pedologist was Blonsky, the well-known author of *The Labour School* who wrote a work called *Pedology* in 1925. Blonsky was considerably influenced by Thorndike, discounted the influence of consciousness in human behaviour, and looked primarily for a biological basis for all individual and social action. Other pedologists were more interested in measuring environmental influences. At the first All-Union Congress on Pedology, held at the end of 1927, and attended by more than two thousand interested participants, Krupskaya spoke of pedology as the new science which attempted to study with exactitude the growth and behaviour of children. In other countries it would have been described as educational psychology with a functional and statistical approach.

The other important current in educational psychology was that of reflexology, notably in the form put forward by Pavlov. It was not easy, though some of the pedologists were also reflexologists, to apply to education the psychological findings of the Pavlovian school, especially as Pavlov showed little interest in human behaviour or the highest mental processes until almost the end of his career. In special schools for handicapped children, however, conditioning was used with some success as the basis for the formation of speech habits and elementary patterns of movement. The principal contribution that the reflexologists made to educational thinking was to demonstrate that deliberate training was important in modifying behaviour.

The tendency of most pedologists was, on the one hand, to dwell upon the limitations placed on education by hereditary factors, and, on the other, to try to assess the effect that environmental influences had on a child's progress in learning. In the many experimental stations in the U.S.S.R. during the 1920's a great amount of data was accumulated on these influences. They were also interested in acquiring information on children's motives and interests. In this they tended to study the nature of existing interests, rather than the way in which interests might be trained and modified. They were interested in reshaping society and held the opinion that the children's motives and personality would be conditioned by the material conditions of their existence. Environmentalism was an important feature of Marxist-Leninist thinking, and it was part of the pedological platform at the end of the 1920's. 'For us, there is no quarrel,' wrote one, 'over the existence of social differences in manifestations of intelligence ... since in every circumstance an

---

[43] He was not seriously reconsidered for another quarter of a century when, in the late 1950's and 1960's biographies and collections of his work began to appear.

associated reflex is formed under the influence of the stimuli of the environment.'[44] Through environmentalism of that kind it was possible to explain why, for example, children of the working class scored less highly on intelligence tests. Pinkevitch, a leading educator at the time, wrote: 'And let us say once more that the whole aim of education consists in the organization of the appropriate environment'.[45] The viewpoint tended, however, to overemphasise the automatic effect of environment, and to underplay the role that might be played by deliberate training and by conscious effort on the part of the learner. It meant also that when psychological tests were used as a basis for selection or advancement in school, civil service, military forces, or industry, they tended to favour individuals from the richer environments, and thus to contribute to the perpetuation of social inequality.

Pedology was at its most popular between 1928 and about 1932, but criticism began to mount in the early 1930's and came to a head in 1936. It was a part of the stabilising process that had been proceeding in the schools since the beginning of the first Five Year Plan, a process of disciplining that in the 1930's spread throughout all areas of soviet life.

On 4 July 1936 the Central Committee of the Communist Party issued a decree 'On the Pedological Deviations in the System of the Ministry of Education'. It made eight decisions on the matter, of which the following were the most significant:

- Teachers and the study of pedagogy are to be completely restored to their rightful place;

- Positions for pedologists in schools are to be abolished and all pedological textbooks to be removed;

- The study of pedology as an independent discipline is to be discontinued in Pedagogical Institutes and Technicums;

- All published works of modern pedology are to be publicly censured as false;

- Schools for atypical children are to be carefully examined and the majority of the children transferred to normal schools.

In the following year, as a consequence of that decree, the Ministry of Education for the RSFSR discontinued its model and experimental schools.

In a lengthy introduction to the decisions, the Central Committee explained its reasons for condemning pedology. Pedologists had become unduly powerful throughout the school system and tended to dominate all aspects of the teaching program. That situation was undesirable because their tests were based on the faulty premise that the behaviour of school pupils was determined by social and hereditary factors. The use of them, therefore, was more suited to the preservation of a capitalist class

society than to the development of a Soviet one. The pedologists, furthermore, by their deterministic attitude moved too many children into special schools and classes on the ground that they could not be effectively taught alongside normal children. Their basic fault, in effect, was that they did not pay enough attention to the importance of the teacher and of his deliberate efforts to educate, as a positive influence in moulding the life of school pupils. Henceforth, soviet educational theory was to emphasise that factor: the importance of deliberate teaching and training. Bauer has brought out the essence of the position very well: 'a"three-factor theory", the determination of the child's personality by inheritance, environment, and *training*, was introduced.'[46]

Henceforth psychological tests were banished from the schoolroom, the teacher regained a dominance in the classroom that he had not enjoyed since pre-revolutionary times, and educational psychology had to shift its grounds into what was to turn out to be a positive and important contribution to the understanding of child development.

At the very time that pedology was at its height and heading for its fall, the foundations were being laid for a more lasting approach to educational psychology which would synthesise ideas from several of the conflicting schools of thought. It leaned less on objective measurement and more on intensive observation and analysis; and in studying the learning process it took due account of the influence of nature and the environment, but also underlined the place of teaching and co-operation in the development of intelligence.

The new approach was the work of Vygotsky and his associates.

VYGOTSKY (1896-1934), AND EDUCATIONAL PSYCHOLOGY

Vygotsky was born in 1896 and was a student at the University of Moscow during the 1917 Revolution. He acquired a wide knowledge of literature, social science, philosophy, and the arts, and in 1924 turned his attention

[44] R.A. Bauer, *The New Man in Soviet Psychology*, Harvard University Press, Cambridge, 1959, p. 84.

[45] A.P. Pinkevitch, *The New Education in the Soviet Republic*, p. 70. A.P. Pinkevitch (1884-1939) began his career as a geologist and in 1909 moved into teaching. He became principal of a progressive secondary school for boys in St Petersburg, and, after the revolution, head of the Hertzen Pedagogical Institute. In 1924 he was made rector of the Second Moscow University and director of the Research Institute of Scientific Pedagogy. He wrote many books and articles on education, notably *Pedagogy*, (2 vols), of which vol. 2 was *The Labour School* (1924-5). Two works have appeared in English, a translation of his lectures on education, *The New Education in the Soviet Republic* (1929) and *Science and Education in the U.S.S.R.* (1935). He lost favour after the Communist Party's decree on pedology in 1936.

[46] R.A. Bauer, *The New Man In Soviet Psychology*, p. 126; for the decree, see O. Anweiler & K. Meyer (edd.), *op.cit.*, pp. 227-31.

to psychology. Ten years later, in 1934, he died of tuberculosis, at the age of thirty-eight.

He had an intimate knowledge of the ideas and activities of his leading European contemporaries, Stern, Claparède, Piaget, the Gestaltists, and the members of the Würzburg school. He was well acquainted also with the work of the American pragmatists, with Thorndike, and with Watson and the behaviourist school. In his interests and in his approach he comes closest to Piaget. He was principally concerned with the psychology of language, with the processes involved with language learning, with problems such as aphasia, and, above all, with the relationship of the

development of language to the development of intelligence. In 1938 a collection of his articles and essays were put together and published under the title *Thought and Language*. This work, paralleling, supplementing, and contradicting the work of Piaget, summed up the contribution of Vygotsky and his collaborators. It plotted the course of intellectual development in young children, relating it to the development of language and the roles played by teaching and by consciousness. Vygotsky's work was kept alive and extended by associates such as Luria and Leontiev, and, since 1950, in association with a revived interest in Pavlov, has been of central importance to Russian psychologists and educators.

(i) Mental Development and Learning

In studying the relationship between mental development and learning in children, Vygotsky suggested that there were three current theories of importance. The first, whose chief exponent was Piaget, held that development and learning were independent of each other, that development was essentially a matter of maturation, and that learning activities had to wait until the child had matured sufficiently to be ready for them. Learning therefore always lagged behind development. The second approach identified learning with mental development, and was associated with the work of James, Thorndike, and the contemporary Russian school of reflexology. Intellectual development was simply an accumulation of habits or of conditioned reflexes, and learning was the same thing. The third theory, characteristic of the Gestalt school, regarded intellectual development as a combination of maturation and learning. Both maturation and learning were independent processes, and it was their interaction that produced mental development. Vygotsky saw points of interest in each of the three theories but agreed completely with none of them. His own position was an interactionist one like that of the Gestaltists, but he placed more importance on the role of learning, especially on structured learning that comes through effective teaching. Learning must be in harmony with the level of development, but it also in some measure leads development. The central thought here is that human effort to learn and master is the most important feature of man's progressive development.

(ii) Zone of Potential Development

Vygotsky strikingly illustrated his point of view by introducing the idea of the zone of potential development. He suggested that it is possible to determine two levels of a child's development. The first is the actual development which may be measured by specific accomplishments; it is, for example, the level of development which is measured by intelligence

Lev Semenovich Vygotsky (1896-1934), became a leading and original researcher in developmental and educational psychology during the 1920's and 30's.

tests and by a variety of achievement tests. Suppose, however, that there are two children with a tested mental age of seven. If they are each given problems harder than they can manage on their own and provided with some slight assistance, such as a leading question or a pertinent demonstration, it may be found that one child can solve problems designed for nine year-olds, and the other cannot go beyond seven and a half years. 'The discrepancy,' wrote Vygotsky, 'between a child's actual mental age and the level he reaches in solving problems with assistance indicates the zone of his proximal (potential) development.'[47] In the example, the zone is two years for the first child and six months for the second. The two children have obviously two different levels of mental development. The child with the larger zone of potential development is likely to do much better in school, and this measure of potential development is a much more helpful indication of the extent and direction of his possible future progress than are the tests of independent achievement. 'What the child can do today with adult help,' wrote Vygotsky, 'he will be able to do independently tomorrow. The zone of potential development enables us, therefore, to determine the child's next steps...'[48]

Good teaching takes advantage of the zone of potential development. Makarenko would have said it makes use of perspectives. It does not base itself on development already achieved but on possibilities for the future. 'Therefore the only good kind of instruction,' wrote Vygotsky, 'is that which marches ahead of development and leads it; it must be aimed not so much at the ripe as at the ripening functions.'[49] The basis of good teaching is a knowledge of the child's present readiness for instruction, a recognition of the most appropriate next steps to be taken, and a systematic approach to the development of his potential.

(iii)   Systematic and Conscious Learning

Systematic learning comes from adequate motivation, and a consciousness of the meaning of what is being learnt. Consciousness is an awareness of the activity of the mind. To be fully aware implies a perception of the meaning of an activity; this suggests a degree of generalisation and some awareness of the process of what we are doing. We must abstract aspects of our thought and synthesise them so that they appear to us as a generalisation that conveys to us the meaning of our activity. The generalisation may be a very simple one, such as a single noun or verb, or it may be a more complicated mathematical formula or scientific law. Whatever its degree of complexity, it is evidence of the consciousness of our learning. Generalisation, in turn, implies the existence of concepts of various levels and degrees of generality, and the

possibility of developing a system of relationships between them. Conscious thought thus tends towards systematisation, and is in turn facilitated by exposure to systematically arranged and presented material.

Teaching at school is an important agent in the development of systematic thought. It should contribute to the process of generalisation and help to make the child conscious of his own mental processes. It is through systematic thought that an individual acquires mastery over his mental activities. Good teaching is characterised by methods which promote the learning and practising of the processes of intellectual mastery. 'Consciousness and deliberate mastery,' according to Vygotsky, are the 'principal contribution of the school years'.[50]

(iv)   Language and Thought

In the development of systematic thinking language plays an important part. Intelligence and language follow separate but related paths in their development. In the speech development of children there is an early pre-intellectual stage, and, similarly, in their thought development, a pre-linguistic stage. Up to a certain stage speech and thought follow different lines which subsequently meet at a point where thought becomes verbal and speech rational. The junction of thought and speech is the initiation of a new form of behaviour. It is the point at which, in Stern's words, the child 'makes the greatest discovery of his life', that 'each thing has its name'.[51] This is the 'crucial instant,' wrote Vygotsky, 'when speech begins to serve intellect'.[52] Despite dramatic descriptions of the occurrence, Vygotsky suggests that the junction of thought and speech is not necessarily sudden and that the discovery of the relationship may be a gradual one. Whatever the circumstances, it brings about an important change in the child's general mental development. Speech begins slowly to turn inward and to serve as verbal thought. It passes through three stages: from external speech, to egocentric speech in which the child in talking aloud to himself helps himself in understanding and directing his activities, and finally, to inner speech into which egocentric speech has faded as the child begins to think words instead of vocalising them. Thus,

[47]   L.S. Vygotsky, *Thought and Language*, trans. E. Hanfmann & G. Vakar, Massachusetts Institute of Technology, 1962, p. 103.

[48]   L.S. Vygotsky, 'Learning and Mental Development at School Age' (1934), in B. & S. Simon (edd.), *Educational Psychology in the U.S.S.R.*, Routledge and Kegan Paul, London, 1963, p. 30.

[49]   L.S. Vygotsky, *Thought and Language*, p. 104.

[50]   L.S. Vygotsky, *Thought and Language*, p. 102.

[51]   Quoted in L.S. Vygotsky, *Thought and Language*, p. 43, from W. Stern, *Psychologie der Frühen Kindheit*, Quelle and Meyer, Leipzig, 1914, p. 108.

[52]   L.S. Vygotsky, *Thought and Language*, p. 43.

'the speech structures mastered by the child become the basic structures of his thinking'.[53] The conjunction of language and thought in this way means that the child's intellectual growth is dependent on his mastery of language. The content and process of thought come to have an intimate association with the meanings, the relationships between meanings, and the structure through which they are expressed, in the language of human communication. Now, since language is thoroughly saturated with social experience and shaped by it, thought too cannot avoid being fundamentally affected by social factors.

In studying the higher nervous processes, Pavlov had come to see language as a second signal system distinctively human and social. Vygotsky, in developing Pavlov's ideas, saw signification, i.e. the creation and use of signs, as a characteristic feature, too, of intelligent human behaviour. Behaviour, initially built up by an interrelated mass of conditioned reflexes, becomes subjected to a new regulatory principle, signification — a mental tool developed in the course of an individual's social life. It extends and directs mental activity and makes it possible for man to control and reshape his environment.

The late 1920's and the early 1930's were a critical period for soviet psychology and education. The 'battle for consciousness' was in progress, the problem of building new men and new minds was becoming more acute, and the demands of the Five Year Plan emphasised the need to produce active men capable of mastering and reconstructing their environment. Vygotsky rose to the challenge of his times. His demonstration that conscious thought is the prerequisite to the mastery of intellectual activities, his indication that through language, a human-made tool, intellectual growth can be actively expanded and controlled, and, above all, his affirmation of teaching as a decisive motive force in intellectual development, was a distinct stimulus to his fellow-workers in education and psychology. From that time on, his influence and his views have been of great importance in deciding the lines of psychological thought and research in the U.S.S.R.[54]

STABILISING THE SCHOOL

After almost ten years of experimentation, impeded by civil disturbance and economic difficulty, it was becoming apparent that the Russian educational system was not achieving some of the basic objectives of all educational systems. Lenin had said, in his address to the Komsomol Congress of 1920, that a good communist had to be a well-educated person. By the mid-1920's there was beginning to be some doubt as to whether the educational system was producing well-educated persons. In 1926 the RSFSR Ministry of Education voiced the opinion that: 'Our schools are not catering for the most elementary needs. There is not

enough emphasis on reading, writing, and reckoning. The pupils are not getting a solid knowledge of natural science, geography, history and mathematics. All the schools, including those at the highest level, suffer from these deficiencies... The great mass of Russian working men are grievously feeling the effects of the fact that the schools are lagging in their task.'[55]

In 1927 an attempt was made to stabilise the work of the Unified Labour School by pooling the experience of a large number of teachers and schools in a substantial and authoritative revision of the 'complex' program. The new statement emphasised careful planning by the teacher, clarity in deciding on the subject-matter to be taught, and adherence to a properly balanced timetable, and it listed the minimum standards to be reached in basic knowledge and skills. It was an attempt to put together and systematise the experience gained in the previous years of experiment, and it was meant to bring order, substance, and security into the work of the teacher. At the same time, traditional subjects were to be taught along with the 'complex' program. They had been reintroduced in some measure in 1924, and, since then, had increased in their share of the school timetable, especially in the middle and secondary grades. Lunacharsky, in 1926, was even moved to remark that the majority of teachers mostly taught by the old pattern of separate subjects, using the 'complex' method only as a veneer.

Criticism, however, for their lack of thoroughness in the teaching of fundamentals continued to be levelled at the schools. A change of attitude began to take effect about 1929, the year described by Stalin as the year of decisive change and the first year of the first Five Year Plan which got under way in October 1928. In 1929 Lunacharsky was dismissed as head of the Ministry of Education for the RSFSR. He was replaced by Bubnov who had been head of political affairs in the Red Army.[56] This move was indicative of the changing educational climate. Henceforth there was to be a closer association of education with the economic requirements of society as indicated in the successive Five Year Plans, and there was to be a much more traditional and disciplined approach to education in the general conduct of schools, in curricula, and in methods of teaching.

---

[53] *ibid.*, p. 51.

[54] A.N. Leontiev and A.R. Luria, "The Psychological Ideas of L.S. Vygotskii" in B.B. Wolman, *Historical Roots of Contemporary Psychology*, Harper and Row, New York, 1968, p. 367.

[55] Quoted in L. Volpicelli, *op.cit.*, p. 89.

[56] The succession of Commissars of Education in the R.S.F.S.R. up to World War II was: Lunacharsky, 1917-1929; Bubnov, 1929-1937; Turkin, 1937-1939; Potemkin 1939-1946.

    A.S. Bubnov (1883-1940) became a revolutionary in 1900, and was an enthusiastic supporter of Lenin. He was a member of the first Politburo in 1917, took an active part in the civil war before becoming political head of the Red Army, and was the editor of *The History of the Civil War in the U.S.S.R.* In his nine years as Commissar for Education he effectively closed off the experimental period and helped to restore traditional methods.

EDUCATION AND THE FIVE YEAR PLANS

The Five Year Plan was a kind of 'operation bootstrap'. It was an effort to break loose from western capitalism by means of a vast industrial and agricultural revolution that had no precedent in history. Its aim was a massive multiplication of heavy industry, a rationalisation and relocation of industrial centres, and the mechanisation of agriculture. It involved both incredible hardship and prodigious achievement in the course of which agriculture was collectivized, large numbers of peasants were expropriated, populations were moved from one centre to another, consumer goods were restricted to mere survival level, and a three-year famine crippled the nation. Many industrial targets were nevertheless fulfilled and a substantial start made on the industrialisation of the country. At a time when the Great Depression hit the western countries, the U.S.S.R. too, suffered from its economic program; but mixed with the distress there was exhilaration, spurred by the sight of tangible achievements, and a determination to exert even greater effort in the subsequent Plan.

To carry through successfully the ten years of industrial expansion called for under the first and second Five Year Plans (1928-37) required unusual devotion to the interests of society, well-disciplined behaviour, and a strong measure of unified planning. These were the qualities that Bubnov sought to impart to the business of education.

For the first time in the history of education, national economic planning and the development of education were brought firmly together. Education was not merely to be concerned with the building of a new society, as it had felt itself to have been since 1917; it was also to be tied to the specific requirements of a specified new society designated by the state's Five Year Plans. This situation gave a new tone to all aspects of Soviet education.

In 1930 Stalin declared: 'The main thing now is to change over to compulsory elementary education. I say "main" because such a change would mean a decisive step in the cultural revolution. And it has long been high time to begin this because we have today all that is necessary to introduce universal elementary education in the vast majority of districts of the U.S.S.R.'[57] Accordingly, the party decreed that education should be compulsory for eight, nine and ten year olds beginning from the school year of 1930, that in 1931 full four-year elementary schooling should be compulsory everywhere, and that seven-year schooling should be enforced in large towns. These decisions had a dramatic effect on enrolments. The number of children in school in 1931 was double that of four years earlier, and between 1931 and 1933 the number of teacher training institutes and technicums also doubled. In 1935 Bubnov announced that four-year schooling was effectively in force, and that seven-year schooling was operating in the large towns; it became universal in 1943.

The party's next step was to look into the four- and seven-year schools, and to complete the stabilisation of them. Consequently, from 1931 to 1936, a thorough reorganisation was undertaken through five successive decrees of the Central Committee of the Communist Party, viz.

5 September 1931 : General reform of elementary and middle schools
25 August 1932 : Curriculum and discipline
16 May 1934 : General organisation of schools
3 September 1935 : Detailed reorganisation of schools
4 July 1936 : Pedology.[58]

The definitive decision of 5 September 1931 'On the Elementary and Middle School' set the tone for the subsequent development of education in the U.S.S.R.; it also marked the formal end of the experimental period in Soviet education. Polytechnical education was to continue but was to be subordinate to solid grounding in the traditional subjects. The experimental methods of teaching and of designing curricula developed in the 1920's were to be discontinued. The three central statements of the decision were:

- 'The instruction in schools does not provide a sufficient amount of general knowledge; and it meets inadequately the task of preparing for the Technicums and Higher Institutes well educated people properly grounded in the sciences (Physics, Chemistry, Mathematics, mother-tongue, Geography, etc.)';

- 'In the school programme a definite syllabus for the systematic study of the mother tongue, mathematics, physics, chemistry, geography, and history must be laid down';

- 'The Central Committee demands that all educational authorities place their work on a new basis which will be responsive to the growing requirements of socialist reconstruction.'[59]

The Central Committee thus asserted the need to raise the level of achievement in schools, especially in the pupils' grasp of systematically arranged knowledge. It therefore decreed an end to the project method,

---

[57] O. Anweiler & K. Meyer (edd.) *op.cit.*, p. 172.

[58] These decrees are reproduced in O. Anweiler and K. Meyer eds, *op.cit.* In I.L. Kandel, "The Educational Merry-go-round in Soviet Russia", *The Kadelphian Review*, 14, 4 May 1935, 327-34, there is an English translation of the decree of 25 August 1932, and others in M.J. Demiashkevich, *An Introduction to the Philosophy of Education.*

[59] O. Anweiler & K. Meyer (edd.), *op.cit.*, pp. 178ff.

and, with it, all remnants of the 'complex' curriculum, and resolved to introduce, from the beginning of 1932, the standard subjects of the traditional curriculum. It recognised the importance of polytechnical instruction as an essential part of communist education through which pupils became acquainted with the main branches of production, and it requested the ministries of education to increase immediately the provision of workshops in schools, but it went on to emphasise that productive work in schools must be subordinated to the educational aim of the school.

Krupskaya stated her agreement with these decisions. She expressed the view that polytechnical education had not been a great success so far because of the inadequate preparation of teachers for its unusual demands, and she was confident that the decision was not a renunciation but the foundation of more effective polytechnisation in the future.[60] It was, however, the end of a train of thinking in the Lenin-Blonsky tradition. The great design of the new soviet education had been to produce a curriculum that would reflect the Marxist conviction of the prime importance of the productive forces in a society, a curriculum that would put productive work at its centre and provide opportunity for the pupils to study and experience various kinds of work and the social consequences of being brought up in a proletarian culture. It was to be the basic general education for all the primary and secondary level schools. It was a revolutionary approach to the curriculum; but practice was never able to match theory. The teachers and the curriculum planners were never able to develop clear, consistent, and intellectually demanding programs, nor were the administrators able to produce the equipment and enough trained teachers to put the new ideas effectively into practice. The decision of 1931 had the effect of making a distinction between general and polytechnical education that had not previously been intended, at least in the minds of the advocates of polytechnical education such as Krupskaya, Blonsky, Shatsky, and Lunacharsky. Henceforth polytechnical education ceased to be thought of as the central feature of the educational program. It was an addition to general education, and sometimes an addition even to vocational education. Three main types of education were henceforth offered in the schools: general, polytechnical, and vocational.

The subordination of labour education to general education was effected by a series of decisions made by the Ministry of Education in the RSFSR during the course of the 1930's. In 1931 it took measures to restore academic respectability to the subjects of general education. The workshops, however, and the courses associated with them lingered on for several years, but there were criticisms that their work was formalised, that it had not kept pace with the techniques of current industrial development, and that it took up time and energy better applied to the basic subjects. Eventually in several decrees in 1937 the Ministry ordered the abolition of the teaching of labour and manual work as independent subjects in elementary and middle schools, the closing of all school workshops, and the transfer, as far as feasible, of teachers of productive labour to the teaching of science and mathematics. A decree of 1936

N.K. Krupskaya (1869-1939), wife of Lenin and a leading educator in the U.S.S.R.

---

[60] O. Anweiler & K. Meyer (edd.), *op.cit.*, article by Krupskaya, November 1932, pp. 199-201.

required rural schools to transfer most of their holdings to state and collective farms.

A polytechnical approach, however, was encouraged and could be maintained in the science subjects. It was a matter of familiarising pupils with the materials and processes used in industry, and of linking the work in science, as often as was reasonably possible, with the economic, industrial, and agricultural growth of the nation.

Back to solid foundations, and service to society by meeting the demands of the Five Year Plans, were the two principal policies henceforward for the schools.

The primary and secondary school should not become an appendage to a factory; it should be stabilised in its traditional role of teaching the basic subjects, and effectively providing the mathematical and scientific foundations for later vocational education.[61] A succession of decrees throughout the 1930's stabilised the school firmly around the orthodox threesome of class teaching, prescribed textbooks, and formal examinations.

In 1932 a beginning was made with the publication of new programs of work. The Central Committee of the party set out in a decision of 25 August 1932 the main lines of development, emphasising, in particular, the special importance of the study of science and mathematics. Soviet educators had always thought it important to study science and to develop a scientific attitude in their pupils, but science had not been dominant in their scheme of things. The decisions of the early 1930's, in the mental environment of the Five Year Plan, brought science and mathematics into a place of prominence that they have ever since retained. There was no attempt to give to them an undue share of the school timetable — it was kept judiciously balanced — but henceforth the first care of schools was that the science program should be good, the thoughts and ambitions of pupils were turned towards achievement in the sciences, and the concern of educational authorities or party committees was to see that teaching in science did not flag. The school programs provided a common syllabus of work throughout the Soviet Union, replaced projects by formal subjects, and restricted polytechnical activities. Standard textbooks were written in all subjects and published in great quantities.

The central administrative machinery was streamlined, and the Scientific Council of Education (GUS) which had been founded in 1919, which Krupskaya, Blonsky, Shatsky and Pistrak had faithfully served, and which had had a powerful voice in the design of curricula and in the statement of general educational principles, was abolished in 1932.

On 16 May 1934 a definitive decree, the most significant since 1923, was signed by the Central Committee of the party and the Council of People's Commissars. It established a school structure that with little change was to last to the present time. Henceforth there were to be three types of general schools: four-year elementary school (Classes I - IV); seven-year middle school (Classes I - VII); and ten-year secondary school (Classes I - X).

In the following year, on 3 September 1935, by a decision of the same bodies, the internal functioning of the schools was reorganised, confirming in some instances reforms that had already taken place. A common school year for the Soviet Union was established, together with a common curriculum and timetable. A common system of promotion from class to class was set up; examinations were formalised, and the pre-1917 style of five-point assessment was re-introduced, viz.: 1, very poor; 2, poor; 3, average; 4, good; 5, excellent. The powers of pupil self-government were reduced, and in particular, the role of the Komsomols was diluted and they were bidden to concentrate their attention on learning their schoolwork. The teachers' disciplinary powers were, in consequence, strengthened, and the school classroom became much more teacher-centred and tractable. By 1936 the pupils were to be in uniform.

The new school tone was also highly patriotic. As in Western Europe and the Far East, the 1930's was a time of increasing national fervour, so too in the Soviet Union the building of 'socialism in one country' became a source of great national pride. In its earliest years the country had had to withstand a serious invasion by outside forces, and the sense of threat remained in the minds of many people, to be intensified by the build-up of Nazi German power, militantly anti-communist, in the 1930's. This situation strengthened the patriotic feelings that already had been stimulated by the collective discipline imposed by the requirements of the Five Year Plans, and the enthusiasm generated by successful achievement. In the schools, the new patriotism was most clearly evidenced by a change of policy in the teaching of history. Throughout the 1920's the approach to history had accorded closely with the attitude of the country's leading historian, M.N. Pokrovsky,[62] a Bolshevik who became deputy commissar of education in the RSFSR in 1918. History was written in impersonal Marxist terms, the centre of the stage was occupied by the Bolshevist Party, and all Russian history before 1917 tended to be regarded as a period of unrelieved oppression lightened occasionally by the exploits of revolutionaries. As a separate subject in schools it even ceased to exist between 1929 and 1935, becoming a part of a wider study of society. Pokrovsky died in 1932, and in 1934 a special commission was appointed to prepare new history textbooks and to establish a new approach to the subject which would give identity and colour to the national past, and

---

[61]   O. Anweiler, *Geschichte der Schule und Pädogogik in Russland vom Ende des Zarenreiches bis zum Beginn der Stalin-Ära*, pp. 428ff. has an excellent discussion of the trend of this period.

[62]   M.N. Pokrovsky (1868-1932) joined the Bolshevik party in 1904. In 1918 he became chairman of the Moscow Soviet and deputy Commissar for Education. In 1920 he wrote the first Marxist history textbook for schools, and during the 1920's completed several more well-known school textbooks.

would engage the pupils' interest in historical personages and significant events. In the textbooks that followed this recasting of ideas, there was an encouragement to the pupils to take a pride in their Motherland, to be interested in the persons and contributions of all who, in the past, had helped to build Russian culture and Russian power, and to pay attention to the heroes of the Bolshevik Revolution, noting especially the achievements of Lenin and Stalin. The new style was exemplified in 1938 by the *History of the Communist Party of the Soviet Union (Bolsheviks), Short Course*, edited by a commission of the Central Committee of the party, and described in its introduction as 'the study of the heroic history of the Bolshevik Party'.

The disciplinary and patriotic tendencies were sharpened in the course of World War II, named the Great Patriotic War.

VOCATIONAL EDUCATION

Associated with polytechnical education but distinct from it was vocational education. In the very earliest days of the Soviets, many educators thought that the polytechnical education of the Unified Labour School could take care of the lower levels of vocational education, and, in consequence, existing vocational schools were discontinued and no new ones were established until 1921. On the other hand, there was a school of thought which held that vocational preparation was the real core of education, and that general education should grow out of it. This viewpoint had an opportunity to show its worth in the Ukraine where vocational schools replaced schools of general education after the level of the seven-year school. They persisted, apparently to good effect, until the general reorganisation throughout the U.S.S.R. in 1931-4.

In 1920 vocational education became compulsory for all workers between the ages of eighteen and forty in the RSFSR, and in 1921 a concerted effort was made to establish effective vocational education.

By the beginning of the first Five Year Plan, the following pattern of full-time vocational education had developed:

- Lower level training for skilled workmen — Vocational Schools: These were created in 1926. Entry to them followed four years of Unified Labour School. The vocational school offered a four-year course with a strong practical bias and some continuation of general and polytechnical education.
- Middle level training for technicians — Technicums: Entry followed normally seven years, but sometimes four years, in the early period, of the Unified Labour School. The technicums offered a three-four year course, and usually specialised in one field of

training. Vocational training was supplemented by courses in science and in general and polytechnical education.

- Higher level training for professionals — Higher technical institutes and universities: Entry followed completion of the nine years Unified Labour School, or a course at a technicum. After the Revolution many universities were discontinued; those which survived acquired a strong vocational bias or were deliberately converted into professional training schools similar to higher technical institutes offering four-five year courses in the area of their speciality with a strong theoretical content and a reasonable breadth in the sciences.

Beyond these levels, training in post-graduate scientific and technological research was made available in Higher Scientific Research Institutes.

Vocational education was a corollary to the literacy campaign. In building the new society, technical literacy was as important as verbal literacy, and the vocational campaign similarly absorbed a great deal of national attention and interest. The need for trained workmen was great in the initial stages of reconstruction and throughout the period of the New Economic Policy; it became clamant once the first Five Year Plan got under way, and remained urgent as industrialisation proceeded in the 1930's through the second and third plans.

The strongest and clearest statement of the basic need for vocational training came from Stalin, first in 1928 when he announced to the Komsomols: 'We must create at a greater rate new cadres of specialists from men of the working class, from communists, and from Komsomols'; and again in 1935 when he tellingly declared: 'You must understand that in our present circumstances "cadres decide everything".' Trained manpower obviously came from technical training institutions; hence in the 1930's there was a great strengthening of vocational education at all levels. The need was felt to be so pressing that for two years 1931-2 the upper grades (eighth and ninth), of the Labour School which since 1924 had had about a quarter of their time given over to vocational training, were turned over almost completely from general to vocational education only to revert once more, in the ensuing reorganisation, to general education when the value of the study of mathematics and science was realised as a basis for sound vocational training in the technicums and higher institutes.

There were two features in the development of vocational education that were worthy of particular note.

- It was a two-pronged campaign. On the one side there was a systematic build up of pre-job training institutions, viz. vocational schools, technicums, and higher institutes; and on the other, there was concerted and widespread action to improve the qualifications of workers on the job. 'Both industrially and educationally,' an observer wrote in 1931, 'Soviet Russia's policy is a gigantic exercise according to Samuel Butler's principle: "Learn by doing". The population are being pitchforked into new factories and institutes and being made to get on as best they can.'[63] To assist with the process of practical training, at both the lower and middle levels, there was extensive provision for the training of those who were already at work.

In 1921 the first of the factory schools for working youths that were to become the principal means of part-time vocational preparation at the lowest technical level was established. By 1930 they were catering for more than half a million pupils. Entry was available on completion of the four-year elementary school, and the course consisted of two to four years of half-time work and half-time general school-work at the factory. In 1933 when it was possible to demand higher entrance qualifications, and it was urgent to produce trained workmen speedily, their program was drastically changed. They took only pupils who had completed the seven-year school, and gave them a six-month or one-year highly specialised and practical course. In the course of time a number of similar schools developed for adult workers who wished to raise the level of their qualifications. These were further supplemented by the development of numerous short courses in factories and institutes, and by a great range of correspondence courses that have remained an important characteristic of Soviet education.

Part-time evening courses in technicums for second level training also became popular. It was possible through these courses to qualify for admission to higher technical institutes. Various measures were adopted to assist deserving students to attend the higher levels of vocational training. For example, in 1918 entrance examinations and fees for universities were abolished. Student numbers immediately increased, but many students were too ill-prepared to manage university-level courses. To cope with this situation a new institution, the Rabfak, came into being towards the end of 1919. The Rabfaks were schools of secondary level associated with and preparatory to many universities and higher technical institutes for workers and peasants, usually between the ages of eighteen and thirty, whose education had been neglected and who aspired to higher education. The course lasted three years and was a streamlined general and political curriculum designed to bring the students up to university entrance level. By the beginning of the first Five Year Plan in 1929, there were 164 Rabfaks with fifty-three thousand students.

- The key institution in the whole pattern of vocational education was the technicum. The schools were taken over from the pre-revolutionary period and reorganised in 1923; by 1930 they were training about a quarter of a million students, and, by 1950, nearly two million. In 1932, at the time of the general schools reorganisation, the importance of the technicums was reaffirmed, and their curricula revised. They thus remained a constant, sturdy institution throughout the 1920's and 1930's, and have continued on in the same basic pattern to the present time. Their growth has been steady and vigorous, and they have adapted themselves to the economic and educational needs of the U.S.S.R. and the developments of modern technology from time to time in a workmanlike and unspectacular way. They covered a wide range of occupations throughout industry, agriculture, and commerce, and they trained primary school and kindergarten teachers and many of the persons needed for the lower levels of the public service. The technicums were 'the most important of the Russian schools'[64] in the sense that they were the pivot of the vocational system; they were the backbone of the soviet work force, and they, more than any other single type of institution, provided the solid educational basis on which the U.S.S.R. entered and flourished in the world of modern science and technology.

During the course of the second Five Year Plan the numbers of students in the factory schools and technicums dropped considerably, e.g. in factory schools, from 975,000 in 1931-2 to two hundred thousand in 1938-9.[65] On the other hand, the number of pupils in the ten-year school increased, as did also the numbers attempting professional courses in the higher technical institutes. There was some anxiety that too many professionals and not enough lower level technicians were being trained, and it appeared that in many cases highly trained persons had to leave their profession to obtain employment.

In 1940, therefore, the next logical step in educational-economic planning was taken by setting up a system of labour reserves by which trained labour could be directed to appropriate work and required to remain for a statutory period in the allotted job.

[63] J.G. Crowther, *Industry and Education in Soviet Russia*, Heinemann, London, 1932, p. 6.

[64] L. Volpicelli, *op.cit.*, p. 72.

[65] *ibid.*, p. 189.

EDUCATION FOR LEADERSHIP

The aim of the Soviet government has been to transform socially, politically, and economically a vast country of many cultures, industrially and agriculturally retarded, into an advanced, integrated economy, communist in mind and spirit. To do this it has felt it necessary to develop a select group, members of the Communist Party and young aspirants for membership, who should have power and responsibility as the vanguard of the Revolution, who should lead, control, and educate the mass of the people, and who should themselves, as far as possible, excel in political understanding, in disciplined behaviour, and in devotion to work.

Two principal means were adopted to produce this vanguard. A sequence of courses was set up outside the ordinary school system to provide more adequate political education for potential recruits and members of the Communist Party. Secondly, an extensive program was developed for the training of children and youth, under the close sponsorship of the Communist Party, in youth organisations in which there would be opportunity to gain experience in leadership and to acquire a grounding in political and social doctrine.

(i) Party Schools

Four levels of political courses were gradually developed by the mid-1920's and provided effective service for approximately the next twenty years.

In factories, political teachers could approach the workmen through clubs, canteens, and special centres; in villages, reading-rooms were set up for discussions, lectures, and the distribution of literature. Often these centres were supervised by members of the youth organisations who thereby gained some active experience in political leadership.

Promising adults and youths, candidates for party membership and those in need of political education, attended schools of political grammar. An extensive network of these schools was set up to provide the elements of Communist theory and policy through short courses of a few weeks or months, run usually in the evenings or by correspondence.

A more extensive and demanding program was offered in the graded Soviet Party schools. These schools had two stages. The lower Party School prepared leaders for posts in the small administrative divisions of the Soviet Union, the higher ones for work in places of greater responsibility such as in urban areas. Political education in the lower school carried on from the political grammar schools; the higher school presupposed both a substantial theoretical grounding and successful experience in responsible political work. The object of the Party Schools was to train political leaders to become skilled in discussion, knowledgeable in doctrine, and capable in organisation. The courses were usually of two years' full-time, systematic work in Marxist-Leninist theory, current social, political and economic policy, and supervised practical work.

Above the Party Schools were the Communist Universities of which the largest and most important was the Sverdlov Communist University established in Moscow by Lenin in 1918. The Communist University of the National Minorities of the West founded in 1921, and the Communist University of Sun Yat Sen for students from east Asia soon followed. By the mid-1930's there were seventy-nine Communist Universities with an enrolment of approximately forty thousand students. The usual course was a three-year full-time program of advanced work in Marxist-Leninist theory and history, a selection of social sciences, and practical administrative and political work.

During the 1930's, as the need for trained technologists became more pressing, a number of these universities were converted into higher technical institutes for training specialists in various branches of agriculture and industry. This, in effect, indicated a new dimension in leadership training. Twenty years after the Revolution, with a stabilised school system and a flourishing youth movement, it was possible to leave much of the political instruction to the established agencies such as the schools and youth groups, and to concentrate on developing leaders of intellectual and technological excellence whose political sophistication could be assumed, or could be thought to require, at most, only a small supplementation. Henceforth as universities and higher institutes expanded in the 1930's and in the post-World War II period, the path to leadership lay through the normal institutions of tertiary education. Leadership came to mean not merely expertise in political theory and practice and a devoted effort to the cause of the Revolution, but the possession of scientific knowledge and technical skill coupled with adequate political understanding. There still remained, however, a place for those with a special knowledge of party policy and theory, and for those who could apply this knowledge to understanding and teaching the social sciences. In 1946, accordingly, the system of Party Schools was reorganised to provide for the training of such people, and to channel into the Academy of the Social Sciences the most promising students, from whom would come leading theoreticians and teachers of the social sciences in higher institutions.

(ii) Youth Organisations

Lenin wrote in 1908: 'We are the party of the future, and the future belongs to youth.'[66] In 1918 the Communist League of Youth, called Komsomol for short, was founded, and was to become a powerful organ

[66] R.T. Fisher, *Pattern for Soviet Youth*, Columbia University Press, New York, 1959, p. 1.

A laboratory lesson of a Rabfak (Workers' School) in the 1920's in the U.S.S.R.

New Era, vol. i, no. 33, January 1928, p. 30.

of the party. Its function was to act as a training and recruiting ground for the communist party, and to join with the party in its various campaigns and tasks, especially where they concerned youth and education. 'Youth, as the most active and revolutionary part of the working class,' the first program of the Komsomol stated, 'moves in the front ranks of the proletarian revolution'.[67]

The Komsomol League accepted members between the ages of fourteen and twenty-three,[68] and became the spokesman, organiser, and leader of youth. In the early years of its existence, potentially rival youth organisations were eliminated and the Komsomols were left as the only substantial, organised group. Tasks to be undertaken by youth, such as that of sharing in the literacy campaign, were channelled through the Komsomol League, which took over the direction of youth activities. Through the structure of the organisation, culminating in a powerful central executive committee, young leaders for youth in the new society were educated for their responsibilities, under the tutelage of the party. While the Komsomols were learners, however, they were also teachers. It

was their duty, by the example of their behaviour, by discussion, and by other deliberate means, to teach the youth of Russia to understand the political philosophy, to adopt consciously the stern discipline, and to practise the collective loyalty through which the new society was to be forged. In respect to society in general the league was an activator, working on behalf of the party, to stimulate political consciousness and economic progress throughout the Soviet Union.

To strengthen its work with youth and particularly with the schools, it founded a junior youth organisation, the Young Pioneers, in 1922, for children between the ages of ten to sixteen. In the following year this was supplemented by the Little Octobrists for younger children of primary school grade, from about seven to eleven years of age. The Little Octobrists were distinguished by wearing a red star on the chest; the Young Pioneers wore a red scarf and were proud of their motto 'Always

[67] *ibid.*, p. 17.

[68] In 1936 the age limits became 15-26, and were subsequently changed to 14-26 in 1942, and 14-28 in 1954.

'Full steam ahead, Pioneers!'

ready', similar to the 'Be prepared' of the Boy Scouts whom they superseded in the U.S.S.R. The three groups interlocked in age range and in leadership. Komsomols led the detachments into which the Pioneers were organised, and Pioneers were made responsible for the Octobrists; at the top of the pyramid a number of Komsomols were members of the communist party and some were persons of importance in it and in political life in general. In 1937, for example, the general secretary of the Komsomol League, Kosarev, was elected to the Presidium of the Supreme Soviet. The connection with the party was always a tight one and party officials from the beginning exercised a close control over the activities of the youth groups. Some leading party members such as Krupskaya and Lunacharsky took a keen interest in all that concerned the Komsomols, Pioneers, and Octobrists, and made a point of attending the Komsomol general congresses that were held annually up to 1922, then every two years until 1928, and irregularly after that. Some of the most important statements on educational policy and purposes were made in speeches to these congresses, notably by Lenin in 1920, Krupskaya in 1926, Stalin in 1928, and Bubnov in 1936.

In her 1926 address Krupskaya undertook to define 'the principles on which work among Young Pioneers should be based'. These were four lines: 'developing comradely solidarity, a social approach to each and every question, ability to work collectively and co-operatively, ability to acquire knowledge'.[69] This was a social, political, and pedagogical process. The Young Pioneer, accordingly, through his organisation, enjoyed a range of social and recreational experiences in Pioneer palaces and camps that strengthened his collective behaviour, learnt to become the younger political limb of the Communist Party through classes in communist history and theory and through active participation in socially useful work, and was expected to show a devotion to work in school in accordance with Lenin's exhortation in 1920 to the youth of Russia to learn, learn, learn.

The political aspirations, comradely spirit, social responsibility, and eagerness for learning that were cultivated among the Pioneers were well brought out in their five basic laws printed in the 1925 edition of *A Guide for Young Pioneers*: 1. The Pioneer is true to the cause of the working class and to the precepts of Lenin. 2. The Pioneer is the younger brother and helper of the Komsomol and Communist. 3. The Pioneer is a comrade to Pioneers and to the workers' and peasants' children of the world. 4. The Pioneer organises other children and joins with them in their life. The Pioneer is an example to all children. 5. The Pioneer strives for knowledge. Knowledge and skill are power in the struggle for the workers' cause.

The Pioneers and Octobrists grew in numbers to a joint total of about one million in 1925, three million by 1930, and thirteen million by 1940. The Komsomol League grew rapidly from its inception in 1918, was checked for a while in 1921-22 as morale sagged with disappointment at the introduction of the New Economic Policy, and then once more increased rapidly to a membership of one and a half million (about six per cent of the age group) by 1925, three million by 1930, and ten million by 1940. In 1926 the name was changed to the All-Union Leninist Communist League of Youth.

In 1922 a Komsomol publishing house was established to take care of the periodicals that were already being issued by the league. It became one of the largest publishers in the U.S.S.R. producing editions, in millions of copies, of books and pamphlets to cater for the interest of young people to further the political and economic causes of the league. In 1925 *Komsomolskaya Pravda* was founded. It was a daily newspaper that eventually developed a very wide circulation and became an authoritative voice for Russian youth and a general newspaper of considerable reputation.

---

[69] N.K. Krupskaya, *On Education*, Foreign Language Publishing House, Moscow, 1957, p. 117.

The Komsomol contribution to the social and economic reconstruction of the country was a significant one. Komsomols provided leadership, usually effective but not always popular, in modernising and collectivising agriculture, and in improving the health and living conditions of the peasantry. They began, in 1922, a system of patronage, first with the Red Fleet whose loyalty and vitality had suffered through the Kronstadt uprising of 1921, and later with the Red Cossacks and Red Air Force and other bodies. The object was to brace flagging morale, or to spur on new enterprises by serving in an exemplary way, for example in the Red Fleet, by attending to the welfare of the families involved, and by improving the political and general education of the men and women working or serving in the institution. In the case of the navy, a recruiting drive was so successful that in 1924 it was reported that forty per cent of the entire personnel of the navy were Komsomols, and in 1928 a submarine was financed and built out of contributions by Komsomols and Pioneers.

On the industrial front, the contribution by the youth organisations became most apparent from 1928 on, with the beginning of the Five Year Plans. The league sent out shock groups to stimulate production where it was unsatisfactory, or to help with special jobs that needed quick completion. The first such group was formed in 1926 at the Red Triangle factory in Leningrad; with the development of the Five Year Plan they became a common practice. As the country moved out of the NEP into the first Five Year Plan a great spirit of optimism, eagerness, and determination was aroused. With the Komsomol this often reached heroic proportions and was given a military flavour as their shock troops attacked their objectives, and stormed their way through to success. One of their principal methods was that of mobilising their members, sometimes in hundreds of thousands, for special projects. For instance, the Komsomols made a large contribution to the building of Magnitogorsk and the Dnieper dam, and in 1932 undertook successfully the construction of a new industrial city, Komsomolsk on the Amur, in the Far East. The Pioneers, too, were not behindhand. In a delightful and inspirational book written for twelve to fourteen year old children, Ilin described the Five Year Plan, and the part the Pioneers were playing in it. 'Every one of you', he wrote, 'can be a builder of the Five Year Plan.

'The Pioneers of the Lisvensky factory constructed a water and a windmill and started a dynamo.

'On the Briansk road sixteen kilometers from Moscow in the village of Peredelkino, the Pioneers of the Khamovnichesky region electrified their camp. They dammed a small river, set up a water wheel, attached to it a small dynamo from a cinema apparatus...

'The youngsters of Ribinsk while studying their own region found deposits of lime which is entirely suited for use as fertilizer.'

The author went on to suggest ways in which children could contribute:

'You thus see how children can help achieve the Five Year Plan. Fulfil your own little plan and then the big plan will be fulfilled before the assigned time ...
Here it is — Your Five Year Plan:

1. To discover beds of lime and phosphorus.
2. To gather useful junk: rags, ropes, wool, bones, scraps of metal, and so on. All these things will come in handy in our factories. Every Pioneer should collect not less than twenty kilograms a year.
3. To build radios and loud-speakers...'

The author lists twelve ways in which Pioneers can contribute to the country's growth in industry, agriculture, and health.[70]

The greatest and the continuing contribution of the youth organisations was in the field of education. Soon after their foundation in 1921 the factory schools came under the sponsorship of the Komsomols who encouraged attendance at them, and set up a teacher training centre for them in Moscow. They were specially active in the illiteracy campaign, both in eliminating illiteracy from their own ranks, and in mobilising a large force to liquidate it from the whole country.[71]

During the course of the 1920's the league became convinced that if Komsomols were to be leaders of youth they would have to be well-educated. This was the theme of Lenin's address to them in 1920, and it was reiterated by Stalin in 1928 on the eve of launching the new economic expansion.

'The working class,' Stalin told the Komsomol Congress: 'cannot become the real rulers of the country unless it extricates itself from educational indifference, unless it creates its own intelligentsia, unless it masters science, unless it can direct the economy on a scientific basis...

To construct, you must know something, you must master science. But to know something, you must learn — learn persistently and patiently, learn from everyone, from both enemies and friends, especially from enemies. You must learn, clenching your teeth without being afraid that the enemies will laugh at us, at our ignorance, at our backwardness. Before us stands a fortress. Its name is science with its many branches. We

---

[70]   M. Ilin, *New Russia's Primer: The Story of the Five Year Plan,* trans. G. Counts and Nucia P. Lodge, Houghton Mifflin, Boston, 1931, pp. 159-62.

[71]   See above, p. 198.

must take this fortress at any cost. Youth must take this fortress if it is to be the builder of the new life, if it really wishes to take the place of the old guard...

   We now need whole groups, hundreds and thousands of new cadres of bolsheviks who are masters of the various branches of knowledge.
   To master science, to forge new cadres of bolshevist specialists in all branches of knowledge, to learn, to learn, persistently — that is now the task.
   A mass campaign by revolutionary youth for the conquest of science — that comrades, is what we now need.'[72]

The league hoped to produce the new intelligentsia within its own ranks. To do so both Komsomols and Pioneers had to give special attention to political education and to general education in school. Special circles and study groups were established through which the members could learn the fundamental ideas of Marx, Engels, Lenin, and Stalin, and the history of the Communist Party, and could study current events and conditions.

   In school they were expected to play leading roles in the government and organisation of the institution, and they were expected to set an example by their discipline and their devotion to their studies. The demand, however, sometimes proved to be too much. Komsomols had to be reminded that every one of them should complete a secondary education; and that to do this they needed to concentrate on their school-work. In 1932 the party warned that the overloading of Pioneers with politico-social tasks should be carefully guarded against. And in the school reforms carried through at that time the organisational efforts of the pupils were restricted in the interests of greater application to their studies. Nevertheless, the youth organisations continued to play a significant part in the discipline and government of the schools, and came to be regarded as sources of responsible activity and centres of youth leadership in the national effort throughout the 1930's to reach educational and economic respectability.

SUMMARY

In summing up his account of education in the first fifteen years of Soviet education, Anweiler called it a classical example of a period of revolutionary transition begun by a radical break with the past, and ended by a resumption of the tradition in a changed form.[73]
   Rejection of the conservative tradition and experimentation with the new characterised the first ten years of the period. There was, however, a

continuity with the pre-revolutionary period; it was a continuity of thought and practice with the progressive educators and experimental psychologists of the time, many of whom, such as Blonsky, Shatsky, Pistrak, and Pinkevitch, became influential under the new dispensation. Contact was maintained also with progressive educators in Western Europe and America through books, correspondence, and frequent visits. The great importance of Russian education in the 1920's was precisely that it was a vast experiment, trying out progressive methods and programs on a larger scale than anywhere else at any previous time in the history of education. The principal interest lay in developing integrated curricula, accenting productive work, co-operation, and scientific knowledge, in developing a new morality and discipline through collective self-government in the schools, and in developing political consciousness. Hence the appearance of the labour school, polytechnical education, the complex and project methods, the Dalton Plan, schemes of pupil self-government, and the youth organisations. At the same time the tasks of coping with illiteracy and producing skilled industrial workers were undertaken. This program lasted throughout the period of War Communism (1918-21) and the New Economic Policy (1921-27).

   With the beginning of the first Five Year Plan and throughout the 1930's a new set of circumstances came into being to change the pattern of education. The plan itself was the most important new factor. For the first time in educational history, education was made a part of a systematic economic plan of development. In the plan economic progress was paramount, and education became its servant. In the course of the ensuing industrial and agricultural growth, urbanisation was rapidly intensified, the school population greatly increased, and the demand for trained factory workers pressed more than ever. Educational experimenta-tion ceased to be the fashion, flexibility declined, and conformity grew. The new mood suited the political situation. Stalin had come to power and throughout the 1930's was consolidating his position by establishing a new orthodoxy intolerant of opposition and deviation.

   The 1930's, therefore, saw a stabilising of the school very much along conventional lines. There was a rejection of the experimental period but there was also some measure of continuity with it. Radical curriculum reforms were abolished, innovations in educational psychology were discontinued, and student influence in school government curtailed. But the earlier interest in science and in technical training, the all-age comprehensive nature of the ten-year school, the emphasis on collective behaviour, and the training for political leadership through the youth

[72] O. Anweiler & K. Meyer (edd.), op.cit., pp. 160-1.

[73] O. Anweiler, op.cit., p. 453.

leagues were retained. For the attempt of the educators of the 1920's to unite Marxism with progressive education was substituted a close party supervision which paid attention to both educational theory and practice. Party concern was primarily with economic development and political orthodoxy, and its care for the schools reflected this interest.

On 2 October 1940, Kalinin, speaking on the twentieth anniversary of Lenin's celebrated speech to the Young Communist League, summed up the task of communist education at the end of the inter-war period on the eve of the U.S.S.R.'s involvement in World War II. The young generation who were summoned by Lenin to build the new society had become the established citizens 'playing an active part in the work of socialist construction'.[74]

'At bottom,' according to Kalinin, 'the tasks of communist education set by Lenin twenty years ago' remained the same and retained their urgency.[75] Fundamentally the aim was to help produce a politically conscious nation cresting forward on a ground swell of proletarian culture to the realisation of a full and collective life. To achieve this aim, five matters were of particular importance:

- Education must help in the struggle toward a high level of labour productivity, both by providing appropriate training and by instilling an abiding consciousness of the importance of hard work of a high quality;[76]
- Pupils must learn to place public interest above private interests, and to cherish and safeguard public property and the society's resources;
- Patriotism, a pride in the accomplishments of the Russian past and the Soviet future, must be cultivated as an inspiration to the working classes 'who are transforming the world along new lines';[77]
- Education should seek to ensure the introduction of collective behaviour into every aspect of work and everyday life;
- And, finally, education should aim to raise the general level of culture throughout the U.S.S.R. so that it may keep pace with and provide adequate backing for the country's economic and technological development.

Education, in effect, was the handmaiden of 'the great proletarian revolution [which] not only effected tremendous destruction, but also laid the basis for creative work on an unparalleled scale.'[78]

In the twenty years following the Revolution, the Soviet Union had conducted a great educational experiment, the enthusiasm of which it had eventually tempered. It had succeeded in providing mass education for both the illiterate adults and the children of primary school age and was well on the way to establishing effective secondary and higher education. It had yoked education to the demands of the Five Year Plans and produced a mass of trained manpower; and it had enthused the rising generation with the thought of the new collective society and the importance of education and disciplined work in achieving it.

To an observer in the 1930's 'the entire country seemed to be a vast school'.[79] Throughout the 1930's there was an unprecedented hunger after knowledge, as teachers taught pupils, pupils taught parents, Komsomols taught Pioneers, Pioneers and Komsomols taught villagers and workmen, authors taught readers, artists taught viewers, and the party set the pedagogical pattern. The U.S.S.R. was an immense, disciplined, didactic society. It was a country also in a state of war, literally because of the extraordinary measures taken against the threat of both internal and external enemies, but figuratively, too, in its concerted fight for education and economic progress.

The climate of struggle, of disciplined aspiration, and of collective effort, suited the Ukrainian educator, A.S. Makarenko, who throughout the 1920's and early 1930's painstakingly wrought out in practice the educational ideas that his writings were to make widely known in the mid-1930's. He expressed admirably the mood of the disciplined but optimistic collective round which educational ideas were henceforth to crystallise.

[74] M.I. Kalinin. *On Communist Education*, Foreign Language Publishing House, Moscow, 1950, 'On Communist Education', Speech at a Meeting of Leading Party Workers of the City of Moscow, 2 October 1940, p. 125.

M.I. Kalinin (1875-1946), a leading Bolshevik revolutionary, became a member of the Central Committee of the Communist Party and of the Politburo. From 1938 to 1946 he was chairman of the Supreme Soviet of the U.S.S.R. He had an abiding interest in education, and became one of the most well-known and influential speakers on a variety of educational questions.

[75] *ibid.*, p. 133.

[76] *ibid.*, p. 139, '... we have not yet caught up with the highest productivity of labour in Europe, let alone America. This means that we have to make a greater effort to increase labour productivity ... But, comrades, by higher productivity of labour we mean not only the quantity but also the quality of the output.'

[77] *ibid.*, p. 153.

[78] *ibid.*, p. 151.

[79] K. Mehnert, *Youth in Soviet Russia*, trans. M. Davidson, Allen and Unwin, London, 1933, p. 25.

CHAPTER 8

MAKARENKO AND EDUCATION FOR A COLLECTIVE SOCIETY

A.S. Makarenko (1888-1939), an influential teacher and advocate of education for a collective society in the U.S.S.R.

SUMMARY

Life of Makarenko

    (i)   Early Career
    (ii)   Director of Colonies
    (iii)   Literary Career

Makarenko's Character and Vision

The Aim of Education

The Collective

Makarenko's Socialist Humanism

Moral Education

Productive Work

The Growth of Makarenko's Influence

The early years of the Soviet Revolution in Russia were years of great excitement. Physically, existence was precarious and full of tension; intellectually many were buoyed up with the hope of building a new co-operative society, and with the possibility of providing new creative opportunities for the human mind. The poet Mayakovsky in the dark year before the Revolution prophesied the coming of 'the man of freedom', and twenty-two years later Makarenko reaffirmed this faith from his experience of two decades of optimistic but painful human engineering in the education of neglected children: 'We are living on the summit of the greatest pass in history, our day has seen the beginning of a new order in human relations, a new morality, a new law, the foundation of which is the victorious idea of human solidarity.'[1]

How to provide an education to match the changed mood and circumstances, and how, through it, to rear new men for the new collective society was the problem that excited the imagination of many educators in the 1920's. For one of them, A.S. Makarenko, it was an unremitting concern.

Makarenko's work is important for four reasons. First, he succeeded in providing for the many outcast and neglected children, with whose education he was concerned in the 1920's and 1930's, a highly satisfactory program of education which led to the rehabilitation of several thousands of them and was used effectively in institutions other than his own. Secondly, in the course of building new social attitudes into his outcasts, he developed educational ideas and methods admirably fitted for the new soviet society. In practice and in theory he demonstrated how to educate the collective man. This was Makarenko's foremost interest. It was an original and substantial contribution to communist education, and it has proved to be the most distinctive contribution made by communist education. Thirdly, not only did he produce an education fitted for a collective society, he also met the needs of the new society in further important ways by indicating the need to plan a new secular morality and new life style, and by demonstrating the appropriate educational process.

---

[1] Vladimir Mayakovsky, 'War and the World', 1916; A.S. Makarenko, *A Book for Parents*, trans. R. Daglish, Foreign Language Publishing House, Moscow, n.d., p. 407.

He thus provided for soviet life an educational basis tailored to the new circumstances — a rationale, an aim, and a set of procedures that were recognisably associated with the needs and aspirations of the growing soviet state.

Makarenko was a practical educator who prided himself on working out his educational science not by abstract thought but in the actual educational arena, 'in the vital actions of people within a real collective'.[2] An important part of his appeal, nevertheless, was his unflagging idealism — his vision of the untold possibilities of the great soviet collective, and of the life of achievement and well-being that was to come through struggle, hard work, and enlightened education. This inspirational quality of his work is the fourth source of his importance. His work, as it was described and analysed in his writings, was a successful combination of commonsense, practical ability, and deep sensitivity, in the service of an ideal optimistically and hard-headedly pursued. It is this compelling mixture of vision and practicality that has appealed to his many readers, and has cemented his influence on soviet education.

LIFE OF MAKARENKO

(i) Early Career

Anton Simeonovitch Makarenko was born in a village in the Ukraine near Kharkov in 1888. His father was a painter at the railway workshops and the family moved with the workshops to Kremenchug in 1900 where the young Makarenko attended a four-year school. This was followed by a one-year teacher training course, and, at the age of sixteen, in 1905, he started teaching in a school at Kryukov, near Kremenchug. There he remained until 1911. In his first teaching year he witnessed the 1905 Revolution; the young man sympathised with the revolutionary cause, and started to read Marxist literature. In the subsequent years of reaction he became attracted to the works of Gorki in which he saw and admired 'the unusual urge for life, the inexhaustible optimism, the belief in mankind, and the unshakable confidence in a bright future'.[3] From 1911 to 1914 he taught primary school children at Dolinskaya, a village near the mouth of the Dnieper. There he started to experiment with ways of organising a school collective, and introduced a variety of out-of-school activities for his pupils. In 1914, at the age of twenty-six, he entered the Poltava Teachers' Institute, graduating three years later in 1917 with a gold medal and a reputation as an outstanding student and a first-rate teacher of history and Russian. For the next two years he was back again at Kryukov in charge of the elementary school. Soon after his arrival at the Kryukov school, the November Revolution took place. It was for him

an exhilarating time: 'After the Revolution,' he later wrote, 'great prospects opened out before me. We teachers were dazzled by their scope.'[4] Within his school he extended his experimental activities, foreshadowing several of his later extra-curricular practices. In 1919 he was transferred to the directorship of an elementary school in Poltava where he became interested in developing agricultural work along with the school-work and in organising his school into working detachments with various semi-military insignia and ceremonials.

(ii) Director of Colonies

In 1920 he was invited to open a colony for neglected children at a deserted farm-school six kilometres out of Poltava on the Kharkov road. Henceforth his teaching career was to be spent in institutions of that kind.

Makarenko's task was to re-educate the *bezprizornye*. These were homeless children abandoned or orphaned in the disturbed conditions of World War I, the ensuing Civil War (1918-21), and the famine of 1921-22, children whom 'the whirlwind of war has scattered throughout the land'.[5] Many were delinquents; others, waifs and homeless strays. All were in desperate need of care and education. In the 1920's they were a serious social problem in the U.S.S.R., and especially in the Ukraine. Estimates of their numbers varied, during the 1920's, from two to seven million, and they remained a substantial problem until well into the 1930's. They roamed the countryside, living by begging, theft, violence, and prostitution. Filthy and poorly clothed, they lived in cellars, hayricks, and on the roofs and in the goods wagons of trains. In age they might be anything from eight to eighteen. For the most part amoral, illiterate, and irresponsible, they were swept up from time to time into homes and colonies for delinquents whose directors were often unable to control them or even keep them on the premises.

To provide a viable colony was no easy task. Makarenko did more; he developed an institution which became an example not only for work with delinquent children, but for education in general.

The start was unpromising. The site was poor, the buildings dilapidated, the equipment minimal, and the winter early and severe. Makarenko began with three members of staff and six seventeen to

[2] A.S. Makarenko, *Learning to Live*, trans. R. Parker, Foreign Language Publishing House, Moscow, 1953, p. 198.

[3] A.S. Makarenko, *Werke*, Volk und Wissen, Berlin, 1963, 7, pp. 312-3.

[4] Y.N. Medinsky *et al.*, *Makarenko, His Life and Work*, trans. B. Isaacs, Foreign Language Publishing House, Moscow, p. 11.

[5] M. Gorki, *Across the Soviet Union*, 1928, reproduced in Y.N. Medinsky *et al.*, *op.cit.*, p. 52.

eighteen year old delinquents. The armies of Wrangel and the Poles were not far off, and law and order was precarious. For some time Makarenko's charges were unresponsive, spending their time in criminal activities in Poltava or on the Kharkov road, until, losing patience, Makarenko indignantly struck one who had insulted him. Zadorov, the boy struck, was physically much larger than Makarenko and could have retaliated with greater force. He and his comrades, however, were impressed by the 'punch in the jaw' as evidence of Makarenko's intense feeling of concern for them. The incident marked a turning point in their relations, and henceforth it was possible for Makarenko and his staff to get some measure of co-operation from their charges. Having established a serious emotional contact, Makarenko then set about building it into a co-operative relationship that would in time become a genuine collective spirit.

The Gorki Colony.

Photograph by A.S. Makarenko in his book *The Road to Life*, Foreign Languages Publishing House, Moscow, 1951.

The significance of his work at this Gorky colony, which he named in honour of his literary hero, lies mostly in a study of the way in which he built the colony into a collective.

Having got the colonists' attention and interest, he gradually built up a series of shared responsibilities and adventures that would be undertaken by all members of this collective colony and not just by one individual. When one of them, Taranets, for example, went fishing with some stolen nets, brought his catch back, and cooked and presented a fish to him, Makarenko would have nothing to do with it. He explained that it was not his; and that it should have been given to the whole collective; Taranets had used the collectives' oil, he had used the collectives' fuel, and he was showing an undesirably individualistic spirit in acting in that way. The colonists were given the responsibility by the local authorities for policing the neighbouring forest and stopping the illegal felling of

pine trees. They had to join together into an adventurous and joyful posse to guard the road as they moved backwards and forwards along the six kilometres to Poltava. In this way, by sharing in significant work and finding enjoyment in their achievements, they gradually built up a sense of collectivity amongst themselves.

The next step was to get them to share in the judgments they made of one another, especially when they met with delinquency within the colony. When one of them, Burun, stole from the housekeeper, his action was considered by all the colonists and the punishment was meted out by them. The colony thus began to feel itself responsible for looking after and judging its own behaviour.

Gradually the colonists built up their own executive and legislative machinery. Makarenko in summarising the development of the colony in 1925 described how the first step was taken: 'At the end of 1921, the colony had no firewood, and the children had no footwear to go into the forest to fetch wood. We had to do something exceptional to combat the cold. For this purpose we detached ten of the thirty pupils who were then in the colony. They were given all the footwear the colony had, and ordered to get us 1,000 poods of wood a week. The oldest of these lads was Kalabalin. The group did the job brilliantly. I don't know how it came about, but in the colony the group came to be known as "Kalabalin's detachment".'[6] Soon the whole colony was divided into permanent detachments, each having its own appointed commander and numbering between seven and fifteen children. Membership of detachments was based on the kind of work done by each colonist, e.g. all who worked in the piggery would be in one detachment, and similarly those in the forge, the vegetable garden, and the carpentry shop. The detachment usually covered the full age range of the colony, had its own dormitory area, and was responsible not only for the work production of its members but also for their general conduct. It was a contact or primary collective, a basic and vital cell within the colony. Each developed its own characteristics, and newcomers were carefully allotted to a detachment according to their needs and the strengths and weaknesses of the detachment. Some detachments proved to be remarkably enduring. Makarenko records that one lasted seven or eight years with only three changes in the membership of twelve.[7] Often, for special tasks, mixed detachments of varying size were formed of colonists chosen from various detachments, and were placed under the control of a boy or girl who was not a permanent commander. In this way opportunity was given for a wider number to experience the responsibility of command, and for the commanders from time to time to be subordinates.

[6]   A.S. Makarenko, *Werke*, 1, 762.
[7]   A.S. Makarenko, *Werke*, 5, 268; Y.N. Medinsky *et al.*, *op.cit.*, p. 247.

The permanent commanders met together with the director, Makarenko, to form a powerful executive-legislative body known as the commanders' council responsible for the day-to-day running of the colony. In turn it reported its conduct to the general assembly of all the colonists which became the principal organ of self-government in the colony. The general assembly made the fundamental policy decisions. For example, when it was suggested in 1926 that the colony might move to Kuriajh near Kharkov and take over the premises and inmates of another colony in a state of decay, it was not the director who made the decision. The colonists themselves sent their representatives to look over the situation and then the general assembly collectively considered the prospect and made the decision to move.

At the same time as they developed those procedures, they strengthened their *esprit de corps* by building up a series of traditions and routines, many of them with a military flavour such as bugle-calls, marching to a brass band, and saluting.

Having built up a collective spirit within the colony, they proceeded to associate it with active communist organisations outside the colony so as to become an integral part of the greater soviet collective of the U.S.S.R. Makarenko became a member of the Poltava town soviet in his first year at the Gorky Colony, and the colonists developed close relationships with a nearby village soviet, with the Komsomol organisation, and with the local Cheka.

Throughout the whole of their activity and basic to it, there was a program of disciplined productive work and formal school education related closely to the general conduct and aspirations of the community in a way in which Lunacharsky had spoken of it in 1918. They had their farming, dressmaking, blacksmithing, carpentry, and eventually, some light industrial work through which they gained a sense of worthwhile productive achievement. In all their tasks they were made conscious of an objective to be reached, and, if possible, exceeded. They developed a sense of constant progression, of building, of moving onwards and upwards. 'A standstill,' wrote Makarenko, 'can never be allowed in the life of a collective.'[8]

Thus, from working and judging and deciding together, and from sharing common traditions and routines and aspirations, and from linking their work and their perspectives with those of social groups who were similarly-minded, they forged a collective.

Makarenko grew with his collective. 'What has the colony given to you?' a friend asked him in 1923. And he replied, 'It has given me more than you could dream of. I have acquired a precise line, an iron will, steadfastness, boldness, and, finally, self-confidence.' His self-confidence came from his growing conviction that he was doing something of educational significance, something of a wider significance than merely educating delinquent children. Already the colony had been recognised as a training school for students, and his work was discussed in the press. He saw himself engaged in an important educational experiment which would contribute something fundamental to the development of communist education.[9] At a later stage he still maintained the validity of his early judgment when he declared, 'I'm profoundly convinced that here, in the colony, we have real Soviet pedagogics.'[10]

In 1923 the Gorky Colony moved a short distance away to more spacious farming quarters at Trepke on the banks of the Kolomak River where it grew into a thriving community during the next three years. In 1926 the colony, 120 strong, moved once more, this time to Kuriajh, the site of a former monastery, eight kilometres from Kharkov, to take over an existing, unsuccessful colony of some 280 children that occupied the site. It was a critical trial of the strength of the Gorky collective. They decided to explode upon the old colony and take it by storm. After careful reconnaissance by an advance party, the whole Gorky Colony made an impressive entry, announced a plan of work, and speedily incorporated the Kuriajhites into joint reconstructed detachments. By insisting on collective work and discipline they succeeded in transforming the establishment within the space of a few months into an efficient continuation of the Gorky colony.

The colony's methods and conduct, however, did not meet at all times with the approval of the local educational authorities. Makarenko found himself in dispute with the educational administrators at the ministry, chiefly on the matter of the discipline and routines that had developed in the Gorky Colony. In 1927 the security police, the Cheka, built a new and substantial colony on the outskirts of Kharkov, named it in honour of their first head, Dzerzhinsky, and invited Makarenko to help run it. Some of his Gorky colonists transferred across to start it, and in 1928, when his disagreement with the central administration reached its climax, Makarenko took the opportunity to move also to a full-time directorship of the new venture. He remained at Dzerzhinsky until 1935. His new establishment soon became self-supporting. It established and ran two thriving factories for the making of electric drills and FED cameras, and developed from a small collective of boys and girls up to the age of fifteen-sixteen into a substantial show place of about five hundred children and youths up to the age of twenty with a sizeable Komsomol organisation and a large staff of teachers and technicians for the factories. The communards, as the boys and girls were called, worked four hours a day in school, and

8 A.S. Makarenko, *The Road to Life*, trans. I. and T. Litvinov, Foreign Language Publishing House, Moscow, n.d., 2, p. 277.

9 A.S. Makarenko, *Werke*, 'Brief an A.P. Sugak', 7, pp. 479-80.

10 A.S. Makarenko, *Road to Life*, 2, p. 224.

Gorki Colony: a detachment in the Gorki Colony about to set out for the fields.

Photograph by A.S. Makarenko in his book *The Road to Life*, Foreign Languages Publishing House, Moscow, 1951.

four hours in the factories, and many of them qualified for further academic education and higher technical training.

During the sixteen years that Makarenko directed his colonies he was responsible for some three thousand pupils. His parting advice to the leavers of 1935 summed up his attitude to his work:

> 'Today you go off into life, seventy of the best communards. You are Komsomols, trained and educated men...
>
> 'Bear in mind always that only iron discipline, the complete unity of our life, our efforts and exertions can lead to victory. I hope you will always realize that self-interest, egoism, stupid thinking, beliefs based on ignorance, and disregard for the interests of the collective are opposed to the policy of our Party.
>
> 'Your road must always be a straight road, and your life will then be fine and useful. Above all, in every move you make, be a citizen of our great homeland! Stride ever forward with our Party, and be, at all times, loyal, sincere, and ardent Bolsheviks.'[11]

Makarenko's pupils moved into every field of life. Some became airmen, engineers, and doctors; many served with distinction in World War II. A substantial number entered the teaching profession; some of these became university professors, others found their vocation in continuing Makarenko's work in the youth colonies. Wherever they were, 'they are all people of the collective',[12] and they retained a profound affection for Makarenko and a respect for his work. When, in 1939, a literary reviewer wrote that Makarenko's account of the Dzerzhinsky colony in *Learning to Live* was only 'a sentimental and syrupy fiction', a group of them indignantly replied that 'Makarenko has not only accurately depicted the colony but, inspired by the Party and as a true pupil of Lenin, he has also created it. We are the fortunate pupils of this collective.'[13]

(iii) Literary Career

In 1935 Makarenko left Dzerzhinsky for Kiev to become assistant director of children's labour colonies in the Ukrainian Ministry of Education, and for several months in 1936 he ran a colony at Brovary near Kiev. Early in

[11] A.S. Makarenko, *Werke*, 2, pp. 458-9.

[12] Y.N. Medinsky *et al.*, *Makarenko, His Life and Work*, 'The Life Patterns of Makarenko's Pupils' by Faina Vigdorova, p. 151.

[13] A.S. Makarenko, *Werke*, 3, pp. 488ff.

1937 he went into semi-retirement in Moscow. There he concentrated on writing, and lecturing, and for the next two years he produced a great many educational essays, social and political studies, and literary sketches, and completed some of his most important books. He died in 1939 at the age of fifty-one.[14]

He carried into the literary career of his final years the same dedication that marked his educational practice. His work was a part of the social realist movement in the literature of the 1930's, and he thought of writing as another aspect of the forming of the collective society. Stalin's definition of social realism fitted his views precisely. 'Socialist Realism, being the basic method of Soviet artistic literature and literary criticism, demands of the artist a truthful, historically specific depiction of reality in its revolutionary development. Moreover, truthfulness and historical specificity in the depiction of reality must be combined with the task of ideologically remaking and educating the toilers in the spirit of socialism.'[15] Makarenko in all his literary and educational work was engaged in ideological reconstruction and committed to the task of building the new socialist man. He was characteristic of the dedicated intelligentsia that the change in educational climate, begun by the first Five Year Plan, nurtured throughout the 1930's. In acknowledging the award to him of the Order of the Red Banner of Labour, he wrote in 1939, 'The work of the writer is by no means a tranquil occupation, and its field of occupation is the whole front of the socialist offensive.'[16]

MAKARENKO'S CHARACTER AND VISION

Makarenko was a man of many parts and of one transcendent conviction. He was a talented writer, was interested in a wide range of literature, could act effectively in drama, and turn his mind to the details of a factory machine or the development of a vegetable garden. Every one of these activities, various as they were, he managed constantly to relate to the development of the new soviet society. The central theme of his life was the building of a collective society. It gave purpose to everything he did, and it was the link between all his activities. He was an all-round-the-clock educator, conscious that, in school, factory, committee meeting, conversation, writing, and general behaviour, he was teaching, advocating, or exemplifying some aspect of collective behaviour. He had a passionate, integral, and visceral conviction of the desirability of a collective society. He was very aware of the twentieth century as a new dispensation in the history of mankind and of soviet society as the pioneer of a new way of life. He rejoiced to be part of this, and he gave his whole mind to the furthering of it. He was not fanatical or obsessed by his conviction; he was simply absorbed in his idea, and made it central in his life and educational work.

His dedication was reinforced by an abiding optimism, a necessary characteristic of great innovators or revolutionaries. He had a confident expectation that his vision would be fulfilled, and that he was not working in vain but that he was contributing in some measure to the realisation of the new world. To this he joined a great faith in the possibilities of human achievement, and tried constantly to build his faith into the constitution of his fellow-teachers and colonists. His perspective made him consistent in his thinking, and persistent in his actions. His stubborn endurance during the early years of the Gorky colony was remarkable; it involved considerable self-denial, constant devotion to work, and produced a disciplined, almost puritanical, outlook on life.

At the same time, he showed a remarkable empathy with his pupils. He entered with uninhibited enjoyment into their games, he understood the nuances of their individual behaviour, and he treated them with sensitivity and a deep concern for their future development. While respecting his pupils as human beings of dignity and independent spirit, he made great demands on them as on himself, and his expectations were seldom disappointed. He aroused an abiding enthusiasm for his ideas in his pupils and staff, and they reciprocated his affection and comradeship. He was, like many good teachers, a little theatrical in the use of his voice and in the staging of some of his encounters with his pupils. Perhaps also a little pretentious in his semi-military dress, he was, nevertheless, clearly a man of deep conviction, sincerity, and genuine feeling for his pupils.

One of the chief inspirations of Makarenko's life was his association with the great writer, after whom he named his first colony, Maxim Gorky. As the revolutionary movement broke out, faltered, and grew

---

[14] The principal source of the history of the Gorky Colony is Makarenko's autobiographical novel, *The Road to Life*, the first volume of which was published in 1933. He described the work of the Dzerzhinsky commune in *Learning to Live* which he completed just before his death. His other major work was *A Book for Parents*, published in 1937, the first of a projected four volumes which he wrote jointly with his wife whom he had married when he was at Kuriajh in 1927. She was Galina S. Salko (1891-1962) who worked at Kuriajh, and, after Makarenko's death became the principal editor of his works. The most important of Makarenko's short pieces for understanding his work are: *Search for a Method for Work in a Labour Colony for Children*, which was a preliminary sketch made in 1932 for a book on educational method that he hoped eventually to write; *Method of Organizing the Educational Process*, a booklet published in 1936 which summarised his views on the structure of a collective in a children's colony; eight *Lectures on the Upbringing of Children* given on Moscow radio in 1937; *Problems of Soviet School Education* which were a distillation of his ideas and experience into a series of lectures given in 1938; a *Letter to the head of the Department of Social Education of the Ukrainian Ministry of Education* in 1928 defending the main lines of his educational credo; The Aim of Education, an article published in *Izvestia* in 1937; and two lectures, *My Experience* (1938) and his last public speech, *From My Own Practice* (1939).

[15] R.M. Hankin, 'Soviet literary controls', in E.J. Simmons (ed.), *Continuity and Change in Russian and Soviet Thought*, Cambridge, Massachusetts, 1955, p. 448.

[16] A.S. Makarenko, *Werke*, 7, p. 187.

again in the early years of Makarenko's teaching career from 1905 on, he found in Gorky's work compelling inspiration. He was moved by the stirring plea to 'Let the storm blow louder', and he saw in Gorky's work a genuine understanding of proletarian life and its aspirations. At his colonies in the 1920's, he encouraged his pupils to read especially *The Lower Depths* and *My Childhood*, hoping that the readers would get from them something of the optimism, determination, and faith in man's potential that he found characteristic and attractive in Gorky. Makarenko and the colonists kept up a correspondence with Gorky from 1925, and he gave Makarenko great reassurance and encouragement in his educational efforts. He visited the Gorky Colony at Kuriajh in 1928 and was impressed with its activities. He read *The Road to Life* in manuscript and stimulated Makarenko to further literary work, even, at one stage, offering him financial assistance. Gorky was the first person of importance to recognise the significance of Makarenko's work. He spoke of Makarenko as an educator of a new type, took a lively share in discussing his educational principles, and gave him his whole-hearted support.[17]

Makarenko did not succeed in writing a definitive treatise on the nature and methods of communist education as he had several times expressed the wish to do. He was not, in fact, a systematic thinker. He was a first-rate practitioner, he was a sensitive and skilful writer, and he was a spirited controversialist, but he was no educational philosopher. In several of his essays, however, he developed at some length various aspects of his ideas; in a number of speeches and memoranda he summarised his general principles; and at various places in his novels and articles he theorised for a page or two about aspects of his work that he regarded as important. From these indications, although there is no single comprehensive treatise, it is possible to get a reasonably clear picture of what he regarded as the main principles of his educational work.

THE AIM OF EDUCATION

Educators, according to Makarenko, must get their aims from a study of the needs of society. 'Wherefrom can the aims of education arise? From our social needs, of course...'[18] In the last speech of his career, in looking at the task of education, he declared, 'I consider education to be the expression of a teacher's political credo',[19] and a teacher in the U.S.S.R. should believe in the cause of the Bolshevik revolution and form part of the struggle to achieve a really collective society. The resources of education should be used in the campaign to create a new type of man in a new society.[20] The aim of his own educational work was 'not putting two or three hooligans or thieves straight but rearing a definite type of citizen'.[21]

Makarenko outlined the characteristics of the task and the new man as follows: 'We want to educate a cultured soviet worker. Consequently we must secure for him an education, preferably a secondary education; we must give him vocational education; we must teach him discipline; he must be developed politically, and become a devoted member of the working class, a Komsomol, and a Bolshevik. We must develop in him a sense of duty and an idea of honour; in other words, he must be made aware of his obligations to his class. He must know how to obey a comrade as well as give an order to a comrade. He must be capable of being polite, stern, kind, and relentless according to the conditions of his life and struggle. He must be an active organizer. He must be tenacious and steeled, he must be self-controlled and able to influence others; if the collective punishes him, he must respect both the collective and the punishment. He must be cheerful, confident, and disciplined, capable of fighting and building, and capable of living and loving life. He must be happy. And he should be such a person, not merely in the future, but also today, on every single day.'[22]

Education therefore must be intellectual, vocational, political, and moral; its product should be a politically knowledgeable, militant, and active person, with a firm communist outlook on life; in character he should be self-disciplined, well-balanced, purposeful, and forward looking, living a full and enjoyable life, morally bound to the purposes and conduct of the collective within which he lives and to which he contributes.

The aim of education is to give persons the kind of experience which will lead to the development of a collective society in which all persons will put their knowledge, skill, and character harmoniously, wholeheartedly, and purposefully at the service of the collective. 'We must send out from our schools energetic members of the socialist society ... Our pupil ... must always principally appear as a member of his collective, as a member of the society, one who is answerable not only for his own deeds but also for the acts of his comrades.'[23]

[17] A.S. Makarenko, *Werke*, 7, pp. 312-402, 542.

[18] A.S. Makarenko, *Problems of Soviet School Education*, trans. O. Sharke, Progress, Moscow, 1965, p. 32.

[19] A.S. Makarenko, From my own practice, Y.N. Medinsky *et al.*, *op.cit.*, p. 273.

[20] A.S. Makarenko, *Learning to Live*, p. 195

[21] A.S. Makarenko, *Problems of Soviet School Education*, p. 100.

[22] A.S. Makarenko, 'Educators shrug their shoulders', first published for the fifth anniversary of the Dzerzhinsky Commune in 1932, *Werke*, 2, pp. 439-40. The characteristics given in this passage are developed at greater length in *The Problems of Soviet School Education*, especially in the introductory section entitled 'Theses'.

[23] A.S. Makarenko, 'The Aim of Education', *Izvestia*, 28 August 1937; *Werke*, 5, p. 373.

THE COLLECTIVE

The key idea in Makarenko's life and educational work was that of the collective.[24]

'We must simply understand to the full,' he wrote, 'the place of the new man in the new society. Socialist society is founded on the principle of the collective. In it there can be no isolated individual, now standing out like a pimple, now crushed to dust in the street, but only a member of the socialist collective.

'In the Soviet Union no individual can live outside the collective, and there can be, therefore, no separate personal destiny, no personal course, and no personal happiness that is opposed to the destiny and happiness of the collective.'[25]

A collective should have the following characteristics:

• It should develop a common aim, not a chance combination of private aims that might be found among the passengers of a tram or in a theatre audience, but one worked out in common by the whole group and held securely by it.

• The common aim directs the common work of the collective. A distinctive characteristic of the collective is that its members work together on a common task useful to the collective, and that they work together, not necessarily or precisely on the same operation but on a task that is shared between them and is seen by them to depend for its success upon the efforts of all.

• Common work requires a common organisation. It is not just a matter of living together in neighbourly harmony; it is a complicated experience of purposeful activity which requires organs and methods through which the collective can consult together, share responsibility, reach mutual agreement, arrange the relationships of subordination and command, determine appropriate disciplinary measures, and regulate its connections with other collectives. Makarenko's *The Road to Life* described how it was effectually maintained, and sketched its impact on various members of the collective.

Makarenko seems to have favoured the development of a series of collectives of different sizes operating at different levels. The society in his colonies, which he regarded as a model, if not for society in general, at least for educational establishments, was a three-layered collective.

At the base were a series of primary collectives, called detachments, small in size, usually from seven to fifteen persons, so that close contact could be maintained among the members. They were based on productive work, i.e. the members in each one were engaged in the same kind of work, for example, as workers in the fitting shop, piggery, or foundry. Similarly the teachers, too, formed a collective. Care was taken to ensure that each primary collective had in it a range of age groups and of activists and non-activists.[26] It was 'a small Soviet cell faced with big social tasks'. It acted 'as the primary cell in social work and life'. Everyone, irrespective of his personal contribution, benefitted or suffered according to the performance of his detachment, and each individual was thought of primarily as a member of a detachment.[27] The primary collective and its purpose and activities must therefore be in harmony with those of the larger collective. In Makarenko's view, it should have a one-man management, a permanent leader who would be its spokesman, act on its behalf, and feel himself especially responsible for maintaining the highest tone within the primary collective.

At the second level came the large collective. 'Collective education cannot be achieved through primary (contact) collectives only, because the unity of such a collective, where children see each other all day long and live in friendly co-operation, engenders nepotism and leads to a type of education that cannot be called quite Soviet education. Only through a large collective, whose interests come not from simple association but from a more profound social synthesis can the transition be made to a broad political education where the word 'collective' means the whole Soviet society.'[8] The larger, central collective was, in Makarenko's experience, the whole colony whose numbers eventually grew to five hundred; for most children passing through the ordinary educational system, the central collective would be the school. The evolution of the collective at that level is the main concern of Makarenko's *The Road to Life*, and has been described above. It must have effective machinery for co-ordinating the views and activities of the primary collectives; in the case of the Gorky and Dzerzhinsky colonies this consisted of the day-to-day executive, the commanders' council, and the supreme policy-making body, the general assembly. Members of the collective took part in the discussions and in the making of decisions mainly but not

24 L. Froese, *Ideengeschichtliche Triebkräfte der Russischen und Sowjetischen Pädagogik*, Quelle and Meyer, Heidelberg, 1956, p. 182, refers to the idea of the collective as the *Angelpunkt* of his educational system.

25 A.S. Makarenko, 'The Aim of Education, *Werke*, 5, p. 370.

26 A.S. Makarenko, 'Method of Organizing the Educational Process', *Werke*, 5, pp. 13-16.

27 A.S. Makarenko, *Problems of Soviet School Education*, pp. 90ff., and 'My Experience' in Y.N. Medinsky et al, op.cit., pp. 246ff.

28 A.S. Makarenko, *Problems of Soviet School Education*, pp. 89-90.

exclusively through their detachment leaders. The object of the central collective was to develop a purposeful single-mindedness that would harness and expand the resources of the whole group, widen the perspectives of the primary collectives, and direct the activities of each for the benefit of all.

In turn the central collective provided a transition to the third level collective, the Soviet Union. It should connect itself with other collectives in towns and factories and other educational institutions, and see itself as a contributing part of the greater Soviet collective, the U.S.S.R., serving its purposes and contributing to them under the leadership of the communist party.

• Out of the sharing of common aims and common tasks arises the necessity for a common discipline throughout the collective. The discipline consists in constantly and deliberately trying to develop a common consciousness, in recognising the worthwhileness of each member of the collective, in demanding the fullest contribution from each, and in placing the interests of the collective above all else. Only in a properly organised collective, Makarenko contended, could one find persons who are at once the most disciplined and the most free.[29] Disciplined, in the sense that they are in full control of their abilities, sensitive to the requirements of their fellows, and serving a higher and wider purpose beyond their personal gain; and free, in the sense that their range of possible accomplishments has been increased by collective support, and they have gained a power to achieve and a buoyant confidence from the strength of the common human effort that uplifts them.

• Makarenko suggested further that each collective should develop a style of living. It is an approach to life that lends a distinctiveness to the behaviour of the collective, and an adhesive that helps hold the members together.

'Style and tone,' he wrote, 'have always been ignored in pedagogical theory, but in reality these qualities come under one of the most important headings in collective education. Style is a delicate and perishable substance... The failure of many children's institutions may be attributed to the fact that they have created neither a style, nor habits and traditions...'[30]

Style is a combination of outward form and inner feeling.

Outward form may involve the establishment of traditions and routines. Makarenko's colonies worked to a routine of bugle-calls, and developed several other semi-military practices, not because they were militaristically inclined but because they were convenient procedures attractive to the members of the collective. One of their traditions was that the colonist who was the duty officer for the day and responsible for the smooth running of the whole establishment should have his commands obeyed by all unhesitatingly, and have his final report in the evening accepted without question. This was a convenience to enable a busy person to undertake his day's work efficiently, but it also forced him to be scrupulous and honourable in all his dealings. Makarenko contended that traditions such as these led to respect for the continuing life of the collective, and engendered a special pride on the part of the members in belonging to it. 'Cultivating traditions,' he wrote, 'and instilling respect for them is an extremely important part of educational work.'[31] Especially important for the morale of the community was it that there should be a tradition of outward smartness of dress and movement, and that the environment should be both well-cared-for and attractive. Hence in his colonies there was always much work put into the cultivation of flower-beds and the beautification of the grounds.

Outward elegance without inner grace, however, was a poverty of style. Makarenko's principal emphasis, therefore, was upon the development, in each pupil, of sensitivity to the meaning of collective life, and the cultivation of attitudes that would make the most of its possibilities. There should be a feeling for form, so that his behaviour was always fitting to the occasion and in the interests of the collective. There should be a sense of security, whereby each member merely by virtue of his being a member feels a confidence that his contribution counts in the organisation and progress of the collective. Out of the sense of security there should develop a sense of dignity, of quiet, controlled pride, designed to uphold his own sense of significance and to underline his feeling of the importance of the collective. Through his consciousness of the importance of the collective, he should develop an awareness of his environment, an ability to feel what is happening around him, a sensitivity to current needs, an alertness to changes in the general tone of his collective life. Further, each member should feel that the collective is on the move, that he and his fellows are constantly improving in school, in productive work, and in daily life, that there can be no standstill but only an advance in a 'springy, rapid, precise tempo'.[32]

Attitudes such as these engender high spirits: 'constant good cheer, no gloomy faces, no sulky expressions, a constant readiness for action, and ... a happy buoyant mood...'[33] Collective life, for Makarenko, was no constant round of dull committee existence; it was an exciting and

---

[29]   A.S. Makarenko, *Werke*, 1, p. 698.

[30]   A.S. Makarenko, *The Road to Life*, 3, p. 263.

[31]   A.S. Makarenko, *Problems of Soviet School Education*, pp. 45-7.

[32]   A.S. Makarenko, *The Road to Life*, 3, p. 263.

[33]   A.S. Makarenko, *Problems of Soviet School Education*, p. 143.

bracing life. A collective with a good style was a place full of aspiration and of creative thinking backed by solid, satisfying achievement.

Makarenko summed up his views in a discussion in Leningrad in 1938. 'What then is a collective? You are not really speaking of a collective when you merely think of it as the sum of a number of individuals. The collective is a social, living organism. As an organism it possesses powers and responsibilities, and a pattern of reciprocal and interdependent relationships. Without these it is no collective, it is only a crowd or some gathering or other.' He explained that the educational problems of constructing a living collective had been his constant preoccupation. 'For the whole sixteen years of my active life as a soviet educator, I have devoted myself to the task of solving the questions: "How must a collective, how must its particular parts be constructed? How must the system of power and responsibility be created in the collective?"' [34]

The living, vital colonies that he developed were his practical answer to his questions. Life in them was, as he rightly remarked to his detractors, 'a genuine Soviet socialist education'. [35]

MAKARENKO'S SOCIALIST HUMANISM

By the time of the first Five Year Plan it had become the practice in education to speak of socialist humanism, a concept paralleling that of social realism more generally used in the arts. It was an apt description of Makarenko's activities, and his educational work virtually defined the concept.

Makarenko's socialist humanism had four main features:

- The first was singled out and described in his reminiscences by Ferre, the agronomist for many years at the Gorky colonies, as a sincere understanding of and consideration for the human being in the child. [36] It is a child-centredness that is not exclusively so. Although it does not derive its aims and purpose from the child's needs and interests, education is sensitively oriented to the child. Children are regarded with affection, and a careful study is made of their present condition and future possibilities. Further, and more importantly, they are respected as persons living here and now, not merely as potential, partly-formed adults. In consequence, they are trusted to behave responsibly, and, in response to this treatment, may be expected to gain in self-respect and human dignity. One important way to show respect for an individual is to have high expectations of him, and in consequence to make heavy and exacting demands on him to work to fulfil his potential. What Makarenko reiterated in several of his lectures as his fundamental

principle expresses very well the flavour of this approach: 'The greatest possible respect for a person must be combined with the highest possible demands upon him.' [37]

- An interest in promoting sociality in behaviour was the second main feature of socialist humanism. The general tenor of education was towards social-mindedness, towards building both the formal structures and the mental climate of collective responsibility. Makarenko referred to this, in his description of the Cheka men, as 'that precious substance for which I could find no better name than "social adhesive" — that feeling of common perspectives, that awareness of each other at any stage of the work, of all members of the collective, the perpetual consciousness of one high common goal...' [38] Behaviour of this kind was quietly and firmly underpinned by a confident recognition of one's own social worth, and of the social significance of one's work.

- Socialist humanism is the expression of a belief in the great possibilities for achievement by individuals working freely and devotedly together on common tasks. Hence it is characterised by optimism and cheerfulness. It is oriented to the future. Optimism and collective enthusiasm were the order of the day in the years of the Five Year Plan, and Makarenko's work and writings admirably caught the spirit of the times. The contemporary themes of construction and industrialisation also fitted well. Men's energy could be channelled through machines to create a free and happy new world. It was a special brand of soviet happiness, lyrically described by Makarenko, [39] to be achieved by determined human effort. 'Socialist humanism,' he wrote, [40] 'is based on an optimistic conviction' in the future happiness and freedom of mankind.

- The belief in human progress by human effort carried with it the conviction that it was possible to change human beings significantly by changing their environments. 'Man is bad only when he is in a bad social situation and in poor conditions,' Makarenko wrote, and went on to describe how he had transformed the most difficult children by changing their conditions of living, and conversely that 'the best of boys can easily

[34] A.S. Makarenko, 'A Few Inferences from my Educational Experience', *Werke*, 5, p. 241.

[35] A.S. Makarenko, 'Letter to the Head of the Department of Social Education of the Ukrainian Ministry of Education', *Werke*, 7, p. 440.

[36] Y.N. Medinsky *et al.*, *op.cit.*, p. 104.

[37] A.S. Makarenko, *Werke*, 7, p. 182; 5, p. 238; 5, p. 288.

[38] A.S. Makarenko, *The Road to Life*, 3, p. 386.

[39] A.S. Makarenko, 'Happiness', *Werke*, 7, p. 43.

[40] A.S. Makarenko, *Werke*, 7, p. 165.

become wild beasts in the environment of a poorly organized collective'.[41] This environmentalist approach to education confers on education a great power; it is regarded as one of the principal agencies for the transformation and uplift of society. There is, in consequence, a great responsibility placed upon teachers to understand the best interests of society and to use their power wisely. But a mere change of environment is not enough. Planned re-education must accompany it. Educators must become social engineers. Olesha, a well-known writer of the time, summed up this aspect of socialist humanism with the words, 'I want to be an engineer of human material', and Makarenko, echoing this statement in *The Road to Life*, puzzled about ways to develop a technology of educational practice through which a teacher's work might approach more closely to that of an engineer in building the new type of person required. In his view this engineering process required a careful assessment of the raw material, detailed specification and planning, and a program of measurement to check the process of production. It is a little strange, therefore, to find him uncompromisingly opposed to the principles and practice of pedology, the scientific movement in educational measurement. He saw it only as a movement which, committed to hereditary determinism, condemned his *bezprizornye* as hopeless. He joined loudly in uncompromising condemnation of the movement which was formally banished from the schools of the U.S.S.R. in 1936, when one might have expected him to see the possibility of transforming it into a more effective instrument in support of the objects of socialist humanism.

Those four features: respect for human personality, social-mindedness, an optimistic belief in man's potential, and a disposition towards human engineering, were the characteristics of an approach to education that Makarenko consistently displayed through his career and managed to blend tactfully and skilfully into a practical form of socialist humanism.

MORAL EDUCATION

One of the principal problems of soviet education was to think out a basis for the teaching of moral behaviour, and to devise a means for putting it into practice. Traditionally the church had been the source of moral authority, and the family, with some support from the schools, the main vehicle for the teaching of morals. With the severing of contact between the church and education, and the development of an active anti-religious

campaign, and with the uncertainty that surrounded the activity and authority of the family in the 1920's, those instruments of moral education had lost much of their effectiveness. It was necessary to find new moral foundations.

The new soviet state was not meant merely to be a change of government, it was meant also to be a change in a way of life. The change was to be economic, political, social, and, above all, moral. If the change in the fabric of life was to be genuine and lasting there had to be a conversion in the inner life of the people — a change in the motivation of their behaviour, an acceptance of a new form of moral authority, and the adoption of new criteria for approving or disapproving their own and their neighbours' actions.

Makarenko faced this problem in an extreme form in trying to remodel the lives of his *bezprizornye*. It is to his credit that he saw his work as largely that of moral reconstruction, and that he saw it as applying not merely to his handful of delinquents but to the whole of the Soviet Union.

The new morality, in Makarenko's view, had to be secular, exacting, consistent, collectivist, work-oriented, participatory, and communist. Writing in *A Book for Parents* towards the end of his career, he confessed that the dialectics of communist morality had not yet been fully mastered, and that there was a good deal of intuition rather than precise thinking in his views. Nevertheless, he was convinced that 'Our morality grows up out of the real solidarity of the working people. Communist morality, simply because it is built up on the idea of solidarity cannot be a morality of abstention. In demanding from the individual the abolition of greed, and respect for the interests and life of his comrades, communist morality demands solidarity in everything else, especially in struggle.'[42]

The basis of morality, then, was to be found in the conditions and habits of collective living. Whatever contributes to the solidarity and advancement of the collective is good, whatever disrupts and retards it bad. Makarenko is certain of the final authority of the collective, but did not specify which collective. There were, for example, three levels of collectives in his colonies: the detachments, the whole colony, and the soviet union, mediated at Dzerzhinsky by the Cheka. Sometimes the judgments of the different collectives conflicted. In general, the judgment of the middle-level collective, the colony as a whole, prevailed even on one important occasion against the conviction of the Cheka men.[43] The relationship between the various levels and types of collective was a part of the incomplete dialectic of the problem. At all events, the essence of moral

[41] A.S. Makarenko, 'On Educational Literature', *Werke*, 5 p. 381.

[42] A.S. Makarenko, *A Book for Parents*, p. 410.

[43] A.S. Makarenko, *Problems of Soviet Education*, pp. 62-6.

education was found to lie in constructing and accepting the responsibilities, and the discipline associated with them, in collective living.

These responsibilities are to work and to co-operate. A collective without work is an amoral organism. It must have a task, and it must be a task freely agreed upon in common. The task gives direction to the collective, and is the justification for its existence; it is in the full sense a working man's society. A work-task fully and freely agreed upon sets the tone and pattern of behaviour. There is a moral obligation to work, and not merely to work, but also to plan purposefully the most effective way to accomplish the task, to work to capacity to complete it, and to work in the interests of the whole collective.

Co-operation is the essence of collective living. It implies that each member should be respected to the extent to which his contribution matches his capacity; it implies that all members should act honourably and openly with every other member, altruistically having at all times the interests of the others in mind; it implies personal freedom and security to work, speak, and participate in the life of the collective, provided that these activities are in the interests of all; and finally it implies a recognition that the interests of the collective come first at all times. This is a morality of forward-looking, disciplined altruism.

A disciplined person is one who has learned how to work and how to co-operate. A thoroughly moral person is a thoroughly disciplined person, and an undisciplined person is an immoral one. Discipline is the face of the collective, the expression of its inner cohesiveness and drive.

Makarenko explained that discipline must be conscious and that a person must be taught to accept a set of principles such as the following: that the interests of the collective are paramount; that when an offence is committed it is an offence against the collective; that it is the collective, though it may act through an individual, which accuses and punishes an offender; that the higher a person stands in the collective the more is demanded of him; that discipline is really shown when a person does with pleasure a task normally regarded as unpleasant; and that discipline has a clear purpose and is associated with a clear-cut task which the pupil can see requires appropriate discipline for its completion. In essence, Makarenko suggests, a pupil must be taught that discipline is a prerequisite to successful action, and disciplined action is morality. Disciplined action is not merely obedience to a set of rules and regulations. It is a state of mind and body of well-tested habits. It comes as a result of long and concerted educational effort.

How does one educate to produce a disciplined person? Makarenko suggested a variety of methods. Emulation is useful, both in the sense of setting an example and of striving to surpass a competitor. Makarenko and his teachers meticulously guarded their own behaviour in the colonies as an example to their pupils, and encouraged the study of soviet heroes such as Gorki, and the Arctic explorer Otto Schmidt. Within the colony, detachments were continually assessed, groups of workers vied to surpass their production quotas, and outstanding workers were proudly congratulated on formal ceremonial occasions, in anticipation of the Stakhanovite movement. Rewards and punishments were sometimes useful methods, but Makarenko did not place great store upon them. Sometimes the reward for the best disciplined group was a difficult or unpleasant job such as cleaning the lavatories, to demonstrate that the best group had earned the honour of tackling the hardest job or of taking on a piece of extra work. Similarly, the hardest punishment was given to the most virtuous, as a mark of respect for their worth, and as an indication that they had the heaviest responsibilities to bear. Punishment must be varied to suit the state of development of each group and individual; it should have agreed-upon rules and traditions, and it should always be seen as the expression of the disapproval not of a teacher or other individual but of the collective.

Besides traditions in punishments, Makarenko thought it important to establish traditions of behaviour. Customary forms of procedure adopted in the discussions in the general assembly, routine ways of inducting new members of the colony, ceremonial festivities on important occasions, traditional ways of showing respect for the officers and symbols of the collective, were considered by Makarenko to be of great help in habituating pupils to proper ways of behaving, of impressing on them the importance of certain aspects of their common life, and of conveying to them a sense of the dignity and continuity of the collective.

Life governed by tradition, however, unrelieved by the prospect of future advancement is stagnation; and inactivity is tantamount to immorality. Hence for Makarenko the opening out of what he called new perspectives was very important. 'The true incentive of man's life,' he wrote, 'is tomorrow's joy.'[44] One of the most vital matters in running an educational institution is to develop a series of activities with short-, medium-, and long-range perspectives. Every individual should have short-range perspectives which provide him with an incentive to overcome difficulties and bring to him the satisfaction of achievement; the collective should plan ahead with objectives to be attacked and reached on a longer-term basis; and as a distant perspective all should look forward to their future life of achievement in the great collective of the Soviet Union. Their perspective may be that of qualifying for the Rabfak or a higher educational institution or it may be that of service in the Red Army or the factory. Wherever it is to be; the anticipation of it links the outlook of the individual and the advancing collective with the forward movement of the Soviet Union.

---

44 A.S. Makarenko, 'Perspectives', *Werke*, 5, p. 78; *The Road to Life*, 3, p. 283.

Perspectives successfully achieved mean joy and satisfaction, and encouragement to plan more advances; but they also imply difficulties to be overcome, and discipline to be imposed. The drive to achieve should bring discipline 'hard as iron, serious discipline, Stalin discipline'.[45] It is not learned easily or quickly. Makarenko suggested that in his colonies he started the process by making resolute demands upon his pupils, while at the same time respecting, trusting, and loving them. This process was a kind of 'exacting affection'. In time it was gradually transferred to the collective which began to make the demands and set the disciplinary and moral pace for its members. Finally, in the third stage, each member of the collective 'will adopt an exacting attitude towards himself',[46] and a well-disciplined life will become habitual with him.

The process should not, in Makarenko's view, be left entirely to the school. It should be initiated and reinforced in the home. An exacting affection should be characteristic of home education also, and through it each child should acquire a sense of being in a collective, and the qualities that go with a healthy collective life, such as awareness, the ability to plan his time and resources, and a sense of responsibility for his actions.[47]

All the methods that might be used to build soviet morality in each member of the collective are subordinate to the one overriding condition that the members must be engaged in productive work. 'The accomplishment of joint tasks, mutual-assistance and dependence on work of communal importance, these conditions alone make possible the creation of really effective moral relations between the separate members of a community.'[48]

PRODUCTIVE WORK

Work in itself, in Makarenko's view, was not educative. It should be productive, and it should be collective. Early in the 1920's he accepted the current fashion that children should learn various labour processes and his colony was equipped accordingly with the usual shoemaking, joinery, and sewing shops. This exposed the children to a number of elementary skills, but did not enable them to produce anything worthwhile. Similarly he tried to tie his work processes in with school-work but found it impossible to integrate them in any sensible way. Henceforth he maintained a strict separation between school and factory, holding that each had important work to do and that they should not be confused by fruitless attempts to relate them to each other. He was able, in due course, to develop his own factories within the colony, turning out products of importance for the contemporary soviet economy. The factories were owned and run by the collective, and through them the colonists learnt what production really meant. It involved the setting out of an exact,

detailed production plan, the establishment of standards of tolerance and standards of quality, and the co-ordination of the work of the supply, mechanical, optical, assembly, and commercial departments. It brought an income sufficient to run the colony and plan for expansion. The operation was a genuine experience of modern industrial activity, and it engaged the whole of the colony in collective planning and collective production.

Productive work, when it was of that kind, Makarenko contended, had a substantial effect which permeated the life and character of every colonist. The operation demanded of everyone reliability, accuracy, responsibility, and concerted effort; it built into the community habits of organisation, and the discipline of collective striving towards a difficult but definite goal; and it tied the collective effectively into the pattern of interests and needs and into the tempo of life of the general collective society of the soviet union.

THE GROWTH OF MAKARENKO'S INFLUENCE

Makarenko's work was the principal experiment that survived from the 1920's and exercised an influence on the subsequent thought of educators in the U.S.S.R. The change in the educational climate that began with the first Five Year Plan, and became characteristic of the 1930's, was a trend towards more exacting programs of work. It began to establish a pattern that has persisted to the present day. In that decisive period of soviet education Makarenko's educational approach proved very acceptable. In the early 1920's there had been a trickle of visitors to his embryonic Gorky colony; by the mid-1930's there was a constant daily stream to the Dzerzhinsky commune. The attractiveness of his writings spread his influence more widely towards the end of the 1930's. In the 1940's his principal works had sales running into millions of copies, and he became the favourite reading of many parents and teachers. The publication between 1950 and 1952 of his complete works under the auspices of the Academy of Pedagogical Sciences of the RSFSR set the seal on his popularity. From that date on he became well-known to all trainee teachers in the U.S.S.R. and was widely read and discussed by educators in many countries of the world.

---

[45] A.S. Makarenko, *Learning to Live*, p. 310.

[46] A.S. Makarenko, *Problems of Soviet School Education*, p. 75.

[47] A.S. Makarenko, 'Radio Talks on the Education of Children', *Werke*, 4, pp. 367ff.; *Conseils aux Parents*, trans. I. Lézine, L'Association France-U.R.S.S., Paris, n.d.

[48] W.L. Goodman, *Anton Simeonovitch Makarenko, Russian Teacher*, Routledge & Kegan Paul, London, 1949, p. 88.

Makarenko has obvious affinities with several overseas progressive educational movements. His colonies resembled the experimental work with delinquents in the George Junior Republic in the U.S.A., and Homer Lane's Little Commonwealth in England. There was a common concern with building new attitudes and a new approach to society — on the one side, for living in a western democratic environment, and, on the other, for life in a collective society. Makarenko's use of productive work aligned him with the *Arbeitsschule* movement of educators such as Lay, Kerschensteiner, and Blonsky, and he was familiar with the literature in that field. But none combined, as he did, a school with a factory collectively owned and run by the pupils of the school. The Gorky colony on its first site and at Trepke could be regarded as a residential country-boarding-school similar to those established by Hermann Lietz and inspired by the reformed English Public Boarding School, Abbotsholme. The purposes and ultimate pattern were very different but some of the early practices were similar. Again Makarenko's ideas had some clear similarities to the socially-minded educational theorists such as Natorp and Dewey, with their emphasis on conjoint activity and social relevance in educational practice. It is probable that Makarenko studied each of these movements and schools of thought; it is hard to see how he could avoid doing so in his Kharkov teacher training course during World War I and in the pedagogical reading he undertook in the climate of the early 1920's.

Makarenko, nevertheless, was, in essence, independent of contemporary educational movements and influences. He appears to have worked out and elaborated his own practices, sometimes logically, sometimes by intuition, but always with a somewhat utopian vision of the soviet society in mind. He once remarked, in reviewing the educational achievements of the U.S.S.R. that 'Education has been gradually converted from an erudite instrument helping to enjoy life into a tool helping to build life.'[49] He himself proved to be, for the U.S.S.R., one of the chief architects of that educational transformation.

---

[49] XXX International Conference on Public Education, Geneva, 1967, *Public Education in the Soviet Union*, Moscow, 1967.

Military style marching formed one of the standard exercises of Hitler's youth:
Jungvolk **on a cross country march.**

CHAPTER 9

THE TOTALITARIAN INTERLUDE: EDUCATION IN JAPAN, ITALY, AND GERMANY, 1919-39

During the 1920's and 1930's in most countries the relationship between education and politics was zealously cultivated. The relationship was, as we have seen, particularly close in the U.S.S.R. It was also deliberately encouraged and highly developed in a group of countries whose ideologies were very much opposed to communism. Those countries were totalitarian, nationalistic, expansionist, charismatically led, and inclined towards militarism. The three most prominent, in their desire to commit education to the ideology and requirements of the totalitarian state, were Japan, Italy, and Germany, the three countries which eventually concluded a tri-partite alliance and fought World War II against the U.S.S.R. and the western democracies.

JAPAN AND THE GROWTH OF NATIONALISM, 1919-45

The Imperial Rescript of 1890 has been formulated out of a desire to find a way in which to blend traditional Japanese thought and practice harmoniously with the Western influences that were rapidly penetrating into the country. The Rescript was a temperate but firm reaffirmation of the Japanese spirit. All countries in the twentieth century experienced the impact, at once stimulating and disturbing, of the scientific and technological revolution. The challenge of scientific thought and method to accepted beliefs and habits, the redistribution of resources, the redeployment of the work force, the shifting of the balance from agriculture to industry, the expansion of commercial and service activities, and the growth of mass population in cities were fundamental innovations that affected every nation and led from time to time to a reassessment of its educational objectives and practices. They bore with all the greater force on Japan because of the rapidity with which she moved into the stream of the technological revolution.

By 1920 Japan had achieved spectacular results from the westernisation of her industry and commerce. It was clear also that, along with western technology, she had been steadily importing western thought and culture. Some had been deliberately introduced such as the French, German, and Anglo-Saxon educational practices that had been encouraged with the importation of teachers from those countries; others had been the necessary or accidental accompaniment of industrial and business progress. Whatever the means of introduction, there was no doubt that, by the 1920's, significant aspects of western intellectual, social, moral, and religious culture had thoroughly seeped into Japanese life. The movement did not go unnoticed. It was a source of continuing comment and reaction.

One of the principal tasks of educators in the 1920's and 1930's was to find some means of bringing about a compatible marriage between Japanese and Western culture in a context of escalating industrialisation. The main line along which they proceeded was to try to maintain a staunch adherence to Japanese spirit on the one hand, and a solid pursuit of western learning on the other. The area of Japanese spirit included the conduct of social relationships, filial piety, reverence for the emperor, morality, and patriotic regard for the nation. Western learning was mathematics, science, vocational and professional preparation for business, industry, and administration, and modern foreign languages. The distinction between spirit and learning could not always be clearly maintained. Literature and the arts had something of both, often inextricably mixed, and business principles and industrial activities were often built on adherence to some kinds of moral and spiritual beliefs. Nevertheless, for Japanese educators and their political masters the distinction was regarded as sufficiently valid to be of use in educational discussion and in planning the school's activities.[1] Moral education and useful learning were the two necessary and contrasting aspects of the school's curriculum, and from time to time one or the other assumed superior importance. The educational history of the period from World War I to World War II is largely concerned with the increasing weight given to moral education and the nationalistic spirit that came to dominate it.

(i)   Japanese Education in the 1920's

World War I accelerated the progress of industrialisation in Japan. Her shipping and the products of her factories were greatly in demand during the war, and she built up markets, especially in Asia and the Pacific, that she was able to sustain and expand during the 1920's. Agriculture, which in 1910 accounted for half Japan's gross national product, in 1920 accounted for only a quarter; industry had forged ahead, and, with it, the middle class. Secondary, vocational, and university education, in consequence, received a considerable impetus.

In 1915, six per cent of male students of secondary school age were enrolled in secondary schools; in 1925 the proportion had risen to thirteen per cent and the number of secondary schools continued to multiply. The five-year secondary middle school curriculum by the end of the 1920's had been diversified, to cater for the increased and varied demand, into arts, science, and vocational strands. Girls' high schools also developed parallel to the boys' middle schools, expanding rapidly in the early 1920's and by 1925 attendance at them was equal to that in the boys' schools. Vocational

schools were upgraded in standard during the 1920's in an effort to put them intellectually on an equality with secondary middle schools. Higher secondary schools, hitherto regarded as preparatory to universities, were also slightly diversified and increased in number. It still remained difficult, however, for middle school students to enter higher schools and only seven per cent of them succeeded in gaining entry out of the thirty per cent who tried. In the twenty years from 1910 to 1930 the number of universities increased from three to forty-six and the output of university graduates quadrupled. Japan, in effect, by 1930, had matched the advanced countries of Western Europe in provision for higher education, and, like them, found that, when the demand for professionally trained persons declined in the early 1920's and again in the severe depression of the early 1930's, she had an embarrassing surplus of highly educated and unemployed young persons.

The success of the Russian Revolution and the spread of communist ideas in the early 1920's led to a reassertion of the importance of teaching traditional Japanese morals in the school curriculum. National and social responsibilities were re-emphasised, but though important, they were not a dominant part of the elementary or secondary school curriculum at that time.

Japan had by then become a literate, business-oriented, industrial society in a mould apparently similar to that of the western democracies. Forty years before, her people had for the most part been illiterate and agricultural. In the mid-1920's, 99 per cent of children between the ages of seven and thirteen inclusive were in regular attendance at elementary school,[2] and were anxious to pass on to secondary vocational or general schools that would help equip them for positions in the growing industrial and business world. In this context of business expansion and the general spread of education, democratic ideas were nourished and tentative moves were made towards social and political reform. The modest liberalism, characteristic of the U.S.A. and Western Europe in the 1920's, began to make an impact in Japan.

In 1927 an economic recession shook the country, and subsequently merged in 1930 with the world-wide depression which hit Japan with considerable force. The period of economic crisis changed the complexion of political thinking. It reanimated conservative and nationalistic thinking, and discredited the trend of freer economic and liberal political

[1] Makoto Aso and Ikuo Amano, *Education and Japan's Modernization*, Ministry of Foreign Affairs, Tokyo, 1972, pp. 55ff.

[2] R. King Hall, *Education for a New Japan*, Yale University Press, 1949, pp. 322-36, discussed at length the level of literacy in Japan in the 1930's, and suggested that probably not more than 40 per cent of those who completed only the six years of compulsory elementary school could manage to read the daily newspapers.

Japanese children of the 1930's hoisting the national flag before school.

(ii) State of Education in the Early 1930's

In 1930 the Ministry of Education created a bureau of student control concerned with the investigation and guidance of the thought of pupils and students.[3] The bureau had the double task of detecting and prosecuting those who harboured 'dangerous thoughts', and of creating and disseminating propaganda through which to direct pupils' thoughts. It was a substantial and important instrument of control which penetrated into all the schools and informal educational agencies, operating both through the central administration and the local government bodies. The new establishment was part of a drive to eliminate left wing thinking and to reduce the influence of the more liberal teachers and students. Around 1930 professors and teachers with Marxist leanings were dismissed, and in the following years the liberal and democratic teachers lost their positions. The budding democracy of the 1920's was severely curtailed and reactionary and ultra-nationalistic forces tightened their grip on Japanese life.

The 'Manchurian Incident' of 1931 was a turning point. In that year the Japanese army seized the city of Mukden and began to overrun Manchuria. It was the beginning of a commitment to military aggression on the Asian mainland that led subsequently to war with China, involvement in World War II, and ultimate defeat in 1945. The 'Incident' and the immediately successful exploitation of it roused much patriotic enthusiasm in Japan. It also marked the beginning of the military domination of the Japanese government that was to continue until 1945. From 1932 to 1936 there were a series of assassinations, attempted coups, and finally a serious army mutiny in Tokyo which increased tension and led to greater police and military surveillance. In 1936 Japan entered an alliance with Germany, by 1937 she was at war with China, and the whole nation was placed on a war footing; four years later she had entered World War II, siding with Germany and Italy in a triple alliance of fascist-like countries.

School activities reflected the growth of militarism. Concern for cultivating Japanese spirit inexorably took precedence over learning. As early as 1925 army officers had been attached to schools to develop cadet work; they also helped in the courses in military arts, swordsmanship, and judo which were part of gymnastics, and which aimed at developing both physical and moral virtue. In 1929 a Social Education Bureau was established in the Ministry of Education to organise and supervise throughout the community, especially among young persons and adults, the kind of national cultural movement that would promote Japanese

thought that had led up to it. In particular, it nurtured the development of extreme political and economic views among junior officers of the army who began to give substantial support to the idea of some form of state socialism under the direction of a military dictatorship. That form of Japanese fascism was never fully implemented, but, in the course of the 1930's, continued to be attractive to groups of army officers, and helped to reinforce the authoritarian nationalism that characterised the war years after 1937.

---

[3] Japan, Ministry of Education, *Fifty-Seventh Annual Report* (1929-1930), Tokyo, 1935, p. 1. Later, in 1934, it became the Bureau of Thought Supervision.

morality and national spirit. Since 1923 the education department had organised systematic adult education courses in which considerable emphasis was laid on civics. The department had also assisted young men's and young women's societies, whose membership by 1930 was more than four million, to cultivate good health and citizenship. The bureau within the department became responsible for the general encouragement of a large number of social cultural bodies which aimed 'at the promotion of the national spirit through a clear, firm assertion of the fundamental character of the Japanese Empire'.[4] By regular community meetings of the families in towns and villages, by formal adult courses and informal social and cultural activities, a widespread, though somewhat unsystematic, campaign was developed to preserve and strengthen the tradition, 'that the Imperial family is the head of all families of the people constituting this Empire', and that 'the whole nation is one great family bound together with a lasting and inseparable tie'.[5]

(iii) Education in the Japanese Spirit

In 1935 an Education Reform Council was set up to advise the Minister for Education, and in particular to suggest ways of developing 'a clear consciousness of the Japanese spirit'.[6] It suggested an intensification of nationalism in schools, and its successor, the Education Council established in 1937, made recommendations of the same kind during the next four, wartime years. The first most notable act of the committees was the production in 1937 of the *Cardinal Principles of the National Entity of Japan*. It was a substantial booklet setting forth for teachers and pupils an ultra-nationalistic version of the official philosophy of state Shinto.

Shinto was the series of rituals and beliefs by which the Japanese celebrated and supported a common national life.[7] Citizens were bound by law to adhere to the official tenets and comply with the requirements of the rites, and schools were required to perform its ceremonies and teach its beliefs.

It was held that the land of Japan was divine, created by the gods; the emperor was divine, a direct descendant of the sun-goddess; and the people of Japan were divine, offspring of the gods and united in one family with the emperor. A poem in a primary school reader expressed the relationship between emperor and subject and the sentiment that accompanied it;

> 'Great Japan! Great Japan!
> Our seventy million citizens
> Look up to the Emperor even as to God
> And love and serve him even as a parent.'[8]

Shinto was centred in the emperor, not as a charismatic leader like the *Führer* in Germany or the *Duce* in Italy, but as a divine and inviolable representative of an everlasting dynasty which, with paternal goodness and wisdom, had guided the Japanese people successfully throughout the 2,500 years of their history. Especially in the twentieth century had the Japanese nation gone from success to success in difficult times. And, in the stresses of the wartime to come, it was essential to close ranks and to unite in devoted service to the emperor and nation. In fostering loyalty and patriotism through the schools, great importance was attached to the divine origin of the emperor and the nation, and to the need to show reverence by worshipping at the shrines dedicated to the great emperors and their divine ancestors. In that way the school authorities attempted to build 'a bulwark of impregnable sentiment'[9] about the existing order of political absolutism and military predominance.

The Cardinal Principles was an important instrument in the process of intensifying patriotism — a sentiment kindled in 1931, intensified in 1937, and brought to a climax in 1941. The book was produced in 1937 by a committee working for the Bureau of Thought Supervision in the Ministry of Education, and was distributed to all teachers. During the next six years approximately two million copies were printed, extracts appeared in many textbooks, and it was reproduced by many private presses. It was studied in schools and teacher-training institutions, and constantly referred to on public occasions in schools.[10] The purpose of the book was to trace the origins of the Japanese people and empire, demonstrate their uniqueness, reveal the falseness of European ideologies, and provide an authoritative guide to moral and patriotic conduct in the Japanese spirit. Consequently the book reviewed the founding of the nation and 'the boundless Imperial virtues'. It explained the totalitarian nature of the state in which, unlike the citizens of western countries who regarded themselves as individuals supporting a ruler for their common benefit, the subjects of the Japanese emperor were of the same essence with him united together in a common divine origin. It reviewed

4 Japan, Ministry of Education, *Fifty-Seventh Annual Report*, Tokyo, 1935, p. 472.

5 Shintaro Sasai, Regular Community Meetings, in World Federation of Education Associations, *Proceedings of the Seventh Biennial Conference*, Japanese Association, Tokyo, 4, 1938, p. 18.

6 Makoto Aso and Ikuo Amano, *op.cit.*, p. 55.

7 For an extensive analysis of Shinto and its various sects, see D.C. Holtom, *The National Faith of Japan*, Kegan Paul, London, Trench, Trubner, 1938.

8 *ibid.*, p. 79.

9 *ibid.*, p. 138.

10 For an extensive analysis and reproduction of the *Cardinal Principles of the National Entity of Japan* see R. King Hall (ed.), *Kokutai No Hongi*, trans. J.O. Gauntlett, Harvard University Press, 1949; see also R. King Hall, *Shushin: The Ethics of a Defeated Nation*, Teachers College, Columbia University, New York, 1949, pp. 39-61, and R.S. Anderson, *Japan. Three Epochs of Modern Education*, U.S. Department of Health, Education, and Welfare, Washington D.C., Bulletin 1959, 1, p. 16.

Figure 9.1: Japan: Material in Textbooks on Morals by Year of Textbook Revisions.

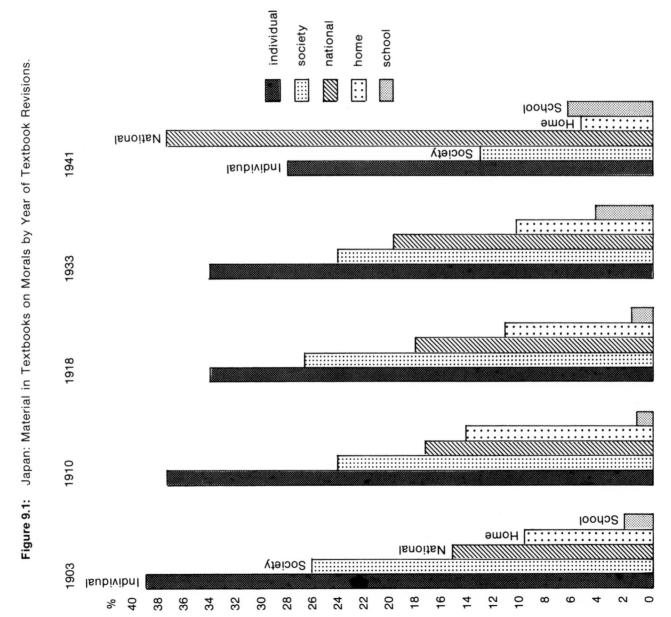

Graphed from Karasawa Tomitaro, 'Changes in Japanese Education as Revealed in Textbooks', *Japan Quarterly*, 2, 373, July–September, 1955.

Japanese history 'as an unfolding of the single course of the great spirit', and indicated that education did not aim at individual cultivation and self-realisation but saw its 'mission in guarding and maintaining the prosperity of the Imperial Throne' by following the Way of the national entity. The *Cardinal Principles* concluded with a forward-looking note. Western ideas had flooded into the country in the past seventy years, setting up an undesirable distinction between scholarly pursuits and education — between scientific thinking and the moral and national entity of the Japanese people. 'Our present mission', therefore, 'is to build up a new Japanese culture by adopting and sublimating western cultures with our national entity as the basis' — an entity immutable, steadfast, and embedded in service to the Imperial Throne 'which is coeval with heaven and earth'.[11]

The *Cardinal Principles* were thoroughly reinforced by the official textbooks that were used in morals lessons in primary and secondary schools. In a systematic and interesting way the textbooks translated into school lessons and reading material the ideas on individual and social behaviour, on loyalty and filial piety, and on the national entity and destiny that the *Principles* enunciated. An analysis of the changes made in the content of primary school morals textbooks from 1903 through four revisions to 1941 demonstrates the dramatic change that occurred in 1941, growing out of the ultra-nationalism of the late 1930's. In particular, nationalism which had been steadily growing during the earlier years of the century became predominant, almost 40 per cent of the topics in the courses being primarily concerned with the cultivation of patriotism.

Teaching in all the subjects of the curriculum supported moral education in some measure. History was specially capable of such adaptation. It was used to show the divine origin of the Japanese and the expression of the national entity throughout the progress of the Japanese nation, so that the children would come 'to realize the lines along which the Empire is destined to achieve its illustrious mission'.[12] School assemblies, excursions to worship at shrines, and ceremonies on special occasions served also to create an atmosphere and add a compulsive emotional content to the teaching.

(iv) The Reforms of 1941

In 1941 a National School Reform was announced. Up till that time, Japanese schools had expanded greatly, but had changed little in form since the beginning of the century. There was a six-year compulsory elementary school with a two- or three-year higher elementary school. Secondary education had three types of schools roughly parallel to each other: a four- or five-year middle school for boys, a similar girls' high school, and a range of secondary vocational schools. Beyond the

secondary schools there was a three-year higher school for boys preparatory to higher education. The universities offered three to five year general and professional courses, and beside them there were technical institutes of slightly lesser prestige offering higher vocational education for a similar duration. The reform transformed the elementary and higher elementary school into a National School of eight years, raised the level of compulsory education to eight years, and increased the nationalistic content throughout the curriculum. Five-year compulsory part-time education following compulsory elementary education was recommended, and also the expansion of scientific and technical education. The reforms, implemented in part in 1941, eventually became inoperative as increased demands for manpower by the military forces and the wartime economy pressed on the schools and universities and caused them progressively to shorten the length of their courses.

In 1941, also, the Ministry of Education followed up the *Cardinal Principles* with a shorter booklet entitled *The Way of the Subject*. It had a similarly wide distribution and constituted, with the Imperial Rescript of 1890, and the *Cardinal Principles* of 1937, one of the three principal and official statements of what the schools should teach about the Japanese spirit. Its object was to 'establish national moral principles which make service to the State their primary concern'.[13] It emphasised Japan's divine mission to incorporate East Asia within its empire and, in stronger language than its predecessor, condemned western influence and put forward the Japanese traditional way as the more significant element in the culture that was to emerge out of the mixture of east and west. To achieve the desired end of national success and prosperity, Japanese children must learn that their proper duty, as subjects, was 'To render service to the Emperor under the influence of his graciousness wherein He cares for the well-being of all peoples — this constitutes indeed the essential qualities of an Imperial subject. The way in which one follows and serves the Emperor is the Way of the Subject.'[14]

FASCISM AND EDUCATION IN ITALY, 1922-43

The march on Rome in 1922 by Mussolini's followers from Milan was the beginning of the fascist regime in Italy. It lasted until the end of World War II. The fascists brought order out of the confusion that had plagued the post World War I years in Italy; they brought efficiency — the trains of

---

[11]   R. King Hall, *Kokutai No Hongi*, pp. 79, 105, 153-5, 178, 183.

[12]   World Federation of Education Associations, *op.cit.*, 4, pp. 403-4.

[13]   R. King Hall, *Shushin: The Ethics of a Defeated Nation*, pp. 68ff.; see also O.D. Tolischus, *Tokyo Record*, Hamish Hamilton, London, 1943, pp. 134ff.

[14]   R. King Hall, *Shushin: The Ethics of a Defeated Nation*, p. 70.

Italy ran on time was their boast; and they brought a high sense of patriotism. With these virtues came devotion to a single party and its leader, suppression of opposition, greater centralisation of administration, close regulation of industry and industrial workers, agricultural and industrial expansion to achieve self-sufficiency, and a somewhat dangerous military adventurism. Fascism, according to Mussolini, was an aristocracy of those best fitted to lead, not by virtue of their birth or wealth, but by virtue of their personality and understanding of what renascent Italy needed. It was social reconstructionism of the right — firm, uncompromising, and anti-liberal. Education and propaganda were obviously to be of importance in building a close-knit, forceful, yet tractable body of citizens for the fascist state.

(i) Gentile Reform, 1923

The first Minister of Education under fascism was Giovanni Gentile,[15] then one of Italy's leading philosophers, who had as his director of primary education, Lombardo-Radice,[16] well-known for his interest in progressive education. Together, in 1923, they planned and put into operation a reform of education.

Compulsory education was extended to the age of fourteen and included five years of primary and three of pre-vocational education. Primary education could be followed by eight years of secondary education taken in one of several parallel schools of various types. In both primary and secondary divisions the Gentile reform reduced vocational education and replaced it by a greater emphasis on general education through traditional subjects. The classical *ginnasio-liceo*, largely a university preparatory institution, was confirmed in its dominance of secondary education and, being merely a school for the upper middle classes at that time, gave a somewhat elitist cast to the educational system.

To control the content and quality of the program throughout the system, the reform introduced state-wide, state-controlled examinations to be taken by the pupils in both public and private schools at the conclusion of the various secondary school courses. The state also had the responsibility for prescribing the content of the courses studied in schools, and was soon to start producing textbooks in which the ideas and sentiments expressed were of the kind that would support the sort of reconstruction the fascists were carrying out for Italy. In these ways the structure was established through which the schools could readily be brought into the service of the state.

In curriculum and methods of teaching, the Gentile reform placed emphasis on expressive activities. Language in its various forms — grammar, composition, speech, song, literature, ancient and modern languages — was the principal study at all school levels; coupled with it were creative activities in art, and an encouragement to pupils not only to learn how to express themselves but also to educate themselves. Interest by the educational authorities in developing expressiveness and auto-education attracted Montessori who associated herself with Italian education in the 1920's and, until spontaneity of expression became less favourably received, in the early 1930's. Gentile was a keen nationalist, and he expected his teachers and schools to express the heightened nationalistic spirit of the new Italy. He opened the way for the schools to teach more overtly than ever before a particular national political line. In the same vein he also re-introduced the teaching of the Catholic religion into the schools, believing that it would provide a basis for disciplined character building, and that it was an important part of Italy's national heritage.

The main lines of the Gentile reform, a preference for traditional general education over vocational education, an increase in state control, and a greater encouragement of expressive work — were not radical, and some of the structural changes were short-lived. But the general trend of the reform and its spirit were a move in a new direction which fitted well with fascist thinking.

An article on Fascism attributed to Mussolini in Gentile's *Encyclopedia Italiana* emphasised three principal ideas in fascism:

- Fundamentally, fascism was 'a discipline of the whole person'.[17] The fascist state was an expression of personality which permeated 'the will no less than the intellect'.[18] Fascism was not merely a state of mind, it was also a visceral commitment. The whole conduct of a person was regulated by his inward and complete acceptance of fascism which acted as an ethical and directive force on his activities.
- Fascism was totalitarian. Mussolini's repeated formula was 'everything in the State, nothing against the State, nothing outside the State'.[19] The keystone of the Fascist doctrine was its conception of the state not as a mere governing body but as the manifestation of the highest and the best in the spirit of the people; it was therefore above and beyond the will of any individual and had an

---

[15] G. Gentile (1875-1944), a long-time collaborator with Benedetto Croce in the neo-idealist school of philosophy, became a convinced supporter of Fascism.

[16] G. Lombardo-Radice (1879-1938) was an experimentally-minded secondary school teacher who became a professor of pedagogics in the University of Rome. He edited several influential educational journals. He consistently advocated the need for free expression and activity in schools. After only one year in the Ministry of Education he returned to academic life.

[17] B. Mussolini, *Fascism: Doctrine and Institutions*, Ardita, Rome, 1935, p. 13.

[18] *ibid.*

[19] *ibid.*, p. 40.

omniscient authority over all spheres of life. It was absolute, 'a spiritual and ethical entity for securing the political, juridical, and economic organisation of the nation...'[20] A fascist had a complete commitment to the state, conceived in this way, which he believed to be the truest expression of the twentieth century, 'the century of authority, a century tending to the "right", a fascist century'.[21]

- Fascism was an activity. It was not just a conviction and a feeling, it was an active struggle in which thought and action were potently combined. 'Inactivity is death,' wrote Mussolini.[22] Fascist activity was of two kinds. 'Life for the Fascist is continuous, ceaseless fight'[23] to achieve the concrete objectives of the fascist state, to promote the social, cultural, economic, and industrial reconstruction of the country, to struggle against divisive tendencies and factions, and to expand the nation's ambitions and territories 'in the present period of dynamism'.[24] It was also an educative kind of activity. A fascist must promote fascism; he had the task of educating others to see the virtues of the fascist way of life. He was engaged in refashioning not only the environment, but also the mind and character of his fellow-men. Therefore, schools, youth work, adult education, and propaganda were of considerable importance for the development and maintenance of the fascist state.

It was the realisation of the significance of educational activity for the future of fascism which led Mussolini with some exaggeration, to describe Gentile's reform as the most fascist of all fascist reforms.[25] It was a mild dose, devoid of the castor oil with which the fascists were accustomed to purge their opponents. It was, nevertheless, a systematic beginning and Gentile in his writing and speeches at the time attempted to provide an educational philosophy consistent with the fascist position.

(ii) Gentile's Philosophy of Education

Gentile's central notion was that of actual idealism. Action and thought were, for him, intimately related. Reality consisted of and was created by pure acts of thought. The real world was a world of ideas or rather of acts of thinking which were permeated by a spirit revealed in some measure through them. To seek for truth meant to seek to know some aspect of the spirit and to try to probe closer to its essence. Man's history was the imperfect expression of the action of the spirit and represented at times his striving towards the more perfect realisation of it.

In the social sphere the complete expression of the spirit was to be found in the absolute national state. 'The nation is that will, conscious of

itself and of its own historical past, which, as we formulate it in our minds, defines and delineates our nationality, generating an end to be attained, a mission to be realized. For that will, in case of need, our lives are sacrificed, for our lives are genuine, worthy and endowed with incontestable value only as they are spent in the accomplishment of that mission.'[26] Nationality was the consciousness of a common collective personality; and the personality was shown concretely and actively in the form of a state. An individual realised his full personality only by being educated to become an integral part of the greater collective personality. There, ideally, everyone fitted harmoniously into his most suitable place; everyone contributed fully to the national interest; and everyone was a part of a unity of spirit expressing itself in the national will.

Gentile saw the world as a tissue of interrelated ideas striving to become a unity, and conceived the ideal human life as one in which each person was consciously committed to being an integral and willing part of a larger whole. The man of culture was one who did not simply look after his own interests but acted in the interests of the community, not necessarily as they were at a particular time but as they ideally should be. Hence educators should encourage pupils to enter into the great heritage of mutual respect and responsibility that had been built out of centuries of human thought and conscience. 'The essential task of education is to produce good citizens, and the good citizen is one who hears the voice of "The State" within him.'[27]

Gentile's main concern in education was with the education of the personality. He did not neglect academic work, and acknowledged the importance of thorough grounding in the traditional disciplines, but he shifted the emphasis to the education of character, and the development of persons fitted in spirit and attitude to take up the challenges of the twentieth century and make something of them. The study of history was always the study of the present; it was the examination of the spirit working itself out in various ways with various materials but always the one spirit whose highest expression was to be found in the state, especially as exemplified in the fascist state in Italy.

[20] ibid., p. 27.
[21] ibid., p. 26.
[22] ibid., p. 13.
[23] ibid., p. 36.
[24] ibid., p. 36.
[25] H.S. Harris, *The Social Philosophy of Giovanni Gentile*, University of Illinois, Urbana, 1960, p. 162.
[26] Quoted in I.L. Kandel, *Studies in Comparative Education*, Harrap, London, 1933, pp. 68-9.
[27] H.S. Harris, *op.cit.*, p. 25; see also G. Gentile, *The Reform of Education*, trans. D. Bigongiari, Benn, London, 1923.

(iii) Youth Movement

The principal instrument for attaching young Italians to the fascist movement was not the school but the youth movement. In the 1920's the schools did not change much; they blossomed much more as centres for the development of fascist enthusiasm in the 1930's. The youth movement, on the other hand, from its inception in the early 1920's and formal legal establishment in 1926, was a significant fascist activity. The party paid special attention to young people and was at pains to preserve for itself an image of youthfulness and vigour. 'The régime is, and intends to remain, a régime of the young', the party secretary proclaimed in 1930.[28]

The National Balilla Organization, named after a Genoese boy-hero of the eighteenth century who lost his life in a revolt against the Austrians, catered initially for two age groups of boys: *Balilla* from eight to fourteen years old, and *Avanguardisti* from fourteen to eighteen. Those groups were soon supplemented by the *Piccole Italiane* for six to twelve year old girls, the *Giovani Italiane* for the twelve to eighteen year old girls, and the Wolf Children for all children six to eight. For the older youth of both sexes from eighteen to twenty-one, the party also established in 1930 the Young Fascists. In 1929 the youth movement up to the age of eighteen became the responsibility of the Ministry of Education and by 1931 had become the sole youth organisation in Italy. Membership, initially voluntary, became compulsory in 1937, and, in the same year, the GIL, the Italian youth organisation, was established to take over on behalf of the fascist party all the activities of the young people from fourteen to twenty-one years old.

The *Balilla* and *Avanguardisti* were designed 'to give moral and physical training to the young, in order to make them worthy of the new standard of Italian life'.[29] Six kinds of activities were listed in the *Balilla* regulations:

'1. teach the young the spirit of discipline and of military
      training, and give them:
2. pre-military training;
3. physical training through gymnastics and sports;
4. spiritual and cultural training;
5. professional and vocational training;
6. religious teaching.'[30]

A girl was to be prepared 'worthily for life' as 'the future mother of the family of new generations'.[31]

In the activities of the youth groups three things were emphasised:

- The main functions were physical. An extensive health program was started, and a great variety of sports, especially team games,

camping, mountaineering, gymnastics, and dancing were offered, and proved very popular. Through them, fitness, good health, companionship, and team discipline were encouraged as virtues desirable in a good fascist.

- The general tone of the movement and some of the principal activities were militarily oriented. The *Balilla* wore a uniform like that of the national militia, and the *Avanguardisti* resembled the Black Shirts of the fascist party. Every Saturday afternoon there was a parade in uniform for all boys and girls for drill, pre-military training, and physical education. The *Balilla's* motto was 'Believe, obey, fight', and to bolster their martial spirit they had their colours and banners to protect and their patriotic songs to sing. The final verse of the Hymn of the *Balilla* went:

> We are clouds of seeds,
> We are flames of courage
> For us the streams sing
> For us May shines and sings;
> But if one day the battle
> Sets Alps and seas aflame,
> We shall be the bullets
> Of Holy Liberty.[32]

The budding fascist had to learn that life was an active struggle in which he should be fit and armed to take his place at his leader's call. 'Remember also,' said Mussolini to the first gathering of Young Fascists in 1930, 'that Fascism does not promise you honours, or jobs, or rewards, but only duty and fighting.'[33]

- There was a special effort to direct the children's loyalty to Mussolini, *Il Duce*. 'In the name of God and Italy,' ran the *Ballilla* oath, 'I swear to follow the orders of the *Duce* and to serve the cause of the Fascist revolution with all my might, and, if necessary, with my blood.' A somewhat blasphemous unofficial creed, which nevertheless found its way into some primary school textbooks, ended with the words, 'I believe in the genius of Mussolini, in our Holy Father Fascism, in the communion of its martyrs, and in the resurrection of the Empire.'[34] The nation's leader was to be

---

[28] A. Starace, quoted in H. Finer, *Mussolini's Italy*, Gollanz, London, 1935, p. 416.

[29] Regulations for the Enforcement of the Law of 9 April 1926 on the Balilla Organisation, Article 1, in B. Mussolini, *op.cit.*, p. 270.

[30] *ibid.*, p. 272.

[31] C. Leeds, *Italy under Mussolini*, Wayland, London, 1972, p. 62.

[32] *ibid.*, p. 63.

[33] H. Finer, *op.cit.*, p. 447.

[34] C. Leeds, *op.cit.*, pp. 63-4.

cherished and obeyed, and, similarly too, all the other leaders of legions, cohorts, centuria, maniples, and squadrons into which the youth movement was organised, so that the life of the young people would be within a network of leadership firmly guiding them to a disciplined and thorough commitment to fascism.

The flavour of the youth movement eventually spread to the schools. By the early 1930's much of the teaching and propaganda associated with the *Balilla* was to be found in the schools, and many of the primary and physical education teachers were also youth group leaders.

(iv) Education in the 1930's

Gentile stayed in office as Minister of Education for only two years. His conservative and potentially fascist system remained little changed until the end of the 1920's. Then its potentiality began to become actuality. In 1929 all school teachers had to take an oath of loyalty to the fascist regime and in 1931 the loyalty oath was applied to university teachers. By 1933 all newly appointed teachers had to be members of the fascist party and were required, twelve months later, to wear uniform on all official occasions. In the early 1930's the state began to publish its own textbooks and exclude others from the schools. Fascist symbols and fascist culture became more pervasive in schools. Every classroom had a portrait of *Il Duce*; children, in their expressive exercises, were taught to imitate Mussolini's style; state textbooks, attractively produced, explained the program of national regeneration that Mussolini had undertaken, extolled his virtues, and exacted from the pupils unswerving obedience to him as the leader of the omniscient state and the emblem of the solidarity of the Italian people. In 1935, in the midst of enthusiasm for the Ethiopian war, military instruction was introduced into secondary schools and universities, and an increasing amount of material on the military and naval prowess of Romans and modern Italians, on the Mediterranean sea as *mare nostro*, and on the future imperial destiny of Italy began to appear in school textbooks and children's literature. The intensity of patriotic and fascist propaganda declined as the pupil moved up the educational ladder. Primary schools were the most heavily affected, and the younger primary school teachers turned out to be among the most active and devoted adherents to the regime. At the upper secondary school level and at university, fascist influence had little impact on school-work, and was exerted principally through the activities of the youth groups.[35]

Until Bottai's School Charter of 1939, Italian fascism made little serious attempt to think through the functions and possibilities of education in reconstructing the new state. Gentile, and the educators who followed him, freely expressed the view that education had an important role to play, but in action they preserved most of the existing fabric and its conservative ways, giving it a thorough injection of fascist culture but not altering it in any systematic way that would enable it to assist in building a modern fascist society. In this matter, secondary education was crucial. Gentile, in 1930, had criticised both education and the nation for their lack of fascism: 'the problem of making the schools Fascist is the problem itself of making the nation Fascist ... It is necessary that the Fascist should think, and will, educate himself, and form himself, and collaborate for his part in the construction of the new potent Fatherland ...'.[36] The concentrated political campaigns in the schools and the youth movement during the 1930's produced enthusiastic followers and party members, but they did not produce a sufficient number of persons adequately educated to transform Italy agriculturally, industrially, economically, and socially as the fascist regime was hoping and endeavouring to do, and as their rivals in the U.S.S.R. had successfully started to do by harnessing their schools intelligently to their program of reconstruction. Because the Gentile reform had limited secondary education to a largely humanistic and elitist program, had rejected any effort to move towards secondary education for all, and had not built, upwards out of the primary school, secondary institutions with a wider technological program that might lead to a rich range of vocational training, the fascist educational system remained unsuited to its reconstructive work.

(v) Bottai's School Charter, 1939

It was Bottai, Minister for Education in 1936, aided by Volpicelli, professor of education at the University of Rome, who grasped the need to connect education in a more integral way with social and economic life.[37] Bottai expressed the view in 1937 that the schools had had enough of mere rhetoric on fascist ideals; the country needed engineers, not lawyers and

[35] The most extensive treatment in English of this period is to be found in H.R. Marraro, *The New Education in Italy*, Vanni, New York, 1936, and L. Minio-Paluello, *Education in Fascist Italy*, Oxford University Press, 1946. For a detailed contemporary treatment, see Ministero dell' Educazione Nazionale, *Dalla Riforma Gentile alla Carta della Scuola*, Vallecchi, Roma, 1941.

[36] H. Finer, *op.cit.*, pp. 469-70.

[37] G. Bottai (1895-1959) was a foundation member of the party. He was on the party's left wing and interested primarily in industrial and social questions. As Minister for Corporations he introduced the Charter of Labour in 1927 that was to have been the basis on which the interests of workers and employers would be harmonised in a corporative fascist state. He was governor of Rome 1935-6. He had held a professorship in corporative law at Pisa for some time and in 1936 became a professor at the University of Rome. From 1936 to 1943 he was Minister of Education.

L. Volpicelli (1900-) was a secondary school teacher in Rome in the early 1930's, interested in J. Dewey's educational views and also in the possibility of a more functional fascist education. He became a professor of education at the University of Rome in 1935. He wrote extensively on current problems of Italian education, on the history of education, and on comparative education.

orators. Secondary and higher education still clung to an outmoded literary education, redolent of middle class values; when the masses entered secondary school they needed vocational education and applied science that was in touch with the workaday world. He produced a School Charter in 1939 which somewhat vaguely set out the main lines along which education should be rethought and reorganised.

In the light of Bottai's criticism of existing education, the School Charter and associated measures were disappointing. They were the beginning rather than the whole substance of a reform. They effected various minor administrative adjustments, they completed the process of state control by setting up a body to take charge of all catholic and non-state schools, and they proposed to make primary and secondary education more realistic by introducing courses of manual work and social service. Life is work, and work in all its forms contributed according to the Charter 'towards shaping character and intelligence'.[38] Productive manual work was to be a feature of the upper primary school which, reminiscent of the U.S.S.R., was to be renamed the Labour School. The one substantial change in the Bottai reform was the introduction of a three-year common middle school. Except for those who moved to a low-level vocational school, all pupils completed primary education at about eleven years of age and proceeded to a sort of junior high school from which, after a three-year course, they might go on to any one of a number of separate types of secondary school. The middle school was a substantial break with the existing elite pattern. It was an encouragement to the children of the working man to enter on a secondary education, a first step towards providing secondary education for all. The middle school started in 1940. World War II, however, inhibited any radical development of its curriculum, with the result that its work did not differ much from that of the traditional courses. World War II, in fact, circumscribed the whole of Bottai's attempt to readjust the educational system, and within a few years, in 1943, brought an end to the fascist regime in Italy.

EDUCATION IN NAZI GERMANY, 1933-45

'Zwingli St. A cold, dismal, empty Sunday morning... He saw knives flash, and felt several wounds... Herbert rushed up to a laundry which he knew and had often used. The door was shut. At the entrance beside the laundry Herbert collapsed ... In the hospital the doctor saw that help had come too late. Herbert Norkus would wake no more. The doctor closed the boy's eyelids.'[39]

The heroic life and death of the fourteen year-old Herbert Norkus, killed in a brawl in Berlin in 1932, was one of the powerful myths

developed by the Hitler Youth of Germany. He was a symbol, as the head of the youth movement put it, of youth's readiness to sacrifice.

The older youth, too, had their hero. They looked to Horst Wessel, 'student and worker', the new German man, who dedicated his whole life 'to the fight for freedom',[40] and whose career and death in 1930 inspired the Horst Wessel song, the favourite of the Hitler Youth.

The Horst Wessel Song[41]

Raise high the flag! With ranks closed tight as ever
Storm troops march on with calm and steady step.
Comrades shot dead by Red Front and reaction
March still with us in spirit as before.

Keep clear the streets now for the brown battalions!
Keep clear the streets for storm detachment men!
The swastika has drawn to it the hopes of millions,
The day of freedom and for bread is near.

The clarion call draws all the men together,
We stand prepared to go and fight.
Soon will the Hitler flags fly high throughout the streets
The end of slavery is drawing nigh!

Raise high the flag! With ranks closed tight as ever
Storm troops march on with calm and steady step.
Comrades shot dead by Red Front and reaction
March still with us in spirit as before.

(i) Hitler Youth

Like Italian fascism, nazism's main educational thrust was in its youth movement. The Hitler Youth were the symbol of the vigour and dynamism that the national socialists tried hard to display. They symbolised also the togetherness of the ordinary German people, and were a dependable reservoir of ready support in the campaigns that had to be fought to install the party in power in 1933 and to keep it in authority for the next twelve years.

The Hitler youth movement was started in 1922 and, by 1933 it numbered one hundred thousand. Soon after the national socialists came to power, most other youth organisations were discontinued, and in 1936

[38] L. Minio-Paluello, *op.cit.*, p. 206.

[39] A. Littmann, *Herbert Norkus und die Hitlerjungen vom Buesselkietz*, Steuben, Berlin, 1934, pp. 126-8. 1934, pp. 126-8.

[40] E. Reitmann, *Horst Wessel, Leben und Sterben*, Steuben, Berlin, 1933, p. 11.

[41] Trans. Vija Sierins, University of Sydney.

membership of the Hitler Youth became almost universal. 'The entire German youth,' ran the law of 1936, 'outside of their homes and school, is to be educated in the Hitler Youth physically, spiritually, and morally in the spirit of National Socialism and for service to nation and national community.' By the outbreak of World War II almost every young person between ten and eighteen was a member. From the age of ten to fourteen boys joined the *Jungvolk* (Young People) and girls the *Jungmädel* (Young Girls group); from fourteen to eighteen, boys joined the Hitler Youth proper (HJ) and from fourteen to twenty-one girls were members of the German Girls' League (BDM). Beyond the age of nineteen young men were eligible to join the Storm Troopers, with whom the youth movement had a very close association.

The youth movement of nazi Germany built on to the practices and traditions of the pre-war *Wandervögel* and the post-war *Bünde*. It maintained their interest in physical and outdoor activities and their love of the countryside, it took over their songs and symbols, and it adopted and extended their programs of work service. The ideals of leadership, self-discipline, acceptance of responsibility, and service to others that the Country Boarding Schools had shared with English Public Schools, and had encouraged in the pre-national socialist youth movement, also found an important place in the Hitler Youth. Compared with the middle class *Bünde*, recruits to the Hitler Youth came in larger proportions from the working class, and they tended to be more interested in holding meetings and parades in city streets and in political agitation. There was, however, no clear and abrupt break. The activities and principles were not obviously changed, yet they were, in time, fundamentally transformed. Activities were given a precision and a soldierliness they had previously eschewed, symbols and songs took on a more partisan and racial tone, leadership became loyalty to Adolf Hitler, and ideological teaching became an increasingly important part of their procedures.[42]

The Hitler Youth focused people's attention on the selective German tradition favoured by the national socialists. They were taught to revere the nordic race and nordic culture, and they were encouraged to regard themselves as the fighting heirs of that tradition. 'Blood and soil' was the catchphrase that summed up the essence of German culture. Peoples of nordic blood and race, the young people learnt, had been the creative force throughout human history, founding empires and dominating other peoples until by intermarriage the purity and power of their blood failed them. Germany was the centre and homeland of the nordic race. It was essential, therefore, for young Germans to cherish the soil which nurtured them, to take pride in the past achievements of their race, to keep German blood free from taint and, under the direction of their leader, to fight against all the circumstances and influences that held Germans back from expressing and enjoying their true destiny.

Jungvolk **at a rally in Berlin in 1933.**

The life of the Hitler Youth was immersed in symbolism designed to reinforce the 'blood and soil' doctrine. 'Flags are suspended from chains' ran the description of a group's meeting place, 'there is a wreath, a dented steel helmet, a photograph of a Hitler Youth killed in battle, guttering candles, and the text of the "Horst Wessel Song" is emblazoned on a large poster surrounded by a votive slogan.'[43] In camps and rallies the ceremonial and symbolism were even more intense. This was supported by instruction in racial biology and race citizenship, by reading books such as L.F. Clauss's *The Nordic Soul*, Alfred Rosenberg's *The Mythos of the Twentieth Century*, and, of course, Hitler's *Mein Kampf*, and by exhortation to fight against Versailles, the communists, and the Jews.

Within the pervasive racist and nationalistic environment of the youth movement, young Germans learnt four basic lessons:

---

[42] See H.W. Koch, *The Hitler Youth*, Macdonald and Jane's, London, 1975, Chapters 6-9, and W.Z. Laqueur, *Young Germany, A History of the German Youth Movement*, R.K.P., London, 1962, chapters 29 and 20.

[43] *Völkischer Beobachter*, 10 February 1935, quoted in Richard Grunberger, *A Social History of the Third Reich*, Weidenfeld and Nicolson, London, 1971, p. 281.

- Physical activity was more important than intellectual in producing a good national socialist. As in the Italian *Balilla*, the principal occupation of the Hitler Youth was in some kind of sport — ball games, gymnastics, skiing, hiking, camping. All such activities helped to develop healthy bodies, build stalwart character, and generate a sense of comradeship, so that the German youth of the future might become in Hitler's words 'slim and slender, swift as greyhounds, tough as leather, and hard as Krupp steel'.[44]

- Solidarity among the German people was vital for their future life and growth. The common Germanic heritage was stressed, both of the early heroic and mythological and of the cultural, political, and military accomplishments of more recent centuries. Germany had 'one people, one state, and one leader' (*ein Volk, ein Reich, ein Führer*). It was the task of young people to help knit even closer the bonds of the organic, integrated, totalitarian state by joining together in fellowship and in unselfish acts of social service, such as the winter relief campaigns, by sharing common pastimes and tasks with other youth, and finally, if need be, by sacrificing their lives as Herbert Norkus and Horst Wessel had done in battle for their cause.

- The highest expression of the human spirit was war. Conscription was reintroduced in 1935, and a soldierly tone pervaded much of German life and especially the activities of the Hitler Youth. War was one of the principal ingredients of nazi literature and film. Ernst Jünger, a leader of the martial school throughout the 1920's and 1930's, who in *Storm of Steel* wrote of war as a spiritual experience, was immensely popular, but he was only one among many who supported the national socialist apotheosis of war in which the German people might be seen to show an unmatched comradeship and superb heroism for the glory of the Third Reich. 'War the father of all things', declared Jünger, 'is our father too; it has hammered us, chiselled us, and hardened us to what we are.' Firm discipline with martial exercise helped to toughen and prepare German youth for struggle at home and war abroad.

- Proper leadership was essential for the youth movement and the country to achieve their aims. 'Youth leads youth' was one of the slogans of the Hitler Youth which prided itself on developing and training its own leaders free of adult officials though in close association with other arms of the nazi party. Beyond their day-to-day activities, the youth and all Germany were led by the great leader, Hitler himself.

The *Führer* was endowed with supernatural qualities. He was the great statesman, general, artist, and above all the great understanding, tireless, immaculate father of the German people. 'Hitler loves every member of the German nation, and forgives each one of them everything that is fallible in them. He loves you and me. He loves the whole German people, and it is this love that forces them all towards him. He knows no hell and no purgatory through which he would have them pass in order to be worthy of him,' said Robert Ley, the nazi labour front leader.[45] The leader was the embodiment of the collective and totalitarian spirit of the nation. For everyone, in some measure, the feeling of being within the *Führer's* ambit was renewed over and over each day every time he used the customary and obligatory greeting, *'Heil Hitler!'* The *Führer* was especially close to the nation's youth. In an introduction to a collection, made for the Hitler Youth, of addresses by Hitler to and about youth, Baldur von Schirach, leader of the Hitler Youth from 1931 to 1940, admonished the youthful readers to 'preserve these timeless words in your reverent and gallant hearts',[46] and Hitler, in a moving speech at a great youth rally at Nürnberg in 1936, let it be known that he thought them, the handsome, slender, disciplined youth, to be 'the greatest wonder of our time'.[47]

From the ranks of the Hitler Youth, young people passed into the labour service which became compulsory for boys in 1935 and girls in 1939. Six months' service between the ages of nineteen and twenty-five was required to be done in agricultural work of public importance. It was a service of economic value to Germany, but, equally, it was significant as a part of the continuation of the moral and social training of Germany's youth. The spade then gave way to the sword, and civic service was followed by military service in the national militia which became compulsory in 1935. The national socialists thus established a link between youth, productive manual labour, and service in the people's army, 'the great school of the nation ... a school of discipline, camaradarie and solidarity, where the character of young generations is formed'.[48] A similar pattern was to be established later by the Chinese in the 1950's to serve a different purpose and a different ideology.

---

[44] Adolf Hitler on Reichparteitag, 1935; see N.H. Baynes, (ed.), *The Speeches of Adolf Hitler*, Oxford University Press, 1942, p. 542, and *Adolf Hitler an seine Jugend*, N.S.D.A.P., Berlin, 1937.

[45] Quoted by R. Grunberger, *op.cit.*, pp. 87-8.

[46] *Adolf Hitler an seine Jugend*, N.S.D.A.P., Berlin, 1937.

[47] *ibid.*

[48] H. Lichtenberger, *The Third Reich*, trans. K.S. Penson, Greystone, New York, 1937, p. 176, reporting the views of the Minister for the Army, General von Blomberg.

(ii) Ernst Krieck

The national socialist view of education was systematically expounded by Ernst Krieck. He was an educational philosopher whose forceful but somewhat woolly-minded writings were widely read in Germany.[49]

Krieck saw national socialism creating a new society, a totalitarian national community, and a 'new unified form of common existence'.[50] The totalitarianism rested on a general Teutonic consciousness of sharing a common blood and soil which set Germans apart from other peoples as a race with a special destiny to purify western civilisation, and to assume the leadership of all other races, with a special obligation to keep itself uncontaminated, and to intensify its own sense of mission.

The state provided direction, organisation, and discipline. It curbed disruptive individualism, and fostered the fundamental values and cohesiveness of the people. The state was the great trainer of the people's character; it was responsible for the development of their political attitudes; and it formulated and expressed the people's collective will. Because education and propaganda were an important part of its business, the state had to take good care to develop organs appropriate to its purposes, to supervise its educational apparatus thoroughly, and to ensure that the marriage between education and politics was consummated.

The national socialist state was to be seen as a total, all-inclusive educational state. Education, according to Krieck, was inextricably part of the social fabric and all aspects of social life had educational functions. Everyone was continually and inescapably teaching everyone else, partly through intangible influence, partly through deliberate example, and partly through formal educational institutions. Educators must make use of all avenues and influences to produce men and women devoted to the new society and the new political ideals that were emerging. Intellectual education was therefore not the first consideration. Physique and character ranked ahead of it. Healthy, handsome, and pure-blooded bodies were the first concern. Closely following was the development of trustworthiness, devotion to national welfare, bravery, unquestioning obedience to authority, and willingness to sacrifice. School, family and youth groups were all expected to join in inculcating such virtues, and in placing the highest value upon them. The ideal product of education was the political soldier. Education was political and politics was educational. It was a politics which aimed at developing a disciplined soldierly people.[51]

Intellectual training was no longer to emphasise critical thinking and objectivity. ' The period of pure reason, and value-free science is over' were the opening words of Krieck's most popular work.[52] Objectivity, he suggested, was not detachment but sincerity and realism. It meant that one did one's best within existing limits and possibilities. These bounds were determined by current society. Intellectual training, and the work of intellectuals such as scientists, must have regard to the needs and interests of society. All intellectuals have, in fact, an ethical duty to see that their work contributes to 'the formation of man and the creation of a national living order according to the character and national laws of the community concerned'.[53]

The most important aim of education was to build up and consolidate a sense of national community which would have its pattern and ideals established by firm guidance from the state and from its leader who was the 'incarnation of the people's will'.[54] To achieve his purposes the leader had to have the support of a dedicated and thoroughly trained elite.

(iii) Schools for the Elite

Krieck put forward the idea that the elite to be trained should be a carefully selected political-military group 'rigorously disciplined, and bound together by a common national idea, devoted to a life of honour, valour, loyalty, and preparedness for service and sacrifice... and committed to the values of national, military, and political life'.[55] The idea was shared by other influential nazi party members. The new leaders who combined military virtue with a deep political consciousness and a determination to build a new Germany in their image, were to be chosen from all ranks of pure Germans and given special training. Various schemes for their education were proposed but none was ever clearly worked out and thoroughly put into effect.

---

[49] Ernst Krieck (1882-1947) became a primary school teacher, and from 1933 to 1945 professor of education at the universities of Frankfurt and Heidelberg. For several years he was also rector at Heidelberg. He began writing in 1910, eventually became accepted as the leading educational theorist of national socialist education, and, when World War II came to an end, he was interned and died in prison. His principal book in support of national socialism was *Nationalpolitische Erziehung*, Armanen Verlag, Leipzig, 1932.

[50] E. Krieck, *Völkisch-politische Anthropologie*, Armanen Verlag, Leipzig, 1938, 1, 97, quoted in G.F. Kneller, *The Educational Philosophy of National Socialism*, Yale University Press, New Haven, 1941, p. 28.

[51] Cf. A. Hitler, *My Struggle*, Paternoster, London, 1936, pp. 160-1.

[52] E. Krieck, *Nationalpolitische Erziehung*, Armanen Verlag, Leipzig, 1939 (1932), p. 1.

[53] E. Krieck & B. Rust, *Das Nationalsozialistische Deutschland und die Wissenschaft: Heidelberger Reden*, Hanseatischer Verlag., Hamburg, 1936, trans. in G. F. Kneller, *op.cit.*, p. 226.

[54] E. Krieck, 'The education of a nation from blood and soil', *International Zeitschrift für Erziehung*, 3, 3 (1933-4), p. 309.

[55] E. Krieck, *Nationalpolitische Erziehung*, p. 83.

A start on the program was made in 1933 with the establishment of small secondary boarding schools, national socialist political educational institutions, the Napolas, which some observers interestingly but loosely compared with English public schools. Pupils were selected rigidly, tested during their training for character and physical development, and culled from time to time to leave only the fittest to complete the program. The schools, though state institutions, had a close association with the political police (SS). Most of them followed the usual curriculum of a non-classical secondary school; a few, however, were *Gymnasien* and *Aufbauschulen*. As boarding schools they tried also to provide a form 'of total education in a tightly-knit community', a 'political education... which moulds the individual and forms the team'.[56] By 1944, thirty-seven of these schools were in operation, two of them for girls.

In 1937 an even more exclusive system for boys was developed, from some of the *Aufbauschulen* of the Weimar Republic, in the form of the Adolf Hitler Schools run outside the state school system, initiated by the labour ministry in connection with the youth movement and the party apparatus.[57] They were six-year secondary boarding schools intended to be established in each of the administrative districts of Germany to take 600 boys free of charge from the age of twelve to eighteen. Perfect health and physique, and demonstrated ability for leadership were demanded and constantly examined. The boys selected for the schools were all regarded as outstanding young people and became members of the Hitler Youth organisation. General secondary education was supplemented by substantial political instruction and physical education, and there was an emphasis throughout on practical ability, perseverance, and the exercise of leadership. At the age twenty-five, graduates of the schools could apply to enter for a further four-year course of leadership training given in successive years at four specially designed castles. Places in the castles were available for only a quarter of the number of those who successfully completed the Adolf Hitler secondary schools. The experience offered in this elite program was described by Hitler:

'My education is hard. Weakness has to be hammered out of them. In my castle of the Teutonic Order a youth will grow up before whom the world will tremble. I want a violent, domineering, undaunted, cruel youth. Youth must be all that. They must bear pain. There must be nothing weak and gentle about them....

'I will have no intellectual training. Knowledge is ruin to my young men. I would have them learn only what takes their fancy. But one thing they must learn — self-command! They shall learn to overcome the fear of death under the severest tests. That is the intrepid and heroic stage of youth.'[58]

During the war, after 1941, the elite schools received close and special attention. By the end of the national socialist period there were twelve

Adolf Hitler schools, several of which had graduated groups of students,[59] and the four castles had been set up and equipped, but none of them had begun their programs as originally envisaged. A final superior institution, a kind of party university at Chiemsee, was also planned to take a limited number of the graduates from the castles to complete their training for leadership. It was, however, never brought into being.

(iv) Educational Reorganisation

Krieck's philosophy and the inclinations of the party were put into operation between 1933 and 1945 in a gradual and unsystematic way. The changes moved, nonetheless, in an unmistakable direction — towards centralisation, towards elitism, and towards the politicising of education in the interests of developing and maintaining the totalitarian state.

Throughout their period in power the nazis increasingly unified the educational system, using Prussia as the example for the other state systems until the abolition of the states in 1934. An extensive program of in-service training was undertaken to ensure that teachers understood and could competently teach along acceptable nazi lines. This tendency was helped by the party's popularity among teachers. By the outbreak of World War II, ninety per cent of teachers belonged to the national socialist Teachers' Association, and about thirty per cent were actual members of the party, a proportion probably higher than that of any other profession. Furthermore, many ex-schoolteachers occupied positions of importance in the party organisation and helped both to attach the schools to the regime and to ensure a substantial degree of uniformity of outlook and program in the schools throughout the country.

Little change was made formally in the schools during the first year in which the national socialists were in power. A start, however, was made to bring the teaching profession to the support of the party. Jewish teachers were dismissed, and all other teachers were encouraged to read Hitler's *Mein Kampf* and to study nazi ideology.

In 1934 Bernhard Rust, a national socialist teacher, became national Minister of Education. From this appointment three tendencies developed

[56] The quotation comes from a speech by A. Heissmeyer, a senior S.S. officer in charge of the schools; reproduced in R.H. Samuel & R.H. Thomas, *Education and Society in Modern Germany*, R.K.P., London, 1949, p. 52. See also *International Educational Review*, 1937, 3, 'The German Nationalpolitische Erziehungsanstalt and the English Public School', pp. 162-73, and D. Schoenbaum, *Hitler's Social Revolution*, Weidenfeld and Nicolson, London, 1967, pp. 277-84.

[57] Occasionally, the name Adolf Hitler school was conferred as a special distinction on other schools. There was, for example, an Adolf Hitler elementary school.

[58] H. Rauschning, *Hitler Speaks*, Thornton Butterworth, London, 1939, p. 247.

[59] H. Scholtz, *Nationalsozialistische Ausleseschulen: Internats-Schulen als Herrschaftsmittel des Führerstaates*, Vanderboeck & Ruprecht, Göttingen, 1973, p. 209; see also H.J. Gamm, *Führung und Verführung: Pädagogik des Nationalsozialismus*, List, München, 1964.

which could be turned to totalitarian purposes. First, Rust had become the first national minister, and represented a centralising move that steadily grew in educational administration throughout the period, undermining the influence of the states and building up the authority of the central ministry; second, it marked the beginning of serious planning for the simplification and rationalisation of the school system; and third, a start was immediately made on putting politics into school and university textbooks and remodelling syllabuses to express the views of the new society more adequately.[60]

(v) Elementary School Education

In 1937 an extensive statement was made on the reform of the elementary school curriculum, and was supplemented by a further guide to studies in 1940. The elementary *Grundschule* was thought of by nazi educators as the real national school, the school for the masses, the school which laid the foundations of a common national consciousness. It was the first half of the eight-year national school *(Volksschule)*, starting at the age of six. It provided a uniform education for all children for four years; thereafter the majority continued for four years in its upper division, and the remainder entered secondary schools.[61] The progressive reforms introduced into the elementary school curriculum in the 1920's were retained but altered in spirit. The core of work was the study of the local environment, by means of which the pupil would learn to know and love the homeland. It was the foundation for further geographical, historical, and cultural study, and it was also the setting for the first lessons of devotion to 'blood and soil'. The mother-tongue, reading, writing, arithmetic, music, drawing, and physical education were the other subjects of the curriculum, as they were in most elementary schools in most countries. In the national socialist school, emphasis was placed on the subjects of physical education and German.

Physical education emphasised four things: health, physical achievement, military preparedness, and race consciousness. It was thus as much psychological as physical in its intention. School activities were supported by a strong national organisation of sports and gymnastics carefully and enthusiastically directed by leaders in each administrative district. The program of physical education had its supreme demonstration and reinforcement in the spectacular presentation of the Olympic Games staged at Berlin in 1936.

Elementary school German illustrated the tendency to politicise the content of school subjects even at the most junior level, but it also provided evidence of the regime's interest in modernisation. The party, in the process of building solidarity and national pride in the German people, laid stress on tradition and on its early Teutonic heritage, but it also prided itself, as the Italian fascist party did too, on being the party of youth, the party interested in future accomplishments, the party that was up-to-date in its thinking and its methods. Consequently, its military weapons were the latest, its military tactics were revolutionary, its methods of communication and propaganda made use of the latest technological advances, and its leader travelled by aircraft at a time when foreign leaders were still moving about by ship and train and motor car. Its image was that of the maker of a renascent and contemporary civilisation. So, too, in education. Wherever progressive ideas and methods did not conflict with national socialist ideology, they were continued and encouraged in the schools; thus the interest the progressive educators had shown in using film, radio, and other audio-visual means of teaching, in an integrated curriculum, in the development of aesthetic taste, in activity methods, in linking the school with the community, and in the reform of language teaching, they took up. But they did not countenance such innovations as co-education, individualised methods of teaching, or improved methods of intellectual training.[62]

In teaching German in the elementary school, teachers were encouraged to use the most effective, up-to-date, and interesting methods; they were issued with attractive textbooks of which, after 1941, the party had a monopoly, and they took the opportunity to link their teaching of language and literature with the everyday life and work of contemporary society. At the same time, they were instructed to remember that German was their own and their pupils' mother-tongue, that it was a central part of their national heritage, that contemporary society which the language reflected was nazi society, and that the most appropriate literature for study was that which helped to develop enthusiasm for the party and devotion to the *Führer*.

The attitude was strikingly illustrated in the use, in the 5th and 6th classes, of a reading book which featured a symbolic and inspirational story, *A Flight through the Storm*, in which Hitler, to keep faith with a waiting rally, undismayed by the hurricane which swept the countryside

---

[60] A brief summary of the initial changes is to be found in J.W. Taylor, 'Education in the New Germany, in the Light of National Socialist Legislation', *International Educational Review*, 1933-4, 3, . 318-31; a useful collection of documents is to be found in H.J. Gamm, *Führung and Verfuhrung*, *op.cit.*

[61] In 1936 a law completed what the Weimar Republic had begun by abolishing the remaining preparatory schools *(Vorschulen)* attached to secondary schools through which pupils had an alternate fee-paying and privileged path into secondary schools.

[62] There are a considerable number of first-hand descriptions of life and work in German schools in the 1930's; one of the most interesting is Anna Dane, 'The education of nazi women', in J.D.G. Medley *et al.*, *Australian Educational Studies*, Melbourne University Press, 1940, pp. 167-208, which describes the experience of teaching in a girls' boarding school which preserved the somewhat progressive tradition of the *Landerziehungsheime*.

Figure 9.2: Nazi Germany: School System after 1938.

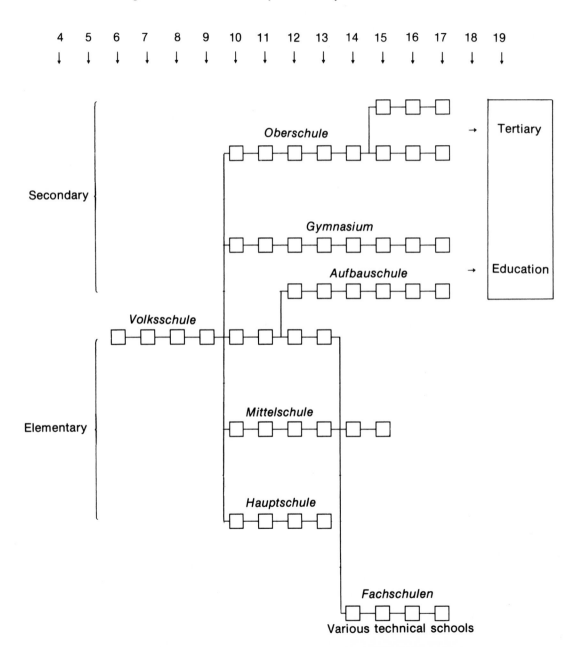

and had grounded all commercial flights, took off in his aircraft and rode out the storm. 'This is no longer flying, this is a whirling dance which today we remember only as a faraway dream. Now we jump across the aerial downdrafts, now we whip our way through tattered clouds, again a whirlpool threatens to drag us down, and then it seems that a giant catapult hurls us into steep heights.

'And yet, what a feeling of security is in us in the face of this fury of the elements. The *Führer's* absolute serenity transmits itself to all of us.'[63]

The other major subject of the elementary school curriculum, arithmetic, followed the general lines for the teaching of German without lending itself quite as readily to political and national purposes. It was possible, however, to include in textbooks examples and exercises which would orient students towards the interests and objectives of the national socialist party.

After four years of elementary education selected pupils could transfer to a secondary school. If they were not selected for secondary education they could move into a middle school whose function remained the same as in the Weimar period. It provided six years of higher elementary education for pupils who had no great academic pretensions but, wished to continue a general education which included a foreign language.

In 1941 another type of higher elementary school, the *Hauptschule*, was introduced, particularly into the occupied territories, and was eventually to replace the middle school. Adopted from the Austrian school system, it was a four-year school intended to provide more advanced facilities for brighter children who might aspire subsequently to transfer to a secondary school.

On the completion of eight years of elementary education, at about the age of fifteen, nine months' rural service in a Land Year, introduced in 1934, was required for all pupils in urban schools. General and political education was continued during that period, and the young people, billeted in camps, would become familiar with rural life, and 'experience the blessings derived from an unselfish, corporate life'.[64]

Following the Land Year, the ex-elementary school students would start a compulsory minimum of three years' technical training in a large variety of vocational schools.

(vi) Secondary Education

In 1937, the same year in which the directions on elementary education were published, a decree was issued which simplified the system of secondary education, and, in the following year, 1938, a detailed statement of policy and guide to the secondary school curriculum was published by the national ministry.[65]

The 1938 reform superseded the Weimar school plan of 1925 which had provided the basis for the school structure since that date. The system was simplified by reducing the course of studies from nine to eight years and the five main types of secondary schools to two, the *Gymnasium* and the *Oberschule*, the principal secondary school, being, in the nazi view, the *Oberschule*.

The ordinance of 1938 on the reorganisation of secondary education was important, not merely because it set out the new program for the schools, but also because it outlined the place and function of the school in national socialist society.

'In any period of history,' it stated, 'the school rests upon the basic forces of the times, but life is always ahead of the school. The school transmits to pupils the spiritual content of its time...' The school on that view did not stimulate or engineer social change, it consolidated, when appropriately controlled, the changes brought about by political forces. The ordinance criticised the authors of the Reform of 1925 for setting their own political goals and seeking to create, through education, a new citizen and a new and more responsible society. To the question which contemporary educators in America were debating, Dare the School build a New Social Order?, the answer was a firm negative. Politics had priority over pedagogics. 'Political action,' the ordinance declared, 'is the foundation of a new order.' Education was to be established in the image of the new political and social order.

National socialist education had evolved not in the schools but in political struggle. The discipline and comradeship of the fight by military-political groups hammered out the new ideal and the concept of the man and citizen that educational agencies should seek to produce. As the nation came to see its mission under the guidance of those who struggled through to successful political action united and inspired by their leader, so education could begin to form a clear idea of its task.

The school, nevertheless, according to the ordinance, was not to be a mere transmitter of tradition. 'The German youth which today goes to our schools has its face turned towards the future.' The school, too, looked forward. Its task, however, was not to try to produce something of

[63] *Deutsches Lesebuch für Volksschulen, Fünftes und Sechstes Schuljahr*, vii, Gemeinschaftsverlag, Braunschweiger Schulbuchverleger, n.d., p. 366, quoted in G.L. Mosse (ed.), *Nazi Culture: Intellectual, Cultural and Social Life in the Third Reich*, Allen, London, 1966.

[64] B. Rust, 'Education in the Third Reich', in J. von Ribbentrop *et al.*, *Germany Speaks*, Thornton Butterworth, London, 1938, p. 108.

[65] Germany, Reichsministerium für Wissenschaft, Erziehung, und Unterricht, *Erziehung und Unterricht in der Höheren Schule*, Weidmannsche, Berlin, 1938, 265 pp. English translations of sections of this publication can be found in I.L. Kandel (ed.), *Educational Yearbook 1938*. Teachers' College, Columbia University, New York, 1939, pp. 179-95, and M. Demiashkevich, 'The reform of secondary education in Germany', *The Educational Forum*, 2, November 1937, pp. 82-9, and 'More on the reform of secondary education in Germany', *ibid.*, 3, November 1938, pp. 81-95.

its own construction, but to serve the nation by supporting the new ideals and training youth physically, morally, and intellectually according to the wisdom of the political leaders. In Germany all educational agencies had one common aim, 'the formation of the National Socialist man', a disciplined, virile, patriotic, politically alert, and devoted follower of the nation's leader. To do this it had to step behind its intellectualist traditions; it had to educate the whole man, so that each individual would develop in physique, in character, and in mind, in the ways which would enable him best to use his energies in the service of the nation.

To achieve the school's aim, the teaching processes should be a judicious blend of pupil activity and teacher direction. Teaching should grow out of the pupil's experience; it should be seen by him to be interesting and useful, and it should involve his feelings and his will as well as his intellect. Activity work should stimulate self-active learning and make use of study groups and group discussion. So that it should have depth and purpose it should involve the pupils in personal experience, evaluation, and the making of decisions. The goal-oriented activity process recommended for German schools — study, discussion, experience, evaluation, and decision — no doubt pleased the Deweyans and other progressives among German educators.

Two further suggestions, however, would have been less congenial. Control and discipline were always close at hand; it was a discipline of order and subordination. The ideal was obedient and soldierly behaviour that permeated all activities. The injunction: 'Order and neatness in every kind of work ... must be valued and relentlessly developed', was difficult to reconcile with the views on creativity that progressive educators had associated with activity methods. The other practice distasteful to progressives was the restriction of education available for girls.

The ordinance quoted the *Führer* as saying: 'The goal of feminine education must be fixed as the education of the future mother.' In consequence boys and girls were to be educated separately, and girls' education was to take its content and tone from the nature and the destined occupation of women. When the nazis came to power in 1933, one-third of the German work force was female, and despite strenuous efforts to confine women to domesticity the proportion steadily increased during the 1930's as women entered many industrial and commercial occupations that had previously been almost entirely male.[66] From 1934 the proportion of places available for women in universities was restricted to 10 per cent and in 1938 entry to higher education was made even more difficult by providing for girls only a single type of secondary school..

The 1938 ordinance decreed that the girls' secondary school should be an eight-year *Oberschule*. Entry was after four years of elementary school at approximately the age of eleven years. After five years of a common secondary course of physical education, German civilisation, natural sciences, mathematics, household arts, English, and religion, the girls could follow one of two streams for the final three years:

- home economics which added gardening, handicrafts, nursing, vocational guidance, and practical social service to the common program; or
- foreign language which enabled girls to take a second modern foreign language and Latin rather than home economics.

A shorter special form of the *Oberschule* was also kept on a small scale. It was the six-year *Aufbauschule* entered after the completion of six years of elementary education; it had boarding facilities and was intended for gifted girls from rural districts.

Important though the firm separation of girls from boys was under the 1938 ordinance, the main significance of the law was the establishment of a common secondary school, the *Oberschule*, which the great majority of secondary school pupils would attend in either its boys' or girls' version. The great variety of schools previously characteristic of German secondary education was reduced to two: the general *Oberschule*, and the specialist classical *Gymnasium*, supplemented by the *Aufbauschule*. All kinds were available for boys; girls henceforth would have difficulty entering a *Gymnasium*.

Secondary education was not intended for all children; it was for a minority. The majority continued beyond the age of ten in the elementary system through the four higher classes of an elementary school or a middle school which led to a variety of vocational schools. Selection for entry to secondary education, usually after four years of elementary school, was based on school performance and national fitness, which was judged by a child's contribution to his youth group, his general conduct, and his possession of Aryan blood.

Of the pupils who did receive a secondary education, over 80 per cent moved into the *Oberschule* which was intended to be a common school providing a comprehensive education for those selected for secondary work. The program for the first five years allowed for no electives, and consisted of physical education, German civilisation, natural sciences, mathematics, foreign languages, and religion. In the final three years boys' schools offered a choice of specialising in science and mathematics or foreign languages, girls' schools in household arts or foreign languages.

Of all the subjects of the curriculum the one that called for the most distinctive treatment was history, which formed part of the German civilisation group. The approach to history had been clearly outlined in a

---

[66] International Labour Office, *Yearbook 1938-1939*, Geneva, 1939, p. 317.

series of ministerial suggestions for history textbooks in 1933,[67] and had been developed by various writers of method books or textbooks since that date. The 1938 ordinance listed the topics for each year. For the first five years of the common secondary program the following were taught in sequence:

- Stories of national heroes of all ages, e.g., Adolf Hitler, Hindenburg, Blücher, Maria Theresa, Otto I, Widukind, Arminius;
- National history from earliest times to Charlemagne;
- The First Empire to 1648;
- German history from 1648 to 1871;
- From 1871 to the present.

For the final three years at the upper level of the secondary school the topics were:

- Prehistory up to the end of the Middle Ages;
- From the Baltic Settlements to 1850;
- From Bismarck to the Third Reich.

History was German history; its study would burn 'the idea and feeling of race through instinct and reason into the hearts and brains of the young people'. Contact with the lives of great heroes would help pupils approach history through their emotions. Prehistory would steep them in the mythological lore of the original Nordic peoples. The history of German settlements beyond the present boundaries of the Reich would emphasise the point that Germans, e.g. in Austria and in Baltic countries, were one people. Above all, a detailed treatment of the most recent period would help establish the right attitudes in pupils and awaken an understanding of the needs and tasks of the present. 'If the formation of political will is our aim, we must take up a clear and decided attitude ... Thus we do not speak of the "Peace Treaty" but of the "Dictated Peace" or the "Shameful Treaty"; not of "Reparations" but of "Tribute", of land robbery, dishonouring, and disarming.'[68] The pattern was incorporated in school textbooks such as *The Eternal Road*, written for *Hauptschulen* during World War II, which has been described as 'the climax in the evolution of the Nazi history textbook'. Put together with the collaboration of leading academics and teachers, its volumes followed the 1938 syllabus, attractively emphasising the heroic accomplishments of the German people and their leaders, and the need to preserve the purity of blood and heritage.[69]

History was not to be a dull, intellectual study. It must live. Class discussion, the reading of sagas and patriotic poems, the use of pictures and slides, and visits to museums, festivals, and other places of interest were to add life and emotion to the lessons, the object of which was to produce persons who really felt themselves to be part of an ever-growing German nation, rejoicing at its triumphs, suffering its disappointments, and taking heart and inspiration from the example of its great leaders. History was clearly a political instrument. The history teacher was primarily a moulder of character, and he must choose content and methods accordingly. One well-known educational writer put succinctly the problem that sometimes faced his fellow-teachers: 'In forming the national will, is objective science or the myth of greater value?'[70] History was an excellent vehicle for teaching race, blood and soil, patriotism, and the martial virtues. Geography by concentrating on geopolitics reinforced the work of the history teacher.

Among the sciences biology was given a special place, being compulsory for all age levels. In it pupils were taught that, step by step, they must grasp the biological laws that regulate life. Nature was to be seen as a systematic totality in which each life form struggled to draw its needs from its surrounding life space. Existence for individual forms was fleeting; it was the life of the species or race that was enduring. Life secured the continuance of its unique and common forms by inheritance through reproduction. Mankind was involved in this process in which the highest form was the nation, united by blood and common destiny. Men, to succeed in life's struggle, must know the facts of heredity, race, and population growth. The nature of race and the laws of heredity must be taught from the very first class in the school, so that they are thoroughly absorbed. It must be made clear that the German people were of the nordic race and that their future welfare and success depended upon the maintenance of the biological purity of their nordic heritage. And the pupils must be determined to keep it so.

(vii) University Education

In the 1920's several central European countries were troubled by their inability to provide employment for the intellectuals produced by their universities and upper secondary school classes. With the onset of the

[67] For a translation of the suggestions see I.L. Kandel, 'The making of Nazis', in *Educational Yearbook*, 1934, Teachers' College, Columbia University, New York, 1934, pp. 480-5.
[68] Wilhelm Rödiger, *The Teaching of History — its Purpose, Material, and Method*, trans. from *Geschichte: Ziel, Stoff und Weg*, Klinkhart, Leipzig, 1934, p. 70.
[69] For a brief description of some leading national socialist school textbooks, see R.H. Samuel & R.H. Thomas, *op.cit.*, pp. 82-8.
[70] W. Rödiger, *op.cit.*, p. 57.

great depression of the early 1930's the problem of adjustment between higher educational preparation and economic opportunity became even more acute. The difficulty was especially appreciated in Germany where many of the enthusiastic recruits to the party had come from secondary school and university students. Accordingly, in their first years in power, 1933-4, steps were taken to reduce drastically the number of university entrants by curtailing the number of places available to Jews and to women, and by giving preference to candidates who had characteristics attractive to the party, such as physical excellence and a record of activity in the Hitler Youth.[71] University student numbers fell from approximately 120,000 in 1931 to fifty thousand in 1939, and rose, when restrictions on entry were relaxed, to eighty thousand in 1943.

In 1935 the centralising tendency of national socialism was expressed by bringing all universities under the authority of the national Minister of Education, and by forming for all university staff a single national socialist staff organisation, and similarly, for all students, a nazi student league.

The intellectual world of the 1920's and 1930's in Germany was one of discontent, scepticism, and detachment. The primacy of rational thinking had been under challenge for the past half-century. In the late nineteenth century Nietzsche had forcefully argued that reliance on rational intelligence was restrictive, and could be destructive of creativity, which springs out of irrational sources. Langbehn in his popular and incoherent *Rembrandt as Educator* preached in 1890 that German scholarship had overburdened the intellect, and had inhibited the power of action. What was required was a more courageous commitment to the emotions. To become a man, one needed education in character and feeling, and contact with a great personality. Spengler, who published his widely read *The Decline of the West* in 1918, resumed the attack on intellect. Instinct and intuition, not analytic thought, were the underpinning of creativity. If there was a way out of the decline for Germans, it was by reliance on strong and impulsive action. Spengler matched the mood of desperate pessimism of the Germany of the 1920's, and, by his substantial popularity among students, confirmed their steady move towards irrationality. Rosenberg's *The Mythos of the Twentieth Century*, published in 1930, was the capstone. It was a systematic exposition of irrational racism. His fundamental concept was a mysterious supra-rational spirit which infused the German people, making them one community and one blood, instinctively finding expression of themselves through an inspired leader. The myth, he claimed, provided truer and more powerful guidance than any attempt at rational thinking.[72]

In the 1920's the impact of Bergsonian and psychoanalytic theories also drew attention to the importance of non-rational motivation in human behaviour. These growing and unsettling movements, when combined with the uncertainty of the economic and political future of the Weimar experiment, made a deep impress on literature, art, and intellectual life in general. It was an age of expressionism, its latent emotionality typified by Munch's painting, *The Cry*, which brought a mass of primitive energy and feeling vibrating to the surface and confronted the viewer with 'the great cry ringing through nature'.[73] Its tensions and dilemmas were portrayed in Kafka's nightmarish stories of human situations wavering between irrationality and ungraspable profundity. And its search for philosophical explanation turned favourably towards Heidegger's existentialism which attempted to define man from the inside, giving voice to an 'inner feel' beyond and below the processes of logic. It was an atmosphere in which dream and reality merged, and intellectuals began either to lose their traditional conviction of the efficacy of intellectual methods or, on the other hand, to cling more strenuously to their hard-won disciplines and progressively to become more and more detached from current life.

The German learned class had not managed to bring their traditional literary culture to terms with the technological revolution that had been remaking Germany and the world since the late nineteenth century. They tended to think of themselves as the elite guardians of a culture that industrial progress and mass political power threatened to undermine. They were therefore a little estranged from the world of the 1920's and 1930's, and perhaps slightly bewildered by it. Though immensely patriotic, they had a distaste for political activity and cherished their non-utilitarian approach to learning. Nevertheless, the growing evidence of

[71] The appropriate laws are given in I.L. Kandel, 'The making of nazis'. *Educational Yearbook*, 1934, Teachers' College, Columbia University, New York, 1934, pp. 517-19.

[72] F.W. Nietzsche, (1844-1900) was professor of philosophy at Basel 1869-1879 and thereafter wrote in retirement. His best known works were *The Birth of Tragedy* (1872), *Thus Spake Zarathustra* (1883-4), and *Beyond Good and Evil* (1886).
   A. Julius Langbehn (1851-1907) wrote extensively and anonymously on literary and aesthetic topics. His *Rembrandt as Educator* created a great stir in the 1890's, and was still being reprinted in the 1920's. His patriotic spirit appealed specially to members of youth groups among whom his writing was very influential.
   O. Spengler (1880-1936), the German Cassandra of the twentieth century, was a schoolteacher who retired in 1911 to live and write on private means. His *The Decline of the West* appeared in two volumes in 1918 and 1928, and became the centre of unprecedented discussion and controversy throughout the 1920's and 1930's.
   A. Rosenberg (1893-1946) was the ideologist of the national socialist party. Born in Lithuania, he joined the party in 1920 and became one of its leading members. In 1934 he was made head of the party's ideological office, and during the war in 1941 became minister for the eastern occupied territories. *The Mythos of the Twentieth Century* was widely read and regarded as a definitive statement of national socialist views.

[73] E. Munch (1863-1944), a Norwegian, for some time lived in Berlin and influenced German art in the first three decades of the century by his stark, psychological look into the depths of human experience.

the importance of irrational factors in human behaviour, the increasing prestige of technological skill and knowledge, and the more intensive involvement of students in political disputation which characterised the pre-national socialist decade caused much heart-searching. Their predicament bred uncertainty and division. The younger academics tended to be more amenable to the press of current change and in many cases became readily and favourably involved with the new forces. Most intellectuals, however, tended to remain indeterminate and reluctant to take any firm stand.

In the climate of the time, when Hitler came to power in 1933, it did not prove difficult for many members of the academic community to combine the non-rational and patriotic approach of nazism with their habitual methods of working. Before the election in March of that year three hundred university teachers signed an appeal to electors on Hitler's behalf. In that same year the philosopher Heidegger joined the party, became rector of Heidelberg University, and exhorted the students and staff to work in the spirit of national socialism 'to experience and endure the abyss of existence' under the courageous guidance of their *Führer*.[74]

During the period the number and quality of university staff changed. Jewish professors and opponents of national socialism were dismissed or migrated to other countries in the early and mid-1930's; by 1939 it is probable that almost half of the staff in office in 1933 had been replaced, and university staff and students were substantially in support of the regime.

Some scholars found either from the beginning or after a short trial that they could not reconcile their ideas and their training with national socialist ideology. Among these were educational leaders such as Spranger, the educational psychologist, and Litt, the educational philosopher; these two resigned their posts. On the other hand there were well-known educators such as Krieck, Petersen, the Jena progressive, and Wilhelm, editor of the *International Educational Review*, who accepted the new dispensation with varying degrees of enthusiasm. In some departments, the dismissals or resignations caused serious dislocation. This was particularly the case in some scientific and technological faculties. Göttingen for instance, celebrated in the 1920's for its extraordinary collection of internationally known mathematicians and scientists, was denuded in the 1930's. A further handicap to scholarship in 1933 was the public burning of learned books in various university towns; it was the beginning of a voluntary and state censorship that restricted the universities' traditional freedom to learn and to teach.

Two other developments were of particular note. There was a development of 'militant scholarship' throughout the universities. This meant that university studies and university teaching became more positive and committed to the support of national socialist society. Every

subject was applied politics. Physical education became important, race science became a study in its own right, and also entered into many other subjects, and fields such as law, political science, history, philosophy, and economics took on a nazi colour. It meant, too, that much more time and importance was given to youth, party, and military activities. There was also a movement of students into technological subjects. Amid the general decline in student numbers, the decrease in students in technological courses was less than that in other courses during the first five years of the period, and thereafter there was a steady increase.

Hitler placed little store by the work of intellectuals and often expressed his contempt for them. The tone set by the *Führer* pervaded society. In consequence, there was less encouragement than in the past for students to proceed to universities, and for academics to pursue the work of scholarship and research. There was, however, no sudden break with tradition. The universities did continue their traditional role, and in many fields managed to sustain work of their usual quality. It was probably true to say, nevertheless, that of all the country's educational institutions, the universities adapted least well and suffered most throughout the national socialist period. They had been primarily self-directive intellectual institutions and, in the climate of the time, independent intelligence did not flourish.

From another point of view, however, the nazi interlude represented an important and positive break with academic tradition. It was a way of bringing the German universities firmly and abruptly into the twentieth century. It put forward and enforced several new ingredients in the idea of a university, e.g., that education was intimately involved in the political interests of the state, that universities had a duty to respond to current social needs, and that, both in research and teaching, applied knowledge was not inferior to pure. Such views, hitherto debatable if not actively repulsed, became axiomatic in most countries after the 1930's. There were, of course, many different shades of application and interpretation over the years and in different places but, as states became increasingly interested in planning the welfare and education of all their citizens, tertiary institutions were inevitably drawn into and felt the impact of political, economic, and social policies undertaken by governmental authorities.

---

[74] M. Heidegger, *German Existentialism*, trans. and ed. D.D. Runes, Philosphical Library, New York, 1965, pp. 42, 43. There are many analyses of the role of university teachers and other intellectuals in nazi Germany; an interesting summary may be found in a chapter, 'Professor NSDAP' in J.C. Fest, *The Face of the Third Reich*, trans. M. Bullock, Weidenfeld and Nicolson, London, 1970. For an extensive analysis of the attitudes of German literary academics in the pre-nazi period, see F.K. Ringer, *The Decline of the German Mandarins. The German Academic Community 1890-1933*, Harvard University Press, 1969; and for an early detailed study, see E.Y. Hartshorne, *The German Universities and National Socialism*, George Allen, London, 1937.

(viii)   Technical Education

The party came to power in an unexampled economic depression at a time when about a third of the work force were unemployed. It had to set itself to restore confidence, resuscitate industry, provide opportunities for work and establish its interest in training people for more efficient labour service in and for the total society. The supply of well-trained manpower at all levels was important for Germany's recovery from the depression, and for the image and prestige of the party.

German technical education, therefore, long studied and envied by foreign educators, remained intact. Its reputation was undiminished. The interests of the party, the utilitarian inclinations of educators and administrators, and the expanding demands of industry and war ensured that facilities for training middle and higher level technicians through technical schools and technical universities were maintained in adequate numbers and quality. Entry into apprenticeship was strongly encouraged and the numbers were steadily increased throughout the 1930's. By special competitions and scholarships many pupils who had not received a secondary education were encouraged to attend technical schools, and to proceed, in some cases, to technical universities.[75] Throughout the cities there was a well-developed system of compulsory vocational schools operating in conjunction with the apprenticeship system, and in the rural villages efforts were made, from 1935 on, to raise the level of attendance and proficiency in agricultural and other vocational courses.

OVERVIEW

The three totalitarian countries, Japan, Italy, and Germany, obviously had much in common politically and educationally, and they provide interesting examples of similar but differing degrees and ways of relating politics to education.

Japan had long since planned the development of its public education system with a view to the nation's prosperity and speedy westernisation. The planning, however, was neither tight nor thorough, and there were grave difficulties in reconciling traditional beliefs and patterns of behaviour with western knowledge and ideas. In the 1920's and 1930's Japan emerged clearly as a major world power. The work of the schools was an important factor contributing to her emergence. They had provided her with the skilled and educated manpower on which her prosperity rested, and they had helped to maintain a depth of national solidarity which produced enthusiastic and patriotic support for the expansionist activities of the Japanese government. Her military successes in the 1930's bred a high degree of nationalist feeling. Henceforth the most prominent feature of the program in her schools was the nurturing of Japanese patriotism and solidarity with a religious zeal which centred round the divine figure of the emperor.

Of the three, Japan provided the strongest example of a country at the highest pitch of nationalism and of a country in which education was harnessed to the task of cultivating and maintaining the national spirit. By and large it was a conservative and backward-looking spirit. Though Japan was rapidly modernising and was conscious of the need to develop a new society out of the mixture of traditional ways and western innovations, her educators did not go far towards achieving a synthesis. They tended to concentrate rather on ensuring that the power of traditional moral beliefs should be maintained with a minimum of deviation.

In Europe, Mussolini's Italy and Hitler's Germany had a stronger sense of beginning something new, of starting a new form of society. The philosophers of the new dispensation, Gentile and Krieck, endeavoured to show how the various educational agencies and influences could be brought to the support of the new political and social regimes. Education, however, was not fully harnessed to social reconstruction. In Italy it was hardly harnessed at all. The schools and the youth movement helped to develop a high level of patriotism, they generated much devotion to the *Duce,* and they encouraged great expectations of the capacity of the fascist party to improve Italian life. But politics and education were never really married; it tended to be a casual liaison, at times warm and colourful but never allowed to ripen and mature.

It could be said that fascist education suffered from a lack of clear definition. In Gentile it had a philosopher who could expound its ideals and ambitions, but who could not see the full practical implications of his philosophy. The schools had many good and effective character educators, but the system lacked planners. The enthusiasm and effort generated by attractive propaganda activities was never coupled to a well-thought-out educational plan. Educational development during the twenty years of fascism was, in consequence, piecemeal and unproductive.

In Germany the union was more complete. The Nazis had a stronger sense of mission. As a result, the school and the other educational agencies became thoroughly politicised. 'Up to 1933 the German school was a Herbart school'[76] according to a contemporary apologist. The national socialist period of reform was a modest, though sometimes violently executed, revolt against established Herbartian custom. The tradition, sometimes misconceived, against which nazi education

---

75   R. Grunberger, *op.cit.,* p. 343.

76   R. Grunberger, *op.cit.,* p. 343.

struggled, was one which valued intellectual skill, individual excellence, and methodically organised schooling. The national socialist approach lowered the traditional importance of the school, and gave a much more significant place than previously to the youth movement, to community influence, and to active participation in social and political work. It replaced the primacy of intellectual training with an attentive care for physical achievement and the cultivation of visceral, inner conviction and expression. It made a point of criticising traditional education for its lack of a compelling ideal, and summoned German youth to rally to the inspiration of their Leader.

Above all it deliberately and clearly demonstrated, what one of its firmest opponents quickly recognised, that 'politics and the mind, politics and civilisation, can no longer be separated'.[77] Education was not something with a life of its own that individuals might or might not pursue; it was intimately related to the social and economic life of the country, something bound up with the life of the community, something, in short, whose task was 'identified with that of politics'.[78]

Nevertheless, in nazi Germany as in fascist Italy the educational system was never planned into the development of society to the extent that it was in the U.S.S.R. The nazi and fascist totalitarians, for all their political rhetoric on the importance of youth and the schools, simply did not realise, as the soviets did, that education was an integral part of, and a powerful tool in, the process of social and economic reconstruction.

[77] Institut International de Cooperation Intellectuelle, *La Formation de l'Homme Moderne*, Paris, 1935, contribution by Thomas Mann, trans. in I.L. Kandel, *Educational Yearbook*, 1941, 'The End of an Era', Teachers College, Columbia University, New York, 1941, p. 17.

[78] G. Gräfe, The conditions and content of the new order of German education, in *Year Book of Education*, 1939, Evans, London, 1939, p. 267.

Pirate Ilond. By J.B.W. Aged 12.

Frontispiece to H. Caldwell Cook, *The Play Way*, William Heinemann, London, 1917.

CHAPTER 10

INDIVIDUAL DEVELOPMENT AND SOCIAL RECONSTRUCTION: THE CONTRIBUTION OF THE PROGRESSIVES AND THE EDUCATIONAL PSYCHOLOGISTS IN THE 1920's AND 1930's

SUMMARY

The New Education Fellowship and the Progressive
  Education Association

Progressive Educators of the 1920's and 1930's
    (i)   Creativity and the Artist Educators
    (ii)   Psychoanalysis and the Progressives
    (iii)   Individual Progress: Dalton and Winnetka Plans
        (a) Dalton Plan
        (b) Winnetka Plan
    (iv)   Community Building through Community Schools
    (v)   Social Relevance and the Rugg Curriculum
    (vi)   Purposefulness through Project Work
        (a) The Project Method
        (b) Cousinet and Free Groups
        (c) Petersen and the Jena Plan
    (vii)   The Lincoln School

Review of Progressive Education at the End of the 1920's

Impact of the Economic Depression on Education in the U.S.A.

The Virginia Curricula

The Social Frontier

National Education Association and Social Reconstruction

Conservative Influences

The Eight Year Study

The Contribution of Educational Psychology
    (i)   Educational Measurement
    (ii)   Statistical Methods in Educational Research
    (iii)   Developmental Studies
    (iv)   Motivation and Non-Cognitive Studies
    (v)   Social Orientation in Educational Psychology

The progressives were not merely critics. They were the makers of a new tradition — a tradition which stood alongside and in various ways impinged on established educational ideas and practices. It was a rich and varied offering that strengthened during the inter-war period and was gradually absorbed into the mainstream. Progressive educators in Europe continued to flourish and to grow in numbers and schools, but it was in the United States that the principal advances were made.

In education the 1920's and 1930's belonged to the Americans. They expanded their schools more rapidly, they enrolled a high proportion of students at all levels, they experimented more widely with school organisation, curricula, and teaching methods, they created practical teaching materials more prolifically, and they thought more deeply and wrote about educational theory more thoroughly and more excitingly than anyone else in the world. During the twenty-five year period from the publication of Dewey's *Democracy and Education* in 1916 to the end of the Eight Year Study in 1941 the world's educators tended to look to America for leadership; and the kind of guidance they received had a distinctly progressive flavour.

The great contribution of that period was threefold. There was an extensive and seminal exploration of ways of developing individual talent and creativity through changed methods and content of teaching; there was a serious awakening to the school's social responsibilities, intense discussion of the function of education in a democracy, and consequent reform of curricula; and there was a sustained effort to bring educational psychology into the service of education to provide suggestive ideas which educators might develop and, through research, to offer an evaluation of ideas and practices that educators might propose in their pursuit of individual development and social responsibility.

THE NEW EDUCATION FELLOWSHIP AND THE PROGRESSIVE EDUCATION ASSOCIATION

A group of progressive educators, mostly Montessorians, met in England at a conference on New Ideals in Education in 1914, and held annual meetings thereafter. Out of their decisions and their association with a group of reformist theosophical educators led by Beatrice Ensor, there emerged a desire to establish an international fellowship of progressively-minded educators of all persuasions. Consequently, in 1921, 100 persons of interestingly diverse views from fourteen countries met at Calais to discuss the conference theme 'The Creative Self-Expression of the Child', and to explore the possibility of an association. They decided to establish three co-operating journals for the English, French, and German speaking worlds

— *The New Era, Pour l'Ere Nouvelle,* and *Das Werdende Zeitalter.* All subscribers to the journals were to become members of the New Education Fellowship under the informal leadership of the three editors, Beatrice Ensor, Adolphe Ferrière, and Elizabeth Rotten. In each issue of the journals a statement of principles, generally acceptable to the members, was published from 1922 until 1932 when a new statement was put forward. It was decided also to make an effort to hold an international conference every two years and, between the wars, eight such conferences were held in various European centres, and two overseas, in South Africa and Australia-New Zealand. The New Education Fellowship was a modest and durable organisation. It established branches throughout Europe, in several countries in Asia and Africa, and in most parts of the English-speaking world. In 1966 it changed its name to World Education Fellowship, and continued to function much as it had for the previous half-century.

A group of American progressives established the Progressive Education Association (PEA) in 1919 at a meeting in Washington D.C. Among its early leaders were Marietta Johnson of the Fairhope Organic School, Eugene R. Smith, principal of the Park School, Baltimore, and Stanwood Cobb, a creative teacher of English and later principal of a progressive school. The association grew rapidly in numbers and by 1930 had a membership of 7,400. In 1924 it established a journal, *Progressive Education,* which appealed both to innovative school teachers and educational theorists, and became a forum for the discussion of many important educational issues until it ceased publication in 1957. The PEA became affiliated with the NEF in 1932, changed its name to American Education Fellowship in 1944, changed back to Progressive Education Association in 1953, and was dissolved in 1955.

The two associations (NEF and PEA) performed similar functions in the progressive movement. Through their journals they became useful clearing houses for progressive ideas and information on current practices. They reported the local and international scene, they provided digests of important experiments, reports, and conferences, and they published informed comment on significant issues. The journals kept their readers up-to-date and offered them interesting and stimulating material. The associations were a kind of informal focus for the progressive education movement. Their very existence was an acknowledgment that there was a movement from which innovators might obtain some comfort and support or, if they wished, an opportunity for disputation. There was an opportunity to come together with other educators in study groups, to attend lectures, and to take part in local, national, and international conferences. Some of those were large and exciting occasions, as, for example, the NEF international conference at Hamlet's castle, Elsinore, in 1929 which attracted 1,800 participants for a two-week study and discussion of 'The New Psychology and the

Curriculum', and the 1937 conference in New Zealand and Australia in which a group of twenty-one distinguished overseas educators, who included Beatrice Ensor, Susan Isaacs, Harold Rugg, Arthur Lismer, and Pierre Bovet, spent twelve weeks in conference in the main cities examining the issues involved in educating in a democratic society. In the two countries, nine thousand teachers enrolled as full participants, and some twenty thousand came to attend the public lectures. It was an event in the social and educational history of both nations which touched off in them a deep and lasting impulse to reform.

Both the NEF and PEA had difficulty in formulating a statement of their interests and principles. In 1920 the PEA issued a seven-point statement which it enlarged in 1929, and the NEF produced a list of seven principles in 1922. The NEF statement was shorter and more inspirational, the PEA one more carefully expressed and somewhat Deweyan in tone. Both statements laid emphasis on activity of two kinds. The freest and fullest development of the individual, was, for both associations, the first and most emphasised aim of education. Encouragement to children to express their individuality creatively, a careful use and cultivation of their interests, constant study of and attention to children's development, and greater freedom for children to develop naturally were the ways in which teachers contributed to the full development of each pupil. The other principal emphasis was on co-operation. There should be co-operation between teachers and parents, co-operation rather than competition among pupils, and, in the NEF manifesto, collaboration between the sexes based on co-education. Learning to co-operate in school was seen as part of the process of learning to be a socially responsible person.

In the 1920's the members of both associations appeared to be mainly interested in promoting creative work and individual development. The themes of each of the first four international conferences organised by the NEF were concerned with some aspect of self expression, freedom, and the creative powers of children, and the journals of the two associations were well-supplied with articles on practices and experiments in creative work.

Early in the 1930's there was a distinct change. The onset of the economic depression in 1929 was the dividing line, and the establishment of the nazi government in Germany in 1933 accelerated the trend. From that period the members of the NEF and PEA became more conscious and outspoken about the schools' social responsibilities, a theme not neglected but underplayed in the 1920's. There was much more interest henceforth in teaching pupils the ways of democracy, in devising activities that would strengthen democratic attitudes, in strengthening the links between the school and community, and in building an improved sense of community both within the school and throughout the whole of society. In the United States the movement in that direction was dramatised and brought to the

THE PRINCIPLES OF PROGRESSIVE EDUCATION

I FREEDOM TO DEVELOP NATURALLY.
The conduct of the pupil should be governed by himself according to the social needs of his community, rather than by arbitrary laws. Full opportunity for initiative and self-expression should be provided, together with an environment rich in interesting material that is available for the free use of every pupil.

II INTEREST, THE MOTIVE OF ALL WORK.
Interest should be satisfied and developed through: (1) Direct and indirect contact with the world and its activities, and use of the experience thus gained. (2) Application of knowledge gained, and correlation between different subjects. (3) The consciousness of achievement.

III THE TEACHER A GUIDE, NOT A TASKMASTER.
It is essential that teachers should believe in the aims and general principles of Progressive Education and that they should have latitude for the development of initiative and originality.
Progressive teachers will encourage the use of all the senses, training the pupils in both observation and judgment; and instead of hearing recitations only, will spend most of the time teaching how to use various sources of information, including life activities as well as books; how to reason about the information thus acquired; and how to express forcefully and logically the conclusions reached.
Ideal teaching conditions demand that classes be small, especially in the elementary school years.

IV SCIENTIFIC STUDY OF PUPIL DEVELOPMENT.
School records should not be confined to the marks given by the teachers to show the advancement of the pupils in their study of subjects, but should also include both objective and subjective reports on those physical, mental, moral and social characteristics which affect both school and adult life, and which can be influenced by the school and the home. Such records should be used as a guide for the treatment of each pupil, and should also serve to focus the attention of the teacher on the all-important work of development rather than on simply teaching subject-matter.

V GREATER ATTENTION TO ALL THAT AFFECTS THE CHILD'S PHYSICAL DEVELOPMENT
One of the first considerations of Progressive Education is the health of the pupils. Much more room in which to move about, better light and air, clean and well ventilated buildings, easier access to the out-of-doors and greater use of it, are all necessary. There should be frequent use of adequate playgrounds. The teachers should observe closely the physical conditions of each pupil and, in co-operation with the home, make abounding health the first objective of childhood.

VI CO-OPERATION BETWEEN SCHOOL AND HOME TO MEET THE NEEDS OF CHILD LIFE.
The school should provide, with the home, as much as is possible of all that the natural interests and activities of the child demand, especially during the elementary school years. These conditions can come about only through intelligent co-operation between parents and teachers.

VII THE PROGRESSIVE SCHOOL A LEADER IN EDUCATIONAL MOVEMENTS.
The Progressive School should be a leader in educational movements. It should be a laboratory where new ideas, if worthy, meet encouragement; where tradition alone does not rule, but the best of the past is leavened with the discoveries of today, and the result is freely added to the sum of educational knowledge.

The first statement of principles by the American Progressive Education Association in 1920.

The Progressive Education Association, *Progressive Education*, vol. iii, no. 4, 1926.

front by a forceful speech from G.S. Counts to a PEA meeting in 1932 on *Dare the Schools Build a New Social Order?*[1] In Europe, the change became strikingly apparent at the NEF conference in Nice in 1932, for which the theme chosen was 'Education and Changing Society'. The speakers at the conference were very aware of the current social and economic crisis for which they thought education had to bear some part of the responsibility. Schools had kept social classes apart and had divided nations from one another. They had to set about the task of changing the pattern of human relationships so that a co-operative new social order based on a democratic spirit might come into being. To achieve such an end the main suggestions put forward were to enlarge the study of society in the school curriculum, to increase group work, self-government, and experiences of co-operation in the school activities, to introduce controversial political and social issues for systematic study in the classroom and, somewhat idealistically, to try to build within each nation and the world a common culture which while encouraging creative self-expression, would unite mankind in a new humanity. Out of the Nice conference came a new statement of NEF principles. Something of the change in attitude that had occurred can be seen by comparing the principle listed first in the 1922 statement with the one placed first in 1932.

In 1922 the first of the principles read:

'The essential object of all education should be to train the child to desire the supremacy of spirit over matter and to express that supremacy in daily life.'

In 1932 it read:

'Education should enable the child to comprehend the complexities of the social and economic life of our time.'

Throughout the 1930's both associations established working-parties and held many discussions on the role of the school in society. NEF members and the schools in which they taught became increasingly interested in teaching about public affairs, in involving pupils in community activities, and in cultivating democratic attitudes. Occasionally also NEF members might raise the question of the possibility of schools deliberately trying to build a new social order. That kind of reconstructive function was more widely canvassed in the U.S.A. where in the 1930's and 1940's it became an important issue in the PEA and led to a recasting, with a stronger social orientation, of the basic principles of the association, first in 1941 and then more substantially in 1947.

Among the progressives in the inter-war period there were six overlapping groups.

[1] See below, pp. 289ff.

PROGRESSIVE EDUCATORS OF THE 1920'S AND 1930'S

(i) Creativity and the Artist Educators

The role of the creative artist-teacher was to develop a fresh dimension in children's education. In the ordinary and traditional view of education, the schools prepared for adult life and taught various fundamental skills, values, and bodies of knowledge. The idea of what constituted the fundamentals was considerably extended during the twentieth century, particularly in the science and social science fields; and although the extensions were often the result of work by progressive educators, they tended still to be justified by their utilitarian and preparatory value.

The contribution of the artist-teachers was an innovation of a different kind. Education, in their view, might have some concern with the future, but primarily it should be focused on the present; it should be a way of encouraging children to express their own ideas, feelings, and experiences. By expressive work of various kinds they could learn what sort of persons they were, and they could learn how to develop and improve what lay within them. In the hands of good artist-educators the pupil's expression was not haphazard or careless; it was a spontaneous but disciplined creation, and above all it was sincere. It was a demanding exercise in making an art form that brought out the apt expression of a genuine and whole-hearted feeling or idea.

Artist-teachers were found in three main areas: in fine arts, dancing, and literature.

In the fine arts the most notable educator was Franz Cizek who first opened free art classes for children from five to fourteen in Vienna in 1908, and continued to teach until the early 1940's.[2] He provided no models and gave no lessons; he encouraged his children to express what they saw and felt, commenting on their work and helping them to probe their own personality and to acquire their own technique. Cizek's approach to art teaching steadily grew in popularity in the 1920's and 1930's, and there were many reports of its impact in the pages of *The New Era,* and *Progressive Education.*[3]

The impact that the Cizek kind of approach could have was illustrated in the career of one of his admirers, Arthur Lismer, an Englishman who migrated to Canada. Lismer became one of the Group of Seven painters who revolutionised Canadian art in the 1920's. In 1927 he became educational supervisor of the Toronto art gallery, and in 1941 moved to a similar position in Montreal. 'In the new education' he wrote, 'art is not a subject nor a profession but a way of life.'[4] Like Cizek he ran classes for children at the art galleries. But his educational activities were

not confined to children. His work cascaded around and about the gallery through an extension program, country art centres, community art projects, and musical, choral, and artistic pageants which became notable annual events in Toronto and Montreal. The gallery became a great workshop of creative activity through which the ordinary adult could become more conscious of the beauty of his environment and could have an opportunity to express himself through art.

A Czech artist-educator and contemporary of Cizek's also had a similar reputation. Frantizek Bakule established, in 1913, a school for crippled children in which they learnt to make their living as creative craftsmen working at tasks such as furniture making, wood carving, basket weaving, and book binding through which they built up self-respect, self-confidence, and creative skill.[5]

In the field of creative dancing, a Swiss teacher, Emile Jaques-Dalcroze was the best-known figure.[6] Dalcrose developed a system of teaching the appreciation of music through rhythmic activity which combined music and bodily movement. Eurhythmics, as it was called, consisted of regular gymnastic exercises to music, and improvisation of both music and movement in a free and creative way. The Dalcroze approach was a training in the translation of mental impressions from music into a physical response, and thus to the development of a deeper sensitivity and a greater ability to express feelings in general.

In the use of literature as a vehicle for creative expression, during the inter-war period there were many gifted teachers of whom two were probably the most widely known: an Englishman, H. Caldwell Cook, and an American, Hughes Mearns. Caldwell Cook[7] held the view that the essence of the educational process was to be found in the absorbing and

---

[2] Franz Cizek (1865-1946) taught in various parts of Austria, and after 1897 settled in Vienna as an art teacher in various technical schools. In 1908 he established a free children's class, and soon after enlisted the support of a group of distinguished artists. In the 1920's his classes became world-famous, and his views widely discussed.

[3] See Gertrude Hartman and Ann Shumaker, *Creative Expression,* Day, New York, 1932, a collection of articles and illustrations published in *Progressive Education* on the development of children in art, music, literature, and dramatics up to 1931.

[4] A. Lismer, 'Creative art', *The New Era,* 13, 11, December 1932, p. 360. See also J.A.B. McLush, *September Gale. A Study of Arthur Lismer of the Group of Seven,* Dent, London, 1956.

[5] F. Bakule (b. 1877) was a Czech teacher whose program was based on children's needs and natural development. His institute for crippled children, established in 1913 in a hospital, was abandoned in 1919, refounded independently near Prague, and became a centre of great educational interest during the next twenty years. It became widely known by the quality of the work, the talented children's choir that developed, and by the extensive tours undertaken by Bakule and the choir.

[6] E. Jaques-Dalcroze (1865-1950), musician and composer, developed his system about 1912 at Hellerau near Dresden. It became very popular in the 1920's in physical education circles.

[7] H. Caldwell Cook (1886-1937) was a teacher at the Perse School, Cambridge before World War I. He wrote *The Play-Way* during war service in France, and returned to teach at the Perse School until 1933.

intense activity which he called play. 'To do anything with interest, to get at the heart of the matter and live there active — that is Play.'[8] The junior secondary boys whom Caldwell Cook taught entered whole-heartedly and critically into the production of literature, giving Littleman lectures on subjects which they had genuinely experienced, drawing fanciful Ilonds, and filling chapbooks of verse and prose describing the happenings on the islands. It was an activity program which required honesty of feeling or creative imagination; the pupils' work was to be done with zest and purpose, free of cliche, affectation, and grammatical nicety.

Similar in outlook but probably a little sharper and more appreciative of contemporary styles, was another original mind, the American Hughes Mearns, a teacher of English at the Lincoln School in New York from 1920 to 1925. His aim was to encourage sincere, disciplined, and creative written expression. Creativity, for him, was the expression of an inner impulse, a sincere effort of the imagination to express a personal experience. Creative work was exacting, absorbing, and unique. The teacher's function was 'a nice balance between instruction and the work of the artist. Art may not be coerced, but it may be enticed.'[9] Mearns gave no formal lessons in poetry writing and original composition, and never suggested the themes on which the pupils might write. Instead he encouraged them to look hard and deep into their own experience: 'So', he wrote, 'we drive them back upon themselves, drive them to search within, a boundless field and rich beyond expectation.'[10] Or, as Caldwell Cook had said, 'Every boy is full of Ilonds.'[11] For both of them the new education was 'the wise guidance of enormously important native powers'.[12] Mearns' classes studied a wide range of poetry and prose, and were especially interested in contemporary works. By reading and discussion, and by practice out of their own experience, taste was built up — 'a knowledge of differences, of textures, of values, and of levels'.[13] Gradually discrimination developed and a feeling for quality pervaded the work of the students. To distinguish the commonplace from the work of the artist was essential. It required hard work and experience. It was not creative simply to have children write as they please. They must write with taste, sincerity, and imaginative power.

E. Jaques-Dalcroze (1865-1950), combined music and physical movement into a form of expression known as eurhythmics.

[8] H.C. Cook, *The Play-Way*, Heinemann, London, 1917, p. 9. See also D. Shayer, *The Teaching of English in Schools 1900-70*, RKP, London, 1972, p. 52.

[9] Hughes Mearns (ed.), *Lincoln Verse, Story, and Essay*, The Lincoln School, New York, 1923, p. xiii-xiv. Hughes Mearns (1875-1965) was an educational psychologist at Harvard 1902-20. He joined the staff of the Lincoln School in 1920 and taught the senior English classes till 1925. In 1926 he was appointed a professor of education at New York Universtiy. He became a well-known literary critic and author.

[10] H. Mearns, *Creative Youth*, Doubleday Page, New York, 1925, p. 35.

[11] H.C. Cook, *The Play-Way*, p. 143.

[12] H. Mearns, *Creative Youth*, p. 28.

[13] *ibid.*, p. 81.

Eurhythmics: Pupils of Jaques-Dalcroze.

New Era, vol. iv, October 1923, p. 242.

The end product of the work of educators such as Mearns, Cook, Dalcroze, Bakule, Lismer, and Cizek was not merely a collection of first-rate poetry, stories, art, and craft; it was also a group of young people with confidence, self-knowledge, and unerring taste.

(ii) Psychoanalysis and the Progressives

The psychoanalysts did not have much direct effect on education in the pre-World War II period. In the 1920's implications for education from the views of the various psychoanalytic approaches were beginning to be drawn, and several notable figures began to describe aspects of child development in psycholoanalytic terms; but in the schools the main impact was to be seen only in the work of a few of the progressives.

The most flourishing and most clearly oriented to the new theory was Margaret Naumberg's Walden School. In her view, existing schools, even those affected by the progressive movement, were unduly restrictive of individuality. 'The constriction, repression, and misdirection of the original power and spontaneous energy of thousands of school children,' she wrote, 'is something I am prepared to denounce as a menacing evil of orthodox education.'[14] As a consequence of her conviction, she founded

[14] Margaret Naumberg, *The Child and the World: Dialogues in Modern Education*, Harcourt Brace, New York, 1928, p. 4. The book was a series of somewhat stilted and inartistically written dialogues expressing the author's criticisms of other schools, describing much of the work of the Walden School, and expounding the psychoanalytic, principally Jungian, views that she was endeavouring to apply in the school. See also R.H. Beck, Progressive Education and American Progressivism: Margaret Naumberg, *Teachers College Record*, LX (1958-9), pp. 198-208. Margaret Naumberg was a graduate of Columbia University who had had Montessorian training, was influenced by Dewey's views, and became interested in Jungian psychoanalysis.

the Walden School in 1914, originally named the Children's School, in New York's Greenwich Village. Starting with a nursery group aged two or three years, it gradually expanded through primary and high school level, building up to about two hundred children in the mid-1920's.

Walden School put much effort into the study and development of the personality of its pupils. The unconscious emotional life of the children, their family background, and their social adjustment were important considerations. The school was originally started 'with the purpose of applying the principles of analytic psychology to the education of normal children'.[15] In pursuing the aim there were two basic tasks, sublimation and release. The first was the channelling of the dynamic life force of each individual and group into some positive expressive work. In this sense the school was fundamentally a sublimating agency, and education was to a large extent a process of sublimation. But it was something more than this; it was also an analytic and releasing agency. This was its second task, to free the children from excessive bondage to their parents, to encourage them to express their subjective inner life, and to promote their emotional, intellectual, and physical expansion.

The school curriculum covered somewhat the same material as was to be found in traditional schools, but it used different methods and emphases. Its atmosphere was warm and relaxed, its timetable was highly individualised to fit the needs of the children, and it made extensive use of the rich and artistic human resources of Greenwich Village. There was, throughout the school, an insistence on intellectual rigour and an encouragement of creative activities. A specimen of such activity which joyously caught the spirit of the school was the following poem by an eleven-year-old girl:

What the Child of 1825 Thinks
I heard a sound
I looked around
I couldn't see a thing
But now I know
It's truly so!
It was the fairy king!

What the Child of 1925 Thinks
Oh! something stirred!
I'm sure I heard
A movement of some kind
O, ding bust gosh!
That's lots of bosh!
'Twas my subconscious mind![16]

It was not a school in which each pupil did as he pleased, but one in which the pupils learnt something of the range of their own possibilities, and the way in which they could be best disciplined and expressed. The outcome that the Walden School hoped for was the development of pupils who would show independence of thought, originality in expression, and a devotion to work and disciplined activity. It was the most planned and probably the most successful of all the psychoanalytically oriented schools of the era. It went far to demonstrate that pupil freedom and creativity could be successfully combined with self-discipline and responsibility.

In Europe, by the 1920's, many progressives had begun to show interest in the application of psychoanalytic theory to education. It was difficult, however, to find a school like the Walden School based fundamentally on a psychoanalytical point of view. The tendency, rather, was to incorporate some analytic insights into a mixture of practices from various sources, or to use psychoanalytic theory to justify some existing practice or idea, such as the importance of freedom for the full and healthy development of children. In Switzerland Hermann Tobler applied his knowledge of psychoanalysis to the education of adolescents in his country boarding school, Hof Oberkirch;[17] in England two schools became particularly well-known for their psychoanalytic learnings. Susan Isaacs from 1924 to 1927 ran a short-lived experimental school in Cambridge, the Malting House Garden School, in which she brought psychoanalysis to bear on the education of a small group of intelligent young children from three to ten years, and managed very astutely to combine it with her equally deep interest in both Montessori and Dewey.[18] Out of her experience at Malting House she wrote two books on intellectual and social growth in young children that had a profound effect on education in England. The other school that was to become well-known was Summerhill. It was a co-educational boarding school for children of all ages, and was founded by A.S. Neill in 1924. He had been much influenced by Homer Lane, an American who had run a psychoanalytically oriented Little Commonwealth, a school for delinquents in the south of England from 1913 to 1918. Neill had undergone extensive analysis, and found in Freud's work a theory which admirably

[15] M. Naumberg, *The Child and the World*, p. 45.

[16] Agnes de Lima, *Our Enemy the Child*, Arno, New York, 1969 (1926).

[17] H. Tobler (1872-1933) was educated in Switzerland and England, and founded the *Landerziehungsheim* of Hof Oberkirch in 1907 near St. Gall. He became a leading member of the N.E.F.

[18] Susan Isaacs (1885-1948) studied psychology at the universities of Manchester and Cambridge, was principal of Malting House School 1924-7, head of the department of Child Development at the Institute of Education, University of London 1933-43. From 1931 on she was a psychologist in the London Clinic of Psychoanalysis. Her main publications were *The Nursery Years* (1929), *Intellectual Growth in Young Children* (1930), and *Social Growth in Young Children* (1933).

supported his views and practical efforts towards freedom in education. His school, never large, continued under his direction until his death in 1972. Neill wrote extensively about his school experiences in a witty, humane, and commonsense style that gained him many appreciative readers. Freedom, self-government, and a minimum of programming characterised the school. For many years he sensitively conducted a form of psychotherapy, which he called Private Lessons, with individual, troubled children in order to free them of repressions, to assist in the re-education of their self-confidence, and 'to lop off all complexes resulting from morality and fear'.[19] But he discovered that the formal techniques of psychotherapy were not important and he gave them up; what was important for the happiness and healthy development of children was 'love, approval, and freedom to be true to self'.[20]

In the 1920's and 1930's the progressives were in search of an educational psychology. Psychoanalysis had come of age during World War I, was fashionable among artists and novelists in the 1920's, and was seeping into popular literature and everyday speech. Few progressives took it up whole-heartedly, but many were attracted by it and helped to spread its influence cautiously and more generally into educational thinking.

Psychoanalysis appealed to progressive educators on several grounds. It was a dynamic psychology; it explored a realm of inner drives and impulses in whose expression and shaping most progressives were vitally involved. It was developmental; psychoanalysts put forward the view of a child as a being whose growth proceeded through a series of stages which should emerge in a recognisable and significant sequence. It was concerned primarily with feeling; the progressives, in their opposition to an over-intellectual influence in traditional schools, could welcome a psychological theory which raised the importance of the emotional life, and helped them to argue for a more balanced and all-round development in children's education. In particular, the affective emphasis in psychoanalysis helped to justify and reinforce the interest taken by most progressive educators in the importance of motivation in the educational process, provided evidence of the crucial effect of love on the growth of children, and underscored the need for sincerity in the teacher's relationship with his pupils.[21] It emphasised the importance of the very early years in the development of children, and in that way helped many progressives, whose work tended to be with younger children, to understand their task better and to gain a greater appreciation of its importance. And, finally, it gave attention mainly to individual problems and individual differences; the progressives' concern with freedom for the individual to develop was reinforced by psychoanalytic theory, and their leaning towards individual counselling and individual programming received support from the methods and ideas of psychotherapy.

(iii) Individual Progress: Dalton and Winnetka Plans

(a) Dalton Plan

In 1920, at a high school in Dalton, Massachusetts, Helen Parkhurst, who had trained as a Montessorian teacher, successfully tried out a method of teaching for elementary and secondary schools which would enable each individual pupil to become largely responsible for the rate and manner in which he could proceed through a prescribed curriculum.[22] It was a form of individualised auto-education.

To implement the plan it was necessary to divide the proposed year's work for the school grade into a number of topics corresponding usually to the number of months in the school year. Each month-long topic was regarded as a job to be contracted for by each student. Within each contract there might be a number of assignments that had to be completed by each individual within a specified time.

At the commencement of each contract, a pupil would be issued with an outline of the topic, the time allowed for studying it, and the number of credit points that it represented in the whole program. Each assignment was broken up into a number of problems through which the pupils had to work their way. It had to be written attractively so as to motivate the pupils to research and learn, and it characteristically contained 'pockets of interest' that many of the pupils might find stimulating. On the assignment sheet there would usually be a list of reference material, suggestions as to how a pupil might go about his work, and a statement of the kind of report that was expected on completion of the assignment.

Classroom teaching was eliminated and the classrooms became workshops or laboratories in which materials relevant to a particular

[19] A.S. Neill, *That Dreadful School*, Jenkins, London, 1937, p. 92. A.S. Neill (1883-1972) was a Scot who taught in the local state schools, had some experience of progressive schools in Germany and Austria, helped to edit *The New Era*, and began his own school, Summerhill, in 1924. His most well-known books were *A Dominie's Log* (1915), *The Problem Child* (1926), *That Dreadful School* (1937), and *Summerhill. A Radical Approach to Education* (1962).

[20] A.S. Neill, *That Dreadful School*, p. 84.

[21] In a remarkable and seminal book in 1935 the psychoanalyst I.D. Suttie made love and companionship the central forces in human development, and pointed out the significance of cultural and educational factors in the various stages of children's growth proposed by psychoanalysts. It was a book that progressive educators who were seeking to reconcile their social and altruistic views with the attractive insights of psychoanalysis found very congenial. I.D. Suttie, *The Origins of Love and Hate*, Kegan Paul, Trench, Trubner, London, 1935.

[22] Helen Parkhurst, *Education on the Dalton Plan*, Bell, London, 1923, p. 30. 'It is of the essence of the Dalton Laboratory Plan that pupils should progress each at his own rate, for only so can the work be assimilated thoroughly.' See also C.W. Kimmins and Belle Rennie, *The Triumph of the Dalton Plan*, Nicholson and Watson, London, 1931; R.J.W. Selleck, *English Primary Education and the Progressives 1914-1939*, RKP, London, 1972, pp. 40-3. 150-6

Susan Isaacs (1885-1948), was a progressive teacher and professor at the University of London who brought insights from psychoanalysis into the study and education of young children.

topic could be found together with the teacher-adviser who had been assigned to that topic. Teachers offered formal conferences to help pupils plan their work at the beginning of their assignments, and again, from time to time, for groups who might have encountered a common difficulty. They were, otherwise, immensely busy on the very demanding task of devising attractive and challenging assignments, answering pupils' questions, and assessing reports.

Pupils had a range of assignments to complete in each of their subjects, and, within the time limit set, could choose the order in which they might do them and the amount of time they might give to them. Assignments were often designed in two parts: the first indicated the work required of all pupils for its satisfactory completion, the second was optional additional and enriching work that might be done by brighter and more interested pupils when they had sufficient time.

The Dalton Laboratory Plan was the most popular and successful innovation of the 1920's. It became well-known in the United States though it was never widely used there. It was taken up enthusiastically in England where by the mid-1920's it was claimed to be operating in two thousand schools and it was still spreading in the early 1930's. It was experimented with and firmly adopted for many years by a substantial number of schools in the English-speaking world in the 1920's and 1930's. It spread throughout Europe and the U.S.S.R., and eventually was probably to be found in some form in most countries. Even in the 1970's, fifty years after its first development, it was possible to find it in use in various modified forms in a sprinkling of schools throughout the world.

The Dalton Plan appealed to a number of interests that were prominent in the 1920's. Primarily it capitalised on a central desire of most progressive educators to allow more freedom to individual children to direct their own pattern of growth. The work of the pioneering educational psychologists had made many educators very conscious of the range of individual differences among children. The Dalton Plan was a way in which teachers could cater effectively for individual differences, and encourage pupils, within a carefully designed framework, to develop at a pace which suited their ability and aptitude. The method of writing assignments made a strong appeal to teachers who were aware of the importance of interest and motivation in the educational process; and the significance of the pupils' research on problems that they were required to solve and their use of materials in laboratories appealed to popular interest in science. The Plan commended itself also to the many administrators interested in improving the efficiency of schools; with the use of words such as contract, jobs, workshops, budgeting, time schedules, it sounded business-like, and its detailed analysis of topics, its programming of the year's work, its regular requirement of reports from pupils, and its careful system of recording were ways of insuring that the business of education could be readily assessed, and, if at times rather demanding on teachers, could be made to proceed competently and efficiently.

Enthusiasm for the Dalton Plan had waned by the end of the 1930's. Teachers found difficulty in dealing with dull or lazy pupils and with ensuring that the pupils' work was original and not copied. They began to modify the system, keeping pupils in the one classroom, setting aside history or geography corners instead of whole rooms as laboratories. They gradually introduced more classroom teaching, and, as the demands of external examinations increased, they edged the Plan back into the top forms of the primary school. There it managed to leave a considerable deposit, continuing in partial and occasional use as one of a number of means used to individualise the process of learning, though it vanished from use in most schools as a complete system.

(b) Winnetka Plan

In commenting on the Dalton Plan, Carleton Washburne[23] wrote that it lacked self-instructive teaching materials, research, scientific construction of curriculum, and techniques for group and creative activities. The Winnetka Plan included them. It was started in 1918 in a well-to-do suburb of Chicago in an effort to break away from the standardising effect of class teaching into a more individualised procedure. It incorporated both individual and social work. On the individual side, the characteristic techniques were self-instruction, self-correction, diagnostic testing, and individual rates of progress.[24] Tool subjects such as reading, spelling, formal language, and arithmetic were analysed and the fundamental knowledge and skills that were required to master them were carefully set out and arranged in sequence. Texts and materials were devised on which pupils could work independently. At appropriate points in their work, when they were ready, they would take tests to determine whether they had fully mastered the process under examination. If they fell short, self-corrective exercises were available to prepare them for a further test; if they succeeded, they pushed ahead individually at their own pace to the next stage. A considerable amount of research was done in the Winnetka schools, at the elementary and junior high school level, on diagnostic and achievement testing, on record keeping, and on the preparation of materials for individual learning. Gradually, other subjects such as science and the social sciences were similarly analysed and adapted in large part to a program of individual learning.

Creative and social work were also important parts of the carefully designed and well-balanced curriculum. They provided opportunity for pupils to fulfil their interests, develop their personalities, and experience the processes and satisfactions of social interaction. Approximately half the school time was spent on creative and social activities. Class projects, dramatic plays, musical performances, farming and business enterprises, a school newspaper, clubs, sports, and school self-government provided extensive opportunities for co-operation and self-development.

The Winnetka schools maintained their experimentation even after Washburne left in 1943, and continued to revise and redevelop their materials and ideas and to give a practical lead to improvement in all aspects of the primary and secondary school curriculum. Teachers, trained at Winnetka, moved into positions of responsibility elsewhere in the U.S.A. and in several overseas countries; and textbook materials produced by the Winnetka staff were published and widely used in the U.S.A. Self-corrective, programmed instruction on the Winnetka model was used in many schools as part of a wider teaching process; and ideas about the sequence of essential skills, methods of integration, creative activities, and the use of community resources were gradually spread to many schools from the research and practical experimentation of the Winnetka staff. Winnetka's great virtue was that, from its beginning and throughout its history, it was more than an ingenious plan for schoolteaching. It was a small, but valuable and sensitive educational intelligence centre, 'a convergence of many influences (that) have come in continuously: from Freud, Adler and Jung; from Piaget and Gesell; from William H. Kilpatrick; from European pioneers in the "activity school"; from Decroly and Montessori; and from innumerable researchers in psychology, sociology and anthropology.'[25]

(iv) Community Building through Community Schools

The original progressive country boarding schools had been very much concerned with developing a strong community spirit and structure within them and they continued the tradition. Bedales and Odenwald were probably the most notable of them in that regard in the inter-war period. In both schools, the idea of fellowship was a leading characteristic: it was a fellowship through which it was expected that all pupils and teachers would share in intellectual, social, and aesthetic activities, all would take responsible parts in organising the school's program, and all would be united in mutual respect and affection. Experience in the school community, it was hoped, would produce individuals who would be interested in extending their experiences beyond the school for the improvement of the community at large.

---

[23] Carleton Washburne (1889-1974) was the superintendent of schools for Winnetka, Illinois, from 1919 to 1943. Subsequently he became professor of education and director of Teacher Education at Brooklyn College of the City University of New York. He was a leading member of the Progressive Education Association, and wrote *A Living Philosophy of Education* in 1940.

[24] C.W. Washburne & S.P. Marland, *Winnetka. The History and Significance of an Educational Experiment*, Prentice Hall, Englewood Cliffs, New Jersey, 1963, p. 75.

[25] C.W. Washburne & S.P. Marland, *Winnetka*, p. 157.

A notable community school, the Workshop Community (*Werk-plaats*), was founded in 1926 by Kees Boeke and his wife in Holland, and was run by them until his seventieth birthday in 1954. Girls and boys from three to nineteen years of age came each day to the school, which, by the 1950's, had an attendance of 850 and was supported by the Dutch government. Pupils worked individually with work cards and self-correcting materials in a manner similar to the Winnetka system. It was a school run without the use of compulsion or punishment in a relaxed but workmanlike atmosphere. Its central institution was the weekly Talkover, a meeting of all pupils and staff to discuss informally their plans and their grievances, at which no voting took place but a unanimous sense of the meeting was reached and summed up by the chairman. As the school grew in size it had to operate through several committees and respresentative general councils for senior and junior schools but in each committee it managed to maintain Talkover principles. It was a school with a warm community feeling, and from time to time the feeling was extended to help members of the outside community when they were in need, but it did not undertake to build the same community spirit throughout its neighbourhood or feel impelled to try to remodel it.

Some of the community schools did feel an obligation of that kind. They had something of a missionary spirit and tended to have a connection with an underprivileged area or group. An interesting and successful elementary school was developed by E.F. O'Neill in the north of England within the local public system. The Prestolee school was in a polluted, begrimed, industrial valley not far from Manchester; its task, in the view of its new headmaster, was 'neither more nor less than to create a new people and a new world'.[26] O'Neill started in 1918 to convert a drab, traditional institution into an exciting free school community. He remained for over thirty years, until the 1950's, as its headmaster.

His work had four features. At Prestolee there was a minimum of structure. There was no fixed curriculum and no firm timetable. Each child, from three to fifteen years of age, worked individually, and there was little class teaching. The pupils were taught to be literate and to be able to do 'such arithmetic as is involved in buying things in everyday life'.[27] The school offered also all the usual elementary school subjects, but O'Neill did not care what kind of further knowledge the pupils acquired provided that they followed their interests and their learning was uncoerced. Freedom was the first characteristic of the school, freedom from the constraints of structure and academic requirements.

The second feature of the school was the enrichment of the children's environment. The school was decorated internally with art work, and externally with thriving gardens; fish tanks, natural history collections, and an extensive supply of materials for use in various activities eventually transformed the appearance of the classrooms; a school camp

in the unspoilt countryside was built and extensively used by the pupils. The school 'tried to substitute *stimulation* for *coercion*'.[28] By surrounding the pupils with beauty and usable materials, the school was able to ensure the truth of an observer's description of it, that 'learning by doing has taken the place of learning by swallowing'.[29] That was its third characteristic. It was an activity school in the best progressive tradition. Interest, self-discipline, self-reliance, the satisfaction of felt needs, and problem-solving were all part of the school's program of creating new people. Individual freedom went hand-in-hand with co-operation as the fourth characteristic in the new dispensation at the school. It became a place of warmth and interest in which activities could be freely shared among pupils and staff. The concept, however, extended much further. O'Neill brought the community into the school and gradually made it, like the Cambridgeshire Village Colleges, a child and adult centre where all could find 'cultural interests, healthy amusement, companionship, and warmth'.[30] The school became a gentle and pervasive agent in the transformation of the village.

What Prestolee became was summarised by O'Neill when, on one occasion, he stated the features of his ideal school.[31]

'A school should be:
    a place for lectures and teaching
    a workshop for young and old — of both sexes
    a den of hobbies and indoor games
    a studio for drawing, painting, and plastics
    a music studio
    a hall for song and dance
    an educational shop-window
    a reference library
    a picture gallery
    a museum
    a reading-room
    a bookstall for magazines and newspapers

[26] E.F. O'Neill, *Une Ecole Active en Angleterre*, Lamertin, Bruxelles, 1924, p. 45, trans. of a letter written to A. Ferrière, There is also a description of the school in Margarita Comas, *Las Escuelas Neuvas Inglesas*, Angel, Madrid, 1930.
E.F. O'Neill (b. 1890) was trained as a primary school teacher, and spent all his teaching life in schools in and around Manchester. He was leading member of the NEF in the 1920's and 1930's.

[27] C. Washburne, *New Schools in the Old World*, Day, New York, 1926, p. 62. Washburne described Prestolee as the most radical experiment in England and one of the three most radical he saw in Europe in the mid-1920's.

[28] C. Washburne, *New Schools in the Old World*, p. 53.

[29] G. Holmes, *The Idiot Teacher*, Faber and Faber, London, 1952, p. 55.

[30] *ibid.*, p. 143.

[31] *ibid.*, pp. 193-4.

a club
a place for parties
a refreshment bar
an orchard
a zoo
an aquarium
a vivarium
a home for pets
a playing field
a gymnasium
a bathing place
a fair garden
a kitchen
a dining place
a laundry
a first-aid post
a cleansing department
store sheds for raw materials.'

An interesting school was established by the New York State Federation of Labour in the early 1920's. Labour unions had become particularly conscious of the part that education might play in building a more co-operative society. 'The organised labor movement', reads a statement on Schools of the Future in 1924,[32] 'regards education as the key to a better life.' Accordingly, to implement their standing resolution to establish experimental schools and as an example of the new education, a school was opened in 1924 on a 177-acre farm at Manumit, Pawling, New York.[33] The school was advised by leading progressive educators and trade unionists. It was co-educational and residential for children from nine to fourteen, and had its own farm. Co-operative self-government shared by pupils and teachers was a feature of it, and it stressed community living in which individual freedom and social responsibility were brought together to the task of caring for the farm and maintaining the life of the residential school. Subsequently the school lost its labour affiliation during the 1930's and became an experimental school 'enrolling children largely from the professional intellectual group', and emphasising intercultural activities, community work, and individual guidance. The school put much effort into developing a community life that was wider and deeper than that of the usual school group. It was something of a rural community and it took an interest in the affairs of its rural neighbourhood. It was, in the long run, interested in improving society by the subsequent work of the persons it produced; it did not, however, work for the reconstruction of the society in which it was placed. That was a task that was accepted and enthusiastically undertaken by the rural schools organised by Elsie Clapp.

Elsie Clapp's Community School, Arthurdale, West Virginia. The school centre building contained school cafeteria and kitchen, home economics and community canning kitchen, doctor's office, school bank, bookstore, typewriting room, and director's office.

Photograph by W.J. Miller in the journal *Progressive Education*, vol. xv, no. 4, April 1938, p. 260.

The connection between school and community was intimate and direct in the rural community schools, of which Elsie Clapp, a staunch follower of John Dewey, was the principal from 1929 to 1938.[34] They were public schools which participated in all the phases of building a new life for a depressed community; they concerned themselves with community betterment in all matters of health, government, occupation, and recreation from nursery to adulthood. The community's ongoing experience became the subject-matter of the school curriculum, and the schools took on responsibilities such as organising a labour exchange, conducting the country fair, developing a co-operative market, and setting up a community fire brigade. Each school merged with the community to become a much esteemed centre of the community's transformed life.

(v) Social Relevance and the Rugg Curriculum

A popular and constant theme of educational reformers from the beginning of the century was that of the need and necessity to make the content of education more relevant to contemporary society. It was a favourite line with the progressives. With few exceptions they took steps in their schools to see that their pupils were brought into some

---

[32] Agnes de Lima, *Our Enemy the Child*, *op.cit.*, p. 241.

[33] New York State Federation of Labor, *Official Proceedings*, Sixty-second Annual Convention, 1925, p. 189.

[34] Elsie R. Clapp was principal of a rural community school in Kentucky 1929-1934, and in West Virginia 1936-8. She described her experiences in *Community Schools in Action* (1939), and later wrote *The Use of Resources in Education* (1952).

meaningful contact with their social environment. It was particularly the case after World War I; and the increased interest at that time gave a greater importance to the study of the social sciences and to efforts to develop more socially relevant courses either in the separate social sciences or in some integrated form.

The most sustained and successful effort to produce a socially relevant course in social studies was that of Harold Rugg who commenced his research in 1920's on what was to be an epic contribution to the field of curriculum development.

Rugg was a man of unusually wide interests, an incisive and flexible mind, and a strong sense of mission. He was initially trained as a civil engineer, worked in industry for a short while, and in 1911 began an academic career at the University of Illinois, first in engineering and then in education. In 1919 he moved to New York as a professor at Teachers College, Columbia University, and a staff member of the College's recently established experimental Lincoln School.

In his work at the Lincoln School be became engrossed in what he regarded as the major educational task of the time, that of closing the gap between school and society and, in particular, that of devising social studies programs adequate to meet the requirements of the twentieth century age which he described as that of the Great Technology.[35] His greatest contribution to this field came from an immense and continuous program of co-operative research and writing on the social studies curriculum that he started at the Lincoln School in 1920 and carried on for many years. In 1936 he described these efforts: 'For about sixteen years I have worked with little interruption at two major tasks: first, the painting of a portrait of industrial-democratic culture for our young people; second, the interpretation of its use by educational workers.'[36]

It was an extensive and carefully planned assault, developed in a number of overlapping phases. First, a large number of studies were made of the characteristics of contemporary society and its future possibilities. Rugg, and his team of workers, selected from contemporary writers in all the social sciences a number of 'frontier thinkers', men regarded by their colleagues as persons of insight and intellectual influence. The contributions of these men were analysed to establish the main concepts that they used in dealing with present-day society. 'Democracy', 'war', 'unemployment', 'income', 'trade', 'social conflict', and 'leadership' were examples of some of the concepts which were listed. The frequency with which they were used, and the importance of them to the writer had also to be assessed. The next step was to discover and list the main generalisations the writers made in using the concepts, e.g. 'As populations grow, rents rise'; 'Rivers are poor boundaries'; 'A good government must secure the responsibility of legislators and officials to the people'. These were some of the 888 generalisations which one

member of the research team isolated. To these were added a formulation of the more significant problems of political, industrial, social, and international problems of contemporary society, and, finally, a list of central themes such as 'the progress of democracy', 'the rise and spread of economic imperialism', and 'the emancipation of women with resulting modifications in family life'.

On the basis of those concepts, generalisations, problems, and themes, a social studies curriculum was devised. The themes provided central organising threads within which problems arose and could be studied effectively when the generalisations and concepts appropriate to the situation had been grasped. Next, within this framework, a mass of facts, diagrams, statistical tables, and striking and pertinent episodes had to be collected and arranged from all the social sciences.

Out of the analyses a rounded picture of contemporary society was built, made intelligible by stressing the overriding themes. The whole work was then braced throughout by an emphasis upon the skills and values of a scientific and democratic community. With the help of several thousand administrators and teachers in nearly 400 schools throughout the United States, the materials were tried out for some seven years. Their grade-placement level, and the best methods of teaching them were experimented with and readjusted. Eventually they were arranged in a series of integrated social studies units, and published between 1929 and 1932 as the Rugg Social Science Course, consisting of six school textbooks for junior high school classes, supplemented by a pupil's workbook of directed study, and a teacher's guide for each of the textbooks. The workbooks and the guides provided an abundance of individual and social activities and skilfully devised tests to try to ensure that every pupil had some active experience of the skills of problem-solving and of democratic procedures, and through them, more thoroughly grasped the meaning of the social science concepts incorporated in the course. From 1932 on, Rugg turned his attention to the elementary school and produced a series of eight volumes for grades three to six.

His course was widely used throughout the United States and widely studied by educators in many other countries. It did not, however, go unchallenged. In the mid- and late 1930's it met with a growing opposition among the more conservative groups of the community. Hostility reached its peak during the tense early years of World War II before America's entry into the conflict. Rugg was accused of trying to engineer through the schools a new socialistic society by 'a complete

---

[35] In 1933 Rugg published *The Great Technology*, John Day, New York, 1933, on the flyleaf of which he wrote, 'We stand at the crossroads to a new epoch: in one direction lies the road to the Great Technology; in others lie various pathways to social chaos and the possible destruction of interdependent ways of living.'

[36] H.O. Rugg, *American Life and the School Curriculum*, Ginn, Boston, 1936, p. v.

system of indoctrination cleverly camouflaged as an educational course'. He was taken to task for his criticism of the existing economic and social system, for his failure to treat American history patriotically, and for his endeavour to build up among pupils a critical attitude and an 'expectancy of change'.[37] Articles and letters of protest appeared in national and local newspapers, hearings were conducted by school boards and various public bodies, and in several places the Rugg books were solemnly and publicly burnt. For the most part the attacks were unsuccessful, and the Social Science Course continued to enjoy a considerable popularity until its content became outmoded in the 1940's.

(vi) Purposefulness through Project Work

(a) The Project Method

In 1918 W.H. Kilpatrick, a close associate of John Dewey at Columbia University, wrote an important article summarising the features of a recently developed educational method known as a project. It was an activity based on pupils' interests and undertaken by them with a firm purpose of broadening their experience and learning something seen by them to be worth the pursuit. Kilpatrick suggested that there were four kinds of such purposeful acts:

- the embodiment of some idea or plan in external form such as building a boat or presenting a play;
- the enjoyment of some experience like a picture or symphony concert;
- the solution of some intellectual problem such as whether or not dew falls or how New York outgrew Philadelphia;
- the acquisition of some degree of skill or knowledge.

The project was not meant to be just an interesting occupation that pupils might take up; it was intended to be an educational instrument that translated into school practice the ideas and principles that Dewey and his followers had formulated. Ideally each project should have had four features. It was an activity that required a measure of co-operative planning; it was not simply thought up by a teacher but was something which emerged from the pupils' interests in discussions between pupils and teacher who then, together, set about planning how to achieve their purpose. It was to be centred round a problem, and the process of examining and solving the problem were to be the heart of the project. It was to be a productive activity, in which those involved would be actively engaged in building up ideas, skills, and resources following stimulating leads that might emerge and working towards a culminating point which could be seen to be a satisfying completion to the project, and which

would be subject to careful evaluation to determine whether the end product was of a sufficient standard and whether it tallied with the original purpose. And finally, it was to be a determined and purposeful exercise, an example of zestful and interested learning at its best; above all a project was an exercise for the pupils in the selection and successful realisation of purposes. 'Purposeful activity in a social situation,' Kilpatrick thought, was essential for worthy democratic life and should become the typical unit of school procedure.[38]

It was possible for the project method to become a means of organising all or most of a school program. One of the best examples of the extensive use of project work was given by Collings in a four-year experiment in a rural American school. He pointed out that the pupils' project curriculum involved them in a wide range of activities: constructing, observing, investigating, playing, experimenting, communicating, and artistic expression, and that they could still perform well when tested on conventional material.

The project method was very quickly taken up. By the 1930's there would have been few primary schools in the English-speaking world that were not affected by it in some way; and many junior classes in secondary schools were making some use of it. It also moved gradually into western Europe and the U.S.S.R., and eventually found an important place in the curricula of many of the underdeveloped countries. For the most part it was an auxiliary to the main curriculum from time to time, or an occasional change in the method of dealing with some part of a school subject. It seldom fulfilled all the criteria of co-operative planning, problem-solving, productiveness, and purposiveness, but it often did manage to include one or more of them, and in various modified forms it found itself a reasonably permanent place in schools throughout the world. It was, in origin, a product of Deweyan thinking on education, and it proved to be an effective means of conveying some important aspects of Dewey's ideas, if sometimes attenuated and recast, to a world-wide audience of teachers and pupils.

(b) Cousinet and Free Groups

A form of purposeful activity which was a variant of the project method was developed in France in the 1920's by Roger Cousinet. Taking advantage of the tendency of children between nine and twelve to be

---

[37] Augustin G. Rudd, Hamilton Hicks & Albert T. Falk (edd.), *Undermining Our Republic. Facts about Educators*, Guardians of American Education Inc., New York, 1941, pp. 20, 42. In his book, *That Man May Understand*, Doubleday, Doran & Co., New York, Rugg related the story of his twenty years of research and writing on the social science course from 1920 to 1940, and of the attacks that were made upon the series.

[38] W.H. Kilpatrick, 'The project method', *Teachers College Record*, 19, 4, September 1918, pp. 320, 335. The above summary is based on Kilpatrick's theoretical article, and the practical experimentation reported in E. Collings, *An Experiment with a Project Curriculum*, Macmillan, New York, 1923.

William Heard Kilpatrick (1871-1965), a keen supporter of John Dewey, made the project method widely known to teachers.

interested in forming small groups and clubs, Cousinet, an inspector of schools who was much influenced by Dewey, encouraged teachers of elementary children of that age range to base their school program on projects put forward by the pupils at which they could work in a small group of about six children. The method of free group work, as it came to be known, combined interest, activity, and co-operation. Its central feature was group work. Individual activity was not neglected, and pupils were encouraged to contribute in ways that developed each individual's interests and abilities. The framework was not one of individual assignments, as in the Dalton Plan, but of group occupations through which 'the children observe, search, find, design, classify, and by degrees explore the universe', and learn to apportion tasks, work accurately, and share common problems and purposes.[39]

(c) Petersen and the Jena Plan

Somewhat parallel to Cousinet's work was that of Peter Petersen, a German progressive educator who, in the university practice school named after Rein at Jena, developed a project method of learning through group activity.[40] Petersen's Jena Plan was designed to revolutionise the organisation and teaching of the elementary school. Its core was in its group work through which pupils learnt to develop group spirit and group solidarity, and they learnt to exercise leadership and responsibility for directing their own group work. Basic intellectual skills were taught in the traditional way and occupied about a quarter of the program. The rest of the school time was given over to group projects and school clubs. Petersen's work was a stage beyond that of Cousinet. Where Cousinet saw group work as the most effective way of developing the pupils' interest and intellectual education, for Petersen the purpose was not primarily intellectual but social and emotional. Group activity was for the sake of experiencing and learning the skills and attitudes of living in a close-knit group.

In a short insightful essay a young German educator in 1930 drew attention to a vital element of the learning process that Dewey had continually emphasised. The author, Friedrich Copei[41] made an analysis of what he called the 'productive moment', in which he indicated that

[39] R. Cousinet, *Experiments in French Primary Schools*, Bulletin No. 12, PEA, 1922, p. 7. See also A.E. Meyer, *Modern Europèan Educators and their Work*, Prentice-Hall, New York, 1934, pp. 53-64. R. Cousinet (b.1881) was a primary school inspector from 1910 to 1941. He wrote *Une Methode de Travail Libre par Groupes* (1945), and *L'Education Nouvelle* (1950).

[40] P. Petersen (1884-1952) was associated with progressive educators from his earliest years, and from 1924 to 1952 was professor of education at Jena. During the 1930's he, surprisingly, supported nazi educational proposals.

[41] F. Copei (1903-1945) a primary school teacher, wrote *Der Fruchtbare Moment im Bildungsprozess* (1930) as his doctoral thesis. In the 1960's it was still being reprinted. He taught subsequently in several universities and was killed in World War II.

fruitful thinking emerged out of problem-solving that was purposefully followed through to the point of illumination — the productive moment. The teacher's task was to watch for the moment and assist the pupil to achieve this breakthrough in understanding. The book was well received by leading German educators, and was seen to bring out very neatly the essence of intellectual education as the progressives saw it. Though not directly concerned with the project method, Copei's essay did show that current German educational thinking was compatible with the intellectual side of the project method.

The six headings under which progressive education has just been described should not be regarded as mutually exclusive. They were trends, many of which were found within a single school. Prestolee, for example, was interested both in freedom for the children and in widening the horizons of the village community; the *Werkplaats* combined individual progress in an all-pervading atmosphere of co-operation; Mearns and Lismer united disciplined spontaneity with social and personal relevance; and Washburne showed how freedom, creativity, purposiveness, and social responsibility could come together effectively in a school program.

Probably the best example of balance and catholicity was to be found in the Lincoln School attached to Teachers College, Columbia University. It was a hard-headed experimental school with an imaginative, versatile, and progressively minded staff who were interested in testing out the possibilities of the activity school.

(vii) The Lincoln School

The Lincoln School was established in 1917 and continued for thirty years until 1948 as an experimental school to produce a modern curriculum taught in a modern spirit. Its distinctive function was 'that of adventuring beyond accepted practice into areas where educational practice and theory are in the process of formation'.[42] A fundamental duty to be undertaken by the practitioners of progressive education was to take up the leads given by the pioneers such as Dewey, Kilpatrick, Meriam, and Marietta Johnson, and put the ideas into practical, workable form. That was the kind of contribution that the school set itself to make. One of the Lincoln School teachers summarised the task by asking the question of herself: 'Must the theory fall down in practice because there were so few to point the way, to show how to do successfully the thing in which we believed?'[43] The school was a co-educational, private, fee-paying establishment of several hundred pupils in New York, organised into elementary, junior high, and senior high school divisions. In its work the school was for the most part moderately progressive, and

because of its temperance it was able to affect public education more widely than more radical schools could.

Undoubtedly, the Lincoln School's main contribution was to the design and practice of curriculum making. Its founders viewed that as its main task, and it lived up to their expectations. The general effect throughout the school was the development of an approach similar to Decroly's Centres of Interest and to the Method of Complexes used in the U.S.S.R. In the Lincoln School it emerged as a core grouping of units of work for each grade.

The units were designed to provide a central integrating experience for the work of a particular class, and to tap into each group's particular stage of development. A second grade teacher summarised the unit-maker's viewpoint: 'All children are fundamentally scientists, craftsmen, actors, and artists.'[44] Each unit provided an all-round education in which the children could observe and solve problems, could construct interesting things, could dramatise some of their experiences, and could express themselves creatively and artistically. The principal units were large centres of interest that might last for an extended period, even up to a full year, and might be accompanied by shorter units sometimes related to the larger ones. Much of the work in formal subjects might arise out of the work on the main unit, but some of the work required of the pupils might be unconnected with it. A good example of a unit was one tried out with eleven year-old children. It was a study of how man has made written records. Taking its start from the pupils' interest in producing a magazine, it led to a study of symbols, methods of recording and books through the ages, and involved the reproduction of earlier materials and methods and the printing of a school magazine.

The staff of the elementary school eventually set out seven criteria for the selection and design of units:

- Does the material come near enough to the child to be real to that child? The making of a school magazine was an example of an expressed interest that was real and sustained by the class throughout the year.

- Does the unit give opportunities for the pursuit of problems, purposes and interests on the child's present mental level? The sixth graders were able to make a play out of a mediaeval manuscript, manufacture paper, and present to a school a review of their work on a demanding level.

[42] *Thirty Schools Tell Their Story*, Harper, New York, 1943, p. 459.

[43] Martha M. Porter, *The Teacher in the New School*, World Book Co., Yonkers, New York, 1930, p. 9.

[44] Avah W. Hughes, *Carrying the Mail. A Second Grade's Experiences*, Bureau of Publications, Teachers College, Columbia University, New York, 1933, p. 3.

- Does the unit stimulate many kinds of activities, creative, intellectual, and social, providing both for individual differences and for the integration of diverse activities? The records unit provided limitless opportunities for handwork, drawing, group discussion, excursions, reading, vocabulary extension, and historical research.
- Does the unit bring about growth from the present level to the next step both in individuals and groups? Is there an effective way of measuring achievement and progress that will enable the teacher to insist that the standards in manual and intellectual work were above those of previous years in both quality and quantity?
- Does the unit stimulate a desire on the part of the individual to proceed on his own initiative and to take responsibility in widening his interests and understanding? Many of the children in the unit on books became interested in working further at the design and practice of bookmaking and magazines, and even in timber getting and the manufacture of paper.
- Does the unit help meet the demands of society and help clarify social meanings? The unit on human records encouraged a scientific attitude in dealing with reference material, deepened an appreciation of differences in languages and modes of expression and raised for discussion questions such as freedom of the press, and the effect of modern technology on methods of recording.
- Does the unit lead to desirable intellectual, social, and moral habits? These were virtues such as perseverance, co-operativeness, open-mindedness, good judgment, self-direction, and initiative.[45]

From the beginning of the 1930's´ the sixth criterion, the social emphasis in unit making and teaching, gained considerably in importance. When in 1935 the school staff published a statement on their approach to curriculum development, they put forward the view that to attempt to change curricula by studying the child's nature and needs or by refining techniques or broadening the scope of subject-matter was inadequate without first understanding the nature of the emerging society. The social changes brought on by the great depression and the deep and serious public interest in the condition of society was having its impact on educational thinking and educational practice. The Lincoln School staff responded by suggesting that a teacher's experience 'must be leavened by new meanings developed from a study of the present social scene if the curriculum is to become more functional in the lives of both teachers and pupils.'[46] They themselves undertook such studies and in consequence began to reorient the school's curriculum, especially at the secondary level, developing more integrated courses, and emphasising the study of western and contemporary society.

During that period, beginning in 1933, the high school took part in the Progressive Education Association's Eight-Year Study. Throughout that experience the school deepened its commitment to integrated courses to such an extent that by 1935 five of the six grades of the high school devoted approximately half of their time to such courses, and in the following years the tendency was extended even further. Invariably those general courses had a substantial content from the social sciences.[47]

The school had a wide influence. Throughout the 1920's and 1930's it helped to establish or to consolidate in American education many of the practices for which the progressives stood. The list of criteria for units was a summary of progressive education. Well-prepared units made appropriate use of research on child development and educational measurement; they posed intellectual problems for solutions; they offered possibilities for creative work for independent activities, and for the integration of subject-matter; they were relevant to the children's interests and to his social environment; and they provided opportunity both for the development of individual initiative and co-operative work. It was a catalogue of the new education and many teachers in America and abroad became involved in it and learnt how to go about it from the publications and reports of the Lincoln School.

REVIEW OF PROGRESSIVE EDUCATION AT THE END OF THE 1920'S

There was some evidence in the 1920's that progressive ideas were penetrating through into the general run of public schools. In 1929 *Progressive Education* published a number dealing with new trends in public school education which indicated that from wide areas of the country there was interest and an effort to introduce some of the features of progressive education. The Los Angeles school system, for example, published an activity course of study in 1924 and established a demonstration school in order to assist teachers to grasp the new ideas and practices. In Michigan, at Grand Rapids, an elementary school had developed a child-centred approach and was using integrated units. In Seattle, schools with a range of children from lower to upper middle

[45] This summary is a modification and combination of the statements contained in Emily A. Barnes & Bess M. Young, *Children and Architecture*, Bureau of Publications, Teachers College, Columbia University, New York, 1932, and James J. Tippett *et al, Curriculum Making in an Elementary School*, Ginn, Boston, 1927.

[46] The Staff of the Lincoln School, *Lincoln School Studies Society: A Study Outline for School Staff Meetings*, Bureau of Publications, Teachers' College, Columbia University, New York, 1935, p.4.

[47] *Thirty Schools Tell Their Story*, p. 461.

social class and of mixed nationalities were working to reconstruct their curricula in the direction of activity work, and at Denver, Colorado, beginning in 1922, a very substantial reappraisal and reconstruction of school curricula and teaching methods from kindergarten through to senior high school had been taking place.

It would be true to say, however, that by 1930 the ideas and practices of progressive education were not yet generally accepted by the schools of the United States. They were becoming familiar to elementary teachers and were being practised more frequently as the years went on; some impact had been made on the junior high schools, but the senior high school had not moved very far. An educator pointed out that in 1930, of the twenty-two thousand high schools, twelve thousand had enrolments of less than one hundred students and the teachers in them had very little concept of education beyond the traditional.[48] Throughout the 1930's the Progressive Education Association was to seek ways through its Eight-Year Study to demonstrate the relevance and effectiveness of progressive ideas at the high school level.

Through art, a group of eight-year-olds in New York rediscover their city.

Progressive Education Association, *Progressive Education*, vol. xiii, no. 4, April 1936, p. 260.

At the end of the 1920's assessment was in the air.

In 1928 Rugg and Shumaker made a substantial appraisal.[49] They were enthusiastic supporters of the progressive movement which they regarded as of great importance, but they were critical of several of the current practices in American progressive schools. An over-concern with freedom from imposition sometimes tended to minimise constructiveness and intellectual rigour, and led to a lack of careful design and sequence in curricula. The literature produced by progressive educators tended to be descriptive and to a certain extent self-congratulatory rather than critical and constructive. There was, for example, as yet no serious analysis of creativity, nor was there any fundamental analysis of the way in which the school should relate to society. One final shortcoming of the American progressive schools of the 1920's was that with few exceptions they tended to be schools for upper middle class children. Manumit was the obvious exception, but most of them were private fee-charging institutions or public schools such as Winnetka and Bronxville which were established in the wealthier areas.

In two successive annual addresses to the Progressive Education Association in 1928 and 1929 two leading progressives, John Dewey and Alexander Meiklejohn, added their assessments. They reinforced much that Rugg and Shumaker had written, and called for a concerted effort on the part of the progressives to provide positive and constructive leadership in education. They saw the present as the end of a phase of progressive education that had been one of necessary protest and innovation. If they were to be free, not to do as they liked, but to do as they thought best, then teachers had to provide help and guidance in such a way that growth and freedom might flourish with a positive emphasis. For that to occur, progressive schools needed not merely a set of methods and a range of attitudes, but also a course of study of which the essential characteristics were that it should have a substantial and demanding intellectual content. It should connect the school with the outside world; it should be related to the life work of everyday men and women in the society in which the pupil lives; and it should aid the pupil's growth and freedom while involving him in a critical examination of the qualities of life in the culture in which he was a participant. That did not mean that the progressive teacher must necessarily be a social revolutionary; but it did mean that the school curriculum should develop out of a vital interest in the fundamental issues of human life and should be an encouragement to the pupils to think those issues through.

[48] American Educational Research Association, Official Report of the 1935 Meeting, *The Application of Research Findings to Current Educational Practices*, AERA, Washington D.C., 1935, article by C.G.F. Franzen, pp. 224-5.

[49] H. Rugg and Ann Shumaker, *The Child-Centred School*, World Book Co., New York, 1928.

In the 1920's a substantial start had already been made in the directions indicated by Dewey and Meiklejohn. There had already been a greatly increased interest in the serious study of contemporary society. *The Cardinal Principles of Secondary Education* in 1918 had proclaimed social efficiency as the prime aim of education, and the social content of school curricula had been steadily growing. Notably, Rugg had been at work starting to modernise teaching in the social sciences. In 1927 the National Society for the Study of Education published a yearbook reviewing curriculum trends and making suggestions for future lines of development. It was the most comprehensive study made, up till that point, of curriculum theory and practice, and it helped, by directing attention to the need for a more solid connection between the school, the child, and society, to set the stage for one of the most stimulating and fruitful periods in educational history.

The yearbook committee, after much discussion among its members, whose viewpoints ranged from conservative to ultra-progressive, agreed upon a statement of the principles that should guide curriculum-makers in their next steps forward. Overall, the clearest emphasis in the committee's recommendations was upon the need to study contemporary society, to understand it, to analyse it, and to derive from it the materials and the skills that can be taught in schools in such a way that children will be able to master it, to enjoy its opportunities, and contribute to its improvement. 'One of the chief intellectual purposes of the school is to develop understanding of the institutions, problems and issues of contemporary life.'[50]

For the progressives the beginning of the 1930's marked a distinct change of orientation. It was a change that could be seen both in the U.S.A. and in Europe. The 1920's were the heyday of those interested in individual freedom and creativity. In the 1930's the weight of discussion was on the school's social responsibility.

In 1929 Percy Nunn, whose views had had substantial influence in England since the end of World War I, made an assessment of the new education. He found its goal was 'the perfection of the individual', and the cultivation of his 'creative spirit'.[51] Three years later, at the Nice Conference, the NEF's principal concern was with the role of the school in society and the most effective ways of studying social and political issues. In the U.S.A. the 'new leaven' in 1928 for Stanwood Cobb, a founder and early president of the PEA, was the educational effort 'to discover the essential child, and to aid it to that development which is normal to its individuality'.[52] By 1932 the main topic of discussion was the role that the school might or might not play in reconstructing society.

The change in emphasis was more distinct in the United States, and the controversy accompanying the change was more widespread than elsewhere. It marked an important new stage in the politicising of education in the democratic world.

The school's relationship to society had traditionally been a conservative one. Its role was that of contributing to stability and continuity. It reflected rather than led society and its job was to see that the tradition was adequately handed on. The Deweyan revolution, however, at the start of the twentieth century initiated a different view of the relationship between the school and society.

Dewey and his followers expressed the view that there should be a close and strong connection between school and society. The school's interest should be in the actual existing society, and it should be the subject of close study by children in school. Insistence on critical thinking and problem-solving meant that children became interested and involved in looking not merely at institutions and everyday behaviour, but also at social issues and problems. The educator's fundamental commitment to activity meant that social issues would be examined to see what action could be appropriately taken about them. In Dewey's view education was a form of social action and in the long run the fundamental method of social progress and reform. In order to act effectively, children had to learn the importance of co-operation and the means of co-operating; they also had to learn to make up their minds about the social values they wished to accept and use as a basis for their behaviour. In that kind of education, there was therefore, an almost inevitable tendency to interest pupils in social reform and to orient schools towards policies and programs that favoured some kind of social reconstruction. It was the great economic depression of the 1930's that made the tendency more explicit.

IMPACT OF THE ECONOMIC DEPRESSION ON EDUCATION IN THE U.S.A.

The depression started with the collapse of the New York Stock Exchange in 1929 and rapidly spread throughout the country and overseas. In 1930 four million Americans were unemployed and by the end of 1931 the number had risen to eight million. Wages were cut, numerous banks failed and the business world was shattered. Gradually the worst of the depression was overcome in the United States by the effluxion of time, by

---

[50] National Society for the Study of Education, *The Twenty-sixth Yearbook, The Foundations and Technique of Curriculum-Construction, Part II, The Foundations of Curriculum-Making*, Public School Publishing Co., Bloomington, Illinois, 1927, pp. 21-2.

[51] T.P. Nunn, 'The basic principles of the new education', *The New Era*, pp. 207-8, lecture delivered at the NEF Elsinore Conference, 1929.

[52] S. Cobb, *The New Leaven*, Day, New York, 1928, p. 251.

the pragmatic efforts of individuals in government, and by the tentative collectivism of Roosevelt's New Deal.

From the point of view of education four effects of the depression were of particular importance. First, the sheer grinding poverty and extensive unemployment affected school funds, slowed down the expansion of school facilities, and restricted many school programs. Secondly, the difficulty of obtaining any work led many of the older students to stay on at school in the higher grades; that was one of the important reasons why there was no slackening in the rate of increase in the number of high school students during the 1930's. The percentage of fourteen to seventeen year olds enrolled in high schools rose from 28 per cent in 1930 to 52 per cent in 1940. The greatly increased number and diversity of senior students made it necessary to rethink the traditional program of senior high school to make it more relevant to the experiences of the pupils and to their probable future destinations. The development of programs in the study of contemporary society was one important way in which the schools endeavoured to make the work of older adolescents more relevant. Thirdly, it intensified the general demands for social justice, and in particular it raised the level of interest in the welfare of youth. This social conscience was given practical effect by the development of greatly increased provision for pre-school education and for adult education, and, particularly, by the creation of two new organisations for youths, the Civil Construction Corps and the National Youth Administration. The fourth significant effect of the depression was a widespread interest in social and economic questions. The depression and the New Deal generated many studies and much discussion in those fields. There was considerable bewilderment at the economic inequalities that were revealed and at the inability of existing mechanisms to provide an equitable distribution of goods and to solve the anomalous situation of great poverty continuing at a time when goods and foodstuffs were being deliberately destroyed. The critical examination of existing practices and circumstances led to a search for and a consideration of ways of building a new society.

The depression, according to a committee of educators, 'revealed many evidences, among adults and children alike, of social, political, and economic illiteracy'. There was a widespread ignorance of significant forces currently at work in society, the school was doing little or nothing about these things, and, although it was not entirely a new problem, it was clear that the depression had thrown it into new and startling relief.[53]

In the elementary schools and the high schools it was an era of curriculum reform. The depression had the effect of eliminating from many school systems all but the subjects regarded as fundamental. Art, music, household arts, health education, and similar activities and their teachers were drastically retrenched so that the depression-time programs looked somewhat like those of the 1890's before the great curriculum

expansion of the twentieth century. In particular, the reformers of the 1930's who took up the challenge and the suggestions of the educational theorists were interested in recasting the social sciences program.

The study of society and its possibilities and the ways in which schools might deal with contemporary ideals and problems was the special concern of the Commission on Social Sciences set up by the American Historical Association in 1929. The following five years until the publication in 1934 of its Conclusions and Recommendations it engaged the efforts of many of the leading scholars and educators of the United States, and was responsible for a substantial series of important volumes on many aspects of social sciences.[54]

The purpose of teaching the social sciences was to equip young people to understand the realities, the forces, and the changes, and to enable them to act intelligently and in the common interest in dealing with the issues as they developed in American society. The commission was a lively, forward-looking body and its members expressed their views of the contemporary scene accordingly, urging the view that schools should prepare pupils for a less individualistic society, and for a positive and creative attack on social problems.

For most educators the social orientation in their thinking meant that the school in its program should pay close attention to the society which it was designed to serve and should try to ensure that the pupils were socially and politically knowledgeable. For others, and this included some members of the American Historical Association's Commission on the Social Studies, Dewey's invitation to education to aim at the reconstruction of man in society, meant that the school should take steps not merely to adjust more effectively to existing society but to enter actively into the process of trying to build a new and more desirable democratic society.

One member of the commission who thought in that way was George S. Counts. At the beginning of 1932 he gave three addresses, one of which was to the Progressive Education Association, and combined them for publication into a rousing pamphlet called *Dare the Schools Build a new Social Order?* Counts argued against defining the task of the school as that of preparing individuals to adjust to social change, and proposed

[53] The Educational Policies Commission, *Research Memorandum on Education in the Depression*, Bulletin 28, Social Science Research Council, New York, 1937, p. 77.

[54] Those with the most influential and immediate bearing on the teaching of social sciences in schools were: Charles A. Beard, *A Charter for the Social Sciences in the Schools*, Scribner's, New York, 1932; Charles A. Beard, *The Nature of the Social Sciences in Relation to Objectives of Instruction*, Scribner's, New York, 1934; Rolla M. Tryon, *The Social Sciences as School Subjects*, Scribner's, New York, 1935; Leon C. Marshall and Rachel M. Goetz, *Curriculum-Making in the Social Studies. A Social Process Approach*, Scribner's, New York, 1936; George S. Counts, *The Social Foundations of Education*, Scribner's, New York, 1934; and Merle E. Curti, *Social Ideas of American Educators*, Scribner's New York, 1935.

that the school should help society to direct the process of social change. 'Education,' he wrote 'as a force for social regeneration must march hand in hand with the living and creative forces of the social order. In their own lives teachers must bridge the gap between school and society and play some part in the fashioning of those great common purposes which should bind the two together.'[55] Teachers should be responsible for thinking thoroughly about the lines of future development of their society. Their concern was even more with the future than it was with the past. They had a duty to their pupils and to their society to formulate a vision of their future society through which the younger generation could be inspired to acquire the means to realise it in their future activities. 'Schools would then become centers for the building, and not merely for the contemplation, of our civilization'.[56]

In the ordinary course of their activities, teachers had to impose on their pupils by arranging their pupils' learning environment, and making decisions about what was to be taught; they should, therefore, not be afraid to use the imposition they already practised in the interests of a program of social teaching that would lead to a better society. Progressive education was in need of a new purpose — a purpose which came not from vague individualistic cultivation but from a firm commitment to develop a more worthy society. It should centre its efforts henceforth not on individual development but on social reconstruction.

Support for Counts' viewpoint came from the President's Committee on Social Trends which had been set up in 1929 and reported in 1933. After an extensive review of the current situation the authors stressed the need for economic and social planning, and they looked for the development of new and emergent values upon the basis of which the society of the future could be reconstituted.

Counts' strongest backing came from fellow progressive professors of education. The most prominent of them to adopt a reconstructionist viewpoint was Kilpatrick. In an important lecture at the end of 1932 Kilpatrick indicated that he thought that civilisation might be at one of its great turning points, and that the time for the old frontier individualism and competitive business was past. The American business system which had made and was continuing to make a deep impression on American education was outworn and anti-social. It must be challenged and remodelled. The school had an important part to play in the future work of reconstruction. The school must study current social problems as close to life as possible. It must get involved in controversial issues and must encourage its students to work at socially significant undertakings. In those ways it would build in its pupils an attitude of social responsibility. It would encourage the development of social intelligence, and it could hope to take some effectual part in remaking the social structure.[57] In the following year Kilpatrick edited a book, The

Social Frontier, in which leading progressive educators analysed questions associated with the school's responsibility to society. They argued that it was false to oppose individual to social, that society was individuals-in-their-relations, and that for the sake of individual development education must promote some forms of community life and must work against others. The school therefore could not be indifferent as to the kind of social organisation that existed around it, but must give a deliberate preference to and must work for its choice of social order. The writers' choice was for a social order in the democratic tradition which, instead of developing haphazardly and with a view to private interest, made use of intelligent, co-operative planning.[58]

The educational profession was uncertain about the role it should play in social reconstruction. Discussion on the matter was further sharpened by the appearance in 1933 of A Call to the Teachers of the Nation published by a sub-committee of the Progressive Education Association. It was a follow-up to Counts' Dare the Schools Build a New Social Order? and was written in the same vein. Education, the call claimed, 'cannot be neutral toward the great issues of life and destiny'. Teachers 'owe nothing to the present economic system, except to improve it; they owe nothing to any privileged caste, except to strip it of its privileges. Their sole duty is to guard and promote the widest and most permanent interests of society. Teachers therefore cannot evade the responsibility of participating actively in the task of reconstituting the democratic tradition and of thus working positively toward a new society.'[59]

THE VIRGINIA CURRICULA

All educators agreed that there was a need for understanding society and that the task of the school was to develop programs which would contribute to that end. But how far was understanding to go? It could be an understanding of the structure and organisation of society and of the principles and ideals through which it should function. That is what was traditionally taught in history and social studies courses; but for many teachers it was not good enough. They would like pupils to see society as

[55] G.S. Counts, Dare the Schools Build a New Social Order? John Day, New York, 1932, pp. 30-1.

[56] ibid., p. 37.

[57] W.H. Kilpatrick, Education and the Social Crisis, Liveright, New York, 1932.

[58] W.H. Kilpatrick (ed.), The Social Frontier, Century, New York, 1933. The other contributors were John Dewey, John L. Childs, R.B. Raup from Columbia University. Boyd H. Bode, and H.G. Hullfish from Ohio State University, and V.T. Thayer from the Ethical Culture Schools in New York. An account of the reconstructionist movement can be found in C.A. Bowers, The Progressive Educator and the Depression: the Radical Years, Random House, New York, 1969.

[59] The Committee of the Progressive Education Association on Social and Economic Problems, A Call to the Teachers of the Nation, John Day, New York, 1933.

it really was, warts and all. They would like them to understand that politics was more concerned with power than with high ideals, and they would like them to see the corruption and self-interest of society as well as its finer sides, its problems as well as its accomplishments, its mistakes as well as its successes. Those teachers did not wish their children merely to accept and to adjust to society as it was but to gain a thorough knowledge and to develop a critical understanding of their contemporary world. To achieve an objective of that kind many argued that it was necessary for their pupils to interact in some significant way with society. In any case, there was a substantial school of thought, among progressive educators particularly, that understanding and action were indissolubly interrelated and that education was incomplete when it fell short of considered social action. But what sort of action was necessary? The commonest procedure was to select some aspect of social life, to observe it, to collect data on it, and to analyse it; many of the units at schools such as the Lincoln School adopted that kind of approach.

On a more extensive scale were the Virginia Curricula published in 1934. They were probably the most extensive, thoughtful, and radical revisions of school programs undertaken up to that time in the United States. Each curriculum was prefaced with a statement that it was based in general on several stated principles which included the view that: 'The school is an agency of society for its perpetuation and recreation. Growth processes in individuals and in society are resultants of continuing interaction between individuals and society.' In 1940 a Commission appointed by the governor of Virginia to report on the curriculum reiterated the earlier statements and recorded with pride the view expressed by a well-known American educator that: 'Most state programs organized since 1931 are based on a core curriculum similar to that of Virginia.'[60]

The core curriculum was developed to cover all grades of the elementary and high schools as 'an educational program which orients the pupil to social life.'[61] It covered the social studies, the language arts, science, and general mathematics, building them together into a co-ordinated and integrated pattern based upon 'centres of interest' which were described as 'pivotal points in social life, about which activities group'.[62] Eleventh grade, for example, included such centres of interest as: 'How can nations through social planning guarantee to all the protection of life, property, and natural resources? How can nations plan for the establishment of proper economic interdependence by apportioning the production of goods and services, and by distributing these more equitably to the consumer? How shall social groups plan to provide for their preservation and reconstruction through education?'

The work involved a wide range of socially relevant activities. Some were directed towards finding out facts and practices, such as attending local council meetings and holding one of their own on some community

problem. Other activities involved the pupils in investigations of aspects of community life, such as an examination of the operation of insurance companies which led to case studies of individuals, interviews with insurance agents, and the study of state laws and various types of insurance policies. The Virginia curricula did not go so far as to suggest that the schools should deliberately work to reconstruct society, but they did suggest content and methods of study that would lead to the development of young citizens with a critical understanding and an interest in the betterment of the community.

A further and final step in committing a school to interact with society was that of actually entering into and taking part in society's affairs. Schools might do this by providing educational facilities for areas of society's concerns where they were needed from time to time, or they might go further, and become involved, as some community schools did, in programs for the improvement of society. Many schools were willing to have their pupils involved in the government of the school and in its improvement but stopped short of involving the pupils in similar activities for the general society outside the school.

'THE SOCIAL FRONTIER'

The full commitment of the community school approach was consonant with the views of Counts, Dewey, and Rugg, who together with Kilpatrick and several other similarly minded educators, formed an association to produce a new and fascinating journal called *The Social Frontier*, which ran from 1934 until the end of 1943. Counts was its first editor. In launching the journal, Kilpatrick, the chairman of its board of directors, declared: 'Its founding is definitely related to the new spirit of creative social enquiry which has been apparent among American educators and teachers during the past three or four years. If the hopes of its founders are to be realised, this new journal must become the expressive medium of those members of the teaching profession who believe that education has an important, even strategic role to play in the reconstruction of American society.'

In its opening editorial, Counts indicated that the journal accepted the analysis of the Report of the Commission on Social Studies of the American Historical Association which stated that: 'The age of

[60] The State Department of Education, *Public Schools in Virginia*, Bulletin, State Board of Education, vol. XXII, no. 4, Richmond, Virginia, January 1940, p. 15. The quotation was from L.T. Hopkins *et al.*, *Integration. Its Meaning and Application*, Appleton, New York, 1938. Other notable core curricula organised around social demands were to be found in the state programs for Mississippi and Kansas.

[61] Tentative Course of Study for the Core Curriculum of Virginia Secondary Schools, Grade 8, State Board of Education, Richmond, Virginia, 1934.

[62] *ibid.*, p. 15.

individualism and laissez faire in economy and government is closing and a new age of collectivism is emerging.'[63] That, he declared, was 'the central and dominating reality to the present epoch', and the journal would 'devote its pages positively to the development of thought of all who are interested in making education discharge its full responsibility in the present age of social transition'.

During the course of its ten years' existence the note of urgency and social reconstruction which characterised its foundation in the depression period was gradually quietened, and in 1939 it became a journal of the Progressive Education Association, changed its name to *Frontiers of Democracy*, and toned down its policy. Nevertheless, throughout its existence the journal gave an opportunity for educators such as Dewey, Kilpatrick, and Counts to argue the case for more extensive social planning and for school teachers to take a more active part in it. For several years Dewey ran a monthly column dealing with current issues and on one occasion engaged, over a series of numbers, in a celebrated debate with Hutchins, the vigorous but traditionalist young president of the University of Chicago. *The Social Frontier* was sympathetic to the social legislation of the New Deal, to its development of enterprises such as the Tennessee Valley Authority, and to whatever tendencies it showed toward national planning. It was, in effect, a vehicle for the expression of socialistic views on politics, economics, and education, and helped to keep before the public the reconstructive ideas of a group of virile and socially sensitive educators.

NATIONAL EDUCATION ASSOCIATION AND SOCIAL RECONSTRUCTION

The NEA's department of superintendence weighed in with three successive yearbooks from 1935 to 1937 on the social reconstruction theme. Only four years earlier it had produced a yearbook on the five unifying factors in American education of which community relationships was listed as one. It was a fairly matter-of-fact technical analysis with no hint of the school's possible interest in investigating the community and working for its reconstruction. The yearbooks of the mid 1930's appear to have come out of a different world. They showed an intense interest in social trends and problems and in the school's concern for them. As might have been expected the line pursued by most contributors was neither the thoroughly reconstructive one of Counts and *The Social Frontier* nor a completely neutral one. It fell between the two.

The school superintendents had, for a generation past, accepted and acted upon the view that the aim of schooling was social efficiency. This had usually meant, as it did in the 1931 yearbook, that the organisation of the schools should be seen to be efficient and that the product of the schools

should fit effectively into current society. That the functioning of society itself might be fundamentally questioned had not been seriously considered. It was precisely this that the three yearbooks did. Between them they presented the variety of views that were abroad concerning social change, the role of educators, and the issues that had to be faced in the present critical period, and suggested guiding principles for the refashioning of education to help further the increasing social emphasis that the authors saw developing in contemporary school programs. Social planning sustained by appropriate education was a necessity, but the nub of the problem was 'how to produce an educational system devoted to modifying or abolishing the present social order and yet have it supported by those most loyal to the existing order'.[64] The key group were the teachers; they had to be re-educated and provided with a stronger organisation which could effectively resist conservative pressures. The yearbooks undoubtedly raised the crucial operational issue, but the authors were to be disappointed of a speedy realisation of their hopes. Neither the conservative weight of public opinion nor the teachers were re-educated in the short term. It is interesting, however, that a contemporary piece of research[65] showed that secondary school teachers considered themselves much less conservative than had been supposed, and that over the years from the early 1920's to the mid-1930's they appeared to be growing steadily more radical.

In 1937 the NEA's committee on social-economic goals, whose chairman in 1932 had expressed his approval of Counts' pamphlet, eventually produced its report, reinforcing the views of the recent yearbooks. It argued that substantial time should be spent in school on social and economic questions and that they should be treated with realism and freedom so that pupils might come to see that changes in social conditions might demand the rethinking of traditional ideals and government practices. A supplementary report demonstrated the growing popularity of social interests by listing and annotating some two hundred new courses in social-economic education which had been developed in schools in the United States between 1928 and 1935.[66] The schools, in the committee's view, were to be agencies for building an ever better social order. They were to do this not by agitation and intervention, though teachers should more and more become community leaders of thought, but by building understanding, skills, and attitudes in their pupils.

[63] American Historical Association, Commission on the Social Sciences, *Conclusions and Recommendations*, Scribner, New York, 1934, p. 16.

[64] NEA, Department of Superintendence, *The Improvement of Education. Its Interpretation for Democracy*, Fifteenth Yearbook, NEA, Washington D.C., 1937, p. 102.

[65] W.H. Kilpatrick (ed.), *The Teacher and Society*, First Yearbook of the John Dewey Society, Appleton-Century, New York, 1937, Chapter VIII.

[66] National Education Association, *Creating Social Intelligence: A Descriptive Bibliography*, Research Bulletin, 13, 3, May 1935, Washington D.C.

It was a middle road to reconstruction that was favoured by the spokesmen for the teaching profession and school administrators. The teachers and those who wrote their NEA yearbooks were neither far to the left nor far to the right. They were greatly interested in extending the social curriculum of the school, and they welcomed some measure of social change. But they did not see the schools leading and directing the process of social reconstruction, nor did they see themselves merely as followers and reflectors of the course of social change. They saw their main task as that of producing the kinds of persons who were capable of living actively, intelligently, and flexibly in a time of great social change, individuals who would express their differences but who would do so in ways that were 'co-operative and socially contributory not self-centred and egoistic'.[67] If they were not to be active leaders in the reconstruction of society, nor merely passive followers, they might at least be well-informed and intelligent guides pointing the way toward social betterment.

The movement in the 1930's to persuade teachers to commit themselves to a more penetrating form of teaching about society and to a point of view about its future development was a demonstration of the growing connection between politics and education that was becoming characteristic of the twentieth century. The relationship had been clearly and firmly established in both communist and fascist countries during the 1930's. In a western democracy such as the U.S.A. it was less easy to define what the relationship should be. None of the educators ever denied the desirability that pupils and teachers should have a whole-hearted commitment to democracy; but how much objectivity was there to be in the study of social problems? Could a teacher legitimately use the school directly or indirectly to change existing political, economic, and social structures? These were perplexing questions that were seriously raised and widely discussed throughout the 1930's. They were not firmly answered by most teachers, but there was no doubt that from that period teachers became much more aware of the role that schools played and might play in society.

The reconstructionist sequence of Dewey, Rugg, Counts, and *The Social Frontier* led on to Brameld, who was already writing in the 1930's. More conformist groups prepared the way for the conservative Basic Education group of the 1950's. The broad middle path widening out in the course of the inter-war period became broader still in the post-World War II period. The study of current society became accepted as an important part of general education; the orthodox educator became more knowledgeable about current social issues and problems; and students of education became increasingly interested in educational sociology and social dynamics.

One measure of the difference between the educational literature of, say, 1910 and 1950 is the extent to which the later writing was impregnated with social reference. Whether the reconstructionists, who spearheaded the movement, succeeded in getting their viewpoint accepted or not, they did at least ensure that education henceforth was to be numbered among the social sciences.

CONSERVATIVE INFLUENCES

Progressive education and the general trend towards the democratisation of education were inhibited by the normal conservatism of the teaching profession and the inertia of public educational authorities. They were also actively opposed by educators and educational authorities with firm, contrary convictions. The grounds for opposition were practical, theoretical, and sometimes religious.

To many, for whom Julien Benda could have been the spokesman, modern reform, undermining the classical curriculum and embodying the vitalism of Bergson, had an undesirable anti-intellectual trend.[68] Benda wrote *The Betrayal of the Intellectuals* in 1927, in which he argued that intellectuals had betrayed their true role of disinterested criticism by becoming linked with political causes, by allowing sentiment to turn their reasoning into rationalisation, and by neglecting the ideal for the practical. What was needed was concerted effort to restore classicism, order, and intelligence to the place usurped by emotion and political realism.

The theme was taken up and enlarged in a more telling way by Ortega, whose *The Revolt of the Masses*, published in 1930, deplored the advent of modern mass man in whose hands the government and future development of civilisation rested. The mass man could be found in all social classes. He was the kind who was self-satisfied, philistine, mediocre, and intellectually vulgar. He did not understand the painstaking care and effort that had been exercised in the past and still had to be exercised to produce and preserve the level of culture which he had inherited. What was needed was an education that would produce men who understood the culture, 'the system of vital ideas which each age possesses', and who were 'at the height of their times'.[69]

Like Ortega, the English classical scholar Livingstone saw the period to be time of unrest and crisis in which old values were unappreciated and new ones had not satisfactorily emerged. There was need for some secure

---

[67] NEA, Committee on Social-Economic Goals of America, *Implications of Social Economic Goals for Education*, Washington D.C., 1937, p. 12.

[68] J. Benda was born in 1868 in Paris, and became a well-known essayist. *La Trahison des Clercs* (1927) was his best known work.

[69] J. Ortega y Gasset, *The Revolt of the Masses*, Norton, New York, 1932, (1930), *passim*, and *Mission of the University*, Princeton University Press, 1944 (1930), p. 81. Ortega (1883-1955) held a chair in philosophy at the University of Madrid 1910-36, and thereafter spent his life in writing and travel.

direction 'to find a principle to rule life'. It was difficult but still possible to achieve that aim because there were certain persistent values running throughout human history that provide guidelines for all times. They were to be found by searching for what Livingstone called the 'first rate' in ideals and conduct, 'what always, everywhere, and by everyone' had been judged to be superior. Education, then, was not so much a matter of discovery and creation as a process of disclosure and reproduction, a presenting of a vision of greatness which the pupil should absorb by constant and thorough association.[70]

In the United States, Hutchins put that line of thinking into a basically conservative educational theory with his statement: 'One purpose of education is to draw out the elements of our common human nature. These elements are the same in any time or place ... Education implies teaching. Teaching implies knowledge. Knowledge is truth. Truth is everywhere the same. Hence education should be everywhere the same.'[71] Human nature, in Hutchins' view, did not change, and its essence was to be found in human reason. The unchanging purpose of education was the cultivation of the intellect of which the chief requirement was 'correctness in thinking'.[72] The main vehicle, at the higher education level, was to be found in the 'permanent studies' which consisted of the great classic books of all ages, English grammar, rhetoric, logic, and mathematics. Studies such as those contributed to the disciplining of the mind by helping to build up intellectual habits.

Hutchins' views were taken further and given a supernatural warrant by some educators whose theories had a religious basis. The most influential statement of that kind in the 1930's was the Encyclical of Pope Pius XI, *The Christian Education of Youth*, issued in 1929. The purpose of education was to form 'the true Christian, the product of Christian education ... who thinks, judges, and acts constantly and consistently in accordance with right reason illuminated by the supernatural light of the example and teaching of Christ'. Family, church and state were the three principal agents in education and should work in harmony under the general supervision of the church. The school was an intellectual agency supportive of and complementary to the moral and religious functions of the home and the church. Progressive educators who encouraged children to mould their own characters, who used activity methods 'exclusively based on the powers of nature', and who favoured co-education, were to be condemned.[73] The central feature of the school's intellectual offering was a training in right reasoning through the study of classical literature, relevant general knowledge, and sound philosophy. On the relationship of school to society, the trend of such thinking was to insist on the primacy of the school's responsibility to individuals and their develop-ment, to acknowledge the importance of the social context of their education and to accept the obligation to transmit the social heritage. It

was social transmission not social reconstruction. A new social order should be built not by the direct intervention of teachers, but by their concentrating on building better and wiser human beings.

When the reconstructive function of the school was seriously propounded in the early 1930's in the United States by Counts' speeches and the subsequent *A Call to the Teachers of the Nation*, it was strenuously opposed by a group of conservative educators. 'Should teachers,' wrote one of them, 'remain neutral in times like these? As teachers they can do nothing else.' They can teach pupils to consider all the facts of the situation but they must themselves remain neutral. They interpret societies, they do not build new ones. 'The school does not precede the cultural transformation but follows it.' To help consolidate that viewpoint the name Essentialists was coined in 1935, and a committee was formed three years later, largely through the efforts of W.C. Bagley, a colleague of Counts, Rugg, and Kilpatrick at Teachers College, Columbia. Bagley had earlier criticised the use of creativity, interest, and liberty as teaching methods by progressives at the expense of discipline and hard work, 'stalwart' virtues that, in his view, the unstable times required more than any others. Associated with interest and freedom was a tendency towards immediacy, towards studying the present in the false belief that it was more useful and relevant than the permanent, which was always relevant because it provided the insights and tools which enabled individuals to transcend immediate situations. The Essentialists, Bagley stated, were 'the advocates of an educational theory which placed relatively heavy emphasis upon the induction of each generation into its social heritage as the primary function of education as a social institution ... and affirms the chief concern of education to be the transmission to each generation of the most important lessons that have come out of this experience...'[74] Their theme was to be taken up again in the 1950's by a newly formed Council for Basic Education.

Thus it could be said that although they had their own independent views on education and its purposes, the conservative educators of the

[70] R.W. Livingstone, *The Future in Education*, Cambridge University Press, 1941, and *Education for a World Adrift*, Cambridge University Press, 1943, pp. 92-3. Born in 1880, Livingstone became president of Corpus Christi College, Oxford University in 1933, wrote a defence of classical education in 1917, and in the mid-1930's began publishing the essays on education that were developed in wartime into the above two books.

[71] R.M. Hutchins, *The Higher Learning in America*, Yale University Press, 1936, p. 66. Hutchins, (b. 1899) was president of the University of Chicago 1929-1945, and in 1953 became president of the Fund for the Republic established by the Ford Foundation. His main publications on education were *The Higher Learning in America* (1936), and *The Conflict in Education in a Democratic Society* (1953).

[72] R.M. Hutchins, *The Higher Learning in America*, p. 67.

[73] Encyclical Letter (Divini Illius Magistri) of Pope Pius XI, on *The Christian Education of Youth*, 1929, pp. 69, 120.

[74] W.C. Bagley, 'The significance of the Essentialist movement in educational theory', *Classical Journal*, 24, 6, March 1939, 326.

inter-war period converged on three aspects in opposition to the ideas and practices of the progressives. The progressive movement was seen as a part of the anti-intellectual trend of the twentieth century. Their schools, by their increased interest in the artistic, emotional, and social development of children, were failing to give the emphasis and care to that intellectual training that was the basic element of a sound education. Intellectual standards in the community would be diminished by the lowered priority given to intellectual work and by the dilution resulting from the popularisation of education if firm steps were not taken to correct the trend. Secondly, progressive education was regarded as insufficiently disciplined. Because of their attention to the felt needs and interests of children, progressive teachers allowed pupils to indulge too much their own pleasure and immediate satisfaction. Effective education, on the contrary, was a disciplined occupation. It required determined effort, perseverance, and constant practice, out of which lasting accomplishment could be built. In the third place, the progressives, because of their obsession with change and the present crisis, paid too little attention to the importance of traditional and perennial values. Their purpose was to help individuals merely to manage and adjust to current change, rather than to get a fundamental understanding and to absorb wisdom from the accumulated experience of the ages.

The progressives' most effective defence of their own tradition was the Eight Year Study.

THE EIGHT YEAR STUDY

Progressive education up to 1930 in the U.S.A. had mostly been an affair of the elementary school and junior high school. Experimentation in the upper secondary school had been restricted by the interests of subject-matter specialists and the requirements of college entrance. In some cases a formal examination was the practice, in others the accrediting authority prescribed the subjects and number of units that had to be studied in each subject. In the early 1930's the Progressive Education Association was able to persuade some three hundred colleges and thirty high schools to co-operate in an experiment to investigate whether the students who followed other kinds of secondary courses could succeed as well in college.

The experiment began in 1933 and continued until 1941. The schools involved in the work came from all parts of the country; some were public and some private, some large and some small; not all of them were progressively inclined but on the whole they tended to be less traditional than most schools. Each school was free to devise whatever program it wished and to have its pupils accepted for higher education on the recommendation of the school principal. In undertaking their new task the schools encountered four interesting problems.

The problem of deciding on educational aims. Hitherto the schools' work had been directed largely by the need to meet college entrance requirements. Once this objective was removed they had to think through their purposes, and justify their existence on more fundamental educational grounds. It took many of the schools several years of hard and concentrated thinking before they achieved a satisfying statement of their objectives. The five public high schools and ten junior high schools in Denver, Colorado had been involved in curriculum revision since 1922, and when they joined the Eight Year Study they were somewhat used to thinking about and justifying their educational aims. Their eventual statement was a good example of the kinds of ideas that the experimental schools were trying to put together:

The chief function of the schools in a democracy is to conserve and improve the democratic way of life. The Denver Public Schools maintain that they can best undertake such a responsibility by:

1. Making the life concerns of pupils and central theme of the curriculum.
2. Recognizing that individual concerns and social concerns are interdependent.
3. Making functional guidance an integral part of all educational activities.
4. Evaluating the school program in terms of the personal and social growth of pupils.
5. Organizing the school program to reveal the essential relationships of learning.
6. Providing a close, direct, working relationship with the community.

This philosophy has guided the Denver schools in setting up the objectives of their program. The ultimate goal is the development of individuals who deal with their problems more and more effectively in terms of their own good and the good of society.'[75]

The problem of setting up appropriate administrative practices. New courses and methods were planned by the different schools in various ways, the most effective of which were those in which all the teachers were involved and committed to a continuous program of planning, assessment, and replanning. To help the schools with their work the Progressive Education Association set up advisory bodies, the most significant of which were the curriculum associates, the evaluation staff, and the college follow-up staff.

---

[75] *Thirty Schools Tell Their Story, op.cit.,* pp. 157-8.

The problem of the selection and arrangement of new content and teaching methods. The schools varied greatly in the liberty that they took with the traditional curriculum. Some preserved the conventional subjects, merely remaking some of their content, sometimes in interesting and ingenious ways. Other schools leaned towards a broad fields approach in which they fused together several related subjects; following that approach, courses in general language, social science, general science, and general mathematics were popular.

The most radical departure from convention in curriculum design was the core curriculum. It was characteristic of many of the schools, and was their most significant contribution to curriculum planning. Many started by widening the scope of a broad fields program, e.g. by fusing English in with social science, or mathematics in with general science. After two or three years of experimentation most schools became dissatisfied with the practice of putting subjects together however skilfully it might be done. They moved to a more generalised basis. Several groups, for example, used an adolescent-needs approach, planning their content around the problems arising from the personal-social activities of adolescents, and using a sequence of units covering areas such as personal living, immediate personal-social relationships, social-civic relationships, and economic relationships. The curriculum associates sub-committee spent much time and effort with schools in helping them develop their general idea of core curriculum, in assisting them to analyse their broad concepts into feasible classroom activities, and in advising them on the construction of the source units which the new curriculum required.

A source unit was a somewhat new device which henceforth was to be an important and commonplace part of a teacher's equipment. The source units developed during the Eight Year Study were aids to the teacher, which, for a given topic, outlined such things as: the student needs that were to be met, the problems and concepts involved, possible ways of dealing with the problems, individual and group activities, suitable reference material for both students and teachers, possible outcomes from studying the topic, and suggested ways of evaluating the work. Many of the source units and of the ideas for core curricula were developed in workshops organised by the curriculum associates for the in-service training of teachers in particular schools or groups of schools.

The rationale of the core curriculum generally implied a reorientation in teaching method. Hence the experimental schools tended to put more emphasis on the pupils' use of reflective thinking and on co-operative planning between students and teachers. The school programs tended to embrace a wider and deeper range of interests, often involving extensive community and vocational studies, attention to the creative arts, and a search for understanding, balance, and personal discipline.

The problem of adequately testing the new aims and outcomes. Existing tests designed for conventional material were soon found to be inadequate. The evaluation committee helped the schools to analyse their objectives more rigorously, and during the course of the experiment devised two hundred tests of a wide variety of processes and objectives. Many of them proved to be useful instruments, e.g. for assessing competence in the interpretation of data, or ability to use logical reasoning or skill in dealing with social problems, and subsequently found a wide use in many schools not associated with the Eight Year Study.

The final testing of the experiment came through an appraisal of the students' competence when they reached college. For five successive years from 1936 on, the graduates of the thirty schools entered various institutions of higher education. How well did they succeed? Could they match or surpass the performance of those who had had to meet the conventional entrance requirements?

A committee of university teachers and administrators formulated the criteria on which the students were to be judged. These covered intellectual competence, cultural development, practical judgment, philosophy of life, character traits, emotional balance, social fitness, sensitivity to social problems, and physical fitness. The students from the experimental schools who went to college were matched with students from other schools over a wide range of items, such as scholastic aptitude scores, sex, age, socio-economic factors, size and type of school attended, and vocational intentions; 1,475 such pairs were arranged and compared. The results were a vindication of the experiment.

In their performance in the subjects taken in college, the experimental group surpassed, slightly but consistently and significantly, the comparison group from other schools. In one subject area only, foreign languages, the experimental group came out slightly below their rivals. On the more intangible criteria of personal and social skills and achievements, the progressive school graduates also made a slightly better showing. When a comparison was made of the results of the six most experimental with the six least experimental schools, it was found that the graduates of the most experimental schools were the more successful and that the margin of their superiority over the comparison group was greatly increased. In the light of those results, the Eight Year Study had demonstrated that the traditional course of preparation for higher education was not the only safe and successful method. From a considerable variety of other high school programs students were able to succeed equally as well in college. One important consequence was that a number of universities did modify their entrance requirements so as to allow high schools more flexibility in constructing their courses.

The full impact, however, that might have been expected from the Eight Year Study was denied it by the involvement of the United States in World War II just as the study was reaching its conclusion. It became, to a large extent, a wartime casualty as other and more pressing interests took the attention of educators and politicians. Something of its effects, nevertheless, could be seen later in the 1940's and 1950's. When the principals of the thirty schools and some associates met subsequently in 1950, they found that for the most part their schools had lost much of their progressiveness with the inevitable staff changes that had occurred, and that there was no continuing urge for experimentation. The Eight Year Study had neglected to involve parents, community, and boards of education in the work and had had too little contact with teachers' colleges who did not sufficiently appreciate it and consequently did not train teachers in the new ways to carry on the work of the study. On the positive side, however, in the 1950's it could be said:

- that the practice of in-service workshops had become popular;
- that some of the new approaches to evaluation were being employed and extended;
- that many of the curriculum innovations, especially the work on the core curriculum and the development of source units, were being tried out and were creating considerable interest, bringing to progressive ideas a more congenial reception in the high school;
- that staff participation in all aspects of school policy and practice was more frequent and active;
- that relationships between college and high school were closer and more flexible to the extent that some of the leading universities had decided to give up the practice of holding entrance examinations.[76]

It could be said that the Eight Year Study had no direct and obvious follow-up, but it had brought forward such a pertinent array of ideas and had so effectively crystallised them into workable practices for secondary schools, that a reviewer in 1950 after looking over the literature of the previous three years was probably correct in his estimate that 'the prevailing principles and practices of secondary education derive their inspiration, it would seem, from the results of the Eight-Year Study.'[77]

THE CONTRIBUTION OF EDUCATIONAL PSYCHOLOGY

In the debate between progressives and conservatives both sides received support from the work of the educational psychologists in the 1920's and 1930's. During that period there were five major trends in educational psychology:

- An expansion of the already established interest in the measurement of mental abilities, and an extension of it into other fields;
- A refinement and expansion of statistical methods;
- A continuance of developmental studies;
- An examination of motivation and non-cognitive aspects of teaching and learning;
- A growing interest in the social psychology of the educational process.

Each trend was discernible throughout the whole period, but they tended, broadly speaking, to form something of a succession. Mental testing was the most popular topic in the early 1920's, developmental and motivational studies were well established in the middle of the period, and social influences came strongly into consideration in the latter part of the 1930's. During the same period three new schools of psychology — behaviourist, psychoanalytic, and Gestalt — made their presence felt and were loosely associated in that order with the successive trends in educational psychology.

(i) Educational Measurement

Mental testing was well established by 1920. Binet's tests had been adapted and standardised by then in many countries and a notable start had been made during World War I on the use of group intelligence testing. The Binet test and its derivatives were regarded as tests of general ability. It was soon realised that general ability might contain a number of groups of special abilities such as verbal, numerical, spatial, clerical, and reasoning abilities. Tests for them were devised and were sometimes referred to as aptitude tests; they might also cover fields such as aptitude for studying various school subjects, for mechanical work, or for art. There were, too, a multitude of special abilities for which tests were constructed, such as sensory discrimination and motor abilities.

The various kinds of ability tests were used principally to predict and to select. They were useful in endeavouring to assess whether a pupil was likely to succeed at a particular kind of vocation or at a particular level of work, or even at particular kinds of academic subjects. They were used extensively to assist in vocational guidance, and the placement of students

[76] The Eight Year Study was described in a series of volumes called *Adventure in American Education*: W.M. Aikin, *The Story of the Eight-Year Study*, Harper, New York, 1942; H.H. Giles *et al.*, *Exploring The Curriculum*, Harper, New York, 1942; E.R. Smith, *et al.*, *Appraising and Recording Student Progress*, Harper, New York, 1942; D. Chamberlin *et al.*, *Did They Succeed in College*, Harper, New York, 1942; *Thirty Schools Tell Their Story*, Harper, New York, 1943. See also J. Hemming, *Teach Them to Live*, Heinemann, London, 1948, and F.L. Redefer, The Eight Year Study ... After Eight Years, *Progressive Education*, 28, 2, November 1950, 33-6.

[77] W.W. Brickman, 'The Secondary School', *School and Society*, 72, 1859, 5 August 1950, 90.

in particular courses and schools. In England, for example, a test of general mental ability became one of the group of assessments used to select pupils at the age of 11+ for entry to secondary grammar school.

Three other kinds of tests became popular in the 1920's and 1930's. Achievement tests in science, mathematics, language, and various other subjects were devised at all levels. Many tests were standardised and distributed commercially. Their popularity was greatly increased by making them objective and easily scored. Similar tests were used for the diagnosis of learning difficulties. In particular, diagnostic tests in the 3R's became, towards the end of the 1930's, the basis for the systematic and carefully designed courses in remedial work which began to develop, at that time, for pupils who were 'backward in the basic subjects'.[78]

Scores on intelligence tests were found to have an imperfect correlation with a pupil's results in school as measured by their achievement tests. The discrepancy appeared to be related to some trait of the pupil's characteristics. Personality tests were designed to throw some light on the non-intellectual factors in an individual's make-up. They covered a very wide range of behaviour and were the beginning of an interesting program of systematic investigation into areas such as temperament, attitudes, interests, moral judgments, and social reactions that matched and supported the growing interest of progressive teachers in the wider aspects of children's behaviour and was to be more considerably explored by educators in the post-World War II period.

The current interest in testing spread to an investigation of school examinations, culminating in an international inquiry in 1931-39, which produced some of the best analyses of the uses, techniques, and effects of examinations ever written.[79] From as early as 1912 there had been substantial studies in the U.S.A. which demonstrated the unreliability of marking of the usual essay-type examinations. In the international inquiry of the 1930's French and English researchers probed the same area, and showed up remarkable divergences between different examiners in the marking of *baccalauréat* papers and school certificate papers even in the seemingly more exact subjects of mathematics and science. In Scotland and in Pennsylvania, U.S.A., a longitudinal study of a large sample of children was kept throughout their secondary and further education with a continuous recording of their ability and achievements for a period of up to eight years. In Germany, Finland, and Sweden educators undertook a similar but less ambitious review of examinations throughout the secondary school. In all of the studies there was evidence of a considerable lack of reliability in existing examination techniques, and there was also a serious questioning of the validity of the examinations. The use of entrance examinations as predictors of success in secondary or tertiary work was called in question, and a relationship between social class and success in selective examinations was demonstrated in several countries.

Throughout the investigation, experiments were made with objective tests. An objective test item was one which required an unequivocal answer that tended to be in the form of a single word or the completion of a diagram. Objective testing concentrated therefore on factual material rather than on requiring students to reflect, organise, and apply their knowledge. Greater reliability could be achieved than was possible with essay-type questions, and when objective tests were combined with a continuous account of a pupil's school-work on a systematically organised record card it was found that both the reliability and the validity of the assessment were greatly increased. From that time the popularity of objective tests and school record cards as bases for assessment, selection, and promotion increased considerably. When, towards the end of the 1930's, successful efforts were made to show that it was possible to devise objective items in most subjects which did require students to assemble data, think, and draw inferences, the future of objective testing in the classroom was assured.

Much of the agitation for the reform of examination techniques came from progressive educators who had done much to stimulate the international inquiry.[80] Many thought that a change in techniques and a break in the existing systems of examining would give teachers better opportunities to use progressive ideas in the classroom. The outcome, however, did not necessarily favour the progressives. Examining techniques were modified in many cases, but there was no relaxation in the importance placed on examinations. Many of the educators who were concerned with improving the methods of testing merely desired to improve the efficiency of the schools. They did not want to relax or change existing programs but to increase their effectiveness. It was very much in that spirit that research on the teaching of school subjects was conducted in the 1920's and 1930's.

In the United States the outstanding contributor was E.L. Thorndike.[81] His talent lay in the breaking down of complex processes into

[78] See G.T. Buswell & L. John, *Diagnostic studies in arithmetic*, Supplementary Educational Monograph, University of Chicago, 1926, 30; C. Burt, *The Backward Child*, University of London, 1937; and F.J. Schonell, *Backwardness in the Basic Subjects*, Oliver & Boyd, Edinburgh, 1942.

[79] See C.W. Valentine, *The Reliability of Examinations*, University of London, 1932; P. Hartog and E.C. Rhodes, *An Examination of Examinations*, Macmillan, London, 1935, and *The Marks of Examiners*, London, 1936; I.L. Kandel, *Examinations and their Substitutes in the United States*, Carnegie Foundation, New York, 1936; O. Bobertag, *Schülerauslese*, Berlin, 1934; Commission Française pour L'Enquête Carnegie, *La Correction des Epreuves Ecrites dans les Examens*, Maison du Livre, Paris, 1936. The following countries were involved: England, Finland, France, Germany, Scotland, Sweden, Switzerland, and the U.S.A.

[80] One of the most readable and effective publications of the period was a booklet issued by the NEF, *The Examination Tangle and the Way Out*, 1933.

[81] E.L. Thorndike (1874-1949) taught educational psychology at Teachers College, Columbia University from 1899 to 1939. For a detailed biography see Geraldine Joncich, *The Sane Positivist. A Biography of Edward L. Thorndike*, Wesleyan University Press, 1968.

simple entities that could be measured and experimented with. Intelligence for him was the mean of a large number of specific abilities, and he made many detailed and useful studies of them. His work on the teaching of school subjects was similarly meticulous and analytic. In elementary arithmetic, for example, he pointed out that there were several thousand processes that had to be performed, and in his work on the psychology of arithmetic he discussed in detail the way in which the multitudinous mental connections could be built up into a sound grasp of the subject.

Thorndike was an associationist who tried to reduce all human behaviour to psychological connections made by a process of stimulus and response. His principal contribution lay in his analysis of the process of learning. Early in his career he enunciated three basic laws:

The Law of Readiness: when any conduction unit is in readiness to conduct, for it to do so is satisfying; when any conduction unit is not in readiness to conduct, for it to conduct is annoying.

The Law of Exercise: when a modifiable connection is made between a situation and a response, that connection's strength is, other things being equal, increased.

The Law of Effect: when a modifiable connection between a situation and a response is made and is accompanied or followed by a satisfying state of affairs, that connection's strength is increased.[82]

'The Law of Effect', wrote Thorndike, 'is the fundamental law of learning and teaching'.[83] The main laws were supplemented by a number of subsidiary principles which took account of contemporary views on the importance of attitudes, and by 1930 he had come to place little emphasis on any but the law of effect. His impact on education in the U.S.A. was considerable; but it is doubtful whether his connectionism had much impact elsewhere. The educational implications of Thorndike's laws that a learner should be ready, should practise diligently, and should receive satisfaction from his, task, could be derived from the views of most other schools of psychology.

Thorndike's indefatigable research and publication on practical educational problems ensured that his views were widely known and acted on in the U.S.A. where his efforts to make education exact, scientific and efficient met, in the 1920's and 1930's, with a favourable response. The whole bent of his mind was to analyse and quantify. 'Whatever exists, exists in some amount' was the foundation of his thinking.[84] His great industry and influence ensured that most educational psychologists in the U.S.A. would follow his lead for the first half of the twentieth century. By the 1950's it had become apparent that the atomistic approach had little to offer beyond the trivialities of measuring simple skills,[85] and, at that stage, a substantial reaction set in.

In the 1920's and 1930's, however, a substantial interest in careful, detailed investigation and controlled experimentation was built up. A number of important studies were made; for example, in the teaching of reading W.S. Gray estimated that by 1960 some four thousand careful, scientific studies had been made into various aspects of it, of which a substantial number were studies made in the 1920's and 1930's in the U.S.A., England, Belgium, France, and Germany. Of them, notable studies were made by Judd, Buswell and their colleagues early in the 1920's on the physiological and psychological factors in reading, by Dottrens and Elise Margairaz in 1930 on methods of teaching, and by Schonell late in the 1930's in England on the diagnosis of reading difficulties.[86]

(ii) Statistical Methods in Educational Research

During the inter-war period statistical methods used in educational research were considerably improved. Educational measurement, it was said, moved in the 1930's 'from adolescence into maturity'.[87] Statistical procedures in four main areas of educational measurement: central tendency, significance, correlation, and test construction, were handled with increasing sophistication during the period.

In trying to get the most out of their data research workers in the 1920's and 1930's had four main problems to deal with which became the subject of investigation by statisticians in more or less chronological order. The first was that of arriving at a norm or standard. What, for example, was the level of performance usually reached by a class of ten-year-olds in long division? Most of pre-World War 1 educational researchers reported their findings by stating average or mean performances. To that expression of central tendency, they sometimes added an indication of the extent to which the scores were spread out by calculating a standard deviation, which, Rugg wrote in 1917, was then 'coming into common use in educational measurement'.[88] There was also a general inclination to assume that most measurements were and ought to be distributed in the form of the bell-shaped normal probability curve in which the scores

[82] E.L. Thorndike, *Educational Psychology*, Vol. 2, New York, Teachers College, Columbia University, 1913, pp. 1-4.

[83] E.L. Thorndike, *Education*, Macmillan, New York, 1912, p.97.

[84] E.L. Thorndike, Measurement in education, *Teachers' College Record*, 22, November 1921, 379.

[85] The phrase comes from Shelley Phillips, *Thinking about thinking*, unpublished Ph.D. Thesis, University of Sydney, 1972, vol.1, p.157.

[86] G.T. Buswell, *Fundamental Reading Habits, A Study of their Development*, Supplementary Educational Monograph 21, University of Chicago, 1922; R. Dottrens and Elise Margairaz, *L'Apprentissage de la Lecture par la Methode Globale*, Delachaux et Niestle, Neuchatel, 1930; F.J. Schonell, *Backwardness in the Basic Subjects*, Oliver & Boyd, Edinburgh, 1942.

[87] W.S. Monroe, Educational measurement in 1920 and 1945, *Journal of Educational Research*, 38, 1945, 334-140.

[88] H. Rugg, *Statistical Methods applied to Education*, Harrap, London, 1917, p. 168.

clustered about a mid-point and fell away in a known proportion on either side of it.

The second important problem was to decide whether some given score was significantly different from the mean score. If two groups have been tested in algebra, is it possible to say that one class is significantly better than the other, or that both are better or worse than the normal? The answer is found by taking account of both the difference that there is between the two means, and the extent to which the scores in each group spread out from their mean, denoted by the standard deviation of the scores or by its square, the variance. A means of deciding how well two sets of scores agreed with or deviated from each other had been discovered by Pearson in 1900 and was known as the chi-square procedure; another procedure was Student's t which was developed in 1907. Neither type of test of significance was used much in educational research until the 1930's, then chi-square gradually became the more popular. Another more sophisticated test of significance, analysis of variance, was developed by Fisher in the early 1920's and came into use by educators in the 1940's.

The third problem was one of establishing relationships. If an examiner was studying students' marks in history, what was he really contemplating? The outcome of the performance might have depended on students' knowledge of historical facts, their literary ability, their perseverance, the form which the examination took, or several other factors. What was the importance of each of them and how were they related to one another? A score on a general intelligence test might have an even more complicated basis, and it would undoubtedly be interesting to establish the relationships between scores in intelligence and scores in history. A method, called correlation, of deciding the degree of relationship between different sets of scores with normal distributions had been worked out by Galton in 1888. Several other methods were developed early in the twentieth century, and the technique was extensively used in the 1920's. During that decade a big step forward was taken into factor analysis. It arose mainly out of intelligence testing. By correlating together a number of measures of mental ability Spearman found a common element and several specific ones. His *The Theory of Two Factors* was published in 1914 and was followed by thirty years of intense work and rivalry in the analysis of mental test scores and great interest in the processes of factor analysis. Thurstone in 1932 and Hotelling in 1933 simplified the procedure and introduced two new approaches which became speedily accepted in the U.S.A. Factor analysis was applied not only to the task of identifying various mental abilities; it was used also in the search after the dimensions of personality. By the end of the 1930's factor analysis was being applied to much of the experimental work that was being done in many different areas of educational research. It was a tool of great consequence which in the post-World War II period, was to be part of the standard armoury of the educational research worker.

The fourth question concerned the organisation of the material used in tests. The educational researcher was interested in much more than testing knowledge or measuring intellectual ability. Once the progressives' influence was felt, it became important also to assess emotional and personality factors. The principal pre-war instrument of the Child Study Movement, the questionnaire, was not always suitable and was certainly not suitable without substantial modification for the new tasks. The research worker's resources were therefore greatly extended during the 1920's and 1930's by a variety of interview techniques and by an extensive development of many different kinds of tests, e.g. non-verbal, artistic ability, projective, manual dexterity, social intelligence, and interest inventories. At the same time the technique of scaling was introduced into questionnaires. It was, for the most part, not difficult to devise questions that required a yes/no answer, but many educational questions called for a more graduated sort of answer. To the question, Do you like French? it would be more useful if a pupil could choose between a range of answers such as: very much, not much, not at all, and don't know. Or, to take the matter further, suppose a researcher wanted to assess how liberal-minded the parents of a particular school might be, he would need to ask them perhaps twenty questions on four or five topics, each probing a different shade of liberalism. To handle the answers effectively he must somehow give his questions a score so as to be able to add them up, find means, and correlations, and perhaps factorise his data. In short, he must be able to regard his questions as being of equal value and he must develop his material into some sort of a numerical scale.

Much thought was given to scaling procedures in the 1920's, and in 1929 Thurstone and Chave produced a means of scaling questionnaires on attitudes, and Likert in 1932 developed another and simpler attitude scale.

Scaling was applied to all kinds of data. In order to use the standard statistical procedures, data not only had to be put into an acceptable numerical form, it had also to be brought into relationship with the basis upon which most statistical work of the period rested, the normal curve. The scaling of the data therefore often took the form of transforming it so that it yielded a distribution fairly normal in its form. 'For many generations in education the normal distribution has been enthroned and has held supreme sway,' two researchers wrote in 1959.[89] Already, however, in the mid-1930's there were serious efforts to develop procedures that did not conform to the normal probability curve and in the post World War II period that 'supreme law of Unreason', as Galton

[89] P.O. Johnson and R.W.B. Jackson, *Modern Statistical Methods: Descriptive and Inducive*, Rand McNally, Chicago, 1959, p.63.

had called it, while still of central importance, could on some occasions and with some ingenuity be bypassed.

(iii) Developmental Studies

The third trend in educational research was a continuance of the Child Study movement of the pre-World War I period. For the most part it was more systematic and was characterised by a number of important long-term studies based on a number of different measures.

Terman in 1921 began a longitudinal study in California of gifted children who, more than fifty years later, in the mid-1970's, were still under investigation. In a series of volumes under the general title, *Genetic Studies of Genius*, he showed that children selected because of their high IQ were superior in virtually every kind of performance. They were stronger and healthier than average, their school and university results were better, they were more highly motivated, they were temperamentally better behaved, they had a wider variety of interest, and, subsequently, in employment they earned more money. Terman's studies stimulated interest in the education of gifted children and reinforced the moves in the 1920's and 1930's towards individualising educational programs and the divisions of pupils into ability groups. Many further investigations of children of high intelligence were made, and in the socially conscious 1930's and post-World War II period some of the research suggested that many of the physical and temperamental traits that Terman found to be characteristic of his gifted group might be attributable to socio-economic class factors.[90]

Experimental and longitudinal studies of young children, later extended into childhood and adolescence, were begun by Gesell and his associates in the United States in 1911 and were greatly expanded in the 1920's.[91] The work was characterised by a detailed analysis of the day-by-day behaviour of normal children, by careful experimentation to determine the precise age and extent of a child's mastery of particular tasks, and by a meticulous plotting of the developmental sequence of children's behaviour. The sequence was arranged in stages based on an assessment of children's motor, adaptive, language, and personal-social growth; it was regarded as a progressive patterning of children's behaviour in a rhythmic sequence that tended to repeat itself with increasing degrees of sophistication at various intervals throughout childhood and adolescence: e.g. 'The relative equilibrium of 5-year-oldness gives way to the impulsiveness of Five-and-a-half and the creative thrusts of Six, and these in their turn lead to the inwardness of Seven, the expansiveness of Eight, and self-motivation of Nine, and the balanced poise of Ten.'[92] The progression from five to ten had already been seen in much the same sequence from two to five, and it would recur from eleven to sixteen. As the research progressed, social

factors were given increasing emphasis, and in the late 1930's and 1940's, the previous predominantly biological orientation of the studies was somewhat modified by a greater concern with social experiences.

In England, Susan Isaacs' work at the Malting House School led to studies of the intellectual and social growth of young children that were continued in a department of child development within the University of London. Her work was suggestive and insightful, especially in her study of children's play and their 'loving and hating', and in the practical conclusions that she drew for teaching. She had a mistrust of any theory of child development which viewed it as a series of fixed stages, and was a keen advocate of activity school programs.

Charlotte Bühler assisted in starting in 1925 a research centre for child psychology in the University of Vienna, and in 1928 produced a systematic analysis of the stages of normal psychological development through childhood and youth.[93] In her research she used a great variety of sources and instruments. She was a keen observer and experimentalist, she devised mental tests for young children, and made particular use of children's diaries and other expressions of their personal feelings and experience. She managed to combine in her work the techniques and ideas of the psychoanalysts and the behaviouristically inclined child psychologists, and to produce a rich and penetrating view of the process of child development. Her insistence on the importance of play and social education made her writing attractive to progressive educators and she was in demand at meetings of the NEF.

Piaget also began his influential series of child studies in the 1920's in Geneva, publishing between 1924 and 1932 five volumes of his investigations into children's reasoning, language, moral judgment, and conception of the world.[94] In that work he laid the foundations for his later more highly developed views of child growth in which the

---

[90] L.M. Terman (ed.), *Genetic Studies of Genius,* 5 vols., Stanford University Press, 1925; May V. Seagoe, *Terman and the Gifted,* Los Altos, Kaufman, California, 1975; J.L. French(ed), *Educating the Gifted,* Holt, Rinehart and Winston, New York, 1959. L.M. Terman (1877-1956) was a professor at Stanford University from 1910 till 1942. He was responsible for several important revisions of the Binet tests of intelligence and for the still continuing study of the gifted.

[91] The studies were the basis for the eventual establishment of an institute of child studies in 1950. An extensive list of publications emerged from Gesell's research, beginning with *The Mental Growth of the Preschool Child* in 1925. A Gesell (1880-1961) was a professor at Yale University. He studied under G. Stanley Hall and was a fellow-student and lifelong friend of Terman. His principal contribution to scholarship lay in his extensive studies of child development.

[92] A. Gesell, L. Ilg & Louise B. Ames, *Youth. The Years from Ten to Sixteen,* Hamish Hamilton, London, 1956, p. 4.

[93] Charlotte Bühler, (b. 1893), wife of a well-known psychologist, K. Bühler, was a professor in Vienna 1923 to 1934, and subsequently moved to the University of California at Los Angeles. She published her classic *Kindheit und Jugend* in 1928.

[94] For a more extended analysis of Piaget's contribution, see Chapter 13.

sequential stages which he suggested took account not only of children's achievements at various ages but also, and most particularly, of the nature of their activity and the actual mental process which was involved in their activity.

The developmental studies just mentioned were not isolated investigations; they were the most widely read examples of a large body of similar research. Other large-scale investigations into aspects of child growth were reported, for example, by Kaminamura (1932) in Japan, Bechterev (1925), Nechayev (1928), and Blonsky (1930) in the U.S.R.R., Marbe (1931) in Germany, Decroly (1932) in Belgium, and Burt (1925 and 1937) and Valentine (1942) in England. And, underpinning the larger studies, there were innumerable smaller pieces of research throughout the 1920's and 1930's into almost every avenue of child behaviour.

The developmental studies helped to make popular the idea that children passed through a succession of discernible stages in their growth, that the detailed characteristics of each stage were recognisable, and that the processes and activities of each were a necessary part of maturation upon which subsequent development was built. That view gave great support to teachers who regarded education as a means of promoting children's growth, and who thought that a school's program should be closely related to the needs of children as they emerged in the course of the different stages of their growth. It also supported educators in their use of the notion of readiness: that a close study of a child's development should be made to see that ideas and materials were available to him only when he had reached the stage appropriate to them.

The studies of the 1920's and 1930's also increased teachers' awareness that there were important factors in children's development outside the intellectual and physical that they tended to concentrate on. Interests, emotions, attitudes, and social experiences were given an increased importance both in their own right and for the sake of their impact on mental growth. Furthermore, their possible significance could be seen in a fresh and different light as the new psychoanalytic and social insights of psychology began to become a part of the equipment of the researchers into child psychology.

As a consequence of the child growth studies, there was often a tendency towards greater flexibility in teaching methods and in the content of school curricula; but such an effect was by no means inevitable. The careful division of children's growth into stages encouraged some teachers to regard the performances characteristic of each stage as norms to be used in assessing the progress of a child's development. The detailed analysis made by some of the research studies and the means used to establish levels and kinds of performances generated tests and testing materials that were used to straitjacket rather than to loosen up teaching procedures.

(iv) Motivation and Non-Cognitive Studies

Motivation was to become one of the popular words with educators in the 1920's and 1930's. Nunn, whose book *Education: its Data and First Principles* was the most widely read educational text in England for thirty years from the time of its first appearance in 1920, wrote that our children 'have in them a creative power which, if wisely encouraged and tolerantly guided, may remould our best into a life far worthier than we have seen or than it has entered into our hearts to conceive'.[95] The creative power was 'a pulse of energy which is the very stuff of life',[96] and which could be seen as a drive or striving towards individuality. Education's task was to provide the stimulating conditions and the social atmosphere in which individuality could best flourish. That implied that much of a teacher's task was motivational, and that in undertaking it he would get substantial help from studying the views of the newer, dynamic schools of psychology that were beginning to claim considerable attention.

In the 1920's the literature and everyday language of the western countries had begun to be noticeably affected by ill-digested ideas and terms picked up from psychoanalysis. None of the psychoanalysts had any substantial influence at that time in education except on a few progressive schools. They did, however, strengthen the position of the many educators who were urging teachers to take more account of non-cognitive factors. Personality became the subject of much closer study and teachers became more interested and more knowledgeable in its formation, realising the importance of unconscious motives in human behaviour and the effect of emotional factors on the process of learning. The teacher's task could be redefined as that of trying 'to establish a reasonable agreement between the child's ego, the urge of his impulses, and the demands of society'.[97]

Psychoanalysts, however, were not alone in arguing the case for some fundamental and internal drive, 'some cause acting within the individual',[98] as the basic motivating factor in human behaviour. Thorndike, other neo-behaviourists, the Gestaltists, and the non-psychoanalytic personality theorists admitted the importance of wants, interests, and attitudes, and began in the 1930's to develop theories of learning in which 'goal-oriented' behaviour was the central feature. By the end of the decade it caused no surprise for a psychologist to write that 'Without

[95]   T.P. Nunn, *Education: Its Data and First Principles*, Arnold, London 2nd ed., 1930, p.253. T.P. Nunn (1870-1944) became professor of education at the University of London in 1913 and was director of the Day Training College, later the Institute of Education, from 1922 to 1936.

[96]   *ibid.*, pp. 12-13.

[97]   Anna Freud, *Psychoanalysis for Teachers and Parents*, trans. Barbara Low, Beacon, Boston, 1963 (1930), p. 84.

[98]   R.S. Woodworth, *Psychology*, Holt, New York, 1921, p.71.

drives, either primary or acquired, the organism does not behave and hence does not learn'.[99]

(v) Social Orientation in Educational Psychology

Gestalt psychology, originating shortly before World War I, became more widely known in the inter-war period, and began then to be influential in education. It made three important contributions to educational thinking. It regarded learning as a purposive activity; it considered that perception and understanding depended upon the grasping of the whole pattern of a situation; and it placed human behaviour within a field of environmental and social forces to which each individual had to find a satisfying adaptation. Personality was seen to be developed through the interaction between the individual and the forces exercised in his social milieu by the interests and attitudes of other people. Human relationships were key elements in the development of human personality.

In the 1930's interest in the study of social relationships spread and affected the work of many educational psychologists of various schools of thought. Three areas were of particular interest. First, Kilpatrick's observation was widely accepted that children learn not merely what they were being directly taught, but also many 'concomitants' such as attitudes, habits, and knowledge that are absorbed from the situation around them.[100] Much of concomitant learning was social in character, and came from the fact that schools and classes were social groups and children were learning within a structure of group relationships. The classroom climate was seen to be an important part of school learning, and it became the object of careful study towards the end of the 1930's. Secondly, it was clear that a basic determinant of the atmosphere of the classroom was the teacher-pupil relationship within it. Studies were made of contacts between adults and children in a variety of teaching situations and evidence was accumulated to show that achievement in school-work and the personal development of students were affected by teacher-pupil relationships. The most influential piece of research was that of Lewin, Lippitt and White, reported in 1939, which compared the effect, on a number of ten-year-old boys in a youth club, of three different patterns of control: undirected or *laissez faire*, leader-dominated or authoritarian, and group or democratic control. They found that, on the whole, the democratically led groups tended to be the most constructive and co-operative, the authoritarian groups to work hard when carefully supervised and to develop more discontent and misbehaviour, and the *laissez faire* to be the least productive and most frustrated.[101]

The other important social ingredient in learning situations that educators became specially conscious of was the interrelationship between pupils. Thrasher, in a study of adolescents in gangs in Chicago

in 1927, and Moreno with play groups in Vienna at the same time, noted the manner in which group members judged one another and were affected in their activities by group opinion, and how, by changing the structure of the group, it was possible to change the climate and productivity of it. Moreno experimented further in the United States, and developed a simple sociometric technique for discovering and describing the relationships between members of a group.[102] The study of the way in which students at school formed work groups and friendship groups began to interest teachers; and, in particular, the influence of the fairly stable, continuing, small social groups of children or adolescents, called peer groups, on their school-work and general behaviour was found to be a surprisingly strong and important factor in education.

An American psychologist in the mid-1930's expressed the view that 'Accepted psychology, proceeding on mechanistic and atomistic assumptions, has been considerably out of harmony with the methods and materials which have been improvised by artistic teachers and which found a theoretical justification in the philosophy of John Dewey and W.H. Kilpatrick.'[103] The work of Thorndike, who dominated educational psychology, was directed to the improvement and reform of existing methods of teaching, the more efficient placement of students, and the better selection of content; it did not seek for radical change of the kind that many progressives had in view. Nevertheless Thorndike and his associates did adapt their work and theories to the current of progressive educational thought. They became more interested in motivation, they put more emphasis on satisfaction in the learning process, they devised tests of attitudes and personality as well as achievement, and they became interested in longitudinal studies of child growth. In such ways they helped to make teachers more skilled within, very largely, the traditional pattern.

It was the newer schools of psychology, the Gestalt and, to a lesser extent, the psychoanalytic, that gave substantial support to the progressives. By the end of the 1930's it could be said that five ideas had emerged from the work of the 1920's and 1930's that were to gain a firm place in educational procedures for the next generation:

[99] N.E. Miller and J. Dollard, *Social Learning and Imitation*, Yale University Press, 1941, p. 21.

[100] W.H. Kilpatrick, *Foundations of Method*, Macmillan, New York, 1925, p. 103.

[101] K. Lewin, R. Lippitt and R.K. White, 'Patterns of aggressive behaviour in experimentally created "social climates"', *Journal of Social Psychology*, 1939, 10, 2, 271-99.

[102] F.M. Thrasher, *The Gang*, University of Chicago Press, 1927; J.L. Moreno, *Who Shall Survive*, Nervous and Mental Disease Publishing Co., Washington D.C., 1934; J.W. Carr, The relationships between the theories of Gestalt psychology and those of a progressive science of education, *Journal of Educational Psychology*, 1934, 25, pp. 192-202.

[103] J.W. Carr, *op.cit.*, p. 192.

- that education should be related to and should assist the growth of children through a maturational sequence of intellectual, emotional, and social behaviour;

- that learning depended on adequate and appropriate motivation. Children learned best when responding purposefully and actively to an inner drive, when their work was directed towards a desired goal, and when the achievement of it brought satisfaction to them;

- that the effectiveness of education depended considerably on the kind of teaching skill that took account of the child as a functioning whole, and combined emotional, and attitudinal development with intellectual learning;

- that the learning and teaching situation was a social one in which pupil-teacher and pupil-pupil relationships played important parts;

- that it was possible to test with reasonable accuracy and objectivity a great range of behaviour. Deficiencies could be diagnosed and useful information could be obtained on personal as well as intellectual development to assist the teacher in his task.

Most of those ideas came from the work of persons with some sympathy for Gestalt psychology and progressive education.

CHAPTER 11

EDUCATION IN UNDERDEVELOPED COUNTRIES AND COLONIAL TERRITORIES, 1900-40: CHINA, INDIA, AND AFRICA

Rabindranath Tagore (1861-1941), Indian educator, poet, and director of Santiniketan.
Mahatma Gandhi (1869-1948), political and educational leader, and father of Basic Education in India.

SUMMARY

China: The Break with the Past

(i)   End of the Tradition
(ii)   May 4th Movement
(iii)   New Directions in Education
(iv)   Education in the 1930's and 1940's

Education in India, 1900-47

(i)   Curzon Reforms
(ii)   Gokhale and Compulsory Education
(iii)   Educational Growth 1901-21
(iv)   National Enthusiasm for Education in the
        1920's and 1930's
(v)   Basic Education
(vi)   The Last Years of British Administration

Education in Colonial Africa from 1900 to the 1940's

(i)   Missionary Education in the Early Twentieth Century
(ii)   Phelps-Stokes Commission
(iii)   Government Education in the African Colonies
        (a) German Colonial Education in Tanganyika
        (b) French Colonial Education
        (c) Education in the Italian Colonies
        (d) British Colonial Education in Africa
(iv)   Indigenous Educational Efforts
(v)   Overseas Education for Africans
(vi)   General Assessment of Colonial Education in Africa

Beyond the industrialised European, American, and Japanese world, there lay extensive and heavily populated areas where formal education had made little headway among the bulk of the population. The areas were of three kinds.

- There were countries which had managed to maintain their independence of western rule though affected, sometimes deeply, by western policies. China was a leading example of such countries. The Chinese people, at the beginning of the twentieth century, were heirs to a high culture with a long, well-established educational tradition which was not attuned to the modern world into which they were being violently thrust. Educationally, their future lay in rejecting some and adopting others of their traditional practices, and in accepting and speedily absorbing much of what western educators had to offer.

- A few countries were neither independent nations nor colonial territories. Under the control of a western power, they yet had some measure of self-government which they restively tried to extend. India was the most substantial of such countries. A land of several established cultural traditions, it had had a long association with British commercial, political, and military power, and had largely surrendered its indigenous educational institutions. By the beginning of the twentieth century what there was of Indian education was in western style. It needed reform, extension, and adaptation to the cultural, political and economic interests of the country.

- Most of the underdeveloped countries were colonial territories of European powers. They were areas with little or no self-government, and for the most part with no strong tradition of formal education. The African colonies, especially those of France and England, provided typical examples of the manner, direction, and extent of the educational progress made in the colonial world.

The history of the impact made by western educational methods and ideas on non-western peoples is a two-tiered one. The western institution, the school and the university, met with little resistance. It replaced whatever local schools existed, and the old institutions vanished with scarcely a trace; it pioneered new areas where no institutions had existed before, and it took hold usually with a minimum of objection. The western school, whether run by local or western authorities, became universal in the twentieth century and was recognisably the same wherever it was to be found. Western educational influence, however, was more than the importation of an institution. It was a contact with new and usually revolutionary ideas. It was a solvent of established ways. Its possession inspired commercial and political ambition, and eventually conferred opportunity and power. The history of the educational development of each undeveloped country is a history of change in a people's culture, of change in individual personalities, and of change in national status.

CHINA: THE BREAK WITH THE PAST

China, like Japan, had been deliberately studying and absorbing western ideas and practices since the mid-nineteenth century. But where Japan had moved at great speed, China had merely ambled forward. Scholars went abroad to study, translations of western books were made, and a few schools specialising in modern learning were set up; but the pace was slow. Her defeat by the Japanese in 1895, her humiliation by European troops in the Boxer uprising in 1900, and the demonstration of the efficacy of westernisation by the Japanese victory over Russia in 1905 brought about an acceleration in China's policy of modernisation.

(i)   End of the Tradition

The first important educational result was the establishment, in 1903, of a system of education loosely modelled on Japan, and a national ministry of education, in 1905, to supervise it. Next came the abolition of the thousand-year-old examination system which had controlled recruitment to the civil service and had directed most of the energies of aspiring pupils to the study of classical literature. By a series of edicts between 1901 and 1905 the system was modified and finally eliminated. The move took the incentive out of the study of the classics, and was the beginning of 'an active encounter with Western civilization'.[1] It also helped to turn Chinese students in increasing numbers to Japan as the Asian mediator of western culture. In 1906, for instance, there were about thirteen thousand Chinese students studying in Japan.[2] The Chinese, at that time, adopted the current Japanese view that western learning was for technical and practical matters, traditional learning for morals, understanding, and the principles of human conduct.[3]

In 1912 the Ching dynasty came to an end and China became a

republic. For the next thirty-seven years up to 1949 the republic endured an uneasy existence, split by rival warlords for its first fifteen years, united by the Kuomintang's national government for ten, under invasion by the Japanese for eight, embroiled for four years in an open civil war that had simmered for the previous twenty, and finally consolidated into a People's Republic. It was a stormy, transitional period. Military and political disruption went hand in hand with cultural and social transformation as China moved into the modern world.

Japanese influence continued through the early years of the republic, and was apparent in the reform of education that followed the establishment of the republic in 1912. The Japanese pattern of school organisation was retained and strengthened as far as possible, and the teaching of citizenship and republicanism was introduced. Three years later an important change occurred.

(ii) May 4th Movement

Japan, a participant in World War I on the allied side, in 1915 presented Twenty-One Demands by which the Chinese government had to agree to Japanese control over large areas in the north and east of the country. Japanese prestige in China slumped, but worse was to follow. In 1917 China also joined the allies and sent labour battalions to the European front. At the conclusion of the war it was found that the victorious powers were committed to support Japanese claims to the former German territories in China, and the Treaty of Versailles confirmed Japan's position. The decision was made known early in May 1919. 'When the news of the Paris Peace Conference,' wrote a Peking University student, 'finally reached us we were greatly shocked.'[4] The students immediately organised a protest demonstration for the afternoon of May 4th.

The impact on education of World War I and its aftermath was greatest among western countries and particularly in Europe where there had been most involvement in the actual conflict. Its influence, however, was also felt beyond that area. In the world's vast colonial territories vague prickings of conscience occurred, and new policies were formulated and tentatively implemented during the 1920's. In Turkey and the Arab countries, revolution and the reconstitution of the Middle East territories were the prelude to an educational expansion in those areas. In the countries of Far East Asia, with the exception of China, the impact was

[1] W. Franke, *China and the West*, trans. R.A. Wilson, Blackwell, Oxford, 1967, p. 119.

[2] 'Chow Tse-tsung, *The May Fourth Movement*, Harvard University Press, Cambridge, Mass., p. 31.

[3] 'Chinese Studies as the fundamental structure, Western studies for practical use', a summary by Chang Cheh-tung in 1898; cf. 'Japanese spirit, Western skill' coined by Fu Kazawa Yukichi; see Chow Tse-tsung, *op.cit.*, p. 13.

[4] Chow Tse-tsung, *The May Fourth Movement*, p. 93.

not of particular significance. China, however, was profoundly affected. She had, at that time, a quarter of the population of the world but was of negligible international consequence. The May 4th Movement that was sparked by her involvement with the belligerents in World War I was to be influential in changing her cultural, social, and political outlook, and, in the long run, also her international status.

The May 4th Incident was a lively procession by students from all the Peking universities through the streets of the city; they expressed their indignation by placards and speeches and finally by burning the house of one of the government ministers. The Incident was the beginning of a series of demonstrations and strikes throughout the country and a widespread boycott of Japanese goods. The government was forced to resign in June, and China refused to sign the Treaty of Versailles. Henceforth 'school storms' or student protests became a common and sometimes telling feature of Chinese political life.

The Incident was part of a larger May 4th Movement that had begun about 1915 and continued until about 1925. Sometimes called the 'new culture' movement, it was a complex of nationalist and reformist influences with a 'vision of a new Chinese man and society'.[5] It was, fundamentally, an educational movement which drew its main strength initially from the talented staff brought together at the University of Peking under the leadership of Tsai Yuan-pei, chancellor from 1916 to 1926 and Chen Tu-hsiu, dean of the Faculty of Arts and one of the founders of the Chinese communist party.[6] Its ideas were spread by many new magazines and articles, and by innumerable lectures and discussions throughout China. It aimed at a cultural and intellectual transformation that was to prepare the ground for, and underpin, future social and political reform. In 1920 Sun Yat-sen, who had founded the republic in 1912 and was subsequently restricted to the control of South China, wrote, 'After the May Fourth Movement was initiated by the students of the National University of Peking, all patriotic youths realized that intellectual reform is the preparation of reform activities in the future ... as an old saying has it that a renovation of the mind is prerequisite to a revolution.'[7] The Movement had five main intertwined but reasonably distinguishable strands.

It was obviously nationalistic. The incident was motivated by patriotism and in the early stages of the movement much of its drive came from resentment against foreign exploitation of Chinese weakness and an increasingly articulate desire for national independence. Secondly, it was a literary movement. It was an important part of the trend to establish the vernacular as a national language. Under the influence of the Movement, archaic language forms and expressions declined, and the ordinary spoken word came to be widely used in schools and all forms of writing. Literature responded by becoming more realistic and concerned with

current life. One of the leading radical writers, Lu Hsun, declared that the Chinese should live for themselves instead of their ancestors.[8] He emphasised the need not only to make language more usable, but to make it also a vehicle for the study of science and modern ideas.

Modernisation became the third strand of the May 4th Movement. It marked a new stage in the modernisation process. The compromise which kept the classics for one sphere and western learning for another was broken down. 'Confucius and Sons' were to be repudiated; the tradition was no longer applicable. What was needed was not merely the practical skills of the western countries, but the theories and ideas, too, that lay behind them. Distaste for the old and enthusiasm for the new reached a high level, especially among youth, during the course of the Movement. The use of scientific method as a general way of thinking, a utilitarian approach to technical, social, and economic problems, and an encouragement to the greater development of individuality and care for individual welfare were the kinds of characteristics upon which the new culture was to be built.

(iii) New Directions in Education

The refashioning was substantially a task for educators. Educational discussion and activity were therefore a fourth and fundamental strand of the Movement. Nowhere was the transitional nature of the period more apparent than in education. A leading contemporary educator wrote: 'The angry tide is raging, the wandering boat is in its midst; when one looks back at the home country, it has gone out of sight; when one looks ahead to the other shore, it is far off, and cannot be seen; who knows China's future? Who knows?'[9]

[5] Charlotte Furth, *Ting Wen-chiang. Science and China's New Culture*, Harvard University Press, 1970, p. 4.

[6] Tsai Yuan-pei (1868-1940) studied in Germany, became Minister for Education in 1912, was chancellor of Peking University 1916-1926 and first president of the Academia Sinica in 1928. He was a classical scholar of note and a great advocate of western learning. Chen Tu-hsiu (1879-1942) studied in Japan and France, taught at primary and secondary level, was a leading literary figure and a professor at the University of Peking 1917-19, founded in 1915 *New Youth*, the most influential journal of the May 4th Movement, became a co-founder and first secretary-general of the communist party in 1921, was expelled in 1930, and was arrested and imprisoned by the Kuomintang in 1932.

[7] Chow Tse-tsung, *The May Fourth Movement*, p. 195.

[8] Chow Tse-tsung, *The May Fourth Movement*, p. 309, quoted in Tang Ssu (Lu Hsun), 'Random Thoughts', no. 46, *New Youth*, 6, 2, 15 February 1919, p. 212, trans. in Lin Yutang, *The Wisdom of China*, Joseph, London, 1949, p. 503.

[9] Chiang Meng-lin (Monlin), quoted in R.K. Johnson, The New Education: New Tendencies in Chinese Education in the Era of the May Fourth Movement, unpublished M.A. Thesis, University of Sydney, 1973, p. 134. Chiang Monlin (1886-1964) studied at the University of California, and was a student of John Dewey's at Columbia University, founded and edited in Shanghai *The New Education* (1919-25), an influential Deweyan journal, became professor of education and later, from 1931 to 1945, chancellor of Peking University, served as Minister for Education 1928-30, and, from 1948 on, resided in Taiwan. He was a strong advocate of westernization and a prolific writer of books and articles on education.

The new education, according to Chen Tu-hsiuin 1915, should move vigorously towards greater realism, vocational preparation, and democratic teaching. In 1921 it marked a transition, he declared, from pursuing individual greatness to working for the improvement of society, from teaching knowledge by a process of infusion to learning by discovery, and from poring over the classics of ancient China to studying the method and content of modern science. Obviously, the schools were not to be changed overnight or even within a single generation, but in the May 4th period there was, at least, a concerted campaign for reform that had both immediate and long-term consequences.

One of the immediate effects was a shift away from Japanese towards American influence. John Dewey had arrived in China at the precise moment of the May 4th Incident. His stay of two years helped to interest Chinese educators in the progressive side of western education, and to direct their attention more substantially in the future towards America. In 1922 a reform of the educational system was announced which clearly displayed the new trend; it was slightly adapted in 1928 when the Kuomintang managed to unify the country and it became the basic pattern for the rest of the period of the Republic. The new system provided for a six-year elementary school, three-year junior middle, three-year senior middle, and four-year university; it was the American 6-3-3-4 pattern and it made use of a credit system employing a method of calculating points similar to a Carnegie unit.

Outside the national system, missionary education, in which American influence predominated, played a numerically small but significant part. Substantial effort by missionaries was put into the establishment of secondary schools, colleges, and universities and many ambitious young Chinese were attracted to their schools. Sun Yat-sen and Chiang Kai-shek, for example, were both products of missionary education.

Another significant educational innovation was the introduction of teaching in the vernacular in primary and middle schools. The possibility of being able to communicate on paper in everyday language was a great encouragement to adult education, and the foundations for mass literacy were laid through the mass literacy campaigns that the May 4th Movement fostered in the early 1920's.[10] Many schools also, in many parts of China, offered free evening classes for children and adults. Women were admitted to universities, and efforts were made by a variety of new women's organisations to stimulate women's education. The utilitarian mood of the reformers was shown by the expansion of vocational education, and by the inclusion of a greater amount of modern knowledge, such as natural science and social science, in the primary and secondary school curricula. At university level the study of biology, physics, chemistry, and geology expanded, and considerable interest was shown in the study of modern economics, sociology, and government. Education and society came slowly closer together, and the Movement became more conscious of its fifth strand, the regeneration of social and political activity.

Social awareness was one of the virtues that the new education also hoped to develop in the rising generation. It would lead to a juster society in which restrictive social practices would be abolished, and equality of opportunity for men and women of all social classes would be closer to realisation. There was much talk of democracy and good government, and much discussion of the means of getting the country out of its currently disturbed and unsatisfactory state. As the Movement progressed, students' interest in politics increased, and by 1922 many had begun to work seriously within party organisations. Of all the political factions that developed, two emerged predominant by 1925: the Kuomintang which had been greatly strengthened by the May 4th Movement, and the Communist Party which had been founded in 1921 by some of the Movement's leaders. At that stage membership was not mutually exclusive. Each, however, was conscious of the need to educate its political followers in its basic ideas. When, therefore, in 1928 the Kuomintang was in a position to reorganise the schools of the nation, Sun Yat-sen's Three People's Principles became a compulsory subject in all primary and secondary schools. Similarly, political education was not neglected by the communists who established peasants' and workers' institutes and began mass literacy campaigns in which political understanding was regarded as the most important objective.

The May 4th Movement was an exciting affair in modern Chinese educational history. It was the critical period of transference from traditional to modern education. It was a ferment of intellectuals, in which they moved the nation culturally into a new allegiance. It was an intricate blending of cultural, social, and political activities through which China became committed to a program of modernisation, national unification, and educational reconstruction. Its principles remained in vogue in a general way throughout the Kuomintang period up to the revolution of 1949.

(iv) Education in the 1930's and 1940's

No major change was made after the readjustments of 1928, but special efforts were made to deal with some of the more difficult problems. In 1935 a plan was formed to provide compulsory one-year primary education to be raised to two years by 1940, but little was achieved. In 1940 a five-year plan to eliminate illiteracy was decided upon, and national primary schools

---

[10] See Pearl Buck, *Tell the People*, John Day, New York, 1945, for an account of the mass education work directed in the 1920's and 1930's by James Yen.

were eventually to be multiplied throughout the villages. Again there was little result. Educational authorities were bedevilled by the size of the problems presented by a population which had grown to 450 million in the 1940's, by meagre economic resources, and by constant warfare against the Japanese after 1937. Schools were maintained in many places by venturesome teachers behind the lines, and an effort was made in unoccupied territory to provide basic education for children from six to twelve. By 1948, about fifty five universities and 150 tertiary level colleges were in operation with about 150,000 students, and the secondary school population had risen to almost two million;[11] but an educational authority had also to concede that in 1948 while thirty one million children were in school, there were '36 million children for whom education must yet be provided.'[12]

EDUCATION IN INDIA, 1900-47

'It is recorded of the Emperor Aurungzeb,' observed Lord Curzon, the British Viceroy from 1898 to 1905, 'after he had seized the throne of the Moghul Empire, that he publicly abused his old tutor for not having prepared him properly for those great responsibilities. "Thus," he said, "did you waste the precious hours of my youth in the dry, unprofitable, and never-ending task of learning words." This is exactly the fault,' Curzon continued, 'that we found with every phase of Indian Education as we examined it. Everywhere it was words that were being studied not ideas.'[13] Indian education, he reported, was in an unsatisfactory condition — four out of five Indian villages without a primary school, the secondary schools offering a lifeless curriculum taught by incompetent teachers, and universities dominated by examinations and 'the monstrous and maleficent spirit of Cram'.[14]

Yet good and appropriate education was of central importance. 'The man in India,' he held, 'who has grasped the educational problem has got nearer to the heart of things than any of his comrades, and he who can offer to us the right educational prescription is the true physician of the State.'[15]

(i) Curzon Reforms

Curzon's thought for Indian education bore fruit eventually in a Resolution of 1904 entitled Indian Educational Policy.[16] The Resolution briefly reviewed the history of education in British India, and summarised its current virtues and vices. Higher education was too exclusively thought of as an avenue to government employment, too much

prominence was given to examinations, too much emphasis at all levels of education was placed on memorisation and mechanical repetition, and, in a desire for English education, the vernaculars were neglected. On the credit side, however, knowledge had been spread to a formerly undreamed-of extent, new avenues of employment had been opened up, and the character of the public service chosen from educated Indians had markedly improved. Nevertheless it was clear that substantial reform was required.

The need for a much wider extension of primary education was demonstrated by the census of 1901 which showed that only one in ten of the male population and only seven in one thousand of the female population were literate. Primary education was to have the first priority in educational expenditure, and special encouragement was to be given to rural primary schools, not for the purpose of teaching agriculture but to provide a simple fundamental education that would enable the pupils eventually to be more intelligent in their daily work. In the primary schools the vernacular language should be used as the medium of instruction and English should not be used as such until well into the secondary school. More than half a million pupils were in secondary schools and the government was determined that the quality of their education should be improved by a stricter supervision, by supporting the training of secondary school teachers, and by encouraging greater diversification of the curriculum to break down its exclusive literary emphasis. At the university level steps had already been taken to reform the governing bodies of the five universities already established, and a tightening up of inspection policies would ensure that the quality of the teaching in the many colleges throughout India affiliated with the universities would be improved.

Three other educational problems received attention: the education of girls, which currently involved only three per cent of those of school age, was to be stimulated by a greater financial allocation and the establishment of model primary schools; technical education, confined mainly to higher level training for government service, was to be encouraged for trade levels that would provide skilled workmen for the

[11] S.Y. Chu, 'China: Education and its traditions', *ibid.*, p. 609.

[12] Cheng Chi-pao, 'China: Public Education', in *The Year Book of Education*, 1949, Evans, London, 1949, p. 611.

[13] T. Raleigh (ed.), *Lord Curzon in India*, Speech at the Educational Conference in Simla, 1905, Macmillan, London, 1906, p. 352.

[14] *ibid.*, pp. 350-2.

[15] *ibid.*, pp. 347-8.

[16] India, Governor-General in Council, *Indian Educational Policy*, being a Resolution issued by the Governor-General in Council on 11 March 1904, Calcutta, Government Printing Office, 1904, 51p.

development of Indian industries, commerce, and agriculture; and a small group of elite schools for sons of the Indian nobility was to be reformed and staffed with highly qualified teachers, largely of the English Public School tradition, to equip their pupils 'physically, morally, and intellectually for the responsibilities that lie before them'.[17] The Resolution put forward a policy of enlightened but slow extension of education.

Curzon regarded his reforms as the beginning of a 'renascence in the history of Indian Education'.[18] The claim was over-ambitious; but at least the new policies were evidence of a decided interest on the part of the British administration that produced a steady improvement in education over the next two decades.

(ii) Gokhale and Compulsory Education

From 1910 to 1912 Gokhale, a leading Indian nationalist and ex-schoolteacher pressed in the imperial legislative council for the gradual introduction of compulsory primary education. 'With 94 per cent of our countrymen sunk in ignorance,' he declared, 'how can the advantages of sanitation or thrift be properly appreciated, and how can the industrial efficiency of the worker be improved? With 94 per cent of the people unable to read or write, how can the evil of superstition be effectively combatted, and how can the general level of the country be raised?'[19] Education to men such as Gokhale was to be the foundation of national development and the prerequisite for the improvement of the quality of Indian life. But the British administration did not feel the same sense of urgency, and his plea was rejected. Nevertheless, first by the Patel Act in Bombay in 1918, and subsequently before 1921 in most other provinces, Acts were passed enabling municipalities to introduce free and compulsory primary education for seven to eleven-year olds.

Gokhale's effort to introduce compulsory education was the most widely discussed educational aspect of an upsurge of national feeling in the pre-World War I years of the twentieth century. The rise of Japan and her defeat of Russia stimulated new thoughts of greater possibilities and of a more speedy development of them throughout the Asian continent. In India the Swadeshi Movement came into being in an effort to stimulate the nation's own productive resources, and educators looked to the development of national schools that would build upon native Indian culture and technical schools that would give India strength in the modern technological world. From these efforts and aspirations there was little concrete result. The slow and steady expansion of education continued along established lines with the modifications introduced by Curzon's Resolution.

(iii) Educational Growth 1901-21

Between 1901 and 1921 the number of primary school pupils doubled, and the teacher training program was expanded to the point where 38 per cent of primary school teachers were trained, but, in many rural areas, only meagrely so. A missionary report in 1920 pointed out that there were seven hundred thousand villages in India and only 142,203 primary schools, many of which were in the towns, and that even where children were able to attend village schools a high proportion dropped out after the first or second class so that ninety per cent of children were in the lowest classes.[20] Clearly, there were as yet only the merest beginnings of popular education, and as the the population was increasing steadily there was a danger that, although the numbers in school were increasing, the actual proportion of children in school would decline. The race between education and demography started to become a serious matter in all underdeveloped countries from about 1920 on.

Table 11.1: Population of India: 1951 Boundaries (i.e. not including Pakistan)

Census Year	Millions
1891	236
1901	236
1911	252
1921	251
1931	279
1941	319
1951	361
1961	439

[17] *ibid.*, p. 33.

[18] T. Raleigh (ed.), *op.cit.*, p. 357.

[19] D.G. Karve & D.V. Ambekar (edd.), *Speeches and Writings of Gopal Krishna Gokhale*, vol. 3, London, Asia, 1967, Speech on the Education Bill, 1911, p. 92. G.K. Gokhale (1866-1915), of a poor Brahmin family, was educated at Elphinstone College, Bombay, and taught at Fergusson College, Poona, until 1902. From that date on, he concentrated on politics. He became a member of the Bombay Legislative Council 1900 and the Imperial Legislative Council 1905, founded The Servants of India Society 1905, and became one of the leading members of the Congress Party.

[20] A.G. Fraser, *et al., Village Education in India*, The Report of a Commission of Inquiry, Oxford University Press, 1920, pp. 25-7.

At the secondary level, the number of school pupils also doubled between 1901 and 1921, and under more careful supervision the quality improved. During the same period, the five universities became twelve, three of the new foundations having a special national and cultural significance: Benares Hindu University which commenced in 1917, Aligarth Muslim University in 1920, and Osmania University in Hyderabad, in which the teaching was in Urdu, in 1918.

The university expansion was associated with the appointment of a commission in 1917 under M.E. Sadler to look into Calcutta University. The commission studied university education throughout India and recommended a widening of the range of university courses, especially to include more of the applied sciences, the development of the affiliated colleges in such a way that they might look forward to becoming independent universities, the separation of secondary education from the undue influence of university requirements, and the establishment of intermediate schools to prepare for university work and to provide more extensive facilities for vocational training. Little of the Sadler Report was put into immediate effect. It was, however, widely studied and it became a document whose tone and general advice were to seep through the academic structure and affect its general development for many years to come.

By 1921 the number of university students in India totalled sixty-six thousand, and 'the spectre of *educated unemployment* had already raised its ugly head'.[21] Most university education was general rather than professional and there were few professional schools outside the universities. Technical education had developed mainly in response to the demands of government departments and much of the training was associated with them. In the universities, in 1921, there were twelve thousand professional students as against fifty-four thousand general students, and of the professional students, ten thousand were in training for the law, teaching, or medicine. Only 1,600 throughout the whole of India's population of 251,000,000 were in colleges of engineering, commerce, or agriculture, and most of those were seeking government employment. High level training for trade and industry was almost totally neglected. Lower level vocational education was in no better condition.

(iv) National Enthusiasm for Education in 1920's and 1930's

The Montague-Chelmsford reforms introduced a system of dyarchy into the government of the Indian provinces in 1919 by which some powers were retained by the governor and his executive council and others were transferred to the authority of an Indian minister responsible to the elected legislative assembly. Education was a transferred power. In consequence, Indians, when the reforms came into operation in 1921, for the first time obtained control over the education departments in each of the provinces. As, however, most of the senior officers in the departments were British administrators, the Indian ministers' control was somewhat diminished until about the mid-1930's when the British element in the educational service had worked itself out.

The 1920's and 1930's witnessed an unprecedented rise in national consciousness and enthusiasm for education. Even such a staid publication as the central government quinquennial review of education was moved to report: 'A burst of enthusiasm swept children into school with unparalleled rapidity; an almost childlike faith in the value of education was implanted in the minds of people; parents were prepared to make almost any sacrifice for the education of their children.'[22]

It was at this stage that Mahatma Gandhi became prominent in Indian politics and launched the non-co-operation movement. One consequence of it was the development of a number of national schools repudiating western education and endeavouring to build more systematically on to traditional culture. This movement also stimulated more interest in education generally and highlighted its shortcomings. In consequence, a government committee was appointed to examine the current state of primary education. The Hartog Committee reported in 1929.[23] It reiterated the well-known criticisms of Indian education, suggested that expansion had been too rapid and that the consolidation of schools and educational effort to produce quality rather than quantity was the prime need. The committee recommended strengthening and extending the training of primary school teachers. It also felt that the village school should play a larger part in raising the standard of village life by relating its training to matters useful to village life and by providing assistance to the village community, e.g. medical help, adult instruction, attractive recreation. In this matter the committee shared the views of many of the progressive and nationalist educators, but in its opposition to rapid expansion it met with much criticism from Indian educators. Nevertheless the economic depression and the attitude of British educational administrators ensured that the Hartog Committee's views prevailed throughout the 1930's.

[21] S. Nurullah & J.P. Naik, *A History of Education in India*, Macmillan, Bombay, 2nd ed., 1951, p. 512.

[22] India, Education, *Progress of Education in India 1927-32*, Tenth Quinquennial Review, Delhi, Government of India, vol. 1, p. 3.

[23] The committee was an Auxiliary Committee of the Indian Statutory Commission and was chaired by Sir Philip Hartog. P.J. Hartog (1864-1947) lectured in chemistry at Manchester University, and was academic registrar of the University of London 1903-20. In 1907 he wrote an influential textbook, *The Writing of English*. He served as a member of Sadler's Calcutta University Commission, and was appointed the first vice-chancellor of Dacca University 1920. After his committee had reported in 1929 he returned to England and was prominent in investigations on the reliability of examinations. *An Examination of Examinations* (1935), and *The Marks of Examiners* (1936) were the outcome of this work.

Throughout the 1920's and 1930's there was a serious questioning of the British contribution to education. 'I say,' Gandhi stated, 'without fear of my figures being challenged successfully that today India is more illiterate than it was fifty or a hundred years ago, and so is Burma, because the British administrators, when they came to India, instead of taking hold of things as they were, began to root them out.'[24] Gandhi's observation was not too wide of the mark. The British had undoubtedly improved the quality of secondary and higher education, and perhaps also of primary education, but by the 1920's education was still the privilege of a small proportion of the population, a proportion not much larger than that of a hundred years earlier, when indigenous schools had been more widespread. By the 1920's traditional indigenous education had almost ceased to exist. Among the nationalists there were many who wished to revive it. Others, however, sought to marry traditional culture with current Indian needs and western educational practices. In the 1920's and 1930's there were many interesting attempts at such a synthesis.

Early in the century a leading Indian poet and thinker, Rabindranath Tagore, had developed his father's school, known as Santiniketan, not far from Calcutta, into a place which aimed 'to bring to the surface, for our daily use and purification, the stream of ideals that originated in the summit of our past, flowing underground in the depth of India's soil', and to bring them into contact with the healthiest tendencies of the modern world. In 1922 Tagore started to build up a wider centre of several higher level schools of study concerned with Indian languages and culture, Chinese culture, fine arts, music, dancing, and local industry, through which he hoped to build strong relationships between eastern cultures and between east and west. Tagore's ideas found a sympathetic hearing among many contemporary progressive educators in Europe, and he helped to stimulate the work of the New Education Fellowship in India.

Activity methods, especially relating children's experience in the villages to the school, were begun in several centres of which the Vidya Bhawan at Udaipur became well known. There, in an effort to overcome the divorce between intellectual and manual work, students were required to complete a prescribed number of labour units as well as the prescribed academic units; they were taken on school camping excursions to give them experience of corporate living; they were involved in service activities to help the neighbourhood; and they studied projects and centres of interest that were related to Indian concerns.

For Moslems, the Jamia Millia Islamia, established in Aligarth in 1923 and transferred two years later to Delhi, provided various levels of education based on the Islamic heritage. A primary school, developed along progressive lines, a high school, combining academic with art and craft work, and a university, offering work mainly in social science and languages, attracted students from various parts of India and Asia. The centre aimed to develop initiative and a spirit of service. It sought to provide a broad education for the youth of Islamic background who might eventually become leaders of a renascent India.

Most of the growing national spirit and increased interest in education was channelled into the state schools as Indian management and control became more effective in the 1920's and 1930's. In many primary schools there was more effort to give the work a local and rural emphasis, not by attempting to put agriculture into the curriculum but by bringing the school more closely into village life and seeing it as part of a movement for rural improvement and reconstruction.

(v) Basic Education

The principal educational question of the inter-war period in the underdeveloped countries of Asia and Africa concerned the suitability of the current education that was available to them. The Africans opted firmly for unadulterated western education that would provide them with employment opportunities and bring them closer educationally to the European colonists. The colonial authorities preferred a special, diluted mixture designed to suit the colonial situation. In India, once dyarchy had given the direction of education to Indians, the question became for them a serious, practical one. Was the kind of education the state was offering the right kind of education for Indians? Gandhi thought not. 'I am firmly of the opinion,' he had declared in 1921, 'that the Government schools have unmanned us, rendered us helpless and godless. They have filled us with discontent, and, providing no remedy for the discontent, have made us despondent. They have made us what we were intended to become, clerks and interpreters.'[25]

In a series of articles in 1937 Gandhi proposed a scheme of basic education for primary schools. India, a quarter of a century after Gokhale's unsuccessful attempt to introduce universal, compulsory, and free education, was still without it, and was still debating the means of financing it. Gandhi, developing ideas he had earlier expressed on several occasions, suggested a self-supporting form of education which would consist of a seven-year course of general education through the vernacular and a substantial vocational training which would assist in the all-round development of the pupils and also enable the pupil to pay for his tuition through the product of his labour. All the processes of rural handicrafts related to cotton, silk, and wool manufacture, to carpentry, bookbinding,

---

[24] P. Hartog, *Some Aspects of Indian Education — Past and Present*, Oxford University Press, 1939, p. 69.

[25] M.K. Gandhi, *Towards New Education*, ed. Bharatan Kumarappa, Navajivan Publishing House, Ahmedabad, 1953, p. 5.

paper-making, tailoring, weaving, and embroidery, he suggested as suitable areas of vocational education. A conference of educators was called at Wardha in 1937 to consider questions relating to the proposal. The conference endorsed the scheme. And they appointed a committee under Zakir Hussain to prepare a detailed syllabus for seven years of free and compulsory education on a nation-wide scale in the mother-tongue which 'should centre round some form of manual productive work'. They expressed the hope that the scheme might eventually be able to meet the salaries of the teachers.[26]

The report of the Zakir Hussain Committee was enthusiastic, but soberly argued. It emphasised particularly the educational significance of basic education, that it provided a desirable balance between intellectual and practical education and that, if the craft or productive work was carefully chosen by the school, it should become a useful unifying or correlating centre for the curriculum and a vital link between the school and its society. Basic education, the report suggested, implied a new ideal for India, the development of a co-operative community in which the ideal of social service prevails. The scheme might turn out to be self-supporting but teachers should be on their guard against allowing the economic motive to dominate their work.

Between 1937 and 1940 several of the Indian states set up training courses and experimental schools in basic education, and, with experience, wider and more varied schemes of correlation were developed. World War II slowed down the program and little further progress was made until 1945. At that date a further conference looked forward to the expansion of the meaning of basic education.

Gandhi had written, in his original articles, that he thought of his educational plan as 'the spearhead of a silent social revolution' that would improve the relationship between classes, 'check the progressive decay of our villages, and lay the foundation of a juster social order...'[27] Educational policy and practice were to be part of the reconstructive process leading to a more humane and juster society. The 1945 conference took up this theme. Basic education should be widened to apply to all ages, children and adults alike, and it should be regarded not merely as a new form of education but as a means of bringing about a new way of life. For the remaining two years of British rule, basic education expanded in all provinces side by side with a general extension of existing forms of education. In each area its content varied but its ideal was the same — to work towards a society based on co-operation and social equality.

(vi) The Last Years of British Administration

Meanwhile, as a consequence of the Government of India Act 1935, the whole field of provincial administration came under the authority of provincial legislatures in 1937, bringing an end to the system of dyarchy. The autonomous provinces had little opportunity to show their educational mettle. World War II was soon upon them, and then two years later India was an independent nation. Nevertheless in the ten years from 1937 to 1947 several important educational activities took place. The national government revived the Central Advisory Board of Education in 1935 and it began to play an important part in influencing decisions on the goals and ways and means for Indian education. On its advice a university grants committee was established in 1945, and reorganised in 1947, to supervise grants to universities from public funds and to co-ordinate university development throughout the country. By 1947 there were nineteen universities with an enrolment of a quarter of a million students in the area which became India. This was a doubling of university students in the ten-year period. At the lower educational levels, however, expansion was slower; both in primary and secondary education the number of pupils increased at a much slower rate than at any previous time in the century, and although between 1931 and 1941 the proportion of literates rose to twelve per cent according to the census of 1941, because of the greater increase in population, the actual number of illiterates increased by twenty-seven million. One of the achievements of the period was a substantial effort by the provincial governments to remove discrimination against untouchables and to make education more accessible to them. Insistence on their admission to the common schools, and a wider provision of scholarships and other economic assistance for them were steps towards their social and educational awakening that led also to similar measures for the elevation of other backward and depressed classes in India.

The most important educational work that was undertaken in the years immediately preceding independence was the post-war plan for educational development formulated by the Central Advisory Board and known as the Sargent Report after the then educational adviser to the Indian government. The Sargent Report put forward a plan under which India would in forty years' time reach the educational level attained by England at the time of the report. It therefore recommended the development of pre-school education for children from three to six years of age, universal compulsory free primary education along basic lines for children from six to fourteen, selective high schools of two types — academic and technical — for pupils from eleven to seventeen, three-year

[26] *Educational Reconstruction*, Hindustani Talimi Songh, Wardha, 5th ed., 1950, contains Gandhi's articles on Basic Education, and the Zakir Hussain Committee's Report.

[27] M.K. Gandhi, *Harijan*, 10 September 1937, in *Educational Reconstruction*, p. 37. See also K.G. Saiyidain, *The Humanist Tradition in Indian Educational Thought*, Asia Publishing House, London, 1966, p. 105.

university education for the successful high school graduates, an expanded full-time and part-time scheme of vocational education and teacher training, and the elimination of adult illiteracy during the next twenty years. It was the first comprehensive statement of a national educational scheme, but it did not provide a program through which the scheme was to be brought to reality. That was to be the function of the successive Five Year national plans that the Indian government embarked on after 1947. It was the final educational legacy of British administration — an English model for India's education of the future. During the next thirty years under an independent Indian government many of the recommendations of the report were to be brought into being.

EDUCATION IN COLONIAL AFRICA FROM 1900 TO THE 1940'S

'Education,' wrote an African in 1934, 'is one of the keystones of African progress.'[28] He wrote at a time when many educated Africans were beginning to see the possibility in the near future of building modernised and independent nations throughout the continent. Within that vision, western education played an important part as one of the significant factors that would improve economic opportunity, advance social change, and foster a new intellectual approach in African life. Education was to be the midwife of renascent, modern Africa.

Western education, however, had not always been held in such esteem. Initially, in most parts of Africa, in the nineteenth century there was a resistance to it. It was principally a missionary affair, and it was seen to be subversive of custom and tradition and to provide little of obvious value to its reluctant recipients. Most opposition was passive but in some regions such as Uganda it was violent, and in Northern Nigeria the colonial governor had to give an assurance to the moslem emirs that mission education would not be introduced. During the first decade of the twentieth century there was a steady change in favour of the new education and the possibilities that it brought with it, and by about 1910, although resistance continued, there were reports in most colonies of considerable enthusiasm for it. The enthusiasm was lasting. It was not adequately met by missionary effort, nor even by the growth of more substantial interest on the part of the colonial governments in the 1920's, 1930's, and 1940's. It was left to the newly independent states in the 1950's and 1960's, conscious of the national importance of the demand, to make a serious effort to meet it by devoting a high proportion of their income towards its satisfaction.

There were three main periods in the development of education in colonial Africa. First, a period of mission activity in which, with some notable exceptions principally in the colonies in moslem areas and in Tanganyika, missionary societies were almost the sole providers of schools; second, a period, between World War I and World War II, of mixed missionary and government effort, in which governments professed strong interest, formulated carefully considered policies, and developed the nucleus of a government system of education; and third, a period following World War II and leading up to independence, in which government efforts in both the planning and provision of education were greatly accelerated.

(i) Missionary Education in the Early Twentieth Century

Few colonial governments before World War I gave very serious attention to education. They were interested mainly in the preservation of law and order, the imposition of taxation, and the promotion of trade. Education was the province of the missionaries. When, between 1900 and 1910, native indifference passed into such enthusiasm, that some American missionaries in the Belgian Congo described it as 'spreading like prairie fire',[29] the missions found their resources considerably strained.

The motive inducing the Africans to seek out the teaching of the missionaries was the mounting pressure of the new social order. Reading, writing, and basic western knowledge were the keys to a share in the progress of the new civilisation; these keys were held by the mission teachers. Their principal establishment was the 'bush', 'village', or 'out' school.

'The native catechist, of slender intellectual attainments, presiding over the syllabic chorus and interspersing it with crude denunciations of drunkenness and dancing, of polygamy and witchcraft, from beneath the shelter of a wretched hut, has seemed to many European observers a pitiable reflection of western bigotry. To the African villager he was the apostle of the new learning, preaching emancipation from the old law, and opening vistas of a more ideal life which was attainable at least by the young and enterprising.'[30] Education in the bush schools was concerned with the 3 R's, morals, and health. The training of the catechists who ran them had a strong literary cast, centring round the Bible, and the bush schools reflected that tendency. As early as the 1870's Sir Bartle Frere had criticised the missions for offering an education that was too bookish, and his strictures were to be repeated by many observers of both missionary

---

[28] P.G. Mockerie, *An African Speaks for his People*, Hogarth, London, 1934.

[29] Barbara Yates, 'African reactions to Education: the Congolese case', *Comparative Education Review*, 15, 2, June 1971, p. 160.

[30] Roland Oliver, *The Missionary Factor in East Africa*, Longmans, London, 2nd ed., 1965, pp. 201-2. See also A.V. Murray, *The School in the Bush*, Longmans, London, 1938.

and government schools throughout the twentieth century.[31] Efforts were made, especially by some of the Catholic orders, to develop industrial and agricultural education. Some of the missions established successful and well-equipped vocational schools for the teaching of agriculture and trades such as building, cabinet-making, blacksmithing, and printing, and their pupils were usefully absorbed into the work force. The effort, however, was somewhat limited and had little impact on the elementary curriculum of the bush school before World War I. The missions, except in the Portuguese and French colonies, where the practice was forbidden, made a point of teaching in the vernacular in their bush schools, and of encouraging their pupils to become literate in their domestic language into which they often diligently translated the Bible for local use. Short and infrequent attendance, however, made the attainment of literacy an impossible goal for all but a few. Pupils could be expected to attend for two to three years, three or four days a week for two to three hours each day. Their academic attainments were meagre, and after leaving school were largely forgotten.

By the end of the elementary program, to take the case of Tanganyika early in the 1920's, they should have been able to read widely 'up to hard Government notices', and to compose and write to dictation simple compositions in the vernacular; to speak, analyse and parse in Swahili, to do long division and 'hard problems involving the four rules'; to have some knowledge of the economic and human geography of Africa and several other places, and to understand thoroughly the laws of health.[32] Some boys and girls who completed the elementary school program continued their education for two or three years in central boarding schools at the more important mission centres. This higher elementary program had a literary bias and for the most part was designed to produce teachers for the village schools.

There were also a very small number of boys — there were no girls — who managed to proceed from elementary education into an academic secondary education. A few secondary schools were established in the main centres of population throughout the colonies. They introduced the pupils, who may not have previously started to learn it, to the European language of the colonial power, set them to work on as close a model of the *lycée* or grammar school syllabus as could be managed, prepared them for the examinations of the metropolitan country, and tried to give them in every way possible the same type of educational experiences that European boys would have in their own schools.

Up to the 1920's most of the educational work in Africa south of the Sahara was done by missionaries; indeed a British Colonial Office memo of 1923 opened with the words, 'In some of the British Colonies and Protectorates in Africa, the whole, and in most of the others at least nine-tenths, of the native education is being given in mission schools.'[33] The

memo writer later, in a widely read book, explained what the missionaries were trying to do. The purpose of mission education was to teach 'through the kind of school that was distinctively Christian and could therefore exert a creative influence in the life of Africa', to get the natives to look at life in a new way, and to 'help to humanize, enrich, and spiritualize the whole of African rural life'.[34]

How well did they achieve these admirable objectives? The Phelps-Stokes Commission made an assessment.

(ii) Phelps-Stokes Commission

In 1922 the Phelps-Stokes Fund of New York published the report of a commission which had spent the previous year touring western, equatorial, and southern Africa from Sierra Leone to South Africa and Rhodesia. The commission consisted of a small group of American and British persons, some with experience in the education of American negroes, including an African from the Gold Coast, and some with missionary experience in Africa. They investigated government and mission schools for native Africans and educational policies in British, Belgian and Portuguese colonies, and in Liberia and South Africa. In 1925 a second report was issued dealing with their subsequent investigation of the education of the indigenous people of East Africa from Abyssinia to Cape of Good Hope.[35]

The two reports contained extensive discussions of general educational principles, careful descriptions of the geographical and political setting of each country, of the general state of education, of the conduct of government and mission schools, with an account of the work of many individual schools, and concluded with a series of recommendations for the improvement of education in each country. They constituted a comprehensive and influential statement about African education in the 1920's.

The reports were a sympathetic but devastating criticism of existing education. The commission pointed to the evidence of the successful results of mission and government education. There were numerous examples of 'intelligent, industrious, and honest' persons produced by the schools in every colony; almost all the clerical work in government and

[31]   B. Frere, *East Africa as a Field for Missionary Labours*, London, 1874.

[32]   Tanganyika Territory, *Conference between Government and Missions, Report of Proceedings*, Education Office, Dar es Salaam, 1925, Sub Appendix B, pp. 135-6.

[33]   Roland Oliver, *op.cit.*, p. 268, memo by J.H. Oldham.

[34]   J.H. Oldham, & B.H. Gibson, *The Remaking of Man in Africa*, Oxford University Press, London, 1931, pp. 38, 41, 71.

[35]   Thomas J. Jones ed., *Education in Africa, A Study of West, South, and Equatorial Africa*, Phelps-Stokes Fund, New York, 1922, and Thomas J. Jones ed., *Education in East Africa, A Study of East, Central and South Africa*, Phelps-Stokes Fund, New York, 1925.

commercial concerns was done by ex-pupils of the schools, and the railways, boats, and telegraph services were maintained by them. In addition there were a number of successful lawyers, merchants, doctors, ministers and teachers who had risen through the village schools to their profession. But when the commission looked at the quantity of educational provision and the quality of the educational systems it was not happy:

- There was a lack of balance. Some authorities emphasised the training of leaders, others the need for mass education, instead of bringing the two aims into a proper relationship with each other. Education was distributed unevenly. In Sierra Leone, for example, almost all the schools were in Freetown for its population of sixty-three thousand, while the rest of the country with a population of 1.3 millions was neglected. Similarly, in most colonies, schools were concentrated in the coastal areas or in some other favoured parts. There was an imbalance too in the matter of the sexes. Boys' needs were given a strongly preferential treatment, while the education of girls was negligible, and above the most elementary level almost non-existent.

- There was a lack of co-operation between the various interested parties in education. Commercial interests did little, though some provided a modicum of vocational training. The native peoples were not encouraged to participate in educational planning though, presumably, it was their needs that education might be thought to be serving. Governments contributed little to education and in some colonies almost nothing at all. Missions designed and operated their own services, subject to an exacting control in French and Portuguese colonies, but elsewhere with some small government assistance and supervision, and with little relation to the work of other missions.

- There was a lack of intelligent adaptation of school practices to the interests and experiences of the pupils and to the life and needs of the community around them. Educators generally professed their desire to make such adaptations, but in practice reverted to European models with the result described by one of the commission on their visits to schools: '... the pupils were asked to sing any song they pleased. They always brightened up at this request for the African loves singing. The chances were strong that we would hear "The British Grenadiers". Perhaps there was a desire to please the strangers, but when they were asked to sing an African song, a boat song, or any chant used in their own plays, a laugh invariably went through the whole class, and only in a few

instances, even when we declared our love for their own music, could they give us a single African chant. Similarly, if we asked about history, we soon discovered what happened in 1066, but of their own story — nothing.' Such a lack of concern led to an obvious undervaluing of indigenous culture by the pupils and a distaste for it. The commission noted, however, that the educated Africans whom it met approved the westernisation of the schools, and were suspicious that if they were provided with an education adapted to African needs they might be fobbed off with an inferior brand of education.

- There was an appalling lack of skill among the teachers, and lack of modern equipment in the schools. Teaching methods were out of date, teachers were poorly trained, textbooks were unsuitable or non-existent, and modern visual aids were unheard of.

- Then there were criticisms by the commission of the provision and operation of the various types of school, which they divided into: **Bush schools,** the two- or three-year local, vernacular, elementary schools which absorbed most of the educational efforts of the missionary societies: 'The training offered in these schools consists of the merest rudiments — reading, taught very ineffectively, a crude form of writing, and usually not more than addition and subtraction in arithmetic. The majority of teachers rarely have more than the equivalent of three American grades or two English standards. These schools are attended most irregularly for two or three years.'[37] The better local elementary schools, usually found in the main towns, might go up to the equivalent of the American fourth grade, and have a teacher with eleven or twelve years of education, but these schools were rare.
Middle schools, which were usually boarding schools, took pupils promoted from the village schools, provided a higher elementary course from the fourth to the seventh standard, or ninth grade in American schools, and were concerned mainly with producing persons suitable for teaching in the elementary schools and carrying on the religious work of the mission out-stations. The commission regarded these as schools of great promise, provided that they could develop a wider curriculum related more closely to the social and economic needs of the country. At the moment, however, they directed their attention too much to literary and clerical pursuits, and only about 25 per cent of them managed to offer courses up to the seventh standard.

---

36 T.J Jones ed., *Education in Africa*, p. xix.

37 *ibid.*, p. 41.

Secondary schools were of three types. One was for the purpose of training teachers and religious workers, such as that in the Basel mission on the Gold Coast which offered courses beyond the seventh standard for a small number of boarders. The second type provided trade courses, such as in the Hope-Waddell Institution in Nigeria where the entrance requirement was less than a complete elementary education. And the third was the academic type of grammar school, such as could be found in Lagos and Freetown. The commission reported that there were remarkably few of any of the three types and that what was needed was more secondary schools of a comprehensive type.

Higher education was limited to Fourah Bay College in Sierra Leone which had a classical bias and prepared a few students in classics and theology for degrees of the University of Durham, and Fort Hare College in South Africa which had only just started. Most Africans wishing for tertiary qualifications had to proceed for university or higher technical work to America or to a European country. The colonies were clearly lacking in institutions for training the needed scientists, agriculturalists, and medical workers.

In looking at the overall picture of education in each of the African countries the commission offered some general and trenchant remarks. Nigeria, for example, the largest and best equipped of the British colonies learnt that: 'Present facilities for education in Southern Nigeria are utterly inadequate and, with few exceptions, not adequately related to the hygienic, economic, and character needs of the eight million people in the southern provinces. Educational provision for the nine million Natives in Northern Nigeria is practically all in promise.'[38] In the Belgian Congo, where the schools were of a 'primitive and crude character', 'the present facilities are negligible'.[39] The Portuguese colonies were referred to as remarkably backward, and 'Observations in Portuguese Africa and reports from Angola offer practically no basis for hope of any essential improvements in colonial policy.'[40] In Nyasaland, 'the Government has spent eight times as much on police, prisons and lunatic asylums as on the education of the people.'[41] Summing up post-elementary education throughout East Africa, the commission reported:

'There are now only two schools south of Egypt and the Sahara that have any claim to recognition as colleges... Even the number of secondary schools is almost negligible. Indeed there are no schools for Natives in East Africa which in relation to Western standards can be properly described as secondary schools. Nor are there professional schools of either secondary or college standard. While a small number of schools offer agricultural training, the real agricultural schools may be

counted on the fingers of one hand, and these are elementary in standard. Trades are taught in a few schools. Teachers are trained in a considerable number of schools, but comparatively few offer well-planned instruction and practice for the preparation of teachers.'[42]

The percentage of students of school age enrolled at school was extraordinarily low. Taking one-fifth of the total population as representing the proportion of school age, the commission found that the impact of educational services had so far been minimal in most countries. British West African colonies enrolled from three per cent to six per cent of the school population, the Belgian colonies from four per cent to nine per cent, the Portuguese colonies three per cent, and British East African colonies from five per cent to 25 per cent. The most successful colony was Uganda, with an enrolment of 25 per cent of the possible number of pupils, but the commission was careful to point out that nine-tenths of them were in inadequate out-schools and that probably not more than one hundred pupils were at school above the fourth standard.

Besides the detailed recommendations which the commission made for each country, they offered several general recommendations.

Struck by the lack of co-ordination and co-operation in education in all of the colonies, they argued strongly for more generous and flexible support of the missions by governments, and the establishment of boards of advice on which all parties could be represented.

Behind this view was the argument that colonial governments should start to believe and act on their statements that their function was a civilising and not an exploitive one. In the short period of idealism after World War I there came to be a wider realisation that, although commercial profits were not to be neglected, the duty of colonial powers was to assist underdeveloped people by providing them with the opportunity to make the most of their resources, talents, and contacts with the western world. To achieve that aim a vigorous attention to education was necessary. It required, as the commission pointed out, a serious effort to build up a substantial mass base of educated people and to provide facilities for the higher education of leaders. Neither of those tasks had been adequately tackled up to that time in any of the African dependencies.

The commission recommended that the basis of African mass education should be in the adaptation and adjustment of western knowledge to the needs and circumstances of individual and community life in Africa. Taking its lead from the recently published *Cardinal*

[38] *ibid.*, p. 145.
[39] *ibid.*, p. 258.
[40] T.J. Jones (ed.), *Education in East Africa*, p. 314.
[41] *ibid.*, p. 199.
[42] *ibid.*, pp. 43-4.

Principles in the United States, the commission pointed out that the main elements to be considered in developing an educational program were health, the adequate use of the environment, preparation for home life, the use of leisure time, the language of instruction, the command of conventional school subjects, character development and religious life, and the demands of community life. In each of those areas teachers must get to know local habits and customs and adjust their teaching so that it would make a real impact on the life of the pupils and the community. To maintain close touch with the local environment, and to give African children the best opportunity to think effectively, the commission considered that the vernacular should be the language of instruction in the early years of elementary education, that, if there was an African *lingua franca* such as Swahili in some parts of Central and East Africa, it should be commenced in the later years of elementary education, and a European language could be learnt in middle school and used for instructional purposes in secondary school.

Especially was it necessary to pay attention to moral education and character development. As the old society was breaking down under the western impact, it was important for educators to fashion persons of virtue and dependability who could build the new society along sound lines. In addition to character education, particular attention needed to be given to agricultural education, and the education of women. Existing education by its bookish tendency had led to a depreciation of the importance of agriculture. Africa, however, was more dependent on its agriculture than any other people in the world; the improvement of it through scientific education and research was an obvious way to increase the health and prosperity of the country. Similarly there had been a neglect of women's education. One half of the population was thus barely touched by education, a half, moreover, whose interest was vital for the improvement of family and community life. To reduce high rates of infant mortality, improve the hygiene of the household, raise the level of the diet and preparation of food, and provide adequate companionship and support for the newly literate men, it was essential to pay careful attention to the education of women, the persons responsible for raising and educating the families of the community. For the new Africa the African member of the commission was reported to have sagely remarked on another occasion: 'The surest way to keep a people down is to educate the men and neglect the women. If you educate a man you simply educate an individual, but if you educate a woman you educate a family'.[43]

The Phelps-Stokes Commission reports were important documents. They were a frank assessment of education for the Africans south of the Sahara, and they were full of sensible advice on how to improve the situation. They summed up a trend that had been operating in American negro education and had been growing in the minds of African educators

for some time, towards making more substantial adaptations of western education to the needs and conditions of Africans. Perhaps because there was only one African on the commission, there was a less than full appreciation of the newer trend that educated Africans had begun to express and were to emphasise in the next two decades, for more and more massive doses of unadulterated western education that might be able, in a short time, to transform their communities into modern societies.

The commission's reports had a stimulating effect on governments, and led directly to the establishment of an influential British Colonial Office advisory committee which endorsed their ideas. Again, the reports appeared at an opportune moment, when colonial governments, somewhat lagging in educational effort before World War I, were becoming persuaded of the need to expand their educational work. They too, in theory, adopted the general trend which the commission had advocated. In practice the lines of the policy were not always easy to discern.

(iii) Government Education in the African Colonies

The principal need of the colonising power was for intermediaries[44] with the native population. Settlers and traders needed interpreters, foremen, clerks; the missions needed teachers, evangelists, and artisans; and the government needed clerks and minor administrators. Education was accordingly designed to produce those kinds of people to assist the colonisers in their enterprises. But missions, governments, and sometimes commercial companies regarded themselves as agents of European civilisation and, accordingly, were moved to educational policies that did not merely serve their own utilitarian ends. Education was to raise the general level of behaviour and culture for the mass of the people, and it was to produce new leaders who at some future time could play a serious part in developing the professional life and government of the colony.

Before World War I all colonial governments had taken some steps to enter the educational field. The Germans and French had proceeded the furthest, though their efforts were not very considerable.

(a) German Colonial Education in Tanganyika

In Tanganyika, the German government in the 1890's started a secular school system parallel to the missionary schools. Its main purpose was to train up an intermediary group of clerks and administrators, and

---

[43] Edwin W. Smith, *Aggrey of Africa*, Student Christian Movement, London, 1929, p. 139.

[44] This is Margaret Read's useful term. See Margaret H. Read, 'Education in Africa; its pattern and role in social change,' *The Annals of the American Academy of Political and Social Science*, 298, March 1955, pp. 170-9.

agricultural and medical assistants. There were three grades of schools: three-year elementary schools in the villages offering the 3 R's and the first steps in accounting and minor government procedure; three-year central schools in which Swahili and German were taught; and six-year high schools providing junior secondary school-work. The most well-known of the schools was the Tanga Government School established in 1892; it became a day and boarding school offering primary, teacher training, clerical, and trades courses, and from 1905 put much of its effort into secondary and technical work. By 1913 the government had established primary and more advanced schools in nineteen centres throughout Tanganyika with eighty other feeder schools, and had two secondary and three vocational schools, with a grand total of about six thousand pupils, all of whom were boys.

The government educational effort did not at first endear it to the missions, who disapproved of the secular and utilitarian approach and were uneasy about the teaching of Swahili because of its association with Islamic culture and religion. Towards the end of the German colonial period the mission schools received government grants-in-aid and were subject to inspection. Their enrolment increased with the upsurge of African interest, described picturesquely by one missionary in 1911: 'The sea will be swept back with greater ease than the African from pursuing learning',[45] and with the passage of an Act in 1910 requiring all chiefs and their heirs to learn to read and write. The new law was a part of a general German policy, initiated at that time, to accelerate their civilising mission: 'the natives have a right to demand,' the colonial secretary said in 1913, in true Kantian style, 'that they should be regarded by the more highly developed races as an end and not as a means'.[46] In the years immediately before World War I missions and government co-operated to the best of their ability in pursuance of that aim. The educational services of the missions in Tanganyika were among the most effective in Africa and, taken in conjunction with the government effort, probably provided the German colony with the best available for Africans south of the Sahara up to World War I.[47]

(b) French Colonial Education

French West and Equatorial Africa. French educational work in west and equatorial Africa was in aim and practice very similar to that of the government schools of Tanganyika. Its rationale was expressed in several decrees during the course of the first three decades of the twentieth century and summed up in the mid-1930's by the inspector-general for French West Africa at that time.

Colonisation was essentially the transformation of the indigenous society. In that process education played an important role and, if the task

was to be soundly tackled, education must be planned properly and supported adequately. It must be related to political and economic realities, must grow in the native soil, and be nurtured by ideas of European, and preferably French, inspiration. The principal problems to be met were:

- the raising of the cultural level of the mass of the people;
- the development of an educated elite;
- the moral conquest of native customs and ideas, and the creation of a new Franco-African culture.

In dealing with those tasks it was necessary to link together both practical, utilitarian school programs and a broad humanistic type of education. Education was not a matter of assimilating native peoples into a sophisticated French culture; teaching had to be adapted to the native's outlook, to the level of development of the native community, and to the economic needs of the area. The French therefore tackled the three main problems by:

- establishing a common school which was designed to provide the pupils with knowledge and attitudes that would improve their everyday existence, and would introduce them to French civilisation through the French language which was the medium of teaching. It was a self-contained system, designedly terminal for almost all the pupils within it.
- training a native elite, a nucleus of educated Africans, who could fill administrative positions in government, education, and economic affairs, and would be active intermediaries between the old and the new, the French and the native population. The selection of such people must be rigorously and carefully related to the needs of the community. 'In a new country education is not an

---

[45] G.H. Wilson, *The History of the Universities Mission to Central Africa*, University Mission to Central Africa, London, 1936, p. 140.

[46] R.F. Eberlie, 'The German achievement in East Africa,' *Tanganyika Notes and Records*, Dar es Salaam, 1960, 55, pp. 203-4.

[47] For education in pre-World War I Tanganyika see particularly T. Watson, 'Education in German East Africa', *University of East Africa Social Science Conference, Religious Studies Papers*, Kampala 1968-9; John Iliffe, *Tanganyika under German Rule 1905-1912*, Cambridge University Press, 1969; George Hornsby, 'A brief history of Tanga School up to 1914', *Tanganyika Notes and Records*, Dar es Salaam, 58, March 1962, pp. 148-50, and 'German educational achievement in East Africa', *ibid.*, 1964, 62, pp. 83-90; Anthony Smith, 'The missionary contribution to education (Tanganyika) to 1914', *ibid.*, 1963, 60, pp. 91-109; R.F. Eberlie, 'The German achievement in East Africa', *ibid.*, 1960, 55, pp. 181-214; Marcia Wright, *German Missions in Tanganyika 1891-1941, Lutherans and Moravians in the Southern Highlands*, Clarendon, Oxford, 1971.

end in itself; it is based on utilitarian considerations.'[48] There were three kinds of elites, each with its appropriate form of training: those who were trained in vocational schools to fill subordinate posts in commerce and the newly developing European-type industries; those sons of chiefs who had been to the special schools established for them and had thus been able to form a bond between traditional authority and the requirements of the colonial power; and those who had attended higher primary and specialist technical schools to fit themselves for official positions as government or commercial clerks, or as teachers, and medical and veterinary assistants.

- striving for a union of the two cultures, French and African, so that the African did not disown his own inheritance but enlarged and deepened it by contact with French culture. The intention was to enable him to achieve a French consciousness, to order his behaviour by the moral outlook of the superior civilisation, and to be committed to the justice, order, and progress that France had brought to his country, while, at the same time, maintaining his roots in his native cultural soil and striving to effect a fruitful link between the French and African ways of life.

Prior to the twentieth century little serious attention had been paid to education and it was left largely unregarded in the hands of the missionaries. In 1903, coincident with a concerted move at home to increase the secularisation of education, the French governor-general of West Africa issued a series of decrees designed to create a state secular system of education. This character provided for:

- three kinds of primary school: a village or bush school, with a one- or two-year course to initiate pupils into the rudiments of French civilisation; a rural regional school for the best of the bush school pupils, offering a full primary course a little below the standard for the metropolitan certificate and including some agricultural training; and an urban primary school similar in standard to the regional school but offering elementary vocational training for mostly clerical occupations;

- three kinds of schools above primary level, a higher primary school entered by a competitive examination and offering a two-year course to prepare pupils for minor administrative posts in government and commerce, a higher vocational school open to pupils who had completed primary education and who wished to enter a skilled trade, and a teachers' training college for the best

pupils from the higher primary school who would receive a three-year course to become teachers, interpreters, or chiefs.

With minor variations the 1903 charter set the pattern of schooling for the next forty years. It was implemented initially in Senegal, became accepted as the policy for French Equatorial Africa in 1911, and slowly thereafter came into operation throughout French West and Equatorial Africa. During the 1920's and 1930's higher primary schools, sometimes combined with vocational schools, were extended beyond Senegal. A higher primary school in Senegal for sons of Moslem chiefs, re-established in 1908 after an earlier chequered career, was copied in several other centres in order to train officials in legal and governmental administration. The higher vocational schools were extended to include a school of medicine at Dakar for medical assistants, a veterinary school at Bamako, and an engineering school, also at Bamako, to prepare assistants for the public works department. And the teacher training school in Dakar developed into something approaching a regional secondary school. In addition a few Africans attended lycées established for the children of French officials and settlers.

By the beginning of World War II, approximately five per cent of the pupils of school age were enrolled in the schools of the French colonies south of the Sahara; of these pupils about one-fifth were in missionary schools regulated by governmental decree and required to follow the same programs as the official schools.

French North African Territories. North of the Sahara, in the French Mediterranean colonies, there was a much larger migration of French settlers and a closer connection with the metropolitan territory. Algeria, the oldest of these colonies, had become a department of France in 1848, and education was modelled on and in content controlled by the French Ministry of Education. Elementary schools were established specially for native children and in them the standard syllabus was modified according to the pupils' progress in the French language and the need for practical instruction in health, household management, agriculture, or elementary vocational training. In Tunisia an interesting effort at cultural linkage was made by devoting a third of the school program to Arabic language and culture.

On the other hand, the French settlers in Algeria, in the later nineteenth and early twentieth century, argued vigorously for an education for the indigenous population that would be locally oriented

---

[48] A. Charton, 'The social function of education in French West Africa', in W.B. Mumford & G. St. J. Orde-Brown, *Africans Learn to be French*, Evans, London, 1936, p. 108. See also G. Le Bon, *Psychologie de l'Education*, Flammarion, Paris, rev.ed., 1914, pp. 312ff. who complained of the 'lamentable consequences' of current policies, and advocated a policy of slow development not unlike the later views outlined above by Charton.

and vocational, and would not enable its products to compete with them. The French government, however, firmly and successfully insisted on offering as general an education as possible, and one that would enable talented and successful native students to complete their education in the same institutions as the French. Beyond the elementary school, native students were expected to attend the same higher elementary, secondary, technical, and higher educational establishments as French pupils, except that special supplementary courses were available in the larger primary schools to prepare pupils for apprenticeship in a variety of trades.

Despite the closer connection with metropolitan France, the proportion of non-Europeans in school was not noticeably different from that in the west and equatorial areas of Africa. Taking the North African territories as a whole, about 6 per cent (a little more than 1 per cent of the whole population) of the pupils of school age in the native population were in government and mission schools by the beginning of World War II. In these Moslem countries Christian missionary work was minimal; there were, however, a considerable number of Islamic schools, most of which taught their pupils little more than a rote knowledge of the Koran, though some, notably in Tunisia, taught in Arabic, with French as a second language, an elementary school course comparable to that of the public schools. For a few pupils secondary education in Arabic culture was available in a few schools in Algeria and Tunisia, notably in the College Sadiki in Tunis, and higher studies could be pursued in Arabic universities in Tunisia or the Middle East.[49]

The French in their North African territories had encountered an indigenous educational system developed to a much higher level than in the areas south of the Sahara. The introduction of the French system was designed to wean the indigenous people away from much of their traditional culture to a new synthesis in which French would be the dominating element. By about 1920 the influence of traditional teachers had been substantially undermined by a variety of devices, and the French school program had reached such a degree of popularity that the local demand for school places was outstripping the colonial government's ability to supply them. In the inter-war period, Islamic schools were able to maintain an uneasy existence, and became associated with a mild nationalist movement. French schools, however, attracted the elite. The middle and upper classes saw in them the means of advancement through which they might maintain or advance their position. A French education, as it became more widespread, became an indispensable passport to positions in the administration and to professional careers; and the program of studies in French schools was the only way to gain access to modern knowledge and to higher studies in the modern world. Thus, socially, economically, and pedagogically, French schooling became overwhelmingly desirable for those who could manage to secure

it. The Islamic schools tended to become associated with lower classes, poor peasants, and labourers.

The French system therefore was up to World War II very much an elite system, as, indeed, were the schools of all the colonial powers. The French North African schools, however, partly because of economic and administrative demand, partly because they were in competition with a well-established local system, and partly because of the presence of a substantial number of French settlers, managed to develop an education that was more selective and more demanding than elsewhere on the African continent.[50] The indigenous pupils who managed to survive the full process of the *lyceé* or of a *collège* such as Sadiki went to France for their higher education. There they learnt that not all Frenchmen were like settlers and colonial officials, and they returned to Algeria, Tunisia, and Morocco to help staff the professions and to form the nucleus of the nationalist movement which led to the achievement of independence in 1956 for Morocco and Tunisia, and in 1962 for Algeria.

(c) Education in the Italian Colonies

In Libya the Italian educational policy, except for a short period in the early 1920's, was one of gradually assimilating the indigenous people into Italian culture and politics. The Moslem religion and associated customs were respected, and local languages and traditions were not disregarded, though they were not much encouraged. The Italian language was pushed in the elementary schools and the curriculum was designed as closely as possible on the home model with the expectation that educated Libyans would qualify as Italian citizens.

It was not until 1924 that native education in Somaliland, hitherto educationally almost untouched, was entrusted to Catholic missionaries under government supervision. In Eritrea an effort was made to establish separate schools, divided about equally between the government and the missions for the different religious groups in the colony: Coptic, Catholic and Protestant Christians, Moslems, and pagans.

Civilising the natives, the principal colonial slogan of Mussolini's Fascist government of the 1920's and 1930's, meant Italianising them as far as possible. 'Help me, O God, to become a good Italian,' a pupil read in his primer supplied by the colonial government in 1936. The government elementary school was a principal instrument of the

---

49   See I.L. Kandel (ed.), *Educational Yearbook 1931*, Teachers' College, Columbia University, New York, 1932, pp. 201-565; Abdou Moumouni, *L'Education en Afrique*, Maspero, Paris, 1964, pp. 41-132; Robert Cornevin, 'Education in Black Africa' (an historical account), *Africa Quarterly*, 7, 4, 1968, pp. 326-34; Jean Capelle, 'Education in French West Africa', *Oversea Education*, 21, 1949-50, pp. 956-72.

50   Fanny Colonna, 'Le systeme d'enseignement del'Algérie coloniale', *Arch. Europ. Sociol.*, XIII, 1972, pp. 195-220.

civilising mission, and their teachers were described by a leading colonial educator as 'apostles of civilization'.[51]

The mission implied that the school would make efforts to uplift the natives spiritually and morally, to improve their health knowledge and habits, to raise the condition of women, to upgrade local agricultural practices, to produce competent native artisans, to instil a disciplined respect for the authority of the Italian government, and to welcome Italian sovereignty and civilisation. For those purposes the elementary school was not quite enough. It was therefore supplemented by a limited number of trades and agricultural courses, by a few vocational schools, and by a youth movement taking its inspiration from the well-disciplined national *Balilla*.

Attendance at government schools for native children in Libya grew from ninety-nine in 1911, the first year of occupation, to twelve thousand in 1936, representing approximately eight per cent of the children of school age. In Italian East Africa the numbers increased from about 250 pupils at the turn of the century in Eritrea, to 8,500 in 1937 over the whole of the colonial territories which then included Eritrea, Somaliland, and the recently conquered Ethiopia. That figure represents probably less than one per cent of the possible school population. Very little secondary education or teacher training was provided for the indigenous peoples.

(d) British Colonial Education in Africa

British Educational Policy. The British in their colonies worked upon the principle of indirect rule, in which, theoretically, education was of vital importance. The principal exponent of this doctrine in Africa was Lord Lugard, whose long career in the colonies ended with the governor-generalship of Nigeria 1914-19. He explained that Europe had a dual mandate inasmuch as 'Europe is in Africa for the mutual benefit of her industrial classes, and of the native races in their progress to a higher plane',[52] and in pursuance of this task the British should, as far as possible, put the responsibility for governing on the shoulders of educated leaders among the colonial people. Julian Huxley, in an influential and critical book, applied the doctrine neatly to education: 'Then there is a double principle that education should be adapted to the local environment of time and place and yet give the opportunity of transcending that environment.'[53]

Education, Lugard explained, had sometimes been disastrous, as could best be seen in India where educated persons had shown themselves to be a subversive influence out of touch with their proper social environment. To avoid such a catastrophic result, schools should aim to produce persons whose education fitted them specifically for administrative, commercial, or technical jobs, and this preparation should be firmly based on an elementary education that was closely related to their environment, that would emphasise character development, and that would fit the recipients for a useful and happy life in their community. Lugard felt that the ideal educational model was the English Public Boarding School in which the formation of character was placed before the training of intellect.

There was little governmental effort in education in the British colonies before World War I. In 1923 a beginning was made to build an official colonial policy by establishing an Advisory Committee which in 1929 became the Advisory Committee on Education in the Colonies. In 1925 the committee submitted its first memorandum,[54] the initial draft of which had been written by Lugard, a leading member of the committee.

Prior to that statement, the British government had had no defined policy on education. The Advisory Committee was very much aware that education could have a disintegrating and unsettling effect upon the people of a country, and recognised that at the same time the British African dependencies in both East and West Africa had recently experienced rapid material and economic development requiring a corresponding expansion in educational facilities. It suggested that to ease the transition into the more modern world and to produce the most effective form of education, the work of the schools should be 'adapted to the mentality, aptitudes, occupations and traditions of the various peoples, conserving as far as possible all sound and healthy elements in the fabric of their social life'.[55] Education was to be a part of the general governmental policy of advancing the welfare of the colonial peoples. Educators therefore had a responsible task of adaptation and construction. They had to study the characteristics and traditions of the indigenous people; they had to select what was worth conserving or developing; they had to design curricula and methods of teaching adapted to the conditions and prospects of their pupils; they had to encourage and train the people to manage their own affairs and to develop the ideals and morals appropriate to their new form of citizenship; and they had to provide ways of educating worthy leaders of the new society. The ideal

[51] Roland R. De Marco, *The Italianization of African Natives. Government Native Education in the Italian Colonies 1890-1937*. Teachers College, Columbia University, New York, 1943; Rodolfo Micacchi, 'L'Enseignement aux indigènes dans les colonies Italiennes dépendant directment de la couranne', Institut Colonial International, *Rapports Préliminaires de l'Enseignements aux Indigènes*, Etablissements Généraux d'Imprimerie, Bruxelles, 1931, vol. 2.

[52] F.D. Lugard, *The Dual Mandate in British Tropical Africa*, Blackwood, Edinburgh, 4th ed., 1929 (1921), p. 617.

[53] Julian Huxley, *Africa View*, Chatto & Windus, London, 1931, p. 304.

[54] Great Britain Colonial Office, Advisory Committee on Native Education in the British Tropical African Dependencies, *Educational Policy in British Tropical Africa*, H.M.S.O., London, Cmd. 2374, 1925.

[55] *ibid.*, p. 4.

was expressed in another way in the anonymous but widely expressed statement that 'the aim of native education should not be the production of bad Europeans but should be the production of good Africans'.[56]

There were, however, many gradations in that point of view.

As far as financial means would allow, the policy was put into effect in the African colonies where it was well-received by the colonial governments. The British governor of the former German territory of Tanganyika, for example, in opening a conference with missionary educators, declared of the Advisory Committee's report: 'It is the "Charter of Education" for this Territory, to which I commit the Government now.'[57] A principal example of the policy was the establishment of Achimota College in Sierra Leone. Nevertheless, by 1929 the committee found that Northern Rhodesia was spending twice as much on European type education as on African education, and by 1933 the advisory committee was noting a strong tendency in East Africa to favour European education, and in West Africa an increased interest in secondary and higher education.[58]

Similar views on general educational policy were expressed by Belgian and French authorities in their re-examination of colonial education during the hopeful years after World War I. 'The Congo,' wrote the Belgian Commission set up in 1922, 'requires a special school system, carefully adapted to the social environment.'[59] And the French circular of 1920 affirmed that 'education is the very foundation of colonial policy'; that its effect should be to increase colonial industrial output among the masses, provide subordinate leaders in government, industry and the army, and develop an interest in co-operating with French policies; that teaching programs and methods should be adapted 'to local needs and to the mentalities of the different races, since the application of programs on an identical and uniform basis in all situations is a grave error condemned by experience'; and that education, while allowing for the production of a highly selected elite with 'access to the higher spheres of learning and to the complete development of personality', should, for the mass of pupils, above all, be practical and realistic in character.[60]

During the 1930's the British Advisory Committee supported three basic practices that accorded well with their fundamental statement of 1925. They advocated the use of the vernacular as the language of instruction, particularly at the primary school level, and urged the need to develop and multiply text materials in the vernaculars. They argued the case for grants-in-aid for any efficient school, and lent their support to missionary schools as a means of spreading education as widely as possible. And they firmly advised the training and use of indigenous educational officials and committees in the development of as thoroughgoing a partnership between Europeans and locals as it was possible to achieve.[61]

In many British colonies throughout the world it was difficult to insist on compulsory education. In Malaya, Ceylon, and Tonga where compulsion was effective, figures for attendance at school were distinctly higher than those in other colonies. Many colonial administrators felt that there was not enough money to pay for the additional teachers that compulsory education would require, and that general public feeling in their colony favoured voluntary attendance.[62] The Advisory Committee was anxious to work towards the effective introduction of compulsory education for at least a four-year course of primary education in all colonies. They quoted with approval an enigmatic statement of the Punjab government that 'Compulsion can be effective only if it is voluntary',[63] and suggested ways in which the efforts and interest of the local community could be more thoroughly engaged. Local support and sufficient finance were two prerequisites to compulsory education. Governments, however, continued to provide comparatively expensive compulsory education for Europeans without which they would not have been able to attract suitable European staff to the public and private services in the colonies.

In 1935 the Advisory Committee made its second major statement on educational policy when it issued its *Memorandum on the Education of African Communities*. The new statement was consistent with the 1925 policy, and was principally an expansion of its idea of developing native culture and initiative. The school was to be a vital part of the process of social change that was taking place in the colonial communities. Its program was to be 'part of a more comprehensive program directed to the improvement of the total life of the community'.[64] There should therefore be a closer connection between educational, economic, agricultural, health, and other social policies in every colony in order to achieve the most effective rural reconstruction. The school should be

[56] W.B. Mumford, 'Comparison of the colonial policies of the three nations', *The Year Book of Education*, 1935, Evans, London, 1935, p. 846.

[57] Tanganyika Territory, *Conference between Government and Missions; Report of the Proceedings*, Education Office, Dar es Salaam, 1925, p. 3.

[58] Frederick J. Clatworthy, *The Formulation of British Colonial Policy 1923-1948*, University of Michigan, School of Education, 1971, pp. 128, 137.

[59] D.G. Scanlon (ed.), Traditions in African Education, Teachers College, Columbia University, New York, 1964, p. 142.

[60] Paul Crouzet, 'Education in the French colonies', in I.L. Kandel (ed.), *Educational Yearbook 1931*, Teachers College, Columbia University, New York, 1932. pp. 272-6.

[61] Great Britain, Colonial Office, Advisory Committee on Education in the Colonies, *Memorandum on Grants by Government in aid of certain kinds of Educational Institutions*, Misc. no. 417, 1930; *ibid.*, *Memorandum on Educational Grants-in-Aid*. Colonial no. 84. M.H.S.O., London, 1933; *ibid.*, *Memorandum on the Education of African Communities*, Colonial no. 103. H.M.S.O., London, 1935.

[62] Great Britain, Colonial Office, Advisory Committee on Education in the Colonies, *Compulsory Education*, 19/33, 1933, memo., pp. 3-5.

[63] *ibid.*, 2, p. 3.

[64] Great Britain, Colonial Office, Advisory Committee on Education in the Colonies, *Memorandum on the Education of African Communities*, Colonial no. 103, H.M.S.O., London, 1935, p. 2.

related closely to the interests and traditions of the indigenous people and should also act as an interpreter of the change and a handmaiden of the progress that was taking place in colonial society by providing opportunity for new skills to be learned, by providing new incentives, by emphasising the sense of mutual social obligation, and by fostering an intelligent interest in the local environment. Local teachers must be trained to these responsibilities, and a greater emphasis must be placed on adult education and especially on the currently lagging education of women. Fundamental to success was the willing and whole-hearted participation of the native communities and co-operatives whose initiative and self-help must be encouraged. Important also was the special preparation of selected persons in methods of rural reconstruction and research.

Although, as they pointed out, their recommendations were consistent with and an extension of their 1925 memorandum, the Advisory Committee regarded their proposals as an advocacy of a new type of education. 'We have tried to show,' they wrote, 'that a new type of Education is needed involving far-reaching changes in practice.'[65] Their statement was an acknowledgment that their policies were many steps ahead of what was actually happening in the colonies. In a few places such as in Achimota College, and in the Jeanes village school experiments in Kenya, their ideas were operating. And they had come to realise that Africa, through economic pressure, was changing rapidly, and that education would have to take a form and content to match and help direct the reconstruction that was taking place.

The committee took this idea further in its 1944 statement, *Mass Education in African Society*. The committee was, at that time, affected by the urgencies of World War II and was under the persuasive influence of one of its numbers, Sir Fred Clarke, an educator interested in the progressive reconstruction of society by the use of collective and co-operative processes. Community education was the approach to which the committee had declared itself to have been long committed. In the *Mass Education* memorandum it affirmed that, if the life of the community was to be improved, 'measures must be taken for the education of the mass of the community, more systematic and energetic than any which were contemplated in the past'.[66] Schemes of education must cover the whole of the community, the young of both sexes, the adolescent, and the adult; they must be mutually supporting parts of the one program of mass education. The committee was conscious of the great acceleration of the pace of social change and of the need for social and civic responsibility in the development and planning of the changes. They saw too the coming widening of local loyalties into the force of nationalism in the various colonial territories. Hence they concluded the urgent necessity for the following goals:

- Universal schooling for children 'within a measurable time';
- The spread of literacy among adults with widespread provision for libraries and appropriate literature;
- Mass education of the community planned and supported by the local community;
- The co-ordination of welfare and mass education plans.

The committee analysed some of the mass education work in the U.S.S.R, China, India, and the Netherlands East Indies, discussed ways of making mass education a people's movement, suggested techniques for promoting adult literacy, and demonstrated ways of making an integral link between literacy, economic progress, and social welfare.

Education for Citizenship in Africa, published in 1948, was the fourth and final memorandum of the Advisory Committee in the series of general policy statements which enlarged the 1925 concept of adapting education to the needs of the colonial peoples into the rich and comprehensive idea of mass community education suitable for life in the modern world. During the war years and subsequently it had repeatedly been proclaimed that democratic responsible self-government was the aim which Britain had in view for all the colonies. It was necessary, therefore, to attune education to this objective, and that is what the Advisory Committee had consistently urged. In their 1948 memorandum they specifically examined the principles and the techniques for accomplishing that purpose in the African colonies.

The colonial peoples, they pointed out, had to pass through in one generation a development that had taken two full and busy centuries in the western nations. It was not enough to train efficient workmen and professionals. Education had to produce 'men and women as responsible citizens of a free country'.[67] The committee re-emphasised their view that education should be based on local cultural foundations, and that the native heritage should continue throughout all levels of education to play an important part. They emphasised the need to study indigenous institutions, and to show that the western democratic heritage is not that of merely a benign central government monopolising, as it may seem in the colonies, all the important initiatives, but of individual and local effort combining judiciously with central government.

Western culture, trade, and education had been disruptive forces in

[65] *ibid.*, p. 20.

[66] Great Britain, Colonial Office, Advisory Committee on Education in the Colonies, *Mass Education in African Society*, Colonial no. 186, H.M.S.O., London, 1944, p. 6.

[67] Great Britain, Colonial Office, Advisory Committee on Education in the Colonies, *Education for Citizenship in Africa*, Colonial no. 216, H.M.S.O., London, 1948, p. 5.

the colonial areas, and, in particular, had tended to separate the younger from the older generations. Democracy required for its adequate performance a temper of mind which embraced traits such as a respect for the individual, confidence in one's fellow-citizens, a strong sense of public duty as well as a well-informed, practical, and straight-thinking intelligence. These were very largely traits of character, and the committee felt that the first emphasis in citizenship education should be placed on character training. Though 'good citizenship may be described as a way of living rather than as a body of knowledge',[68] basic skills and knowledge were still necessary. These might be acquired by studying local social and economic activities and governmental machinery. In particular, it was important that students of all ages, from infant to adult, should be involved in a practical way in some kinds of public activity. Students should also be encouraged to discuss controversial political questions, to practise and value clear thinking, to study their own traditions and the European impact on their life, to understand the nature and uses of modern science, and to use their knowledge of arithmetic, handicrafts, and health in understanding and improving public and domestic practices. Teachers should encourage and enter into the development of clubs, societies, and youth and adult organisations that might contribute to some aspect of education for citizenship.

Adult courses in democratic government and leadership were of great importance and should be associated with the extension of the responsibilities of local government and the growth of co-operative work for the improvement of the local community. More widespread adult education, and a greater supply of detailed information from government officials were necessary. Above all, the greatest attention should be given to the training of teachers. A great deal was to be asked of them. They had to be well-informed and professionally skilled and, most importantly, they had to have the qualities of mind and character necessary for the democratic citizen so that they could teach both the importance and the nature of good citizenship by the example of their lives.

The Advisory Committee's views, expressed in the four memoranda of 1925, 1935, 1944, and 1948, were before their time, but they were also in an important sense behind the times.

By 1925 the African communities had passed the point where they would be satisfied with the adaptive kind of schooling advocated by the committee. They wanted the western education that western children were getting, not a second-best specially diluted for African children. It was not until the 1960's when the colonies were independent states able to make up their own educational prescription, not afraid of dilution at the hands of European masters, that they came to see, for their present circumstances, some of the virtues of the Advisory Committee's policy and the possibility of marrying its views to their own.

Educational Developments in the British African Colonies, Post-1920. Up to the 1940's there were four principal developments in the British African colonies.

First, as the Advisory Committee suggested, there was increased co-operation between missions and government. Joint educational advisory committees were set up with representatives from the government, missions, settlers, and sometimes Africans, and the colonial government encouraged and supported the missionary effort. Grants-in-aid from the government to the missions in support of their schools had been made in the late nineteenth century in all the West African colonies; in the 1920's financial support of efficient non-government, mainly mission schools became the practice in all African colonies. These schools thereby became subject to government inspection and regulation.

Secondly, government departments of education were built up and government activity in education was expanded. A few government schools and embryonic government departments of education were in existence in the West African colonies before World War I; in the 1920's each of the others followed suit and steadily built up their schools. The government departments tended to use their influence to get the missions to put into operation the policies and practices suggested by the Advisory Committee. Encouragement, for example, was given to the Jeanes school movement that used village schools as the principal centre for the improvement of the educational, medical, and economic welfare of the community. They were introduced, from the southern states of the U.S.A., into Kenya in 1925 and spread through many parts of Africa, and may be regarded as forerunners of the later UNESCO programs of fundamental education. In the matter of establishing their own schools for Africans, government education departments were concerned less with mass and more with elite levels of education. Though government primary schools were set up, the main effort at that level was left to the missions, and in Nigeria during the 1930's a number of government schools were actually transferred to missions. Secondary education was developed slowly and cautiously. In the Gold Coast, for example, although the government had, in 1925, enthusiastically, founded Achimota College as a highly selective, residential secondary school which would combine an African with a European curriculum, and the venture prospered, by 1950 there were still only two government secondary schools. In Uganda Makerere College was started in 1922 as a vocational school, developed general secondary courses, and remained at the end of the 1930's the only school in the whole of East Africa offering a full secondary education.

Thirdly, there was a small expansion in facilities for the higher education of Africans consistent with a mild government interest in the

---

[68]   *ibid.*, p. 18.

matter. By 1940 four colleges in the British territories offered some tertiary level work. Fourah Bay was a missionary college, founded in 1827 in Sierra Leone, preparing students for degrees in theology and arts at Durham University. Of the other three, Achimota in the Gold Coast and Makerere in Uganda, though basically secondary schools, provided courses at various levels and catered for a few university level students. The fourth, Yaba Higher College, was started in 1932 by the Nigerian government and, for very small numbers, offered training in medicine, agriculture, teaching, and engineering at a junior professional level. In most colonies, government departments ran training courses for staff in the areas of public works, health, and agriculture. In Nigeria a number of small specialist colleges were established for that purpose. During World War II a special commission was set up to report on higher education in West Africa. This Elliott Commission reported in 1945 and suggested a moderate extension of university facilities. In consequence, two new university colleges were established, one in the Gold Coast, and the other, incorporating Yaba, at Ibadan in Nigeria in 1948. No other tertiary level institutions were developed in the British colonies before the 1950's.

The other interesting feature of the period was the strange contrast between the reluctance of the colonial governments in educational matters and the enthusiasm of many African groups for expanded and improved educational facilities along western lines. The slow governmental progress in African education was the result partly of low governmental aspirations in the matter. Education before World War II and even up to 1950 was not regarded as a matter of central importance by the government. In the 1930's colonial revenues were hit by the depression, and then subsequently in the early 1940's by World War II. The government Departments of Education, never generously financed, were squeezed more than ever. Grants-in-aid were cut, teachers' salaries reduced, many teachers left the service, and whatever projects a director may have had for expansion were dropped. There was, throughout the whole of the 1930's and 1940's a considerable gap between the goals that the Advisory Committee's memoranda might have stimulated the colonial education departments to seek, and the reality of the social and financial situation.

Education, nevertheless, for the children of British settlers and government officers continued to expand and, where it was undertaken by governments, expenditure on it was maintained at a rate per head much in excess of that spent on African education. In Kenya, for example, in 1936, the 1,800 European children cost the government thirty-three times more per head to educate in their separate schools than did the eighty-six thousand Africans in government maintained or assisted schools, and, by 1950, whereas almost all of the European children were able to gain admittance to an academic secondary school, there were available for the

youth of the nine million African population only eleven secondary schools recognised by the government. It was not until 1948 that government expenditure on African education in Kenya exceeded that on European education.

(iv) Indigenous Educational Efforts

Though, by and large, native reaction to the missions and their attempts at education had initially been somewhat cautious, some well-known groups had welcomed western education from the beginning, e.g. the Buganda, Luo, Kikuyu, and Malawi. The welcome to education led to a welcome to the missions but also to a criticism of them when they could not or would not deliver the desired education. This criticism became apparent before World War I, and in the 1920's was strongly voiced in several areas. The most well-organised expression of it was among the Kikuyu in Kenya. They wanted more English, more technical education to produce skilled artisans, and more secondary schools, and they wanted modernisation to proceed under African control. They believed that missionaries and government were going slow with education. 'They wanted to progress and go ahead like the Europeans,' one of the pioneers of the independent school movement said.[69] But the colonial government at that time was in no hurry. It had a gradualist approach to development and, following the policy of the Colonial Office Advisory Committee, it formulated a philosophy of preserving native traditions and building on them in a manner which seemed relevant to white educators. But the Africans thought a western curriculum of English and science was relevant. There was therefore much black political protest against the adoption of the Advisory Committee's policy, against elementary manual and agricultural work, and against European 'selective giving'. Especially was it pointed out that the government money spent on the education of white children, and the range of education available to them, vastly exceeded the resources devoted to black children.

Thus there developed a campaign characterised by African attempts to gain control of missionary education within the church, African attempts to get government schools established independent of missionary control, and African attempts to establish independent schools free from both missionary and government control. In the 1920's the educationally inefficient catechist teacher and the out-schools which had been established on land granted by the community, often with little association with the central mission station, were discouraged, as central schools were

[69] T.O. Ranger, African Attempts to Control Education in East and Central Africa 1900-1939, *Past and Present*, 32, December 1965, 67. See also J. Anderson, *The Struggle for the School*, Longmans, London, 1970.

improved and concentrated on in a drive for greater educational efficiency. This move deprived Africans of much of the educational influence they had exercised over the conduct of the school in their community. Many communities struggled to retain their schools and enlarge their influence. The conflict made for increased resentment. In some areas, especially among the Kikuyu and Malawi, there was a demand, even early in the century, for the government to take over missionary schools. It was argued that natives paid taxes to the government and they, therefore, expected the government to run the services, especially the schools, for which they paid. In the 1920's when local councils were set up, e.g. in Kenya and Tanga, to encourage local government, some groups of Africans wanted to run schools. A few schools were built under local government control but for the most part did not flourish. The colonial government insisted that they conform to Education Department rules; they were poorly financed, especially in depression times; and they were harassed by the missions. Out of such frustrations came the independent schools which were formed at various times between 1900 and 1939 in most of the colonies, and were often, at the time or subsequently, associated with breakaway religious groups.

In the Gold Coast, which throughout the colonial period was the most educationally advanced of the British colonies, there had been a number of schools founded by Africans before the end of the nineteenth century. Notably, several secondary schools had been started. Because of the continued slowness of the government and the missions during the twentieth century in establishing secondary education, many more African secondary schools, some ephemeral and of varying quality, were brought into being. This was especially the case after World War II when many who had completed primary school were looking for the higher qualifications that employers were then starting to demand. By 1950 there were forty to fifty of these secondary schools.[70]

The most striking of the African efforts was among the Kikuyu of Kenya where independent elementary schools were started in the 1920's in the hope of accelerating their progress in western education. The movement flourished throughout the 1930's and by 1937 had over seven thousand pupils in fifty-four schools. At the time when they were closed by the military emergency in 1953 because of their supposed connection with political activities, there were not less than two hundred, some of which had become junior secondary schools. The most outstanding foundation of the movement was Githungiri Teachers' College, in which Jomo Kenyatta, the future president of independent Kenya, was a teacher; it was founded in 1939 and offered courses eventually in primary, secondary, teacher and adult education. It was a brave attempt to build a system parallel to the government organisation, and many of the future leaders of Kenya were products of it.[71]

At the same time, in all the colonial education departments the number of well-educated Africans who were rising to positions of importance was increasing. The main policy-making and the highest executive posts remained in European hands, but slowly there was being built up a body of middle level administrators within the civil service who matched the Europeans in pedagogical and administrative skill.

(v) Overseas Education for Africans

An important part in producing high level professionals in the colonies was played by organisations and individuals who sponsored overseas study. Eventually also governments were induced to provide scholarships for study abroad. In the course of the twentieth century young men went in increasing numbers to universities in Europe and America to study arts, science, law, and medicine, and returned to a professional and sometimes a political life in their own country. In 1945, for example, there were about 150 Nigerians studying in universities in the United Kingdom. By 1953 the number had risen to seven hundred, and there were just over two thousand students from West and East Africa studying abroad in the universities of English-speaking countries.[72] Abroad they met other young talented people from their own and other colonies and found that they shared common problems. They met a greater range of political thinkers than in their colonial environment and formed alliances that, on their return, the colonial authorities often regarded as radical. They met parliamentarians and civil servants on their home ground and learnt something of the forces that operated and might be manipulated in their home background. They met and studied with people in academic circles who stimulated their questioning, widened the range of their thinking, and taught and encouraged them to examine in depth the nature, aims, and practices of imperial government. They returned to their own countries with greater knowledge and confidence, equipped to make their way, if they so wished, into positions of greater influence. Many did this. And out of the returning students came most of the leaders of the independence movements and of the early independent governments.

(vi) General Assessment of Colonial Education in Africa

When the administrative practices of the various European colonisers throughout Africa are examined, there seems to have been remarkably little

[70] P. J. Foster, *Education and Social Change in Ghana*, Routledge & Kegan Paul, London, 1965, pp. 101-3, 166-70.

[71] J. Anderson, *op.cit.*, pp. 112ff., and J.R. Sheffield, *Education in Kenya*, Teachers College, Columbia University, New York, 1973, pp. 15ff.

[72] C.E. Carrington, 'The growth of an educated class', *International Affairs*, 32, 4, October 1956, pp. 453-4; W. Hailey, *An African Survey*, rev.ed., 1956, Oxford University Press, 1957, pp. 118ff.

difference between them in the impact they made on the Africans.[73] The French, early in the century especially, spoke much of assimilation, and the British of association and then of adaptation. Neither, however, was consistent, and both managed to vary their practices from time to time, from place to place, and from governor to governor, even within the bounds of a single colony. Similarly, between their educational policies there was little to choose, and in their practices still less. Charton, the Inspector-General of Education in French West Africa would have been an admirable member of the British Colonial Office Advisory Committee.

All colonial powers assumed that European education, culture, and morality were of a superior brand, with the result that the more the Africans were exposed to European educational influence, the more they were insensibly adapted into patterns of European behaviour so that, had the system been perfect, the elite, the most complete products of the system, would have become Black Englishmen, Black Frenchman, Black Belgians, and Black Italians. And some did. The system, however was not perfect. It had three flaws or saving graces, depending upon one's basic views. First, there was a body of opinion, expressed especially in policy statements, that, despite what many practising missionaries and government teachers thought and actually did, there were considerable virtues in the African way of life that should be maintained and welded with the European offering into a new tradition. Second, even if the government settlers and missions had been whole-hearted in trying to make Europeans out of Africans, their educational efforts were not efficient enough and their work was so financially starved that they could not possibly have achieved such an objective. In the third place, the principal element by which educators placed most store, moral education, was severely flawed. Clarke in the early thirties drew attention to the 'double mind' in African education. Westerners, he suggested, were prone to assert their brotherhood with Africans and, in practice, to shrink from even the easiest implications of it, to speak of civilising the natives and, in practice, merely to propagandise them, to plead for the conservation and adaptation of indigenous customs and, in practice, to undervalue and undermine them.[74] Moral education, though greatly emphasised in all statements of educational policy by missions and government, was no easy task.

Missionary contact wooed the indigenous people away from their established sanctions for conduct, and in their place put a half-believed religion. Governments overthrew customary and traditional allegiances and legal procedures, and substituted maddeningly paternalistic attitudes and European justice. Both government and missions preached the virtues of honour, humility, and brotherhood and, all too frequently, provided examples of broken promises, arrogant behaviour, and racial discrimination. There were, of course, understanding missionaries and

wise civil servants, but there were many who were not. One of the useful and interesting things found out by the colonial subjects who studied in the metropolitan country was that there were many people there who were not like missionaries or colonial civil servants, and there the young colonial learnt much about socialism, freedom of speech, and trade union organisation that was denied him in his own country.

The moral educator had to induce the African to accept intellectually and to act on a pattern of values which, while they had many features in common, had nevertheless been worked out for an alien and imposed civilisation. Moreover, it was a pattern with which the behaviour of the civilisers themselves was not wholly consistent. It is scarcely to be wondered at, therefore, that in most colonial areas there was tension and sometimes breakdown in moral standards until the time arrived when the indigenous people themselves deliberately sought to bring themselves into the western way of thinking, and actively started to build a reconstructed culture. This seems to have happened in many African colonies towards the end of the first decade of the twentieth century. During the 1920's and 1930's the pace appreciably quickened.

By then there was a small number of well-educated Africans who aspired to a more prominent role in the building of their new culture. They were anxious to see that their fellow-countrymen did not receive an inferior education. 'There is,' wrote one of them, an East African in a British colony, 'a pathetic hunger for education in the hearts of thousands of Africans. If they feel they are being fobbed off with a second-rate or even a second-best education, good enough for blacks but not for whites, there will rightly be trouble.'[75] He pointed out that education had been overwhelmingly in the hands of missions, and that it had been shown in civilised countries that the education of the whole population could not be satisfactorily undertaken by charitable organisations. In many parts teachers had insisted upon using the vernacular, and education had been at a very low level. A determined government could establish a worthwhile system in a short time which would make English, which is the official language, universally known, and provide 'a sound education similar to that given to the children of other races'.[76] At that time, the author pointed out, only about one per cent of the population were literate; in consequence, the people could not read and understand the law, did not send representatives to the legislature, did not elect their own chiefs, although they used to do so before the British arrived, and suffered from a

[73] See M. Semakula Kiwanuka, 'Colonial Policies and Administrations in Africa: the Myths of the Contrasts', *African Historical Studies*, 3, 2, November 1970, pp. 295-315.

[74] F. Clarke, 'The double mind in African education', *Africa*, 5, 2, April 1932, pp. 158-68.

[75] P.G. Mockerie, *op.cit.*, p. 10.

[76] *ibid.*, p. 59.

number of irksome discriminatory practices, not the least of which was the receipt of an inferior and piecemeal education in poorly equipped schools with untrained teachers. The Africans, nevertheless, constituted 98 per cent of the population and contributed in taxation the great bulk of the government's revenue. From West Africa support was given to these views by Nnamdi Azikiwe, who was to become the first president of an independent Nigeria.

The African, he pointed out, 'is human, is intellectually alert just as the average European, Asiatic, or American. What he needs is an opportunity to demonstrate his capabilities.'[77] This was demonstrated by the achievements of Africans in European and American universities during the last fifty years. The notion of placing an emphasis in African education on industrial and agricultural work instead of an academic and literary approach was 'maliciously false and a retrograde tendency'.[78] It implied that Africans should be content with menial tasks and should not seek economic, social, and political equality with the European. The African who was interested in politics was branded an 'agitator', and he was disciplined for stepping out of his place. Nor had he the opportunity for higher appointment in commerce and industry if he should manage to progress to the higher levels of technical training. 'The more widespread education becomes, the greater becomes the black man's antagonism to what he believes to be an economic and political system designed to maintain him in serfdom.'[79]

Education, in Azikiwe's view, should not neglect agriculture and technical education but should be a wholesome mixture of literacy, technical, and moral education; elementary education should be compulsory, and mass education for adults should be encouraged by governments. The existing second-best education was associated with the myth of the mental inferiority of the native races disseminated by racists and pseudo-scientists.

Azikiwe's book *Renascent Africa*, published in 1937, summed up the new aspirations in an appeal to the youth of the continent to make a new and greater future for the African: 'And I see him a changed man. He is a Renascent African. He is no longer mis-educated. He is a man.'[80]

---

[77] Ben N. Azikiwe, 'How shall we educate the African', *Journal of the African Society*, 33,131, April 1934, pp. 143.

[78] *ibid.*, p. 145.

[79] *ibid.*, p.148, quoting from an anonymous source.

[80] Nnamdi Azikiwe, *Renascent Africa*, Cass, London, 1968 (1937).

PART THREE

EDUCATIONAL RECONSTRUCTION AND EXPANSION 1945-75

Students at a modern university in northern Africa. Photograph by Afrique Photo/Picou

An elementary school class in an Andean village in South America. Photograph by M. Vathier

In developing countries in Africa, South America and Asia, a striking contrast is apparent between the rudimentary education available in some parts and the highly sophisticated facilities in others.

Photographs from a series of colour slides produced by UNESCO for International Education Year 1970.

INTRODUCTION

The post-World War II period began, like the post-World War I period, with great aspirations generated by wartime expectations. The comprehensive Butler Education Act in England, the utopian report *Education for All American Youth* and the Langevin reform commission in France were all products of the year 1944, as World War II was drawing to a close. They were among the first examples of the plans for reconstruction and expansion that most nations prepared in the immediate post-war years.

The thirty years following World War II was an era of nation-building. First came the reconstruction of war-devastated areas in Europe and Asia, and the opportunity to build new communist societies in eastern Europe and to recast some aspects of life in the western democracies. Soon afterwards, throughout the 1950's and 1960's, a whole new world of national states came into being. Old colonial territories in Asia and Africa attained independence and began to create their own political, economic, and social structures.

AN ERA OF PLANNING

The world, then, for some two decades, was divided into three main groups: the western democratic nations of Europe and America; the communist bloc of the U.S.S.R., eastern Europe, and, for a while, China; and the third world, aligned with neither of the other groups and consisting mainly of the newly independent countries and the Arab world.

The communist group had long been committed, since the U.S.S.R.'s first five year plan in 1929, to regulating their own development by working to a succession of formal and comprehensive plans. The western nations after World War II began also to plan in looser and less elaborate ways. The third world entered with vigour on a course of planning that left few aspects of life untouched. Education was an obvious subject for planning. As the years proceeded, studies of the relationship of education to national progress multiplied, and constant efforts were made to relate various aspects of educational development to economic growth and

social welfare. Education was seen to be a vital ingredient in the complex process of developing new minds, new skills, new bodies of manpower, and new patterns of behaviour in the many new societies and nations of the second half of the twentieth century.

EXPLOITATION, CONSERVATION, AND EDUCATION

Associated with the widespread interest in national planning was a greatly intensified awareness of the vast increase in the material and human resources of the twentieth century nations. The world's capacity to exploit deposits of fuels and minerals, to improve the production of food, to invent new technological processes, to control disease, as well as to create havoc and destruction and to recover quickly from it, had increased with every passing decade of the twentieth century. It had become particularly noticeable in the post-Depression and post-World War II years and was highlighted by a number of spectacular achievements. In 1945 Hiroshima was devastated by an atomic bomb; twelve years later the first space-ship, Sputnik, was successfully launched in 1957; and in another twelve years, in 1969, man landed on the moon. The rapid material exploitation of new areas in new nations, the development of nuclear power, and the beginning of the exploration of outer space were striking indications of human capacity available to those who had sufficient economic strength and educational resource. Of similar importance was the recognition of the increased capacity, through the control of education and various arms of the mass media, to manipulate the thoughts and actions of human beings.

Exploitation, both material and human, brought its reaction. By the 1960's strong contrary movements had been built up. The first was a conservation movement which aimed at the husbanding of natural resources whose stocks might be depleted by excessive consumption, and at preserving, for reasons of health and recreation, features of the natural environment which was being eroded and defaced in the interests of economic growth. The second was a defence of human integrity, on the one hand, from excessive invasion and manipulation by those who might control the various means of persuasion and indoctrination, and, on the other hand, from insufficient and unequal opportunity for development and expression resulting from positive discrimination or disadvantageous circumstances. Education was called upon by various interested groups to redress the balance in each case. Environmental and social studies became more popular in the programs of formal schools, and were the subject of much attention by adult and informal educational agencies.

NEW STRUCTURES DEVELOPED FOR EDUCATION

In the post-World War II period educators began to break out from the old moulds within which they had hitherto tried to carry through the adjustments and reforms that the conditions and ideas of the twentieth century had imperatively demanded. An important innovation was the development of international educational agencies, of which the United Nations Educational, Scientific and Cultural Organisation (UNESCO) was the principal one. They channelled educational assistance from one nation to another, they brought into general public discussion the principal contemporary educational problems throughout the world, they established training centres and educational experiments to benefit the nations of selected regions, and they encouraged, helped, and guided many of the underdeveloped countries with many aspects of their educational planning.

Literacy was the one overwhelming problem of all underdeveloped countries. Persistent efforts, in the third quarter of the century, were made to overcome it by the rapid spread of primary schooling, and, for adults, by experimenting with a new educational structure, development education, which took the four elements of agricultural improvement, health care, self-government, and literacy education, and built a simple, practical program by relating them together and demonstrating how a better life could be achieved by literate people. At a more advanced level of formal education, the selective tradition, inherited from European models, was abandoned for the most part in underdeveloped countries and a single-track system was substituted of primary school leading to comprehensive secondary school, often closely connected with some form of productive work.

In western Europe the elitist secondary school pattern gradually gave way to comprehensive schools as secondary education for all began to become a reality during this period. The upsurge of students completing secondary education and proceeding to tertiary level brought about the establishment of many new universities, some of which struck out on non-traditional paths in trying to provide their work with greater relevance. In the United States, the Junior College broadened out, some fifty years after its establishment, into a Community College providing vocational, recreational, and general education to increasing numbers of students of a great range of qualifications, attainments, ages, and interests throughout the community which supported the college. In other developed countries a similar institution also began to emerge, between the secondary school and university, working with a wide brief to cope with the varied and increasing educational expectations of modern communities.

At the other end of the scale there was a realisation that many were still being left behind. In the 1960's therefore extensive programs of compensatory education were launched and much research was concentrated on the causes and treatment of educational under-achievement in many countries.

CURRICULUM INNOVATION

The changes in content that the inter-war period had set firmly in train were continued after World War II. The launching of Sputnik intensified the rivalry between the communist and western democratic groups, and led the western countries to question the efficacy of their educational systems. The U.S.A., in particular, initiated a review of the school curriculum, and began to develop new mathematics and science programs. Other countries, western, communist, and non-aligned, followed suit. Within a few years there were numerous programs operating in all subjects and at all school levels throughout the world. In all probability, there has never been as swift a transformation of school subject-matter as occurred in the 1960's. Interest in innovation of the same kind was maintained into the 1970's.

The changes which endured and which teachers tried persistently to put into practice tended to have three characteristics. In the first place, they were an attempt to encourage pupils to discover facts for themselves, to think for themselves as researchers, to seek to define problems and issues and try to work out solutions; in the second place, they did not settle on any one approach but suggested opportunities for exploring the desired content by combinations of individual assignment, group projects, and various other means; in the third place, particular encouragement was given to the pupils to express themselves, on the topics they were studying, by extensive discussion, by creative writing or art, or by whatever was the appropriate form. In short, the heart of the innovatory movement of the 1960's and 1970's lay in its emphasis on problem-solving, on the use of multi-techniques, and on opportunity for active expression by the pupils. They were the characteristics of the kind of teaching that was designed to try to equip students to deal with a world of change.

Citizens of the twentieth century had always been conscious of living in a time of rapid and radical change and none were more sensitive to the need to cope with a changing world than those who lived in the 1970's. Progressive educators from early in the century had perceived the need to develop curricula and educational methods relevant to a changing society, and had been especially interested in encouraging problem-solving, expressive activities, and the mastery of a variety of investigative skills. As a distinct movement, progressive education declined in the 1950's. It is a measure of the progressives' impact and relevance that the essence of their ideas was absorbed into the mainstream of educational activity, and continued to enlighten the next generation.

A Policy for Education in 1975

The conditions of political, social, and economic life in our country today make it necessary to change our general view of the system of education in order to prepare the way to the France of tomorrow. . . .

The schools' most lively critics accuse it of reflecting and reproducing the society of its period. Even if it is true that all educational systems are conceived and do function within the constraints of some kind of society, working in phase with it, one must recognize that there is still a large area of choice within the ideas and practices of the society; there is no country in the world where students and teachers are merely conformists. . . . It is quite impossible to deny the role of the School in the transformation of Society. The men which it moulded yesterday are those who have formed the world of today. . . .

Education is, in fact, a feature of civilization; it is involved in the transformation of the modern world.

Necessarily affected by the changes, but also having an effect on them; how could one imagine that the School could remain unchanging? . . .

In 1975, it is essential to produce a coherent and comprehensive plan through which one can maintain continuity with past development, can settle on steps towards future change, and can leave room for subsequent adjustment. . . .

It is a matter therefore of creating for the last quarter of the century, an educational system which combines adequate opportunity for innovation with judicious control.

M. Haby here sums up the cautiously progressive view of education characteristic of French Education in the 1970's.

René Haby, Minister of Education, France in *Pour une Modernisation du Système Educatif*, Paris, 1975.

CHAPTER 12

REMAKING SECONDARY AND TERTIARY EDUCATION IN EUROPE, U.S.A. AND JAPAN, 1945-75

SUMMARY

Rethinking Secondary Education

   (i)   Sweden
   (ii)   France
         (a) Langevin-Wallon Commission
         (b) Classes Nouvelles
         (c) Reform of 1959
         (d) Collèges d'Enseignement Secondaire
  (iii) West Germany
         (a) Plans for Reform
  (iv) England
         (a) Tripartite Division of Secondary Education
         (b) Grammar School
         (c) Modern School
         (d) Comprehensive Secondary School
   (v)   Secondary Education in the U.S.A.
         (a) Education for ALL American Youth
         (b) End of the Progressive Education Association
         (c) The Conant Reports
         (d) Federal Education Acts
         (e) Expansion of Secondary Education
  (vi) Japan
         (a) Post-war Reconstruction
         (b) Old v. New Values
         (c) Education and Economic Growth
         (d) Reform of School Organisation and Curricula

Redesigning Tertiary Education

   (i)   Growth in Enrolment
   (ii)   Structural Reform in Europe
  (iii) Tertiary Expansion in the United States
  (iv) Student Unrest in the 1960's
   (v)   Issues in Tertiary Education

In the quarter-century following World War II four educational developments in western countries stood out:

- The change in the structure and function of secondary education;
- The expansion of tertiary education;
- The increase in the application of research to education;
- A substantial movement for curriculum reform.

The first two are the subject of this chapter; the other two will be dealt with in the next.

It was widely realised by the 1940's that primary and secondary education were not two types of education but two successive stages in an educational process, with a change of stage at about the age of twelve. It was somewhere about the 1940's that secondary education caught up with the educational thinking of the primary school. For the past twenty years the primary school had been concerned with educating children rather than with teaching particular subjects. Pupils were conceived of as active and expressive persons whose educational development was the teacher's special care. Educational development was more than intellectual cultivation or the mastery of the 3 R's; it involved also physical, emotional, and attitudinal growth. For the kind of teaching that this development required, a wide range of experiences was desirable which would give the children opportunity to learn how to solve intellectual problems and to become involved in social and aesthetic activity.

To achieve education of such a kind at the secondary level there had to be a redefinition of purposes, a replanning of the curriculum and, in the opinion of a growing number of educators and politicians in many countries, a restructuring of the school system. Substantial change appeared to be necessary, also, if the maximum opportunity was to be provided for the intellectual development of all pupils. There was an increasing sensitivity after World War II that all individuals should have as nearly equal chances as possible for furthering their education. Social legislation was rapidly extended in most European nations, and the abundant provision of education became a central part of the movement towards a welfare state. The move, however, was not merely a matter of welfare. Educational expansion was, as it had been argued at the beginning of the century, an important factor in national development. Most countries appeared to be anxious to make use, in the most effective

Figure 12.1:   Sweden: Comprehensive School Organisation (simplified), 1975.

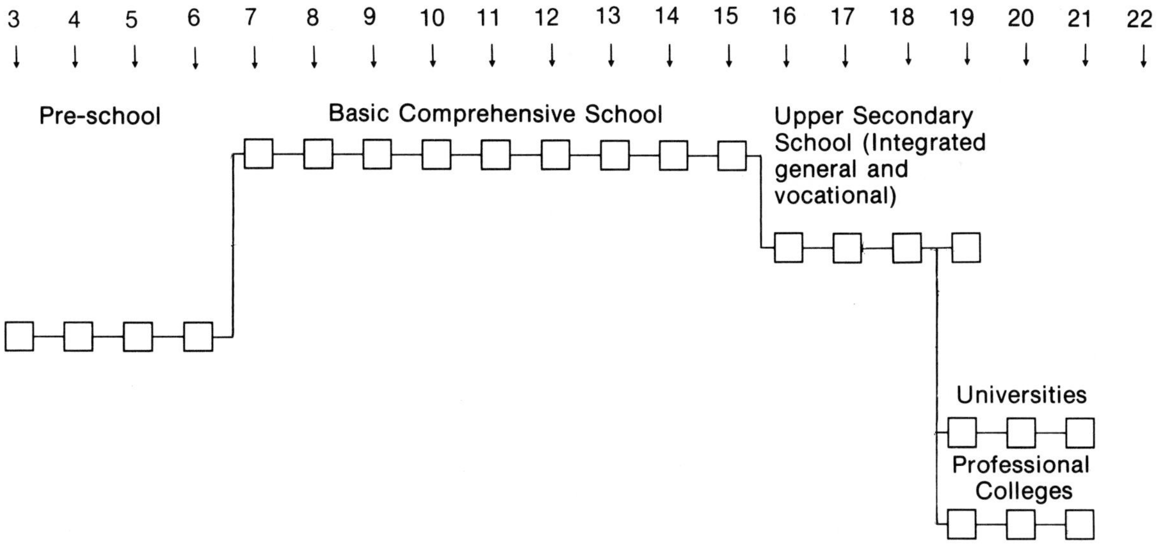

way, of all the resources of manpower that could be made available. It was important, therefore, for national welfare, as well as for social welfare, that secondary education should be extended, that it should be of a kind which would enable all the talent in the nation to profit by it and to develop through it, and that adequate tertiary education should follow it.

RETHINKING SECONDARY EDUCATION

(i) Sweden

Sweden was the pacesetter for Europe in the reform of secondary education in the 1940's and 1950's.

The forty years of discussion and argument that had been proceeding in several countries up to World War II on the desirability and the shape of secondary education for all began to come to practical fruition in the years after the war.

During the 1930's and 1940's, after an extensive reform in 1929, the country had a seven-year primary school from which transfer could be made after the fourth or sixth grade to a four- or five-year middle school, and from there to a four-year general, or three-year technical, or two-year

commercial gymnasium. Parallel to the middle schools and gymnasia was a system of six- and seven-year girls' schools.

A commission was established in 1940 which initiated research, discussion, and experimentation on educational reform, and, in 1946, recommended the establishment of a nine-year comprehensive school for pupils aged seven to sixteen. In 1950 the Swedish parliament accepted the commission's recommendation in principle, and encouraged the continuation of research and experimentation, in a substantial number of school districts, with various modes of organising comprehensive education and with a variety of curricula for the upper grades.[1]

Throughout the 1950's there was considerable dispute over the matter of school organisation. In 1956 the four-year general primary school was universally extended upward to six years, and, in 1962, to eight years with a streamed ninth year above it; the middle schools were eliminated and the gymnasium reduced to three years.

In 1970 the common program was extended throughout the whole nine-year school, and a start was made in 1971, in accordance with an earlier decision, to combine the various types of gymnasia and vocational schools into single multilateral schools. The common comprehensive

[1] For an account of some of the appropriate research see Chapter 13.

nine-year school was free and compulsory for all pupils from the age of seven to sixteen. All students took a common general course with a few electives in the last three years of school. No streaming was practised and all schools were co-educational. The integrated upper secondary school was a combination of academic and vocational schools, either streamed into two-, three-, and four-year courses, or in separate schools under the one administration. The upper secondary school was free and co-educational, and in 1975 accepted some eighty per cent of the pupils from the top form of the nine-year school. Sweden thus by the early 1970's had moved into a single-track comprehensive school system.

(ii) France

In France *Les Compagnons*, starting from World War I, in company with other reformers, had pressed throughout the 1920's and 1930's for *l'école unique* which would be a common primary school followed by a common secondary orientation period of two years. In 1936 the socialist government of Léon Blum, under the influence of Jean Zay, the Minister for Education, raised the school leaving age to fourteen, and in 1937 instituted a number of experimental orientation classes in the first year of secondary education. It was a first, small step towards a more thorough reorganisation leading perhaps to a common comprehensive secondary school. World War II, however, put an end to any further reform and the nazi occupation of France nullified the tentative moves that had so far taken place. Towards the end of the war the French government-in-exile in Algeria set up a commission which recommended compulsory education with a common program for all pupils to the age of fifteen years; on completing a common primary education, all pupils would pass into a first orientation stage of secondary education up to fifteen years, and thereafter into specialist secondary and vocational courses. Moved by that example, the French government established a commission on educational reform, chaired first by Langevin and subsequently by Wallon, which sat from 1944 to 1947.

(a) Langevin-Wallon Commission

The Langevin-Wallon Commission report was a landmark in French educational history. The general structure of the French educational system, according to Wallon, was not democratic. 'The history of France has brought into being two separate systems of institutions — those intended for the education of the bourgeoisie and those for the use of the people... Secondary education is essentially bourgeois education,

planned to suit its own needs.'[2] The problem was to devise means by which the system of primary education for the people and secondary education for the middle classes could be fused. The commission in its report criticised French education for its lack of coherent planning, for its tardiness in catching up with the social changes that had taken place in France during the last half-century, and for the out-of-date methods which it used. The school had lost touch with society and pursued its way in a closed world of its own, giving preference to wealth and the higher social classes. Transfer between primary, secondary, and technical education was difficult, and the proportion of working men's children who reached the university was infinitesimal. The schools had not profited from the developments in educational thinking and technique that the scientific study of education and progressive education had brought about, and did not give sufficient emphasis to the study of social science, critical thinking, and the cultivation of active and responsible citizenship.

The commission recommended that French education should be thoroughly reconstructed so that each individual should have the opportunity to develop his aptitudes to the utmost, that all should obtain the kind of training that would best serve the interests of the whole community, and that the work at all levels should imbue the pupils with a determination to raise the cultural level of the nation to the highest possible level.

The commission, accordingly, proposed that education should be free and compulsory from six to eighteen years of age and should be divided into three levels. After possible attendance at kindergarten between the age of two or three and six, a pupil would enter the first stage, a primary school following a course common to all until the age of eleven. At that point he would move without examination to the second level, a four-year orientation course taken by all pupils, somewhat after the style of an American junior high school. At fifteen the third level commenced. At that point the common program ceased and three types of schools took over up to the age of eighteen: an academic school with four streams — classical humanities, modern humanities, pure sciences, and applied sciences; a technical school with four streams — commercial, industrial, agricultural, and art; and an apprenticeship system of training, combining practical manual work with further general education. Beyond the secondary school level, the commission proposed a

---

[2] H. Wallon, 'The Reform of Education in France', in *France (new plans for education)*, *NEF* Monograph no. 5, London, New Education Fellowship, 1946, p. 5. P. Langevin (1872-1945) was a professor at the Collège de France. He was a distinguished physicist who became a leading member of the New Education Fellowship and chairman in 1944 of the French commission on educational reform. H. Wallon (1879-1962) succeeded Langevin as chairman of the commission in 1945. He was a professor at the Collège de France, and a well-known psychologist.

Figure 12.2: France: Langevin-Wallon Commission Proposals, 1947.

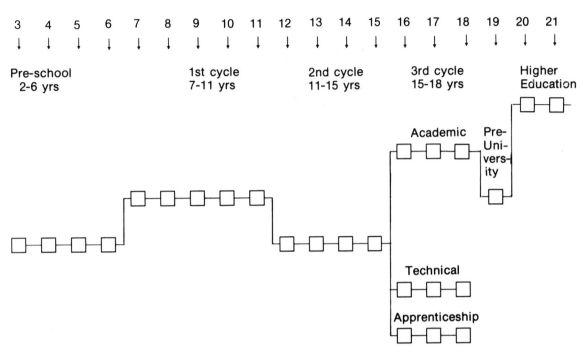

further unspecified period of work preparatory to university entrance, and a reorganisation of higher education. Throughout the various levels, attention was to be given to the diagnosis of each pupil's strengths and weaknesses, to modern methods of individual teaching, to work in small groups, and to the encouragement of creativity and social responsibility.[3]

'Instead of a scientific approach, they have preferred the delight of mere affirmation and *a priori* construction,' wrote one of the opponents in a sarcastic review of the commission's report.[4] He echoed the sentiments of many responsible citizens who continued to prefer the piecemeal tinkering of the inter-war generation to the generous, logical sweep of the commission's new broom. The force for reconstruction generated during the struggle for recovery after World War II was not strong enough, however, as *Les Compagnons* had found twenty years earlier after World War I, to nerve the French to undertake the wholesale rethinking and rebuilding of education that the commissioners declared to be necessary. The report, nevertheless, was widely studied. It was the backdrop to every educational discussion in France for the next fifteen years; it was the inspiration for experimental work with various methods

of teaching and ways of organising secondary education; and eventually it became the basis for a substantial reform that took place in 1959.

During the life of the commission, in 1945, a move had already been made to widen secondary education by converting the existing higher primary schools into secondary *collèges modernes*, and developing a form of primary school extension, the *cours complémentaires*. It was in line with the general move in European countries towards regarding secondary education as a level rather than a kind of education.[5]

(b) Classes Nouvelles

In 1945 the experimental *classes nouvelles* were launched. Three years later there were six hundred classes in two hundred secondary schools of every kind. They started at the bottom of the secondary school with *les*

---

[3] France, Ministère de l'Education Nationale, Commission ministérielle d'étude, *La Réforme de l'Enseignement*, Paris, 1947 (Project Langevin-Wallon).

[4] Pierre Boyance in *Le Monde*, 22 April, 1948, p. 5.

[5] Olive Wykes, 'France: the changing concept of *culture genérale*', in E.L. French, *Melbourne Studies in Education 1961-62*, Melbourne University Press, 1964, 31.

Sizièmes Nouvelles and gradually worked up through the *lycees* and *collèges* until there were a large number of experimental classes at all levels scattered throughout the French secondary school system. In 1953 they became known as *classes pilotes* and a number of experimental secondary schools were developed, to be called *lycées pilotes*. The *classes nouvelles* were restricted in size to twenty-five pupils, and were supported by special teacher training and conference centres, notably at Sèvres where eventually a comprehensive *lycée pilote* was established. The experimental classes provided work in the same subjects and prepared pupils for the same examinations as the traditional classes, but they attempted two things in addition. They sought to rearrange the content of studies, adapting it much more to the interests, level of development, and individual aptitudes of the pupils, and enriching the general program by including more artistic work, manual experience, and a study of the social and natural environment. They also adopted a variety of newer teaching methods; subjects were correlated, and centres of interest were developed, textbooks were eliminated and wide individual reading encouraged, small group work was stimulated, and closer relationships were built between teachers, pupils, and parents. It was a concerted attempt on a grand scale by the governmental authorities to fertilise the teaching profession and the secondary schools with the newer views of education and child development that had been emerging in Europe and America for the past fifty years and had received much attention in the United States, somewhat less in England and Germany, and scarcely any at all in France. The experiment stimulated public and professional criticism of existing secondary school programs, loosened the traditionalists' grip, and prepared the way for reforms in structure, content, and method that were ushered in by the decrees of 1959.

(c) Reform of 1959

The Fourth French Republic ended in 1958, and the reform of 1959 was one of the early acts of the de Gaullist Fifth Republic. In some measure it symbolised the new effort that France was making to come to grips with the modern world. In 1946 Albert Camus had summed up a generation of criticism from *Les Compagnons* to the Langevin-Wallon Commission when he wrote: 'The world changes, and with it mankind and France itself. French education alone has not yet changed. The children of this country are still taught to live and think in a world that has already vanished.'[6]

The 1959 reform demonstrated that the new regime was determined to put French education in touch with the needs of the world of the present without losing continuity with a cherished intellectual tradition.

The double aim inhibited thoroughgoing reform. The school leaving age was raised to sixteen to take full effect in 1969. There was to be a common primary school for pupils from six to eleven years old, who would then enter secondary education via a two-year period of orientation, except for those who were judged not fit to enter secondary education and were to continue with primary and some vocational studies until the school leaving age. After the orientation years secondary education was divided into four parts offered in different kinds of schools: a short vocational course of three years, long vocational courses of four and five years, a short general course of three years, and a long general course of five years. The long general course was a broadening of the university preparatory course offered in *lycées*. Its first two years had three streams — classical, and modified classical, both of which were, in fact, started in the first year of orientation, and modern; for the next two years there were seven streams — three classical, two modern, and two technical; for the final year leading to the second part of the final examination, the *baccalauréat*, there were five streams — philosophy, experimental sciences, mathematics, applied mathematics, and economic and human sciences.

The restructuring of 1959 was a substantial move towards the democratic concept of *l'école unique*, in that it provided for seven years of common education for the majority of pupils. The existence, however, of a primary continuation called terminal education, and the invasion of the orientation years by the classical streams of the *lycées* somewhat undermined the force of the reform. A step forward into the modern world was taken by including a range of vocational offerings in the secondary school sphere, but they were kept segregated in separate schools, and no move was made to establish a comprehensive secondary school, although some of the *lycées pilotes* had been moving in that direction.

By the beginning of the 1960's, therefore, France had responded in a modest way to the increasing demand for secondary education and for its modernisation by providing a greater number of places and a great range of offerings with an opportunity for pupils to explore and select appropriate courses. The orientation years, however, were taken in the various secondary schools to which the pupils elected to go at the end of the primary school. To make a change to another school after two years or at a later stage was, clearly, very difficult. The effect of the orientation years, according to the minister in 1963, was 'feeble', and few pupils had been able to change courses. Furthermore forty-five to fifty per cent of pupils had not entered the secondary orientation years but had remained in the primary division terminal courses. It soon became apparent that substantial rethinking had to be done if French secondary education was to

6   Albert Camus, *Actuelles*.

Figure 12.3: France: Reform of Education (simplified), 1959.

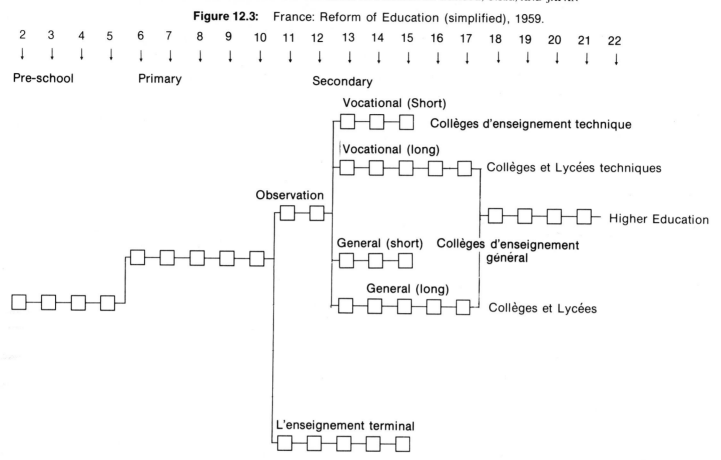

provide the opportunities to the whole community that Langevin and Wallon had envisaged for it.[7]

(d) Colleges d'Enseignement Secondaire

The reform of 1959 was too unwieldy and indecisive to last. Its two-year cycle of observation was found to be too short, and, as it was not a course in a common school but merely the first two years of exploration in schools to which pupils had already been allotted, it was of very limited value. Educational opinion built up fairly rapidly in the 1960's in favour of a common middle school which would offer for all pupils a general orientation for four years as the Langevin-Wallon Commission had proposed twenty years earlier. The groundwork for that kind of institution had been laid by the *lycées pilotes* which in the 1950's had experimented extensively with orientation classes, school counselling, and general education in the pupils' earlier years within the framework of a multilateral school. Accordingly in 1962 a new middle school came into being, the *college d'enseignement secondaire* (CES). Within five years there were 1,500 of them. In many cases they were united with *collèges d'enseignement general* and were beginning to take over from the *lycées*

[7]   Mario Reguzzoni, *La Réforme de l'Enseignement dans la Communauté Economique Européenne*, Aubier-Montaigne, Paris, 1966, and Joseph Majault, *L'Enseignement en France*, McGraw-Hill, London, 1973, provide comprehensive accounts of the French educational reforms of the 1950's and 1960's. See also J.N. Moody, *French Education since Napoleon*, Syracuse University Press, 1978.

A French *Lycée* of the 1970's.

La Documentation Francaise, *Architecture Scolaire et Pédagogie Nouvelle*, June 1975.

the teaching of the lower secondary years. By 1972 eighty per cent of entrants to secondary education went into a CES.[8] Though of central and growing importance for the future development of secondary education, the CES, by the mid-1970's, still remained one of four types of secondary school in France viz., the CES *(collège d'enseignement secondaire)*, the CEG *(collège d'enseignement général)* common in rural areas, the CET *(collège d'enseignement technique)* for pupils concentrating on technical subjects, and the *lycée* many of which were confined to the upper three years of secondary education.

From 1968, extensive experiments were carried out in many CES's with the various ways of grouping pupils that had long been familiar procedures in Anglo-Saxon countries but which so far had had little consideration in France. Within each school three types of groups were set up: homogeneous ability groups for French, maths, and modern languages; homogeneous groups with a wider spread of ability for the

social sciences; and mixed ability groups for science, drawing, music, and manual work. In an evaluation after a five-year trial, it appeared that a greater degree of individual attention to pupils had been made possible by the new arrangement, that there was more individual progress and satisfaction, and that the experimental schools greatly increased their expected holding power. At the same time experiments were also being conducted with ways of developing more independent study by pupils in secondary schools. The objects of the work were to improve teaching and learning techniques by engaging the pupils more extensively in problem-solving and in the need to discover and analyse relevant materials, to increase opportunities for the use of initiative on the part of the pupils, to provide experience in co-operating with others in small groups on tasks of

[8] France, Ministère de l'Enseignement Nationale, *Le Mouvement Educatif en France. Principales Tendances 1971-73*, Institut National de Recherche et de Documentation Pédagogiques, Paris, 1973, p. 47.

Figure 12.4:   France: School System (simplified), 1975.

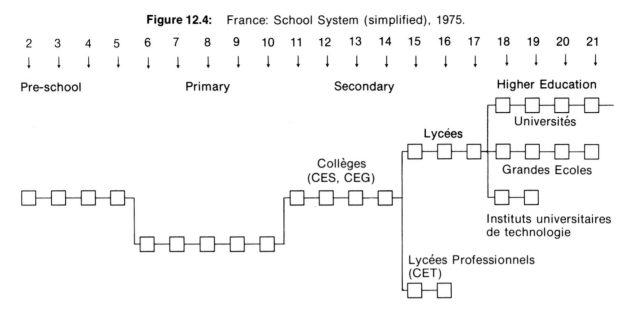

common interest, and to raise the level of the pupils' motivation by using their interests more effectively and by involving them in responsibilities with others in their group.[9]

The French experience in the quarter-century following World War II was of particular interest. During the twentieth century the French had shown themselves to be profoundly conservative in educational matters, especially in secondary education. 'Innovation in our country has always remained a marginal thing, the work of pioneers disputed and decried, tolerated as the product of eccentrics, or rejected as dangerous,' wrote the director of research for the Ministry of Education in 1974.[10] The parliamentary debates, and the laws proposing reforms and adjustments in French education from the beginning of the century until the 1950's, were exercises in futility and intransigence. It mattered little whether a law was accepted or not. The effect on French secondary education was hardly discernible. The change came with World War II and the Langevin-Wallon Commission. The commission had a new spirit and a genuine reform to offer. It envisaged secondary education as a matter of course for all pupils, and it proposed a common basic four-year period of general education and orientation. During the next twenty-five years secondary education in France was reconstructed in that image. Within the highly centralised system experimental stations were deliberately set

up in the shape of *classes nouvelles* and *lycées pilotes*, whose careful developmental work, carried out on a wide scale, contributed to the building up of public and professional opinion favourable to substantial educational change. With the development of the CES a firm basis for change was established. The CES became a comprehensive four-year middle school which, by the early 1970's, was genuinely and firmly changing the nature of French secondary education. It was well disposed towards innovations in teaching practice and was beginning slowly to transform traditional teaching in the lower section of secondary education. It was, also, an institution which provided a new range of opportunities for all pupils, and it conceived its task and the task of secondary education in terms wider than had previously been acknowledged, as nothing less than that of providing a higher level of general culture for all young people in France. The development of the CES and the raising of the school leaving age to sixteen in 1969 meant that French children could be educated together for nine years through

[9]   France, Ministère de l'Education Nationale, *Vers l'Individualisation de l'Enseignement dans le Premier Cycle Secondaire*, Recherches Pédagogiques, no. 58, Institut National de Recherche et de Documentation Pédagogiques, 1973; *Le Travail Indépendant, ibid.*, no. 66, 1974.

[10]   Louis Legrand, 'Objectifs et modalités du travail indépendant', in *Le Travail Indépendant*, p. 7.

Figure 12.5: France: Growth of the School Population.

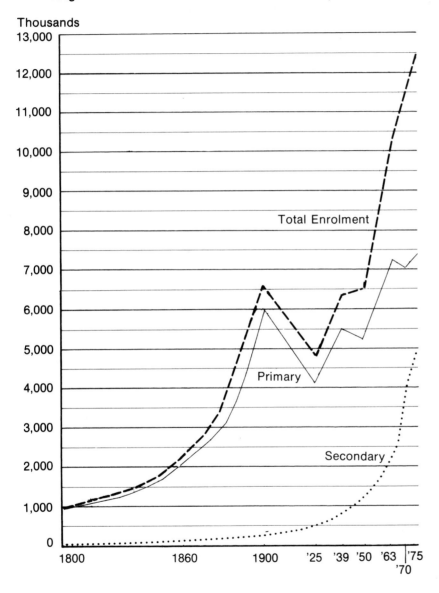

Note the rapid upturn in secondary enrolments 1950-75, from La Documentation française illustré, *Architecture Scolaire et Pédagogie Nouvelle*, June 1975.

primary and middle school, and, as this pattern grew and flourished, the elitist hold on French secondary education was gradually relaxed.

(iii) West Germany

Germany had an educational tradition and school organisation somewhat similar to that of France.

After World War II, West Germany was reconstituted as a federal republic in which each of the eleven states maintained its own educational system. These varied in minor ways throughout the country. In general, it could be said that there was a four-year primary school from which about seventy per cent of the pupils proceeded to a higher primary school of four or five years, ten per cent to a middle school of up to six years with a practical bias, and twenty per cent to an academic *Gymnasium* with classical, modern language, and science streams for nine years. Post-primary education, therefore, had three parallel types of schools, which, as in the French higher primary schools, *collèges*, and *lycées* and the English modern, secondary technical, and grammar schools, corresponded to different levels of ability and social class. In four of the states a closer approximation to France and England was made in the 1950's by the development of a six-year primary school followed by three secondary schools: a three-year practical school, a four-year technical school, and a seven-year cultural school.

The first fifteen years after the end of hostilities in 1945 had been devoted to repair and restoration. In the larger cities up to seventy per cent of the schools had been destroyed. There were millions of refugee children to be accommodated, and there was a shortage of teachers. It was not until about 1960, therefore, that much innovation was seriously considered. From then until 1970, there were many proposals for reform.

(a) Plans for Reform

Much discussion on the possibility of postponing the age of selection for secondary education and extending the years of common schooling led to the formulation of plans of reform in 1959 and 1960. The *Rahmenplan* of 1959 suggested two years of orientation between four-year primary and secondary education, followed by three kinds of secondary schools similar to those in the four reformed states. A second widely discussed plan, the *Bremer Plan*, proposed a four-year primary school, a two-year middle school, and a four-year secondary level of the three kinds of schools or streams, with a substantial common core of subjects in the early secondary

Figure 12.6: West Germany: School System (simplified), 1975.

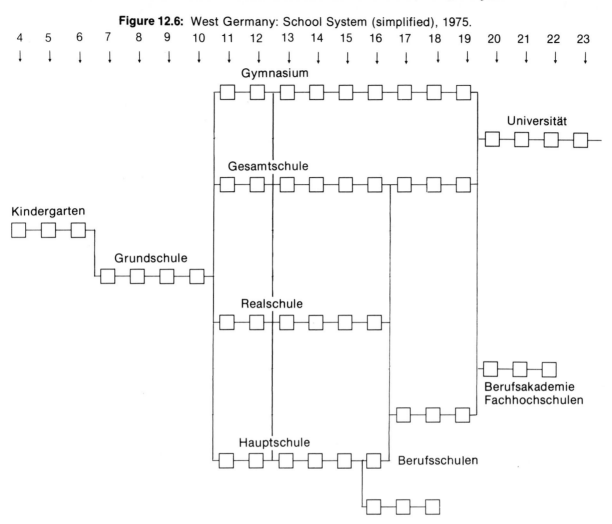

years. The proposal came close to the recommendation of a common ten-year school with specialised extensions for one to three years, something like the Swedish comprehensive system. The first proposal retained the multiple-track secondary system and tried to improve the means of selection for it; the second moved tentatively towards the development of a single-track system.

By 1970, however, little change had taken place. A federal government report issued in that year remarked that 'The structure and

organisation of the present-day secondary school system is fundamentally the same as that during the Weimar Republic. It has been modified but not basically altered.'[11] The federal government was of the opinion that it needed to be modernised and democratised by the development of an integrated comprehensive school to replace the selective multi-track

[11] Germany, Federal Republic of, *Report of the Federal Government on Education*, 1970, Bundesminister für Bildung und Wissenschaft, Bonn, 1970, p. 57.

system, and it was prepared to help the states financially to change over to a comprehensive system in the course of the 1970's. An overall education plan was put forward by a joint federal and states planning commission which aimed at standardising the educational systems of the country, and reforming them in the interests of efficiency and equality of opportunity.

By 1975 it could be said that it had become fairly common practice for a break to be made for all pupils after a four-year elementary school, and a transfer at that stage into one of three kinds of schools: a six-year *Hauptschule* which was previously the continuation of the elementary school; a six-year *Realschule* previously a middle school; and a nine-year *Gymnasium* mostly of the three traditional types but sometimes of a combination of them. In addition, in 1975, there were 180 experimental *Gesamtschulen* (comprehensive schools).

(iv) England

In England, as in France, World War II led to a reassessment of the existing secondary educational pattern. 'We stand at the cross-roads,' declared the educational authority for London in 1944, 'and the opportunity of choosing which path to follow is not likely to recur.'[12]

(a) Tripartite Division of Secondary Education

Secondary education since the Hadow Report of 1926 had grown into a tripartite form. The word secondary was almost synonymous with education in a grammar school offering from the age of eleven plus an academic curriculum preparatory to university studies. A small group of semi-vocational schools known as junior technical schools with an entry at thirteen plus had also slowly come into being. The great majority of pupils, however, were to be found in a third type of school still administered as an elementary school; it could be simply an extension of the elementary school beyond the sixth class to the school leaving age of fourteen, or a special top department of the elementary school known as a senior school, or a collection of pupils from the top classes of elementary schools into a central school. The senior and central schools were sometimes known as modern schools, and that was to be their name after the post-World War II reorganisation.

The tripartite division was encouraged by two widely discussed reports published by the Board of Education in 1938 and 1943. The first, known as the Spens Report, recommended that all pupils should transfer at eleven plus to secondary schools, and that pupils should be allocated to each of the three types on the basis of their tested intelligence and aptitude. The Norwood Report of 1943 equated the three types of schools

with three types of minds in a way which earned the scorn of contemporary educational psychologists but the approval of many practising educators. Four years later, in 1947, a Ministry of Education pamphlet commenting on current development plans and offering advice about secondary education reiterated the Norwood Committee's view that there were three types of pupils who conveniently fitted the three types of existing schools. One kind was interested in learning for its own sake, could 'take a long view and hold his mind in suspense' and flourished on books and ideas in the kind of curriculum provided by a secondary grammar school. A second kind had interests and abilities which lay markedly in the field of applied science, art, or commerce and had resolved at an early stage to pursue towards that end an exacting course such as was to be found in a secondary technical school. And a third kind, which embraced the majority of pupils, dealt more easily with concrete things than with ideas and were more suited to the course rooted in their own day-to-day experience that they would find in a secondary modern school.[13]

In 1944 the British parliament passed its definitive Education Act which replaced the Board of Education by a ministry, raised the school leaving age to fifteen from 1947, and, amongst other things, required every local authority to see that there were sufficient schools 'for providing secondary education, that is to say, full-time education suitable to the requirements of senior pupils', and that the schools should offer to their pupils 'such variety of instruction and training as may be desirable in view of their different ages, abilities, and aptitudes, and of the different periods for which they may be expected to remain at school, including practical instruction and training appropriate to their respective needs'.[14] Throughout the whole of the Act there was no mention of a tripartite division for secondary education nor, indeed, of any kind of secondary school at all.

All local authorities were required, under the Act, to submit to the Ministry of Education plans for the development of education in their area. Most authorities decided to provide secondary education in separate modern, technical, and grammar schools.[15] The largest of them, London,

---

[12] London County Council, *London School Plan*, L.C.C., 1947, Appendix II, Reorganization of Post-primary Education, report of the Education Committee, 19 July 1944, p. 210.

[13] Great Britain, Board of Education, *Report of the Consultative Committee on Secondary Education with specific reference to Grammar Schools and Technical High Schools*, HMSO, London, 1938 (Spens Report); Board of Education, *Curriculum and Examinations in Secondary Schools*, HMSO, London, 1943, pp. 2-4; Ministry of Education. *The New Secondary Education*, Pamphlet no. 9, HMSO, London, 1947, p. 23.

[14] Great Britain, *Education Act, 1944*, 7 & 8 Geo.6, Ch. 31 #8.

[15] Great Britain, Ministry of Education, *Organization of Secondary Education*, Circular 144, 16 June 1947, p. 1.

however, created something of a sensation by deciding to reconstruct its war-damaged system by building comprehensive secondary schools. The Ministry defined the new school as: 'a comprehensive school means one which is intended to cater for all the secondary education of all the children in a given area without an organization in three sides'.[16] In a level-headed and cogently argued document the London authority examined the English tradition and possible alternatives. Comparing the purposes and achievements of English grammar schools with American comprehensive high schools, they observed, 'We tend to love exclusive aristocracies, and when the aristocracy of wealth went out of fashion we created a new one which we were pleased to think was an aristocracy of brains, that is, of those who excel in book learning. We need to create a much wider aristocracy — of those who excel in the art of social living. This, the American school consciously sets out to achieve.'[17] After reviewing the virtues and disadvantages of various forms of organisation the London authority decided that they should aim at establishing a system of comprehensive schools throughout their administrative area.

That was the first substantial break with the tripartite system. Inasmuch as secondary technical schools were developed only to a very small extent, the tripartite system was really a dual one, and, like the French system that Langevin-Wallon struggled to reform, it still retained the overtones of social distinction between selective secondary grammar schools for an elite, and unselective post-elementary education, renamed secondary modern schools. The next fifteen years was a period of educational exploration of great interest and productivity. Educators examined and experimented with the tasks and programs of grammar, modern, and comprehensive schools, broadening curricula, recasting teaching methods, and developing, surprisingly, more and more similarities between them in aims, organisation, and programs.

The movement was accompanied by political and social argument, sometimes of great heat. During the 1940's and 1950's the tripartite system tended to be identified with the conservative political party, the promotion of comprehensive schools with the socialist labour party. Labour ministers, however, when in office continued to favour the tripartite scheme, and were responsible for issuing *The New Secondary Education* which argued its case. Supporters of comprehensiveness wanted education not to mirror the social stratification of the country but to correct it. As in the United States at that period, educators became acutely aware of the connections between education and social class, and the relationship became a favourite topic for discussion and research out of which the discipline of educational sociology had its beginning and initially much of its content. The comprehensive school was a non-selective school for the children of all the community where pupils from all social backgrounds would be educated together. It would lessen social

distinction, and promote social unity. Grammar schools, on the other hand, could be shown to have a social class bias in their attendance, and their very existence was a reproach to genuine democracy. But, argued the grammar school supporters, did genuine democracy imply egalitarian mediocrity? A grammar school education was an essay in excellence. To surrender such a program would be to deprive English secondary education of the high quality which was its pride. Further argument among educators focused on the question of the desirability and possibility of selecting pupils at 11+, at the end of primary education, for a variety of schools with different objectives; on the impracticability of arranging for the transfer and reallocation of pupils from one type of school to another; on the difficulty of establishing parity of esteem between various kinds of school when one of them was specifically designed to cream off the intellectual elite; and on the question of whether children's aptitudes and interests were sufficiently clustered to justify segregation into separate schools.

(b) Grammar School

Grammar school recruitment up until the inter-war period was related more to social class than to the ability of pupils.[18] The grammar school attracted pupils not because of the content of its courses or its methods of teaching but because it was the accepted route to higher white collar positions. Many parents in England tended to choose a grammar school education not because it was thought to have some intrinsic worth or to be the kind of education most suited to their children's abilities, but in exactly the same way as Africans preferred a traditional European kind of education, because that education was the recognised path to the kind of occupation they desired for their children. The Hadow, Spens, and Norwood reports encouraged people to think that as secondary education became more widespread, the grammar school should develop into a school restricted to pupils of high ability. The tendency became more pronounced as the school certificate examination and, subsequently in 1950, the general certificate of education (GCE) became more prominent and decisive in the secondary school curriculum. Those examinations were the means of entry to universities, and although only a small minority actually proceeded from the grammar schools to the universities, the academic bias and university preparatory flavour of the school were accepted by parents, pupils, masters, and mistresses as a

---

[16] *ibid.,* p. 2.

[17] *ibid.,* p. 216.

[18] Olive Banks, *Parity and Prestige in English Secondary Education,* RKP, London, 1955; see especially Chapter 16.

proper form of discipline and general education for the pupils from whom the country's future executives and professional workers would be recruited. After World War II the grammar school became a distinctive school associated with intellectual merit; entrance to it was guarded by the somewhat fearsome dragon known as the 11+ examination, designed to select the intellectually bright, and the exit from it was through a gate marked HSC or after 1950, GCE.

During the 1950's, however, the grammar schools began to lose some of their distinctiveness. Many of the new modern and comprehensive schools had more attractive buildings, and were better equipped than older established grammar schools, and many of their teachers had previously served in grammar schools. Until the 1950's the grammar school curriculum had been characterised by the study of languages, literature, and history. In the 1950's and early 1960's the sciences emerged much more strongly to challenge the primacy of the literary humanities. With the change came a hint of doubt, a slight lack of self-confidence, in the rightness and relevance of the traditional humanities. It was at that time that Snow wrote the first of two essays on the disjunction between the two cultures, literary and scientific.[19] Science, whether pure or applied, took the pupil into the world of laboratories, practical measurement, probability, discovery methods, and experimental controls. Those belonged to a culture with which the traditional grammar school had no great familiarity. It did, however, move speedily into the area, expanded its science and maths teaching staff, and built extensive new laboratories. Gradually the grammar school curriculum widened further still in several directions. As the classics declined, English became more prominent and the choice of subjects broadened. Maths and science increased in importance, several social sciences were offered, more emphasis was placed on music and art, and many schools introduced domestic science, woodwork, metal work, mechanical science, and technical drawing.

In the lower forms of the secondary school the program in many grammar schools could be so wide that it did not differ significantly from that of other types of secondary schools except in the intellectual and academic quality of the work that was done.

What was distinctive of the grammar school was the existence of the sixth form. And it was to be the characteristic of a grammar school education until, in due course, modern and comprehensive schools began to build up sixth forms of their own. English educators have always thought that 'The sixth form is the crown of the grammar school'.[20] In the 1950's it was the top form in which pupils might remain for two or three years and work for high academic results in their Advanced Level General Certificate of Education examinations. It became highly specialised and competitive but, at the same time, like the French *lycée*, also widened the range of its specialisms. From the sixth form the school prefects and other leaders were chosen, and, in the life of the sixth form, the pupils intellectually and socially were to reach their peak. Administrators found it difficult to think of a secondary school without a flourishing sixth form, and when, for example, they calculated the size and organisation of a comprehensive school they invariably estimated the number of pupils of various streams entering in the first year that would be required to enable the school to retain sufficient pupils to make up a sixth form of a reasonable size. The Crowther Report in 1959, dealing with youth aged fifteen to eighteen, devoted much space and thought to a study of the sixth form. The members of the committee approved the high degree of specialisation characteristic of it, disapproved of earlier specialisation that was creeping into the grammar school, and suggested that as the number of sixth form pupils continued to grow in England a wider range of specialism should become available. They summarised the distinguishing characteristics of the sixth form as:

- a close link with the university;
- concentration on study in depth;
- an increased amount of independent work;
- an intimate intellectual relationship between pupil and teacher;
- the growth of social responsibility.[21]

The sixth form for many English educators was the pride of the whole system, perhaps the most important English contribution to contemporary educational practice. By the intellectual merit and sense of social responsibility shown by its sixth form pupils, the real quality of a grammar school was to be judged.

(c) Modern School

The secondary modern school had its roots back in the higher elementary schools of the late nineteenth century and in the senior and central schools of the 1930's, but the Education Act of 1944 gave it the opportunity to expand with such vigour that it became virtually a new institution. The pupils who attended the modern schools, were those who had not been selected for the grammar or technical schools, and, therefore, were not committed to an academic or to a vocational course or to the need to prepare for an external examination. The new school was the

[19] C.P. Snow, *The Two Cultures and the Scientific Revolution*, Cambridge University Press, 1959.

[20] Frances Stevens, *The Living Tradition*, RKP, London, 1960, p. 75.

[21] Great Britain, Ministry of Education, Central Advisory Council for Education (England) *15-18*, H.M.S.O., London, 1959, vol. I, Chapter 21.

Table 12.1: England and Wales: Percentage of Pupils in Various Types of Secondary Schools, 1950-75.

Secondary School	1950	1955	1960	1965	1970	1975
	%	%	%	%	%	%
Modern	55	56	54	49	37	17
Grammar	25	24	22	23	18	8
Technical	4	4	3	3	1	.4
Comprehensive	.4	.7	4	8	28	60
Other Secondary maintained schools	.9	2	6	7	7	7
Independent and Direct Grant	14	14	11	10	9	8

Percentages were calculated from Department of Education and Science, *Statistics of Education, 1975,* Vol. 1, Schools, HMSO, 1976, and earlier tables.

secondary school for the great majority of children as Table 12.1 shows, but what was to be its purpose and function?

In the post-World War II period up to the early 1960's, the modern school developed in interesting ways. In a number of the newly established schools the staff accepted their freedom from the need to prepare for external examinations as a challenge to create a new approach to secondary education. They did not wholly succeed. The modern school did not emerge as a distinctive educational development, but it did manage to produce examples of approaches and practices that had not previously characterised English secondary education. There was a tendency in many schools to emphasise social skills and co-operative work, to look primarily to the interests of the pupils, and to study their development with care. Those tendencies were undoubtedly associated with the fact that modern school teachers were concerned only as yet with the earlier years of secondary education, had had experience, in many cases, in primary school teaching, and were trained teachers. On the other hand, fewer of the grammar school teachers had been trained to teach; in the 1950's about half of the new recruits were accepted on completion of a university degree without teacher training; their interest was often directed more towards history or English or physics than towards the process of teaching, and the attention they necessarily had to pay to the senior school work and the subject-matter of courses aimed at success in

public examinations made them less knowledgeable of and less inclined to use fresh and newer approaches to their work.

The modern school was by no means a hotbed of radical teaching method. In general, it was plodding and unexciting; but it did provide examples of flexibility and innovation, and a few attempts to think out a new pattern of general education for the mass secondary school in a technological age. The Education Act of 1944 had made secondary education mandatory for all, for at least three or four years, and the modern school was the symbol of this achievement. Some of the schools saw that this implied the need to think through and produce a secondary education that was designed for children living in the technological civilisation of the mid-1950's. Some of them, therefore, produced useful courses on the study of contemporary society and redesigned their English courses to give them more relevance to the pupils' contemporary experience, and most schools increased the weight of science and mathematics in the curriculum. But there was no systematic effort to design a modern curriculum for a modern school, and no lead was given from the central authority whose pamphlets and circulars gave the impression that they regarded a modern school as a rather vaguely watered-down grammar school for the less intelligent children.

The modern school's activities seem to have been bedevilled by a seeking for 'parity of esteem' with the grammar school. Many sought to imitate the grammar school and to depart as little as possible from its program. A great opportunity was thus lost of striking out boldly to construct a new school distinctive of the new purposes for which it had been called into being.

Social and economic factors conspired to bring it closer to the grammar school. In the early 1950's eighty-five per cent of the pupils of modern schools as against sixty per cent of grammar school pupils were children of manual workers, 35 per cent of modern school and twelve per cent of grammar school pupils being from the families of unskilled workers,[22] but as the number of unskilled workers declined during the 1950's, the social class band from which modern and grammar school pupils came merged more and more. The great post-World War II increase in service and distributive occupations meant that many of the pupils of both modern and grammar schools were to move into them, competing for somewhat the same places; the increasing social mobility of the population was reflected in the desire to use secondary schools as a means of promoting upward social movement; and the rapid development of new firms and new types of jobs in them and a similarly speedy decline in unskilled jobs during the 1950's placed a premium on vocational

---

[22] Great Britain, Ministry of Education, Central Advisory Council for Education (England), *15-18,* HMSO, London, 1960 (Crowther Report), vol. II, p. 112.

flexibility with a sound basis in general education. Employers were interested in seeing firm evidence of the worth and achievements of competing young applicants, and parents and pupils were not backward in encouraging the schools to take steps to produce the appropriate kind of evidence. Hence modern schools began to prepare their pupils for local and external examinations which would provide the desired certification.

The Crowther Report in 1959 endorsed the tripartite system and recommended that extended courses should be developed more widely in modern schools, but that external examinations should as far as possible be avoided. It argued also for the raising of the school leaving age to sixteen, an event which did not happen until 1972, and it suggested a considerable extension of post-school further education, by means of which it hoped that in twenty years' time at least half, instead of the current tenth, of the modern school leavers would obtain technical training.

Meanwhile modern schools had started, as had some grammar schools too, to introduce semi-vocational courses. In addition, by the mid-1950's, a trend had set in towards the upward extension of the school with a view to preparing pupils for the GCE. Between 1953 and 1960 the numbers from modern schools presenting for the examination rose by more than five times, from approximately four thousand to twenty-two thousand, and the numbers staying on beyond the school leaving age also rose rapidly. The move into the orbit of the GCE examination started a tendency towards more specialisation in the upper forms which was encouraged by a small increase in the recruitment of university graduates as teachers. Clearly, by 1960, the modern school was moving steadily closer to the grammar school pattern.

(d) Comprehensive Secondary School

In 1961 the London County Council returned to the fray to report in detail on the work and progress of sixteen of their fifty-nine comprehensive schools. The London authority showed that more fundamental thinking about secondary education and more innovation in curricula, teaching methods, and school organisation had gone on in its group of schools than probably anywhere else in the whole country, and that it confidently expected that 'the next decade should see a vigorous continuance of the process of constructing a system of secondary education for all which is capable of meeting the challenge of a rapidly changing world.'[23] Among the schools there was a variety of organisational patterns: some were multilateral schools, dividing their pupils into a number of homogeneous ability streams; others used ability groups, and allowed pupils to move into different ability sets within the groups according to their performance in different subjects; others again used homogeneous groups for certain subjects and mixed groups for others, generally arts, crafts, and physical education.

Reallocation of pupils in their streams usually took place at the end of each year. In all schools, for the first three years, there was a common general course which resembled, somewhat, especially in the third year, the orientation years being introduced at that time into French secondary education. In the third year and more widely in the fourth, semi-vocational courses were commenced to introduce pupils to a variety of occupations. From the fourth year on, the schools offered three types of courses: academic, commercial, and technical studies, the first of which would lead on to the sixth form, in which some of the schools were developing a less specialised pattern than that of the grammar schools.

The comprehensive schools had to devise adequate and relevant programs for all pupils, some of whom would leave at fifteen, many of whom would stay for four or five years, and still others go on to the age of seventeen or eighteen. The staffs continually experimented to provide guidance and satisfaction to pupils of all levels of ability and expectation. Most schools were consciously trying to develop a strong corporate life through small study groups, school societies, and an association with the local neighbourhood as a community school. By 1960 the extent of migration from the West Indies, India, and Pakistan was becoming apparent in several areas of London. As the comprehensive schools began to become multi-racial, they started consciously to perform for London the job that the American high school had historically endeavoured to play in cities such as New York, Boston, and Chicago, that of helping the promotion of mutual adjustment and understanding in the changing community.

Throughout the 1950's evidence had been accumulating in England, as also in the United States,[24] of the cultural bias of intelligence tests. It became clear that intelligence testing, on which much reliance was placed in selecting pupils at eleven plus for grammar schools and for streaming them in ability groups in all secondary schools, discriminated against working class children. Pressure to eliminate the eleven plus examination and to expand the provision of comprehensive schools continued to have political associations. During the 1950's when the conservative party was continually in office, comprehensive schools received even less encouragement from the central government than they had under the previous lukewarm labour government. Nevertheless, a growing distrust of the selection examination, the slowly growing

---

[23] London County Council, *London Comprehensive Schools. A survey of sixteen schools*, LCC, London, 1961 p. 71; see also London County Council, *The Organization of Comprehensive Secondary Schools*, LCC, 1953.

[24] See below, Chapter 13.

tendency for the practices of the different kinds of schools to approximate to each other, and the demonstrated successes of comprehensive schools in public examinations and in retaining pupils beyond the school leaving age, started a ground-swell in the early 1960's in favour of comprehensive secondary education.

The movement was reinforced by some timely research along the three different lines, sociological, economic and educational that were pursued in the argument about comprehensive schools. Sociologically, more studies by unimpeachable authorities provided evidence for the unreliability and the class bias of the selection process at eleven plus. Economically, there was great interest, after Sputnik through into the 1960's, in making maximum use of the nation's potential talent. Studies made for the Robbins Committee on higher education indicated that the idea upon which selective secondary education was based, that the nation had a somewhat limited pool of ability of persons capable of profiting by higher education, was without foundation, and that the current tripartite secondary school system was very wasteful of talent that the nation could ill-afford to neglect.

Educationally, evidence from research and the observation of experimental schools suggested that comprehensive schools provided a richer intellectual and social education for all levels of pupils, that deprived and less bright pupils were likely to do best in the wider opportunities and relationships offered by a comprehensive school, and that more pupils would emerge as bright pupils and would reach as high a level of achievement and gain a greater maturity than they would in segregated schools.[25] There was considerable interest in the research and progress made in Sweden in the reorganisation of secondary education and, as an increasing number of local authorities produced plans for ending the eleven plus examination and for developing comprehensive schools, public discussion became widespread and often heated.

By 1965, eight per cent of secondary school pupils were in comprehensive schools. In that year the labour party, recently returned to government office after an absence of thirteen years, issued a circular which gave greater impetus to the comprehensive movement. Circular 10/65 declared the government's intention to eliminate the eleven plus examination and end separatism in secondary education. It requested all local educational authorities to produce plans for reorganising secondary education along comprehensive lines. Six possible forms of comprehensive organisation were cited as existing in England. Local authorities were asked to study and adopt the one best suited to their situation.[26]

It was clear that some patterns were more comprehensive than others. The great majority of schools had adopted some form of streaming; in doing so they had rejected the selective principle in deciding against separate schools, only to reintroduce it with separate streams inside the

comprehensive school where it was found to have somewhat the same social, economic, and educational effects as the selective tripartite school system. Studies published in the early 1970's indicated that comprehensive schools, though still predominantly multilateral, had started to move away from the practice of streaming. Mixed ability groups were increasing in popularity with both pupils and teachers.'[27]

Circular 10/65 helped to increase the pace of secondary school reconstruction. The rather conservatively-minded Incorporated Association of Assistant Masters in Secondary Schools, which in 1960 had issued a tepid and somewhat disapproving report on comprehensive schools, produced in 1967 a more serious and encouraging statement about their possibilities, and many more educators became reconciled to and sometimes interested in the new development. Between 1965 and 1970 the percentage of secondary school pupils in comprehensive schools rose from eight per cent to 28 per cent. At that date, comprehensive schools had one and a half times the number of pupils in grammar schools, and three-quarters of the number in modern schools maintained by local educational authorities.

In 1970, however, the conservative party returned to power, rescinded the circular, and cold-shouldered the comprehensive school movement. Nevertheless, by 1972, thirty-eight of the 146 local educational authorities had completed their secondary reorganisation along comprehensive lines, and 117 had comprehensive schools in some part of their areas.[28] The comprehensive school was slowly climbing in numbers and prestige. In 1974 a new labour party government once more promoted the comprehensive idea. From 1965 numbers in grammar and modern schools had been slowly dropping and those in comprehensive schools steadily rising. In the mid-1970's the change was accelerated, and, by 1975, sixty per cent of secondary pupils were in comprehensive schools.

With many compromises and controversies, and with much reluctance to abandon traditional practice, it looked as if a new structure and a new view of secondary education was emerging out of a half-century of social,

[25] Examples of these various kinds of research are to be found in J.W.B. Douglas, *The Home and the School,* Macgibbon and Kee, London, 1964; Great Britain, *Higher Education,* HMSO, London, 1963-4 (Robbins Report); T.W.G. Miller, *Values in the Comprehensive School,* Birmingham University Education Monograph, 1961; Alice Griffin, Selective and non-selective secondary schools: their relative effects on ability, attainment and attitudes, *Research in Education,* no. 1, Manchester University Press, 1969. An extensive bibliography is contained in T.G. Monks, *Comprehensive Education in England and Wales,* NFER, London, 1968.

[26] Great Britain, Department of Education and Science, *The Organization of Secondary Education,* Circular 10/65, 12 July 1965, HMSO, London, 1965.

[27] J.M. Ross, W.J. Bunton, P. Evison & T.S. Robertson, *Critical Appraisal of Comprehensive Education,* NFER, London, 1972, Chapter 4; C. Benn and B. Simon, *Half-Way There,* Penguin, Harmondsworth, (2nd. edn), 1972, pp. 217ff.

[28] Christopher J. Hill, *Transfer at Eleven,* NFER, London, 1972, p. 27.

Figure 12.7: England: School System (simplified), 1975.

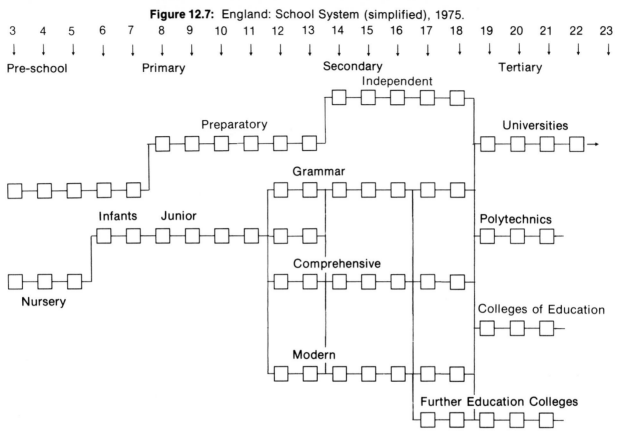

economic, and educational reassessment. It was a movement that was not unique to England, but one which she shared with all developed countries, and of all of them, she and Sweden in the post-World War II period experimented with, researched, and discussed problems and possibilities of secondary school reorganisation the most thoroughly.

(v) Secondary Education in the U.S.A.

Since the beginning of the century the American high school had been a comprehensive school of a multilateral type. 'It is called comprehensive,' wrote an educator in 1959, 'because it offers under one administration and under one roof (or series of roofs) secondary education for almost all the high school age children of one town or neighborhood.'[29] It was a school 'whose programs correspond to the educational needs of all the youth of the community'.[30] The programs were usually arranged as a number of parallel curricula — college preparatory, general, commercial, home science, and vocational, and by 1960 there were principally four types of school: junior high school (grades seven to nine with approximately 25 per cent of all pupils), senior high school (grades ten to twelve, fifteen per cent), junior-senior high school (grades seven to twelve, 32 per cent), and high schools (grades nine to twelve, 28 per cent). There were also a small number of specialised high schools, mostly in large centres of population.

[29] J.W. Gardner, Foreword in J.B. Conant, *The American High School Today*, McGraw-Hill, New York, 1959, p. ix.

[30] J.B. Conant, *op.cit.*, p. 12.

(a) Education for ALL American Youth

Towards the end of World War II the idea that the comprehensive high school for the new era should make a firm effort to provide a common program for all was set forth by the Educational Policies Commission of the National Education Association in a report *Education for ALL American Youth*. Most of the youth were expected to continue through high school and junior college, from seventh to fourteenth grade. A common program in the junior high school with aims similar to those of the 1918 *Cardinal Principles* was to be followed by a study of five 'areas of learning' in the remaining grades. For an urban high school they would be individual interests, vocational preparation, science, common learnings (mostly social science, English, and art), health and physical education. The orientation of the proposal was 'on the present living of youth, on the improvement of community life, and on such practical matters as competence in occupations, citizenship, and family living'. It was a continuation of the spirit of many of the progressives of the 1930's and it was taken up in many school systems. It was a strong bid to break away from college preparatory courses and to make what came to be known as 'education for life-adjustment' the central part of the high school's work.

In 1951 and 1954 reports from federal commissions reinforced the move to life-adjustment education;[31] but many teachers trained in liberal arts and science disciplines found it difficult to move into the new approach, and many parents and academics became perturbed at the threat to traditional disciplines. From 1956 an organisation known as the Council for Basic Education fought the issue strenuously, and in the cold-war McCarthyist atmosphere of the 1950's largely succeeded in its endeavours. Life-adjustment education was temporarily eclipsed by an interest in producing well-considered, carefully tested, and modern versions of academic subjects, beginning in 1952 with the work of the University of Illinois Committee on School Mathematics. Later, in the unrest and disillusion of the mid-1960's, the spirit of the life-adjustment programs was reanimated.

(b) End of the Progressive Education Association

One of the casualties of the period was the Progressive Education Association which was disbanded in 1955. Since World War II its membership had dropped and it had shown little in the way of new initiative. By the 1950's it was not associated much with innovative school practices, but rather tended towards discussion on social issues. The association and its journal were oriented theoretically towards reconstructionism, of which Brameld was the most radical and well-known exponent. Brameld held that human civilisation was in a state of crisis, and that American education should play a creative role in shaping the future. In such a situation the scientific method, reflective thought, and co-operative planning of Dewey were not enough. There was need also of a sense of commitment which would give a positive direction to emerging society; that sense would be achieved through discussion aimed not at compromise and majority opinion but at consensus. Not open-mindedness but an agreed and defensible partiality was the virtue to be cultivated. A similar but more Deweyan line was taken by another group of leading progressives who argued that 'the central task of education' in a democratic society was the development of practical intelligence the method by which individuals and groups in situations of uncertainty could intelligently reach and agree upon decisions on which they were prepared to act.[32] Those ideas, however, though kept alive in various schools and universities, did not flourish in the climate of the 1950's. It could be said, also, that much of the reform in methods, organisation, and school relationships for which progressives had worked was accepted in the schools by the mid-century as a matter of course, and there was no agreement on new directions nor obviously compelling new inspiration from the progressives in the 1950's. The association therefore withered and expired. When progressive schools revived in the mid-1960's, the old association was not resuscitated.

(c) The Conant Reports

The successful launching of the space satellite, Sputnik, by the U.S.S.R. in 1957 led to a questioning of the efficacy of American secondary education, and a demand for evaluation. There was a decided move towards more intellectual rigour. The successor, for example, to the committee that had proposed the life-adjustment program of *Education for ALL American Youth* affirmed in 1961 that 'the central purpose of American education was the cultivation of the rational powers of the human mind'.[33]

[31] U.S. Office of Education, *Life Adjustment Education for Every Youth*, Bulletin no. 22, Washington D.C., 1951; Commission on Life Adjustment Education, *Vitalizing Secondary Education*, Bulletin no. 3, Washington D.C., 1951; Second Commission on Life Adjustment Education for Youth, *A Look Ahead to Secondary Education for Life Adjustment*, Bulletin no. 4, Washington D.C., 1954.

[32] T. Brameld, *Ends and Means in Education: A Midcentury Appraisal*, Harper, New York, 1950; *Toward a Reconstructed Philosophy of Education*, Dryden, New York, 1956; *The Climactic Decades*, Praegar, New York, 1970; R.B. Raup, G.E. Axtelle, K.D. Benne and B.O. Smith, *The Discipline of Practical Judgment in a Democratic Society*, (re-issued as *The Improvement of Practical Intelligence*, 1950), Harper, New York, 1943.

[33] National Education Association, Educational Policies Commission, *The Central Purpose of American Education*, NEAT, Washington D.C., 1961, p. 11.

The principal and most extensive assessment of secondary education was that made by Conant in 1959 and 1960 and, later, in 1967.[34] In a balanced appraisal, Conant saw the high schools discharging three functions: general education for all; college preparation for those proceeding into tertiary education; and vocational education for the others. He reported that no radical change was necessary. The high school had developed along appropriate lines, but it could be improved by eliminating the very large numbers of small and poorly staffed schools which were evidence of considerable inequality of educational opportunity throughout the nation, by discontinuing college preparatory, vocational and other streams so as to ensure that each pupil had his own individualised program, by providing an academic minimum of standard basic subjects to be completed by all, and by giving special attention both to the academically talented and to pupils who needed remedial work. All of Conant's recommendations bore fruit in the 1960's. School systems were consolidated and small and inadequate units gradually vanished, great attention was paid to ways of eliminating inequality of opportunity, high school programs became more individualised, though few schools gave up the practice of streaming, academic curricula were strengthened, and very considerable interest was shown in special education for the gifted, for the disadvantaged, and for the retarded.

An important part of the strengthening of intellectual and academic interests in the high school in the 1950's was a trend to accelerate the progress and enrich the courses of gifted students. A significant influence in that regard was a plan started in 1956 by the College Entrance Examination Board to offer college level courses on the successful completion of which advanced standing up to second year in college was received by the student. The scheme was widely adopted in the 1960's.

(d) Federal Education Acts

The National Defense Education Act, passed in 1958 and further extended in 1964, was a move to strengthen intellectual education in science, mathematics, modern foreign languages, and technology. It provided loans and fellowships for individuals teaching and studying in those fields, and gave substantial aid to educational authorities for research, equipment, building, and various teaching programs. In 1964 the scope of the act was increased to cover also English, social sciences, and reading in elementary and secondary schools. Many projects for the improvement of teaching procedures and curricula were put into effect as a result of the Act. The Economic Opportunity Act 1964 was a further extension of federal government assistance to education in general and to the solution of the problem of unequal opportunity in particular. President Johnson and his supporters in the mid-1960's had a vision of the Great Society in which

poverty and other handicaps to personal and social development would be eliminated 'by opening to everyone the opportunity for education and training, the opportunity to work, and the opportunity to live in decency and dignity'. The Act provided vocational education and work experience programs for youth who had left school, and community action programs to mobilise resources in the attack on poverty. It also provided aid for students to attend college, and initiated a pre-school program, Head Start, for children from low-income families. A third significant Act, the Elementary and Secondary Education Act of 1965, provided substantial funds to states for education, especially to assist the education of children suffering some disadvantage, whether physical, mental, financial, or racial. Considerable remedial and counselling work was undertaken, experimental classes were initiated, and research and development centres were established in conjunction with universities in several different regions to work on selected practical educational problems.

The shift in emphasis in the three Acts was indicative of the change in climate in American education. The social consciousness and relevance to everyday life that characterised the educational thinking of the 1940's, moved in the 1950's and early 1960's to a concern with more rigorous academic performance and excellence in achievement, only to be challenged in the mid-1960's and early 1970's by a renewal of interest in providing courses pertinent to current social issues and conditions.

(e) Expansion of Secondary Education

The thirty-year period from 1940 to 1970 saw an escalation in secondary school enrolment. In 1940, 45 per cent of pupils who had entered the fifth grade completed the twelfth and final grade of high school; in 1970, the proportion had risen to 75 per cent. Figure 12.7 illustrates the rise in the percentage of the five to seventeen year old population at school during the period 1889 to 1968 from 75 per cent to 96 per cent. The slight fall-off during 1900-7 and again from 1940-44 was steadily retrieved in the following years, as the proportion moved up towards one hundred per cent.

The growth and holding power of the American high school is best illustrated in Figure 12.8 showing the number of students completing high school as a percentage of seventeen-year-olds between 1900 and 1970. The proportion rose from seven per cent in 1900 to fifty per cent in 1940 and to 83 per cent in 1970, the two fastest periods of growth being the periods 1930-

[34] J.B. Conant, *The American High School Today*, McGraw-Hill, New York, 1959; *Recommendations for Education in the Junior High School Years* Educational Testing Service, Princeton, 1960; *The Comprehensive High School*, McGraw-Hill, New York, 1967. J.B. Conant (1893-   ) was a distinguished chemist, president of Harvard University from 1933 to 1953, and U.S. High Commissioner and Ambassador to West Germany from 1953 to 1957.

Figure 12.8: United States of America: Ratio of School Enrolment to Population 5-17 Years of Age, 1889-1968.

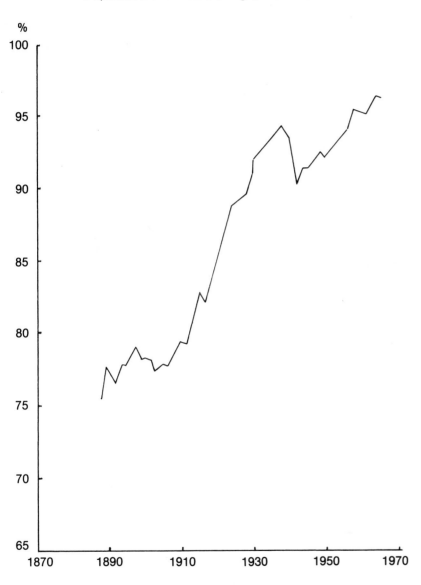

Figure 12.9: United States of America: High School Graduates as a Percentage of 17 Year-olds, 1900-70.

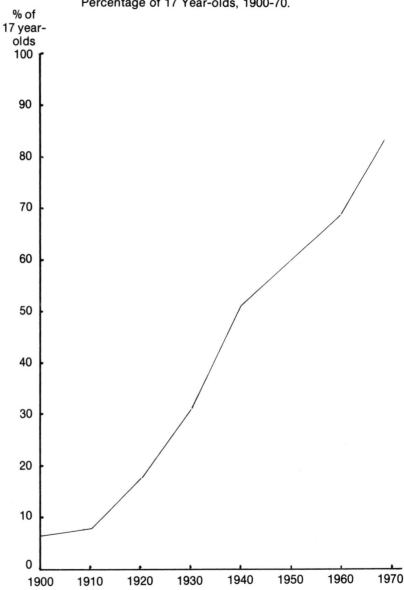

From Abbott L. Ferriss, *Indicators of Trends in American Education*, Russell Sage Foundation, New York, 1969, p. 18.

From Chris A. De Young and Richard Wynn, *American Education*, McGraw-Hill, New York, 1972 (1955), p. 191.

Figure 12.10: United States of America: School System (simplified), 1975.

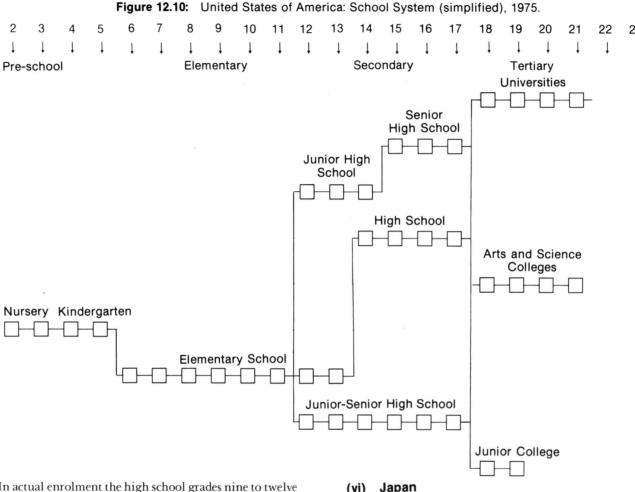

40, and 1960-70. In actual enrolment the high school grades nine to twelve almost tripled in number between 1950 and 1970, rising from seven to twenty-one million students in by far the fastest period of acceleration during the century.

It was clear that the mass high school of 1970 had to face a different task from its predecessor of 1900, when high school graduates were not yet ten per cent of the seventeen-year-old group, or even of 1940, when the proportion was fifty per cent. The school by 1970 had reached the stage of providing a complete secondary education for almost all the youth of the United States, and a rapidly increasing proportion of them were continuing on into tertiary education.

(vi) Japan

(a) Post-war Reconstruction

In 1946 the Fundamental Law of Education and in 1947 the School Education Law established the basis for education in Japan for the next several decades. 'Education,' it was stated in article 1 of the Fundamental Law, 'shall aim at the full development of personality, striving for the rearing of the people, sound in mind and body, who shall love truth and justice, esteem individual value, respect labour and have a deep sense of responsibility, and be imbued with the independent spirit, as builders of the peaceful state and society.'[35] In 1948 the Imperial Rescript that had guided Japanese education for more than half a century was repudiated. The American occupation after World War II ensured that American ideas about aims, organisation, and methods were to have a considerable influence.

In structure Japan developed a single-track system (6-3-3-4) from kindergarten to university with a common, compulsory, and free nine-year schooling, between the ages of six and fifteen, consisting of six years of primary and three years of junior secondary education. Beyond that level a variety of general and vocational secondary schools developed, leading to a junior college on the American model and to university. In 1960 about twenty per cent of pupils studied some vocational courses in the junior secondary, and forty per cent in senior secondary schools. A feature of the tertiary level was the large number of private institutions, which, in the mid-1960's, numbered 270 junior colleges as against forty public, and 185 universities to thirty-four public, and enrolled seventy per cent of all students in higher education.

The new system was not merely a change from a dual to a single-track organisation; it was also a change in spirit. The defeat in the war and subsequent occupation up to 1952 had a crushing effect on the authoritarian and nationalistic society with its paternalistic and close-knit code of ethics. 'Suddenly democracy, individualism, liberalism, and equalitarianism without any social basis poured into Japan and facilitated moral anarchy.'[36] There was a period of social and political disorder, and some confusion in education. Central controls were modified, decentralisation in educational administration was developed, and an effort was made to change the pattern of classroom teaching. Co-education was introduced, social studies substituted for traditional ethics, and a more permissive teaching approach was initiated to encourage individuality and spontaneity.

In the 1950's competitiveness became an increasing feature. A remarkable economic recovery and industrial expansion was mounted which put Japan among the leading industrial nations of the world; it was accompanied by an upsurge in secondary school and tertiary level attendance, and by a fierce competition for scarce places in the higher vocational and professional training institutions. At entrance to high school and at exit from it there developed an emphasis on selection that tended to overshadow many more appropriate educational values and purposes.

(b) Old v. New Values

Japan in the quarter-century after World War II provided an interesting example of a nation endeavouring to strike a balance between the dynamic of individualistic democracy and the tradition of social cohesion. There was strong support in the 1950's for the reinstitution of morals courses which would help to maintain a pattern of common values based on co-operation, respect for authority, and love of traditional culture. In 1958 a course of that kind was reintroduced as a compulsory subject into primary and secondary schools, and, at about the same time, measures were taken to restore some of their lost authority to the central Ministry of Education. Traditional discipline, it was hoped by its advocates, would be strengthened in such ways; but the educational debate with the recently emancipated teachers and students continued with some feeling. Basically, it was a political issue, and was seen as such by an observer who wrote: '*Politics* is an attempt to shape society according to a vision of the world — a vision of how things are, as well as how they should be. *Education*, as commonly conceived, is an effort to teach a vision of the world to human beings, particularly to children. Hence, education is politics, for they are both about how society is and how society should be.'[37] The vision of the conservatives was of a stable and patriotic society expanding in a controlled way somewhat like pre-World War II Japan; the more radically-minded looked forward to a society free of the old establishment, egalitarian, where both individual opportunity and group co-operation could flourish. Between the two there were many further shades of opinion. The difference between the two was brought out by a story told 'about a school class visiting the famous Katsura Gardens in Kyoto, and being told by the left wing teacher about the exploitation of the peasants by their feudal overlords which had made the expenditure on the gardens possible. Those who told the story wished that the teacher had used the occasion for the explanation of the artistic significance of the gardens in an attempt to nurture the students' attachment to their cultural heritage.'[38] Indoctrination in support of traditional forces of cohesion, or, on the other hand, in an effort to abolish exploitation, became a temptation. With the new attitude in education went a tendency to dispense with traditional methods. In the 1950's it was suggested that, as a consequence of the change, scholastic standards had fallen. The question of standards of achievement in basic subjects became a contentious issue between teachers and the more

[35] Japanese National Commission for UNESCO, *National Statements on Educational Goals, Aims and Objectives in the Asian Countries*, Tokyo, 1969, chapter on Japan, p. 2, see also T. Kaigo, *Japanese Education: its Past and Present*, Kokusai Bunka Shinkokai, Tokyo, 1968; and T. Kobayashi, *Society, Schools and Progress in Japan*, Pergamon, Oxford, 1976.

[36] M. Shimbori, 'The fate of postwar educational reform in Japan', *The School Review*, 68, Summer 1960, 239.

[37] J. Galtung, Social structure, education structure and life long education: the case of Japan, in Organization for Economic Cooperation and Development, Japan, Paris, OECD 1971, p. 131.

[38] OECD, *Japan*, p. 51.

conservative and economically oriented Ministry of Education. The subsequent revisions of curricula were designed, in part, to re-emphasise teaching in such fundamentals.

(c) Education and Economic Growth

Japan also faced a related and equally intransigent problem of determining the role to be played by education in the economic development of the country. Since the beginning of the Meiji era education had been used as an instrument of national modernisation, the remarkable effort 'to leave Asia and enter Europe'. It had been regarded as one of the most important factors in the modernising process, and, in the post-World War II period when it began to cut loose from traditional ideology and concentrated on economic success, the promotion of modernisation had come to be regarded as its main purpose. In a *White Paper* in 1962, the Ministry of Education pointed out the extent to which education had contributed to Japanese economic growth and argued for a still greater investment in education. The report suggested that the percentage of the growth of gross national product accounted for by education was:

Japan 1935-55	25 per cent;
U.S.S.R.1940-60	30 per cent;
U.S.A. 1929-60	33 per cent.

A main purpose of education was to increase production: 'If the effect of human ability is highly rated in increasing production, then it should naturally follow that positive effort should be made to increase human ability. And education should play the main role for this purpose . . .' A further report issued in 1966 found that the relationship of education to economic growth was not a simple one, but that, nevertheless, schools should regard it as one of their main tasks to continue to try to offer to industry the best educated labour force that they could. One of the consequences of that view was the introduction of the fundamentals of technical education for all students in the lower secondary schools, an increase in vocational specialisation in upper secondary curricula, and the establishment of technical colleges partly in parallel with upper secondary schools, a move which breached the single-track ideal.

Such a view was being seriously questioned by the mid-1960's. Not economic growth but the quality of human life was regarded by some Japanese authorities, and especially by the many protesting university students of the 1960's and 1970's, as the more significant objective. Smog, polluted water and seafood, traffic hazards, housing dislocations and

shortages, family break-up, delinquency, increased violence, individual indebtedness from excess consumption — all the drawbacks of crowded urban living in an industrial society were painfully experienced and freely aired in the 1960's. Was there a case for rethinking education so as to direct it less towards increasing the people's productivity and more towards improving the humane qualities of their life and assisting them to escape the dehumanisation and rigidities of class and economic structure of which there was widespread complaint?

(d) Reform of School Organisation and Curricula

One of the principal administrative responses to the criticism of rigidity was to move towards the diversification of schools. That was the case at the senior secondary level where there were academic, vocational, and combinations of academic and vocational high schools. But with diversification went increased competition and the need for selection. The fact that each kind had a different prestige rating in the eyes of Japanese parents, and that, even within categories, different schools were variously esteemed, tended to intensify competition for selection to enter the school of one's choice. Diversification was developed also at tertiary level. The Central Council for Education recommended in 1962 and again in 1970, in revised form, that there should be five different types of tertiary institutions: universities with three or four year courses, two or three year colleges, graduate schools with specialised and in-service courses, research institutes, and technical colleges which were established in 1962 and grew rapidly in popularity. The technical colleges offered five-year courses, three at senior secondary, and two at post-secondary level.

In 1968 the courses of studies for primary schools and lower secondary schools were revised by the Ministry of Education so as to strengthen moral education, to consolidate work in basic subjects, to extend work in science, and to adjust the school program more effectively to the abilities of the pupils. The subjects of the lower secondary school, the last three years of compulsory education, were a comprehensive mixture of general and pre-vocational education: compulsory — moral education, Japanese language, social studies, mathematics, science, music, fine arts, health and physical education, industrial arts and homemaking; elective — foreign languages, agriculture, business, fisheries and homemaking, and special activities. A report in the same year on upper secondary education, preparatory to a new course of studies to be introduced in 1972, was concerned that youth were apt to be dehumanised and lose their sense of social solidarity when exposed to the forces of contemporary industrialisation and urbanisation. It suggested therefore a revised program that would pay more attention to personality development, social experiences and extra-curricular activities. By 1970, eighty per cent of the entrants completed upper secondary school

Figure 12.11: Japan: School System (simplified), 1970.

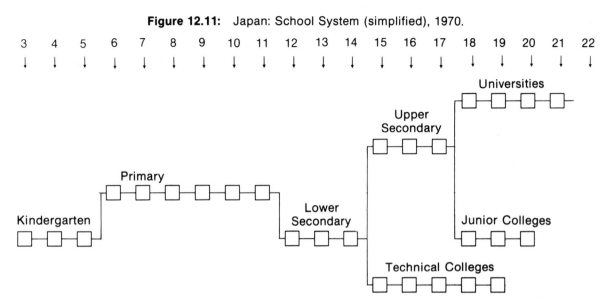

at approximately the age of eighteen. Japan had achieved mass secondary education. Henceforth the upper secondary school could be regarded as part of the common educational experience, and perhaps an important formative influence for almost all youth.

The early years of the 1970's were a period of strenuous debate and experimentation. The Central Council of Education reported to the Minister of Education in 1971 on fundamental policies and measures for the future development of school education. It suggested that consideration be given to changes in the organisation of schooling to possibly a 4-4-6, 4-5-5 or 6-6 system. It proposed a reform in curricula in order to strengthen the basic studies, increase the diversification of subjects at upper secondary level, and establish greater continuity and integration of work between primary, junior high, and senior high schools. And it stressed the need to improve the education and status of teachers. The Teachers' Union between 1971 and 1973 similarly produced a series of reports. In the course of the debates that ensued the Ministry initiated considerable research, commissioned a number of experimental projects, and began gradually to move towards the development of a major general reform throughout the whole system.

As an aid to clarifying objectives, particularly those of upper secondary education, it was suggested that the report *The Image of the Ideal Japanese* written in 1966 should be carefully studied.[39] It did for the 1960's what the *Cardinal Principles of the National Entity of Japan* had done for the 1930's. It set out the characteristics expected of a person

living in a democratic and industrialised Japan in the second half of the twentieth century. As an individual he should possess the freedom which comes from a power to control one's actions and take responsibility for them, the individuality and selfhood that come from a balanced development of abilities, the strength of will that comes from sincerity of purpose, and the sense of awe and respect for the continuity of the human contribution on which the present rests. As a member of a family, he should be expected to make the home a place of love, rest, and education which reaches out to other families and homes throughout society. As a member of society, he should be a devoted worker, with a spirit of social service, with a constructively critical and forward-looking view of society's cultural and productive activities, and with a respect for the core of social norms that lie at the heart of social morality and social order. And, as a national of Japan, he should have an abiding love of the nation, a love and respect for the emperor as the symbol of the state, and a deepening sense of the need to preserve, cultivate, and extend the characteristics and virtues that lie behind the achievements of the Japanese people.

The *Image* expressed the ideal towards which Japanese teachers and their pupils might aspire. It was a careful balance of traditional feeling for the maintenance of the solidarity of Japanese society and the spirit of individual enterprise that Japan's westernisation had stimulated

[39] Japanese National Commission for UNESCO, *op.cit.*, pp. 34-47.

throughout the century. To achieve a viable union between social cohesion without inertia or the exploitation of individuals, and personal initiative without disorder or loss of responsibility, has been a perennial problem of human society. In the 1970's Japan's teachers had become sharply aware of it as a task to which education was expected to make a germinal contribution.

REDESIGNING TERTIARY EDUCATION

(i) Growth in Enrolment

The explosive increase in secondary enrolments in the post-World War II period was followed by a dramatic expansion of tertiary education.

Every country was affected. In the twenty years between 1950 and 1970 the number of students in tertiary institutions increased with great rapidity. In Japan enrolments went up sevenfold, in France and Sweden fivefold, and in most other countries they tripled or doubled.[40] Through the course of the century, from 1900 to 1970, the increase in developed countries was even more impressive. The United States, for example, which led the field in enrolments throughout the period, doubled its number of students every fifteen years, and increased the proportion of the age group at college from four per cent in 1900 to forty per cent in 1970. France had a twentyfold increase in student numbers between 1900 and 1970, from thirty thousand to 650,000; and Great Britain moved forward comparably from twenty-five thousand to 590,000. In non-western countries tertiary education was largely a creation of the twentieth century, and they, too, joined vigorously in the post-1950 expansion.

By 1950 the proportion of the appropriate age groups of pupils completing a full secondary school course had passed fifty per cent in the United States, and was between three and 27 per cent in other western countries. By 1965 the numbers of secondary school graduates had quadrupled, and the proportion of the age group had risen in the United States to 76 per cent, Canada 72 per cent, U.S.S.R. 58 per cent, and ranged in the other developed countries from about seven to thirty per cent. The proportion of tertiary students showed a corresponding increase.

It would appear that by 1965 tertiary education enrolments had reached a point similar to that of secondary education in 1950. Just as secondary education began to move rapidly after 1950 towards secondary education for all in the industrial countries, so too did tertiary education after 1965 move in numbers and in structure towards mass higher education.

Table 12.2: In Nine Countries: Secondary School Graduates as a Percentage of Their Age Group, and Tertiary Education Enrolments as a Percentage of the 20-24 Age Group

Countries	Secondary School Graduates in Age Group		Tertiary Education Enrolments in 20-24 Age Group	
	1950 %	1965 %	1950 %	1965 %
Canada	27	72	8	24
France	5	17	6	17
Germany	4	8	5	10
Japan	16	51	5	12
Spain		7	2	9
Sweden	7	19	5	13
United Kingdom		19	5	12
USA	56	76	20	41
USSR		58		31

This table is based on OECD, *Development of Higher Education 1950-1967*, OECD, Paris, 1971, pp. 68 and 103; *The World Year Book of Education* 1972-3, *Universities facing the Future*, Evans, London, 1972, p. 16.

[40] Organisation for Economic Cooperation and Development, *Policies for Higher Education*, OECD, Paris, 1974, p. 19, indicated that among the twenty-four developed countries having OECD membership the increase in tertiary enrolments from 1950 to 1970 went from four to fourteen million, an increase of approximately three and a half times.

By 1970, however, there was still a considerable distance to go. In no western European country, as yet, did fifty per cent of the appropriate age group complete secondary education; in most countries the proportion was by then somewhere between twenty and thirty per cent. The U.S.S.R. had moved up to about sixty per cent and the north American countries and Japan to about eighty per cent. The pool from which tertiary education drew was growing, but except for two or three countries, universal access was not an immediate prospect. In most countries the proportion of women enrolled in tertiary institutions, though constituting probably fifty per cent of the age group, filled somewhat less than 25 per cent of the places. Tertiary expansion, nevertheless, had been so speedy and extensive that in 1970 more than half the entrants were first generation tertiary students — evidence of a rapidly widening pool of educational aspiration.

(ii) Structural Reform in Europe

In most countries the unprecedented popularity of tertiary education and the problems involved in coping with it led to the establishment of various committees to investigate the phenomenon and make recommendations for future developments. The most substantial reports concerned specifically with tertiary education were those undertaken in England and in the United States. The Robbins Committee in England in 1961-63 and the Carnegie Commission 1967-74 in the U.S.A. produced multi-volumed reports that were widely read in many countries. The Science Council in West Germany also made an impressive series of studies throughout the 1960's, and the Japanese Central Council of Education in 1971 was responsible for an influential review of the whole range, including tertiary education.

In England during the post-war period the three components of tertiary education — universities, teachers' colleges, and colleges of further education (mainly technical colleges) — underwent a substantial change in relationship. In 1944 a process of upgrading the non-university institutions began with a recommendation from a government committee that teachers' colleges should be linked with universities in a new, loose association to be known as an Institute of Education. Within a few years all but one university had established the Institute scheme. In the following year, 1945, another committee, looking at technical education, suggested the need to draw a firmer distinction between the education of the technologist and that of the technician. It could be done by having a selected number of technical colleges concentrate on higher-level technological training to overcome 'the shortage of scientists and technologists who can also administer and

organize, and can apply the results of research to development'. Eleven years later, in 1956, the distinction was reiterated and more closely defined; and several of the technical colleges were converted into higher-order Colleges of Advanced Technology (CAT's).[41]

In 1963, for the first time, a committee looked at the whole pattern of English tertiary education, its interrelationships and its future prospects. The Robbins Committee was impressed with the recent expansion in enrolment and commissioned some useful research on problems of access by students and their ability to cope with higher education courses. It concluded that the pool of ability was much larger than had been supposed by many academics, that there were large reservoirs of untapped ability in the community, especially among girls and socially disadvantaged students, and that, in the interests of both individual and national development, 'courses of higher education should be available for all those who are qualified by ability and attainment to pursue them and wish to do so'.[42] The committee recommended that provision should be made to expand the number of students at tertiary level to approximately three times its current size by 1980. In the event, enrolments during the next ten years far outstripped the targets set by the committee. To cope with the expansion and the need to provide a system of tertiary education suitable for the nation's needs, the committee recommended a substantial strengthening at all levels. Graduate work was to be encouraged to the point where about thirty per cent of university students should be studying at graduate level, several new universities were recommended and established in main centres of population, the CAT's became universities of a type similar to the well-established German *Technische Hochschulen*, teachers' colleges were to become colleges of education capable of teaching to degree level in conjunction with a university school of education, and the various kinds of technical colleges were to be encouraged to maintain several levels of courses and to prepare students for degrees to be awarded by a central Council for National Academic Awards.

The system that emerged for tertiary education during the 1960's, following the Robbins Report, came to be known as a binary one. The universities were one leg of it, the teachers' and further education colleges the other. The pattern was confirmed in 1966 by the establishment of some thirty new institutions to be known as polytechnics which were formed from existing technical colleges. In 1970 polytechnics accounted

---

41 For teacher training, see Great Britain, Board of Education, *Teachers and Youth Leaders*, HMSO, London, 1944 (McNair Report). For technical education see *ibid.*, *Higher Technological Education*, HMSO, London, 1946, (Barlow Report); Great Britain, Ministry of Education and Science, *Technical Education*, HMSO, London, 1956 (White Paper); and *ibid.*, *A Plan for Polytechnics and Other Colleges*, HMSO, London, 1966 (White Paper).

42 Great Britain, Committee on Higher Education, *Higher Education*, HMSO, London, 1963, p. 8 (Robbins Report).

Figure 12.12: Great Britain: Numbers in Full-time Tertiary Education, 1900-70.

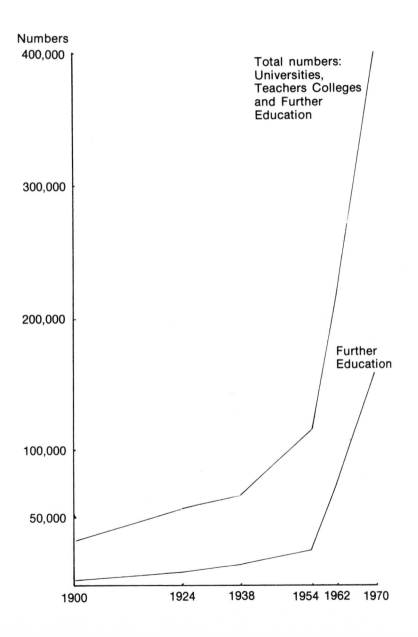

for about half the tertiary level students enrolled in further education courses. They were primarily teaching institutions with a wide range of students studying part-time or full-time in degree courses and in courses below degree level that would usually have a clear vocational purpose. They tended to be closely associated in purpose, administration, and sentiment with a local community and to be interested in providing courses and services of interest and value to the community. The binary system reproduced at tertiary level something like the grammar/modern school distinction at the secondary level. Some educators, sensitive to the favoured position of the universities, had already begun in the 1970's to hint at the creation of 'comprehensive academic communities' which in time might redraw the map of tertiary education in England.[43]

The pressures and ideas apparent in tertiary education in England were to be seen in all the European countries, and the moves to solve them took fairly similar lines. West Germany, for example, founded another seven universities during the 1960's; France added seven also before the sweeping reform of 1968, and Sweden doubled the number of faculties in its universities. Teacher training institutions were linked closely with universities in several of the German states and in others their future was strenuously debated. In France secondary teacher education was part of or closely associated with universities; primary teacher education remained distinctly separate just as it had in England before the McNair Report of 1944, but it was raised to tertiary level status by a reform in 1973. In Sweden the teacher education colleges all offered some university level courses independently or in conjunction with universities. Vocational studies in technical and art colleges in West Germany remained firmly separated from universities and were not raised in status; in 1975, however, a framework for reform was agreed to by the federal government providing for an integrated and comprehensive system of tertiary education, and experiments were initiated in two states to produce three-year technical academies for students who had qualified for university entrance.

In France the vocational *Grandes Ecoles* continued throughout the period to be regarded as the higher end of higher education; in 1966 a small number of University Institutes of Technology, offering a two-year degree and somewhat similar to English Polytechnics, were introduced and subsequently merged in the new tertiary complexes established in 1968. In that year, urged largely by current student disturbances, a new and comprehensive pattern of tertiary education was introduced. The Orientation of Higher Education Act of 1968 provided for two levels of university institutions. First, there were to be the *Grandes Ecoles* as before, and secondly, in place of the old universities, there were to be

[43] J. Pratt and T. Burgess, *Polytechnics: A Report*, Pitman, London, 1974, p. 189.

about forty multi-disciplinary universities made up by various combinations of Education and Research Units (UER's). Each UER was a unit or department in a separate discipline, e.g. economics, business, law, or Latin. In combining with other units to form universities they generally amalgamated into a coherent faculty with a common central theme, e.g. law or modern languages. Thirteen universities were established in Paris alone; some of them concentrated on single areas of study, some were multi-disciplinary, and others combined traditional university departments with institutes of technology and with research institutes, ranging in the level of their work from short-course vocational studies to post-graduate research.

(iii) Tertiary Expansion in the United States

In the development of tertiary education the United States in the course of the twentieth century outdistanced every other country in the size of its enrolments, in the variety of its institutions, and in the conscientious study given to possibilities and problems in the area. One thoughtful foreign observer wrote in 1972 that 'the development of the United States colleges and universities has been a turning point in the history of higher education.'[44]

In 1947, soon after World War II, the President's Commission on Higher Education made its report. It was of the opinion that Americans appeared to have lost their sense of direction and their sureness that they were moving towards a better tomorrow. This, the Commission regarded as a serious matter in a world moving through a period of rapid and revolutionary change. There was a need, it felt, for a reaffirmation of democratic principles and values, for the implementation of those principles and values throughout the field of education, and for the careful teaching of democratic ideas and processes to students at every level. There should be an effort, also, to bring greater understanding and skill into all aspects of human relations. Out of the study of social science should come a positive social policy that would arrest the current drift, and redress the balance between our knowledge of natural science and technology and our proficiency in human relations.

To fulfil the desired aims the commission argued for more two-year community colleges, offering a combination of general and vocational courses, for more careful manpower planning, and for the readjustment of graduate education to provide a better balance of education and preparation for an academic vocation.

The President's Commission saw a much larger role for education in the national life. Institutions of higher education were no longer to be regarded as instruments for the production of an elite, but rather places where all could go to extend their education and as places which

produced persons and ideas of vital importance to the continuing life of the American community.

By the 1960's the United States had developed a distinctive three-tier tertiary system — universities, four-year colleges, and community colleges, with, in 1970, approximately the same number of students in each tier.[45]

The universities numbered about one hundred and fifty and could be either state or private institutions offering a wide range of liberal arts and professional courses leading to bachelors through to doctoral degrees. Some state universities had as many as thirty thousand students on the one campus, others ran only to a few thousand. Many, especially in the mid-west, had been land-grant foundations; they thus developed a high sense of community involvement, and did much in the course of years, through research, teaching, and advice, to raise the educational and productive level of their region. A feature of most universities was the development of the graduate school as a separate administrative organisation for the promotion of research and the education of higher degree students.

At the second level, four-year colleges were somewhat diverse. The central feature of them was that they offered liberal arts and science courses, and in many cases, the kind of professional training closely allied to it, such as teaching, nursing, and business education. The more prestigious, such as Oberlin, Swathmore, and the Claremont Colleges, were private colleges which provided high-quality teaching in small classes. Most were state colleges which had often been teachers' colleges and had broadened out into general work but still retained a strong interest in teacher education. The four-year colleges took the place of undergraduate university work for many students and were preparatory to university professional and graduate schools, but they were also terminal for those who sought an undergraduate professional qualification or a general education. Some of the colleges moved into graduate work, and, in the general expansion of student numbers, were converted into state universities. In 1970 there were about 1,500 colleges, and they enrolled about three million students, about half of all the students studying for degrees in the United States.

The third tier, the community colleges, was the newest and most rapidly growing segment. The junior or community college was the most distinctive contribution made at the tertiary level by American educators during the twentieth century. It was to the twentieth century what the high school was to the nineteenth. The high school was an effort towards

[44] J. Ben-David, *American Higher Education*, McGraw-Hill, New York, 1972, p. 23.

[45] Carnegie Commission on Higher Education, Priorities for Action: *Final Report*, McGraw-Hill, New York, 1973, p. 69.

moving mass general education up into the secondary level. It took three-quarters of a century of experiment, controversy, and slow acculturation before it reached its take-off point early in the twentieth century. The community college was an effort to raise mass education to the tertiary level. Almost three-quarters of a century since the foundation of the first college, it began in the 1960's suddenly to blossom.

In the early years of the century there was much discussion in university circles about the standard of work of the first two undergraduate years. The view was widely expressed that they were more properly part of secondary education and that some steps should be taken to detach them from the university. Although that object was never achieved, sufficient interest was aroused to enable the establishment of an alternative way for students to complete those two junior years. A private junior college was established in 1896 in Chicago, and in 1901 the first public junior college opened near Chicago in Joliet, Illinois in association with Joliet high school. By 1915 seventy-four junior colleges were in existence. They could be regarded as two-year extensions of the high school program, or, where they were independent of high schools, as an amputated segment of the university undergraduate program, or, in some cases, as a two-year consolidation of previously over-extended four-year colleges.

The greatest development, before World War II, took place in California which gave the movement state financial support from 1917 on. Strong high school holding power, absence of tuition fees, an interest in educational experimentation, and, relative to the other states, a buoyant economy, combined in the 1920's and 1930's to favour a substantial development of junior colleges, so that by 1940 California had 47 per cent of the total U.S. enrolment. By then, there were 575 junior colleges in existence throughout the United States with almost two hundred thousand students. The junior college at that time could be described as a two-year institution, sometimes independent, sometimes attached to a university, but, most often, associated with a high school. It was small, with an enrolment usually of less than two hundred. Half the colleges were private institutions, and the other half might be run by state authorities or, more frequently, by local school districts. The task of the junior colleges was to provide, for high school graduates, two years of work equivalent to two years of undergraduate university work, which might be used to gain credit towards a university degree, or two years of terminal work of the same quality and standard.

After World War II, wider functions for the two-year junior colleges became more apparent. They began to be less exclusively designed to serve the purposes of high school graduates; admission was widened to admit those who could be deemed capable of profiting by their courses, and programs in adult education were greatly extended. In those post-war years the junior college took its first steps in the direction of becoming a community college. In that move California again led the way. Adult education enrolments increased rapidly, a stronger demand for sub-professional vocational training emerged, and an interest was developed by many people in extending their general education beyond high school level. Henceforth most junior colleges in the United States started to develop a more complex pattern of functions:

- They continued to provide courses from which students could transfer into universities, and for many students it was a most important though restricting function.

- They enormously increased their vocational offerings, thereby starting to fill a gap in American vocational education for the training of people of technician level that post-war demands were making more apparent.

- They expanded their general and special interest courses to cater for the adults of the local community who sought further education of various kinds at various levels. For that kind of institution the President's Commission suggested in 1947, the use of the name community college.[46]

The name and associated functions steadily gained in popularity until by 1970 it could be said that the junior college had been completely metamorphosed into the community college.

During the 1960's many of the states developed vigorous community college programs. Illinois, for example, in 1965 adopted a master plan for higher education which placed community college education within daily attendance distance of everyone in the state, and encouraged the new colleges to survey the needs and interests of their communities with a view to meeting them as fully as possible. Figure 12.13 shows clearly the spurt in the growth of community colleges in the 1960's when the enrolment quadrupled. By 1970, one-quarter of the total number of students in higher educational institutions were in community colleges. By 1975 their enrolment had increased by a further fifty per cent.

The post-World War II growth and fertility of two-year community colleges provided striking evidence of the great concern with and surge towards providing the widest possible educational opportunities for all citizens.[47] It was a contribution towards equality in education in three important ways:

[46] U.S. President's Commission on Higher Education, *Higher Education for American Democracy*, vol. 3, *Organizing Higher Education*, U.S. Government Printer, Washington, 1947, p. 5.

[47] Carnegie Commission on Higher Education, *The Open-Door Colleges. Policies for Community Colleges*, McGraw-Hill, New York, 1970, p. 2; Leland L. Medsker & D. Tillery, *Breaking the Access Barriers: A Profile of Two-Year Colleges*, McGraw-Hill, New York, 1971.

Figure 12.13: United States of America: Total Enrolments of Students in Higher Education and Enrolments in Junior Colleges to 1970.

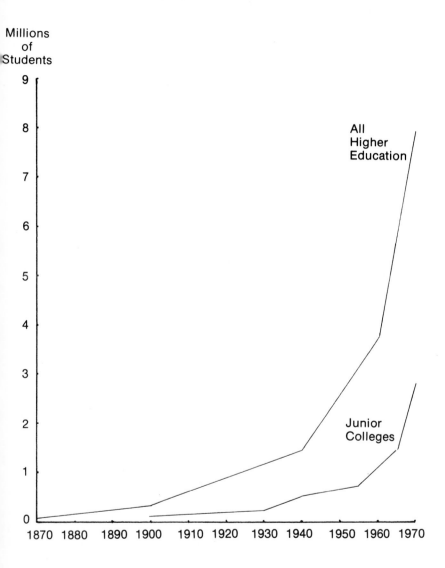

From Carnegie Commission on Higher Education, *Priorities for Action: Final Report,* McGraw-Hill, New York, 1973, p. 84, with additions, and *Community and Junior College Directory, 1973,* American Association of Community and Junior Colleges, Washington D.C., 1973, p. 6.

- The new millions who attended community colleges in the 1970's included many groups of whom some were adults who had previously not had an opportunity to continue their education, and some were adults who had found new interests because the community college awoke an awareness of them. The largest group, about half of all the enrolments, were young people who, in socio-economic status and racial composition, were more representative of the college age population than those in any other type of higher education. By catering extensively for part-time students, who constituted half the enrolment of the colleges, and by facilitating the attendance of persons who wished to have a break in their schooling or to return after a period of employment, the colleges developed a flexible and much appreciated approach to the continuing education of the community.

- The community colleges became the main public avenue for vocational education, ranging the whole alphabet of courses from advertising to wild-life conservation, flexibly adjusting their offerings to the needs of local business and industry, social welfare, and the community situation, employing work-study programs, and part-time and full-time courses to try to make it feasible for as many as possible to enrol. About one-third of all students in community colleges were enrolled in vocational courses.

- By centring the community college on a particular area, where the local community was readily in reach and had the opportunity to be consulted about the program of the college, it was possible to start to mould it into a genuine people's college, which could be looked to for the general cultural enrichment of the community like a Danish Folk High School, or for the general servicing of the community's interests and of the individual needs of all who had left high school.

In 1972 the Carnegie Commission on Higher Education started the second chapter of the summary of its reports with the striking statement: 'In 1900, 4 per cent of the eighteen to twenty year olds in the United States were enrolled in higher education. In 1970, that figure was 40 per cent.'[48] It went on to point out that the five main barriers to equal opportunity were:

- family income — that children of the more well-to-do were much more likely to go to college than those of poor parents;
- ethnic grouping — that the proportion of black students in the usual college age group was only half that of white students, and that other minority groups were even less well represented;

---

[48] Carnegie Commission on Higher Education, *A Digest and Index of Reports and Recommendations, December 1968 - June 1972,* California, Berkeley, 1972, p. 15.

- geographic location — that youth in the deep south had the lowest rate of attendance, and that living within easy travelling distance of a college was an inducement to attend;
- age — that many beyond the traditional college age who could benefit did not attend;
- quality of early schooling — that one's chances of attending college depended in some measure on the quality of one's schooling which varied from district to district.

The commission saw the movement in higher education to be a four-stage one from: elite or restricted access education, such as had characterised higher education in the U.S. prior to World War II but with diminishing effect, to mass higher education which had steadily grown since the formation of the land-grant colleges in the latter decades of the nineteenth century and had burgeoned after World War II with a rush of returning servicemen into courses of higher education, to universal-access higher education, first for those of usual college age and later for persons of all ages, and finally to universal attendance in some form of post-secondary education. The commission hoped by its report and its influence to move higher education forward in a responsible way into the last two stages.

The commission was established in 1967 and during the next six years investigated and reported extensively on the objectives, problems, and possible future development of every aspect of American tertiary education. In addition, it invited a large number of research and reflective studies from selected scholars. The very many highly readable volumes of material constituted 'the most thorough analysis of a nation's higher education that has ever been made'.[49] The commission made many thoughtful remarks, and put forward many detailed recommendations, but did not suggest any startlingly new ideas or fresh departures. The main burden of its advice was for Americans to make a great effort to clarify the purposes of higher education, undertake the 'recreation of a great new sense of purpose', develop guidelines to guarantee the essential independence of institutions of higher education, rethink and restore the approach to general education, and make provision for the greater participation of students in the decision-making process.[50]

(iv) Student Unrest in the 1960's

In 1965 Marcuse wrote that in advanced industrial society 'the productive apparatus tends to become totalitarian to the extent to which it determines not only the socially needed occupations, skills, and attitudes, but also individual needs and aspirations... Technology serves to institute new, more effective, and more pleasant forms of social control and social cohesion.'[51] He argued that the corporative capitalism of western society was inherently repressive both to those outside it and those within it. Its high point, the affluent welfare society, tied the individual by many conscious and unconscious bonds to a life in support of expanding production, insensitive and exploitive development, and competitive activity. In such circumstances, even one of the great virtues of democracy, tolerance, was repressive. What was needed was a radical change in consciousness and a refusal to accept the authoritarian processes and values of current society. A group with a new sensibility could take action to free society, to transmute its values, and to move towards the development of a participatory democracy in which 'for the first time in our life, we shall be free to think about what we are going to do'.[52]

Marcuse's view appealed strongly to groups of radical students in many countries during the 1960's who had been nurtured on a decade of hard-hitting criticism of capitalist society from perceptive sociologists and journalists.[53] It helped them to analyse more deeply the dissatisfactions many of them felt, and it provided some of the more radical with a theoretical basis on which to organise student protest and revolt. Such theoretical awareness was not present in the earliest years of the disturbances; it developed as students began to form a community of protest, started to hold discussions and write manifestos about their aims and methods, and came to see the international dimensions of their activities. The student revolts thus grew into a movement which, though scattered in many countries and concerned with diverse problems, yet had many common techniques and some common ideological interests.

In the 1950's student protest broke out from time to time, and towards the end of the 1950's there were serious disturbances in many places, e.g. Budapest, Warsaw, Madrid, Paris, Göttingen, Buenos Aires, Ibadan, Rangoon, and on several campuses in the U.S.A. The protests, however, were sporadic. There was no continuous simmering of disaffection. It was not until the early 1960's that trouble became widespread and persistent. Beginning in 1960, students in Tokyo signalled their disapproval of the

45 E. Ashby, 'The great appraisal', in *The World Year Book of Education 1972-3, Universities Facing the Future*, W.R. Niblett & R.F. Butts, (edd), Evans, London, 1972, p. 42.

50 Carnegie Commission on Higher Education, *Priorities for Action: Final Report*, McGraw-Hill, New York, 1973, pp. 91-2.

51 H. Marcuse, *One Dimensional Man*, RKP, London, 1964, p. xv. H. Marcuse (1898-1979) migrated from Germany to the U.S.A. in the early 1930's, taught in various American universities, and was professor of philosophy in the University of California at San Diego, 1965-1970.

52 H. Marcuse, *An Essay on Liberation*, Penguin, London, 1969, p. 91.

53 e.g. C. Wright Mills, *White Collar* (1951), *The Power Elite* (1956); W.H. Whyte, *The Organization Man* (1956); Vance Packard, *The Hidden Persuaders* (1957), *The Waste Makers* (1960).

connection with America, succeeded in preventing President Eisenhower's visit to Japan, and showed their distaste for aspects of the 'economic miracle' of Japanese recovery and expansion after the war by disrupting public meetings. In the U.S.A. negro and white students continued their campaign against segregation. In Europe and South America demonstrations were held in protest at the American blockade of Cuba; and in Pakistan and Nigeria students demonstrated about conditions within the universities. At the same time, staffs of several universities in Germany, South Africa, and England staged protests against governmental corruption, apartheid, and nuclear testing. Over the next three years there was a similarly wide range of protests in many countries. In August 1964 students in Karachi, by demonstrating against American policy in the Vietnam War, brought forward an issue that was to be a central one for the remainder of the 1960's. It was expanded in 1965 by students in France, Germany, and all the English-speaking countries.

The American Students for a Democratic Society issued, in 1962, a much-discussed statement critical of the affluent society and seeding the establishment of a participating democracy 'governed by two central aims: that the individual share in those social decisions determining the quality and direction of his life; that society be organized to encourage independence in men and provide the media for their common participation'.[54] Three years later, in 1965, the German socialist students' union (SDS) issued an influential manifesto, *Universities in a Democracy*, which, in Marcuse's style, criticised western society, called for its radical reconstruction, identified universities as institutions of the unwanted society, and summoned students to take the leadership in dismantling and reconstructing the university as a step towards a wider revolution. From about 1964-65 on there was a general tendency for students to link dissatisfaction over local university policies with wider social issues, and to bring a strong political note into student protests. The change was particularly noticeable in a prolonged sit-in in 1964-65 on the Berkeley campus of the University of California in which the well-established tactics of the civil rights movement were used and general issues of civil liberties were brought up. Thereafter, on most American campuses three issues were dominant: involvement in Vietnam, racial equality, and repression and civil liberty. The Berkeley upheaval was the event which students in English-speaking countries regarded as marking the serious beginning of the student movement; it was endlessly debated and analysed.

Throughout 1966 there were widespread strikes in French universities against the government's proposals for university reform, and an increase in demonstrations on political issues in Germany, Italy, and the U.S.A. In that year the Cultural Revolution began in China. The emphasis in it on the importance of political understanding and

participatory democracy in university government was noted and studied by students throughout the world. It was especially welcomed in Latin America where the centuries-old tradition of student political agitation was reinforced. In 1966 the University of San Marcos, Lima, was the scene of violent clashes between rival radical factions, and the University of Mexico was similarly shaken in 1966 and 1968. In Japan, too, where, since the 1920's, students had been involved in protests on issues in national politics, activity was raised to fresh heights.

In 1967 the Vietnam War was the cause of massive protests in the U.S.A. in which the student organisation, Students for a Democratic Society, played a leading and radical part in persuading students to examine and confront the established authorities of society. German students, particularly in Berlin, had sustained and violent clashes with the police and became more and more alienated from the establishment. The Turin Charter was produced by Italian students, reinforcing the revolutionary views expressed earlier by the German SDS and in England the London School of Economics experienced a week-long strike and sit-in by students.

The movement was much more than a political protest. It was felt by many participants to be a new youth movement, cultural and social, as well as political; and they showed their taste for new and uninhibited experiences in unusual dress, speech, drugs, music, art, and poetry. Rock music was very characteristic, and a bearer of much of the movement's farther-out social criticism.

> Why are you crying my son
> Are you frightened what mankind has done?

à propos the dehumanisation of society, sang the Beatles in 1968. And Cat Stevens asked

> I know we've come a long way
> We're changing day to day
> But, tell me, where do the children play?

In some places Free Universities were set up in an attempt to apply what were later called counter-cultural ideas in higher education — breaking down the teacher-pupil distinction, tackling 'real' issues head-on, and forming some kind of learning community based on exchange. Such things and ideas expressed the messianic kinds of feelings widespread in the movement — that this was a new dawn, and that the whole world was opening up.

The year of crisis was 1968. In the early months of the year students in

---

[54] 'The Port Huron Statement' of the American Students for a Democratic Society reproduced in part in P. Jacobs & S. Landau, *The New Radicals*, Penguin, 1967, pp. 154-67.

several German universities protested against a leading German news-paper chain, invading printing plants and harassing delivery trucks. Students in Belgium at Louvain erupted over a language issue and caused the government to resign. At Columbia in New York, students, roused over a racial issue, seized part of the campus and shut down the whole university for the remainder of the semester. In May, the most substantial revolt of all occurred in Paris. From the beginning of May until the middle of June the Sorbonne was occupied by students, and rioting was almost a daily occurrence. For a short while an alliance was formed with workers, barricades were out in the Paris streets, several industrial plants were occupied, and the government appeared to be threatened. Gradually public order was restored, the Minister for Education resigned, and a reconstruction of higher education was promised. Demonstrations and sit-ins occurred in that year in universities in almost every country of the non-communist world, ranging from fairly mild confrontations and student-run programs in England to strenuous and bloody confrontations with the police in Japan.

After 1968 the revolt of university students did not cease but, with some notable exceptions, it proceeded at a reduced tempo. The principal exceptions, in which violence increased and students became more persistent in taking over and shutting down universities, were in Japan and the U.S.A. In 1969 most of the major universities in Japan were occupied by militant students and brought to a standstill. The Japanese radical student movement was probably more widespread and more committed to political revolution in the Marcuse style than that of any other advanced country. Unrest continued on many campuses in the U.S.A. and had its most dramatic expression in May 1970. In that month disturbances at Kent State University, Ohio, over the recent escalation of the Vietnam War, provoked retaliation by local troops sent to keep order. Four students were killed and nine wounded. And in Jackson College, Mississippi, racial clashes led to the shooting of two black students by law enforcement officers.

The movement in the 1960's had been a series of educational, social, and political protests. It had voiced dissatisfaction about university teaching and examining methods, insufficiency of staff-student contact, relevance of courses, and lack of student participation on university disciplinary and governing bodies. It raised a number of social and political issues of which the three outstanding ones came to be the involvement in the Vietnam War, racial discrimination, and nuclear testing. The techniques of protest were most highly developed in the U.S.A. They developed from simple marches, speeches, and strikes to more productive measures such as sit-ins, teach-ins, and the taking over of university teaching programs or the establishment of independent student universities. Students became more disruptive as the years went by and

entered into alliances with various radical worker groups in order to spread the effect of revolutionary ideas and action. The issues that were brought up were seldom single or simple; a bread and butter issue, for example, about examination procedures might involve questions of student power and authority in the university, and extend to the general question of oppression in a capitalist society. In such a way protest about local and institutional matters became opposition to the repressiveness of society, and commitment on the part of the more radical to struggle for a fundamental change.

The student revolts which came to a climax towards the end of the 1960's continued into the 1970's in a somewhat changed but more pervasive form. Overt strikes and demonstrations were still plentiful on issues similar to those of the 1960's, though the end of the Vietnam War in 1975 somewhat defused the movement by depriving it of its most popular international rallying point. Many of the students' demands for participation in university government had also been conceded to the reasonable satisfaction of many of the protesters. The most significant thing that had happened, however, was that the views that had been regarded as somewhat novel when expressed by SDS leaders in the mid-1960's, had by the 1970's become common currency in the academic community. New students and staff and even well-established academics were reading and discussing as a matter of course the varieties of Marxian analyses of contemporary society and social change that had been thrown up during the revolts. Many new topics and new courses on those and associated themes had found their way into university syllabuses, and the ideas were slowly seeping through the consciousness of all members of the university. The revolution, if less obvious and violent, was becoming for many what Marcuse had declared to be the first step in changing social existence, a radical change in consciousness.[55]

Student unrest precipitated university reform in the late 1960's and in the 1970's. Some of the reforms were, as in France and Germany, a substantial recasting of the system; others, as in England and Japan, were a less sweeping but nevertheless significant modification of university government and curricula. In all cases the universities became involved in a thorough questioning and rethinking of the purposes and structures of tertiary education.

---

[55] Useful summaries of occurrences and ideas in the course of the student revolts are to be found in the following: United States, *The Report of the President's Commission on Campus Unrest*, U.S. Government Printer, Washington, 1970; B. & J. Ehrenreich, *Long March, Short Spring*, New York Monthly Rev. Pr., New York 1969; S. Spender, *The Year of the Young Rebels*, Vintage, New York, 1968; F.F. Harcleroad (ed.), Issues of the Seventies, Jossey-Bass, San Francisco, 1970; England, *Report from the Select Committee on Education and Science 1968-9, Student Relations*, vol. 1, HMSO, London, 1969; P. Jacobs & S. Landau, *The New Radicals*, Penguin, 1967; T. Pateman (ed.) *Counter Course*, Penguin, 1972; and the appropriate issues of *Minerva*.

(v) Issues in Tertiary Education

In the quarter-century of expansion and reconstruction in tertiary education that followed World War II the student unrest of the 1960's was the most serious and dramatic problem of the period. There were, however, many others. There were, for example, serious questions of administration, provision of buildings and equipment, finance, student selection, staff recruitment, internal government, external relations, support for research, and expansion of the curriculum. Each was important in the development of universities and other institutions, and many were difficult and recurring. Three, because of their generality and the intense interest which they aroused, stood out from all the others — the nature of a general education was the most studied topic of the 1940's and at various later times; academic freedom became a vital issue in the 1950's; and the function of the multiversity and the other emerging forms of tertiary education received a good deal of attention in the 1960's and early 1970's.

World War II produced a deep consciousness that the world had lost a sense of common values, and that educators should bend their efforts to bring mankind back into an area of common discourse. The title of Livingstone's wartime essay from Oxford, *Education for a World Adrift*, summed up a widespread feeling about the 'age without standards'. A common response in many universities and schools was the effort to devise some satisfying and comprehensive pattern of general studies. The most widely studied statement on the matter was the Harvard University Report of 1945, *General Education in a Free Society*. The authors suggested that the curriculum should provide a basic understanding in three broad areas: natural sciences, social sciences, and the humanities, and that the subject-matter should be taught so as to develop in the mind of the young the abilities 'to think effectively, to communicate thought, to make relevant judgments, to discriminate among values'.[56] For the next twenty years numerous experiments of various kinds were made to provide a common intellectual experience for students through courses based on ideas, problems, and human activities, offered in depth or in survey fashion. The purpose was to build a university which had a sense of being a common intellectual community.[57] In America, the small private four-year colleges such as Sarah Lawrence and Bennington were the most persistent and probably the most successful. In England, a new university, Keele, was established in 1949 with a common first-year inter-disciplinary program followed by a selection of subjects requiring work in both science and non-science areas. Even in Japan, under American occupation, general education of the Harvard Report pattern was widely introduced. Several difficulties were encountered by all the experiments. Science and technology were, until the early 1960's, subjects which clearly had begun to attract large numbers of students and to assume a leading position in the

hierarchy of university studies. Most scientists tended to support general studies especially as it spread a knowledge of science among the humanities students, but few were interested in teaching general science or in putting science into an inter-disciplinary pattern with non-science subjects. There was, too, the perennial difficulty of securing agreement on the best common elements. The problem was increased in the 1960's when students in most countries started to drift away from science towards the social sciences. A new basis for the synthesis became necessary and at that stage the size and diversity achieved by the various tertiary institutions rendered a satisfactory solution even more difficult.

In the 1950's there was an upsurge in government spending on tertiary education which continued to grow throughout the next two decades. At the same time it became apparent that universities by their output in research and trained manpower were important elements in the economic and social development of a nation. Governments therefore became interested in adapting university work to support their developmental plans, and in providing money for the kinds of projects that seemed best to fit their own purposes. It was a challenge to the traditional autonomy and academic freedom of universities. In many countries, particularly in the communist and underdeveloped world, universities whole-heartedly accepted the role of co-operating with governments in the interest of developing a planned economy.

In the western democracies there was also much co-operation but much questioning, too. The European professor who had been 'a government-paid private practitioner', and the American whose salary had come from more varied sources were reluctant to surrender the independence of action and speech that they enjoyed outside the civil service. The position was exacerbated by the development of a cold war of undeclared hostilities between the communist and western democratic groups beginning in the late 1940's. Some aspects of the research undertaken by university staff were related to military or other unrevealable matters. Confidence and free exchange of information among scientists was seriously affected. At the same time challenges were made to the national loyalty of various members of the university staff. Fitness to teach and research in universities was judged by various politicians, especially in the U.S.A. where the movement was led by Senator McCarthy, on the basis of an individual's political beliefs. In consequence many state universities in America required their teachers to take oaths of loyalty, and there were many bitter discussions in university circles on academic freedom. The hysteria of McCarthyism lasted only for a

[56] Harvard Committee, *General Education in a Free Society*, Harvard University Press, 1945, p. 65.

[57] See R. Thomas, *The Search for a Common Learning: General Education 1800-1960*, McGraw-Hill, New York, 1962.

short but harrowing time. The more insidious problem of commitment to secrecy and to political policies from the acceptance of government grants for specific kinds of research and development remained with all universities in the western world, and was one of the serious objections to university policies raised by students during the unrest of the 1960's.

In 1963 Clark Kerr wrote that the University of California had 'operations in over a hundred locations... nearly 10,000 courses in its catalogues; some form of contract with nearly every industry, nearly every level of government, nearly every person in its region ... Over 4,000 babies were born in its hospitals. It is the world's largest purveyor of white mice. It will soon have the world's largest primate colony. It will soon have 100,000 students — 30,000 of them at the graduate level; yet much less than one-third of its expenditures are directly related to teaching.'[58] The institution had become a 'multiversity'. The American university was undergoing its second great transformation — the first, towards the end of the nineteenth century; the second, in the period since World War II. Tertiary education was part of a great 'knowledge industry' engaged in the manufacture, distribution, and utilisation of knowledge. In the process, its institutions had increased vastly in size and in the range of their contacts and interests. No longer were they compact intellectual communities, they were 'a whole series of communities and activities'.[59]

It was clear that by the 1960's tertiary education was no longer regarded in advanced countries as an education for the few. It had diversified into institutions of various levels and of considerable size, and its courses and researches were related to almost every human interest. It had become a knowledge service-station for society. In the course of that process of evolution some of its student and professorial judges believed it had erected an over-elaborate and somewhat impersonal structure and it had lost or watered down its vital and traditional function of independent social critic. Tertiary authorities were not blind to such criticisms. They recognised the great problems of re-establishing cohesion both within a single diversifying institution and throughout a proliferating system. Where the liberal tradition of study associated with a faculty of arts or philosophy was no longer central, could another source of cohesiveness be discovered? Tertiary education, by 1970, had become an important form of public education, planned and monitored by governments, and supported by public funds. There was little room for independence. In what areas, and with what kind of voice could dissent be effectively expressed? It was, nevertheless, true that a healthy spirit of experimentation was alive in the tertiary section of education. For example, new integrations and combinations of subjects suggested some progress towards a new form of general education for the latter part of the twentieth century in recently established universities in England; the Ruhr university at Bochum in Germany was attempting to re-unite technological work with traditional university studies and redesign methods of teaching; and in polytechnics, community colleges, and universities schemes of student participation of diverse kinds were in operation. There were, in effect, few institutions of tertiary level which had not learnt a lesson from the years of student unrest, had not seriously considered the substantial reports of the 1960's and 1970's, and had not begun to take thought about their future development in a much more sophisticated and wide-awake way than ever before.

---

[58] C. Kerr, *The Uses of the University. With a Postscript — 1972*, Harvard University Press, 1972, pp. 7-8.

[59] *ibid.*, p. 1. See also Martin Trow, 'Reflections on the transition from mass to universal higher education,' *Daedalus*, 1970, 1-42, and Martin Trow, 'The expansion and transformation of higher education', *International Review of Education*, 18, 1, 1972, 61-84.

**Bloom's
Taxonomy of Educational Objectives
Cognitive Domain
Knowledge**

1.00 Knowledge
    1.10 Knowledge of Specifics
    1.11 Knowledge of Terminology
    1.12 Knowledge of Specific Facts
    1.20 Knowledge of Ways and Means of Dealing with Specifics
    1.21 Knowledge of Conventions
    1.22 Knowledge of Trends and Sequences
    1.23 Knowledge of Classifications and Categories
    1.24 Knowledge of Criteria
    1.25 Knowledge of Methodology
    1.30 Knowledge of the Universals and Abstractions in a Field
    1.31 Knowledge of Principles and Generalisations
    1.32 Knowledge of Theories and Structures

Intellectual Abilities and Skills

2.00 Comprehension
    2.10 Translation
    2.20 Interpretation
    2.30 Extrapolation
3.00 Application
4.00 Analysis
    4.10 Analysis of Elements
    4.20 Analyses of Relationships
    4.30 Analysis of Organisational Principles
5.00 Synthesis
    5.10 Production of a Unique Communication
    5.20 Production of a Plan or Proposed Set of Operations
    5.30 Derivation of a Set of Abstract Relations
6.00 Evaluation
    6.10 Judgments in Terms of Internal Evidence
    6.20 Judgments in Terms of External Criteria

These are the main headings in the *Taxonomy*: a set of standard classifications of student behaviour upon which statements of educational objectives, analyses of classroom teaching, and the testing of educational achievement could be based. It was in widespread use in the 1960's and 1970's. B.S. Bloom (ed.), *Taxonomy of Educational Objectives*, Longmans Green, N.Y., 1956.

CHAPTER 13

TRENDS IN EDUCATIONAL RESEARCH AND CURRICULUM DEVELOPMENT

SUMMARY

Research in Education
- (i)   Educational Sociology in Action
    - (a)   Education and Society
    - (b)   Education and Social Class
    - (c)   Community Studies
    - (d)   Research on the Comprehensive School
    - (e)   Environment and Educational Achievement
- (ii)   Research on Teaching
    - (a)   Behaviour of Teachers
    - (b)   Reading and Readiness
    - (c)   International Research on Educational Attainment
- (iii)   Child Development
    - (a)   Studies of Adolescents
    - (b)   Mental Testing
    - (c)   Piaget and Cognitive Development

Summary of Trends

Curriculum Development
- (i)   Background to Curriculum Reform
- (ii)   Secondary School Curriculum Reform
- (iii)   Transformation in the Primary School
- (iv)   Pre-School Education
- (v)   Aspirations of the mid-1960's and 1970's

RESEARCH IN EDUCATION

Innovation became an important word in education in the post-World War II period and it was through educational research and projects of curriculum development that innovation was most often proposed and tested. The immense activity and interest generated by the expansion and reform of secondary and tertiary education stimulated and was supported by an increase in educational research, much of it fruitful and suggestive. From early in the 1950's also, substantial projects for curriculum development began and spread through all subjects and all countries during the next twenty years. They brought considerable changes to the schools, not merely in the content of studies but also in methods of learning and teaching and in general outlook.

In the post-World War II period educational research expanded greatly and assumed increased importance. The science of education had steadily progressed from the early days of Meumann and Lay, had improved its techniques, had recruited a number of distinguished practitioners, and had made some useful contributions to the understanding of educational processes, but it had tended to remain somewhat peripheral to the main work of educational administrators and the schools. After World War II wider efforts were made by administrators to look for help and information on educational problems from research teams; and, gradually, in universities, public departments of education, and independent foundations, considerable numbers of trained researchers were engaged and a substantial body of well-researched ideas and information was built up. The services of educational research were used to assist in the making of basic social and educational policies, to provide data for the training and assessment of teachers, to contribute to the deeper understanding of the processes of children's intellectual, social, and emotional growth, and to assist in the development of new curricula for primary and secondary schools.

Within a very wide range of studies undertaken during the post-war period, there were three principal areas of activity:

- the social context of the school and its pupils;
- the nature of the teaching process;
- child growth, especially intellectual development.

George Herbert Mead (1863-1931), American sociologist and associate of John Dewey.

(i) Educational Sociology in Action

A French educational administrator in Morocco, pondering on the relationship of education and society, published, in 1944, a notable historical study of his native village, in which he traced, for a hundred years up to World War I, the manner in which, with varied success, education responded to local needs, and in turn made an impact on the life of the local community as it moved from its undeveloped state into the modern world.[1] His study was a harbinger of the new trend. Historians of education were henceforth to view education much more in its social context, and a sociological interest was to become increasingly apparent in all other areas of educational research.

Rarely before the end of World War II had a serious application of sociological ideas and methods been made to education. The most prominent exceptions were to be found in the work of Emile Durkheim and G.H. Mead, and, later, of Karl Mannheim. Durkheim, one of Europe's leading sociologists, was a professor of education and later, also, of sociology at the University of Paris from 1902 to 1917.[2] Education, for him, was conditioned by its society and was designed to fit individuals to fulfil society's demands. Society was bound together by a social solidarity resting on shared sentiments and shared labour; individuals were constrained by the social bonds and the social trends that grew up in the course of social living. One of the sociologist's main tasks was to study current social constraints and social movements; and the task of the educational sociologist was to demonstrate the contribution education made to social solidarity, without which individuals would disintegrate into a state of personal disorganisation which he called anomie. Educators had a responsibility to try to determine what current social needs were, to take action to see that they were met, and to adapt the school to the changes. Thus, schools were institutions concerned with the process both of mediating society to children, and of helping to reconstruct society.

Mead shared Durkheim's interest in social action. He was a colleague of Dewey's at Chicago who shared his pragmatist philosophy.[3] He was interested principally in the psychological impact of society on man.

[1] R. Thabault, *Mon Village 1848-1914, L'Ascension d'un Peuple*, Delagrave, Paris, 1945; trans. P. Tregear, *Education and Change in a Village Community. Mazières-en-Gatine. 1848-1914*. RKP, London, 1971

[2] E. Durkheim (1858-1917), a product of the Ecole Normale Superieure, taught for several years in *lycées*, became a professor of social science at Bordeaux in 1887, and joined the staff of the University of Paris in 1902. His major works bearing on education were *Education et Sociologie, L'Education Morale*, and *L'Evolution Pédagogique en France*.

[3] G.H. Mead (1863-1931) was educated at Oberlin and Harvard, and taught at Chicago University from 1893 to 1931. Most of his work was published posthumously. *Mind, Self, and Society* (1934) was his best-known book.

Mind and self he saw to be formed from man's social activities, particularly through the action of communication. Meaning arose out of co-operative group action, and education's task was to communicate and to improve group actions and relationships. Mead held, like both Durkheim, and later, Mannheim, that education was the basis of social cohesiveness and that teachers were inescapably concerned with the social organisation of their school, with the social conditions of their pupils, and with the social problems of their times.

Karl Mannheim, pursuing a line of thought somewhat similar to that of Durkheim and Mead, brought education more firmly into the service of social reconstruction.[4] Society, he pointed out, was the total context in which man lived and of which in mind, in knowledge, and in behaviour he was a creature. Education could be understood only when we knew for what society the children were being educated. Contemporary civilisation in the 1930's and during World War II was involved in a critical struggle between democracy and totalitarianism. To succeed, democracy should reject *laissez faire* liberalism and become a planned democracy in which there was freedom, co-ordination, and growth. To achieve such a society and to maintain it education was of central importance. It would have to be an education for children and for adults, an education for the masses and for a democratically trained and selected elite, an education which would produce an educative society.

Mannheim managed to tap the immediate post-war interest in democratic reconstruction, and his views stimulated educators to consider the place of planning in a democratic society. With the work of Durkheim and Mead, his contribution helped to direct attention to the importance of sociology in educational thinking and research.

The post-war years developed something of a sociological climate in which social effects and problems became the popular topics of educational discussion and investigation.

(a) Education and Society

During the course of World War II much thought was constantly given to the kind of social reconstruction that might be undertaken when hostilities should cease. Education was a leading candidate for appraisal and possible redesign. The post-World War II climate had little of the idealism that characterised the immediate post-World War I period. It was hopeful but sober. It looked to educators not to perform miracles, but to find out how education was related to and how it might foster social improvement.

The research problem turned round three questions:

What educational opportunity is there? What difference, for example, did it make to be brought up in St. John's Wood rather than in East London, in Bronxville rather than in Harlem, or in the village of Karla rather than the metropolis of Bombay?

What is the effect on children of the educational opportunity that is offered to them?

What are the best means of achieving the effects desired from the available educational opportunities?

The first two questions were the basis of most of the research undertaken between 1945 and 1960 on the study of the school and its environment. On the third, some research was undertaken in the 1940's and 1950's, mostly in Europe on problems of school organisation. More detailed research on the design and impact of specific educational programs came later, in the 1960's. The three questions were never wholly distinct. Inevitably research on educational opportunity led to investigations of school performance and ways of enriching or modifying it. It is, however, possible, to see the three questions as emphases appearing in various research programs, and broadly characteristic of successive periods of time.

(b) Education and Social Class

The scene was set for research in the area of the first two questions by a widely-read study that appeared in the mid-forties.

In *Who Shall be Educated?* the American authors brought together a substantial body of recent research, from communities in New England, the Midwest, and the South, to show that schooling in the United States was weighted in favour of urban middle class white children. They found that schools tended to preserve existing social class differences among the pupils by using class biased tests of intelligence and achievement to sort and grade pupils, and by reflecting and maintaining the standards and aspirations of the various social classes of American society. They concluded that 'class values are of the utmost importance in the training of children from the moment of birth throughout their growth, and, in fact, throughout their lives'.[5]

Through that study American educators for the first time became

---

[4] K. Mannheim (1893-1947) was born in Hungary and taught sociology in Germany at Heidelberg and Frankfurt universities. In 1933 he migrated to England, taught in the London School of Economics, and in 1946 became a professor of the sociology of education at the London University Institute of Education. *Ideology and Utopia* was published in 1929, *Man and Society in an Age of Reconstruction* in 1935, and rewritten for an English version in 1940, and *Diagnosis of Our Time* in 1943.

[5] W.L. Warner, R.J. Havighurst & M.B. Loeb, *Who Shall be Educated?*, Harper, New York, 1944, p. 87.

generally aware of the pervasive existence of social class in American society and of the school's role in preserving social distinctions and discriminatory practices. Since the late 1930's American sociologists had been producing evidence of social class and caste distinction in American society. Through the studies of Middletown, Yankee City, and Deep South the situation had become familiar to academic readers. In the late 1940's and 1950's it was to be recognised by the nation's educators. The authors of *Who Shall be Educated?* suggested that schools should accept the existence of social class distinctions and should more consciously promote social mobility in order to produce a more democratic society in which social and economic opportunity would be fostered by educational opportunity. 'The School,' they wrote, 'seems clearly to be the instrument best suited for making social mobility a better understood and more clearly defined activity.'[6]

With the development of appropriate sociological techniques, it became fashionable in the 1950's to make the study of social class influences the central feature of any investigation of school achievements and school environment. An extensive study in the American mid-west, at the pseudonymous Prairie City, was undertaken to investigate whether 'the social behaviour of adolescents is related functionally to the position their families occupy in the social structure of the community'.[7] It documented the tendency of social class to be associated with school drop-out, discrimination in the curriculum, academic rewards, and success in a variety of high school activities. Another study, in an industrial New England town, plotted the stages by which elementary school children may become aware of social class.[8] Allison Davis in a series of publications, argued that schools and teachers had become purveyors of middle class habits and attitudes. Because of that class pattern, the schools were responsible for the failure of many lower class and negro children, with contrary expectations and interests, to learn the kinds of things the schools sought to teach.

The Chicago group of researchers found that lower class and black children had difficulty in understanding tests which reflect a middle class culture, and also were unable to cope with school work that was similarly oriented.[9] From their studies Davis suggested that the most important inference to be drawn was the criticism that the American public school curriculum tended to emphasise a range of mental problems and skills that was too narrow for most of the abilities necessary for attainment even in middle class culture itself. 'The greatest need of education is for intensive research to discover the best curricula for developing children's basic mental activities... The present curricula are stereotyped and arbitrary selections from a narrow area of middle class culture...

'We need to start with simple situations, drawn from the daily life of the pupil. As yet, we do not know what these situations are.'[10]

(c) Community Studies

The study of social class effects was the cutting edge of the research in the newly developing field of educational sociology. It was, however, not the only consideration. Research broadened out into a study of the general school setting and produced a number of useful surveys employing and further developing the sociological tools that interest in research on social class influences had made popular. Prairie City, and another similar field research station, Midwest, provided examples of such an extension of interest.[11]

The work in Midwest owed much to the ideas of Lewin and the field theorists in psychology. Since the mid-1930's they had been arguing the need for a closer study of patterns of social relationships and the forces at work within those fields. Their work and that of Barker at Midwest emphasised the connection between the individual pupil and his social environment at school and at home. They brought into fashion studies of school morale and *esprit de corps;* they endeavoured to measure school climate and atmosphere; and they made popular the study of group dynamics. In 1934, Moreno had published an intriguing sociometric study in which he investigated the cohesive and isolating relationships in various social groups, and devised a method of ascertaining and charting them.[12] By the 1950's there was considerable interest among educators in exploring classroom and peer group patterns among pupils, and in training pupils and youth groups in role-playing. Out of that interest came a richer understanding of the social interaction that occurred in school classrooms and a keener perception of the relationship of the social environment to the educational process. It produced also a realisation that classroom situations were more complex than had hitherto been conceived, that they were a dynamic pattern of persons and small groups with needs, expectations, and perceptions influenced by differing social backgrounds.

[6] *ibid.*, p. 147.

[7] A.B. Hollingshead, *Elmtown's Youth: The Impact of Social Classes on Adolescents.* Wiley, New York, 1949, p. 9.

[8] Celia B. Stendler, *Children of Brasstown*, Urbana, Illinois., Bureau of Educational Research and Service, University of Illinois, 1949.

[9] K. Eells, A. Davis, R.J. Havighurst, V.E. Herrick & R.W. Tyler, *Intelligence and Cultural Differences*, University of Chicago, 1951.

[10] A. Davis, *Social Class Influences upon Learning*, Harvard University Press, 1949, pp. 97-9.

[11] See, for example, R.J. Havighurst & Hilda Taba, *Adolescent Character and Personality*, Wiley, New York, 1949; and R.G. Barker and H.F. Wright, *Midwest and its Children*, Rowe, Peterson, Evanston, Illinois, 1954.

[12] J.L. Moreno, *Who Shall Survive? A New Approach to the Problems of Human Interrelations*, Nervous and Mental Disease Publishing Co., Washington D.C., 1934.

The research tools of social survey and social dynamics work were, in general, simple, and could be readily handled by interested teachers. The new social dimension that came through those studies into classroom practice was attractive to many teachers and invited their participation. In consequence, throughout the late 1940's and the 1950's, there were a large number of small-scale researches designed and carried out by classroom teachers, and aimed at increasing their knowledge of the local social environment, or at improving their handling of classroom situations. It recalled the earlier years of teacher participation in research in the heyday of the Child Study movement fifty years earlier, from 1890, to 1910. The new venture became known as action research and had two principal characteristics. First, its advocates held that much research in the past had been fruitless because those who carried it out were detached from the practical arena in which its results might be applied. If research was to have an effect on educational practice, it was important, therefore, that practising educators — teachers and administrators — should be involved in the planning and execution of it. Second, for research to be effective, research projects should be more pertinent to school concerns, and should arise out of current and relevant school situations.

The idea of action research became popular in the 1950's and continued into the early 1960's. It was not confined to research organised by teachers but became an approach widely used by educational researchers in an effort to ensure relevance for their work. Many researchers sought their problems in practical situations in school organisation and classroom teaching.

By the studies of social class and other social influences, by the investigation of classroom dynamics, and by the widespread use of action research, the effect of the environment on educational opportunity was substantially documented in the U.S.A., and a beginning was made towards understanding how social influences work on the educational process and how they might be better managed.

(d) Research on the Comprehensive School

In Europe the investigation of environmental patterns was slower to emerge. When it did, it was associated with post-World War II plans to improve educational opportunity by readjusting the formal structure of education. The research that was undertaken was action-oriented research inspired by current public educational policies. Administrators and politicians were interested in the possibility of developing new types of schools or in reorganising old forms, and a great deal of public discussion was aroused on the topic.

The relationship between environment and education was, among research workers in Europe, connected closely with the kind of secondary education available and the methods used for selecting pupils for secondary school. The move to reorganise secondary education stimulated research particularly in Sweden and in England.

In Sweden several notable large-scale surveys were carried out. A ten-year follow-up of the whole fourth grade in Stockholm was published in 1947, with an analysis of the pupils' school achievement related to their social background. In 1952 a study was published in which all the pupils from ten to fifteen years of age in the whole of the Göteborg educational system were tested for theoretical and practical intelligence, and smaller samples were given achievement tests in various subjects of the school program and special linguistic tests. The data was factor-analysed to produce developmental profiles through which the maturation of pupils could readily be judged. The study was used by educational authorities to help work out the organisation and program of the new comprehensive schools.[13]

Ten years later another follow-up study of the fourth grade in Stockholm was published. The occasion was an interesting one. Nine-year comprehensive schools had been introduced only on the south side of the city; they existed side-by-side with a variety of other patterns of schooling — five-, four-, and three-year secondary schools recruiting from the fourth, sixth or eighth grade of the elementary school. It provided an unusual opportunity for comparing performance in various selective and non-selective school situations. The purpose of the research, therefore, was to find out if there were 'any measurable differences of scholastic achievement' between pupils who had spent given amounts of time in different patterns of schooling.

Where the 1947 study had established that achievement in school was affected by environmental differences outside the school, the 1962 study was designed to look at the effect of environmental differences within the school. The study found that, although minor differences could be found at various levels and for various kinds of pupils, the type of grade or school had no bearing in the long run on the achievement of pupils, that the performance of pupils in highly academic classes did not correlate, except in lower level classes, with the kind of schooling they had previously had, and neither did that of pupils in less selective classes.[14]

In England, several studies were made of the impact of social class on selection for secondary school. A study in the mid-fifties, for example,

[13] J. Elmgren, *School and Psychology, A Report on the Research Work of the 1946 School Commission*, Stockholm, 1952. See also T. Husen, 'Two Decades of Educational Research', *Social Science Research in Sweden*, 1973, and *Problems of Differentiation in Swedish Compulsory Schooling* Norstedt, Stockholm, 1962 for a summary of research on problems connected with comprehensive schools.

[14] N.E. Svensson, *Ability Grouping and Scholastic Achievement*, Almqvist and Wiksell, Stockholm, 1962.

indicated that social class had a substantial effect on the extent to which pupils went to academic secondary schools and remained to complete the full course.[15] There was also a widely read study of school climate complementary to the Swedish work. At the end of the 1950's a comparison was made between comprehensive, selective grammar, and modern schools in three different areas of England to assess the interests, cultural standards, and morale of the pupils. The results tended to show that the comprehensive school may well be 'a more attractive society to live in' than the grammar or modern school.[16]

Further investigations of the way in which school organisation affected pupil achievement continued in many countries. To a large extent they produced inconclusive results. One research worker, in 1970, summarised the work on ability grouping or streaming during the 1950's and 1960's with the remark: 'It would seem that everyone can find evidence in previous research to support whichever side they take on the issue.'[17] She attributed the inconsistency and inconclusiveness of the abundant research that had been done to a lack of attention to some important factors, in particular, to a failure to take account of teachers' attitudes, methods, and responses to the streamed or non-streamed schools in which they worked. Accordingly, in her study, begun in 1963, of the effects of streaming and non-streaming on the personal, social, and intellectual development of primary school pupils, care was taken to examine the teachers' attitudes and classroom practices. It was found, in comparing streamed and non-streamed schools, that 'there was no difference in the average academic performance of boys and girls of comparable ability and social class', and that 'neither school organization nor teacher-type had much effect on the social, emotional or attitudinal development of children of above average ability'. Children of average and below average ability, however, were much better off in several ways in classes run by teachers who preferred non-streamed schools and who adopted a somewhat child-centred approach in teaching.[18]

(v) Environment and Educational Achievement

In the 1950's research moved well into the area of the second major question: What is the effect on children of the educational opportunity that is offered to them? In what ways is their performance affected by the interaction of their environment and their schooling? The studies of the 1940's had tended to place more emphasis on the effect of environment on educational opportunity; the studies of the 1950's and 1960's were more inclined to look at performance and potential within the school. In that area three leading questions emerged: How important is the effect of environment on educational attainment and intellectual ability? How is a pupil's language competence related to environmental factors?

What are the best ways of compensating for environmental deprivation?

There were numerous studies in those areas in European countries such as England and Sweden, and in the United States, and Japan. Most of the research was large-scale survey work. In contrast with the work of ten or twenty years earlier, it was complex and comprehensive. Large samples, many variables, and batteries of questions and tests were involved. Percentages, means, standard deviations, product moment correlations, and simple tests of significance that had served the previous generation of research workers gave way by the end of the 1950's to the more elaborate techniques of factor analysis.

One of the best known and most extensive surveys of the relationship of environment to educational attainment was an English study reported by Wiseman in 1964.[19] He and his colleagues carried out three large-scale surveys in the Manchester area; in 1951 and 1957 investigations of fourteen-year-old secondary school pupils, and in 1963, a study of primary school pupils from ages seven to ten. Tests of reading, arithmetic, and general ability were used in each case, and data was gathered on a wide range of environmental factors in the home, neighbourhood, and school. On analysis, there were substantial correlations between environmental factors and attainment, and even stronger ones with intelligence. The conclusion drawn by one of the researchers was similar to that of Davis in America that: 'On every count, these findings give more weight to the environmentalist than to the genetic viewpoint of the nature of ability required in intelligence tests.'[20] Other significant conclusions of the research were that bad homes and neighbourhoods were more effective in preventing bright children from emerging than they were in producing backwardness; that environmental influences on educational attainment were greatest at the youngest ages, especially up to about the age of eight, and progressively decreased in importance as children grew older; that home influences were much more important than those of neighbourhood or school; and that, of home influences, what mattered most was the attitude of parents to school and to books.

The several major official English reports of the late 1950's and 1960's — *15 to 18* (Crowther Report, 1959), *Half Our Future* (Newson Report, 1963), *Higher Education* (Robbins Report, 1963), *Children and*

---

[15] J. Floud, A.H. Halsey, and F. Martin, *Social Class and Educational Opportunity*, Heinemann, London, 1956.

[16] T.W.G. Miller, *Values in the Comprehensive School*, Edinburgh, Oliver and Boyd, 1961; R. Pedley, *The Comprehensive School*, Penguin, 1963, p. 109.

[17] Joan C. Barker Lunn, *Streaming in the Primary School*, Slough, National Foundation for Educational Research in England and Wales, 1970, pp. 3,4.

[18] *ibid.*, pp. 272-6.

[19] S. Wiseman, *Education and Environment*, Manchester University Press, 1964.

[20] *ibid.*, p. 120.

their Primary Schools (Plowden Report, 1967) — were much affected by the research on educational opportunity and environmental effects on education. Two of them, Robbins and Plowden, actually commissioned some extensive research, relied heavily on the findings, and encouraged publication of the research data and analyses. Wiseman's 1963 study, and the work of Lunn on streaming, were part of the Plowden investigation.

In the United States work in the same field had also become sufficiently extensive and impressive for the U.S. Congress to have a substantial study commissioned. The outcome was a report in 1966 by J.S. Coleman *et al.*, *Equality of Educational Opportunity*, based on a massive survey of approximately 645,000 children in four thousand elementary and high schools. Coleman and his group gathered information on school resources, the training and attitude of teachers, the home background, achievement, and attitudes of students, and the social and political influences at work in the communities where the schools were situated. The Report found that white students and orientals achieved at comparable levels, with Puerto Ricans and negroes well behind. There was a substantial gap between metropolitan whites in the northeast and non-southern negroes in verbal ability, reading comprehension, and mathematics. In assessing environmental effects on achievement the Report held that the physical resources and facilities of the school were of little importance; it was personal relationships that were of the most significance, and, in particular, the social environment provided by the child's family and fellow-students. Coleman concluded: 'Taking all these results together, one implication stands out above all: That schools bring little influence to bear on a child's achievement that is independent of his background and general social context; and that this very lack of an independent effect means that the inequalities imposed on children by their home, neighborhood and peer environment and carried along to become the inequalities with which they confront adult life at the end of school.'[21]

It was clear that there was a correlation between backwardness and poverty, that many bright children were being unduly handicapped by lack of educational opportunity, and that parental attitudes had a crucial effect on a child's educational progress. Moves were therefore made to try to put more educational fire into the environment. To provide improved educational opportunity and more stimulus to educational achievement, a second outcome of the environmental research and the social conscience that accompanied it was the development of programs of compensatory education. They commenced on a substantial scale, in the U.S.A. in the early 1960's as part of the poverty program drive towards the Great Society. Education soon became the main feature of the poverty program in the hope that it could solve many of the accompanying social problems. In particular, a strenuous effort was made to provide more educational

facilities for pre-school and young elementary school children in conformity with the findings of much of the survey research on the decisive influence on educational achievement of educational deprivation in the early years. Wiseman had particularly made that point, and it was supported by Bloom who, in 1964, reported on an examination of about one thousand longitudinal studies of child development. In his view the evidence showed that intelligence grew most rapidly in the early years, that environmental effects were likely to be most important in the first five years of life, and that in linguistic development the pre-school and elementary school period was responsible for establishing three-quarters of the learning patterns.[22] A second feature of the programs was a move to accelerate intellectual progress by teaching ideas and skills, chiefly in language and mathematics, at an earlier age than had previously been thought desirable.

In both England, where the Plowden Report of 1967 was a stimulus to a compensatory program, and in the United States, there was a growing conviction that verbal ability was a key element in scholastic progress, and that the effect of environment on it was of critical importance. Bernstein, in England, took up that basic idea. He showed that the differences between children of differing social classes were bigger on verbal than on non-verbal tests. To explain it he suggested that different classes had different modes of speech. Middle class speech was formal and led to a sentence organisation through which one's experience could be readily verbalised and conceptualised; on the other hand, lower class speech discouraged verbal elaboration and abstraction. Because of the differences in language codes, children of different social classes learned their behaviour, including their language and intellectual skills, in different ways.[23]

The investigation of the influence of language was the beginning of a significant change in environmental studies. The emphasis till then had been on establishing the fact that environment had various important effects on learning, but had not established how the effects were produced. The new trend was to introduce more concern for the mechanism of the process; it was a move from the study of 'what' to the study of 'how'.[24]

A study in the United States admirably demonstrated the new trend. It was a skilful investigation of 'the mechanisms of exchange that mediate

[21] J.S. Coleman, *Equality of Educational Opportunity*, p. 325.

[22] B.J. Bloom, *Stability and Change in Human Characteristics*, Wiley, New York, 1964.

[23] B. Bernstein, 'Elaborated and restricted codes: their social origins and some consequences', *American Anthropologist*, Special Publication, 1964, 66, 6, 2, pp. 55-69; B. Bernstein & D. Henderson, 'Social class differences in the relevance of language to socialization', *Sociology*, 1969, 3, 1, 1-20.

[24] H.E. Jones, 'The environment and mental development', L. Carmichael (ed.), *Manual of Child Psychology*, 2nd. ed., Wiley, New York, 1954, 631-96.

between the individual and his environment',[25] an intriguing study of the way in which negro mothers of different social classes communicate with and teach their young children. Using Bernstein's notion that the various language codes of different social classes structure both what a child learns and how he learns, Hess and Shipman interviewed a group of negro mothers and their four-year-old children from four different social status levels. The mothers were given a variety of tasks such as making up a story for their youngster or preparing him for the experiences of his first day at school, and in addition were asked to teach three simple cognitive exercises in sorting and copying to their child. A comparison of the linguistic behaviour of the mothers enabled the researchers to point out the ways in which the teaching styles of the mothers induced and shaped the learning styles of the children, and led them to conclude that 'the meaning of deprivation is a deprivation of meaning'. Deprivation was seen to be a cognitive environment, in which behaviour was controlled by status rules, in which a child related to authority rather than to rationale, in which he was compliant rather than reflective, and in which he was motivated by immediate reward or punishment rather than by future effects or long-term goals.

The interest in educational processes and the example of projects such as that of Hess and Shipman encouraged researchers to consider seriously the view that research should move more substantially from survey to experimental work.

(ii) Research on Teaching

During the 1930's Lewin and his associates had observed and experimented with groups under different conditions of leadership. The study demonstrated that, with careful observation and systematic recording of speech and action, it was possible to obtain a reasonably objective and full picture of the climate and activities of a group at work. Research workers readily transposed those ideas and techniques to the classroom.[26] In the decade following World War II teachers and researchers were busy learning to regard the classroom as a field of social interrelationships, and the teacher as a leader who, in various ways and for various purposes, had the management of the changing pattern of interactions in his classroom. Lewin and his colleagues had many imitators, and there were a great many studies of teachers as autocratic, democratic, or *laissez faire* practitioners.

The movement drew attention to the various social roles that teachers played, and it reinforced the growing influence of sociological thinking in educational research. An indicator of the type of research that became increasingly popular in the 1950's was an investigation of teacher-parent,

teacher-student, and parent-student relationships made by gathering responses from teachers, parents, and students on their perceptions of all three relationships. The study was notable chiefly for uncovering a great range of misperceptions by all three parties concerning the roles, expectations, and relationships that form an important part of the psycho-social environment in which the school operates.[27]

In 1955 Charlotte Fleming summed up the current position with the view 'that it has been demonstrated that pupils respond in differing fashions to different teachers, that teachers using different methods are reacted to in differing fashions according to the type of social climate they produce; that these changes affect not merely the amount of learning as measurable by tests of attainment but involve changes of attitude and of observable personal responses'.[28]

That kind of research was a substantial move into the area of the third major research question of the period: What were the best means of achieving the effect desired from the available educational opportunities? To probe the question, researchers had to look at the processes that went on in the classroom. What did the teachers do and how effective was it? What was the most appropriate curriculum, and how well did the students cope with it?

(a) Behaviour of Teachers

Prior to the 1950's most of the research on teachers had been concerned with means of judging their effectiveness. From the time when school inspection and teacher training were first taken seriously in the nineteenth century, there had been attempts to assess teachers, and to determine the characteristics of desirable teaching. In the 1930's and 1940's a considerable amount of research was done in relating teachers' characteristics to various criteria of effectiveness. A summary of the research, however, in 1948, pointed to the melancholy conclusion that its findings were contradictory, inconclusive, and of little value.[29]

In the 1950's a concerted effort was once more begun. It was deeply affected by the growing influence of sociological thinking on educational research and in particular it turned the attention of educational research

[25] R.D. Hess & Virginia C. Shipman, 'Early experience and the socialization of cognitive modes in children', *Child Development*, 1965, 36, pp. 868-86.

[26] See above, Chapter 10.

[27] D.H. Jenkins & R. Lippitt, *Interpersonal Perceptions of Teachers, Students, and Parents*, Washington D.C., Division of Adult Education Series, NEA, 1951.

[28] C.M. Fleming, 'The Child within the Group', in University of London, *Studies in Education 7. The Bearings of Recent Advances in Psychology on Educational Problems*, Evans, London, 1955, pp. 36-7.

[29] S. Barr, 'The measurement and prediction of teaching and efficiency', *Journal of Experimental Education*, 1948, XVI, 202-83.

workers to the observation of teacher behaviour. That was, initially, the principal change from earlier research in the area. Flanders, for example, looked at the classroom climate through the interaction between teacher and student and developed categories for analysing it; Ryans made a very substantial study of the various characteristics of teachers based on extensive and systematic classroom observations; and Smith, considering that 'more direct and primitive analyses of teacher behaviour are needed as a preface to correlational and experimental studies', made analyses of the actual language used by teachers. From approaches such as those a start was made in building up a body of information on what a teacher actually did in a classroom.[30] Throughout the 1960's researchers were apparently indefatigable, and many refinements in observation and analysis were introduced.

Two views of the function of a teacher predominated throughout the research. Some saw the teacher as a modifier of his students' behaviour. Taking their lead from neo-behaviourist learning theories they saw the teacher's task as that of managing students' behaviour so that teaching became an instructional process towards a precisely defined behavioural goal. The best example of the approach was to be found in programmed learning. Other research workers thought of the teacher's function as more nearly that of facilitating the intellectual and attitudinal development of his students. They tended to be associated with enquiry methods of teaching, and with an interest in creative and expressive behaviour. The first approach, that of behaviour modification, was the channel through which neo-behaviouristic research on motivation, learning, and reinforcement which for many years had appeared irrelevant, was brought to bear on the educational process. The second approach produced a number of studies comparing discovery with expository methods, and generated an interest in research into the processes of problem-solving, and into the effectiveness of teachers' cognitive activities such as probing, criticising, structuring discussion, and pacing.[31]

In the volume of research on teacher behaviour from the mid-1950's to the early 1970's, there were three principal lines of work:

- An effort to understand as precisely as possible what the teacher was actually doing. Most of the research was concerned with that stage — with observing teachers at work and with devising ways of recording their behaviour as teachers, classroom managers, and school organisers. It was a natural history approach, descriptive and analytic.

- An attempt to assess the effectiveness of the teacher's behaviour. That stage of research was not as widespread as the effort put into the first stage but nevertheless, did produce a substantial number of studies. The principal criterion of a teacher's effectiveness was

the educational achievement of his pupils, and most of the studies were correlational, relating aspects of teaching behaviour to tests of pupil achievement. Rosenshine, in 1971, reviewed about fifty of such studies and concluded that the relationship had not been thoroughly investigated and that 'Educational researchers have *not* provided those who train teachers with a repertoire of teaching skills which indicate to a teacher that if he increases behaviour X and/or decreases behaviour Y there will be a concomitant change in the cognitive or affective achievement of his students.'[32] From all of the research there was little ground for making any normative recommendation.

- An endeavour to devise ways of improving the teacher's performance. That stage of work required experimental classroom studies, but very little was attempted. A number of experimental programs in teacher education were started towards the end of the 1960's and began to stimulate more experimental work in the schools on teaching processes.

Probably the most promising of all the research programs in this field was the work at Canterbury, New Zealand, which involved all three stages. It was a sequence which ran from observational survey, to correlational analysis, and finally, experimentation. The experimental results were fed back to refine the initial descriptive work, and, in turn, to help continually to develop a more productive sequence.[33]

The achievements of that period of research on the behaviour of teachers did not produce firm recommendations and tangible guides for the improvement of teaching, but it did have three important effects: it gave research a greater hope of reaching results of practical significance by bringing it to focus on the relationship of teacher behaviour to student achievement; in consequence it made research workers think more seriously about behavioural objectives and their definition; and it broke the ground for the development of experimental studies both in teacher behaviour and in programs of teacher education.

[30] N.A. Flanders, *Teacher Influence, Pupil Attitudes, and Achievement*, Office of Educational Cooperative Research Monograph, Washington D.C., no. 12, OE 25040, 1965; D.G. Ryans, *Characteristics of Teachers*, Washington D.C., American Council on Education, 1960; B.O. Smith & M.O Meux, *A Study of the Logic of Teaching*, Urbana, Illinois, Bureau of Educational Research, University of Illinois, 1962

[31] B. Rosenshine, *Teaching Behaviour and Student Achievement*, NFER, Slough, 1971.

[32] B. Rosenshine, *ibid.*; and B. Rosenshine and Norma Furst, Research on teacher performance criteria, in B.O. Smith (ed.), *Research in Teacher Education, A Symposium*, Prentice-Hall, Englewood Cliffs, New Jersey, 1971, p. 40.

[33] G. Nuthall & I. Snook, 'Contemporary models of teaching', Chapter 4; and B. Rosenshine & Norma Furst, 'The Use of direct observation to study teaching', Chapter 5, in R.M.W. Travers, *Second Handbook of Research on Teaching*, Rand McNally, Chicago, 1973.

(b) Reading and Readiness

In the improvement of methods of teaching particular skills or content there continued to be a substantial interest. More research was done on the teaching of reading than on any other aspect of the school curriculum. It was therefore a little dismaying to find that a reviewer in an extensive survey of primary school reading, was able to write: 'It soon became clear that the findings of research in beginning reading ... are not an important factor in influencing decisions about beginning reading instruction.'[34]

In research on the teaching of reading, a separation was made between an emphasis on coding and an emphasis on meaning. Various studies done in the 1960's appeared to show that emphasis on meaning enabled a child to read faster in the initial stages of learning but by about the fourth grade teaching with a coding emphasis produced better results overall.[35] Experimentation for earlier and speedier reading programs started to reverse the fashion of the 1940's and 1950's which preferred a more leisurely approach through preparatory readiness programs.

The concept of readiness, in fact, went into a steady decline in the 1960's, and its significance was substantially rethought by the early 1970's. It had been a significant idea in educational thinking since the beginning of the century, and was associated particularly with those who emphasised the importance of biological maturation in child development. Montessori and Gesell were of that mind and so, too, was Piaget whose influence was beginning to be felt. Their popularity and the teacher's practical need to use a sequence of method and content appropriate to the learner ensured its continuance. Research on critical periods and the teachable moment was popular in many countries up to the 1950's.

Copei's idea of 'the productive moment'[36] was a variant of the idea of readiness. Saito, a primary school teacher in Japan in the 1960's, advanced a similar idea. In describing the process of teaching he pointed out that a skilful teacher should watch carefully to seize and develop the occasion when a pupil was coming to a point of 'break through' in understanding and was showing a readiness to appreciate the implications of his insight. Saito spoke of 'the moment for future development'.

Postponement of the teaching of some ideas and processes to a later period when the pupils were ready for them was part of the readiness approach, and was based in some cases on carefully designed experimentation in the grade placement of items such as that in the Winnetka schools under Carleton Washburne. In general, grade placement of content was related closely to mental age; the background of the child's experience also was acknowledged to be a factor, but one, which Washburne in 1939 wrote, was 'a field scarcely explored at all in any thoroughgoing way'.[37] In the 1940's and 1950's two developments changed the picture. The widespread sociological studies of school environment and societal influences on and within the school substantially affected educators' views on the importance of biological maturation. Shortly afterwards programs for deliberately developing readiness in children by a process of educational and environmental enrichment demonstrated in due course that prerequisite learning could be effectively introduced. Once the impact of environment and the possibilities of readiness programs were more widely understood, the older notion of readiness based primarily on maturational sequence crumbled. It was supplemented and remodelled during the 1960's by attention to ideas such as matching and pacing, and by a stronger realisation of the importance of motivation and skill in presentation.[38] Like the once popular word, interest, however, it is hard to see readiness dropping out of use altogether. Research has refined its meaning, demonstrated its complexity, divided it into its component parts, and made it more tangible and usable. Its fate is, in effect, a pointer to the course of educational research in the quarter-century since World War II.

(c) International Research on Educational Achievement

In 1964 the data for a fascinating and comprehensive international study of secondary school achievement in mathematics was collected. In 1960 a Council for the International Evaluation of Educational Achievement, IEA for short, was formed to look at ways of comparing students' achievement in different kinds of educational systems. The IEA resolved to try to identify cognitive and affective factors influencing national systems of education and to try to devise instruments to measure them. A feasibility study was successfully undertaken, and the IEA then decided to look at secondary school mathematics, using a large sample of various secondary school-age groups from twelve developed and underdeveloped countries. In analysing the data, achievement in mathematics was correlated with the many personal, social, administrative, and educa-

34 J.S. Chall, *Learning to Read: The Great Debate*, McGraw-Hill, New York, 1967, p. 288.

35 G.M. Della-Piana and G.T. Endo, 'Reading research', in R.M.W. Travers, *Second Handbook of Research on Teaching*, Rand McNally, Chicago, 1973, pp. 884-6.

36 See above, Chapter 10. F. Copei, *Der Fruchtbare Moment in Bildungsprozess*, Quelle and Meyer, Heidelberg, 1962 (1930); K. Saito, *The Development of Educational Science*, 1969. K. Saito (1911-   ) became the principal of a primary school in 1952 and remained in primary teaching until his retirement in 1969. He was a prolific writer on educational topics.

37 C. Washburne, Introduction, in *Child Development and the Curriculum*, 38th Yearbook of the NSSE, Bloomington, Illinois, 1939, p. 8.

38 See W.D. Wall, 'Teaching methods', in University of London Institute of Education, *The Bearings of Recent Advances in Psychology on Educational Problems*, Evans, London, 1955, pp. 154-7.

tional variables on which information was collected from students and teachers. The exercise was the first large-scale multi-national attempt to measure educational achievement in a way that would enable comparisons to be made between different systems and conditions of education throughout the world. For the first time it was possible to get valid comparative data on performance and, for instance, to look at the achievement of pupils in selective or comprehensive schools in several countries, to examine the effects of co-education, and to compare the variability within centralised and non-centralised systems. It involved many leading educational research workers in much fruitful discussion on hypothesis formation, techniques of sampling, testing, and analysis, and in the joint presentation of results.[39] Following the mathematics study the IEA moved into the study of science, language, and civic education, with larger samples in a wider range of countries.

(iii) Child Development

Interest in the social factors influencing the growth of children and youth emerged strongly in the 1950's and during that period there were several notable studies of adolescence. The impact of Piaget's work, however, began to be felt about the same time, and research effort was turned in the 1960's overwhelmingly towards the investigation of children's cognitive development. That research sometimes had social overtones, but for the most part it concentrated on observations and experiments in which social processes were not of central importance.

(a) Studies of Adolescents

The 1940's and 1950's were notable for a number of studies of child development, the most widely known of which were those by Gesell and his associates at Yale. From the 1920's Gesell had been responsible for a series of influential studies on young children; in the post-World War II years the studies were continued upward into adolescence, culminating in 1956 with a volume entitled *Youth: The Years from Ten to Sixteen*. A comparison of that work with the near contemporary study by Coleman, *The Adolescent Society*, is some indication of the impact of the sociological trend in educational research in that period. Gesell in his post-war studies continued the interest he had shown in the 1930's in longitudinal development. His views were based on a close examination of the way in which individuality emerged from 'the patterning process whereby the mutual fitness of organism and environment is brought to

progressive realization'.[40] In the chapter on interpersonal relationships there was a portrait of an adolescent forming friendships, and reacting to parents, and a note that at times group pressure may be strong, but there was no suggestion that peer groups might be a vital part of an adolescent's life and no analysis of their structure, function, and influence. On the other hand, Coleman's research, conceived in the mid-1950's, was based on an interest in status systems. It was a survey of social climates in high schools, and concentrated on the social relationships of adolescents. Associations, cliques, and peer groups were central to his research, and their structure and impact on values, ideas, and interests was carefully explored in the high school society, 'that cruel jungle of dating and rating'.[41] Gesell's idea of a maturational process directing growth through adolescence was replaced by the suggestion that a teenage socialising culture was the principal influence affecting adolescent behaviour.

(b) Mental Testing

Mental testing and the selection of students for secondary or higher education were among the chief activities of educational researchers throughout the twentieth century. The surveys conducted in 1932 and 1947 by the Scottish Council for Educational Research were among the most widely known instances of large-scale mental testing, in each of which group tests were administered to the complete age group of eleven-year-olds throughout the country. In 1950 Vernon was of the opinion that great progress had been made in the construction of tests of ability and achievement, in the processing of test items, and in the standardising of teachers' estimates.[42] Nevertheless, refining the test instruments, and devising and evaluating selection procedures were the continuing concern of research teams in most countries, and, with the increasing prosperity of the test industry, the size of Buros' mental measurements yearbook continued to grow. The wider use of factor-analytic techniques made for more exactitude, and also increased interest in the pattern of human abilities and their development.

[39] T. Husen (ed.), *International Study of Achievement in Mathematics*, 2 vols., Almquist and Wiksell, Stockholm, 1967.

[40] A. Gesell, Frances Ilg, & Louise B. Ames, *Youth: The Years from Ten to Sixteen*, Hamish Hamilton, London, 1956, p. 25.

[41] J.S. Coleman, *The Adolescent Society*, Free Press, New York, 1961, p. 51. Other notable studies were C.M. Fleming, *Adolescence: Its Social Psychology*, RKP, London, 1948; W.D. Wall, *The Adolescent Child*, Methuen, London, 1948; R. Strang, *The Adolescent Views Himself*, McGraw-Hill, New York, 1957; and C.I. Sandstrom, *The Psychology of Childhood and Adolescence*, Almqvist and Wiksell, Stockholm, 1961.

[42] P.E. Vernon, *Modern Educational Psychology as a Science*, University of London, Institute of Education, Studies in Education 1, Inaugural Lecture, Evans, 1950, pp. 14-15.

Of particular importance was the study of cognitive development. The usual investigation by the conventional tests and measurements of the 1950's was able to yield interesting classifications of mental abilities, and it was possible to chart the development of them by various performance tests, but the method had little to offer for the researchers who wished to understand the process of cognitive development. For this they turned to the work of Piaget.

(c) Piaget and Cognitive Development

Continuing on from the heyday of Binet, Decroly, and Claparède, before and after World War I there had been a considerable effort in educational research in European countries, particularly in Belgium, France, and Switzerland.[43] In each of the centres there was considerable interest in educational testing and in a study of the intellectual processes involved in teaching and learning skills in the basic subjects of the primary school. The work that was done tended to be within the European functionalist tradition in cognitive research and to lean heavily on the language and ideas of biology. European researchers looked for developmental trends, and were particularly interested in the growth of thinking skills in young children, whom they regarded as active organisms involved in processes of assimilating, adapting, and seeking equilibrium. It was an interest in studying the active processes of the mind rather than in quantifying and statistically analysing its output. Dewey, and Baldwin who finally migrated to Paris, were the kinds of American thinkers who fitted well into the European tradition of which Claparède and Stern were well-known representatives. Their successor was Jean Piaget from the Jean-Jacques Rousseau Institute in Geneva. By the 1940's he had become the leading researcher in the European psychological tradition, and had begun to have a pervasive effect on the work and ideas of the other European centres of educational research.[44]

In 1942 a prominent American educational psychologist had deplored the current lack of knowledge of Piaget's work, because, in his view, it provided 'the most illuminating single description of the way in which children attain power in problem-solving'.[45] Another ten years were to pass before the omission was repaired.

Piaget's career falls into three periods. In the 1920's he published studies on various aspects of the development in young children of language, reasoning, moral judgment, physical causality, and of their representation of the physical world. Those early studies were restricted to verbal questions and answers in interview situations and yielded correspondingly limited results. Nevertheless, Claparède writing in 1923 ventured the opinion that 'M. Jean Piaget's studies offer us a completely

new version of the child's mind'.[46] The second period began with his studying the day-to-day behaviour of his own children from the time each was born, and by focussing on children's actions of various kinds as they related to persons, objects, and situations. Throughout his work he always used small samples and studied them intensively. He followed up his research on early intellectual development by studies of older children, and commenced to work out in the 1930's and, in essence, had completed by the late 1940's, a comprehensive theory of the process of thought and of the stages through which it develops in childhood and adolescence. In a series of lectures given in Paris during World War II, and in Manchester soon after the war, he summarised the position he had reached; those lectures were later published in English as *The Psychology of Intelligence* (1950), and *Logic and Psychology* (1957). In his third period, through the 1950's and 1960's, work by the Piaget school in Geneva continued, extending the research on intelligence to adolescent groups, and reinforcing the theoretical position by further studies, such as those on children's concepts of time, space, and probability. From the 1940's on, Piaget and his collaborators also started extensive and carefully devised experimentation on the nature and development of perception. This he related, from time to time, to his work on intelligence. Parallel to his interest in the development of intelligence, he worked on problems of the nature and genesis of knowledge, and eventually managed to bring his three main interests together with the publication in 1967 of *Biologie et Connaissance*.

Out of that more than half-century of observation and experimentation, there emerged an impressive body of description, explanation, and theory dealing with a wide range of intellectual activities.

---

[43] Buyse, one of Decroly's collaborators, developed a flourishing research program at Louvain from the mid-1930's, and in the post-World War II period educational research made good progress at the Sorbonne and in Geneva, where Dottrens built up a substantial reputation.

[44] Jean Piaget (1896–   ) was born in Neuchâtel. A child prodigy interested primarily in biology, he had published about twenty learned papers on molluscs before he reached the age of twenty-one. After obtaining his doctorate in natural science at Neuchâtel he went to Paris to study psychology. There he encountered Binet's collaborator, Simon, who set him to work standardising a set of reasoning tests on Parisian children. This task, for the first time, involved him in a study of thought processes, and helped to set the direction of his future career. In 1921 he returned to Switzerland to work with Claparède in the Jean-Jacques Rousseau Institute which he later helped to affiliate with the University of Geneva. He became a director of the Institute in 1932 and remained there until his retirement. Throughout his career he also taught part-time at the Universities of Neuchâtel, Lausanne, and Paris, and he became the Director of the International Bureau of Education in Geneva. Over the years Piaget and his collaborators built up a formidable body of literature in journal articles, monographs, and books, aimed from first to last at building up a biological theory of knowledge.

[45] W.A. Brownell, Problem solving, *NSSE Forty-first Yearbook*, 1942, pt. 2, *The Psychology of Learning*.

[46] J. Piaget, *The Language and Thought of the Child*, Preface by E. Claparède, Kegan Paul, Trench, Trubner, London, 1926, p. xi.

**Pierre Bovet
(1878-1944).**

**Jean Piaget
(1896-   ).**

**Edouard Claparède
(1873-1940).**

Claparède, Bovet and Piaget were in succession the directors of the J.J. Rousseau Institute in Geneva which has been responsible for much important research in education and child development.

Piaget was concerned mainly in building up a theory about the kind of thinking of which individuals were capable at various stages of their development in childhood and adolescence. He attempted to answer two broad questions: What kind of framework can be used to describe intellectual processes? and, What are the successive stages of intellectual development through which children and adolescents pass?

Intelligence, in Piaget's view, is an adaptive process. An organism and its environment become mutually adapted as the organism assimilates new experiences to its existing pattern of behaviour, or, on the other hand, accommodates its behaviour to take account of experiences that do not fit into accepted ways. Assimilation and accommodation are the conservative and progressive sides of adaptation, and the need to assimilate, and, in the process, to accommodate also, is the motive force behind the development of intelligence. Intelligence develops through a balancing of one against the other. Its growth is marked by a series of equilibria; when the equilibrium is upset there is a movement forward towards the next stage of development to bring about a more inclusive and stable equilibrium. Developed intelligence may therefore be thought of as an adaptive process with a complicated mechanism of equilibrium for the organisation of behaviour. Though it may be intimately associated with physical and affective behaviour, the process is not a physical or affective one; it is cognitive.

All behaviour to some extent acquires an organisation or structure; 'it is this structuring of behaviour that constitutes its cognitive aspect. A perception, sensori-motor learning (habit, etc.), an act of insight, a judgment, etc., all amount, in one way or another, to a structuring of the relations between the environment and the organism. In this way they reveal a certain affinity among themselves which distinguishes them from affective phenomena.'[47] Cognitive functions inject organisation into human behaviour. Intelligence, in Piaget's use of the term, is a superior form of cognitive functioning, a high-level structuring of behaviour; it is 'a system of living and acting operations'. Operations are the patterns of logical thinking by which an individual extends the scope of his behaviour. Fully developed, operational intelligence is characterised by the internal action through which an organism arranges data in systematic forms, e.g. by classification, seriation, or numbering, and reflects on and manipulates those formal relationships.

Piaget in all his writings never ceased to be a biologist. Adaptive action was central to his thinking on every aspect of human behaviour. He was concerned with an organism developing in interaction with its environment, and he saw intelligence as a prolongation of this organic development.

[47]   J. Piaget, *The Psychology of Intelligence*, RKP, London, 1950, p. 5.

Action is an integral part of intelligence. Actions are the raw material of intellectual operations. In infancy they are simple sensori-motor activities. Gradually, intelligent actions become internalised, i.e. they become thought processes that do not develop into exterior actions. As behaviour becomes more complex, thought processes become more organised and abstract. The whole development from the simplest thought to the most complex abstraction is a successive transformation of action from a primitive sensory state to that of a sophisticated, logical, internalised structure. In his view on the relationship between intelligence and action, Piaget resembled Dewey and the educators of the activity school movement to which he gave his wholehearted support.

What are the stages through which an individual passes in the course of his intellectual development? Piaget identified various stages at different points in his research. There appear to be probably four stages, each divided into a number of sub-stages:

- The sensori-motor stage (0-2 years);
- A stage of pre-operational thought (2-6 years);
- A stage of concrete operations in middle childhood (7-11 years);
- A stage of formal operations reached in adolescence and characteristic of adulthood.

The period of sensori-motor intelligence covers approximately the first two years of life. In it, intellectual development starts with simple reflex actions such as sucking, swallowing, and crying; the young child adapts these to the varying circumstances of his environment, and there starts the process of intellectual development.

The origins of operations are to be found in sensori-motor processes but though 'sensori-motor intelligence lies at the source of thought, and continues to affect it through life',[48] there is a long way to go before this pre-verbal intelligence grows into reflective thinking.

Pre-operational thought is a kind of intellectual development marked by symbolic and intuitive thinking. An increasing command of language is the dominating intellectual influence in the first half of this stage, and it fosters the development of symbolic thought. The child's principal achievement during this period, therefore, is his acquisition of the ability to manipulate representations. These are the means by which objects and activities are mentally registered: they are the signs and symbols which stand for various actions and things but do not necessarily resemble them. From about four to seven years of age the child progresses through a sub-stage of intuitive thought. Intuitive thinking is the process of bringing to bear one pattern of thought at a time, and in due course checking or regulating this pattern by another. When this checking becomes instantaneous and systematic, we have the beginning of operational thought.

The period of concrete operations extends from about seven to eleven years of age, and is a consolidation of the pre-operational period. Operations are formed by a kind of thawing out of intuitive structures. During these years the child develops his skills with signs and symbols into a coherent cognitive system with which to deal with the world around him. The system is made up of operations which are networks of related intellectual activities such as the processes of addition, subtraction, multiplication, and division. The structure of his thinking consists of balanced networks of reversible operations through which he can deal coherently with the tissue of objects and activities in which he is immersed. He is usually incapable of using these intellectual processes when separated from objects that he can manipulate. He does not reason in logical propositions: the operations are concrete and not yet formal ones.

Formal operations develop in the adolescent years after about the age of eleven, and are characteristic of adult thinking. It is at this stage that the individual becomes capable of handling logical propositions, of putting forward hypotheses and following a train of logical argument that has no necessary relationship to particular objects or to reality. He can place reliance on the necessary validity of an inference independent of its agreement with experience. It is the kind of thought which does not restrict itself to the immediately observable; it can form hypotheses and it can reflect upon itself. Scientific thinking becomes possible.

Piaget unfolded a progressive scheme of successive levels of adaptation, each developing out of its predecessor. The genetic succession ran from elementary perceptual and reflex interaction through habit formation, sensori-motor intelligence, representative thought, intuitive thought, and concrete operations, to formal operational intelligence. Each level incorporated the previous one, differentiated itself from it, and established a new equilibrium.

Piaget's work affected research, particularly in Europe, in the 1940's and 1950's, but had little impact on educators and school programs until the 1960's. He was a prolific writer, but his writing was difficult and sometimes obscure. His theories ran counter to the prevailing theories in use in schools and in textbooks of educational psychology, and, although he wrote a little on education, he did not spend much time in drawing implications from his position for education. Nevertheless his work had several features that were clearly of interest and importance to educators.[49]

---

[48] *ibid.*, p. 119.

[49] H. Aebli, *Didactique Psychologique*, Delachaux et Niestlé, Neuchâtel, 1951, was the first comprehensive attempt to draw out the implications of Piaget's work for education. In 1969 Piaget in *Psychologie et Pédagogie* (trans. as *Science of Education and the Psychology of the Child*, Longmans, London, 1971) also tried his hand at it.

In the first place, his approach was a developmental one. Like a schoolteacher he saw the process of intellectual growth spread over the years from birth to adolescence and he pointed out, tentatively, stages of growth that might successively interest the pre-school, primary, and secondary school teacher. He showed too that children's thinking was different in quality from that of adolescence and adulthood, with the implication that both the method and content of education might also be different at successive stages. Secondly, Piaget was concerned with intellectual processes. Most contemporary educational psychologists were interested in determining the conditions under which learning took place, or in measuring whether it had been transmitted, or in assessing how well it had been reinforced. Piaget turned his attention to an analysis of the actual process by which intelligence grew and operated. He demonstrated that intelligence was more than a composite of specific stimuli and responses; it grew through a series of complicated structures. His view was that certain cognitive structures were built up, that they had particular ways of functioning, and that they were adaptable. Acceptance of that viewpoint would place more emphasis on fundamental understanding in learning, on cultivating patterns of cognitive functioning in the classroom, and on fostering the processes of adaptation through which intellectual development takes place. Thirdly, he never tired of saying that action was the basis of thought. His examination of the development of intellectual processes reinforced the activity school tradition of the progressive educators. Dewey, Lay, Montessori, Decroly, and Kerschensteiner had argued for and demonstrated the kinds of methods that, in Piaget's view, would develop most effectively the kinds of intellectual processes that his work had revealed. 'The essential functions of intelligence consist in understanding and in inventing, in

Geneva: J.J. Rousseau Institute. Some of the significant research on child development was done at *La Maison des Petits*, the experimental school founded by Claparède at the Institute.

other words in building up structures by structuring reality.' It was not by copying or by making associative responses to stimuli that knowledge was acquired. 'To know an object is to act upon it and to transform it.' If therefore, wrote Piaget, we wish to form individuals capable of inventive thought and of helping the society of tomorrow to achieve progress, clearly we need 'an education which is an active discovery of reality'.[50]

In the 1950's the English-speaking world became aware of conservation and of Piaget's experiments with it. In education an interest in conservation meant an interest in the way in which children came to recognise the invariance of certain relationships and measurements in their spatial environment. Ability to conserve was a key feature in determining whether a child had moved from intuitive pre-operational to the stage of concrete operational thought. For the next decade a seemingly endless stream of research was conducted with young children on the conservation of liquids, solids, number, weight, length, area, time, movement, and speed. In the history of educational research, never has there been a topic so seized upon by so many in so short a time. The stampede had three effects. It focused attention on concept formation and its importance in education; it was for many researchers the beginning of an interest in developmental processes; and it attracted many towards European-based cognitive psychology away from the neo-behaviourism that had long dominated educational and psychological research.

The movement was greatly boosted by the publication in English in 1958 of Inhelder and Piaget's *The Growth of Logical Thinking from Childhood to Adolescence*, which contained not only a theoretical examination of cognitive development through the stages of concrete and formal thinking, but also an account of fifteen experiments underpinning the theory. Throughout the 1960's a good proportion of the research in that area in many countries consisted in the replication and extension of those experiments. It was not, however, the only research. Efforts were made in four areas arising out of Piaget's work:

- On concept formation, with the manner in which concepts are developed, the age at which they are formed, and the order of their attainment.
- On the intellectual processes that occur throughout a child's cognitive development such as conservation, transitivity, perception, classification, and seriation, and on problem-solving processes, on sequence in learning, and the effects of training on the development of cognitive processes.
- On the existence and possible nature of stages in the cognitive development of children consisting largely of a study of Piaget's sequence of stages. Was the order of succession constant? Was one prerequisite to another? What kinds of behaviour were so tied

together that they might be regarded as a stage? What was the structure or pattern of relations in the cognitive processes that characterise each stage? How extensive were individual differences in affecting the age at which stages were entered and the proficiency with which the tasks of each stage were performed? Those questions were the subject of considerable investigation. Lunzer, after reviewing the research evidence on them, concluded, while apparently accepting the order and characteristics of the stages, that 'the acquisition of these ways of processing experience is much less coherent than Piaget would have us believe'[51]

- On the educational implications of research in cognitive development. A number of researchers attempted to apply various findings to the teaching of school subjects, mathematics and science being the most favoured.[52]

In the U.S.S.R. educational psychologists were interested, too, in cognitive development, especially in the relation between language and cognitive development, and in the effect of education on development. Since Vygotsky's formulation, in the early 1930's, of the theory of the zone of potential development which was the difference between the level at which children could perform tasks by their own efforts, and the level they may reach under adult guidance, educators, throwing away intelligence tests, had been working on methods of outpacing development. Educational psychologists in the 1950's and 1960's made a careful study of Piaget's work to explore ways of speeding up cognitive development by education. For both Piaget and the Soviet psychologists, action was the basis and beginning of thought, and much experimental work was done in the U.S.S.R. on the relationship between action and thought, and, in particular, on the role played by orienting activity and conscious control in the process of cognitive development. One educational psychologist, for example, in a conservation experiment, taught children to use a third object as a standard against which they could see and talk about changes in dimensions which made quantities appear different when in reality they were not. By introducing this mediational way of thinking, conservation could be achieved at an age

[50] J. Piaget, *Science of Education and the Psychology of the Child*, pp. 26-9; cf. H. Aebli, *Didactique Psychologique*, p. 14, and pp. 40ff. who summed up the contrast between traditional pedagogy supported by associationist psychology, and the activity school supported by Piaget, in the chapter heading 'L'élément fondamental de la pensée: l'image ou l'operation?'

[51] E.A. Lunzer, 'Children's thinking', in H.J. Butcher (ed)., *Educational Research in Britain I*, University of London, 1968, p. 94.

[52] See, for example, K. Lovell, *The Growth of Basic Mathematical and Scientific Concepts in Children*, University of London, 1966; and D.B. Harrison, 'Piagetian Studies and mathematics learning', in J.W. Wilson and L.R. Carry (eds.), *Studies in Mathematics*, vol. 19. *Reviews of Recent Research in Mathematics*, Stanford, School Mathematics Study Group, 1969, pp. 93-127.

earlier than Piaget had suggested.[53] Galperin reported in 1966 that certain concepts that typically do not appear until the age of ten to twelve were attained by six-year-olds.[54]

One further substantial influence of this line of research was in the study of moral development. Piaget's work suggested that moral development took place in stages and that the stages paralleled those of cognitive development. The principal research was directed to an examination of the modes of thought underlying moral responses. Kohlberg and Turiel, for example, in the United States studied and established a sequence of stages somewhat parallel to and reliant on cognitive development, and they endeavoured to uncover the processes and structures which undergo transformation as children move into successive stages.[55]

SUMMARY OF TRENDS

The overall picture of educational research since World War II was one of varying fashions and emphases. Nevertheless, there were a number of very general trends that emerge with reasonable clarity.

The high interest of the 1940's was undoubtedly sociological. The influential studies were those of social status and its impact on educational opportunity and educational organisation. They were, for the most part, surveys of local school systems or selected groups of schools or classes in which a number of social class or other status variables were correlated with aspects of the pupils' behaviour and achievement at school. Concurrently with that development there was a growing dissatisfaction among many educators with the lack of impact on school programs that the ordinary run of research had had over the years. Out of the dissatisfaction action research was born.

Action research was widespread in the 1950's and at the height of its popularity in the early 1960's. Thereafter, school-based research in some instances died away, and in others merged into the large development programs that school authorities and curriculum committees became engaged in.

During the 1950's status studies continued, but began to break down into more exacting investigations of the processes and mechanisms of education in its social context. A good example was the tendency to move from the study of teacher characteristics to teacher behaviour. Observation moved out of the laboratory into the classroom, and a start was made on working out techniques of observing and recording field behaviour in educational settings.

The 1960's saw a general development of large-scale studies such as the nation-wide Coleman investigation of equality of educational opportunity in the U.S.A., the Robbins Report on higher education in

England, and the curriculum review in the U.S.S.R. The dramatic development of two pieces of technical equipment, optical scanners and computers, made such ventures much more feasible. With the rapid improvement in that machinery and the multiplication of suitable computer programs it became possible to process a multitude of items, to classify and arrange masses of data, and to deal competently with the relations between large numbers of variables. More sophisticated statistical treatments, therefore, became possible, and educational research tended to move from univariate to multivariate analysis. The 1960's saw not only substantial investigations of educational achievement such as the international study of mathematics, but also a number of smaller, penetrating, and complex experimental studies of educational processes which was beginning to make it possible for social scientists to do something like justice to the richness of variables and variety of effects in analysing and experimenting with a segment of human behaviour.[56]

Throughout the period as a whole there was thus a movement from the investigation of status to the study of process; from relatively simple, small and medium-scale to complex large-scale research; and from correlational survey to a more penetrating experimental design, which by the 1970's had taken the investigator closer to an understanding of the actual process of education, and had given him an opportunity to make a helpful and genuinely useful contribution to the work of the teacher.

Associated with research programs and drawing much strength from them was a great upsurge in the 1950's and 1960's of curriculum revision. It had many of the characteristics of the other types of research, and, in addition, was a wide-ranging series of developmental programs that affected teaching methods, school organisation, and teacher education as well as the curriculum of every level of schooling.

CURRICULUM DEVELOPMENT

(i) Background to Curriculum Reform

After World War II educators had some sense of entering a new age. The function of schooling began to take more firmly a shape that had

[53] I.L.F. Obuchova, 'Experimental formation of representations of invariantness in five and six year old children', in *Proceedings of XVIIIth International Congress of Psychology*, Moscow, 1966, pp. 103-8.

[54] P.Y. Galperin, 'Method, facts, and theories in the psychology of mental action and concept formation', *ibid.*, p. 51.

[55] E. Turiel, 'Developmental processes in the child's moral thinking', in P. Mussen, J. Langer, and M. Covington (eds.), *Trends and Issues in Developmental Psychology*, Holt, Rinehart, Winston, New York, 1969, pp. 92-133; and 'Stage Transition in Moral Development', in R.W.M. Travers ed, *Second Handbook of Research in Teaching*, Rand McNally, Chicago, 1973, pp. 732-58.

[56] M.M. Tatsuoka, Multivariate analysis in educational research, in F.N. Kerlinger (ed.), *Review of Research in Education*, Peacock, Itasca, Illinois, 1973, p. 311.

previously been argued and fought for, but not quite realised. Nor was it to be realised immediately and without struggle. Changes in structure were planned immediately after the war and matured unevenly over the next twenty-five years. In curriculum, experimentation and development also got under way and by 1960 had become a substantial movement. By about the mid-1960's the curriculum change could be perceived as a widespread and distinct change of attitude, gathering up some of the developments of the previous ten or twenty years and adding to them other novel and critical elements from the ferment of the 1960's.

Four factors combined to produce the new situation that faced curriculum-makers in the post-war world. Since the beginning of the century, universal primary education in developed countries had provided a wider and deeper layer of educated people throughout western society. The possession of elementary education begot the desire for more and, as the century progressed, the educational tide level moved steadily up into the secondary school. In the years after World War II most of the western countries had started seriously to provide three and subsequently four and more years of secondary education for all pupils. The rising tide of educational expectation among young people was abetted by the increasing expectations of parents anxious that their children should improve their prospects and their standards of living. In the second place, the newer methods of teaching that had developed in the twentieth century and had been most widely championed and publicised by progressive educators were beginning to be accepted by the teaching profession in general. After World War II all primary schools and, in increasing measure, secondary schools, shared in some measure the methods and the ideas on curriculum that progressive educators of the previous generation had introduced to the schools. Thus in the post-war period the academic instructional approach that had characterised secondary education in particular was beginning to crumble. In the third place, there was a conjunction of two explosions. The explosion of the school population, partly a result of a rising birthrate but principally the result of the general rise of expectation, became apparent in western countries: in an increased total enrolment in schools and particularly in the greater numbers of pupils who stayed at school beyond the statutory school leaving age.[57] The schools' increased retention rate had the effect of extending the period of secondary schooling that a country might normally have been expected to provide. It changed the nature of secondary education from something that was offered to a selected few, to an education that all pupils, in the normal course of events, might be expected to undertake and benefit by. Plans for its reorganisation to cope with the new situation were therefore widely canvassed and gradually brought into being, and curricula suitable for the many rather than the few began to get serious consideration. At the same time, the expansion of knowledge, particularly scientific knowledge, had by the 1950's been such that it was also commonly referred to as a knowledge explosion. Dramatic statements that scientific knowledge had doubled itself in the last fifteen years, and that three-quarters of all the scientists the world had ever known had been born within the last fifty years were common at the time. It had become quite obvious that school curricula were not keeping abreast of current advances in knowledge, and that, without a substantial revision of their programs, schools could not hope to produce students who were at least reasonably in touch with modern developments. A fourth factor, implicit in the others, was also of significance: it was the factor of change itself. Not only were knowledge, school population, and teaching methods changing, at times quite rapidly, but the job structure in most countries, material standards of living, and traditional moral and social values were also in flux. The world had never stood still, but it seemed, when after World War II it entered the atomic age and, hard upon that, the space age, that change was at the very heart of contemporary living. 'To equip people to live in a changing society' had been a well-used phrase of progressive curriculum-makers in the 1930's; by the 1950's it had become one of the most common statements in the mouths of all persons who spoke and wrote about education.

In 1950 Ralph Tyler, who had played a leading part in the evaluation of the Eight Year Study, summarised the current state of knowledge and his own preferences about the process of curriculum development in the United States. Four things had to be undertaken by persons engaged in designing a curriculum:

- They had to determine its objectives. Since, in his view, 'Education is the process of changing the behaviour patterns of people',[58] educational objectives should represent the kind of behaviour that is to be brought about in the students.

- They had to decide the kinds of learning experiences, e.g. skills in thinking, acquiring knowledge, developing social attitudes, and developing interests, that might be relevant to the objectives.

- They had to organise the experiences to provide continuity, sequence, and integration within some general pattern such as a subject, a core, or an undifferentiated structure.

- They had to work out means of evaluation. It was necessary to make a careful assessment of the extent to which the objectives had been achieved.

---

[57] Probably the most forceful and widely read statement on this phenomenon was that dealing with France, by Louis Cros, *The Explosion in the Schools*, Sevpen, Paris, 1963.

[58] R.W. Tyler, *Basic Principles of Curriculum and Instruction*, University of Chicago, 1950, p. 4.

Tyler's thorough, commonsense, and slightly progressive analysis of curriculum tasks was an important part of the background of thinking about curriculum development for the next twenty years. Within the general pattern there were, of course, a number of different emphases given by different educators. Two were of particular importance.

Several textbooks in curriculum development appeared between the end of World War II and the early 1960's which were comprehensive, well-written, and widely used in English-speaking countries.[59] Without exception they were progressive in the Deweyan tradition. They cogently introduced Deweyan theory into curriculum construction, and drew heavily on the curriculum practices of progressive school authorities. In that manner the progressive legacy was firmly embedded in American curriculum development and in the many other national systems influenced by American educators.

At the same time a different though not necessarily incompatible influence was at work. Starting with the University of Illinois School Mathematics project in 1952, there was a move to bring school subjects into closer contact with their academic discipline, and to raise the quality of performance in them.

In that period of expansion, transformation, and general popularisation of education, it was thought important not to lose sight of quality. There was a consciousness in western countries immediately following World War II that their future prosperity and prestige depended more than ever before on the fruitful husbanding of their intellectual resources. In the face of the rising numbers and aspirations in the developing nations of the world, the cultural and political influence and the economic survival of the pre-war leading nations were felt to depend upon the cultivation to the full of the talents of their limited manpower. Education for excellence both in general education and in specialised fields was to be seriously considered. The launching of Sputnik in 1957 caused a great deal of reflection by western countries on the question of whether they were falling behind the communist world in the quality of their intellectual and technical culture. It enormously accelerated their search for the relevant and the first-rate in education.

By such a combination of factors, therefore, education was pushed into the reconsideration of old ways and the exploration of new paths. In the 1950's and 1960's the structure changed, producing new relationships between primary, secondary, and tertiary education, and new forms of organisation, particularly at the secondary and tertiary levels. Within the structure, too, innovation was at work, Curricula and methods of teaching were slowly but substantially altered to produce a kind of education where sensitivity to change and democratisation, and concern for quality and relevance were key elements.

(ii) Secondary School Curriculum Reform

At the secondary level curriculum reform took place in all the main areas — mathematics, science, languages (native and foreign), social sciences, and art. Work on the new programs began in the U.S.A. on School Mathematics in 1952, and was followed by the Physical Science Curriculum Study (PSCS) in 1956, the year before Sputnik. Many of the projects that followed in other subjects and in various countries were conceived on a large scale and took a lead from the organisational pattern of the PSCS. It brought together academics in physics and education, educational administrators, and teachers in joint committees supported by state and private funds. It was an attempt to produce statements of aims, principles, and content, and text materials and kits embodying the up-to-date scientific knowledge of the professional scientists, and the educational know-how of the professional educators in a program for teaching physics to senior secondary school pupils. It was soon followed by other projects in the U.S.A. — the Chemical Bond Approach (CBA) 1957, the School Mathematics Study Group (SMSG) 1958, the Chemical Education Materials Study (CHEM) 1959, and the Biological Sciences Curriculum Study (BSCS) 1959. In the 1960's each of the other areas of study started curriculum projects, and all around the world projects multiplied in all subjects.

In Europe curriculum reform followed on the American start, and was heavily influenced by it in the early 1960's. The first projects tended also to be in science and mathematics and to be modelled on the American experience. After the mid-1960's they widened in range and became more distinctive of the particular interests, developments, and situations of the various countries. France began experimental programs with modern mathematics in 1964, and then established a commission to reform the teaching of science and technology. In Germany a survey published in 1972 was able to report as many as 130 curriculum projects in operation, the most popular areas being science, mathematics, social science, and language teaching. In England, with the assistance of the Nuffield Foundation, a School Mathematics Project in 1961 and a Science Teaching Project in 1965 were begun. In 1964 England established a new organisation, the Schools Council for the Curriculum and Examinations, to assist in and to stimulate reforms in school curricula. Three years later the Nuffield Foundation and the Schools Council together started a Humanities Curriculum Project which provided materials and ideas to encourage disciplined discussion among pupils on social and moral issues.

---

59 The best known texts were H. Alberty, *Reorganizing the High-School Curriculum*, Macmillan, New York, 1947; B.O. Smith, W.O. Stanley & J.H. Shores, *Fundamentals of Curriculum Development*, World Book Co., New York, 1950; Hilda Taba, *Curriculum Development. Theory and Practice*, Harcourt Brace and World, New York, 1962.

In the same year, the same sponsors again came together on work on a number of projects relating linguistics to the teaching of English at primary and secondary school level. Over the years, other major projects developed, such as Modern Languages (1963), Science 5-13 (1967), Project Technology (1967), and Sixth Form Mathematics (1969).

Throughout the whole of the movement there were four common features. First, there was a search for relevance. It was a relevance in two senses. Project Technology and the Humanities Curriculum illustrated the first sense, the effort to direct the pupils' attention to material that was related to contemporary life and to the current state of knowledge in the field that was being studied. The importance of bringing the curriculum more into line with recent advances in the academic discipline was emphasised by the mathematicians who pointed out that there had been little change in school curricula for the past fifty years, despite the fact that 'The Twentieth Century had been the golden age of mathematics, since more mathematics and more profound mathematics, has been created in this period than during all the rest of history'.[60] The aim of the Illinois Mathematics Project, the first of the 'new maths', as stated by its director, was to bring schools and pupils mathematically up to date. 'It is an attempt to determine what the teacher must do to bring to the mind of the adolescent some of the ideas and modes of thinking which are basic in the work of the contemporary mathematician'.[61] The curriculum was designed, accordingly, to teach students to understand and be precise in their usage of the terms of modern mathematics, and to encourage them to think mathematically by discovering mathematical rules and principles for themselves. But, in a rapidly changing world, relevant subject-matter also meant the kind of subject-matter that would best enable pupils to cope with and grow with the changes that were bound to confront them. Relevance of that kind came from an understanding of the fundamental principles and the structural framework of the developing subject. The PSCS program was based on that view. Its aim was to enable students to penetrate to the discipline of physics, and to understand the fundamental concepts of the discipline. They would then not only have had a lasting intellectual experience, they would also have the width, the flexibility, and the depth of understanding which would enable them to see the place and significance of future developments in the subject.

Secondly, related to the first feature, there was an emphasis on inquiry and discovery. In the 'new maths', pupils were put to discovering the nature of sets and varieties of number systems. In the Humanities Curriculum the work was built around inquiry, and the search for and judgment of evidence. On almost every project of curriculum reform the pupils were to learn the techniques of inquiring and experimenting, and, by practising them, build up an attitude of critical questioning. In that matter, the curriculum movement was still thoroughly Deweyan —

aspiring to cultivate the exploring mind, the problem-solver receptive to change, the twentieth century citizen at home in indeterminate situations.

Thirdly, the movement put an emphasis on the self-activity of the pupils. They were encouraged to think up their own apparatus for scientific experiments, or, in the new English or new French programs, to express themselves with greater confidence, in a greater variety of ways, and with greater self-knowledge. The new English, wrote a grammar school master, had 'a life not a *belles-lettres* approach'.[62] In France there was a deliberate timetabling of specific periods in the upper secondary school for independent study with self-evaluation and, beginning in 1973, an experiment in which the pupils of a CES equipped with an up-to-date resource centre devoted a third of their time to working independently at a variety of disciplined and original projects in modern languages, technology, and the social sciences.[63] The curriculum reformers were interested in ensuring that pupils not merely acquired knowledge but that they understood it, and that they could express their understanding of it effectively; and, furthermore, that in the process of expression they were adding important dimensions to their own educational development, those of self-awareness and social responsibility. To help in achieving those ends, in all the programs, and especially in the language and social science ones, there was considerable attention paid to oral work, to skill in listening, to ability to converse, explain, and discuss, and to a striving after sincerity and genuineness in the expression of each individual.

In the fourth place, the curriculum reform was accompanied by and made extensive use of current innovations in teaching techniques, most of which were audio-visual. The kits and study units produced by many of the projects contained teaching films, videotapes, strip films, gramophone records, tape recordings, transparencies for overhead projectors, and were supplemented by radio and TV programs. In language teaching, a language laboratory and its accompanying audio equipment or material were usually regarded as necessary.

Starting in the mid-1950's programmed learning continued to be widely experimented with in the 1960's. Although never widely adopted it created sufficient interest to have an effect on the curriculum reform movement in two ways. In order to be effective, a teaching program had to

---

[60] National Council of Teachers of Mathematics, *The Revolution in School Mathematics*, NCTM, Washington D.C., 1961, p. 1.

[61] M. Beberman, *An Emerging Program of Secondary School Mathematics*, Harvard University Press, Inglis Lecture, 1958, p. 44.

[62] Geoffrey Hoare, 'Some English', in Bob White *et al.*, *Experiments in Education at Sevenoaks*, Constable, London, 1965, p. 89.

[63] France, Ministère de l'Education National *Le Travail Indépendant*, Paris, Institut National de Pédagogique, 1974.

be worked out in small steps with great precision; it required, therefore, that close attention should be paid to analysing the objectives of teaching the course or topic, and a concentrated effort to state each objective as a form of behaviour that could be taught and learned. The current popularity of Bloom's timely *Taxonomy of Educational Objectives*, published in 1956 and carried in every curriculum-maker's knapsack of that generation, was reinforced by the concern for behavioural objectives expressed by programmers. It added to the skill and the interest that curriculum teams in every subject had in thrashing out and clarifying their objectives and in ensuring that they were thoroughly practicable. An interest in programmed learning brought with it, also, attention to the idea of mastery. To proceed, as in the earlier and similar Winnetka Plan, from one step to another it was necessary to master the first step. The pupil was able to work through a program only by succeeding at each step before moving on to the next. In that way he built up, little by little, a body of knowledge or skill over which, it was hoped, he had substantial control. The approach highlighted for curriculum workers the need to determine what elements in their projects it was necessary for pupils to achieve a mastery of, to think seriously about the sequence in which items or topics might with most advantage be arranged, and to devise ways of teaching and learning to ensure that pupils mastered the appropriate material. It also made it essential that each curriculum project had some effective method of evaluation built into it. Process studies of what was happening in the classroom, and achievement and attitude tests to assess the extent to which results matched objectives were the usual methods of evaluation.

The other innovation in teaching method that affected the curriculum movement was team teaching. It started in the mid-1950's, and was an effort to use teachers as groups rather than isolated units of professionals, each contributing to the work of the team the kind of thing that he could do best. It was a criticism of existing rigidities in the pattern of schooling — of fixed class size, of inflexible school architecture, of the traditional multi-purpose teacher, and of inelastic timetabling. The curriculum movement, too, developed an interest in modifying each of these. Large lecture groups and small working parties were incorporated in the projects, and flexible teaching spaces to replace standard classrooms followed as a matter of course. A teacher with skills in drama, or group discussion, or field work was to be kept on those specialities while others with different skills were to be used to best advantage throughout the school; class divisions, in consequence, and with them lesson timetabling tended to become more fluid. Those irruptions into traditional teaching practice led to the open plan school that, at primary and junior secondary school level, began to appear in the late 1960's and made a considerable impact on educational thinking in the early 1970's.

The curriculum reform movement in secondary education that started in the 1950's, gathered strength in the 1960's, and widened out in the 1970's was complex and varied in its motives and activities, but, in essence, educationally speaking, it had one direction. It was a move from instruction to education. The traditional teacher-centred instructional mode of classroom procedure characteristic of secondary education in European countries and to a lesser extent in the U.S.A. in the first half of the century was undermined by the new practices and ideas. In its place, the new curricula fostered a means of educating in which pupil and teacher formed much more of a partnership in the process of inquiring, discovering, discussing, understanding, and expressing matters relevant to the state of contemporary knowledge and their life within contemporary society.

(iii) Transformation in the Primary School

The Hadow Report in England in 1931 suggested that 'the curriculum is to be thought of in terms of activity and experience rather than of knowledge to be acquired and facts to be stored'.[64] A reasonable number of teachers in both progressive and traditional schools put the Hadow Report's words into action during the 1930's, and laid the foundation for more extensive reform when the times would be more opportune. But, more importantly, the training colleges became firm advocates of the progressive movement; and progressive ideas, by the end of the 1930's had become established educational theory in discussions on primary education.[65] Depression and war, however, inhibited any substantial practical advance in the schools, and denied the financial support which it required until the later 1940's.

In a report issued immediately after World War II, in 1946, the Advisory Committee on Education in Scotland summarised current criticisms of primary education in a way which was clearly applicable to all western European countries at that time. The content and methods of primary education were laid down several generations back and appeared in parts to be outdated; the division of content into subjects was an adult conception that was not a natural way of learning for children; the whole atmosphere was too academic and divorced from the living interests of children who were required to be passive listeners rather than active participants; the traditional class teaching approach was inefficient; the less able children found little in school and left it as early as possible; the

---

[64]   Great Britain, Board of Education, *The Primary School*, Report of the Consultative Committee (Hadow) HMSO London, 1931, p. 93.

[65]   R.J.W. Selleck, *English Primary Education and the Progressives 1914-1939*, RKP London, 1972, pp. 120-1.

syllabus was overcrowded, and little could be done thoroughly.[66] At about the same time as these criticisms were appearing, steps were being taken in England that would be of considerable importance in enabling a future steady reconstruction to take place.

From 1945 all teachers in England who were not university graduates, and that meant most primary school teachers, had to be trained and qualified to teach. In the 1920's almost all pupils, save the few who were selected for secondary grammar schools, were educated in an all-age school carrying them from five to the school leaving age of fourteen. Gradually the post-primary tops to the schools were sheered off so that by the end of the 1940's only a third of the all-age schools were left, by the end of the 1950's only about one-tenth, and by the mid 1960's they had almost completely vanished, leaving primary schools to concentrate single-mindedly on the education of young children below the age of eleven plus.[67]

During the course of the third quarter of the century, with an improved teaching staff, smaller classes, and manageable primary schools, English primary education was to be transformed to the point where by the early 1970's it had come to be regarded by a considerable body of American educators as a worthwhile object for study and possible imitation.[68]

The English primary school was not unique. Its principal features and the directions of its development were reproduced in many other countries; but, because its activities were particularly well documented and the changes which they represented were spread widely throughout the country, the English primary school may be looked on as a suitable example of the way in which primary education was moving in the three decades after World War II.

In the 1940's teaching in the basic subjects had lost much of its formality, local studies with excursions and associated activities had begun to play an important part in many curricula, and schools were seriously trying to build up their pupils' social experiences and to think of themselves as societies. Throughout the 1950's the process of enrichment and increasing informality was carried further. In 1959, after a lapse of fifteen years, the Ministry of Education issued a further volume of suggestions to primary school teachers in which it summed up the current position as the product of 'years of steady maturing' based on 'the foundation of experience patiently accumulated' in which the schools laid emphasis upon two salient things — a concern with children as children whose needs and characteristics were to be regarded by teachers as an interdependent whole, and a concern for the quality of the children's learning which was to be both interesting and demanding.[69]

That view of primary school development was supported and extended by the Plowden Report of 1967 which made a thorough review

of primary education, spending some three years commissioning research and deliberating on the whole field. The report described a study made by Her Majesty's Inspectors of Schools in classifying all the primary schools of England into categories devised by the committee. They found that approximately a third had developed into schools with a good modern approach, a third were middle of the road schools with some good features, and a third were little affected by the progress of the past fifty years. About 10 per cent of primary school children were in schools of distinctly high quality and about five per cent in really bad schools. The committee's concern was to raise the level of all schooling up to that of the higher categories. To tackle situations of educational and social deprivation, it suggested a policy of positive discrimination towards children severely handicapped by home conditions, not unlike the principle of compensatory education in the U.S.A., through which schools in educational priority areas would receive additional funds and educational assistance. For the general run of schools it advocated the employment of more school non-professional aides to assist teachers, the further reduction of class sizes, the modernisation of school buildings and the more widespread adoption of the methods of the high quality schools, such as small group and individual methods of teaching, non-streaming, and a greater range of activity work.[70]

The Plowden Report was widely read and favourably reacted to. It further stimulated the growing ferment in primary education. In the post-Plowden period of the late 1960's and early 1970's the trend in English primary education was towards the wider adoption of three related lines of activity:

- There was a steady enrichment of the material environment of the pupils. New and imaginatively designed schools were built at a greater rate during that period than ever before. School libraries considerably increased in number, and the range of their reference

66 Great Britain, Scottish Education Department, *Primary Education*, Cmd. 6973, HMSO, Edinburgh, 1946, p. 20.

67 Great Britain, Department of Education and Science, *Children and their Primary Schools*, vol. 1 (Plowden Report), HMSO, London, 1967, p. 98.

68 Beginning in 1971, for example, an Anglo-American Primary Education Project was established through the Ford Foundation in America and the Schools Council in England, to provide, for American teachers in training and the general public, descriptions of the way British primary schools work. By 1974 more than twenty titles had been published. See also C.E. Silberman, *Crisis in the Classroom*, Prentice-Hall, New York, 1971; and G.W. Bassett, *Innovation in Primary Education*, Wiley, London, 1972.

69 Great Britain, Ministry of Education, *Primary Education*, HMSO, London, 1959, pp. 10-11.

70 Great Britain, Department of Education and Science, *Children and their Primary Schools*, 2 vols., HMSO, London, 1967, *passim*. Since 1899 the central educational authority in England has had three different names at different times, viz. 1899-1944 Board of Education, 1944-64 Ministry of Education, and 1964- Department of Education and Science.

material was substantially widened to cater for an increase in the pupils' individual project work. Science materials were also provided much more generously and art and craft areas were well stocked.

- The human environment within the school was slowly transformed into that of a community with a warm and secure atmosphere in which the pupils could more freely expand and learn more effectively to express themselves. There was a growth of pupil responsibility and co-operation; there was increasing informal contact between teachers and pupils; there was a move towards the abolition of ability grouping or streaming; open-plan schools became more popular; and there was a more extensive effort to take care of the whole personality and of the many varied facets of it in each child.

- The teaching-learning environment was gradually recast. Orderly classes became busy, small discussion groups; knowledge was acquired with a purpose to solve problems or to contribute to some constructive work; oral work in English and sometimes in a foreign language vied in importance with written work; expression through music, art, drama, and dance was made the basis for personality development and for fundamental learning; and exacting standards of performance were expected in the arts as in the 3R's. All the subjects of the primary school curriculum underwent revision, most noticeably mathematics, which emerged as a compromise between traditional forms and efforts through the new mathematics to introduce more mathematical thinking into the subject. The activities throughout the whole curriculum 'were designed to emphasise enjoyment, cooperation, reality and achievement'.[71]

In effect, the image of the primary school in that period changed from that of a somewhat austere but reasonably pleasant institution for the acquisition of basic knowledge and ideas, to that of an attractive, warm, multi-resource community engaged in growing up with considerable discernment through an intriguing array of stimulating and exacting activities.

(iv) Pre-School Education

Pre-school education had had its strong advocates early in the century at a time of deepening social conscience. It had continued to grow steadily and unspectacularly thereafter as a form of education regarded as particularly suitable for working class areas, and available also for middle class families who were prepared to pay for the support of a pre-school centre. Play and creative activities, social development, and a close contact with parents and local community were characteristic features of most centres. Those which followed Montessorian lines emphasised sensory education through her self-corrective apparatus. In the 1950's there was a Montessorian revival, and her approach was used mainly in an effort to promote intellectual growth in young children. It was the beginning of a wider interest in early childhood education.

The drive towards equality of educational opportunity, which had characterised the twentieth century and had manifested itself particularly since World War II in the effort to develop comprehensive schools and a diversity of secondary and tertiary level curricula, was to be seen also in the 1960's in the increased effort that was put into providing remedial and compensatory education for socially disadvantaged children. In all western countries pre-school education was encouraged as a means of enriching the social and intellectual environment of children from economically less favoured areas. Project Head Start began in the U.S.A. in 1965 as a special compensatory program for disadvantaged children of pre-school age to assist them to attain a level at entrance of elementary school comparable to that of other pupils in more favoured environments. Largely for the same reason, nursery and infant schools in England, the écoles maternelles in France, and the kindergartens in Germany, Sweden, and Japan also experienced a considerable expansion and increase of public support throughout the 1960's and early 1970's.

The traditional program, in consequence, underwent some modification. Without jettisoning the existing approach, a new emphasis was placed on social and on intellectual development. Particular attention was given to the extension and improvement of the language competence of pre-school children and, to a small extent, to the sharpening of their number concepts. Piaget's work on the intellectual development of young children, and Bernstein's sociological research on class language were an underpinning for the new work of pre-school teachers. To get the maximum benefit from the hoped-for intellectual development of the children, efforts were made to plan a continuing program with primary schools. Though conceived initially with a view to providing compensatory work, the new programs were taken up by all kinds and levels of pre-schools. In the 1960's the number of women from all social levels who joined the work force increased considerably, and so also did a general public sense of the significance of the pre-school years in a child's future development. There was a consequent all-round increase in demand for pre-school centres, and a wider adoption of the new programs.

---

[71]   J.M. Pullen, *Towards Informality*, Macmillan, London, 1971, p. 35.

(v) Aspirations of the mid-1960's and 1970's

In about the middle of the 1960's it could be said that a change in the general climate of education had clearly begun to appear. The stimulus of the curriculum projects of the past decade had been taking effect and much of the work done in them was to be endorsed and continued. It was, however, a beginning of a rethinking of curriculum development, and in particular a reassertion of some of the main ideas of the pre-World War II progressives. The schools of the 1960's and 1970's were different institutions from those of the 1920's and 1930's or even the 1940's and 1950's. The French CES, the English comprehensive, and the Soviet Ten-Year schools, for example, did not even exist before World War II. The new schools were mass schools; they were schools for a space age generation. Old curricula and old methods of teaching had, obviously, to be re-examined. It was, however, much more than a matter of curriculum reform.

An educator, writing in 1965, dramatically caught an important aspect of what she saw as the world-wide change. 'The cat is out of the bag. The simple equation Education equals Power has suddenly been grasped by the masses the world over. Power to choose your career, power to achieve the standard of living you want, power to exploit the resources of the natural world, power to control and manipulate other people — all these are seen to be conferred by Education.'[72] The discovery of the power which might be applied through education was one of the most striking features of the post-World War II rise in the level of aspiration experienced by the youth of the period. By the mid-60's in all countries there was a mass realisation of the importance of education. With the realisation came a measure of disenchantment. Teachers and the youth of the day began to question more seriously than ever whether the effects of the power wielded by the products of contemporary education were desirable. There was a loss of faith in traditional recipes, and there were serious misgivings about currently accepted values that had supported affluent western societies. The most dramatic evidences of it were the Cultural Revolution in China and the world-wide revolts of university students. They were symptoms not just of protest against restrictive, unjust, or misguided practices in education but rather of a refocusing of educational purposes. The new deal had four main features:

- There was a re-emphasis on discovery learning. It was a revival of Dewey's view that the process of inquiry was the heart of intellectual education and a continuance of what had been an important feature of many of the recent curriculum reforms. It was also a recognition that in changing and uncertain times it was not established knowledge and traditions that were important but the skills of inquiring, probing, and assessing through which new ways of living and behaving might be found.

- There was an interest in examining moral values. Established values were found to be sometimes vague and inadequate. Ways were, therefore, developed to clarify them, to assess their relevance, and, where desirable, to formulate new ones. There was the beginning of a move for educators to try to develop individuals who would not simply accept or adjust to the values of current society but who would give them careful thought and would be personally concerned about the humanity and the morality of the activities in which they and their society engaged.

- There was a move towards involving pupils and teachers in greater participation in the management and direction of all aspects of education. Particularly, in the determination of curricula, pupils' needs and interests were not only considered but their views were also taken into consideration. There was the beginning, too, of a widespread move to involve schools, and to train the teachers in them, in adapting existing curricula and designing new ones to suit their requirements.

- There was a great increase in flexibility in school programs. There were some schools which managed to provide such a rich and varied offering that each pupil was able to have his own individual program which scarcely overlapped with that of any other. In most schools the general tendency was for pupils to accept a limited offering, and, within it, to have an opportunity to build programs to their own taste by concentrating on sections or topics of special interest to them. Two aspects of that development were of particular interest in western countries. There was a growth in the tendency to link school subjects with experience in productive or social work in factories or community agencies. Philadelphia's Parkway School without walls was a well-publicised example.[73] It was the use of the long-established principle in Communist education of uniting education and productive work. Western educators found that it brought interest and relevance into the work of western urban school students also. The second aspect of the trend towards flexibility was the effort to give pupils themselves responsibility for choosing and working at programs that would develop their self-confidence, their powers of self-expression, and their sense of humanity.

---

[72] Marjorie Reeves (ed.), *The Problem of 18 Plus*, Faber and Faber, London, 1965, p. 11.

[73] J. Bremer and M. von Moschzisker, *The School Without Walls*, Holt, Rinehart and Winston, New York, 1971.

It was with something of a new spirit that western education moved into the 1970's, a spirit which could also be seen emerging in the developments and reforms of the non-western countries. For the past twenty years educators' efforts had focussed on four things: on the quantitative expansion of education at all levels: on democratising the provision, organisation, and conduct of schools; on diversifying the educational structures; and on modernising the context and methods of teaching.[74] The object of education was to enable societies to make the most out of the conditions with which they were faced. The new trend that appeared to be developing in education was that of 'preparing men for a type of society that does not yet exist'.[75] It was to be an education more open to innovation, more accepting of dissent, more capable of providing for all needs and all tastes in a lifelong education within the learning society of the future where rational efficiency was to be matched with human sensibility.

[74] E. Faure *et. al.*, *Learning to Be*, UNESCO, Paris, 1972, p. 22ff. provided a useful analysis of worldwide trends.

[75] *ibid.*, p. 13.

World: Adult (15+ year old) Population and Literacy Rates.

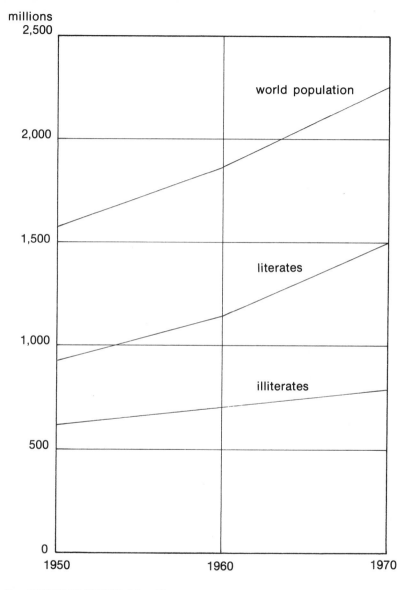

millions

2,500

2,000

1,500

1,000

500

0

world population

literates

illiterates

1950   1960   1970

From UNESCO ED/BIE/34/Ref. 1, p. 29.

CHAPTER 14

EDUCATIONAL REVOLUTION IN DEVELOPING COUNTRIES 1950-75: INDIA AND AFRICA

SUMMARY

Education in India after 1947

    (i)   Education Commissions

    (ii)   Karachi Plan

    (iii)   Kothari Commission

    (iv)   Indian Education in the early 1970's

The Educational Renascence in Africa 1950-75

    (i)   'The African Mind'

    (ii)   Education by 1950

    (iii)   The Educational Explosion of the 1950's

    (iv)   Education in Independent Africa 1960-75

           (a) The Colonial Legacy

           (b) Education and National Development

           (c) Addis Ababa Conference and its Aftermath

                 in the 1960's

           (d) Modification and Modernisation of the

                 Western Pattern of Schooling

           (e) Trends in Enrolment

The tempo of education in dependent developing countries changed with the approach of independence. Commissions on various aspects of education recommended new plans, and governments undertook some measure of expansion to meet the rising aspirations of the population and the new needs that were emerging. After independence there was a noticeable upsurge of enrolments at all levels of education, an influx of new ideas and a greater acknowledgment of the importance of education for the future development of the new nation.

The progress of the developing countries was assisted by new international, inter-governmental agencies that were established immediately after World War II. The United Nations was set up in 1945, and had a number of specialised agencies with strong interests in education in developing countries, such as the World Health Organisation (WHO) and the Food and Agricultural Organisation (FAO) which initiated and supported educational programs in their respective areas. The most important of the specialised agencies in the educational field was the United Nations Educational, Scientific and Cultural Organisation (UNESCO). It was established in 1946 to harness education to the interests of peace and the prevention of further wars: the statement, 'since wars begin in the minds of men, it is in the minds of men that the defences of peace must be constructed', was written into its constitution. UNESCO was interested in assisting with the education of persons displaced by war, in promoting scientific and cultural contacts and developments between nations, and in experimenting with ways of assisting education in underdeveloped areas.

By the mid-1950's, as increasing numbers of independent nations were coming into being, UNESCO interest turned primarily towards the problems of underdeveloped countries. It provided assistance in many ways. It established experimental and training stations on various aspects of education of importance to underdeveloped countries, e.g. an institute for training teachers of fundamental education in tropical countries was established in Mexico in 1951, and an institute of educational planning was set up in 1963 in Paris to advise and train educational administrators. It arranged seminars and working parties on selected educational problems, and it sent experts to advise and work with educators in the countries which requested them. It held large conferences to assist in developing educational plans for various regions, such as Karachi for south and east Asia in 1960, and Addis Ababa for Africa in 1961. It assisted individual nations in preparing their own plans, and in experimenting with literacy programs and with methods and curricula in technical and general education. And when the United Nations set up a special development fund, UNESCO administered that program as well as its own. Grants to underdeveloped countries were also made by the World Bank, and UNESCO assisted in the preparation of submissions to that body. In connection with all those activities UNESCO produced reports, newsletters, pamphlets, statistical analyses, journals, and books that provided information and guidance to educators throughout the developing world in the course of the educational revolution that they were making.

India was the first of the Asian countries to achieve independence after World War II, and, as it had inherited a well-established educational system, its educational activities were mainly to effect an expansion of existing facilities rather than to give a new or radical direction to them. Nevertheless, it inherited huge educational problems contributed to by illiteracy, poverty of resources, and intractable social customs. It required much effort and thought from Indian educators, from UNESCO and from other international sources to try to come to grips with them. In Africa, new states developed speedily in the 1950's and 1960's and, starting from different educational levels, from different basic cultures, and from different colonial experiences, provided examples of varying patterns of development within the same set of fundamental problems. They wanted to become literate, to become economically viable, to express their cultural identity, and to build a sense of national community. Education was an essential instrument for the attainment of all those purposes.

EDUCATION IN INDIA AFTER 1947

The emergence of a country from dependence to nationhood puts it immediately into competition with the rest of the world, and requires it, if it is to develop and flourish, to look to and make the most of its resources. For most countries, manpower is the most important resource; the country's future, therefore, depends very much on the manner and extent of the education that is used to shape its manpower. India in 1947 was one of many countries that had to start to make its way independently in the mid-twentieth century. Its experience may be regarded as reasonably typical of south and south-east Asian countries.

India was a populous country, a composite of varied peoples, languages and traditions, and a country of great historical and cultural achievement. It had, for nearly two centuries, been under the control of an alien colonial power which had given it a taste of western manners and technology but had left it, by 1947, still economically backward and educationally underdeveloped.

(i) Education Commissions

The first move in India was to make an assessment of the educational position. Between 1948 and 1956 three commissions looked respectively at university, secondary, and basic education.[1]

University education was to be expected to provide, it was hoped, a sound and substantial supply of leaders for the new nation, especially in the professional fields where she was weakest.

The secondary schools report, while recommending the strengthening of existing facilities, started to take a somewhat new approach by suggesting the development of comprehensive secondary schools in which vocational studies would be given greater importance. A four-year primary education was to be followed by seven years of secondary, of which the first three years would be a common course leading to specialist courses in the last four forms. The medium of instruction throughout secondary schooling should be the mother-tongue or the regional language. The commission's recommendations were gradually implemented by the successive Five Year Plans that India embarked on from 1951.

The committee reviewing basic education found that this had only just begun to get under way and they looked forward to the time when generations of pupils coming out of basic schools 'can transform India as nothing else can'.[2] Instead of trying to saturate particular areas to demonstrate the worth of basic education, education departments should accelerate the spread of basic education by giving all primary schools a basic slant. The quality of existing basic schools was mixed; some were of high quality but in some the facilities were poor, and teachers had grasped neither the general principles nor the activity method of basic education. The committee recommended that more extensive research and training on all aspects of basic education was needed, and that state governments should unambiguously declare their intention to promote basic schools.

A further and continuing problem for India was the overwhelming incidence of illiteracy. In 1951, 88 per cent of the population over fifteen

---

[1] India, Ministry of Education, *Report of the University Education Commission* (Radhakrishnan), New Delhi, 1949; *Report of the Secondary Education Commission* (Mudaliar), New Delhi, 1953; *Basic Education in India*, Report of the Assessment Committee on Basic Education (Ramachandran), New Delhi, 1956.

[2] *Basic Education in India, op.cit.*, p. 59.

years old was illiterate; in 1961, 72 per cent, and in 1971, 71 per cent. That steady, slow reduction in the proportion of illiterates did not match the general increase in population. Consequently the 176,000,000 illiterates in 1951 grew to 187,000,000 in 1961 and to 387,000,000 in 1971. Such a mass of illiterate population was a substantial hindrance to plans for agricultural and industrial development, to the improvement of health, and to the growth of co-operative institutions.

From the various reviews it emerged that India in pursuit of its new national goals had six fundamental educational problems:

- It needed a greatly increased stock of trained high-level administrative and technical manpower to staff its public and private executive positions, and to develop its agricultural and industrial resources.

- It needed an immense increase in secondary school level technicians to staff the middle-level positions in commerce, industry, and agriculture that the modernisation of the country would require.

- It needed a massive growth in the provision of general primary education to achieve, within a reasonably short time, universal compulsory primary education as the indispensable foundation for economic, political, and cultural progress towards both the attainment of reasonable living standards for all and the development and maintenance of the co-operative democratic society to which its political leaders were committed.

India: Students at an engineering college in Chandigarh.

- For the very same reasons that universal primary education was a necessity, the elimination of adult illiteracy by an effective and continuing form of literacy and social education was also needed.

- It needed to evolve a form of education with appropriate content that would draw upon the educational experience of western countries in the course of their own modernisation, would manage to maintain vigorously the indigenous traditions of the various cultures of the sub-continent, and would also bring to the whole country a sense of sharing a common heritage and a common purpose in respect to the nation's future development.

- It needed to produce trained teachers in sufficient numbers to man the schools and cope adequately with the readjusted and expanded program of education.

From 1951 on, Indian development was guided by a series of Five Year Plans under which education absorbed about seven per cent of the nation's projected financial outlay. A quantitative expansion of education was undertaken in the Five Year Plans to try to meet the country's main educational needs.

Primary education absorbed the most money and effort at all times, as India struggled to achieve universal primary education by 1980. Basic education which had been designed specifically as a form of primary and subsequently secondary education particularly suited to Indian conditions encountered heavy weather. In 1956 at the time the review committee made its report, fifteen per cent of primary level schools were basic; progress continued slowly during the next ten years, and in 1966, the proportion had risen to 37 per cent. A subsequent review in the mid-1960's, found that both the teaching profession and the general public were somewhat resistant, as they were elsewhere, to other forms of progressive education. There was a widespread belief that academic standards were lower in basic schools, and many high schools were reluctant to admit pupils from basic schools. Craftwork was hard for many schools to manage satisfactorily and many disliked it and saw no value in it. The idea that basic schools should be self-supporting had never been widely accepted and by the 1960's seems to have dropped out of serious consideration.

In the initial plan the desire for university-trained personnel was also prominent, but as in the 1950's the economy proved unable to absorb many of the university graduates, support for higher education in general lessened, and the plans concentrated more on first and second level technical education. Nevertheless, by 1965 the number of universities had risen to sixty-four from the twenty that existed in 1947, and the number of colleges of higher education had increased from 340 to 2,360, raising the number of tertiary level students from 266,000 to 1,528,000. The most striking advance was in the technological field. Between 1951 and 1961 five Indian Institutes of Technology were established in different regions offering undergraduate courses and high-level graduate work in a wide range of science and engineering fields, and other institutions were subsequently raised to the same status. Higher level agricultural studies were also boosted by a similar development of a network of specialist agricultural universities which combined teaching and research with agricultural service to the community.

In the early 1960's teacher education, and towards the end of the 1960's literacy too were given increased weight.

(ii) Karachi Plan

In 1960 representatives of the Asian member states of UNESCO, meeting at Karachi, adopted a plan to achieve, by 1980, eight years' universal education up to the age of fourteen. The fifteen nations in the Karachi Plan stretched across southern and eastern Asia from Iran to Indonesia and north to South Korea. The twenty-year program was designed to raise the percentage of the total population receiving primary education from nine per cent in 1960 to twenty per cent in 1980, at which point approximately all the children under fourteen-years-old would be at school. The operation involved more than a mere expansion of primary education; it implied also a considerable development of secondary schools and teachers' colleges through which teachers for the primary schools would be produced, and it involved an increase in tertiary education to provide staff for the secondary schools and teachers' colleges. Administrators and supervisors also had to be multiplied, and an enormous building program entered upon. The whole operation was costed for the fifteen nations and was, for many, found to be beyond their resources. In 1962, therefore, in a meeting at Tokyo, it was decided that each country should prepare its own educational program for development within the limits of its own plans and prospects of economic growth. It was clear that massive aid from developed countries would be needed for most of the countries to have any reasonable prospect of reaching the target for 1980. In India's case the Karachi Plan helped to confirm the country's commitment to the rapid expansion of primary education, and drew attention to the other educational consequences of it, especially to the need for a larger program of teacher training. The Karachi Plan targets were incorporated into India's successive five year economic plans; it was proposed that universal primary education for children from six to eleven years old should be achieved by the end of the Fourth Plan in 1971, and for those from eleven to fourteen by the end of the Sixth Plan in 1981.

The Karachi Plan was an important educational development for the Asian nations. It was the first time that the educational needs of the region had been considered as a whole, and the huge task revealed of raising the educational level of that very large segment of the world's population. The plan helped the fifteen countries define their educational targets, and became a general reference against which the governments could assess their plans and progress.

(iii) Kothari Commission

Soon after the beginning of the Karachi Plan the Indian government set up an Education Commission, which, besides its Indian members, included educators from Japan, U.S.S.R., U.S.A., France, and England. It reported in 1966 on the state of current education, and made proposals for future developments. It was the most substantial investigation in Indian educational history. The commission was thorough in its inquiries, imaginative in its statement of aims, and practical in its recommendations.

With its opening sentence — 'The destiny of India is now being shaped in her classrooms' — the Education Commission declared its sense of the significance of education for the reconstruction and future development of the country.[3]

The population of India, the commission pointed out, was then five hundred million, and half of it was below the age of eighteen; by 1985 the student population of India would be equal to the total population of Europe. For this vast population the education available was too academic, unaware of its function in national reconstruction, poorly related to economic and agricultural development, divisive, elitist, and devoid of social responsibility. 'In our opinion, therefore, no reform is more important or more urgent than to transform education, to endeavour to relate it to the life, needs and aspirations of the people and thereby make it a powerful instrument of social, economic and cultural transformation necessary for the realization of our national goals. This can be done if education

— is related to productivity;
— strengthens social and national integration; consolidates democracy as a form of government and helps the country to adopt it as a way of life;
— hastens the process of modernization; and

---

[3] India, Ministry of Education, *Education and National Development*, Report of the Education Commission 1964-66 (Kothari), New Delhi, Government of India, 1966, p. 1.

— strives to build character by cultivating social, moral and spiritual values.'[4]

The commission envisaged a new shape for Indian education that would combine quality and utility more effectively in the interests of Indian development.

'We need to bring about,' it stated, 'a major improvement in the effectiveness of primary education; to introduce work-experience as an integral element of general education; to vocationalize secondary education; to improve the quality of teachers at all levels and to provide teachers in sufficient strength; to liquidate illiteracy; to strengthen centres of advanced study ... and to pay particular attention to education and research in agriculture and allied sciences.'[5]

India: A class for the little children in the Harijan section of a village in Madras State.

In pursuance of those aims, it recommended a doubling of the percentage of national expenditure on education during the next twenty years. It proposed that during that period primary education, with work-experience of the basic education type, should become available to all, and secondary education should eventually be based on neighbourhood comprehensive schools in which twenty per cent of the lower school and fifty per cent of the top classes should consist of vocational courses. An increased supply of middle level technicians should come from those courses and from the technical high schools of the cities. In all these schools moral and spiritual values should be directly and indirectly

taught, the pupils should be involved regularly in some form of social and community service, and modern science and maths should occupy a substantial place. The commission looked forward to the time when there would be a ten-year common school throughout India, offering, as in the U.S.S.R. and the U.S.A., a free general and utilitarian education for all. At a higher level, there should be a fourfold increase in tertiary students with an emphasis on the production of technologists and agriculturalists through the development of polytechnics, midway between universities and secondary schools. One-third of the increasing number of tertiary students were to be catered for by correspondence education. The other emphasis in tertiary work should be on teacher education, 'a key area in educational development',[6] which was to be encouraged by raising teachers' salaries and upgrading the work of the training institutions'. At the adult level, the commission hoped by a variety of programs to increase adult literacy to eighty per cent by 1976.

Quality, relevance, social responsibility, and the acceleration of the educational program were the commission's special concerns. To improve the level of primary and secondary education, it proposed the setting up of about ten per cent of the schools as quality schools for which the best teachers and pupils would be selected to act as pacesetters for the system. Similarly, at the higher level some half-dozen universities should be declared major universities and given special treatment to raise them to international standard. At all levels, the need to raise economic production and to develop India as a democratic co-operative society should be borne in mind in the selection of the kinds of productive work, the vocational courses, and the general curriculum that the schools offered.

The commission was conscious of the need to preserve the essence of India's heritage while taking steps to move forward into the contemporary technological world. The living tradition of India expressed in literature, art, thought, and spiritual perception was to be married in the school curriculum, to the scientific knowledge and techniques of the progressive western nations. One of the loftiest aspects of the Indian heritage was the great humane tradition of compassion and non-violence, *ahimsa*. 'The greatest contribution of Europe doubtlessly is the scientific revolution. If science and *ahimsa* join together in a creative synthesis of belief and action, mankind will attain to a new level of purposefulness, prosperity and spiritual insight. Can India do something in adding a new dimension to the scientific achievement of the West?'[7]

---

[4] *ibid.*, p.6.

[5] *ibid.*, p. i.

[6] *ibid.*, p. 622.

[7] *ibid.*, p. 22.

Figure 14.1: India: School System (simplified), 1970.

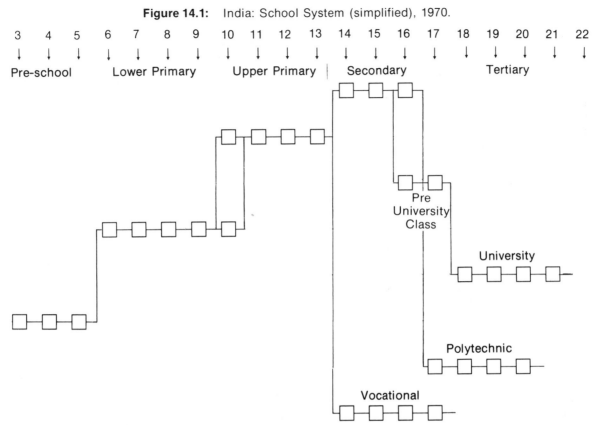

The report concluded on a note of urgency, counselling the importance of immediate, decisive, massive, and sustained action. India stood in great need not only of firm action to reform the whole educational system, but also of a firm determination to orient her education towards effective action, to impress upon pupils their social responsibilities. 'Knowledge and commitment must go together,' the chairman of the commission wrote later. 'How to achieve this is a great and urgent task facing Indian education, and in a sense world education.'[8]

(iv) Indian Education in the Early 1970's

The report of the Kothari Commission provoked considerable discussion but no immediate change in the pattern of education. Several state plans were developed for the general improvement of education, and at the tertiary level firm steps were taken to upgrade the work by selecting and giving special support to about thirty university departments as Centres for Advanced Study and to several Institutes of Technology. In the same vein was the foundation of a high-level, post-graduate, innovative university in New Delhi, the Jawaharlal Nehru University, established in 1965 as a tribute to India's great national leader.

By the 1970's India had a reasonably common pattern of education, though in each of the twenty-two states there were variations in detail. In general a two- to three-year pre-school led to a four- to five-year primary or junior basic, followed by a three- to four-year higher primary or senior basic, and a three- to four-year secondary or higher secondary school, with sometimes a one- to two-year pre-university class or college, leading to universities and institutes of technology. Vocational education could

[8] D.S. Kothari, *Education, Science and National Development*, Asia, London, 1970, p. 76.

Figure 14.2:   India: Increase in Enrolments and General Population Increase, 1901-70.

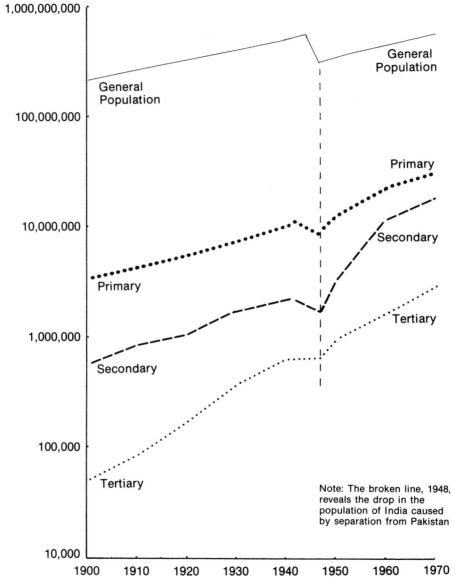

Note: The broken line, 1948, reveals the drop in the population of India caused by separation from Pakistan

begin at the end of the higher primary school; at a more advanced level, polytechnics accepted students on completion of a high school course.

Between 1950 and 1970 enrolments at all levels of education had grown considerably: by 91 per cent at primary level, 279 per cent at secondary, and 391 per cent at tertiary. The accompanying figure shows the slow growth in enrolment from 1900 to 1950, and the steady increase at an accelerated rate from 1950 to 1970.

It was clear that, although school enrolments had continued to grow and plans had been formed to improve the quality of the output, many of the same problems that had plagued Indian education throughout the century remained in the 1970's with scarcely diminished intensity. An Indian educator reviewing the general situation thought that the quality of education was seriously affected by the prevalence of overcrowded classrooms and outdated texts, by the scarcity of good equipment and good buildings, and the continuance of outmoded teaching methods. The heavy incidence of wastage was a considerable problem; some fifty per cent of primary school entrants for a variety of reasons such as malnutrition, distance from school, lack of aspiration, or necessity to join the work force, did not complete five years of primary education and therefore probably failed to attain a level of minimum literacy.[9] While the population grew by 2.5 per cent between 1961 and 1971, the rise in the literacy rate was only .5 per cent. Obviously India was falling behind in the task of eliminating illiteracy, and the problem was being compounded by primary school wastage. The multiplicity of languages and the complications of the caste system also added substantially in 1970, as they had in 1900, to the difficulty of providing effective education for all Indians. 'Illiteracy, ignorance and poverty,' wrote an Indian in 1975, 'are the three main evils facing all developing countries. India, being one of the developing countries, is not an exception to it.'[10]

THE EDUCATIONAL RENASCENCE IN AFRICA 1950-75

(i) 'The African Mind'

Part of the reluctance of colonial governments to embark upon a speedy or extensive program of western education for Africans stemmed from the view, widely held by Europeans at least up to World War II, that the African mind was both different in character and inferior to that of the European. Lévy-Bruhl in the 1920's had learnedly developed the theory that the savage mind operated in a way different from that of the civilised

mind. It was pre-logical, dependent primarily on memorisation and on a feeling of mystical, intimate participation in the surrounding milieu. From the demonstration that it operated in a particular way, the implication was drawn by some readers that it could not operate in any other way, and that it was relatively futile to try to teach Africans to think as Europeans did. Even when there might be apparent success in teaching children to think, they soon reached a ceiling, somewhere about adolescence, and further or higher education beyond that point was a waste of time.[11] To teach an African successfully to be an individual who might seek to control his environment was an unlikely possibility.

The experience of teachers and the results of intelligence testing appeared to demonstrate that the African mind was not only different from the European; it was also inferior. One forthright missionary in the mid-1920's who held a somewhat wowserish view of African customs and traditions exclaimed at a conference, 'Generations of intemperance and incredible sexual excess do not produce brain power, and the results of such a process are here in Africa before your eyes'.[12] And at the same period, the annual report of the Department of Education in Kenya likened the thought processes of Africans to those of mentally defective children in which 'the imagination and the emotions are both highly developed but the development of the reasoning faculties must be slow'.[13] In Nyasaland, in 1932, a regular six-monthly inspection of children was begun. From the records to be kept, the department's annual report stated that 'It should be possible in a few years' time to form accurate estimates as to age at which physical and mental retardation commences owing to the prolonged residence in the tropics.'[14] Mental testing on African children began at the time of World War I in South Africa, and by the 1930's was in use throughout all the colonies. Verbal and non-verbal tests, tests of special skills and of general intelligence led to the conclusion, reached independently by Allison Davis in his research with negroes in the U.S.A. that the tests were culturally biased and that little purpose was to

9   K.C. Mukherjee, 'The classroom in India: the pressures of population and poverty', *Aspects of Education*, 14, 1972, 51-65.

10   T,R, Nagappa, 'The new outlook that is much needed', *Indian Journal of Adult Education*, 36, 7, July 1975, 9.

11   See, for example, Nathan Miller, *The Child in Primitive Society*, Kegan Paul, Trench, Trubner, London, 1928, p. 125, who wrote that mental development was early and precocious, and came 'to a dead halt, however, about puberty', after which children regress to dullness, sexual licence and mental ossification.

12   Tanganyika Territory, *Conference between Government and Missions, Report of Proceedings*, Dar es Salaam, Education Office, 1925, p. 28.

13   Quoted in J. Anderson, *The Struggle for the School*, p. 40, from Kenya Education Department, *Annual Report*, 1926, p. 15.

14   Nyasaland Protectorate, *Report of the Education Department for the Year 1932*, Government Printer, Zomba, 1933, p. 10.

be served by administering to African children tests designed for western children. The only result was to show that black children could not do them as well as white children.[15] By 1950 a number of educators were engaged in adapting the tests and in devising new ones specifically for Africans. In subsequent years studies were made of the main factors affecting intellectual development and the means by which teachers could encourage intellectual growth.[16]

A number of anthropological studies before about 1950 tended to confirm the white educator's unflattering opinion of the educational potentialities of African children. They were found to have a tendency to be unstable, impulsive in the face of new experiences, lacking in power of attention to demanding tasks, intellectually conformist, without personal uniqueness, and to have a rote rather than a rational approach to learning.[17] By the 1950's researchers had begun to challenge those interpretations. A somewhat different picture was emerging, with a greater appreciation of the extent of individual differences between African children, and a greater respect for their personality characteristics and their intellectual adaptability. There was also a stronger feeling that more positive effort to upgrade education and other environmental influences would bring improvement in Africans' scores on tests of intelligence, ability and attainment.[18]

This was the time of 'the cracking myth' of the natural superiority of the European,[19] a time when Africans had become reasonably familiar with western civilisation and many were matching white achievement in a variety of areas.

(ii) Education by 1950

World War II had an important effect on the colonial territories in Africa. During the war there was an increase in propaganda directed at the colonial peoples from both the enemy and the colonial powers in an endeavour to secure their sympathetic support. Such efforts were a stimulus to a wider use of the vernacular and an encouragement to literacy. The same propaganda also gave a boost to nationalism which was further strengthened by the greater attention the colonial powers were forced to give to the interests of the indigenous peoples, and by the encounters that serving colonial troops had with other more advanced cultures and with other groups, particularly in Asia, where there were highly developed independence movements. The economy of the colonies, too, during the war and during the period of stringent rationing in European countries that followed it, made considerable progress. The production of food, raw materials, and minerals was greatly increased to supply the metropolitan powers. The stimulus to production and employment brought with it an increased interest in technical training

and in the elementary and secondary education that underpinned it. The war did not create specifically new educational demands, it accelerated educational progress in areas and along lines that were already developing slowly, and the intellectual and economic stirring that emerged from it led to substantially more educational effort by governments in the post-war period.

In 1940 there was a sign of the new developments to come. In that year the passage of the Colonial Development and Welfare Act by the British parliament broke new ground. It was matched for the French colonies by a government fund set up in 1946 on an even larger scale than the British. Those moves put an end to the policy of trying to develop the colonies out of their own resources. It recognised that adequate health and education services could only be established by the substantial injection of funds from outside. From those sources additional but fairly limited funds became available for all levels of education and for research, and each colony drew up a development plan which helped to promote and guide the educational explosion that eventually took place in the 1950's.

Table 14.1 shows the state of school enrolment in schools for Africans in the dependent territories in 1950.

The number of children being educated effectively in primary schools was undoubtedly much exaggerated and should probably be reduced by half. The number given in the table is the number of pupils enrolled in every kind of school — government, government assisted, and unassisted. Nearly all the unassisted schools were in that category because they were bush missionary schools of such low standard that they did not deserve assistance. In many of the colonial territories they constituted, in 1950, about half the total number of primary schools. For example, in the Belgian Congo, of the 943,500 primary school children given in the table,

---

[15] See, for example, S. Biesheuvel, *African Intelligence*, Johannesburg, South African Institute of Race Relations, 1943.

[16] Judith L. Evans, *Children in Africa. A Review of Psychological Research*, Teachers College, Columbia University, New York, 1970, pp. 9-27. See for example P.E. Vernon, *Cross-Cultural Studies of Abilities*, National Institute of Education, Makerere University College, Kampala, Uganda, 1966.

[17] J.F. Ritchie, *The African as Suckling and Adult (a psychological study)*, Rhodes-Livingstone Institute, Paper No. 9, 1943; J.C. Carothers, *The African Mind in Health and Disease: A Study in Ethno-Psychiatry*, WHO, Geneva, 1953, pp. 108ff.

[18] Arthur G. J. Cryns, 'African intelligence: a critical survey of cross-cultural intelligence research in Africa south of the Sahara', *Journal of Social Psychology*, 1962, 57, pp. 283-301; R. Dogbeh, 'Intelligence and education', *Présence Africaine*, 1961, 9, trans. in Frederic R. Wickert, *Readings in African Psychology from French Language Sources*, African Studies Center, Michigan State University, Lansing, Michigan, 1967, pp. 40-6; Philip E. Vernon, *Intelligence and Cultural Environment*, Methuen, London, 1969, pp. 228ff.

[19] See N. Sithole, *African Nationalism*, Cape Town, Oxford University Press, 1959, Chapter 12, 'The Cracking Myth'.

515,000 (55 per cent) were in unassisted schools, and similarly in Nigeria approximately sixty per cent of the pupils were in unassisted schools. Only in French West Africa was this element eliminated; the entry in the table for that group of dependencies, therefore, indicates only the number of pupils in government approved schools.

It is by no means easy to get accurate figures for school enrolments in colonial territories. It is clear, nevertheless, that none of the colonial powers had any reason to feel satisfied at the contribution it had made to the education of the African peoples. A comparison of the percentage of the population in England and France obtaining formal schooling with that of the African populations is an indication of the comparative lack of interest shown by most colonial authorities in education during the first half of the twentieth century. Their record over that period was not an impressive one. Neither quantitatively nor qualitatively did they achieve much of note.

Primary education in the more favoured colonies was provided for about fifty per cent of the children of primary school age, in the less favoured ones it was ten to fifteen per cent dropping in Angola as low as two per cent, and it varied markedly from district to district within any one colony. Furthermore, the rate of progress was abysmal. The principal of Achimota College in the mid-1930's calculated from the figures in the Gold Coast departmental report that, given the current rate of progress, it

Table 14.1: Africa: Enrolment in Schools in the Principal Colonial Territories, 1950.

Country	Primary		Secondary		Tertiary	Population	% of Pop. in Formal Educ.	Illiteracy 15 yrs and over %
	Total	Girls %	Total	Girls %	Total	Total		
British African Territories								
Gold Coast (Ghana)	271,000	25	9,000	14	437	5,020,000	6	75-80
Kenya	337,000	23	11,500	14	66	6,018,000	6	75-80
Nigeria	971,000	21	28,400	n.a.	2,900	34,330,000	3	85-90
Nyasaland (Malawi)	228,600	35	1,400	5	700	2,289,000	10	90-95
N. Rhodesia (Zambia)	156,000	32	1,200	30	713	2,440,000	7	75-80
S. Rhodesia	232,000	43	9,200	43	990	2,065,000	12	75-80
Sierra Leone	39,000	29	3,100	30	214	2,004,000	2	90-95
Tanganyika (Tanzania)	177,000	37	11,000	19	42	8,310,000	2	90-95
Uganda	238,000	25	9,300	25	30	5,119,000	5	70-75

(continued over page)

Other African Territories								
Belgian Congo	943,500	4	13,800	22	5,524	11,258,000	9	60-65
Rwanda Urundi	469,000	22	1,100	14		3,927,000	12	90-95
Angola	13,568	41	2,277	39	154	4,125,000	4	95-99
Mozambique	174,320	37	8,600	23		5,697,000	3	95-99
Algeria	362,000	34	47,000	n.a.		8,753,000	4	80-85
Fr.Equatorial Africa	108,800	14	5,900	33		4,406,000	3	95-99
Fr.West Africa	189,900	21	8,700	20	2,529	17,368,000	1	95-99
England	5,206,000	49	802,700	42	214,800	43,830,000	14	
France	4,593,500	48	752,300	49	307,100	41,550,000	14	

would take seven hundred years before the whole of the population of those parts would be able to read and write their own language. And the Gold Coast was one of the educationally more advanced colonies in Africa.[20] The children who did attend school remained, in most areas, for only about three years, and received, in ill-equipped schools, an uninteresting education from poorly trained teachers. A Belgian psychologist, experienced in colonial education, expressed the view after extensive testing, that 'at the end of the primary school, the African child ... presents a lack of integration, an intellectual fragmentation, and a kind of instability'.[21] The implication that he drew was that the quality of primary education needed to be enormously improved in regard to its method, its content, and its environment.

Secondary education was highly selective. About five per cent of those who entered primary schools eventually made their way to a post-primary education, which, for most pupils, was a vocational course for commerce, industry, or agriculture, but it could also be a course of teacher training, or an academic course for a very restricted number who might aspire to tertiary level work. Most of the academic schools did not offer full secondary school courses; when they did, they prepared their students to qualify for the secondary school certificate of the metropolitan power.

Girls' education was comparatively neglected. Girls were much fewer in number than boys in schools, and they tended to leave earlier. Of the primary school pupils in the British West African colonies only about 25 per cent were girls, and in East Africa the proportion was little better; in the French Equatorial and West African colonies the percentage was even lower. Their numbers, in all colonies, declined greatly at secondary level, and at tertiary level, where educational opportunities even for boys were rare, they dwindled almost to nothingness.

Tertiary education was embryonic. In 1950 there were no full universities in the sub-Saharan dependent territories. In the British colonies there were four university colleges just in being, with a mere

[20] W.B. Mumford & B.N. Parker, 'Education in the British Dependencies'. A review of the 1935 Annual Reports on native education in Nyasaland, Northern Rhodesia, Tanganyika, Uganda, Gold Coast, Nigeria, and Sierra Leone, *Journal of the Royal African Society*, 36, 142, January 1937, pp. 17-32. The reviewers felt that in some of the East African territories one thousand years would be nearer the mark.

[21] Paul Verhaegen, *L'Enfant Africain*, trans. Frederic R. Wickert, *op.cit.*, p. 313.

handful of students. In the French, Belgian, and Portuguese colonies there were none. Middle-level technical colleges had been established in most of the colonies and took care of most of the tertiary level students. Teacher training was mostly of secondary school level with a few courses offered at post-secondary level.

(iii) The Educational Explosion of the 1950's

The 1950's were the last decade of colonialism for most of the dependent territories in Africa. Their independence was preceded by a burst of educational activity the like of which had not been previously seen or contemplated in the colonial areas, as the gradualist policy was replaced by a near crash program of educational development.

A typical example of the accelerated educational program of the 1950's was the progress made by Nigeria during that period.

The introduction of responsible government in 1951 was the beginning of a tempestuous period in Nigeria's history. Strong political parties emerged, and there was vigorous political manoeuvring as a new constitution emerged every three years from 1951 to 1960. Education was regionalised and the parties in each of the three regions vied with each other to provide the best facilities possible. The overall result was a great thrust forward for education throughout the whole country. 'Educational development is imperative and urgent,' declared the Minister for Education in the western region, 'It must be treated as a national emergency, second only to war. It must move with the momentum of a revolution.'[22] The statement expressed in words the heartfelt feeling of the developing countries, that their future depended upon the speedy extension of sound and effective education and it was a plea for the rapid bridging of the gulf between political attainment and educational development.

Between 1950 and 1960 primary school enrolments in Nigeria increased from 971,000 to 2,913,000 and schools were spread more evenly through the country. Universal primary education, provided at public expense, was introduced into the western region in 1955, and in 1957 into the federal region of Lagos, and, in a modified way into the eastern region. By 1960, ninety per cent of the fourteen-year-old children in these areas were enrolled. It was the first time that free education had been implemented in any substantial part of any African colony.

Secondary education received similar attention. From 1948 to 1960 the number of secondary school places increased tenfold. Middle, modern, secondary commercial and technical, and secondary grammar schools were multiplied and in organisation and curriculum were set up after the style of the English tripartite secondary system.

Technical education had always lagged and continued to do so.

Nevertheless trade training centres were increased throughout the country, and in 1953 a Nigerian College of Arts, Science, and Technology was established with branches in each region to provide middle level technical training. Tertiary level education had received an encouragement with the opening of a University College at Ibadan in 1948. By 1960 it had more than a thousand students, and a commission was preparing a report on the multiplication of Nigeria's institutions of higher education.

The expansion of the 1950's was not unplanned. The passage of the Colonial Development and Welfare Act of 1940 had encouraged the formation of development plans in each of the colonies. In 1946 a ten-year development plan was launched in Nigeria to accelerate economic progress, and expand the social services of the country.

Five years later two study groups were established, one to investigate education in British West Africa, the other for East Africa. Their reports were considered at a conference of African and English educators and published in 1953. The reports, the first such since the Phelps-Stokes Commission thirty years earlier, pointed out the enormous distance that had to be traversed to bring the African countries educationally into the modern world. The abysmal poverty of Africa, its rapidly increasing population, the mushrooming of urban centres, the beginnings of industrial development, the weakening of agricultural life and the social structure dependent upon it, the inexorable demand for higher standards of living and material satisfaction, and the new sense of belonging to an African nation, were powerful factors moving Africa into a new world which, the study groups saw, had to be buttressed by extensive and solid educational foundations. Inadequate provision of schooling at all levels, an inordinate wastage rate, and an insufficient supply of well-trained teachers held back the countries of both West and East Africa. The 1953 report made suggestions and recommendations over the whole range of educational provision, stressing in particular the need for attention to girls' education, for a rethinking of the whole school curriculum, for the development of modern teaching procedures, and for the extensive recruitment and training of teachers. During the course of the 1950's attention was given to these educational needs and much progress was made but it was still possible to point out in 1958 that in Nigeria the secondary school intake was only twelve thousand a year, a third of the number needed to sustain the country's economic progress in the immediate future.

In 1959 another commission was set up to look at Nigeria's needs in higher education. This body, the Ashby Committee, reported in 1960. It was noteworthy for two things. It looked comprehensively at the

---

[22] Western Region, *Debates* (30 July 1952) pp. 463-70, quoted in A.B. Fafunwa, *History of Education in Nigeria*, Allen and Unwin, London, 1974, pp. 167-8.

country's high-level manpower needs for the next two decades, and used this study as a basis on which to recommend various measures of educational development to meet them. The committee's work was an example of the procedure of relating educational to economic planning which was to become a characteristic approach in developing countries during the next decade. Its second principal feature was to make a set of recommendations far more generous and far-reaching than that of any previous committee or policy. It proposed:

- the development of four universities, independent, with degree-conferring powers, and a wide range of professional courses;

- the establishment of several new teachers' colleges and the training of many more graduate teachers in universities;

- a considerable enlarging of facilities for technical training at post-secondary level;

- the speedy expansion of secondary education in order to provide sufficient recruits to fill the places available in the newly established expanded tertiary institutions.

Nigeria became independent in 1960, and the commission's recommendations were put into operation in the course of the 1960's by the new national Nigerian government.

Educational expansion during the 1950's of which the Nigerian experience is an example of what was general throughout the British territories, was similar but not quite so rapid in the French sub-Saharan territories. It was stimulated by the general conference at Brazzaville in 1944, the Development Fund for Overseas Territories, FIDES, and by the smouldering nationalism which the Algerian insurgency fuelled. Primary school enrolments, both public and missionary, trebled during the 1950's. Secondary education was strengthened by the establishment of several new *lycées* and the upgrading of higher elementary schools into secondary *colléges*. Vocational education at secondary level, which the French had always emphasised more than the British, grew rapidly, especially in the fields of commerce and agriculture. Enrolments in both secondary and vocational schools also trebled. Education at the tertiary level was introduced into the colonies for the first time in 1950 with the foundation of the Institute for Higher Studies which became the University of Dakar in 1958. In that year also a Centre for Higher Education was established in Abidjan in the Ivory Coast, and an Institute for Higher Studies at Brazzaville in the Congo.

Clearly, throughout the colonial territories in Africa, there was a decided advance during the 1950's, but the distance to be covered was immense. By 1960, despite the efforts of the 1950's, probably only about fifteen per cent of six to fourteen year-olds were in primary school in the French territories, and thirty per cent in the British.

(iv) Education in Independent Africa 1960-75

The Mediterranean colonies were the first to achieve independence — Libya in 1951, Morocco and Tunis in 1956, Algeria, after eight years of ruinous warfare, in 1962.

In West Africa, Gold Coast, renamed Ghana, was, in 1959, the first of the British colonies to gain independence. Nigeria followed in 1960, Sierra Leone in 1961, and Gambia in 1965. Of the French territories in the same region, Guinea became independent in 1958, and the remainder in 1960.

In East and Central Africa, the movement covered the same years, first Sudan in 1956, then Somalia 1960, Tanzania 1961, Uganda 1962, Kenya 1963, and Malawi and Zambia 1964. The Belgian possessions erupted into independence and violence in 1960 in the case of the Congo, renamed Zaire in 1972, and Rwanda and Burundi in 1962. Angola and Mozambique remained Portuguese territories until 1975.

The new nations' educational heritage from their colonial period was a mixed one. Africa, in 1960, had a population of 273 million, of whom fifty-five million might have been expected to be of school age, between six and fourteen years. There were fifteen million children in primary school, and one and a half million in secondary, vocational, and teacher training institutions, and 150 thousand in tertiary education at home or abroad.[23]

All the countries had high illiteracy rates and low levels of school attendance. Secondary, technical, and higher education were, with the exception of only one or two countries, in their beginning stages. Teachers and teacher training were of low standard. In Nigeria, for example, 73 per cent of the primary school teachers had only a primary education. Many were teaching in unpromising conditions, with fifty to eighty children in a small bare room, with no equipment but a blackboard, a piece of chalk, and a few miserable dogeared texts, with not enough pencils and pieces of paper to go around, and another class within a yard of his ...'[24]

(a) The Colonial Legacy

Colonial education had left a legacy of formalised teaching, characterised by an excess of teacher talk and rote learning, by severe discipline, by a concentration on language learning and a curriculum of literary based subjects, and by consistently unsuccessful attempts to introduce practical

[23] *UNESCO Conference on Education and Scientific and Technical training in relation to Development in Africa,* Nairobi, 16-27 July 1968, 3-7.

[24] C.E. Beeby, *The Quality of Education in Developing Countries,* Harvard University Press, Cambridge, Mass., 1966, p. 76.

work through school gardens and agricultural plots.[25] The contemporary half-century of rich experimentation in progressive education that had been steadily transforming the atmosphere and practice of schools in western countries appears to have had no influence on the schools of colonial Africa. It had, in some measure, influenced the policy-makers, as the tenor of the successive memoranda of the British Colonial Office Advisory Committee demonstrated, but the theories of such bodies were not expressed in the usual practice of the schools. The stated aims and educational suggestions of colonial administrators often echoed the colonial office's up-to-date views on linking education with local experience, on increasing the relevance and utility of the curriculum, and on building new community skills and attitudes through the school, but the local schoolteachers had neither the wish nor the competence to act in those ways, and local opinion was firmly opposed to an education different from the traditional European pattern. It was left to the new, independent governments eventually to see the wisdom of the theorists, and self-confidently to return to and put into effect the kinds of policies that the advisory committee had prematurely advocated in the 1920's and 1940's.

Despite the obvious weaknesses and insufficiency, colonial education did make a significant impact on the African continent. It was a powerful agent of instability. It accelerated the dissolution of traditional society. 'The spread of modern education,' wrote a leading educator and anthropologist in 1955, 'has been one of the most powerful forces in African social change.'[26] Traditional customs such as those involved in sex education, the learning of tribal history and tribal law-giving, and aesthetic education through song, dance, and the decorative arts were discouraged or fell into neglect. The occupational training of intermediaries coupled with increasing European demand for their services, and the introduction of a money economy progressively changed the employment pattern of the African people. The traditional forms of livelihood lost their attractiveness as wider and more lucrative choices became available. The movement of individuals increased as labour left the farms and sought employment in the towns or in the mines. Schooling helped to make mobility more feasible. The literary kind of education fitted the young men for clerical positions in business and administration, and they and their relations heartily encouraged the acquisition of the kind of education that made possible the move out of subsistence farming into more profitable urban employment. And the movement to growing urban centres increased the demand for schools in the towns both for juveniles and adults. Back in the rural areas community development and increased literacy were associated with improved living conditions and aspirations, especially among women. In turn, authority patterns in families and in the villages slowly yielded to the new culture. New groups and personal

relations developed especially among young women in both village and town, altering family patterns and modernising patterns of upbringing.[27]

In a poem, entitled *Conflict*,[28] a Nigerian woman schoolteacher and broadcaster expressed the mingled sense of frustration and expectation that her educated generation was experiencing in the transitional years preceding independence.

> Here we stand
> infants overblown,
> poised between two civilizations,
> finding the balance irksome,
> itching for something to happen,
> to tip us one way or the other,
> groping in the dark for a helping hand
> and finding none.
> I'm tired, O my God, I'm tired,
> I'm tired of hanging in the middle way —
> but where can I go?

Colonial educators left behind them a systematic framework of schools, a ladder from primary to tertiary level and an administrative organisation that the independent nations could readily expand. Vocational schools though not abundant were sufficiently widespread to train a small body of artisans who became the nucleus of a growing commercial and industrial development in each country. The secondary schools managed to turn out small but increasing numbers of young men who went on to tertiary institutions which provided indigenous members of the learned professions. From those men came the national leaders. They were the men whom Lugard had mistrusted and could not comprehend. They were intelligent, hardworking, ambitious, resentful of discrimination, contemptuous of many white administrators, intensely nationalistic, politically radical, and anxious to bring the colonial government to an end. They were a small group, constituting for example, in Nigeria in the early 1950's only about 0.5 per cent of the population.[29] Many of them, throughout Africa, were teachers who contributed at several levels to the eclipse of western colonialism. In quite a number of communities teachers were secretaries of local village and

[25] For arguments about agricultural education see especially P.J. Foster, *Education and Social Change in Ghana*, RKP, London, 1966, pp. 293-5.

[26] Margaret H. Read, 'Education in Africa: its pattern and role in social change', *The Annals of the American Academy of Political and Social Science*, 298, March 1955, 177.

[27] *ibid.*, p. 179.

[28] Mabel Segun, *Conflict*, in Frances Ademola, *Reflections. Nigerian Prose and Verse*, African University Press, Lagos, 1962. Mabel Segun (née Imoukhede) was educated at the CMS Grammar School, Lagos, and University College, Ibadan.

[29] James S. Coleman, *Nigeria. Background to Nationalism*, University of California Press, Berkeley, 1958, p. 142.

town welfare societies and the political parties associated with them; they were prominent in various elected assemblies, and, after independence, formed the largest vocational group in most African legislatures. Of the first group of national leaders in the new states, before the military take-overs of the late 1960's, a surprising number had been members of the teaching profession. Nkrumah in Ghana, Kaunda in Zambia, Kenyatta in Kenya, Senghor in Senegal, Tsiranana in Malagasy, Nyerere in Tanzania, Kasavubu in the Congo, and Keita in Mali, had all been successful academic products of the colonial educational system, had become teachers, and were deeply aware of the importance of education for the future development of Africa.

(b)   Education and National Development

At independence, the task of the new leaders was to harness education to the requirements of national development. Through mass education they aimed to weld their new nations into effective political, cultural, and economic units; through widespread vocational education and service opportunities for youth they desired to fit their young people for the wealth of middle level constructive jobs anticipated in the future; and through high level and specialised education they hoped to create a sufficiently large elite to replace the colonial civil service and to staff the new projects and the expanded services of their developing nations. Their situation was similar to and as challenging as that of the U.S.S.R in the early 1920's and, like the Russians, they came to realise the necessity for careful national planning.

The idea of relating education to economic progress was not new. In Europe and the United States at the beginning of the twentieth century it had been commonly argued that economically advanced countries such as Germany owed much of their advance to the existence of effective educational systems. In the business-minded world of the United States, before and after World War I, calculations had been made of the cash value of an education, that is, the contribution to personal wealth and economic value of various levels of educational attainment. In 1929, the U.S.S.R. formulated the first of its Five Year economic development plans, which, as they became more sophisticated, involved detailed estimates of the contribution that various types of educational institutions could make to the training of the work force of a required quantity and quality. After World War II the other newly-formed Communist nations adopted similar planning procedures. In the post-1950 period the western democracies became more involved in national planning. For the first time they began to consider what economic profit could be channelled out of the increasingly expensive education industry. They began, therefore, for the first time, to make detailed estimates of

manpower needs for particular rates and kinds of economic development, and to plan the kinds of educational institutions and training programs that would meet the desired targets. The Robbins Report in England in 1964 was one of the most widely known examples of that form of planning applied to a particular area, tertiary level education. By the mid-1960's, a UNESCO survey showed that, of ninety-one countries studied, sixty-four had educational plans that formed part of wider national economic plans.[30]

In the developing countries, stimulated by the British Colonial Development and Welfare Fund and the French FIDES, general development plans were drawn up in the 1940's and 1950's. Subsequently, international agencies such as the International Bank for Reconstruction and Development, the United Nations Development Program, UNESCO, national assistance schemes such as the United States Point Four program, and foundations such as the Ford Foundation, encouraged and assisted countries to produce developmental plans by supplying consultants, training courses, and financial help.

The rationale behind the planning movement was clearly and succinctly stated in the Second Nigerian national plan in 1970.

'The concept of education as a capital good is linked with the concept of "human capital" which attaches high premium to human skills as a factor of production in the development process. A corollary of this is that human skill or productivity is just as important an input in the process of development as finance, natural wealth and physical plant. Because education plays a most important role in the creation and improvement of "human capital", its relevance and importance to development is now very well recognized in development planning. Experience of developing countries during the past three decades has indicated that shortage of talents and skills needed for development can decisively retard economic progress.

'Therefore, a country like Nigeria cannot afford to leave education to the whims and caprices of individual choice. Available resources for development are highly limited. Public policies in the field of education must therefore take full account of the needs of the country in terms of developmental manpower and skills.'[31]

Educational plans were mainly of two types: cost-benefit, and manpower requirement.

Cost-benefit analysis was an attempt 'to choose investment projects in order of their benefits per unit of cost'.[32] The object of educational

---

[30]   UNESCO, *Educational Planning. A Survey of Problems and Prospects*, Paris, 1968.

[31]   Nigeria: *Second National Development Plan, 1970-74*, Federal Ministry of Information, Lagos, 1970, p. 235.

[32]   M. Blaug, *An Introduction to the Economics of Education*, Allen Lane, London, 1970, p. 120.

planning was to produce the maximum benefit at the lowest possible cost. Education was regarded as an investment, and was to be managed and supported in such a way that the financial return from its products would make it compare favourably with other kinds of possible investments.

The simplest cost-benefit approach was the ordinary man's view that the payment of school fees and maintenance for his children would result in an education that would get them a more remunerative job, and that the longer the period of education and the more that was paid out, the greater would be the return. Adam Smith pointed out this 'cash value of an education' argument as long ago as 1776. In modern times it was an argument used by parents in England who scraped and saved to send their children to expensive independent schools, by educators in the U.S.A. to induce students to stay on longer at school, and by African villagers who, enthusiastically and often with great financial strain, sent their sons to take advantage of whatever education was available and could be afforded by them.

Education was regarded as a profitable private investment. For private individuals the higher the level of educational attainment the higher was the usual salary at the beginning of employment, the more steeply it rose during employment, and the higher the return it produced on retirement.[33] In a series of studies in the 1950's and 1960's, in both developed and underdeveloped countries, it was shown that length of schooling was the most important determinant of an individual's level of earning, far outweighing the effect of social class or measured IQ.

Education was also a valuable public investment. There was a relationship betweeen the amount of education a person received and his productivity, such that by increasing the amount of education available in a country, a government might also be increasing the country's productivity. It had to be supposed that individuals merited their higher income by reason of their higher productivity. Countries, therefore, by paying to produce more educated people at selected levels might benefit to some extent beyond the cost to them of supplying the education. A substantial study of the economic growth of the U.S.A. from 1910 to 1960 concluded, after a detailed analysis that for the period 1930-60 the diffusion of education accounted for 23 per cent of the annual growth rate, more than that of any other factor.[34] The method used in the study was subsequently applied with similar effect to several other developed and underdeveloped countries. A number of studies of the condition of contemporary societies and of the history of developed nations suggested that steady economic growth cannot be achieved with a literacy rate of less than forty per cent and that the size of school enrolment positively affected the rate of growth of the gross national product during the following decade.[35]

Studies in both West and East Africa of the cost-benefit aspects of the current educational expansion indicated by the mid-1960's the need to relate educational growth to the provision of job opportunities. As primary education was speedily expanded, large numbers of young persons who had completed primary education came on the labour market to find insufficient jobs available for them. In consequence, there was a large pool of unemployed youth, who tended to move into the cities and swell the urban population. Employers who had previously had jobs to offer primary school leavers found enough secondary school pupils to fill the positions, and the government by investing a large proportion of its budget in primary education, had insufficient funds to invest in other projects that might have created more employment. Where employment was available, the productivity of the ex-primary school pupils was higher than that of the less educated both in industry and agriculture, but the cost-benefit analyses of the situation indicated that primary education in both West and East Africa had expanded beyond the capacity of the economy to absorb the products of the primary school, and that, from an economic point of view, secondary education and perhaps some other non-educational investments should have priority.[36]

The most popular approach, used by no less than sixty countries in the mid-1960's, was that of planning educational development to meet the needs of future manpower requirements forecast by economic planners as necessary to attain some economic target. This procedure assumed the commonsense point of view that there was a close link between the level of productivity and the structure of the work force, and between occupational performance and educational preparation. The relationships, however, though broadly true, tended to be imprecise, and to leave a good deal of room for varied forms of training and placement. The three East African countries of Kenya, Tanzania, and Uganda in the mid-1960's embarked upon a series of Five Year Plans which projected their country's development up to 1980. Tanzania's President Nyerere, in introducing that country's plan, explained that it aimed by 1980 at three things: to quadruple per capita income, to Africanise employment so as to make the country fully self-sufficient in manpower requirements, and to raise the expectation of life from the existing thirty-five or forty to an expectation of fifty years. To achieve the second aim, he said: 'This means a carefully

---

[33] ibid., p. 27.

[34] E.F. Denison, *The Sources of Economic Growth in the United States and the Alternatives Before Us*, Committee for Economic Development, New York, 1962; see also M. Blaug, *op.cit.*, pp. 89-100.

[35] Mary J. Bowman & C.A. Anderson, 'Concerning the role of education in development', in C. Geertz (ed.) *Old Societies and New States*, Free Press, New York, 1963, pp. 251-79; M.C. Kazer, Education and economic progress: experience in industrialized market economics, in E.A.G. Robinson and J.E. Vaizey, *The Economics of Education*, Macmillan, London, 1966, pp. 89-173.

[36] G. Hunter, Primary Education and employment in the rural economy with special reference to East Africa, pp. 242-56, and A. Callaway, Unemployment among school leavers in an African city, pp. 257-72, in *The World Yearbook of Education 1967: Educational Planning*, Evans, London, 1967.

planned expansion of education. The expansion is an economic function; the purpose of government expenditure on education in the coming years must be to equip Tanzania with the skills and the knowledge which is needed if the development of the country is to be achieved. It is this fact which has determined Government educational policy.' Education was thus to become firmly and uncompromisingly the handmaiden of economic development. Priority was to go to adult education to ensure that adults would understand and make an immediate contribution to the plan, and it was also to go to the expansion of secondary, technical, and higher education and to teacher training, in order to produce the necessary stock of higher level manpower. Primary education was regarded as of much less importance.[37]

How was one to relate accurately the output of trained manpower from schools to the increasing needs of the growing economy? In the Ashby Report in Nigeria in 1960 Harbison suggested, from his experience, that higher education should grow three times and secondary education twice as fast as the country's gross national product in order to meet the requirements for educated manpower in that developing country. Over the next ten years recalculations of that formula were used in many African development plans. The targets for manpower production had then to be translated into school buildings, equipment, teachers, recruitment policies, and the funds needed to pay for the projected educational expansion.

As the African countries developed their plans, it became apparent that they would face a crippling financial burden. For example, Ivory Coast, the largest of the French affiliated West African nations, spent approximately four per cent, the same proportion as France, of its GDP on education, and in 1963 could manage to provide primary education for only 54 per cent of its school age children, and secondary education for only five per cent . Its poorer Saharan neighbour, Mali, spent 2.2 per cent and had ten per cent in primary and one per cent in secondary education. The whole budget of the Mali nation would, at that time, not have sufficed to provide schooling for all its children.[38] In countries where the standard of living was much lower than in European countries, the cost of educating a person even at primary school level, though much cheaper in actual outlay, could be, in proportion to the national income, up to ten times as much as in a European nation, and secondary education perhaps twenty times as much. Few African nations, therefore, could afford a rapid educational expansion at all levels.

Nevertheless the growth of educational provision in the 1960's and early 1970's far outpaced anything the African nations had previously experienced. It was a substantial growth with important economic and political consequences even if it was still far below concurrent progress in the developed countries.

(c) Addis Ababa Conference and its Aftermath in the 1960's

At the beginning of what the United Nations declared to be the first Development Decade, in 1961 under UNESCO sponsorship, there was a general conference of African nations at Addis Ababa on the development of education in Africa, and in 1962 at Tananarive on the development of higher education. Conferences were similarly held for the Asian nations at Karachi in 1960, and for the Latin American nations at Santiago da Chile in 1963. They were supplemented by a variety of regional conferences which revised targets in the light of the progress made in the three continents.

The enrolment objectives for the three regions for 1970 are set out in Table 14.2.

For Africa, the Addis Ababa conference proposed long-term targets to be attained by 1980, and short term five-year targets up to 1965. For the long term it was expected that, throughout Africa, by 1980, primary education would be universal, free, and compulsory, secondary education would be able to cater for thirty per cent of pupils who completed primary education, and tertiary education would take twenty per cent of those completing secondary education. For the first five years emphasis was to be placed on secondary education. Educational expansion was to be related in all possible ways to economic development, and therefore, for the first five years of the plan, priority was to be given to the cornerstone of productivity, secondary education, to curriculum reform especially by the introduction of more and better mathematics and science teaching in secondary schools, to a greater emphasis on secondary level technical education, and to teacher training. Primary and tertiary education also were to increase and illiteracy to decrease by appreciable amounts. By 1965-6 considerable progress had been made but the plan had not worked out precisely as had been hoped. The following two tables summarise the general lines of achievement.

From Table 14.3 it can be seen that secondary education increased but did not attain its target, that primary education made considerable progress but also fell short of its target, and that tertiary education overpassed its target.

Table 14.4 shows that in secondary education the hoped-for move from general to vocational education did not take place, but that the move was actually in the opposite direction. The problem that had bedevilled the colonial powers, of trying to overcome the reluctance of the African people to invest in vocational education instead of the apparently less

---

[37] Julius K. Nyerere, 'The Five Year Development Plan for Tanganyika, address to Parliament, 12 May 1964, Dar es Salaam, Uwananchi, 1964.

[38] Lê Thành Khôi, 'Problems of educational planning in Africa: countries with a French-type system', in *The World Year Book of Education 1967: Educational Planning, op.cit.*, pp. 347-57.

Table 14.2: Africa, Latin America, and Asia: Enrolment, 1958 and 1963, and Enrolment Objectives 1965 and 1970, by Level and Region.

	Enrolment in Thousands				Percentage Distribution of Enrolment			
	1958	1963	1965*	1970*	1958	1963	1965*	1970*
Africa								
Third level education	13	31	46	80	0.1	0.2	0.3	0.4
Second level education	585	1,140	1,833	3,390	5.9	7.5	10.7	14.2
First level education	9,355	14,105	15,279	20,378	94.0	92.3	89.0	85.4
Latin America								
Third level education	458	711	655	905	1.8	2.0	1.6	1.6
Second level education	3,024	5,132	6,230	11,457	11.7	14.4	15.0	20.5
First level education	22,367	29,869	34,721	43,532	86.5	83.6	83.4	77.9
Asia								
Third level education	1,588	2,418	2,206	3,320	2.0	2.2	1.8	1.9
Second level education	14,231	23,064	14,545	23,064	18.3	20.7	11.4	13.2
First level education	62,042	85,684	110,368	148,716	79.7	77.1	86.8	84.9
Total, all Regions								
Third level education	2,059	3,160	2,907	4,305	1.8	1.9	1.5	1.7
Second level education	17,840	29,336	22,608	37,911	15.7	18.1	12.2	14.9
First level education	93,764	129,658	160,368	212,626	82.5	80.0	86.3	83.4

*   The objectives for 1965 and 1970 are based upon a 6-6 year first and second level duration in Africa and Latin America, and a 7-5 year first and second level duration in Asia. In Latin America, to some extent, and in Asia, to a large extent, the first level duration in 1958 and 1963 varies greatly from country to country but is generally less than the objectives for 1965 and 1970.

The table is reproduced with permission from *The World Yearbook of Education, 1967: Educational Planning*, Evans, London, 1967, p. 393.

vocational academic secondary education, was evidently still with the independent African nations. Similarly, for the countries south of the Sahara the intended shift in tertiary education from literary to scientific and technical courses did not take place; it, too, was decisively reversed. In the Mediterranean countries, however, the hoped-for move towards technology in tertiary work did take place.

It became apparent during the 1960's that four factors continued to inhibit educational progress as they had throughout the whole of the twentieth century.

First, the general increase in population was such as to bring much larger numbers into school but made it difficult to increase the percentage of the age groups at school. The African population rose from 270,000,000 in 1960 by more than one-half to 344,000,000 in 1970. That was the major reason for the inability of many countries to reach their primary enrolment targets.

Second, there continued to be a troublesomely large drop-out of pupils from primary and secondary schools. In primary schools there was a grade-by-grade loss of about twenty per cent, and about thirty per cent of all students in each grade were found to be repeating the grade. In consequence, about seventy per cent of primary school pupils did not progress far enough to complete the fourth grade, the level assumed by the planners to be necessary for literacy. The combination of increasing population and the large drop-out and repeating rate in primary education had the effect of increasing the actual number of illiterates in the population. From 1960 to 1970 the percentage of illiterates fifteen years of age and over decreased from 81 per cent to 74 per cent of the African population, but the actual numbers increased from 124,000,000 to 153,000,000.

Table 14.3:   Africa: Addis Ababa Conference Targets and Achievement, 1960-61 — 1965-66.

	1st level %	2nd level %	3rd level %
Proportion of enrolment to relevant age group 1960-1	36	3	.2
Target figures for 1965-6	47	6	.4
Proportions achieved 1965-6	44	5	.5

Reproduced with permission from R. Jolly (ed.), *Education in Africa: Research and Action*, Heinemann, London, 1969, p. 9.

Table 14.4:   Africa: Addis Ababa Conference Targets and Achievement for Kinds of Second Level Enrolments, 1960-61 — 1965-66.

	General %	Vocational & Technical %	Teacher Training %
Second Level enrolment 1960-1	79	9	12
Target figures for 1965-6	76	12	12
Enrolments achieved 1965-6	83	8	9

Reproduced with permission from R. Jolly (ed.), *Education in Africa: Research and Action*, Heinemann, London, 1969, p. 11.

A third perennial difficulty was in inducing the female half of the population to attend school. Although their numbers increased at all levels of education during the 1960's, the proportion of girls at school still remained well behind that of the boys.

Finally, every country found that it had inadequate financial resources to make the leap forward in the 1960's that the rising expectations of its people pressed upon it. About 4.2 per cent of the national income of the African countries was allotted to education in the first half of the 1960's. It had to be supplemented by international loans, credits, and gifts of money and services, which were estimated to be between thirty and fifty per cent of the total educational costs throughout the 1960's.

The need of the developing countries to harness education to economic progress, and the consequent distortion of the ideal, was neatly pointed out by a leading educator in Tanzania in 1972. 'So long as only 50 per cent or less of school age children in most of our countries go to school, we can never, in all honesty and sincerity, maintain that our education is centred around man, on his fulfilment as a person in the life of the country. For, to be valid, education must be universal, the right of every child. At this point in our development, we must admit that education is more or less controlled by economic factors for economic reasons. Thus our planning of education is discriminative and therefore elitist in nature, rather than comprehensive and egalitarian. The result is that our education can be called relevant and meaningful only in so far as it provides the state with well trained manpower.'[39]

[39]   *Strategies for Educational Change*, Institute of Education, University of Dar es Salaam, 1972, p. 66.

(d) Modification and Modernisation of the Western Pattern of Schooling

There were pedagogical problems also that had to be tackled. A widely discussed view of the basic educational task of the new countries was persuasively put by Nyerere in a statement *Education for Self-Reliance* in 1967. The task, he wrote, before the people of Tanzania, was that of creating 'a socialist society which is based on three principles: equality and respect for human dignity, sharing of the resources which are produced by our efforts, work by everyone and exploitation by none'.[40] It was to be undertaken by the people of a country that would be rural and poor for a long time to come, where the farmers had steadily to work themselves out of poverty by intelligent, co-operative, and determined self-reliant effort. Education's task, therefore, was to encourage community co-operation, build up basic and vocational skills, and help develop a commitment to the fundamental principles of the new life. To achieve those goals education had to be transformed in content and in organisation. The seven-year primary school, which would be the only school for most Tanzanians, should henceforth have priority and should offer an education complete in itself in basic literacy, arithmetic, vocational skills, and in the values, history and government of the country, and it should be free of traditional academic examinations. Similarly, secondary schools should not be mainly preparatory for universities but complete units in themselves, preparing pupils for service to the community.   Schools should be communities and productive centres supported by their own farms or appropriate industry in urban areas. Through engaging in that kind of work pupils would learn to have a responsibility for making significant decisions, would experience the discipline of having to work for their existence in a predominantly peasant economy, and would build up a 'sense of commitment to the whole community'.[41]

It was a concept not unlike that of Makarenko's colonies and the schools of contemporary China. It came at a time when, throughout Africa, the first post-independence flush of euphoria was passing. Many of the original leaders had fallen to military coups, and the one-party socialist states they had set up had passed into military dictatorships. The Congo, Rwanda, and subsequently Nigeria had been convulsed by civil war. It had become apparent that Africa's millennium was neither near at hand nor to be achieved without much blood and sweat, and that it was to be approached, perhaps, by a route different from the one on which most countries had set out. Nyerere's manifesto was, therefore, timely. It was a proclamation of war — a war on poverty, backwardness, and disunity; a war to be fought by hard work, by stern self-denial, and by rejecting the move towards individualistic semi-industrialisation on the western model in favour of a gradually improving semi-collective peasant economy. In the campaign for that form of modernisation, education was to be a key weapon.

Whether or not they fully accepted Nyerere's socialist and rural emphases, all African countries found themselves endeavouring to develop more functional methods and curricula in schools that would relate education more closely to the cultural and economic life of the people. Literacy campaigns in the late 1960's, for example, became more functionally related to vocational training and agricultural extension; national and African history was widely taught; the newly emerging indigenous literature started to find its way into schools through-out Africa as textbook writers and publishers multiplied; and more extensive planning of agricultural education was undertaken in accord-ance with the view expressed in the 1970-74 Kenyan Development Plan of 'the strategy of rural development as the route of national development'.[42]

In the 1960's it could be said that African schools began to come more clearly into the sphere of modern education. Methods imitative of outdated European practices were slowly being discarded as teachers' colleges multiplied and increased the supply of trained teachers educated with some knowledge of current theory and practice.   Research centres were established in universities and departments of education, and although the emphasis on planning led to a multitude of surveys of wastage, pupil aspirations, girls' education and selection for secondary school, there was at least a beginning also of work on teaching method, classroom behaviour, and the processes of learning.[43]

In several countries promising classroom and curriculum reform took place. In the Ivory Coast, for example, the 1971-75 development plan spoke of a comprehensive reform of the content and the introduction of modern methods into primary education, especially by the extension of an

[40] Julius K. Nyerere, *Ujamaa — Essays on Socialism*, Dar es Salaam, Oxford University Press, 1968, p. 50. President Nyerere had read and been influenced by a recent condemnation of current trends and plans in former French Africa. In a forceful book, *False Start in Africa*, René Dumont in 1966 criticised the colonial legacy and took the new national governments to task for inadequately tackling agricultural reform, for slavishly imitating western educational policy and not evolving a more useful and imaginative system of their own. He suggested, among many agricultural and economic reforms, that education should be thoroughly recast. There should be a firmer emphasis on the education of the agricultural peasant with the development of inexpensive farm schools, the introduction of productive manual work into general education at all levels, to help close the gap between the elite and the peasants, and the encouragement of initiative and enthusiasm in achieving the needed revolution.

[41] *ibid.*, p. 52.

[42] Republic of Kenya, *Development Plan 1970-1974*, Government Printers, Nairobi, p. 166.

[43] Judith L. Evans, *Children in Africa: a Review of Psychological Research*, Teachers College, Columbia University, New York, 1970, pp. 113-14.

Table 14.5:   Africa: Enrolment in Selected Countries, 1970.

Country	Primary		Secondary		Tertiary		Population	% of Pop. in Formal Education
	Total	Girls %	Total	Girls %	Total	Girls %		
Ghana	1,419,838	27	99,299	28	5,426	14	9,026,000	17
Kenya	1,427,589	27	137,008	30	4,967(1968)	n.a.	10,898,000	14
Nigeria	3,515,827	24	356,565	32	14,402	14	55,074,000	7
Malawi	355,004	24 (1968)	11,727	28 (1968)	929(1969)	17	4,530,000	8
S.Rhodesia	722,365(1968)	n.a.	43,711(1968)	n.a.	1,001(1968)	21	5,270,000	15
Sierra Leone	155,967	n.a.	30,797(1969)	n.a.	837	18	2,600,000	7
Tanzania	829,169(1969)	24	38,288(1968)	27	1,988(1969)	n.a.	13,273,000	7
Uganda	720,127	28 (1965)	48,911	23	2,953	18	9,810,000	8
Zambia	694,670	34	54,618	33	1,671	15	4,295,000	18
Zaire	2,822,908	n.a.	243,998	23	10,165(1969)	5	21,570,000	14
Rwanda	415,566	23	9,660	33	411	9	3,587,000	12
Burundi	181,758	26	9,243	27	466	6	3,600,000	5
Angola	384,884(19690	n.a.	53,000	39	1,757	39	5,154,000(1965)	9
Mozambique	496,381	n.a.	19,555(1968)	n.a.	1,145	41	6,957,000(1965)	7
Algeria	1,851,416	26	236,884	28	12,929	23	14,010,000	15
Chad	162,333(1969)	n.a.	9,911(1969)	7	n.a.		3,706,000	5
Ivory Coast	506,272	14	68,684	21	3,472	17	4,310,000	13
Senegal	257,708	16	55,212	29	3,049(1969)	19	3,925,000	8
England	5,189,402	76	3,521,443	49	509,501(1969)	32	48,988,000	19
France	4,939,683(1969)	67	4,106,647(1969)	51	615,329(1969)	n.a.	50,775,000	19

ambitious scheme of teaching through television, started in 1968.[44] Similar innovations were in progress throughout the 1960's on a smaller scale in Niger[45] and several other countries. In Kenya, an integrated seven-year primary school curriculum made its appearance in 1967 empha-sising, instead of rote learning, child- and community-centred activities, and an effort was made to overcome the effect of the secondary school entrance examination on primary school work by developing a wider form of certification.[46] In many of the countries work was in progress from the mid-60's adapting to African uses the new mathematics and science courses that were then being developed in Europe and America.

[44] République de Côte-d'Ivoire, *Plan Quinquennal de Développement Economique, Social et Culturel, 1971-75*, Ministère du Plan, 1971; and *Programme d'Education Télévisuelle, 1968-1980*, vol. 1, Républic de Côte-de'Ivoire, Ministère de l'Education Nationale, 1968.

[45] UNESCO: Institut international de planification de l'education, *Les Techniques Modernes dans l'Enseignement: Comptes Rendus de Quelques Expériences*, vol. 1: UNESCO, Niger, Paris, 1967.

[46] Republic of Kenya, Ministry of Education, *A Study of Curriculum Development in Kenya*, Government Printer, Nairobi, 1972; Ernest Statler, *Education Since Uhuru: The Schools of Kenya*, Wesleyan University Press, Middletown, Conn., 1969, pp. 35-57; James R. Sheffield, *Education in Kenya*, Teachers College, Columbia University, New York, 1973, p. 95.

Table 14.6: Africa: Estimated Total Enrolment, 1950 and 1970.

Year	Primary	Secondary	Tertiary	Population	% of Pop. in Formal Education	% of Pop. 15 years and over Illiterate
1950	8,511,000	745,000	71,000	217,000,000	4	84
1970	32,389,000	5,075,000	444,000	344,000,000	11	74
Increase 1950-70	280%	580%	525%	58%		

(e) Trends in Enrolment

The figures in Table 14.5 for 1970 enrolments indicate the great distance that all African countries moved in the first years of their independence. A comparison of Table 14.1 and Table 14.5 shows that the two sub-Saharan countries most educationally advanced in the colonial period, Ghana and Nigeria, increased their primary enrolment between 1950 and 1970 by five and three and a half times and their secondary enrolment by eleven and twelve times respectively while their population was less than doubled; and where no university existed before 1950, Ghana by 1970 had two, and Nigeria five flourishing institutions. In East and Central Africa, where progress in colonial times had been slower, Kenya and Zambia quadrupled their primary enrolment between 1950 and 1970, and improved their secondary enrolment by twelve and forty times respectively; each also had its own university in 1970. In the French-speaking areas, Algeria and Ivory Coast also made similarly spectacular gains.

Between 1950 and 1970, taking Africa as a whole, the number of pupils in formal education increased fourfold, and the proportion of pupils to the total population rose from four to eleven per cent. Primary enrolments quadrupled, and secondary and tertiary enrolments both increased more than sixfold.

It was a remarkable achievement; but it was still a dismal fact in 1970 that only approximately one-third of the African children of primary school age were in school, and that 74 per cent of the African population of fifteen years and over still remained illiterate.

In the 1970's the movement towards nationhood and economic development, and the rapid growth in population continued to affect educational policies. The rate of educational expansion, however, began to slow down after about 1965, a disturbing amount of unemployment appeared among secondary school leavers, and there was an increased questioning of the relevance and quality of the education being offered. There was wide discussion as to whether the economic development policies were along the right lines, and the beginning of a realisation that simple growth was not in itself a desirable objective; it had to be linked with social equity, opportunity for participation by the less privileged, and general employment. In particular it was desirable that the interests of the eighty per cent of the population who worked on the land should be given priority.

In all the developing countries of the world there was an increase in enrolment between 1950 and 1970 of 211 per cent in primary education, 465 per cent in secondary, and 511 per cent in tertiary, and in Africa a considerably greater increase.[47] To effect such increases and to produce skilled manpower for rapid economic development, often more than fifty per cent of the education budgets of developing countries was devoted to the expansion of secondary and tertiary education, which catered for something less than twenty per cent of the total enrolment. The growth thus produced appeared to bring little benefit to the poor who were the overwhelming majority of the population. In all developing countries in 1970, despite the efforts of the previous decades, the proportion of the five to fourteen year age group in school reached only 44 per cent, and the rate of overall literacy was just fifty per cent, but only 26 per cent in Africa.

47   World Bank, *Education*, Sector Working Paper, December 1974, p. 28.

Table 14.7:   World and Regions: Enrolment Ratios by Level of Education, 1970.

Region	Pupils of primary school age at school %	Pupils of secondary school age at school %	Tertiary enrolment as % of 20-24 year olds %
World Total	71	54	11
Africa	48	25	2
North America	99	93	48
Latin America	78	49	6
Asia (excluding China, North Korea and Vietnam)	59	44	5
Europe and U.S.S.R.	97	67	17
Oceania	97	75	14

From UNESCO, ED/BIE/34/Ref. 1, Paris, 27 July 1973.

Clearly, the developing countries had not yet achieved a minimum level of education for the majority of their population, and they appeared by 1970 to be working at about the limit of their financial capability. To involve the mass of people more effectively in improved production and in education, attention had to be given to providing 'low-cost, functional, mass education'.[48] That was the policy that Nyerere had initiated in Tanzania. In the early 1970's more countries were beginning to adopt policies of that kind.

In the maps showing school enrolment in 1900 and 1970, and literacy (Figures 14.3, 14.4 and 14.5) a considerable advance can be seen to have been made, particularly in Latin America and in large parts of Asia; but India, the second biggest country in the world, and much of Africa, remained in 1970 among the least educationally developed areas. It was a sobering fact that in 1970 one-third of the world's population over the age of fifteen was still illiterate. Despite the educational progress throughout the century, the number of illiterates in 1970 was greater than the number in 1950 and was steadily growing larger. (Figure on chapter title page.)

The distance that the underdeveloped countries still remained behind the developed ones, which had also been making considerable progress between 1950 and 1970, can be seen by comparing the figures for Africa and Asia with those of North America and Europe in Table 14.7.

It had become abundantly clear by the mid-1970's that, quantitatively, education in most of the African countries would remain indefinitely well behind that of its western model, and that basic changes in its design and purpose should be seriously contemplated.

An analysis made for the 1976 Lagos Conference of Ministers of Education arranged the African States into four groups in order of school attendance in 1972: seven states mostly in the Saharan region, and including Ethiopia and Mauritania, had been able to enrol only an average of twelve per cent of the six to eleven age group; sixteen states scattered across central Africa and the Atlantic coast, and including Tanzania, Malawi, and Morocco, enrolled 34 per cent; twelve states widely distributed in the continent, and including Egypt, Algeria, Kenya, and the Ivory Coast, enrolled 62 per cent; and the fourth group of eight, of whom Congo, Gabon, and Mauritius were the most successful, enrolled 76 per cent. That grouping and analysis made clear both the great distance still to be covered even in basic education, and the great diversity of educational provision existing among African States. In group one, for example, enrolment ratios rose, between 1960 and 1972, from five per cent to twelve per cent, and in group four from 48 per cent to 76 per cent; and it

[48] *ibid.*, p. 4.

Figure 14.3: World: School Enrolment c. 1900. Percentage of Total Population Enrolled in Primary and Secondary Schools.

15-20%

5-15%

0-5%

Figure 14.4: World: School Enrolment c. 1970. Percentage of Pupils of Primary and Secondary School Age Enrolled (approximately 6-17 year olds).

	80+%
	30-79%
	0-29%

Figure 14.5: World: Literate Proportion of Population over 15 years of age, 1970.

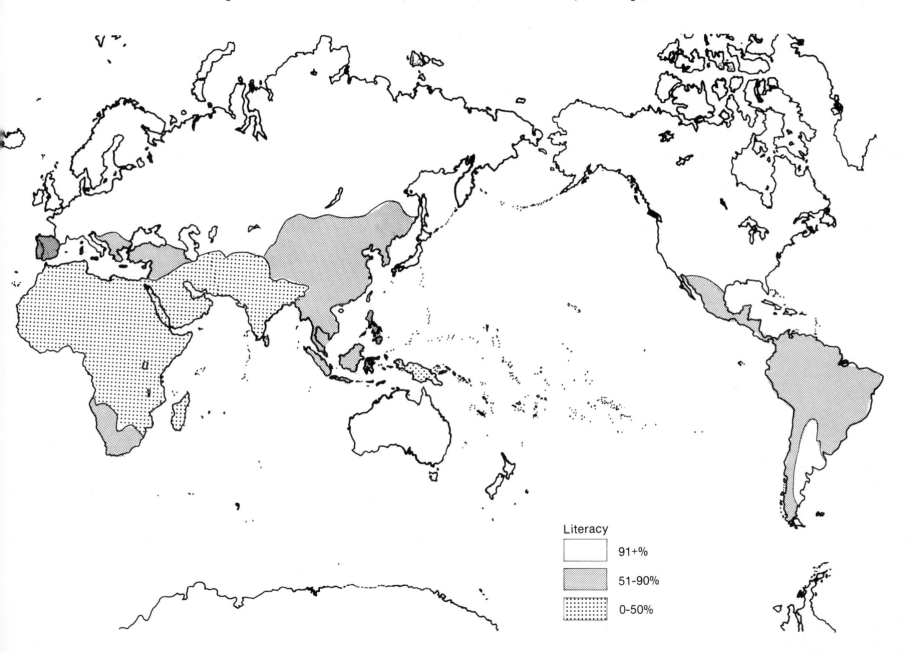

Literacy

91+%

51-90%

0-50%

is probable that by the end of the 1970's about ninety per cent of the children who had reached fifteen years in group one were illiterate, and, in group four, forty per cent.

By 1975, there was a noticeable change in public pronouncements and discussions about education. Nyerere in 1967 had provided an attractive lead in Tanzania, and others, particularly in the more newly independent States such as Guinea-Bissau, Angola, and Somalia took a somewhat similar line. There was 'a search for a new type of education for all', that, at the meeting in Lagos, was regarded as marking a new stage in the development of education in Africa, 'a new mission ... to promote an authentic, modern African society.'[49]

The educational movement was part of a wider social and cultural change. There was a growing trend to reject policies of political and economic reform through which the various States since independence had sought to develop into nations somewhat after a western capitalist model. In the new pattern, social rather than political reform was to be given priority. The new African nations were to be built from the bottom up by improving the social conditions and opportunities of local communities and by reformulating social, political, and economic relationships between the various communities throughout the nation. The primary considerations were social reform and the strengthening of indigenous cultures. In this movement education was given an important role.

The colonial and western pattern of schooling had been found to be inadequate to the needs and resources of the African States, and it did not fit well with the newly projected pattern of social development. It was argued that education must be harnessed more closely to the social revolution by moving from an elitist to a mass education, by linking schools more closely and relevantly with life and productive work, and by strengthening cultural identity through an increase in local and African content in the school's programs. Consequently, a substantial number of educational experiments were undertaken in countries such as Mali, Benin, Togo, Ethiopia, and Tanzania to explore ways in which education might more effectively be connected with social development. The teaching of indigenous languages, development of mass education centres, extension of correspondence education, integration of schools with the environment, and redesign of the content of basic education were the kinds of innovations that were tried out in various places. In the search for African renewal the schools' purpose was to support social reconstruction and to ensure that educational reform took place concurrently and in close relationship with the reform of society. The intelligentsia of the future was no longer to be the westernised product who had master-minded the struggle for independence and its aftermath, but a new breed from a university that is not 'a mirror diffusing a reflected light but a torch that ... is fuelled primarily in the hearths and homes of the people.'[50]

[49] A. Damiba, *Education in Africa in the light of the Lagos Conference (1976)*, UNESCO, Paris, 1977, pp. 45, 49.

[50] Joseph Ki-Zerbo, 'L'Université, tête pensante de la société' p. 52, presented to the Conference of Ministers of French-speaking Afro-Malagasy States in Kinshasa, 13-18 January 1969, quoted in A. Damiba, *op.cit.*, p. 24. See also UNESCO, *Educational Reforms and Innovations in Africa*, IBE series Experiments and Innovations in Education No. 34, Paris, 1978; B. Davidson, *Africa in Modern History — The Search for a New Society*, Penguin, Harmondsworth, 1978; A.A. Mazrui, *Political Values and the Educated Class in Africa*, Heinemann, London, 1978.

CHAPTER 15

EDUCATION IN COMMUNIST COUNTRIES 1945-75: U.S.S.R. AND CHINA

U.S.S.R.: Teaching the new mathematics to young children in a primary school class, 1972.

SUMMARY

Education in the U.S.S.R. from World War II to 1975

The Chinese Educational Experience, 1949-75

EDUCATION IN THE U.S.S.R. FROM WORLD WAR II TO 1975

The Communist tradition hammered out in the bitter experiences of the 1920's and 1930's in the U.S.S.R. was severely tried in World War II. It was reaffirmed in the post-war period when educators became more conscious of their systematic theoretical position as they became more conversant with Makarenko's writings and a growing literature on educational theory and research. In the three decades after the war educational provision rapidly expanded in both the Asian and European republics of the Union, and the characteristic features of communist education, such as the association of education with productive work, the cultivation of collective thought and behaviour, and the centrality of politics in education, gave rise to much discussion and some experimentation. Soon after World War II education, largely based on the work and ideas of the U.S.S.R. was put into the service of a number of communist societies that were established in eastern Europe. There the formal pattern of educational organisation that was set up, the educational theory and principles that were used, and the impact that was made on society were very similar to the experience of the U.S.S.R. It was not quite the same in China, where the Communist Party came to power in 1949. The fundamental principles were the same, and so too were the main practices in the schools, but they were set in a dissimilar social and educational tradition and a very dissimilar situation. The problems, therefore, that the new society encountered, the uses to which education had to be put, and the characteristics that needed emphasis differentiated the Chinese experience from that of the U.S.S.R. It developed, in consequence, a pace, a tone, a program, and a literature through which it made a distinctive contribution to the communist educational tradition.

(i)   The Impact of World War II

During World War II most schools throughout the U.S.S.R. were dislocated; those in the war zone were devastated. In the Leningrad area alone some eight hundred schools were put out of action and many of the pupils who managed to survive had their education for the three years of the siege in underground cellars and air-raid shelters.

Even in unoccupied areas the effects of war placed severe handicaps on the schools through a shortage of teachers and facilities and the running down of the organisation. At the out-break of World War II there were 34.8 million children in school; by 1942 the number had dropped to sixteen million. Over the next few years there was a steady improvement but in 1950 enrolments were still 1.5 million short of the 1940 figure. The sharp drop in the birthrate that occurred during the war years had its impact on enrolments during the 1950's, again pushing them downwards. The lowest level was reached in 1956 with an enrolment of some five million less than that of 1940. By 1960 enrolments had climbed back to the 1950 level, and thereafter increased rapidly.[1]

The war was responsible for several innovations in educational thinking and practice. The first notable change was the introduction in 1940 of a system of fees for upper secondary general education, secondary special education, and higher education. This practice lasted until 1956 and probably helped to divert numbers of children leaving the seven-year schools into industry, agriculture, or vocational education away from academic kinds of education. Children with outstanding records in schools and children whose parents were in the armed forces, or cases of special hardship were exempted from the payment of fees. A second important change was the abolition of co-education in 1943. Until 1954 when co-education was resumed boys and girls were sent to separate schools in urban areas but in most of the country areas co-education remained in force as before.

During the war period several new institutions were established. Two specialised boarding schools were set up in Leningrad for the sons of members of the armed forces — the Nakhimov School for the Red Navy, and the Suvorov School for the Red Army. The schools were initially very fashionable but lost their popularity during the 1960's with the more widespread development of secondary boarding schools.

Another new and potentially important institution that was established during the war years was the Academy of Pedagogical Sciences of the RSFSR which came into being in 1943. The aim of the academy was to become the spearhead of educational research, to be the centre for the diffusion of ideas and knowledge about education, and to be an authoritative advisory body to the Ministry of Education. From the beginning, the academy discharged those functions vigorously. It undertook studies in educational theory and published, in due course, authoritative editions of the work of educators such as Ushinsky, Makarenko, and Shatsky. It undertook research into the methods of teaching at all stages, from kindergarten to university, and was responsible for the production of new textbooks and the periodical

revision of the curricula at various stages of the ten-year school. It developed a number of experimental schools and through them tried out new methods of teaching, and it fostered research on the teaching of handicapped children and on the use of correspondence and evening education. By 1970 the academy had developed ten research institutes in Moscow and one in Leningrad, each dealing with a different aspect of education, such as Theory and History of Education, General and Polytechnical Education, Defectology, and Evening and Correspondence Education. In 1966 the academy became the U.S.S.R. Academy of Pedagogical Sciences.

The constraints of wartime life provided a suitable climate for a stocktaking of the disciplinary side of school life, and in 1943 a code of twenty *Rules for School Pupils* was produced. The Rules were intended both to set the general tone of a pupil's behaviour and to give precise directions about some aspects of his conduct in school. Thus he was exhorted to work diligently for the sake of his country and to respect his teachers. And he was told that diligent work involves being punctual in attendance, arriving at school with all the necessary textbooks and materials, and listening attentively throughout the lesson. Respect for the teacher was shown by greeting him politely, by rising when a teacher or director enters or leaves the room, by standing to attention when answering the teacher, and by being generally attentive to the teacher's words and requirements. The Rules conveyed to the pupil a sense of living in a society in which patriotism, obedience to duly constituted authority, love of parents, consideration for others, helpfulness, self-respect, and diligence were essential moral attributes.[2]

The *Rules* fitted the wartime climate, but also made clear that soviet society expected dedication and seriousness from its students and potential intellectuals. Zhdanov, a leading political figure, addressing the writers of Leningrad in the immediate post-war period, made the same point that the *Rules* and educators such as Makarenko had emphasised: '. . . it is necessary that our literature, our journals should not stand aloof from the tasks of the day, but should help the party and the people to educate our youth in the spirit of supreme devotion to the Soviet order, in the spirit of supreme service to the interests of the people.'[3] Education was not merely a school matter. In building a new society all possible agents had to take part in helping to develop ideological awareness and socialist

[1] N. De Witt, *Education and Professional Employment in the U.S.S.R.*, Washington, National Science Foundation, 1961, pp. 131ff.

[2] A translation and commentary on the rules for school children are to be found in N. Grant, *Soviet Education*, Penguin Books, Harmondsworth, England, 1964, pp. 47-9, and in G.S. Counts and Nucia P. Lodge, trans., *I Want to be like Stalin*, Day, New York, 1947, pp. 149-50.

[3] A.A. Zhdanov, 'The duty of a soviet writer', in J.H. Meisel and E.S. Kozera (edd), *Materials for the Study of the Soviet System*, Ann Arbor, Michigan, G. Wahr, 1950. p. 387.

consciousness. Artists and intellectuals of all kinds, therefore, as well as teachers had a duty to educate the people and further the interests of their collective society.

Wider powers were given to school directors to control both pupils and teachers. And the press towards achievement through examination success was boosted by the institution of school leaving examinations for the elementary and seven-year schools, and by the introduction of gold and silver medals for successful pupils, entitling their holders to proceed to the university without further examination.

(ii) Reconstruction

The period from the end of World War II to approximately the end of the 1950's was concerned with re-establishing and expanding the school system. There was a notable expansion of secondary education in the 1950's, paralleling that in other developed countries. Universal eight-year education was achieved and facilities for higher education of all types were considerably extended.

The extent of the expansion is indicated in Table 15.1. From this table it can be seen that there was a very substantial growth in attendance at pre-school and higher educational institutions of all levels but that the number of pupils in the general school increased very little between 1940 and 1960. Over that period, however, the size of the school age population dropped by almost one-third. The actual proportion of the school age population, therefore, who were attending school rose from 87 per cent in 1939 to 92 per cent in 1959 and 95 per cent in 1970.

Three matters are worthy of special note during the immediate post-war period.

First, there was a continuation of the steady build-up in the provision of general education from the beginning of the Revolution. In the 1920's most children had had a four-year education available to them; in the 1930's and 1940's seven-year education had become widespread and, by 1960, eight-year education was universal. At the same time extra-curricular activities for children of school age were further stimulated. In 1957 the age of entry to the Pioneer organisation was raised to ten years, and great encouragement was given to the formation of Octobrist groups among the younger children. Pioneer and Komsomol camps and other activities were expanded and out-of-school study circles for children interested in academic subjects became popular. In addition to the general eight-year school, special schools which emphasised particular subjects were developed. Thus there were special language schools, in which the teaching of a foreign language would begin in the second grade and continue, with an additional period allowance, through to the tenth grade; in the upper grades, it would be used as the vehicle of instruction in several of the academic subjects. There were also special mathematics-physics, music, painting, and ballet schools, which catered for gifted children in each of these fields.

Another type of school that became popular in the 1950's was the boarding school. There had always been a number in existence, but they had never been widespread. From 1956 on they were deliberately encouraged and for the next ten years they multiplied considerably. By 1970 the initial period of expansion and popularity was over.

Second, there was a remarkable extension of education at the tertiary level. In the twenty years from 1940 to 1960 the number of higher education students increased by almost two hundred per cent. The greatest increase came from part-time and correspondence students. In 1940 they were a little more than a quarter of all higher education enrolments; by 1960 they had become a little more than half. The actual number of institutions showed very little increase, but there was a vast expansion in their facilities and staff to cope with the larger numbers. One notable increase in establishment occurred in Siberia. The Siberian branch of the Academy of Sciences established its headquarters in the early 1950's in a newly built Academy Town some twenty-five kilometres from Novosibirsk in Central Siberia. There the Academy set up some twelve post-graduate research institutes and founded the University of Novosibirsk in 1959. The town also developed its own school system with several general ten-year schools and a special English school, and in 1963 a boarding school specialising in mathematics and physics.

Several new universities were created from pedagogical institutes in a number of autonomous republics. Teacher training institutes were consolidated into:

- pedagogical institutes with, in 1956, a five-year course, reduced to four years in the early 1960's, for graduates of the ten-year school who intended to teach in the upper grades;
- pedagogical colleges offering, for teachers of kindergartens and the lower grades, a two-year course of preparation for those who had completed the ten-year school or a four-year course for those who had only an eight-year general education.

Third, correspondence and evening education was systematically revised and expanded. Secondary level correspondence schools and evening schools for working youth in the 1940's and 1950's became an important means for many pupils of completing their secondary education. In 1956 the U.S.S.R. Ministry of Higher Education systemat-ised procedures for the recognition of correspondence and part-time work in higher education with a consequent boost to part-time enrolments.

Table 15.1: U.S.S.R.: Number of Students attending Kindergarten, General Education, and Higher Education, 1940, 1960, 1970.

	1940	1960	Increase in 1960 over 1940	1970	Increase in 1970 over 1960
School Population					
Kindergarten	1,171,500	3,115,000	166%	8,100,000	160%
10 year schooling	34,800,000	33,400,000	4%	45,085,000	43%
Higher education	811,700	2,395,500	195%	4,600,000	92%
Total Population					
Pre-school population ages 0-6	30,436,000	33,327,000		31,130,000	-7%
School age population, ages 7-16	39,800,000	36,500,000	-8%	47,533,000	30%

Adapted from tables in *Educational Planning in the USSR*, UNESCO: International Institute for Educational Planning, Paris, 1968; N. De Witt, *Education and Professional Employment in the USSR*, Washington, National Science Foundation, 1961; and *Statistical Yearbook*, UNESCO, 1965-77.

(iii) Educational Development in the Central Asian Republics

The educational expansion of this period brought a great increase in the number of pupils and institutions throughout the more developed areas of the U.S.S.R. — it also had a profound effect on the progress of the more backward educational areas. Regions such as Siberia and the five Central Asian republics had begun by 1960 to show clearly the effect of their educational enrichment in the post-war period and to give firm evidence of the kind of substantial future technical and cultural development that would make them important Asian communities.

Typical of the trend was the progress made in the Uzbek SSR, the small state stretching between the Aral Sea and Afghanistan, and the Tajik SSR, lying along much of the northern border of Afghanistan and touching the western edge of China. In the traditional Moslem Uzbek community before 1917 only five to ten per cent of the population over the

age of ten was literate. In the 1920's and 1930's, under the soviets, primary education spread much more widely, and literacy increased to something like 65 per cent by the end of the 1930's. By 1960 two-thirds of the Uzbek population had completed an education of primary school level or better.[4] In the Tajik SSR the literacy rate went from four per cent of the over ten-year-old population in 1926 to 83 per cent in 1939, and 96 per cent in 1959.[5] The youth organisations were specially active in the literacy campaigns to very good effect. In Central Asia, the Komsomol organisation was first established in Tashkent in 1918 and throughout the

[4] William K. Medlin *et al.*, *Education and Social Change: a study of the Role of the school in a Technically Developing Society in Central Asia*, Ann Arbor, School of Education, University of Michigan, 1965, p. 376.

[5] M.M. Shorish, *Education in the Tajik Soviet Socialist Republic 1917-1967*, unpublished Ph.D. Thesis, University of Chicago, 1972, p. 185.

1920's was involved in many, sometimes bloody, struggles with the conservative Moslem establishment.

Three other educational changes of significance took place. First, opportunities for women were immeasurably increased. Improved education and the decreasing influence of Moslem culture led to greater freedom in social behaviour and to better job opportunities for women. Second, the spread of education made possible a higher level and a wider range of intellectual achievement in the arts, sciences, and technology. This in turn opened up avenues for employment at highly sophisticated levels in academic, business, and industrial fields. In 1930 the Tajik SSR was the most backward part of Central Asia; by 1970 one in every three persons had received secondary or higher education, and there was at least an eight-year school in every village. The educated youth of the Tajik SSR appeared to be highly motivated, politically conscious, and assured of adequate employment, except when, as in the early 1970's, the growing migration of educated European workers caused an over-supply on the labour market. And third, more persons from the local communities became capable of handling responsible positions in the civil service and of developing a larger understanding of political questions.

In short, society and culture were brought into the modern world and given a new and wider range of possibilities. These were not only intellectual and practical possibilities, they embraced also a new range of values. The Central Asian peoples learnt a new view of human relationships which valued women equally with men and sought for collective happiness; and they were taught to appreciate the centrality of productive work in the life of a society and to see the acquisition of education as the right and duty of every individual.

The change did not occur overnight. For the first twenty years of soviet administration, 'educational policy concentrated on producing a basically literate population that would be a consumer of elementary information appropriate to the tasks and aims of the sociocultural revolution'.[6] Adult literacy and universal four-year primary education were the basic educational foundations laid by the end of the 1930's. World War II brought a general stimulus to the agricultural economy, the transfer of industrial plant to the region, and a demand for more highly skilled workers. In 1927 in the Tajik SSR ninety per cent of the schools were three- or four-year rural schools. At that time there was only one secondary school in the region; and even by 1939 the number of secondary pupils in grades eight, nine and ten in the whole of Tajikistan reached only one thousand. World War II noticeably raised the demand for educational qualifications. By the 1950's seven-year education had become available for all children, and opportunities for ten-year education and for technical education were rapidly increasing. From Table 15.2 the advance made by both the U.S.S.R. as a whole and the Central Asian republics in the post-World War II period can be seen.

After 1945 throughout Central Asia it was possible to offer secondary schooling, technical training, and university work on a sufficiently substantial scale to enable Central Asians by 1960 to begin to control their own economic and cultural development within the framework of the U.S.S.R. The Central Asian University had been founded in Tashkent in 1920, and the Uzbek State University at Samarkand in 1930. In 1947 the first Tajik university, the Tajik State University, was founded in the capital, Dushanbe. By 1975 there was a small network of tertiary institutions offering courses in arts, science, engineering, medicine, agriculture, and education. By 1960 the larger part of the academic staffs were native born, and the whole pattern of schooling, throughout all levels, approximated to that of a developed country. The percentage of the total population enrolled in tertiary education ranged in the five Central Asian republics from 1.27 to 1.85 per cent in 1970, and compared favourably with that of many western countries, e.g. U.S.A. (1966) 2.82 per cent, France (1966) 1.00, Great Britain (1966) .81, and far outstripped

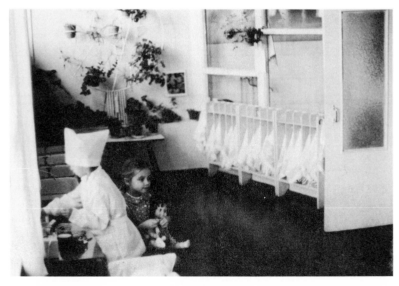

U.S.S.R.: Children playing doctor and patient in a kindergarten in Novosibirsk, 1972.

---

[6]   William K. Medlin *et al.*, *op.cit.*, p. 182.

Table 15.2: U.S.S.R. and Central Asia: Educational Level of Population aged 10 Years and Older

Proportion of population 10 years and older who have 8 years or more of education

	1939 %	1959 %	1970 %
USSR	11	36	48
Central Asia	5	35	45

Adapted from M.N. Shorish, *op.cit.*, p. 372.

that of most developing countries. Neighbouring Afghanistan had managed to achieve a level of .03 per cent by 1968.[7]

Solid efforts by devoted educators, from the 1920's on, promoted the modernisation of the region, and at the same time encouraged native literacy and artistic talent and scholarship to a high level of performance. Education, economic, social and cultural development, throughout all the Central Asian republics, went hand in hand. Technical education was geared to the country's progress, and its graduates were, for the most part, suitably placed in the growing agricultural and industrial economy, and amply rewarded. The bugbear of developing countries, the unemployment of educated youth, was not a vital problem in the Central Asian republics during most of the history of their modernisation. The result was an educational and economic situation which placed the Central Asians, by the beginning of the last quarter of the twentieth century, well ahead of their neighbours in Iran and Afghanistan.

(iv) Polytechnical Education

The reconstruction of education during the 1940's and 1950's led to a renewal of the discussion on the nature of general and polytechnical education throughout the U.S.S.R. The 19th and 20th Conferences of the Communist Party in 1952 and 1956 affirmed the need for more polytechnical education in schools. Many schools, in consequence, introduced productive work experiences into their curricula, experimental programs were developed in several of the republics, and students'

production brigades were established and grew steadily in popularity. The academy of pedagogical sciences during the next five years undertook research in the subject and made recommendations about the revision of textbooks and curricula. In 1958 Khrushchev, then premier of the U.S.S.R., criticised the undue academic emphasis of the schools and their divorce from life.

'We are striving to have our whole youth, millions of boys and girls, go through the secondary school... Owing to the fact that the secondary school curriculum is divorced from life, these boys and girls have absolutely no knowledge of production, and society does not know how best to utilize these young and vigorous people. ...This state of affairs can hardly be considered right.'[8]

He sketched the general lines of the new education policy which were elaborated later in the year in a series of theses published by the central committee of the communist party. In December 1958 the Supreme Soviet passed a law which incorporated the ideas into the educational system.

The Khrushchev reforms required that the complete secondary school should be extended from ten to eleven years, that manual training should begin in first grade so that by the end of the eighth form all pupils

---

[7] E. Allworth (ed.), *The Nationality Question in Soviet Central Asia*, Praegar, New York, 1973, pp. 86-99.

[8] N.S. Khrushchev, 'Strengthening the Ties of the Schools with Life and further developing the system of Public Education', published in English as *Proposals to Reform Soviet Education*, Soviet Booklet no. 42, October 1958, p. 4.

U.S.S.R.: General view of a design for a secondary polytechnical school for 1,000 pupils, in Dubna, Moscow District.

S.G. Shapovalenko, *Polytechnical Education in the U.S.S.R.*, UNESCO, 1963.

should have had some experience of hand tools and machine tools, and should have had some teaching in the fundamentals of production and the relevance of their scientific subjects to industry. From the ninth to eleventh grades additional polytechnical work was to be done, up to as much as one-third of the curriculum, and in this pupils were to spend time working in local factories or in the fields.

The law also required those who left school to spend two years at work before entering a higher educational establishment, except for a small percentage of gifted students who could proceed direct into tertiary education.

(v) Reform in the 1960's and 1970's

The questioning of established practice characteristic of the 1950's was continued into the 1960's. The Khrushchev reforms were implemented by the early 1960's but met with such criticism that, by 1964, they had been very substantially modified. It was found that part-time work in factories for senior students in the eleven year schools was unsatisfactory; schools, factories, and students all disliked it, and found it disruptive. Little of

educational value appeared to result. In 1964 the schools reverted from an eleven to a ten year program, and part-time work in the factories was reduced and reorganised so as not to interrupt school studies. Renewed thought was given to the way in which the other subjects, especially the sciences of the general curriculum, could contribute to a polytechnical education, and labour instruction was reduced to two periods per week for all classes in the ten year school. This subject included the study of labour theory, the development of skill in some handicrafts, and some experience of industrial processes; for the more senior ninth and tenth classes it might involve complicated craftwork such as the building and repair of motor cars, two hours per week in an industrial plant, and a month in the summer holidays full-time in industry. Some factories subsequently developed special students' departments, and in Moscow and Leningrad several labour centres were started in 1970-71 specially equipped to take school pupils for their labour education from a number of neighbouring ten year schools.

These revisions of school organisation and practice became universal in the U.S.S.R. with the establishment in 1966 of the U.S.S.R. Ministry of Education. Henceforth the Ministry was to be responsible for determining educational policies throughout the whole of the U.S.S.R., and the

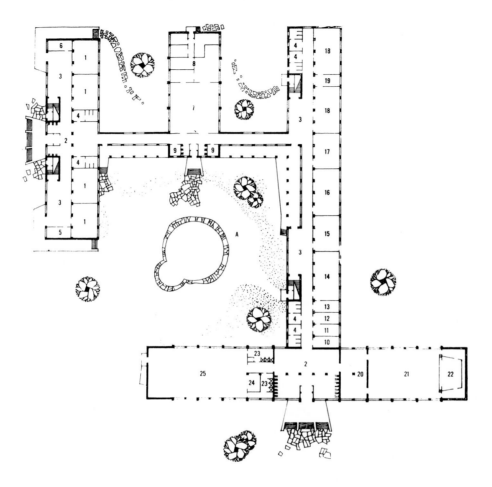

U.S.S.R.: Plan of ground floor of the Dubna Secondary School, Moscow District: (1) classrooms for junior classes; (2) vestibule and cloakrooms; (3) recreation rooms; (4) toilets; (5) staff room; (6) radio announcements room; (7) dining room; (8) kitchen; (9) wash rooms for dining room; (10) doctor's office; (11) headmaster's study; (12) office; (13 and 14) biology room; (15) domestic-science room; (16) engineering room; (17) specialised technology room; (18) woodwork and metalwork rooms; (19) tools and equipment room; (20) lobby; (21) assembly hall; (22) platform; (23) changing rooms with shower; (24) apparatus room; (25) gymnasium; (A) recreation ground.

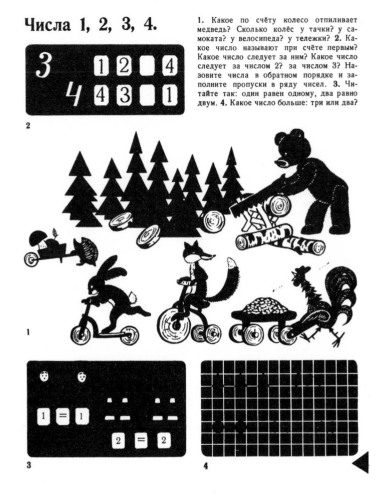

Числа 1, 2, 3, 4.

1. Какое по счёту колесо отпиливает медведь? Сколько колёс у тачки? у самоката? у велосипеда? у тележки? **2.** Какое число называют при счёте первым? Какое число следует за ним? Какое число следует за числом 2? за числом 3? Назовите числа в обратном порядке и заполните пропуски в ряду чисел. **3.** Читайте так: один равен одному, два равно двум. **4.** Какое число больше: три или два?

U.S.S.R.: Learning the numbers 1 to 4: a page from an elementary arithmetic book of the 1970's.

In the years of the early 5-year plans we introduced universal 4-year education. In the new 5-year plan we shall *complete the introduction of universal secondary education* ...

'Those who will enter schools during these years will be developing the country's economy and culture in the 90's and in the beginning of the 21st century. The curricula and teaching methods in general and technical schools and higher educational institutions must even now increasingly take into account future scientific and technological developments.'[9]

(a) Curriculum Review

To fit the schools more effectively for the role of providing ten-year general and polytechnical education for all, an extensive review of the curriculum was initiated in 1964 under the direction of the Academy of Pedagogical Sciences. A large committee was formed consisting of scientists, administrators, and teachers to direct a program of review and research on the curriculum. The committee recognised that the existing curriculum was mostly, with some adaptation, a product of the 1930's and that the pupils of the 1960's were, in general, much more advanced than those of the earlier generation, especially in their acquaintance with the achievements of modern science. The curriculum had been designed for a seven- or an eight-year school and it often involved unnecessary repetition for pupils in the ninth and tenth grades. What was needed was a curriculum which would be abreast of modern thinking, especially in mathematics and science, which by its thoroughness and timeliness would make demands on present-day pupils, and which would follow a properly graded and economical sequence, from first grade right through to the tenth.

Details of possible programs were worked out in the research institutions of the Academy of Pedagogical Sciences, and over a period of two years were tried out in a number of experimental schools associated with the academy. Examination of the results and a conference with teachers led to a modification of the proposed program and a rewriting of textbooks. The new programs were then tried out in a sample of ordinary schools in an industrial region, an agricultural region, and a town in Siberia. After an evaluation by administrators, teachers, researchers, and textbook writers, the revised program was tried out in all the large towns of every republic of the Union. A final evaluation was then made, and it was passed on to the U.S.S.R. Ministry of Education for approval and adoption. It became effective in the schools in 1971. The new curriculum introduced principally four changes:

Academy of Pedagogical Sciences, which was given all-Union status at the same time, was to be its principal instrument for evaluation, research, and innovation.

From the mid 1960's, ten-year education for everyone became the major objective to be achieved by the end of the ninth Five Year Plan in 1975. The premier, A. Kosygin, in a report in 1971 stated:

9 A. Kosygin, *Directives of the Congress of the 24th Communist Party of the Soviet Union for the 5-year economic development plan of the USSR for 1971-1975*, Novosti, Moscow, 1971, p. 70.

- The primary school years were reduced from four to three. The experimental work of this aspect of the curriculum, undertaken principally in the Moscow region, and subsequently checked in all republics, demonstrated that children could reach a higher standard, especially in mathematics, with the new three-year program, than they had previously attained with the old four-year program. In consequence, secondary specialised work, after 1971, was begun in the fourth grade.[10]
- The sophistication of the textbooks and program in mathematics and science was considerably increased throughout the whole of the ten-year school, but most noticeably in the primary grades.
- The sequence of work in all subjects was greatly improved, e.g. in history the program moved from historical stories in fourth grade through ancient history in fifth, medieval in sixth, Russian in seventh, modern in eighth, pre-revolutionary history and up to 1936 in ninth, to contemporary Russian history and civics in tenth. The course in civics, sometimes referred to as social science, offered in the final year of the ten-year school, was revised in the early part of the 1960's and a new textbook was produced to provide a summing-up and an authoritative statement of the principles of Marxist-Leninism and the work and history of the Communist Party and its accomplishments in the twentieth century.
- The course of studies retained, as formerly, a large number of compulsory subjects studied in each year. The new program, however, provided a little time also for some electives beginning with an hour a week in seventh grade and extending to four or five hours in the tenth grade, in this way it was possible for pupils to study a number of topics offered by the school staff outside the regular syllabus, e.g., logic, physiology, aspects of psychology or history.

A further reform which took place towards the end of the 1960's was the beginning of the absorption of the nursery school into the kindergarten. Combined nursery schools, taking children in their first year, and kindergartens, up to the children's sixth year, were gradually established. For six year-olds, experimentation was begun with more formal work in preparation for work in the first year of the ten-year school.

Table 15.3 lists the subjects and the time allowance per week that were first approved by the RSFSR Ministry of Education for use in the ten-year general school in 1972. The other Union republics adopted similar timetables with some adjustments to allow for the teaching of national languages.

Figure 15.1 represents the school system of the U.S.S.R. as it had

Novosibirsk Pioneer Palace: Salute of Pioneer Committee at the beginning of a meeting to plan the year's program.

evolved by 1975. It can be seen that the general structure of education in the U.S.S.R. was little altered in the 1960's and 1970's. The substantive changes were in the content of education. They reflected recent advances in knowledge, and they took account of the fact that pupils, as in most other countries, were remaining longer at school, and that therefore a larger and more varied population had to be catered for. Attendance at technicums and vocational schools also continued to rise, and their programs, too, were modified, particularly by the inclusion of more general education. By 1975 approximately ninety per cent of pupils in the U.S.S.R. were completing ten years of schooling in either a ten-year school or a technical or vocational school.

(b) V.A. Suchomlinski on Education

The reform and expansion of education were accompanied by a renewed interest in and discussion of fundamental educational principles. Makarenko's works were widely read and became basic texts for teacher

---

[10] For an account of the primary school reform see B. Schiff, *Die Reform der Grundschule in der Sowjetunion*, Osteuropa-Institut an der Freien Universität, Berlin, 1972.

Table 15.3:   RSFSR: General Ten-year School Timetable in Hours Per Week, 1975.

	I	II	III	IV	V	VI	VII	VIII	IX	X
1. Russian lang.	12	11	10	7	6	5	3	2	—	1
2. Literature	—	—	—	2	2	2	2	3	4	3
3. Maths	6	6	6	7	6	6	6	5	6	6
4. History	—	—	—	2	2	2	2	3	4	3
5. Civics	—	—	—	—	—	—	—	—	—	2
6. Nature study	—	1	2	1	—	—	—	—	—	—
7. Geography	—	—	—	—	2	3	2	2	2	—
8. Biology	—	—	—	—	2	2	2	2	1	2
9. Physics	—	—	—	—	—	2	2	3	4	5
10. Astronomy	—	—	—	—	—	—	—	—	—	1
11. Technical drawing	—	—	—	—	—	—	1	2	—	—
12. Chemistry	—	—	—	—	—	—	2	2	3	3
13. Foreign language	—	—	—	—	4	3	3	2	2	2
14. Art	1	1	1	1	1	1	—	—	—	—
15. Music	1	1	1	1	1	1	1	—	—	—
16. Physical education	2	2	2	2	2	2	2	2	2	2
17. Labour instruction	2	2	2	2	2	2	2	2	2	2
18. Preparatory Military training	—	—	—	—	—	—	—	—	2	2
Total	24	24	24	25	30	31	30	30	32	34
19. Work practice in days	—	—	—	—	5	5	5	—	24	—
20. Optional studies	—	—	—	—	—	—	1	2	5	4

education courses. During the 1950's and 1960's he became established as 'a modern education classic'.[11] His more important writings were translated into most of the languages of the U.S.S.R. and eastern Europe; and he became known and studied in non-communist countries. His ideas were taken up and extended by a new writer and educator, V.A. Suchomlinski, whose school was extensively visited and studied in the 1960's, and whose books and articles were widely read and highly regarded throughout the Soviet Union.[12]

The general tenor of Suchomlinski's work can be judged from the title of his principal book, written in 1969 near the end of his life, *I Devote My Heart to Children*. His school became known as the School of

Happiness, and was a place in which children gained an enthusiasm for their work and maintained it throughout their whole school-life.

---

[11] O. Anweiler, *Leben, Werk und Bedeutung A.S. Makarenkos. Einführung zu A.S. Makarenko, Ein Pädagogisches Poem*. Ullstein Buch, Frankfurt am Main, 1972, p. 7.

[12] V.A. Suchomlinski (1918-1970) was a Ukrainian teacher who, like Makarenko, was trained in the Poltava Pedagogical Institute, graduating in 1939. After a period of war service in which he was badly wounded he became the principal of a school at Pavlish where he was to remain throughout his career. He published his first substantial book in 1956 and continued for the next fourteen years to contribute articles and books on his general educational ideas and his experience in the Pavlish school.

Figure 15.1: U.S.S.R.: School System, 1975.
(simplified diagram)

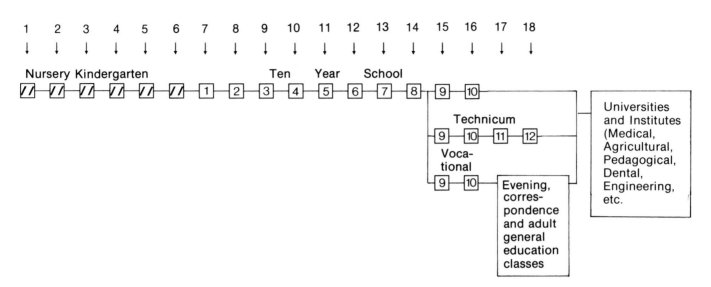

Suchomlinski's main interest lay in trying to improve the process of teaching. He held that, to learn effectively, children have to experience the pleasure of continuous success in tasks on which they have had to overcome difficulties. 'All our intentions, all our attempts and achievements turn to dust if the pupil does not wish to study. And the wish to study is derived only from success in study... This apparent paradox contains the whole complexity of pedagogical work. Interest in learning is only to be found where there is inspiration that comes from successful study.'[13] Interest, and eventually understanding and conviction, came from experience. An experience which gave rise to a problem was the beginning of mental activity, and it was through successful mental activity in which the child was interested that true happiness and satisfaction was to be gained. Suchomlinski emphasised the uniqueness and creativity of each child. 'Every child is a world,' he wrote, 'a perfectly special, unique world'.[14] The educator's task was to build a unity of interest and feeling between himself and each child, to seek out the tasks through which each child could make his unique contribution, to provide the experiences which the child could see to be of value and which would challenge the child to work with zest and intelligence, and to guide and encourage him to succeed at his task. Suchomlinski's approach to teaching was in the activity tradition. It was characterised by

an encouragement of aspiration and striving in children. Constantly teachers should provide children with opportunities to do creative work, to write, to draw, to solve problems, and to pose them. He had a keen sense of the need to care for the personal development of each individual within the collective so that each person might be able to make a full and rewarding contribution both to his own all-round development and to the life of his fellow-workers.

(c) **Informal Education**

It is important to realise, however, that the school system, though central in the education of the children and youth of the U.S.S.R. has by no means been the sole medium through which public education is conveyed in the U.S.S.R. The Soviet Union has been one of the closest of all present-day countries to the educative society. The object of the state has been to produce better people in the sense conceived of in communist thought. All the agencies of public life have had the serious educational task of contributing to this aim. The news media, therefore, not only

---

[13] V.A. Suchomlinski, *On Education*, Politizdat, Moscow, 1973, p. 78.

[14] *ibid.*, p. 7.

inform, they also instruct; the trade unions associate themselves with schools and with youth groups, and provide educational facilities for their members and for the children of their members; slogans in the street exhort their readers to improve their production, their behaviour, and their understanding of their country's way of life.

For children and youth the activities of the youth organisations have grown over the years and have been enriched by a range of supplementary clubs offering additional educational opportunities through hobbies, sports, and technical skills. For adults large numbers of Houses of Culture have offered facilities of a community centre and an extensive range of technical, cultural, and recreational activities for all adults. Twenty-five thousand People's Universities with five million students in factories, offices, and institutions throughout the whole country have, since their establishment in 1960, provided technical, political, literary, and art courses wherever there has been an interest or demand. The work of the People's Universities and of the many other clubs has been assisted by the Society for the Propagation of Knowledge. Every region has developed such a society to provide speakers and courses on a wide range of topics for the meetings at clubs and institutions which wish to make use of the facilities.

The educative society of the U.S.S.R. is the concrete expression of a great faith in education. It has been a consistent belief of the country's leaders and educators since the days of the revolution that, by continual nurture in an educational atmosphere and through constant study and training, the new soviet man can be produced — the man of scientific knowledge and moral responsibility. The conviction that this faith in education has been justified has been well expressed by one of the leading historians of education in the U.S.S.R., N.K. Goncharov:

'A new and superior morality has grown out of the relationships between men in the course of building the new society... The characteristics of the soviet man are a spirit of collectivism, love of work, consciousness of social duty, a spirit of internationalism and soviet patriotism, and uprightness and devotion to the discharge of his duties.'[15]

THE CHINESE EDUCATIONAL EXPERIENCE, 1949-75

Pre-1949 China was a Confucian society, but one whose beliefs and structure had been threatened and eroded for the past hundred years. The Confucian ideal was a hierarchical society in which everyone knew his place and what was expected of him. It was a conservative society looking for inspiration to a golden age of the past, and ruled by a benevolent elite which by the mid-twentieth century exercised neither a benevolent nor an effective power of rule. In a country where family loyalties were strong and respect for position was an important stabilising influence, social relations tended to be based on status rather than on worth and social contribution. But the hollowness of the relationship was becoming more and more apparent as the bureaucracy and intelligentsia showed themselves progressively less capable of dealing with the economic, political, and military crises that beset twentieth century China. In a land of peasant farmers, the larger part could eke out only a minimal subsistence that, with periodic flood and famine, deteriorated into widespread starvation. Among the poorer peasants kinship ties were lessened, relations with the governing classes became ineffectual, and the Confucian value system crumbled.

Theoretically, if not always in practice, human history, in the Confucian view, was part of a rational and harmonious natural order in which there was a stable but flexible hierarchy. Where conflicts arose they were to be settled by concession and compromise, and a search for the mean between the disputants. Within this world of balance and harmony where nothing was done to excess, and where all was subject to the mean, the guides and governors of society were the literati, persons of superior education and moral capacity who sought to maintain the stability of the social order.

To them the modern vice of constant acquisitiveness was distasteful. Economy and careful husbanding of resources rather than a constant drive for mounting production represented the judicious mean. Their view enjoined frugality upon everyone according to his class and circumstances. Existing status would thus be preserved from the disruptiveness that resulted from money-making and social climbing. Society was not, however, at a standstill, it was subject to change and development. Change did not involve the construction of a new society but the repair of the old. It looked to the removal of grievances and the restoration of harmony and stability in accordance with a long-established pattern. Society was held together by social usage. Change was not to be a change in values or in the principles of social usage, but a change in the ways of practical action and practical relationship, taking advantage of contemporary knowledge and modern development in order to put traditional values into better operation. Innovation was not opposed — it was moderated. It should be piecemeal and gradual, not sweeping and revolutionary.

Harmony, stability, and the doctrine of the mean were the traditional beliefs that were buttressed by a moral authority 'that proceeded from above

───────────────

[15] N.K. Goncharov, *Public Education in the U.S.S.R.*, Report made at the International Seminar in Tashkent, April, 1961, pp. 9-10.

and was accepted below', and by a policy of gradual adjustment to change.

For the past hundred years the synthesis had been breaking down. Attempts at repair had been unsatisfactory. One of the attractions of communism was that it held out the promise of a new and satisfying synthesis of institutions and values. It was one, however, that differed radically from traditional Confucianism.[16] To harmony it opposed class-struggle, to stability the law of contradiction, to the mean the dictatorship of the proletariat, to elite authority the wisdom of the people, and to gradualness the idea of continuous revolution.

The communist revolution drew its strength from a land-short peasantry in a condition of massive poverty. Exploitation and injustice on the part of the richer classes, and the inability and unwillingness of the governing elite to make effective reforms made the poorer peasantry ripe for revolutionary change. The Japanese invasion and occupation in the 1930's and the first half of the 1940's accentuated the country's instability and heightened its receptivity to a new order which promised greater economic, personal, and social satisfaction. The communists provided hope, justice, and efficiency. Their new society was to be a people's republic run in the interests of the common man; they had built up in their military campaigns a reputation for just and equitable dealing with the villagers whose houses they occupied and whose stock they requisitioned; and they had shown in more than ten years' experience in Yenan that, where they had charge, they could run their affairs with reasonable efficiency.

(i) The Yenan Experience

After the Long March from south-eastern China in 1934-5, the communists established their base in Shensi province in the north-west, and made Yenan their headquarters. There, for the next ten years or so, they consolidated their position, expanded their efforts, and worked out in detail and in the practical situation the ideas that were to guide their activities when eventually they assumed control over the whole of China in 1949. Yenan was a strenuous and creative period which produced, among other things, a characteristic and enduring approach to educational theory and practice.

There was a conscious effort to cut themselves off from many contemporary principles and practices of education, from the reforms that had taken place in Chinese education, and from overseas educational ideas. That kind of education was regarded as a product of capitalist thinking, suitable perhaps for highly developed countries, appropriate for urban rather than agricultural communities, operative in times of peace but not in the current wartime situation. The education that should

be developed was to be fundamentally different. It was to serve two needs — the need for the broadest mass of the people and the need for cadre education.

Mass education should enable every worker to participate in guerilla warfare, organise labour power, and gain cultural knowledge and eventually higher level knowledge. Because of widespread adult illiteracy and lack of political awareness, and the need to raise the level of adult contribution to the war and to production, mass education should stress the education of adults before that of children, and it should be centred on the villages and run by the villagers. Cadre education should produce leaders in war and in production, and should have the government's first priority because sound and properly educated leaders were the most urgent necessity in the existing situation. But leaders must remember their fundamental relationship to the masses. In 1943 the *politburo* issued what was to become the classic statement on this matter: 'In all the practical work of our Party, correct leadership can only be developed on the principle of "from the masses, to the masses"... The basic method of leadership is to sum up the views of the masses, take the results back to the masses so that the masses give them their firm support and so work out sound ideas for leading the work in hand.'[17]

In respect to method and curriculum, the two guidelines were: simplify and apply. A short concentrated curriculum was the best. The number of subjects and the length of schooling were to be reduced to sheer essentials, and the subjects were to be taught with great thoroughness. They should also be taught in their application. 'For example, literature and mathematics have always been considered important courses, but very often middle school students who had studied for five or six years were unable to act as reporters for a wall newspaper or keep accounts for a co-operative. This is because the old educational policy was aimed at training minor litterateurs and mathematicians, not at training propaganda and accounting workers who knew how to function in real life.'[18]

Political education, through which to cultivate a revolutionary view of life, and a commitment to Marxist-Leninist thought, was to be

[16] For an elaboration of these points see Mary C. Wright, *The Last Stand of Chinese Conservatism*, Stanford University Press, 1957, and Arthur F. Wright, 'Struggle vs. Harmony, Symbols of Competing Values in Modern China', *World Politics*, 6, 1, October, 1953, pp. 31-44.

[17] 'The problem of transforming general education in the base areas', *Liberation Daily*, 7 April 1944, reproduced in Peter J. Seybolt, *Revolutionary Education in China, Documents and Commentary*, IASP, White Plains, New York, 1973, pp. 349-54, and 'On regulations and curriculum in general education', *Liberation Daily*, 27 May 1944, *ibid.*, pp. 355-64; see also A. Doak Barnett (ed.), *Chinese Communist Politics in Action*, University of Washington Press, Seattle, 1969, Chapter 3, Mark Selden, 'The Yenan legacy: the mass line', p. 149; and M. Lindsay *et al.*, *Notes on Educational Problems in Communist China 1941-47*, Institute of Pacific Relations, New York, 1950.

[18] P.J. Seybolt, *op.cit.*, p. 363.

dominant in all school curricula. Applied knowledge should also be a central concern of the teaching program, and its connection with production and the war should be continually apparent.

School organisation, similarly, should be adapted to the needs and activities of the people, by the use of a variety of forms such as winter schools, half-day schools, night schools, short-term training classes, work-group and practical study systems, and whatever other ways proved to be a suitable combination of production with education.

It was difficult to provide effective education in the communist-held areas. Resources were meagre and existence was precarious. Schools had sometimes to be evacuated at a moment's notice. Teachers were scarce and difficult to recruit. Books were hard to come by, and what equipment there was for vocational training had mostly to be improvised.

Nevertheless, throughout the Yenan period, various educational institutions were established with varying degrees of success. The Yenan city primary school, for example, eventually developed a successful focus on production and family life, by introducing work in accounting, letter-writing, map-making, contract writing and the abacus, and by encouraging pupils to help at home with manual work and to join in hygiene campaigns. Two other primary schools worked out specific programs which combined productive labour with school work.

The most prominent examples were provided by the Yenan University, and the Resist Japan Military and Political University (Kangta), both of which were designed to train cadres, the first through study in administration, science, literature, art, and medicine, the second mainly through military study. These universities emphasised the unity of theory and practice, the study of a few essential courses, and the development of self-instruction. Content consisted principally of a substantial political segment, of various aspects of the needs and experiences of everyday life considered in a practical way and gradually raised to a theoretical level by a study of the problems and the intellectual processes to which the practical activities gave rise. Much time was occupied in productive work which would be of service to the local area, and might involve students in about three months' practical work in the countryside each year. Methods in the universities encouraged informal relationships between teachers and students, stressed the desirability of an enthusiastic revolutionary spirit, and emphasised the importance of independent study for which provision was specifically made in the timetable. Mutual assistance among students was encouraged and examinations were redesigned to try to eliminate competitiveness, to stimulate students to further study, to help them improve their methods, and to provide further opportunity for co-operative work in the solution of useful problems.

The Yenan legacy in education was important in several ways:

- It established the primacy of the mass line in education, though there might be some lingering feeling that in some circumstances cadre training should rank first;
- It demonstrated that political and ideological education was a fundamental basis for the new society where politics was to be in command;
- It emphasised the connection between education and productive work and built up a commitment to practical, essential, and streamlined courses.

These were the ideas and practices that educators were to strive to introduce throughout China after 1949. They represented the Maoist line in education, which in the 1950's and early 1960's was not always in full favour, until the Cultural Revolution in 1966 brought the people back to the spirit and style of Yenan.

(ii) The Tasks of Chinese Communism

When the communists came to power in 1949 they had four basic tasks to undertake.

First, they had to provide a new governmental structure and a form of leadership which would embody their ideas on the role of the masses in the new society. What they were trying to do was to produce a new man and a new society.

The new man was to be a person who was selfless, one who had lost or had been educated out of his individualistic selfishness, and who was trained in loyalty to the people, to serve their needs and interests. He was to be a person, also, who was interested in active participation, who strove not just to understand but to take an active part in the new society and to further its development. He was to be class-conscious, sensitive in detecting differences in class structure and ready to take steps to try to eliminate them; and he was to be a person with scientific skill, trained to be rational and interested in investigation.

The new society was to be a mass society. In Mao Tsetung's view, it was to be a socialist society dependent for its government and its development on the collective will of the people; and it was to be a revolutionary society, one that believed in constant revolution. To effect the changes, the new society had to eliminate the old hierarchy and set up in its place some way in which the needs and the interests of the masses could be expressed and could be responsible for the regulation of the government.

In building a socialist society most countries have followed broadly one of two lines. One approach has been to try to develop a new elite, a new group of experts who know where to go, and can produce the instruments and ideas to lead the society along the new path. The other approach is one in which a call is made primarily upon the wisdom and the interest of the mass of the people. The speed of social and educational change is the speed at which the mass can move and can find proper ways of expressing itself and satisfying itself with the new society that is being set up. The second is the Mao Tsetung approach, the first is what the Chinese regarded as the Russian approach. In the pre-revolutionary period in Yenan the Chinese Communist Party largely adopted the mass approach; during the 1950's they tended very much to follow the other approach until, in the 1960's, they became disenchanted with it, and during the Cultural Revolution deliberately turned away from it back to the mass approach.

The second kind of change that had to be made was a change in land holdings throughout China. China was a land of peasants and a million villages. Before the revolution, in 1949, eighty per cent of the population worked on the land, and somewhere between sixty per cent of the peasants were on the breadline or just below it. One of the first jobs of the new regime in looking at the needs of the people was to redistribute the land so that all would have a measure of security. This was done in the early part of the 1950's. The landlords were dispossessed, the richer peasants lost some of their land and the landless peasants and the poor peasants gained some. But it was not enough. It was necessary at the end of the 1950's and into the 1960's to work out ways in which the peasants in their new role could come together and work in a collective way for the new society. In the early 1960's the landholders, in some cases already in co-operatives, were combined into communes, which were collections of villages working together under the one committee planning its operations collectively for some thirty thousand to sixty thousand people as one unit.

Thirdly, it was necessary also to modernise. Much of the disruption of the past hundred years had been associated with the difficulties of modernising and the contact with western society that accompanied it. The new regime was determined to remain firmly and uniquely Chinese while moving into the modern era and learning the technology of the west. It had to proceed in such a way as to avoid a major disruption of its peasant economy or a too-close attachment to western ideas and practices.

Finally, the next necessity was to change the kinds of relationships that existed in society. To organise a successful revolution and to maintain it, a revolutionary party must become vitally and fundamentally involved in the business of changing attitudes and social relationships. In China it was particularly necessary to change the established relationships between the peasants and the bureaucracy or intelligentsia that had previously held the power. The peasants had to be made to some extent intelligentsia by improving their education and by encouraging them to take on jobs which previously they would have left to experts. On the other hand, it was necessary to bring the intelligentsia into closer contact with the peasants, so that those who had a good education might link that education with the workers, and spend some time at work with them. They had to learn to be peasants as well as members of the intelligentsia, and to refer their activities to the needs of the peasants.

Beyond the peasant-intelligentsia relationship it was necessary to engineer an overall change of attitude throughout the country. A society with an ingrained Confucianist tradition had to be transformed into a Marxist society. It was an attitudinal change of daunting proportions. It was the fundamental task that the schools were asked to accomplish. They were developed as instruments for promoting social change and for developing in the new Chinese not only the appropriate attitudes but also the appropriate skills for the new society — skills of being a collective person, technological skills, and scientific skills that went with the modernising and the building up of the new society.

The task of education was to serve, in every way possible, the attitudinal, social, political, and economic transformation that was taking place.

(iii) Mao Tsetung's Theory of Education

Mao Tsetung was a school teacher by profession and always thought of himself as a teacher.[19] He began his training as a teacher in the normal school at Changsha in 1913 and after a short period in Peking returned to Changsha to teach in the primary school at the training institution. At the same time he became involved in adult education and during the 1920's worked extensively to improve the education of the peasants of central China. He was involved in educational work in the army during the Long March and later, from 1935 on, in Yenan.

Education, according to Mao, had an important role to play in changing society. Ideas generated by education could influence the behaviour of the masses and could affect the form of society that revolutionary forces were bringing about. Marx, an exile who had not lived

---

[19] Mao Tsetung (1893-1976) was born of a peasant family in the village of Shaoshan in Hunan, and trained as a teacher in the nearby city of Changsha where he taught for some years. In 1921 he became a foundation member of the Chinese Communist Party, and worked in Shanghai, Canton, and throughout Hunan until 1927 when he established a revolutionary base in the Chingkang mountains in Kiangsi. Open fighting followed against the Kuomintang. In 1934 the Long March began from Kiangsi west and north to Yenan where a centre was established in 1935 for the next twelve years. From 1949 when the People's Republic of China was established, Mao Tsetung was the country's leader both charismatically and in practice, and held office as chairman of the Communist Party and from time to time as chairman of the People's Republic. He wrote extensively on political issues, and his thought has been widely studied and applied in all situations throughout China.

to see the success of the revolution, had concerned himself mainly with an analysis of capitalist pre-revolutionary society. Lenin, who had helped to engineer a revolution and its immediate aftermath, added authoritatively to ideas about the nature of the revolution and the first stage of transition to the new society. Mao, who directed a successful revolution and also spent more than a quarter of a century guiding the course of post-revolution development, contributed uniquely to the theory and practice of ensuring the continuation, maintenance, and deepening of the revolution.

Mao saw Marxism not as a body of revealed thought, but as a developing theory with a core of basic principles. It should change and expand as new minds and new circumstances were brought to bear on it. It was a body of theory that was meant to be put to practical use as a guide to action. It must therefore be adapted to circumstances, and it should be regarded primarily as a method of analysing social phenomena. Marxism was a practical tool concerned with the 'concrete analysis of concrete conditions'.[20]

For Mao, four things were of the greatest significance in the Marxist methods of analysis.

Since, for Marxism, the central feature of a society is its productive activity, the knowledge, ideas, and behaviour of the people in a society will be closely related to the kinds of productive activities in which it is involved. To understand society it is necessary to study its mode of production, and it is necessary to do this by engaging in practical productive activities. The combination of practice and reflection is the first important feature of Mao's view of Marxist method. Knowledge is acquired through activity and it is verified by activity. Participation by the learner in productive work is the fundamental method of acquiring knowledge. 'If you want knowledge,' Mao wrote, 'you must take part in the practice of changing reality. If you want to know the taste of a pear, you must change the pear by eating it yourself.'[21] The most fruitful forms of activity are those which are both social and productive. These are the source materials of human thought. 'Where do correct ideas come from? Do they drop from the skies? No. Are they innate in the mind? No. They come from social practice, the struggle for production, the class struggle, and scientific experiment. It is man's social being that determines his thinking. Once the correct ideas characteristic of the advanced class are grasped by the masses, these ideas turn into a material force which changes society and changes the world.'[22]

Secondly, in studying any activity the student must look for the problems that need to be solved, and in the problems he will find a number of contradictions emerging which will require his attention. Communist society moves forward by the resolution of contradictions. They are to be settled among the people not by force but by persuasion so that new and stronger bonds can be built up in society. To resolve the

contradictions and to provide an answer to the problems of which they are a part, proper investigations must be undertaken. Mao was insistent that everyone must learn how to investigate, to become aware of what the state of affairs is in order to have a proper basis for understanding and action.

Thirdly, investigation was not to be conducted in a vacuum. Since society and culture were concerned with human relations, they were inevitably political matters. Politics is the practical expression of man's wishes and interests in matters of common concern. It is therefore an integral part of life, and it is vital that it should be the expression of a policy that is in the interests of the masses. In every investigation and in every activity there must be a political involvement. Mao Tsetung wrote that it was necessary in education to put proletarian politics in command.[23] This must be done so that in all activity the interests of the masses will be placed first, and the direction of the people's revolution maintained.

Fourthly, continued re-examination, criticism and rectification of public and private thought and action were necessary. Revolution is not a single event but a continuous struggle. Constant vigilance must be maintained to see that public authorities do not take the wrong turning, and that private individuals do not lose their sense of direction or their enthusiasm.

The four methods, involvement in productive activities, resolution of contradictions, politically controlled investigation, and continuous reassessment, were for Mao Tsetung essential parts of the behaviour of all people who were committed to a Marxist way of thinking and to the development and maintenance of a communist society.

One of the principal functions of education was to teach these methods and to make the masses conscious of the necessity to learn to use them.

Education was not confined to school-work. The whole people, adults as well as children, peasants and workers as well as intellectuals, had to learn what the new life meant. And, on the other hand, teachers had to learn from the people. The new society was a society of the

[20] Mao Tsetung, 'Our study and the current situation', *Selected Works*, Foreign Language Press, Peking, 1967, vol. 3, p. 165. The expression is a quotation from Lenin. I am indebted to Mrs G. Louie, whose doctoral thesis is on Chinese educational thought, for substantial guidance on Mao Tsetung's educational thinking.

[21] Mao Tsetung, 'On practice', *Selected Works, ibid.*, vol. 1, p. 300.

[22] Mao Tsetung, 'Where do correct ideas come from', (May 1963) *Four Essays on Philosophy, ibid.*, 1968, p. 134.

[23] Mao Tsetung, 'Scientific and Technological Training', *Peking Review*, 2 July 1968; see J. Chen ed., *Mao Papers: An Anthology with Bibliography*, Oxford University Press, New York, 1970, p. 154, quoted J.N. Hawkins, *op.cit.*, p. 78. Cf. 'All work in schools is for the purpose of transforming the students ideologically', Mao Tsetung, quoted J.N. Hawkins, *op.cit.*, p. 76.

common people; its culture stemmed from the life of the peasant, the worker, and the People's Liberation Army man. Teachers and intellectuals had to learn what this culture was; they had to learn from the people what their needs and aspirations were; and they had to learn the habit of mind, the down-to-earth commonsense, and the strengths of character that the masses possessed. Intellectuals in the new society must in some measure become peasants, and peasants intellectuals. Teachers must learn from the people, and in turn teach the people so that they might become clearer in mind, more skilful in action, and more dedicated in purpose. 'We must', said Mao, 'teach the masses clearly what we have received from them confusedly.'[24] It was the apotheosis of a common man. But teachers had other learning to impart too. The new society was to be a practical and scientific one, and it was to be politically conscious. Teachers had to use their skill and knowledge to make the masses literate. They had to supplement the people's culture with the scientific skills and ideas that would widen their horizons, modernise their living, and increase their production. And they had to explain with clarity and interpret with conviction the ideas of Marxism and the policies of the Chinese leaders.

The aim of education before a successful revolution was to prepare for the revolution; the aim after the revolution was to help to maintain and extend it. In essence the aims were the same, but they differed in emphasis. The most significant contribution that education could make to pre-revolutionary society was to develop a social and revolutionary consciousness. In that phase of development, educators should seek particularly to make the masses aware of their social, economic, and political position and of the means of changing it. They should be taught how to investigate, resolve their problems, weld together common political ideas, and realise the importance of seizing control of the productive forces of society. Education could not revolutionise society, but it could help to create an appropriate revolutionary climate for the introduction of the new order.

After the revolution the task of maintaining and extending the revolution made important demands on educators. The maintenance of the revolution required that the kind of contribution made in the pre-revolutionary period should be continued. Every avenue of education had to be used to continue to develop workers with a socialist consciousness. Fundamentally the new society must draw its strength and its support from the attitude of the masses. While the skills and attitudes of the supporters of the revolution must be confirmed, generations of 'worthy successors to the revolutionary cause of the proletariat'[25] must also be prepared principally by the appropriate education of the youth of the country. They should be committed to Marxism, ready at all times to serve the people and listen to the people, be skilled in working co-operatively and be modest, prudent, and self-critical.[26] In the post-revolutionary period

Mao Tsetung as the charismatic leader and teacher. This is a picture from the museum in Shaoshan of Mao in the early years of his career.

the revolutionaries would control the resources of education and could freely and openly turn it to their purposes; they were therefore in a position to undertake the extension of the scope of the revolution. This in Mao's phrase was to be done by building, through the educational agencies, a society which was 'red and expert'.[27]

The new society needed expert scientists, engineers, technicians, and administrators. It had to ensure that they were trained in sufficient numbers and that they were politically educated. Those who 'neglect ideology and politics can become directionless economists and technicians and that is very dangerous'.[28] The new society was to be an educative society

[24] André Malraux, *Antimemoirs*, trans. T. Kilmartin, Penguin, London, 1970, p. 410, reporting a conversation with Mao Tsetung. See also Mao Tsetung *Talks at the Yenan Forum of Literature and Art, Selected Works*, Foreign Language Press, Peking, 1967, vol. 3, pp. 84-5. 'Only by speaking for the masses can he educate them and only by being their pupil can he be their teacher.'

[25] Mao Tsetung, *Quotations from Chairman Mao Tsetung*, ibid., 1966, p. 277.

[26] ibid., pp. 276-7

[27] Mao Tsetung, 'Instruction on the question of redness and expertness', 31 January 1958, trans. *Current Background*, 8 October 1969, reproduced in T.H. Chen, *The Maoist Educational Revolution*, Praegar, New York, 1974, p. 218.

[28] Mao Tsetung, 'Mao Tsetung on Education', *Chinese Education*, 6 (1974), p. 20.

and a society of commitment. The redness of the expert intellectual was necessary not only to ensure that he himself worked with a commitment to the new society but also that his work might be seen and accepted by the people as an appropriate contribution to their way of life. Any possible divergence between the expert and the masses was to be minimised, on the one hand by the ideological education of the expert and by immersing him in the life of the people, and on the other, by raising the level of expertness and increasing the opportunities of the ordinary worker. For Mao it was important at all times to 'serve the people'; it was equally important to have faith in the people's capabilities.[29] It was part of the general education of the worker and peasant that they should be encouraged to undertake tasks that previously were left to specialists and intellectuals. The improvement of machinery, the development of new work techniques, the construction of dams, and the remodelling of villages were projects to be undertaken by the people with a minimum of expert guidance. Work of that kind provided an opportunity to bring out the workers' latent special knowledge, bolstered their confidence, and confirmed the idea that the new civilisation was one that was being built by the common man.

Mao summed up his view of the aim of education in a statement made in 1957: 'Our educational policy must enable everyone who receives an education to develop morally, intellectually, and physically, and become a worker with both socialist consciousness and culture.'[30]

From Mao Tsetung's view of the aims of education and his analysis of Marxist methods, the kind of emphasis that should be introduced into the curriculum and teaching methods of schools followed.

The school curriculum should be reconstructed so that there would be substantial opportunity for the pupils to engage in productive work. A program of productive work should be a significant thread running throughout kindergarten, primary, secondary, and tertiary education, providing school pupils with experience of practical work in industry or agriculture, and bringing home to them its relationship to other school studies, and its fundamental importance for understanding and controlling the development of society. The curriculum should also be re-examined to ensure that the matters studied by pupils were relevant to present and future life in a communist society in China. It was necessary, for example, to look at the content of language, mathematics, science, history, geography, art, and physical education courses in order to prune traditional elements, to introduce appropriate new facts and ideas, and to re-orient the material and its interpretation so that pupils would absorb the kind of knowledge and attitudes that were thought best suited to the development of their new society. An important addition should also be made to the curriculum by the deliberate teaching of politics. Politics should be the controlling element in education as in life. Therefore, each subject should be impregnated wherever possible with ideology and with

political analysis, and the curriculum should be supplemented at appropriate age levels by a systematic treatment of politics as a subject in its own right.

The methods of handling such a curriculum should be, in essence, the same as those of Marxist analysis. Teachers and pupils should see much of their work in the form of problems and should co-operate in seeking out the contradictions and the ways of resolving them. They should enter into and learn the best ways of conducting social investigations, and of relating all their subjects to the realities of life and to politically desirable developments.

(iv)   The Early 1950's

The Chinese Communists after they came to power in 1949 moved slowly in education. The country had been divided and disrupted for many years and needed consolidation. Initially, therefore, steps were taken to restore and re-establish schools and universities, and to encourage teachers, while continuing much as they had before, to begin to learn about and absorb Maoist ideas.[31]

The most decisive step taken in 1949 was the consolidation of the youth leagues. Various Socialist Youth Corps had met together in 1922 for the first time in an all-China conference, and in 1926 became the Communist Youth Corps whose object was to win over and educate the youth of China in Marxist-Leninism. The Corps was active in student work with trade union groups, and in the Shanghai Uprisings of 1926 and 1927. A children's corps, later called the Young Pioneers, was also formed with members between the ages of nine and fourteen. In the 1930's the Corps provided groups of picked youths who fought with distinction with the Red Army and, during the Japanese war, combined their efforts with those of the large number of other anti-Japanese youth groups that sprang up during the conflict. This co-operation encouraged many

29   Mao Tsetung, Serve the People, Selected Works, Foreign Language Press, Peking, 1967, vol. 3, pp. 177-8.

30   Mao Tsetung, 'On the Correct Handling of Contradictions among the People', in On New Democracy etc., ibid., Pocket ed., 1967, p. 202.

31   For the development of Chinese communist education the following references are useful: Education in Communist China, Proceedings, vols. 1 and 2, Centre d'Etude du Sud-est Asiatique et de l'Extrême Orient, Bruxelles, 18-19 February, 1969; S. Fraser (ed.), Chinese Communist Education, Records of the First Decade, Vanderbilt University Press, Nashville, 1965; S. Fraser ed., Education and Communism in China, Pall Mall, London, 1971; R.F. Price Education in Communist China, RKP, London, 1975; Chiu-Sam Tsang, Society, Schools and Progress in China, Pergamon, Oxford, 1968; L.A. Orleans, Professional Manpower and Education in Communist China, National Science Foundation, U.S. Government Printing Office, Washington D.C., 1961; R.H. Solomon, Mass Revolution and the Chinese Political Culture, University of California Press, Berkeley, 1971; T.H. Chen, The Maoist Educational Revolution, Praegar, New York, 1974; K.E. Priestley, Education in China, Eurasia, New Delhi, 1963.

Chinese youths to join the communist armies in resistance to the Japanese. After the defeat of the Japanese, in 1946 groups called Democratic Youth Leagues proliferated, and turned their energies to reconstruction and the overthrow of the Kuomintang.

These groups were united in 1949 into the China New Democratic Youth League (NDYL) whose objects were to support the war of national liberation, to promote the study of Marxist-Leninism, to lead the masses of youth in support of the People's Government, to engage in social service, and to build a new democratic society. In the early years of the new regime the youth league played a substantial part in helping to get schools and universities re-established, and in winning teachers and community leaders over to the communist cause. In 1957 the NDYL changed its name to Communist Youth League. It then had three levels of membership: Communist Youth, over the age of seventeen, whose numbers increased from 190,000 in early 1949 to more than twenty-five million in 1960; Young Pioneers, between thirteen and seventeen years of age, whose numbers increased from about five hundred thousand in 1949 to fifty million in 1960; and the Children's Corps for those between the ages of seven and twelve.[32]

One of the first moves of the communist government was to give a great impetus to spare-time education. It is probable that on the eve of liberation more than 85 per cent of the people over the age of ten were illiterate and less than forty per cent of school-age children were at school.[33] Spare-time classes in enormous numbers were organised in factories and on farms to provide literacy training, political education, and general information. They were supplemented by radio classes, study groups, and the widespread distribution of posters, leaflets, and elementary level books written in the simplified characters that were introduced during the 1950's for general use. In 1960 the Ministry of Education reported that one hundred and thirty million peasants and thirty-eight million industrial workers were currently in attendance at spare-time classes.[34] Spare-time schooling became an integral and enduring part of Chinese education for adults. By the 1970's almost all factories and communes were organising regular spare-time classes for the peasants and workers and China had become very much a nation continuously at school.

A further supplement to existing schooling was the development, particularly in response to directives in 1958, of half-work, half-study vocational schools. These part-time schools were aimed at youth, covered a wide range of subjects, and were a popular substitute for a middle school education.

In 1951 a campaign, centred on Peking and Tientsin, was started for the ideological remoulding of the intellectuals. They were required to begin the serious study of Marxism, attend criticism sessions, and write confessions. Universities were brought under the control of communist party committees and political reliability began to become a more important criterion for promotion than academic quality. Teachers, above all, had to learn the vocabulary and ideas of Maoist Marxism and to build up their political consciousness. The campaign continued throughout the early 1950's parallel with the reform and re-education of the public service through what was known as the three anti- and the five-anti campaigns against corruption and bureaucratisation.

A substantial degree of elitism still remained in the Chinese educational system. It could be seen particularly in secondary education. Entrance to secondary education was by means of a selective examination, and continuance in it dependent on the passing of formal examinations. The school curriculum was academically oriented towards tertiary education and was prescribed by the central Ministry of Education in Peking. Most students left school after an elementary education and, if they wished to further their education, would continue through a part-time vocational course.

In these years also, missionary schools were discontinued and the foreign teachers connected with them were repatriated. Their influence, which for half a century had been considerable, came to an abrupt end. The missionary schools and universities were financed from abroad and were regarded as symbolic of the interference and indignity that China had suffered for a hundred years at the hands of western powers. With liberation in 1949, the feeling of nationalism was intensified, and it became possible to express more effectively the new sense of aspiration and self-confidence that was building up inside China. The Korean War (1950-53) deepened Chinese hostility to western influences and increased their enmity to mission activities. Mission schools were seen as examples of cultural aggression on the part of foreign powers, and as private ventures in the new socialist state. Their elimination was speedily accomplished. By 1953 they had vanished.

The Chinese began to look, instead, to Russia for inspiration and example, especially after the signing of an agreement with the U.S.S.R. on scientific and cultural co-operation in 1954. Throughout the 1950's many Chinese went to study in the U.S.S.R. instead of in Western Europe

[32] see Klaus H. Pringheim, 'The Functions of the Chinese Communist Youth Leagues (1920-1949), *The China Quarterly*, 12, October-December 1962, pp. 57-91. The League had two widely circulated journals, *Chinese Youth* started in 1923 and, from the 1950's on, aimed at the more well-educated youth, and *Chinese Youth Journal* started in 1951 as a general youth newspaper; see A. Doak Barnett (ed.), *Chinese Communist Politics in Action, ibid.*, Chapter 9, James Townsend, 'Revolutionizing Chinese Youth: a study of Chung-Kuo Ching-nien', pp. 447-76.

[33] S. Fraser (ed.), *Chinese Communist Education*, pp. 111-12.

[34] T.H. Chen, *op.cit.*, p. 79, and M. Bastid, 'Mass Education', in *Education in Communist China, Proceedings*, vol. 1, *op.cit.*, p. 73.

or the U.S.A., and many Russians taught and acted as advisers in China. Russian became the most popular foreign language in universities and secondary schools; higher education was pruned and remodelled into universities and professional institutes, and part-time tertiary work was greatly extended following the example of the U.S.S.R. The curricula of primary, secondary, and university education began to approximate to those of Russia, to develop a more strongly scientific and practical bent, and to make extensive use of Russian textbooks. In 1960 the association with the U.S.S.R. was abruptly terminated when relations between China and the Soviet Union broke down.

(v)　A Hundred Flowers Bloom

> 'Let a hundred flowers bloom
> Let a hundred schools contend'

was the invitation issued by Mao Tsetung on 27 February, 1957.[35] He believed that a communist society could be developed in China not by relying on force but by the power of education and persuasion. Constant ideological education and rectification campaigns were waged from 1949 until the end of 1955, and for the next two years there was a relaxation while the move to collectivise agriculture and nationalise commerce and industry was carried through in 1955 and 1956. A similar indulgence was apparent at this time also throughout most communist countries in the readjustment period following Khrushchev's condemnation of Stalinism early in 1956.

In mid-1956 suggestions were made that China's intellectuals should be encouraged to show greater initiative and variety in their contributions to the country's cultural life within the limits of the new ideology: 'Since they serve the workers, peasants, and soldiers, literature and art should sing the praises of the new society and positive characters as a matter of course. At the same time, they should criticize the old society and negative characters. They praise progress while criticizing what is lagging behind. Therefore the themes of literature and art should be very broad.'[36] Soon after, Mao Tsetung began a rectification campaign to improve and humanise the style of work of party and bureaucracy members. By May 1957 it was decided to seek the views of the people, particularly the scholars and artists, on the conduct of the new society. It was, in Mao Tsetung's view, a mass society whose leaders had the task of finding out the opinions and needs of the people, and, armed with this information, putting appropriate policies into action.

The result was unexpected. The criticisms lasted for six weeks from 1 May to 8 June. Like their counterparts in Poland and Hungary who, also in 1956-57, had provided a stimulus to disaffection with the established

communist government, the Chinese intellectuals were often severe in their criticism and provocative of revolt. Various scholars objected to the neglect of their talents and specialities, and chafed under the bureaucratic and dogmatic leadership of party members, and those trained in western countries deplored the restrictions placed upon their use of knowledge gained in non-communist academic circles. Some schoolteachers complained that they had difficulty mixing freely with other teachers who were Communist Party members, and suggested that various democratic parties should share school management with the Communist Party. Some students seemed to think that 4 May had come again and they tried to revive the 1919 spirit of revolt. Not only were they interested in rectifying educational abuses such as alleged favouritism for party members, and incompetence in university and school administration, they agitated also for the reform of the government, freedom of the press, and the abolition of censorship. Some serious rioting occurred. Peasants and workers in a number of instances criticised the bureaucratic inefficiency of some party members, and, in several cases, went on strike.

The danger of possible widespread rioting and the fomenting of anti-communist feelings brought a speedy end to the blooming and contending period. Its chief importance was the clear indication that a substantial segment of the intellectuals had not yet become thoroughly committed to the new regime. In consequence, a large number of senior party members were transferred to responsible posts in universities and secondary schools, political education was intensified, and the program of rustication increased.[37]

Throughout 1957-58 probably as many as a million cadres and intellectuals were transferred to manual work alongside the peasants in the countryside, and in 1958 it became obligatory on all government officers in rotation to spend a month in physical work each year. The desired effect of the experience was recorded in verse in an English-language Peking journal:

> After ten months I wasn't the same,
> I left with much more than I came.
> I filled in the gap of my school education,
> Learnt that labour makes the nation.
> Today it's· back to the city once more,
> An intellectual who now knows the score.[38]

---

[35]　Mao Tsetung, 'On the Correct Handling of Contradictions among the people', op.cit., p. 207.

[36]　S. Fraser (ed.) Chinese Communist Education. Records of the First Decade, op.cit., p. 232, Speech by Lu Tingyi, 'Let All Flowers Bloom Together, Let Diverse Schools of Thought Contend', May 1956.

[37]　Roderick MacFarquhar, The Hundred Flowers Campaign and the Chinese Intellectuals, Praegar, New York, 1960.

[38]　S. Fraser, op.cit., p. 57, extract from Peking Review, 11, 6 (10 February 1959).

(vi) The Great Leap Forward

The years 1958-60 were those of the Great Leap Forward in which China made a concerted effort to expand her production at a much more rapid pace than before. There was an encouragement to produce needed goods in as great a quantity as possible by formal and informal methods and there was an intensification of political education. Factories were expanded and backyard workshops were multiplied.

The principal task of education was seen more strongly than ever to be the production of persons who were 'red and expert'. Consequently, strenuous efforts were made to establish factories in schools and universities, and to set up schools and universities in factories. Thousands of school-factories and factory-schools were established at that time and were a foretaste of the greater expansion during the Cultural Revolution in the late 1960's. Half-work, half-study programs were encouraged in order to produce practical-minded technicians and to boost production.

The renewed interest in relating productive work to education coincided, interestingly, with a similar move in the U.S.S.R. with the implementing of the Khrushchev reforms of 1958. In China, from 1958 all pupils were required to spend some of their school time on jobs allocated to them by the school authorities. Jobs were to be done at school or in local factories or farms, and gradually increased in complexity and time with the maturity of the pupils. For the next two years experiments were conducted in various ways of combining education with productive work, and in 1960 it was proposed by the Minister of Education that the hours given to productive work should be increased 'because the co-ordination of education with productive labour is the central task in the educational revolution'.[39] He suggested, at the same time, a reduction in the length of school courses. A number of experiments had continued, since the early 1950's, to trim the primary school from six to five years, and the secondary school to five years also. By integrating the school program more effectively and, in particular, by modernising content and methods in mathematics and science, and by eliminating much deadwood in all subjects, a considerable saving, it was hoped, could be effected. During the next few years experimentation in these matters continued, but no general change was effected. It was left to the Cultural Revolution eventually to bring about a firm and universal change in the length and content of schooling and in the emphasis to be placed on productive work.

Figure 15.2 shows the growth in enrolment in Chinese education since the beginning of the century. The rapid spurt at all levels of education during the 1950's, following the Communist Revolution, is clear. It was interestingly matched by a similar acceleration earlier in the revolutionary period surrounding the foundation of the republic in 1912.

Throughout the 1950's the formal structure of the regular education system remained, except for some adaptations from Russian influences, much as it had been before the Communist Revolution. The content of it, however, was steadily being changed, and a much wider range of informal and spare-time education was being developed to provide basic schooling for large numbers and to accustom people to extensive and continuous political discussion and education. In those ways education was gradually emerging with a new appearance and style. But by the 1960's the Yenan example had by no means yet been fully put into operation throughout the educational system. That was to be the function of the Cultural Revolution.

(vii) The Great Proletarian Cultural Revolution

'Under the direct leadership of Chairman Mao Tsetung and the Central Committee of the Chinese Communist Party, a great mass proletarian cultural revolution without parallel in history is swiftly and vigorously unfolding with the irresistible force of an avalanche.'[40] The Cultural Revolution was the culmination of many preliminary rumblings for several years over the extent to which the country was deviating from the true line of Mao Tsetung's thought. It was a sustained, nation-wide rectification campaign which started in 1966, continued in full force till 1968, and lingered on into the early 1970's.

In 1962 Mao Tsetung had launched a socialist education movement to intensify the political development of youth and to purify the country's administration.[41] Two years later the People's Liberation Army began a Mao-study campaign and produced, in 1964, the little red book of *Quotations from Chairman Mao Tsetung* which attained great popularity throughout China during the next five years.

Towards the end of 1965 the vice-mayor of Peking was attacked for anti-Marxist expression in a historical novel that he had written. Over the next six months other similar disputes emerged and escalated. Literary and artistic differences had been simmering for some time. If, in every aspect of life, service to the people and to the revolution was to be the touchstone of behaviour, then leisure activities and the arts could not hope to escape the general rule. The traditional arts of Peking opera and ballet therefore came under scrutiny, and moves were taken in the 1950's

---

[39] Robert D. Barendsen, 'The 1960 Educational Reforms', *The China Quarterly*, October-December 1960, 4, 58.

[40] *Red Flag*, Editorial, no. 8, 1966.

[41] See R. Baum and F.C. Teiwes, *Ssu-Ching: The Socialist Education Movement of 1962-1964*, Center for Chinese Studies, Berkeley, 1968.

Figure 15.2: China: Growth in Primary, Secondary and Tertiary
Enrolments, 1905-65.

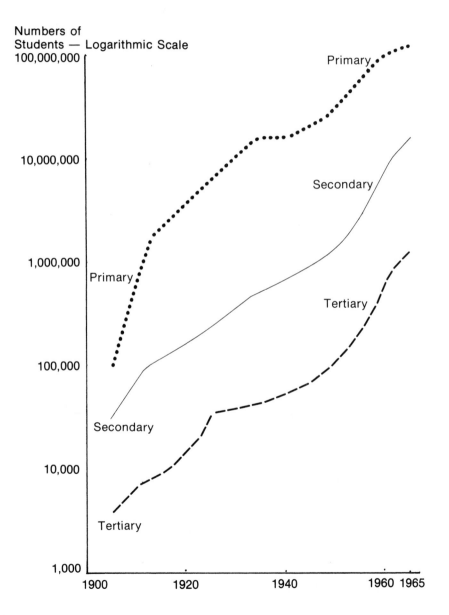

and early 1960's to change them into vehicles of political education. New
ballets were written such as *The White-Haired Girl*, and new operas such
as *The Red Lantern* based on recent events in the civil war or the war
against Japan in which the people and the communists showed to good
advantage. Productions of such a kind were revised from time to time, and
the theory was held that creative works should be modified by their
authors and producers in as artistic a way as they could to meet the
political requirements of the day. Disagreements arose whenever
modifications were to be made, especially among traditional writers and
composers who did not accept the theory. The early months of the Cultural
Revolution was a period of intense intellectual dispute on artistic matters
in which university and secondary school students took a vigorous part. In
February 1966 the central committee of the Chinese Communist Party
issued a circular exonerating the vice-mayor of Peking but after several
months of argument, on 16 May, firmly repudiated its earlier decision.
This action pointed to divisions within the party and encouraged criticism
of the authorities.

A poster, expressing student discontent with the activities of the
principal of Peking University, was put up on 25 May, and widely
broadcast through the radio and press on 2 June 1966. It was generally
regarded as marking the beginning of the Cultural Revolution. The
movement quickly spread to other universities, and was taken up by Mao
Tsetung, who signalled his leadership of it and his opposition to the
more conservative members of the government by writing his own poster
on 5 August with the title 'Bombard the Headquarters'.

On 8 August the central committee of the party formally adopted the
Cultural Revolution as its policy and issued Sixteen Points as guidelines
for it. The committee declared that the Cultural Revolution marked a
significant new stage in the socialist revolution in China. It was a
concerted attempt to transform the cultural, educational, and administrative superstructure to conform to the change that had already taken place
in the country's economic base. Tendencies towards elitism in education,
revisionism in ideology, bureaucracy in administration, and selfish,
reactionary policies in various walks of life were to be firmly quashed. To
achieve success the revolution must bring the masses and especially the
young people into the centre of the struggle, 'putting proletarian politics
in the forefront and Mao Tsetung's Thought in the lead'. The aim of the
movement was 'to revolutionize people's ideology' and to deepen their
socialist consciousness. The outcome would be a more solid conviction of
the correctness of Marxist-Maoist thinking, a greater ability on the part of
the masses to participate in management and government, and higher
productivity in all areas. The battle was to be waged by persistent
argument through posters, pamphlets, debates, and self-criticism, and it
should be concentrated on party members, government officials at all

levels, management in factories, and teachers. People with special skills in science and technology should not be molested.

Education was a particularly important target. In every kind of school and university Mao Tsetung's policy 'of education serving proletarian politics and education being combined with productive labour' was to be thoroughly applied. The central committee recommended also that schooling should be shortened, courses should be fewer and better, and that students should take part in industrial work, farming, military affairs, and the political struggles of the Cultural Revolution.

The committee's directive was a blueprint for the movement over the next two years, and a clear indication of the strenuous drive that was to be made to politicise more thoroughly all forms of education.

Student groups from secondary schools and universities were organised loosely into companies known as Red Guards who for the rest of 1966 undertook the leadership of the revolution, causing some disruption in most towns and cities, though the countryside remained largely free from their influence in the early stages of the movement. Early in their campaign the Red Guards displayed particular hostility towards evidences of traditional practices and individualistic activities. Some public and private treasures were confiscated, defaced, or destroyed, and some opponents were ill-treated. For the most part, however, the movement relied on massive debate, lengthy discussion, and persuasion. The general formula was struggle, criticism, and transformation. In the latter part of 1966 they held mass meetings in Peking, and in January 1967 participated in disruptive agitation in China's main commercial city, Shanghai.

At the end of 1966 and early in 1967 the industrial workers, hitherto only mildly engaged, became heavily involved, especially in Shanghai, Canton, and Peking. At about the same time a third important body in the Cultural Revolution, the People's Liberation Army, also began to play a more important part.

The PLA was regarded as a 'people's army' which performed the usual military duties and also worked in many civilian occupations assisting in communes, factories, and schools, and undertaking many civil construction jobs. In the establishment of communism in China it had played a fundamental role militarily and ideologically. Early in the movement, in June 1966, a call to the PLA had been made in an article entitled 'Raise high the great red banner of Mao Tsetung's thought and carry the Great Proletarian Cultural Revolution through to the end'. It exhorted the members of the army to become thoroughgoing revolutionaries in the great revolutionary undertaking without precedent in human history 'that reaches into the very souls of people ... to create and cultivate among the masses an entirely new proletarian ideology and culture, and entirely new proletarian customs and habits'.[42] The army was

to become a great educational agency, 'a great school' of Mao Tsetung's thought,[43] which would

> 'launch many-sided cultural activities which are rich in revolutionary educational significance, read revolutionary books, sing revolutionary songs, perform revolutionary plays, see revolutionary films, tell revolutionary stories, listen to revolutionary broadcasts...'[44]

In January 1967 the PLA firmly espoused the cause of the revolutionaries, and henceforth became the chief vehicle of Mao's policies and the controlling influence in the movement.[45] Its central role was underlined by Mao Tsetung's directive of 7 March 1967: 'The army should give military and political training in the universities, middle schools, and the higher classes of primary schools, stage by stage and group by group ... Sending army cadres to train revolutionary teachers and students is an excellent measure. It makes a world of difference whether there is such training. Through this training, they can learn from the Liberation Army.' In consequence, PLA men set up study groups in schools, reconciled various revolutionary factions, and helped to restructure the organisation and administration of the country's schools.

In the early months of 1967 a new form of organisation began to appear, the revolutionary committees. They were small groups representing various revolutionary elements in the area or establishment where they were formed. Gradually they took over provincial and local government, and the management of institutions such as communes, factories, and schools. In schools they were likely to consist of representatives of the PLA. Communist Party, Red Guard, teachers, and local workers or peasants, and they were responsible for the day-to-day conduct of the school.

Towards mid-year in 1967 serious disturbances occurred in Szechwan and in the city of Wuhan. They were followed by clashes among Red Guards of varying degrees of radicalism, often involving units of the PLA, in the major cities of Shanghai, Canton, and Tientsin. The disturbances marked the end of the predominance of the Red Guard. Thereafter the Cultural Revolution stabilised itself under the influence of the PLA and the mixed revolutionary committees whose number and influence increased greatly throughout 1968, a year that was devoted

[42] *The Great Socialist Cultural Revolution in China (5)*, Foreign Language Press, Peking, 1966, p. 23.

[43] Mao Tsetung, 7 May 1966, 'The May 7 Directive', trans. *Issues and Studies*, 6, 4 (January 1970) 86. It is also reproduced in part in T.H. Chen, *The Maoist Educational Revolution*, Praegar, New York, 1974, p. 233.

[44] *The Great Socialist Cultural Revolution in China (5)*, p. 24.

[45] *Liberation Army Daily*, 25 January 1967, reproduced in K.H. Fan (ed.), *The Chinese Cultural Revolution: Selected Documents*, Monthly Review Press, New York, 1968, pp. 203ff.

mainly to an effort to bring life back to a somewhat less tempestuous condition.

The Cultural Revolution might be said to have ended with the meeting of the 9th Congress of the Chinese Communist Party in April 1969 which elected a new central committee, adopted a new party constitution and reaffirmed the thought of Mao Tsetung as the central guide to China's development. In particular, it reasserted Mao's views on the need for continuous revolution, and saw the Cultural Revolution as a successful phase of it.

(viii) Effects of the Cultural Revolution on Education

The impact of the Cultural Revolution on education was considerable.[46] Its general effect was to make the ordinary person more sensitive to political ideas and political behaviour. It demonstrated to him that, for the future health of the new society, ideological conviction was more important than managerial skill, and it showed him that he had the power and the duty to become involved in an effective way in running public affairs.

On formal schooling the effect of the Cultural Revolution was particularly important. The intended direction of the thrust was outlined in the 7 May directive written by Mao Tsetung on that date in 1966. Students as well as workers and peasants, administrators, and party members, should, as well as their usual studies, learn industrial, agricultural, and military work; they should deepen their class-consciousness and bring to an end the domination of their schools by bourgeois intellectuals; and they should shorten the period of schooling and revolutionise education.

The first enthusiastic supporters of the Cultural Revolution were the university students of Peking; it then quickly spread to universities elsewhere and to schools. By mid-1966 classes in most schools and universities had been abandoned, and teaching ceased for some time to come. Many students joined the Red Guard, and both students and staff busied themselves with rethinking the curriculum, with self-criticism, with discussions on Mao Tsetung's Thought, and, in many cases, with work in factories or agricultural communes. In universities, a large proportion of the staff continued with their research work.

One of the prime purposes of the Cultural Revolution was to re-educate the intellectuals, of whom teachers and senior secondary and university students were a large and vital part. They had to be converted to the view that political conviction was more important than knowledge of the usual school subjects, and that they should learn to be genuinely a part of the common people and to value the wisdom and skill of the masses. Accordingly, all teachers had to re-examine their convictions and traditional practices, and many had to submit to prolonged and searching interrogation by Red Guards. In this process they gradually remade their ideas. In the course of re-education some moved too far to the left and had to be restrained and further rectified.

The most widely known struggles took place at two universities in Peking with adjacent campuses, Peking University and Tsinghua, a science and engineering university. When the movement started at Peking University on 2 June 1966, the Tsinghua students came across to study the posters and protests and decided to revolt against their administration, too, of whom the head was also Minister for Higher Education. Their principal objection was to the university's emphasis on examinable expertise and on competence in theory rather than in practical work. The students of both universities looked for more study of current political thought, more attention to marxist methods of investigation, and more workshop experience. Work teams were sent to the universities by the central committee of the party, but were repudiated by the students who, with Mao Tsetung's approval, formed their own committees which took charge of the universities, became the spearhead of the Red Guard movement, and began to spread the revolution to the campuses of other universities. During the next few months splits developed within the committees and dissension continued throughout 1967. Many Red Guards from other cities and country areas crowded into Peking, camped for months in the streets, and filled the great square before Tien an Men with rallies and mass meetings. In mid-1968 a team of several hundred PLA and industrial workers arrived at each of the universities to try to reconcile the contending factions. A violent three months' struggle ensued at Tsinghua before the fighting was finally brought to an end, and revolutionary committees were set up under which the universities were eventually able to resume teaching. In the midst of the disturbances university staff and students began to co-operate with workers' propaganda teams in an effort to evaluate and reconstruct every university department. They made serious efforts to rethink their past behaviour, to read and discuss marxism more extensively, and to study university experience in Yenan and decide the ways in which it might be applied in their own universities.

46 For the Cultural Revolution and its aftermath in education the following references are useful: T.H. Chen, *The Maoist Educational Revolution*, Praegar, New York, 1974; J. Robinson, *The Cultural Revolution in China*, Penguin, Harmondsworth, 1969; D.W. Fokkema, *Report from Peking*, Hurst, London, 1970; W. Hinton, *Hundred Day War: The Cultural Revolution at Tsinghua University*, Monthly Review Press, New York, 1972; Tsien Tchchao, *L'Enseignement Supérieur et la Recherche Scientifique en République Populaire de Chine*, LGDJ, Paris, 1971; J.N. Hawkins, *Mao Tsetung and Education*, Linnet, Hamden, Conn., 1974; S. Fraser and J.N. Hawkins, 'Chinese Education: Revolution and Development', *Phi Delta Kappan*, 53, 8 (April 1972), pp. 487-500; W.F. Connell *et al.*, *China at School*, Novak, Sydney, 1974.

The progress of the Cultural Revolution in the universities in Peking, though somewhat more violent, was typical of the pattern that occurred in schools and universities throughout China. First came moves to seize power, then a long process of rectification and reconstruction interspersed with factional fighting. By 1969 the disruptive side of the revolution had for the most part run its course. Most schools were back at work, some in October 1967, others during 1968; and the universities, closed since June 1966, were planning to resume classes by 1970. The early years of the 1970's were spent in solid discussion and experimentation on the best means of putting into practice in education the insights gained in the course of the revolutionary struggles.

There were six important effects of the Cultural Revolution on education:

- Schooling was seriously disrupted. Formal education at primary and secondary level was discontinued in many areas of China for up to two years, and at university level for about four years. The disruption slowed down the production of literate and trained workers of all grades, but it did make possible a radical rethinking and replanning of school work.

- It led to a more thorough politicising of the school curriculum. Teachers who previously had seasoned their academic expertness with the redness of communist theory and practice found that henceforth redness was to be dominant. Education was to be ideologically centred. This meant that the curriculum had to be rethought and textbooks in every subject re-written so that they might express more adequately and thoroughly the moral and political content and thought of Mao Tsetung. Schools and universities were to serve the people more completely; students for selective courses such as universities were to be chosen by university authorities after they had had work experience and had been selected for higher education by their workmates on the basis of their devotion to the proletarian cause, the responsibility of their character, and their intellectual ability.

- Curricula were extensively modified by the introduction of more time for productive work in them. School factories became more common; up to two months a year was spent working in neighbouring factories or agricultural communes, and programs of substantial productive labour became integral parts of all curricula from kindergarten to university.

- The school and university program was considerably shortened. Primary school became five instead of six years, secondary four or five instead of six, and university courses, including professional courses such as medicine and engineering, were reduced wherever possible to three. The content was correspondingly reduced, and much experimentation with the streamlining and adjusting of all school subjects was undertaken in the early 1970's. Methods of assessing pupils became more varied. Traditional examining lost some of its force, and teachers began to make more use of examinations as diagnostic and teaching tools.

- School administration was overhauled. More authority was given to provincial and local educators to determine curricula, to produce text materials, and to organise their schools. The revolutionary committees started in the Cultural Revolution were maintained in all schools as the governing authority. The committees provided a collective leadership for each school, demonstrating by their existence the importance placed on collective thinking and socialist consciousness. As a consequence of their mixed lay, professional, and party membership they were able to ensure that schools maintained a close connection with local, proletarian, and party interests.

- Most importantly, there was a powerful effect on the general tone and conduct of education throughout China. The Cultural Revolution was a great reaffirmation of the faith and a herculean effort to convert the uncommitted. By the mid-1960's, after almost twenty years of communist government, some of the original revolutionary fervour had been dampened, and there were still people to be found in positions of importance and in the teaching profession who were prepared to accept and work within a communist framework but who fell short of total involvement. The Cultural Revolution was an effort to restore revolutionary vigour, to emphasise the view that revolution was a continuous phenomenon, and to remake the minds of those who were to guide and educate the revolutionary generation to come. The following reading passage from a textbook in the teaching of English used in the early 1970's is a demonstration of the way in which the leadership and political thinking of Mao Tsetung had come to penetrate the classroom.

> Chairman Mao, Chairman Mao
> You are our great teacher
> We are your good pupils.
> We love you
> We follow your teachings,
> And make revolution forever.

It was a triumph for the mass line. The Cultural Revolution had strenuously maintained the view that ideas and decisions in the new society were to come from the people, and that everyone should be a committed participator in forming them. The new citizen that schools, youth groups, and study circles were attempting to shape was one who could take a point of view, speak out in support of it, and act upon it, one who could submit his behaviour and his ideology to scrutiny by his fellow group members, and one who had learnt to subordinate his personal preferences to the welfare of his group and to the leadership of the party and Mao Tsetung.

Physical exercise has been an important part of the school curriculum, and it has been usual for the whole school to take part in mass exercises. Nankai Middle School, Tientsin, provides two fifteen minute periods for exercises each day, and the students here are exercising in a temperature of about four degrees below freezing. A school student leads his school fellows. (December 1972)

(ix) Education in the 1970's

By the mid-1970's Chinese education had settled into a reasonably firm pattern. Schools in China were run by local authorities such as municipalities and counties under the general guidance of the provincial authorities, of which there were twenty-two, and the national ministry. Consequently, although there were differences between schools in different districts in matters such as school organisation, timetabling, and textbooks, there was sufficient similarity to justify reference to a Chinese system of education. The general pattern is given in Figure 15.3.

After a four-year kindergarten, there was a five-year primary school, followed by a four- or five-year secondary school divided into two or three years of junior, and two years of senior school; university and full-time vocational training followed secondary school with an interval for work experience. Besides the full-time program of schooling, there was a rich variety of spare-time courses and institutions.

Primary school started at the age of seven and had five grades. In most parts of the country, Chinese educational authorities reported, all children by 1975 had the opportunity to complete a primary education; in some cities such as Shanghai, Sian, and Kwangchow, seven years of education to the end of the junior middle school was common. The primary school curriculum usually consisted of Chinese language, mathematics, politics, common knowledge, painting, singing, and physical education. Much of the time in the Chinese language class was taken up with learning Chinese characters, three thousand of which had to be learnt in the primary school course. A foreign language, usually English, was often started in the fourth or fifth year. The subject common knowledge included natural science, history, and geography. Most primary school teachers were prepared in normal schools which offered courses of various lengths up to two years for students who had completed a junior or senior middle course and had subsequently spent some time in productive work.

Secondary education continued to spread. It was co-educational and non-selective, and had a fairly standard curriculum of Chinese language and literature, politics, mathematics, physics, chemistry, biology, hygiene, history, geography, revolutionary art, music, and literature, industrial or agricultural work, physical education, and military training.

The Cultural Revolution had disrupted university work. When classes resumed in 1970 and 1971 they were small and the students tended to be academically under-prepared. Students, not all of whom had completed a full secondary course, were accepted on the recommendation of workers' and peasants' groups after they had spent several years at work. In consequence, universities had to modify their curricula and their methods. With small student numbers there was a surplus of staff and therefore opportunity for much experimentation in teaching and for close co-operation between staff and students. Small group teaching, field research in historical and literary studies, student participation in teaching and research, and a large variety of short and bridging courses made life in the university lively and unusually interesting. The idea of a university was expanded, and the range of tertiary level institutions increased. They varied from the well-known multi-faculty universities such as Peking to highly specialised institutes of medicine or agriculture or engineering or teacher education. They included vocational training

Figure 15.3: China: School System, 1975.
(simplified diagram)

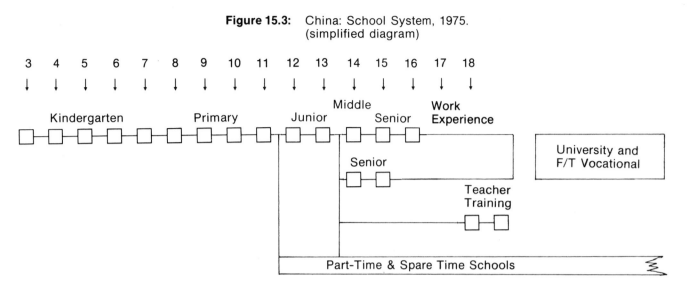

establishments for workers and peasants set up by large factories for the higher training of workmen in, for instance, silk manufacture, or machine tool production.

The model for the workers' and peasants' tertiary colleges was the July 21st Workers' College established at the Shanghai Machine Tools Plant in 1968, to 'create technicians from among the workers'. It offered a three-year full-time course for its own employees who had had several years of work experience, and in some cases, no more than a primary education. The curriculum covered aspects of engineering, electricity, mathematics, a foreign language, and politics. The teachers came mostly from among the technicians already in the plant; the work was closely related to the activities of the factory, and the examinations were exercises in design or practical construction. Mao Tsetung drew the country's attention to the desirability of encouraging tertiary institutions of that type when he stated 'it is essential to shorten the length of schooling, revolutionize education, put proletarian politics in command and take the road of the Shanghai Machine Tools Plant in training technicians from among the workers. Students should be selected from among workers and peasants with practical experience, and they should return to production after a few years' study.'[47]

A further important foundation of the post-Cultural Revolution period was the May 7th Cadre Schools. They began in 1968 and spread subsequently throughout China. They were established for the in-service ideological training of government and business administrators and white-collar workers, such as the trade union officials and teachers. The schools offered experiences of varying lengths of time in agricultural work and political study. An alliance between intellectuals and peasants had always been an important element in securing any lasting reform in social conditions in the course of Chinese history. Mao Tsetung sensed that the intellectuals were getting out of touch with the peasants and took steps in the Cultural Revolution to mend the situation. His pronouncement of 7 May 1966, had made it clear that workers, peasants, and intellectuals should all become involved in politics, industry, and agriculture. The May 7th Schools put the policy into practice for the intellectuals by making them, in some measure, peasants for a suitable time. The schools were in the countryside where the students could work with the peasants for half of their time and actually live with them for a short while. For the other half of their time they studied the classics of Marxist-Leninism and the principal works of Mao Tsetung, and held discussions on current topics of significance. The peasants, for their part, were encouraged to undertake, out of their own resources, difficult jobs such as dam-building, for which they would previously have expected expert intellectual help. By such means the division of interest and understanding between intellectual and peasant was steadily lessened as the intellectual gained personal experience of manual agricultural work, and the peasant became, to some extent, an intellectual.

---

[47] Reported in *Peking Daily*, 21 July 1968.

Schools in China suffer many of the problems of city schools elsewhere. This aerial view of a secondary school at Kwangchow reveals the congested nature of the city, and of the school playground. The students are at an assembly, undergoing political instruction given by a member of the school's Revolutionary Committee. (December 1972)

Particular attention was paid in the 1970's to the development of youth activities. Most of the drive and enthusiasm for the Cultural Revolution had come from the students and youth of China, particularly through the activities of the newly-formed Red Guard. Subsequently, the youth movement was vigorously maintained and reconstituted with new names under the guidance of revolutionary committees. Nearly all the primary school children in the upper grades became Little Red Soldiers; most secondary school children joined the Red Guards; and a smaller, selected number of teenagers of fifteen years and over obtained membership of the Communist Youth League. The principal tasks of the youth groups were to provide ideological education and to help organise their members to undertake responsible community tasks. In many cities there were Children's Palaces for seven to sixteen year olds to reinforce the work of the youth groups. The palaces provided a wide range of extra-curricular activities, trained leaders, and organised political education for the children.

There were also many other spare-time institutions available. Spare-time physical education schools coached specially promising children and youth in a number of sports and in gymnastics. Spare-time schools run by factories, communes, and by the state provided almost every kind of vocational training, and a wide variety of general education courses for adults. They added a richness to the educational scene, brought education closer to the people, and were a means of making up the great educational backlog that China still had to overcome.

In 1973 a further rectification movement was launched, known as the Anti-Confucius campaign. In schools, it was a reinforcement of the strenuous politicising of the Cultural Revolution.

If communism was to become fundamentally and unshakeably the way of life of the Chinese people, it was clear that the long tradition of Confucian thought and attitudes had to be firmly grappled with and overcome. For almost a quarter of a century the clash had been avoided. There had been skirmishes from time to time and there had been a steady build-up of loyalties to Marxist-Maoist thought, but no deliberate and protracted effort to eradicate the underlying conservative tradition. A concerted attack on Confucianism was to be a feature of the mid-1970's. Hierarchical order, male superiority, self-restraint, love of traditional forms, individual benefit, and fatalism were identified with Confucius who, in turn was seen to be the inspiration of contemporary as well as traditional enemies of the common people. To build the new society it was necessary to oppose the wisdom of the people to bureaucracy, equality of the sexes to dominance by men, continuous revolution to moderation, creative proletarian culture to immemorial ways, collective betterment to personal advantage, and determined human effort to the will of heaven. The campaign was used to mount a general criticism of reactionary thought and practice, and to encourage the development of a progressive revolutionary spirit by the inspiration of which the working people would become 'the makers of history'.[48]

(x) Ideology and the Teaching Process

In November 1975 a major education debate was initiated at Tsinghua University in Peking. Starting as a local discussion on whether university standards could be maintained in the light of current admission and teaching policies, the debate spread throughout the whole educational structure of the country and became an evaluation of the educational changes that followed the Cultural Revolution. The main immediate effect was to reaffirm and strengthen working class leadership and work participation by students at all levels in all schools. In the later 1970's a considerable reaction was to set in against the views and achievements of the Cultural Revolution.

The debate was concerned with the justification of the educational practices that had been developed out of the turmoil of the Cultural

48 *China Reconstructs*, 24, 2 (February 1975), 14.

Revolution, but it inevitably moved into a discussion of the ideology upon which the educational methods were built.

It has not always been clear that ideology necessarily has any important effect on the teaching and learning processes in educational institutions. Throughout the course of the twentieth century it has been apparent that progressive methods can exist at times quite happily in conservative regimes, and traditional practices can readily serve the purposes of radical governments. One of the principal features of the Chinese educational experiment was to show that an ideology, if taken thoroughly and seriously as the principal influence on human activity, would have a close relationship to and an important effect on methods of teaching and learning in schools.

The primacy of the Maoist ideology that proletarian politics should be put in command brought about a fairly constant and consistent pattern of teaching which involved four elements: simplification, systematisation, application, and saturation. They were not necessarily four successive steps, but aspects of the teaching process that were in constant use, sometimes separately and sometimes in conjunction with one another.

To assure understanding and to induce commitment, moral, social, and political material was put in its simplest and most straightforward form. Simplification was applied also to all other material to enable persons with minimum educational qualifications to progress up the educational ladder as far as possible, and to demonstrate the feasibility of lay and proletarian control over the educational process.

For all knowledge and for all educational activities, consistency with Mao Tsetung's thought was essential. Whatever choices, therefore, were made in the curriculum, and whatever experiences were offered to the children were scrutinised by conscientious teachers to see that they fitted the Maoist system. China, as a planned society, had to hold together spiritually as well as economically, and the educators, in the service of the people, were guardians of the nation's present and future intellectual and cultural consistency.

Because theory arose out of practice and had value only by contributing to the improvement of practice, emphasis was placed upon knowledge whose practical application could be seen. A central aspect of the learning process was the experiencing of practical activities, and pupils were taught to seek for the ways in which knowledge might be applied to practical use.

The development of political conviction in all pupils took precedence over every other aspect of education. It penetrated every subject of the curriculum and every educational activity. The school was saturated with this objective and the very saturation became a teaching technique. Especially for political education but also for other subjects,

constant repetition and re-examination of the material to be learnt, in many different guises and at many different times, and frequent exercises, discussions, and reminders about it, were designed to keep pupils continually aware of it and to ensure its absorption, by thoroughly saturating them in it.

Within the overall approach defined by those four factors there was room for a variety of teaching techniques as occasion demanded. Pupils were taught by experience, by example, and by instruction; they might be drilled, exhorted, and admonished, or set to work constructively, imaginatively, and creatively. Throughout China there was great variation in the methods used by different schools and different teachers.

The general approach, however, was universally maintained, and within it three other practices were commonly adopted which had been strongly reinforced by the Cultural Revolution and regarded as particularly relevant to Maoist ideology. First, schools and universities adopted an 'open door' policy by which they encouraged the community, particularly the workers, peasants and PLA to enter the institution and take part in its government and in the actual teaching; and they sent their students off for substantial periods to gain experience in investigating and working at various jobs in the community. Secondly, there was an endeavour to teach the techniques of problem-solving, and to encourage

These students at the Fung Cheng No. 3 Primary School, Shanghai in 1972 were engaged in the manufacture of transformer parts for use in local factories.

EDUCATIONAL RECONSTRUCTION AND EXPANSION 1945-75

students to tease out the contradictions in their ideas and activities and to resolve them in the framework of Mao Tsetung thought. Thirdly, working, planning, and judging together in groups rather than as individuals was an important part of the teaching and learning process in schools. Participating in group discussion, learning to accept group decisions about one's work, and sharing both routine and creative jobs with others, formed an important part of a student's education.

In the twentieth century the movement of education has everywhere been away from a teaching process that is centred in the classroom, is concerned principally with the study of books, and gives the teacher the sole responsibility for planning, directing, and conducting the pupils' education. The classroom-, book-, teacher-centred education has been attacked from several points of view, notably by the progressives and the communists. The progressives endeavoured to move the pupil from the classroom into the social and natural environment, to replace the world of books by the world of experience, and to diminish the central role of the teacher by concentrating on the needs of the pupil or the needs of a democratic society. In China, the communists, especially in the concentrated ideological campaigns that followed the Cultural Revolution, widened the pupils' classroom to the factory, countryside, and society, raised practical experience above book learning, and invited workers and peasants as teachers into the school and on to controlling committees in order to implement the view that the interests of the proletarian society were paramount in education.

In such ways students and institutions were developed which resembled those of the western non-communist countries in many ways, but which showed the deliberate impact of a different ideology and which gradually built up distinct characteristics of their own. Proletarian politics ruled them and changed the nature of their task, the orientation of their curriculum, and the flavour of their methods.

Index

Tregear, P., 373n
Trepke, 231, 241
Trotsky, L., 80n
Trow, Martin, 370n
Tryon, Rolla M., 289n
Tsai, Yuan-pei, 308
Tsang, Chiu-Sam, 444n
Tsien Tchchao, 450n
Tsinghua university, 450
Tsiranana, P., 412
Tuft, James H., 78n
Turiel, E., 388
Turkin, 214n
Tyler, Ralph W., 375n, 389-390

U

U.S.A.
the Dalton Plan in, 139, 191, 277-279
economic depression and education in, 288-290
education in, 3-35 *passim*, 37-39, 47, 48, 50-51, 60, 68, 69, 93, 95, 97-100, 101, 105, 107, 108-116
Federal Education Acts in, 354
Herbartian influence in, 61-63
the high school in, 190-194, 352, 354
attendance, 192, 289
characteristics of, 192-194
curriculum change, 191-193
holding power of, 354-356
progressive education in, 71-89, 120-124, 270-272, 274-279, 281-283, 285-288
the Project Method in, 120, 191, 283
school surveys in, 98-99
secondary education in, 352-356
curriculum reform in, 390, 391
expansion of, 354-356
social sciences in, 281-283, 286
tertiary education, expansion of, 363-366
vocational education in, 364, 365
the Winnetka plan in, 122, 191, 279
youth organisations in, 289
U.S.S.R.
Academy of Pedagogical Sciences, 427, 434
common curriculum in, 217
common school year in, 217
curriculum review for the ten-year school, 434-435
education in, 10, 12, 14, 15, 60, 68, 79, 195-241, 426-438
Dewey's view of, 204

educational research in, 427, 434
expansion of, in Central Asian Republics, 429-431
and the Five Year Plans, 215-218, 224, 225, 412, 434
informal, 437-438
Khrushchev reforms, in, 431-432, 447
for leadership, 220-224
Makarenko and, 225-241, 426, 427, 435-436
period of experimentation in, 203-211, 214, 215, 224, 238
polytechnical, 14, 197n, 204, 206-208, 215-217, 218, 224, 240, 431-432
pre-soviet awards in, 428
reconstruction of, after World War II, 428
reform of, in the 1960's and 1970's, 432, 434-438
Suchomlinski and, 436-437
vocational, 218-219
impact of World War II on, 426-428, 430
educational policy, 196-197, 200, 204, 222, 430
educational psychology in, 211-214, 387-388
Five Year Plans in,
First, 198, 199, 200, 203, 204, 207, 208, 211, 214, 215-218, 223, 224, 233, 237, 240, 332
Second, 199, 200, 214, 215-218, 219
Ninth, 434
foreign language teaching in, 428
liquidation of illiteracy in, 197-200, 221, 223, 224, 429-430
school and society in, 80, 426
the new Soviet man in, 233, 234
system of education in, 201-203, 217, 428
reform of, 432, 434-435
universal compulsory education in, 200-203, 206, 215, 428, 430, 434
youth organisations, 220-224, 428, 438
U.S.S.R. Ministry of Education, 432, 434
U.S. President's Commission on Higher Education report, 363, 364
Ufer, Christian, 55-56, 61, 66
Uganda, education in, 315, 318, 326
underachievement, 333
unemployment
educated, 312, 400, 419
and educational expansion, 413
UNESCO, 3n, 333, 398-399, 412
conferences, 410n, 414-416

fundamental education programs, 326, 398
statistical data by, 420, 429
United Nations Development Program, 412
United Nations organisations, 326, 333, 398-399, 412
United States Point Four Program, 412
universities, 9
in China, 308, 440, 448, 450-451, 452-453
control of
by the people, 450-451
state, 264-265, 369-370
in England, 25, 361-362, 369
enrolments in, 312
in France, 48, 368
multidisciplinary, 363
reform of, 175, 362-363
Free, 367
in Germany, 25, 48, 258, 265, 362, 367-368, 370
in India, 312, 399, 400, 403
in Japan, 34, 35, 245, 249, 366-367
multiversities, 369, 370
state control of, 264-265, 369-370
student revolt in, 15-16, 308, 358, 366-368, 395, 448, 450
technical, 25, 48, 202, 218, 266
in the U.S.A., 25, 48, 363, 367, 368, 369-370
in the U.S.S.R., 202, 203, 218, 219, 220, 430
People's Universities, 438
during the war, 164
university, the
and the community, 363
as a community, 369
university education
in Africa, 331, 408, 409, 410
in China, 446
reconstruction of, 450-451, 452-453, 454
expansion of, 312, 314, 333, 361-363, 400, 403, 410
general studies in, 369, 370
in Germany, 263-265, 362
in India, 310, 312, 314, 400-401
in Japan, 245
in Nazi Germany, 263-265
reform of, 310, 368, 446
university entrance requirements, 295, 296, 297, 428, 451, 452
university government
student participation in, 367, 368, 370
University Grants Committee, 178
university grants committee, India, 314
University Institutes of Technology (France), 362

University of Dakar, 410
University of Durham, 318, 327
University of Illinois Committee on School Mathematics, 353
University of Illinois School Mathematics Project, 390, 391
University of London, 50
University of Novosibirsk, 428
University of Paris, 48
University of Peking, 308, 448, 450, 452
university tradition, 265
urbanisation, 2, 21, 97, 224, 358, 411, 413
Ushinsky, K., 427
utilitarianism, 47, 308
in education, 168, 190, 309, 320

V

Vaizey, J.E., 413n
Vakar, G., 213
Valentine, C.W., 298n, 302
Valentiner, Th., 159n
Van Liew, C.C., 57n, 58, 61, 62n
Van Liew, Ida J., 56n, 58, 60, 61, 62
Veblen, Thorsten, 11, 22n, 77n, 88
Veckenstedt *Landerziehungsheim*, 130
Verhaegen, Paul, 408n
Vernon, P.E., 109n, 382, 406n
Vial, F., 44n
Victor, E., 158n
Vidya Bhawan, Udaipur, 313
Vigdorova, Faina, 232n
Violas, P., 88n
Virginia Curricula, 290-291
Viviani Bill (France), 169
vocational education, 3, 7, 12, 15, 20, 25, 26, 39, 46, 216, 309, 321
in China, 309, 445, 452-453, 454
in colonial Africa, 316, 317, 408, 410
compulsory, 218, 249, 266
in England, 48, 50, 169, 177, 182
in France, 48, 49, 50, 169, 175, 183, 340
in Germany, 47-49, 140-141, 142, 168-169, 171, 183, 260, 362
in independent African countries, 411, 412, 414-416
and literacy campaigns, 417
in India, 312, 315, 402, 403, 405
and industrialisation, 245
in Italy, 250, 252, 254
in Japan, 245, 249, 357
and occupational levels, 47